AF361304

SPAIN, THE SECOND WORLD WAR, AND THE HOLOCAUST

History and Representation

SPAIN, THE SECOND WORLD WAR, AND THE HOLOCAUST

HISTORY AND REPRESENTATION

Edited by SARA J. BRENNEIS and GINA HERRMANN

UNIVERSITY OF TORONTO PRESS

Toronto Buffalo London

© University of Toronto Press 2020
Toronto Buffalo London
utorontopress.com
Printed in Canada

ISBN 978-1-4875-0570-7 (cloth)
ISBN 978-1-4875-3250-5 (PDF)
ISBN 978-1-4875-3251-2 (EPUB)

Toronto Iberic

Library and Archives Canada Cataloguing in Publication

Title: Spain, the Second World War, and the Holocaust : history and
    representation / edited by Sara J. Brenneis and Gina Herrmann.
Names: Brenneis, Sara J., editor. | Herrmann, Gina, editor.
Series: Toronto Iberic.
Description: Series statement: Toronto Iberic | Includes bibliographical
    references and index.
Identifiers: Canadiana (print) 20190203862 | Canadiana (ebook) 20190203900 |
    ISBN 9781487505707 (hardcover) | ISBN 9781487532505 (PDF) |
    ISBN 9781487532512 (EPUB)
Subjects: LCSH: Jews – Spain – History – 20th century. | LCSH: Holocaust,
    Jewish (1939–1945) – Spain. | LCSH: World War, 1939–1945 – Spain. |
    LCSH: Spain – Ethnic relations – History – 20th century.
Classification: LCC DS135.S7 S63 2020 | DDC 946/.004924–dc23

This book has been published with the assistance of the Oregon Humanities
Center and the College of Arts and Sciences at the University of Oregon and
the Amherst College Faculty Research Award Program, as funded by The H.
Axel Schupf '57 Fund for Intellectual Life.

University of Toronto Press acknowledges the financial assistance to its
publishing program of the Canada Council for the Arts and the Ontario Arts
Council, an agency of the Government of Ontario.

Contents

Part Three: Spanish Exiles in France

Part Four: Spanish Republicans in Nazi Camps

Part Five: Propaganda

Part Six: The Blue Division

Part Seven: Nazis in Spain

Part Eight: The Holocaust in Contemporary Spanish and Ladino Culture

Part Nine: Afterlives: Holocaust Appropriations in Spain

List of Illustrations

Acknowledgments

What began as a panel at the 2012 Kentucky Foreign Language Conference on Spain and the Holocaust has grown into a decade-long collaboration and friendship. The editors would like to thank the following individuals and institutions for their generous support of this volume, from its formative stages through to the final publication: Theodore Zev Weiss, Paul B. Jaskot, and the faculty of the 2013 Holocaust Educational Foundation Summer Institute on the Holocaust and Jewish Civilization at Northwestern University; John K. Roth; Haim Avni; Jo Labanyi; Alejandro Baer; Pedro Correa Martín-Arroyo; Bernd Rother; Josep Calvet; Benton Arnovitz, Director of Academic Publications at the United States Holocaust Memorial Museum; the Amherst College Faculty Research Award Program as supported by the H. Axel Schupf '57 Fund for Intellectual Life; the National Endowment for the Humanities; the Oregon Humanities Center; the Amherst College Spanish Department; the University of Oregon Departments of Romance Languages and Judaic Studies; our translators, Neil Anderson, Kate Good, and Sarah Booker; our research assistants, Leah Kim and Monica Cardenas; our indexer, Do Mi Stauber; and Mark Thompson, Frances Mundy, and Matthew Kudelka, our editorial team at the University of Toronto Press.

Our utmost gratitude to all of our contributors, from whom we have learned so much and who have demonstrated great patience and goodwill as the volume came together.

Our deep appreciation to our families: Mike, Lena, Rafael, Eric, Charlie, and Malcolm.

SPAIN, THE SECOND WORLD WAR, AND THE HOLOCAUST

History and Representation

Introduction

SARA J. BRENNEIS AND GINA HERRMANN

Spain, the Second World War, and the Holocaust: History and Representation is a response to the questions that students and fellow scholars have posed to us when they hear about our research interests, namely, "What was Spain's role during the war?," and "Wasn't Spain neutral?" We have discovered that addressing these questions is a far more complex matter and speaks to broader and more multidimensional themes than we could have imagined when we began to solicit contributions for this collection. This book is the first to engage critically with the interdisciplinary implications of the two key paradoxes that mark our understandings of Spain during the Second World War and the Holocaust: that Spain declared itself neutral yet played a role in the Second World War; and that Spain has long promulgated the myth of the Franco regime as saviour of Jews, when in fact Spain also hastened the destruction of European Jewry. These contradictions have inspired us to examine in a single volume the situation of Spain during the Second World War from multiple angles, bringing the historical antecedents and consequences together with the representational legacy of the era.

This volume evaluates the Second World War and the Holocaust – both their history and their later representations – through the case study of Spain. The chapters here, which have been contributed by international experts representing the fields of history, literary studies, cultural studies, political science, sociology, and film studies, clarify the historical issues in and related to Spain and also demonstrate the impact of such an inclusive treatment on theories of memory. Moreover, select essays explore the way the Holocaust has been made visible and is now regarded in Spain by unravelling how the facts, memories, and representations of the Second World War and the Shoah are interrelated in the Spanish context. Many of our contributors have done extensive archival research with an eye towards bringing new information and perspectives to the table. Many of the chapters analyse primary and secondary materials previously unavailable in English and often unknown to non-experts. Spanish, Catalan, and Ladino quotations throughout the volume are provided in the original language with the English translation; quotations in all other languages have been translated into English, often for the first time.

We have attempted to be comprehensive in our selection of topics, but we also recognize that we have left out some particular themes, historical events, and disciplinary approaches that merit inclusion.[1] As new revelations and scholarly investigations continue to emerge regarding Spain's role during the Second World War and the Holocaust,[2] we anticipate our readers will find further lacunae; it is our sincere hope that such observations will inspire additional discussion, debate, and research.

Within Spanish historiography and cultural studies, a robust bibliography has contributed to our understanding of these historical events and their after-effects. This research has informed our own inquiry; however, none of it puts themes and methodological approaches into dialogue the way we do here.[3] Many of the contributors to this volume have written pioneering studies in the fields and subjects we address in the pages ahead, and we invite readers to consult our extensive bibliography to grasp the depth and the breadth of the knowledge and expertise accumulated in these pages.

Spain and the Second World War

When the Spanish Civil War broke out in 1936, there were only a few thousand Jews in Spain. The fratricidal conflict pitted Republicans – a loose band of communists, socialists, and anarchists, all protectors of the democratically elected Spanish Republic – against Nationalists, supporters of the Catholic Church, the military, and the bourgeoisie headed by General Francisco Franco. Although antisemitism was not a principal tenet of the Nationalists, Franco consistently pointed to a Judeo–Masonic–Bolshevik conspiracy as the root of Spain's dysfunction.[4] With the superior military strength of Italy and Germany on his side, Franco's Nationalists soon defeated the Republicans. The war in Spain was a staging ground for the world conflict that was to explode just weeks before the official end of the Spanish Civil War, on 1 April 1939, with Adolf Hitler's invasion of Czechoslovakia on 15 March of that year. Franco's victory in Spain thus proved to be a convenient distraction for Hitler's dismantling of Czechoslovakia and the beginning of the Second World War.[5]

Spain stood officially neutral – later "non-belligerent" – during the Second World War. Notwithstanding the uniquely religious overtones of Franco's Catholic-military dictatorship (1939–75), Spain shared nearly all the basic characteristics of a generic fascism. Spanish Falangism, Nazism, and Italian Fascism shared the perception that they were under threat by common enemies, and the de facto alliance and ideological proximity of Franco, Hitler, and Benito Mussolini would shape the course of world politics for almost forty years. Ángel Viñas has argued that the Spanish principle of *caudillaje*, in which the Caudillo (Franco) was the "primary source of law ... not bound by any constitution, nor by any laws deriving therefrom," was modelled on the Nazi *Führerprinzip*.[6] The Spanish Falange was in line with German fascism, imitating the National Socialist combination of force, ideology, and the promise of material rewards. What distinguished the Falange from the Nazi Party was its adherence to Catholic dogma, which Hitler found abhorrent.

As head of the Spanish state, Franco was the ultimate authority through whom all laws, regulations, and policies passed. During the war, Franco and his government made it a practice to backtrack on official measures while keeping others under a cloak of secrecy.[7] Ramón Serrano Suñer was Spain's Minister of Foreign Affairs from 1940 to 1942; he was replaced by Francisco Jordana in September 1942; Jordana served until 1944, when he was replaced by José Félix Lequerica. These three men were integral in the crafting of Spanish policy towards Nazi Germany. With differing levels of autonomy and success, they orchestrated Spain's continued flirtations with the Axis and Allied powers under Franco's aegis. Franco and his ministers kept up a steady stream of correspondence with Hitler and his associates – including with Heinrich Himmler, head of the SS – that in the early stages of the war (1940–1) mainly concerned Franco's interests in expanding the Spanish empire in Morocco and Gibraltar as well as Hitler's desire for Spain to enter the war on the side of Nazis. The Franco regime must be viewed as supporting the Axis cause in both its rhetoric and its actions during the Second World War. As Paul Preston has explained, this support included "the devotion of the Spanish press to the Axis cause, the refuelling and supplying of U-boats, the provision of radar, air reconnaissance and espionage facilities within Spain, [and] the export of valuable raw materials to the Third Reich – [which,] although diminished by the spring of 1944, were never entirely halted until the end of the war."[8] This cooperation also included a face-to-face meeting between Franco and Hitler in Hendaye on 23 October 1940.[9] Hitler did not acquiesce to Franco's specific demands; however, the two men did sign a secret protocol that essentially made Spain a member of the Axis, reaffirmed if only verbally Spain's intention to eventually join the war, and consolidated Spain's accord with Germany and Italy under the 1939 Treaty of Friendship and Alliance.[10]

In the years after Hendaye, Hitler continued to press Franco to join the war. Franco and Serrano Suñer made vague promises but never agreed to a specific date for formalizing Spain's involvement, aiming to put off Spanish belligerence until it appeared clear that England had been considerably weakened. That moment would not come. What is more, given Spain's precarious economic state after its Civil War, Franco became increasingly aware that the country's participation in the world conflict would damage Spain's infrastructure.

While these heads of state were negotiating potential alliances, a few unique members of the Spanish diplomatic corps in Germany and in German-occupied France, Hungary, Greece, Romania, and Bulgaria worked – often in opposition to official policy – to usher scores of Jews to safety. Historians agree that although Spain eventually provided safe passage for thousands of Jews, with an earlier, more systematic approach and defined humanitarian goals, Franco could have helped many more.[11]

At the same time that Jews from all over Europe were journeying south to escape the Nazis, half a million Spanish Republicans were fleeing Franco by crossing north to France after the Republic's defeat. When Hitler's Germany occupied France in 1940, thousands of Spanish refugees found themselves at the mercy of the collaborationist Vichy regime. After Franco's government denied them recognition as citizens, some ten thousand Spaniards – most of whom were Republican veterans who had enlisted in the French Army or had joined the Resistance, or were forced into militarized labour units – were deported to Nazi concentration camps, including Mauthausen, Ravensbrück, Buchenwald, and Neuengamme.[12] Consequently, the significance of Nazi crimes in Spanish Republican memory is indisputable. Of all the sinister destinations intended for the Spanish partisans, Mauthausen would prove the most lethal, with more than forty-five hundred of approximately seven thousand men perishing there.

Spaniards also fought alongside the Nazis on the Russian Front. More than forty-five thousand, many of whom were Spanish Civil War veterans, comprised the Blue Division. They spent 1941–4 deep in Soviet territory; some five thousand died fighting under German command. Although they were not witnesses *per se* to the Holocaust, these Blue Division soldiers, many of whom expressed anti-Judaic sentiments in their memoirs about the war, hovered on the margins, seeing both the prologue to the Nazi genocide and its aftermath in territories where Jews had been murdered en masse. Spanish Republican exiles were also in the Soviet Union; they included the leaders of the Spanish Communist Party in exile in Moscow, and when war broke out, many of these men fought alongside the Soviets. Spaniards, Republicans and Nationalists alike, can be counted among Stalin's victims in the gulags.[13]

Spain and the Holocaust

How Spanish historical events, circumstances, and phenomena came to bear on the Holocaust – the genocide of approximately six million European Jews by the Nazis and their allies – justifies our claim that Spain must be considered among the nations connected to the Shoah.[14] And as we have seen, Spain actively participated in the war.

Although Spain had been essentially "free of Jews" for centuries, ideological inconsistencies among the Spanish regarding the perceived superiority of the Sephardim – Jews descended from the Iberian Jewish community expelled in 1492 – did not go unnoticed by German authorities. Historian Haim Avni, author of the first major study of Spanish wartime policy towards European Jews, reveals that in 1941, German Ambassador Eberhard von Stohrer, reporting on his dismay at the lack of anti-Jewish legislation in Spain, wrote that "insofar as the people are concerned, and insofar as the official ideology of the State is concerned, there is no Jewish problem."[15] After the war, Spain would cite its distance from German antisemitism in its efforts to end the country's isolation. Indeed, hatred of Jews was not codified in Spanish law during the Second World War: Spanish Foreign Minister Ramón Serrano Suñer replied to an inquiry from a Romanian official on 19 December 1940 that "en la legislación española no existe discriminación alguna en relación con los judíos que residen en España" (there is no discrimination in the Spanish laws against Jews living in Spain).[16] However, as political scientist Antonio Marquina Barrio has argued, the Nationalist slogan that "Communists, Jews, and Masons" were enemies of Spain and prevalent anti-Judaism among government ministries and in the Falange fuelled the larger public's perception of Jews during the war.[17]

Franco actively courted Hitler's favour during the early part of the war, but in later concessions to the Allies he burnished his false reputation as a protector of Jews while at the same time limiting the number of Jewish refugees permitted to remain in Spain at any one time. After Hitler's January 1943 ultimatum to neutral countries that they either repatriate their Jewish nationals or leave them to their bleak fate with the Nazis, the Spanish government's policies towards Sephardic Jews living in occupied Europe who possessed Spanish citizenship shifted opportunistically between February and March 1943.[18] Nevertheless, in spite of these draconian and mercurial policies towards refugees, of the approximately eighty thousand who fled the Nazis through Spain between 1939–44, including French resistance fighters and Allied and Axis soldiers, at least fifteen thousand were Jews.[19] Many of these illegal and legal refugees were able to move through Spain, into Portugal, and on to safety in the Americas or Palestine.

Historians have estimated that between fifteen thousand and twenty-five thousand Jews were aided through diplomatic means largely independent of Madrid as they travelled by sea or crossed the Pyrenees from France to Spain, legally or not. The statistics vary primarily as a function of the communities (Ashkenazi or Sephardic) or the geographies under study and the archival focus of the research. These archives include oral histories, documentation from French and Spanish consulates and civil governments of Spanish border provinces, records from the American Joint Distribution Committee, War Ministry archives, customs records, and passenger ship manifests.

To this day, these archives offer accounts of the purely selfless valour of a number of Spanish diplomats who provided passports and letters of protection for thousands of Jews, most famously in Hungary. These efforts at rescue rely on historical fact even while indulging in a form of myth-making that has allowed marginalized Spain to partake in a wider European culture of memory that depends on a coming to terms with each nation's implication in the Holocaust. While for decades historians have been working in archives to collect evidence regarding what actually occurred in the context of Spain's interventions on behalf of Jewish populations in Europe, the court of public opinion has in many cases already found Spain not guilty and, indeed, laudable for its actions during the Holocaust. The image of Spain as a rescuer of Jews, polished by television documentaries, miniseries, commemorations, and news reports, has blinded Spaniards to far more complex and often contradictory regime positions and individual official decision-making that determined whether Jews would escape Nazi terror or would be murdered.

Haim Avni has asserted that any examination of Spain's position regarding the Jews during the Holocaust must keep present the fact that the Expulsion of 1492 (not officially revoked until 1968) and the Inquisition that followed "etched a deep scar on the national memory" and as the centuries passed would be felt as a historical blunder.[20] Many of the Sephardic Jews residing in the nation-states formed after the demise of the Ottoman Empire at the end of the First World War would be at risk during the Shoah, which wiped out the primary

Judeo-Spanish population centres and led to the almost complete disappearance of their traditions and language, Ladino. Spain's re-evaluation of the Expulsion after a series of crises – including the loss of its colonies in 1898 – its bid for modernity, and the era of Jewish Emancipation, which coincided with the Enlightenment, help explain the general tenor of paradox that has shaped Spanish positions towards the Sephardim. Those positions include Primo de Rivera's 1924 decree permitting individuals with Spanish heritage abroad – implicitly Sephardic Jews – to apply for citizenship. This order, which allowed applications only until 1930 and required thorough documentation of Spanish ancestry, was motivated largely by international diplomacy that would later have implications for Jews seeking repatriation to Spain during the Holocaust. Thus the Spanish philosemitism celebrated by some Spanish intellectuals during the early twentieth century did not translate into a massive national effort to protect Sephardic Jews. As journalist and historian Jacobo Israel Garzón has stressed, distinct geographically delineated communities of Jews received different treatment, and the failure to grasp this has led to variability in perceptions among historians.[21] The vast majority of Jews who attempted to pass through Spanish territory en route to a third nation were Ashkenazim who found themselves at the mercy of rapidly shifting Spanish policies towards refugees. Sephardic Jews, most of whom resided in the Balkan nations or in small communities in France and Italy, often stayed where they were, hoping that their official or unofficial ties to Spain would offer them a measure of protection.

Spain did not realize its full potential regarding the number of Jews it could have saved during the Holocaust, Sephardic and Ashkenazi alike. The regime could have loosened its rules governing transit visas; it could have aided, rather than hindered, the various Jewish rescue organizations eventually permitted to operate on Spanish soil; and Franco conceivably could have thrown open Spain's doors to Jews fleeing persecution from all over Nazi-occupied Europe. Avni concludes: "Because of Spain's position during the war, the Spanish government could have rescued some groups of Jews, but it refrained from taking full advantage of the opportunity ... Although knowing that abandoning its Jewish nationals and other Jews was tantamount to annihilation, the Spanish government confined its operations to what seemed the most expedient at the time."[22] In 1941 the government sent a solicitation for the collection of an "Archivo Judaico" (Jewish Archive): a census of all Jews within Spain's borders. Whether or not this information reached Himmler, as is presumed,[23] its mere existence at a moment when Spain's entry into the war was an open question demonstrates the existential danger in which Spanish Jews found themselves: they were at the mercy of the Franco regime.

Spain never questioned Nazi policies, and Franco was committed to protecting the country's wartime economic interests with both Allied and Axis powers. Despite the Allies' repeated attempts to embargo Spanish wolfram (tungsten), Franco continued to supply the Nazis with this element, which was vital to armament production, through legal and illegal trade channels well into 1944. The steady flow of wolfram and other materials from Spain into Germany prolonged the war and implicated the former as "quasi-perpetrators of the murderous Nazi terror."[24]

In his study *Franco y el Holocausto* (2005), Bernd Rother offers a final accounting with regard to the Franco regime's responsibility for the persecution and murder of European Jews. Notwithstanding that it had declared itself a "non-belligerent" nation, the Franco regime acted as an ally of Hitler's Germany. Spain did not support the National Socialist program of persecution of the Jews, nor did it promulgate regulations pertaining solely to Jews. Spain's goal was to bar Jews from Spanish territory by requiring byzantine proof of nationality, looking to other countries to take in Jews in transit, and accepting new groups of refugees only after those on Spanish soil had moved on. As Josep Calvet has shown, at certain points during the war, in concert with the shifting pressures the Spanish state faced in its dealings with the Allies and the Axis alike, thousands of Jews were turned back at the border, some of them directly into the hands of the police of their countries of origin, who then handed them over for detention or for deportation to concentration camps.[25] Spain's efforts after the war to present itself as a refuge for Jews can be attributed to fear of public opinion, particularly in the United States, and to efforts to preserve its economic relations abroad. As we have noted, on a number of occasions Jews were rescued through Spanish diplomatic patronage and protection, but this was on the initiative of the Spanish legations themselves and was not the result of any directive from Franco.

These observations about failures and refusals to help save Jewish lives must be placed in the context of what the Franco regime actually knew about the extermination of European Jewry. By 1944 the government in Madrid had received various reports that Jews were being exterminated at Auschwitz. A delegation of doctors to Poland and Austria in December 1941 filed a secret report to the Ministry of the Interior about euthanasia as well as the forced transfer of Jews to the ghettos of Warsaw and Krakow. This account eventually reached Franco's hands. Soldiers of the Blue Division, returning from the east, complained to the Dirección General de Seguridad about the mass exterminations on the Eastern Front. In March 1943, a Spanish lawyer overheard in Berlin that captured Jews were being asphyxiated by gas.[26] Communications from Spanish consuls and ambassadors warned that if Jews were not allowed to be "repatriated" (itself an ironic usage, since no Jews were allowed to remain in Spain but were, rather, required to transit through to another nation), they would be sent to extermination camps. Clearly, then, the Franco government was receiving information that Jews were very likely to be murdered should they be deported. On 24 July 1944, Ángel Sanz Briz, the attaché to the Spanish Legation in Budapest, sent Madrid a detailed report about the Auschwitz camp that had been in circulation among embassies in Europe. Having received this communiqué, the regime in Madrid would have been aware of the mass slaughter of Jews, including at Auschwitz-Birkenau.

To further assess what the Franco regime knew about the Shoah, we must also take into account the continually thwarted efforts of Jewish relief agencies to establish offices in Spain. These agencies' entreaties supply further evidence that the Spanish government understood very well the dire plight of European Jews. Yehuda Bauer, in his history of the American Jewish Joint Distribution Committee (the "Joint"), writes that the Spanish leadership steadfastly refused to allow any *Jewish* relief organizations to operate in Spain. Moreover, non-Jewish aid associations had to try to function via makeshift and temporary agreements, including one that finally, in 1943, permitted the Quakers to represent the aid groups.[27] The impact of these efforts was quite limited. When David Shaltiel, Haganah representative from Palestine, arrived on the Iberian Peninsula in September 1944 to help organize the rescue of Jews, he reported back to his superiors: "There is nothing to do here; we came two years too late."[28]

Spanish Republicans witnessed first-hand how Jews were treated in French concentration camps and later in the Nazi camps. Spanish Republican testimonial accounts cannot be described as replete with memories of the torture and murder of Jews in those camps where these inmate populations crossed paths; nonetheless, Spanish prisoners of the Nazis saw and heard about (and would later write about) the systematic violence against and murder of Jews in camps where they themselves were being imprisoned and tortured. Spanish camp survivors, many of them associated with anti-fascist resistance units and ideologies, understood the radical difference between Jewish victims and themselves in the eyes of the Third Reich – that is, that their internment was the result of a *choice* to fight against fascism rather than the outcome of a policy to annihilate an entire "race."

At Mauthausen, Spanish deportee Raimundo Suñer witnessed from the garages where he worked the arrival of a transport of some two hundred Jews in October 1942. Typically, only Spaniards in Mauthausen who had been granted privileged working conditions – in the garages, the photography lab, the Gestapo offices, and so on – would ever have the chance to spot Jews, many of whom were murdered soon after they entered the camp. Suñer watched as this group of Jews, naked and arranged in three lines, marched towards the washroom. He overheard their cries as the SS viciously beat them, and noticed that by the next day, they were all gone. In a chilling description, Suñer writes: "Después de las nueve de la noche se oían gritos y ruidos, y es que los SS se divertían con ellos con palos, vergajos y hasta con los picos. A la mañana siguiente no quedaba ninguno vivo y cuando salimos al trabajo ya estaba todo limpio." (After nine at night, cries and noises could be heard, and what happened was that the SS were amusing themselves with them with sticks, whips, and even with picks. The next morning none of them were left alive and when we left for work everything was entirely clean).[29] Suñer's account displays a desire to record intimate details of scenes that most Spanish prisoners would not have witnessed, painting a grotesque portrait of the treatment of Jews within Mauthausen's walls.

Mercedes Núñez Targa, a Spanish member of the French resistance, recounted the excruciating memory of Jewish mothers and children interned with her at the Ravensbrück camp for women. She wonders whether the little Jewish children, frozen with terror and hunger, who clung to their mothers' legs during an endless roll call, "saben lo que les espera bien pronto, lo adivinan?" (do they understand or guess what awaits them? [the gas chamber]).[30] Her writing underscores the radical experiential and existential difference between prison populations in the camp – "el recuerdo de aquellos niños judíos es como una herida permanente, nunca curada, para nosotras, las deportadas" (the memory of those Jewish children is like a permanent, forever gaping wound in us, the political deportees). The politicals inhabited the same physical space but existed in a world apart from the genocidal universe of Jewish mothers and children.[31]

The memoirs and novels of Spanish-born writer Jorge Semprún, prisoner #44904 at Buchenwald, are haunted by Jewish prisoners whose experiences in the camps were far more shattering and who could not frame their deportation, as Semprún could, as the outcome of free will and political agency. Semprún remembers coming upon a dying Hungarian Jew who was chanting the Kaddish. Overwhelmed by the sight, Semprún thought: "No one can put himself in your place ... or even imagine your place, your entrenchment in nothingness, your shroud in the sky, your fatal singularity."[32] In her discussion about the problematic way in which Jewish victims become abstractions in Spanish camp writing, Ruth Wisse, scholar of Yiddish literature, has remarked how "all other nationals were treated relatively better than the Jews, the survivors among them feel that they have to defer to the arch-victim in their suffering." Spanish deportees would have had few encounters with Jewish people over the course of their lives and would have known little if anything about Judaism.[33] Thus despite the tendency to "abstract the Jew rather than to seek to know him," Spanish memories of the camps speak to the testimonial will to give first-hand evidence of the extermination of European Jews.[34]

Of course, these Spanish prisoners had no means to inform the world about the murders of Jews they witnessed at Buchenwald, Mauthausen, Ravenbrück, and other camps. The Spaniards had been abandoned as early as 1940 by Franco, who allowed them to be transported to Nazi camps as "stateless" prisoners even while he began to consider the administrative and diplomatic benefits of visa policies that would allow Jews to transit through the peninsula.

From History to Representation

Spanish philosopher Reyes Mate considers the relationship between history and memory in the context of the Holocaust using language that evokes the scholarly disposition that grounds our book:

> History has focused on the reconstruction of the facts, and memory on the building of the present sense. One works with testimonies, the other one with files – two different views that continue to merge and contaminate one another ... The historian Saul Friedländer takes both approaches in *Nazi Germany and the Jews*. In the first part, he uses the files to study the ideology and structure of Hitlerism; in the second part, he resorts to the testimonies of the victims in order to understand the meaning of that historical moment "from the inside." Using the methods of history, we can find out how many crimes were committed; using memory, we can learn about the experience of the victims. Talking about crimes without mentioning the victims is not the same as talking about the victims of the crime.[35]

The contents and organization of *Spain, the Second World War, and the Holocaust: History and Representation* respond to Mate's directive to reconstruct the facts of Spain's wartime behaviour and to attend to how the consequences of those actions would be felt and remembered by individuals who witnessed, rescued, failed to act against, or perpetrated crimes – as well as those who fell victim. Memory and representation – in the form of literature, film, and other visual media – are thus linked in this volume: we understand these cultural representations as the tangible manifestations of how the past is, has been, and will be remembered over time.

The past two decades have marked a watershed for Spain's acknowledgment of memories of the Spanish Civil War and the Franco dictatorship. From the establishment of the Asociación de la Recuperación de la Memoria Histórica in 2000 to the passage of the Ley de Memoria Histórica in 2007, a movement has arisen to re-examine Spain's Civil War and dictatorship in the interest of probing the divisions between victors and vanquished that have marked the country for decades. This groundswell now encompasses the memory of Spain's role in the Second World War and the Holocaust. Spain's relationship with fascism and Falangism has been as convoluted as it has been prolonged, and it is important to stress that Spain – from before the Civil War, through the Second World War, and throughout Franco's thirty-six-year dictatorship (1939–75) – boasted the longest anti-fascist resistance in Europe. As our contributors attest, the cultural production inspired by this resistance, traditionally studied in reference to the Civil War, today extends to the Second World War and the Holocaust.

The stories in this volume can be thought of as a series of interlocking dramas that develop simultaneously on different stages. The characters include Jews from across Europe whose lives are linked to the Spanish regime's choices; lone-wolf diplomats who rescue Jews; cultural representatives transporting antisemitic propaganda between Spain and other countries; leaders in the Catholic Church who espouse Jewish-Masonic-Bolshevik conspiracy theories; Blue Division soldiers; anti-fascist resisters; Spanish Republican victims and survivors; Nazis advising Franco's government after the war or fleeing to Spain with Nazi hunters at their heels; and artists and writers trying to shape the nation's memory of the aforementioned. The stages are set not only in Spain but also in Germany, North Africa, the United States, Austria, France, Greece, Russia, Hungary, and other parts of Eastern Europe as people and ideas move across geographical spaces, political ideologies, and cultural discourses. The scripts emanate from history and artistic representation: camp intake records, Church newspapers, diplomatic communiqués, letters among survivors, memoirs, oral histories, fiction, photographs, documentary film, poetry, theatre, monuments, textbooks, and new media.

The chapters in this volume that deal with representation further problematize, recontextualize, visualize, and pay homage to the ways in which Spain was implicated in the Second World War and the Holocaust. Moving from the analysis of early oral histories and testimonies that provided immediate feedback after the war on the conflict and its human toll to recent interpretations in narrative, poetry, theatre, film, and new media of a more remote historical period, our understanding of representation as complementing history is a rejoinder to the injunctions of Holocaust scholars such as Theodor Adorno and Berel Lang. This volume argues that representations of the Holocaust and the Second World War, far from banalizing and distorting events, enhance our understanding of how the historical memory of this period has shifted in Spain through the decades. As Andreas Huyssen points out, the Holocaust and the Second World War appear now inextricably linked to their cultural manifestations in our collective consciousness: "Popularizing representations and historical comparisons are ineradicably part of a Holocaust memory which has become multiply fractured and layered."[36] This becomes patently clear in the case of Spain, where public conceptions of the Holocaust, as sociologist Alejandro Baer has reasoned in his work, tend to be diffuse and incomplete. In Spain, Baer has observed, "the weakness of [the] link [between Spain and the memory of the Holocaust] is not historical but cultural."[37] He argues that in a country known for its poor reception of the history and the memories of the Holocaust, one must interrogate the omissions and prejudices that continue to mould ideas and knowledge of the Shoah in Spain alongside more constructive representations.

The sheer volume and variety of literary, cinematic, and digital interpretations contained in this volume stands as proof that representations of the Holocaust and the Second World War are conjoined with their historical underpinnings in the contemporary Spanish imagination. For example, twenty-first-century Ladino poetry exploring a recovered language and past reflects how the fate of Sephardic Jews during the Shoah is remembered in Israel; a Twitter account portraying the agony of a Spanish Republican imprisoned at Mauthausen keeps the memory of the deportation alive for a new generation; and a contemporary Spanish play based on the International Red Cross's 1944 visit to the Terezin concentration camp informs Spanish theatregoers of a history little studied in Spanish curricula. Meanwhile, contemporary Spanish novels that engage with Nazi persecution of political prisoners and Jews alike evince blind spots in terms of their historical accuracy; recent Spanish poetry trained on the Holocaust uses Anne Frank as an imprecise synecdoche for the suffering of millions; and Spanish documentary films problematically position Spanish Republicans as heroic victims whose experiences can be compared directly to those of the Jews. As we ask ourselves what the Second World War and the Holocaust mean today to Spain, these works of art assume a formative role in creating and sustaining a Spanish vision in all its complexity – inaccuracies and exclusions notwithstanding – of a past shared with the rest of Europe.

Organization and Scope of the Volume

Our volume is organized thematically and, where possible, chronologically. Each section brings together diverse scholars writing around a central concept, event, or geographic region. Although each chapter provides the reader with sufficient fundamental background historical and contextual information that it can be read in isolation, together the chapters that comprise this volume offer a complementary panorama of the history and representation of Spain before, during, and after the period that encompasses the Second World War and the Holocaust.

Haim Avni's prologue opens our volume with an overview of Hitler's rise to power and the diplomatic and military negotiations between Germany and Spain. Avni interprets specific intersections between Jewish and Spanish histories and peoples during the twelve years of the Nazi regime, including Jewish and Spanish opposition to the 1936 Nazi Olympic Games in Berlin, the joint incarceration of Spanish Republicans and Jews in French concentrations camps, and the Spanish Blue Division forces that moved through decimated Jewish communities on the Eastern Front during the war. His chapter serves as a prelude to the in-depth examinations contained throughout the volume, which pinpoint the many moments of overlap between Jewish and Spanish history during the war and the Holocaust.

The first section, Legacies of Antisemitism in Spain, focuses on Jewish populations in Spain and Sephardic Jews abroad. Jewish people on the Iberian Peninsula were subjected to long-standing anti-Judaic sentiments, while Jews in transit through Spain suffered the regime's uneven treatment. Israeli historians Martina L. Weisz and Raanan Rein (chapter 1) anchor our collection with a look back to the nineteenth and early twentieth centuries in order to understand how notions of antisemitism and philosephardism in early-twentieth-century Spain shaped the ideas of Spanish officials who cast Jews alternatively as heroes and monsters throughout the Spanish Civil War and the Second World War. Gonzalo Álvarez Chillida (chapter 2) follows with a review of philosephardism (also discussed in Isabelle Rohr's chapter in the next section) and antisemitism during the crucial decades preceding the Second World War and throughout the years of the conflict itself. His chapter points to the role of the Spanish Church (examined by Graciela Ben Dror in chapter 19) in casting Jews as the sinister power behind a world conspiracy to destroy Christianity, foment liberal revolutions, and control international capital. Philosemitism simultaneously developed in Spain during this same span of time and included a successful campaign to celebrate the Sephardim abroad. During the Second Republic, sympathy for Spanish Jews manifested itself more as intent than as action; then the Civil War fuelled right-wing animus against Jews, which was further inflamed by propaganda arriving from France and Nazi Germany. These two opening chapters establish the background for Spain's legacy of its treatment of Jews, bringing us to the gates of the Second World War.

The second section, Spain and the Fates of Jewish Communities, takes readers on a geographic journey through the diverse populations of Jews in Europe and North Africa affected by Spain's deeds during the Second World War. Jacobo Israel Garzón (chapter 3) opens with a portrait of four distinct populations of Jews inside and outside of Spain, each of which faced varying treatment in light of Franco's policies, the goal of which was always to keep Jews from settling on Spanish soil. This section continues the theme of Franco's manipulations of philosemitism – previewed by both Chillida and Weisz and Rein in Section I – with Isabelle Rohr's (chapter 4) discussion of Jews in the Spanish protectorate of Morocco. Rohr examines the opportunistic nature of the Franco regime's policy towards the Jews of North Africa and its decision to keep the doors of Spanish-occupied Tangier shut to Jewish refugees. North Africa as a locus of Spanish involvement in the war is addressed as well in chapters by Weisz and Rein and Robert S. Coale. Josep Calvet's (chapter 5) and Tabea Alexa Linhard's (chapter 6) complementary essays move the geographical focus north, navigating the border crossings through the Spanish Pyrenees by primarily Ashkenazi Jews fleeing Nazi persecution and seeking refuge or transit via Spain. Through readings of personal testimony and archival documentation, Calvet describes the political, diplomatic, and charitable phenomena that determined how and when refugees could escape across the Pyrenees. He also gives a riveting account of Jewish refugees hidden by Catalan and Spanish civilians during the war. Linhard's chapter looks at these same border crossings through the lens of cultural studies, treating human rights as a way to explore the representational and memorial valences carried by the criss-crossing routes of displaced Jews. A number of chapters in this volume – including the contributions of Calvet, Israel Garzón, Maria Fragkou, and Pedro Correa Martín-Arroyo – deal in detail with relief agencies and aid to refugees operating in or in relation to Spanish territory.

Maria Fragkou's chapter 7 directs the story of persecuted Jews towards the larger Mediterranean, specifically to Salonika, Greece, the location of the most significant settlement of Sephardic Jews in Europe. The situation of a group of Jews of Salonika – the "little Jerusalem of the Balkans" – who were deported to the Bergen-Belsen concentration camp during the war includes an important anecdote about 367 Spanish Sephardic Jews who were helped by the relentless efforts of Athens-based Spanish consul Sebastián Romero Radigales. His intervention allowed these people to be held in a section of the camp set aside for "neutrals" as they awaited repatriation to Spain. Fragkou's emphasis on the destinies of Salonikan Jews pairs well with Shmuel Refael's study of the poetic legacy of this Ladino-speaking community in Section VIII. Closing this section is José Antonio Lisbona's chapter 8 about the fates of Jewish communities, in which he meticulously traces the decisive role played by a number of Spanish diplomats in Hungary, Greece, France, Romania, and other locations in rescuing Jews from persecution and deportation to the death camps. There was no single model of rescue, and diplomatic protections led to different outcomes depending on the country of action. Lisbona's compendium of diplomatic interventions pairs with Calvet's chapter on escape routes, and together these two contributions encompass the broad scope of Spanish efforts to save European Jews. Lisbona clarifies the line between myth and reality in the narratives of the consuls, who have become part of a highly manipulated legacy of magnanimity associated with Franco's regime (see Pedro Correa Martín-Arroyo's chapter on the evolution of the Franco myth).

The third section, Spanish Exiles in France, tracks the movements of Spanish Republican refugees from the end of the Civil War in 1939 through to the liberation of the concentration camps in 1945. Geneviève Dreyfus-Armand (chapter 9) describes and assesses the various wartime roles filled by Spaniards in French territory from the moment of the *retirada*, the massive refugee crisis that brought nearly a half million Spaniards to France in 1939 in the wake of the Nationalist victory, through to their internment in French camps. Her chapter then turns to the Spanish participation – as labourers, conscripts, or resistance fighters – in the Second World War in France, and finally as the first units under General Philippe Leclerc to enter Paris to liberate that city from Nazi occupation. In chapter 10, historian Robert S. Coale traces the destinies of three Spanish Republican exiles, the Camons-Portillo brothers of Santander, Spain, from the harsh French internment camps, to concentration camps in Oran in French Algeria, and then to the deportation of Spanish combatants from the French Foreign Legion and Labour Companies to Mauthausen. This chapter encapsulates the risks and opportunities Spaniards encountered as they took up positions in military, forced labour, or resistance units in wartime France (others who study the movements of Spaniards in France during the war in this volume include Avni, Lisbona, Gina Herrmann, and Soledad Fox Maura). To close this theme, Juan M. Calvo Gascón (chapter 11) writes about the monument to Spanish Republicans deported to Mauthausen that was erected at the camp in 1962. Calvo's examination of a single memorial structure demonstrates how Mauthausen survivors in France and Spain both individually and as a collective negotiated issues of national identity, memorialization, and the politics behind the attempts to regulate how groups bent to an identity-relevant past in national-social contexts in the 1950s and early 1960s. In other sections of the volume, Sara J. Brenneis, Marta Marín-Dòmine, Rosa Toran, Marilén Loyola, and Isabel Estrada also discuss the significance of Mauthausen.

The contributors to the fourth section, Spanish Republicans in Nazi Camps, flesh out the travails of exiled Spanish Republicans who were deported to Nazi concentration camps. Gina Herrmann (chapter 12) investigates how women fared during the Republican exile to France and the circumstances in which Spanish women resisters were captured and deported to Nazi camps alongside French anti-fascist women. Herrmann focuses on female political prisoners used as Nazi slave labour and on the limited opportunities factory work offered for the continuation of resistance through the sabotage of armament manufacturing. The chapter draws on the personal histories of two now well-known Ravensbrück survivors who had been active in the rural French resistance: Mercedes Núñez Targa and Neus Català. Mauthausen, Buchenwald, and Ravensbrück remain the camps most associated with the Republican deportation; however, Andrea Hepworth (chapter 13) studies the deportation of hundreds of Spaniards to the Nazi concentration camp at Neuengamme, focusing on the survivor testimony of José López, whose orally transmitted memories of incarceration Hepworth discovered in the KZ Gedenkstätte Neuengamme Archive. These studies by Herrmann and Hepworth coincide in their observation that the full scope of the Spanish victimization in the Nazi camps will likely never be fully understood because so many deportees entered the camps with false French identities. Continuing the exploration of Nazi camps with significant Spanish Republican prisoner populations, Sara J. Brenneis (chapter 14) offers a detailed look at the Austrian concentration camp Mauthausen, the destination for more than seven thousand

Spaniards during the war, over 60 per cent of whom were killed by the Nazis. Brenneis analyses how this camp in particular has occupied a place in Spain's collective memory since its liberation in 1945, becoming the inspiration for seven decades' worth of narratives – written by survivors and non-survivors alike – published in Spain. As this impressive textual body has evolved from first-person accounts to new media narrative interpretations of the Spanish experience of Mauthausen, Brenneis follows the development of a contemporary consciousness about the Nazi camps in Spain that risks becoming dehistoricized.

Republicans' experiences of deportation produced some of the finest imaginative, autobiographically inspired literature composed by twentieth-century Catalan and Spanish writers. The next two chapters are close readings of the literary works of two survivor-writers: Joaquím Amat-Piniella and Jorge Semprún. Marta Marín-Dòmine (chapter 15) composes a meditation on Amat-Piniella's foundational 1963 novel, *K.L. Reich*, a fictionalized approximation of the Spanish experience of Mauthausen that explores the hierarchy of international camp prisoners and their Nazi captors.[38] Her reading interprets Amat-Piniella's narrative as complementary to the photographs of Mauthausen that have become the contentious centrepiece of the Spanish visual imagination of the deportation of Spanish Republicans to Nazi camps, a theme also present in Isabel Estrada's chapter. Soledad Fox Maura (chapter 16) follows with an account of the chameleonic Jorge Semprún, arguably the only Spanish survivor whose writings have been elevated to the Pantheon of canonical Holocaust authors. The Spanish-born, French-schooled intellectual's novels and memoirs about his deportation to Buchenwald and his account of the tribulations of Spanish communism place him among the most important European public intellectuals to publish on Nazi oppression and the legacies of Stalinism. Fox addresses how Semprún's encounters with Jews during and after the Holocaust shaped his own identity as a deportée-witness to the Shoah whose own survival ethically obliged him to speak "in the name of" Jewish victims.[39] Rosa Toran (chapter 17) concludes this part of the volume with an appreciation of Montserrat Roig, a Catalan journalist whose groundbreaking oral history, *Els catalans als camps nazis,* released in 1977, introduced Catalans and Spaniards to the history of the deportation and whose work, more than any other, fuelled the growing consciousness in Transition-era Spain of the presence of Spaniards in Nazi camps. Roig's foundational work with Catalan survivors underscores the centrality of orally transmitted memory for the history of Spain during the Second World War; oral texts are also analysed by Herrmann, Hepworth, and Boris Kovalev in their respective contributions.

The fifth grouping of essays, Propaganda, provides readers with an unusually strong collection of studies on wartime propaganda produced by the Franco regime, the Spanish Church, and the Nazi state. Together the chapters produce a dialogue about how German and Spanish information campaigns came to influence each other; they also explain the reasons for the persistence of Franco's reputation for helping the Jews. Javier Domínguez Arribas (chapter 18) discusses the causes of violent and ubiquitous antisemitic propaganda circulating in Spain during the Second World War. The author argues that the Jewish common enemy provided cohesion among diverse groups within the Francoist constellation. In chapter 19, Graciela Ben Dror studies the multiform reaction to wartime European antisemitism and the persecution of Jews by scrutinizing the platforms of various Catholic organizations and entities in Spain, including Acción Católica Española and the Jesuits, particularly through their print news media. The role of the Catholic Church is also discussed in chapters by Álvarez Chillida, Mercedes Peñalba-Sotorrío, and David Messenger. Pedro Correa Martín-Arroyo's contribution (chapter 20) describes how Franco's propagandists manipulated the rescue organizations operating in Spain, in part by professing an exaggerated humanitarianism towards Jews through the state-controlled press. Correa lays out how the Franco regime, in order to improve the nation's international standing in the post-war years, attempted to whitewash its Second World War antisemitic record and exploit the myth that Spain had rescued Jewish refugees. Next, Mercedes Peñalba-Sotorrío (chapter 21) appraises the little-studied German propaganda that circulated in Spain during the Second World War, and finds that it was not resolutely antisemitic but rather relied on denunciations of the country's other enemies of the time: namely, Western plutocracy, Freemasonry, anti-Christianity, and communism. Finally, in chapter 22, Marició Janué i Miret investigates the promotion of Spanish culture in Nazi Germany by prominent Falangist intellectuals, who were invited to travel to Germany as representatives of a doctrine of Spanishness that coincided with Hitler's aims to promote an ideology of racial purity rooted in colonial expansion. Later chapters by Joshua Goode, David A. Messenger, Isabel Estrada, and Stacy N. Beckwith examine the post-war presence of Nazis in Spain while also looking at questions of German/Spanish cultural exchange addressed in Peñalba-Sotorrío and Janué i Miret's contributions.

Turning the volume's spotlight to the Russian Front, the chapters comprising The Blue Division, section VI, consider the history and autobiographical writings of the pro-Axis Spanish volunteers who fought as part of the Wehrmacht in the Soviet Union. Boris Kovalev (chapter 23) looks at the presence of Spanish volunteer forces fighting alongside the Germans at the Russian front during the Second World War, relying on archived testimonial accounts from Soviet civilians who recounted their interactions with and impressions of members of the Blue Division, translated into English here for the first time. Macarena Tejada López (chapter 24) builds on Kovalev's background to explore diaries and memoirs of Blue Division soldiers alongside two works of fiction with the Blue Division as protagonist. Her chapter examines how shifting social and political contexts (from dictatorship to democracy) informed the thematic and self-representational choices made by these soldiers and authors as they revisited and recorded their experiences on the Russian Front. Where Kovalev and Tejada López address how the Divisioners felt about Jews, their observations can be read alongside Peñalba-Sotorrío's examination of German antisemitism in Spain, as well as the first section of the volume dealing with Spanish antisemitism. These two chapters can likewise be paired with Avni's prologue, which also addresses the División Azul from the vantage point of Spaniards working in military hospitals in the German-administered Ostland territory around Riga.

The seventh section, Nazis in Spain, follows the paths and influences of Nazi cells during and after the war in Spain. The authors of these two chapters take up questions about how Germans used Spain as a base of operations as the war unfolded and as a refuge from denazification during the post-war period. In chapter 25, Joshua Goode takes measure of the phenomenon of Nazis residing in Spain who enjoyed affiliation with the Franco regime and thus were able to avoid extradition back to Germany. He focuses on the case of Otto Skorzeny, a former Waffen SS officer famous for liberating Mussolini in 1943 as well as a public figure celebrated in the Spanish press. In Spain, he positioned himself as a prescient anti-communist, an incarnation of a new Germany, and a successful businessman who furthered Spanish financial interests. David A. Messenger's chapter 26 details the wartime espionage activities of Germans in Spain – including the "werewolf" Nazi cells – while providing an account of the Gestapo presence and influence in the country. Messenger's chapter tracks these errant Nazis from their active involvement supporting the Nationalists during the Civil War through to their clandestine activities in the post-war period as they waited in vain for an international resurgence of pro-Hitler sentiment.

The Holocaust continues to inspire Spanish and Ladino poets, filmmakers, dramatists, and novelists in the contemporary period. The eighth section, The Holocaust in Contemporary Spanish and Ladino Culture, reviews the cultural and educational production in Spain and among Ladino poets interested in the Holocaust as a trope and as a catalytic, catastrophic historical moment. Our contributors unpack how the Holocaust continues to influence contemporary representations at a temporal and cognitive distance. Marilén Loyola's chapter 27 bridges the divide between the events of the Holocaust, the Second World War, and historical memory debates in contemporary Spain through a study of twenty-first-century Holocaust theatre. Loyola assesses plays by Juan Mayorga that link the persecution of Jews and the Holocaust to Spain as well as *El triángulo azul* by Laila Ripoll and Mariano Llorente, a piece that dramatizes the history of the photographic evidence of Nazi terror salvaged by Spanish prisoners and others working in the Mauthausen clandestine camp resistance. Loyola's interpretation of the latter thus links to chapter 28, Isabel Estrada's study of documentaries about Spain and the Second World War, including a film about Francesc Boix, who was largely responsible for the rescue of the condemning photographs. Counterposing Boix's heroism with Nazi villainy, Estrada also analyses a documentary about Paul Maria Hafner, a former SS who enjoyed fifty years of exile in Spain, a story that complements the chapters on Nazis by Goode and Messenger. Estrada contends that recent documentaries are responsible for sustaining a particular and problematic visual memory of the deportation and Holocaust in the Spanish imagination, with all its contingent historical pitfalls. Stacy N. Beckwith's chapter 29 considers prose fiction, looking at four successful historical novels by Spanish and Catalan authors that grapple, with varying degrees of nuance, with the persecution of Jews from medieval Spain to the Third Reich. Beckwith's analysis turns on how, for novelists and readers alike, the fictional and historical worlds in contemporary novels by Chufo Llorens, Antonio Muñoz Molina, Juana Salabert, and Clara Sánchez reckon with diverse Holocaust and Nazi camp memories, via the notion of "Sepharad" as a cultural and ethical void that continues to indict the modern Spanish nation. The treatment of the Sánchez novel, *Lo que esconde tu nombre* (*The Scent of Lemon Leaves*), dealing with the intrigues surrounding a sinister group of former SS living on the Spanish coast, places Beckwith's contribution in an interdisciplinary conversation about Spain as a haven for Nazis as discussed by Goode, Messenger, and Estrada.

Paul Cahill follows with chapter 30 on three contemporary Spanish poets who draw on the figure of Anne Frank (whose legacy is also addressed in Linhard's chapter) in order to reflect on questions of poetic composition, generational identity, and human suffering in verse primarily concerned with the process of writing itself. Examining the recent works of José García Nieto, Antonio López Luna, and Jorge

Urrutia, Cahill shows how the poetic repertoire positions Frank as a frequently employed, if overly simplified, emblem of Holocaust memory. Next, Shmuel Refael (chapter 31) provides a historical consideration of Ladino poetry composed in response to the Shoah. He then delves into the innovative work of C. Yacob Nahmias (himself a child of survivors), whose single collection of poems, published when he was nearly eighty, captures the nostalgia and incomplete memory of a second generation of Jews of Salonica. Refael reads Nahmias's imagery and use of the Ladino language through notions of forgetting and a conscientious recuperation of a nearly lost culture. In the section's concluding entry, Marta Simó (chapter 32) argues that whereas generations of Spanish school-age students benefit from increased classroom access to the history of the Holocaust, stereotypes about Jews and misconceptions about the Shoah continue to shape what and how Spaniards think about their country's place in the Second World War. Simó's chapter thus explores the possibilities and limitations for Spanish youth to engage on any meaningful level with the country's own history and its relevance to Holocaust Studies in an era marked by growing antisemitism and neo-Nazi activity in Spain.

Afterlives: Holocaust Appropriations in Spain brings the volume to a close by considering the memorial continuity of the Holocaust in Spain from a sociological perspective. Alejandro Baer and Natan Sznaider (chapter 33) understand the Holocaust as a paradigm of memory that has provided new generations of Spaniards concerned about the criminality and repression of Francoism with a vocabulary and historical filter through which to publicly articulate Spanish victim identities and traumas. *Memoria histórica*, the authors maintain, cannot be separated from the impact in Spain of a globalized Holocaust discourse.

NOTES

1 How, for example, have the arts helped enrich the history and memorial practices associated with wartime Spain? (See, for instance, Daisy Fancourt, "Spain's Musical Politics during World War II." [n.d.], http://holocaustmusic.ort.org/politics-and-propaganda/spains-musical-politics-during-world-war-ii). Our collection likewise would have benefited from a chapter about the Spanish anti-fascist exiles in the Soviet Union, where they received military training and fought with Russian troops (see Pike, *In the Service of Stalin*; and Arasa, *Los españoles de Stalin*). Still another subject we have not examined in detail here relates to Spain's economic accommodations with the Allies in return for oil and other commodities

and to what Christian Leitz describes as "the intense economic warfare" between Spain, Germany, and the Allies over Spanish wolfram. Spain's so-called neutrality did not extend to trade and economic questions: these are details of a larger history of Franco's late wartime disposition to adjust its stance in response to the Anglo-American embargo of 1944. See Leitz, *Economic Relations*; see also S. Payne, *Franco and Hitler*, regarding Spain's economic concessions during wartime.

2 The recent declassification of documents in Britain's National Archives attesting to Hitler's role in a planned German takeover of the Canary Islands in 1940, reported in *El País* in June 2017 ("Cuando Hitler se planteó conquistar Canarias"), the publication of photographs showing the presence of Nazis and fascist iconography in Barcelona during the Second World War (Vilanova Vila-Abadal and Capdevila Candell, *Nazis a Barcelona*), and Samuel O'Donoghue's study of how Spanish publisher Carlos Barral endeavoured to promote and disseminate knowledge of the Holocaust among Spanish readers of a variety of Spanish publishing ventures in the late 1950s ("Carlos Barral and the Struggle") are three examples of these ongoing investigations.

3 Earlier works that have shaped the issues under study here include Avni, *Spain, the Jews, and Franco*; Rother, *Franco y el Holocausto*; S. Payne, *Franco and Hitler*; Baer and Garzón, *España y el Holocausto*; Gómez López-Quiñones and Zepp, eds, *The Holocaust in Spanish Memory*; and Guttstadt et al., eds, *Bystanders, Rescuers or Perpetrators?*

4 Our spelling of "antisemitism" without a hyphen throughout this volume follows the practice of the Vidal Sassoon International Center for the Study of Antisemitism, as explained in Almog, "What's in a Hyphen?"

5 Bergen, *War and Genocide*, 107.

6 Viñas, "Natural Alliances," 144.

7 Ibid., 150.

8 Preston, "Franco and Hitler," 1.

9 Just three days earlier, Himmler had visited Madrid, where he likely discussed the details of a November 1937 accord regarding the creation of a kind of fascist Interpol whereby Francoist police and the Gestapo would exchange information and tactics. See Leitz, *Nazi Germany and Neutral Europe*, 114–42.

10 S. Payne, *Franco and Hitler*, 92.

11 Avni, *Spain, the Jews, and Franco*, 198–9; Rother, *Franco y el Holocausto*, 410.

12 Bermejo and Checa, *Libro memorial*. See also that book's accompanying online database, sponsored by Spain's Ministry of Culture (http://pares.mcu.es/Deportados/servlets/ServletController), which provides information on the origin, date of birth, Stalag or prisoner-of-war camp, transfer to Nazi camp, and date of death or liberation for the thousands of Spaniards deported to Nazi concentration camps.

13 See Iordache, *En el Gulag*.

14 Weinberg, "Two Separate Issues?," 379; Bergen, *War and Genocide*, 1–3.

15 Qtd in Avni, *Spain, the Jews, and Franco*, 71.

16 Ibid., 72, 215.

17 Marquina Barrio, "La España de Franco y los judíos," 192.

18 On these shifting policies see Avni, *Spain, the Jews, and Franco*, 133–41.

19 Calvet, *Las montañas de la libertad*, 131–5; Calvet, "Spain and Jewish Refugees," 113–22 in Guttstadt et. al., eds, *Bystanders, Rescuers, or Perpetrators?*, 114.

20 Avni, *Spain, the Jews, and Franco*, 3.

21 Baer and Israel Garzón, *España y el Holocausto*, 15.

22 Avni, *Spain, the Jews, and Franco*, 199.

23 See Reverte, "La lista de Franco para el Holocausto."

24 Leitz, "Spain and the Holocaust," 81.

25 Calvet, *Huyendo del Holocausto*, 57–67.

26 Rother, *Franco y el Holocausto*, 125–7.

27 Bauer, *American Jewry and the Holocaust*, 49, 207.

28 Qtd in Avni, *Spain, the Jews, and Franco*, 194.

29 Suñer Aguas, *De Calaceite a Mauthausen*, 249 (translation by Sara J. Brenneis).

30 Núñez Targa, *El valor de la memoria*, 174 (translation by Gina Herrmann).

31 Ibid.

32 Semprún, *L'écriture ou la vie*, 240; *Literature or Life*, 249.

33 Wisse, "The Individual from the Ashes," 31.

34 Ibid.

35 Reyes Mate, "From History and Memory – and Back," 15–30, trans. Elena Valdés Luxán, in López-Quiñones and Zepp, eds, *The Holocaust in Spanish Memory*, 30.

36 Huyssen, *Twilight Memories*, 256.

37 A. Baer, "The Voids of Sepharad," 114.

38 Amat-Piniella's novel has been translated into English by Finley and Marín-Dòmine.

39 Semprún, *The Long Voyage*, 63.

Prologue: Jews and Spaniards at Meeting Points of Their Histories during the Nazi Era

HAIM AVNI

The Nazi Era

It all began within the legal bounds of Weimar democracy, playing by the rules. On Monday, 30 January 1933, Adolf Hitler, founder and Führer of the National Socialist German Workers' Party, marched into the office of Field Marshal Paul von Hindenburg and accepted the post of chancellor of Germany. This was the third time he had been offered that position. Over the course of 1932, a tumultuous year that saw four electoral campaigns – two parliamentary and two presidential – the Nazi party had emerged as Germany's strongest political force. Earlier, a reluctant Hindenburg had offered Hitler the chancellorship, but with standard prime ministerial authority attached. This time, however, he yielded to Hitler's repeated demands for extraordinary, almost dictatorial powers, which were inscribed in the Weimar Constitution but reserved for times of emergency. The 30th of January 1933 was an ordinary day for most of Europe and the rest of the world, but in retrospect, it marked the beginning of an era: the Nazi era, with Adolf Hitler at its epicentre. The regime would last for twelve years and ninety-eight days, until 8 May 1945, the day of the Third Reich's surrender to the Allied armies.

Hitler's immediate political and military ambitions were clear for all to see: to void the punitive peace agreements imposed on Germany after the Great War; to regain all the lost territories populated by Germans that had been annexed by surrounding states, and to restore Germany to ascendancy among the powers of Europe. Somewhat less plain was his intention to extend German dominance far beyond the prewar borders, particularly in Eastern Europe. He was determined to achieve these goals by cunningly undermining Germany's international obligations under the Treaty of Versailles, tapping into the weariness and indecision of the Western governments. First, however, he would set out to dominate his own people, the Germans, by eliminating his political opponents – including the communists – and inspiring the masses with his anti-democratic rhetoric.

He seized upon racist antisemitism as the perfect tool for this purpose, and it became a pillar of the regime. His racist ideology gave all Germans, even the most humble, a sense of innate superiority, and invited them to persecute the now defenceless Jews. Hitler's rise to power was followed almost immediately by the systematic "legal" persecution of German Jews, who found themselves ejected from German academic, cultural, artistic, economic, and social life. Jewish physicians, lawyers, industrialists, and merchants lost their Aryan patients, clients, and customers and were forced to emigrate, leaving their property behind. Shunning and oppression of the Jews was based on a "scientific" doctrine: the "natural" inequality of human beings from birth and the existence of a biological hierarchy in which the Aryans were at the top, the "Semites" (and blacks) were at the bottom, and the other races – including Iberian Latinos – were in between. This racist theory was applied universally to all Jews and persons of Jewish descent throughout the world – including those who fell under German control after the invasion of the Soviet Union in June 1941 – as well as to the Slavic peoples of Eastern Europe. The policy of expelling the Jews from the Third Reich and the occupied countries in Western Europe evolved into a plan to methodically exterminate Jews wherever they could be found. This plan would remain in place until the very last days of the Nazi regime, with the gaunt survivors of the extermination camps forced to embark on "death marches" even while the Reich was collapsing and the Red Army advanced.

Nazi policies against the Jews gained Germany the sympathy of antisemites around the world. These people usually belonged to the most nationalistic and conservative elements in their societies and were viewed as the most zealous defenders of their countries; their admiration for Germany's treatment of its Jews transformed them into collaborators with Germany even before Hitler turned against their nations. This was evidently the case in Vichy France as well as in other countries defeated by the Nazis or allied with them.

The rise of the Nazis soon became a prominent factor in international relations. Yugoslavia and Czechoslovakia, two new federative states created by the League of Nations, which had formed the Little Entente together with Romania to defend themselves against their former oppressors, Austria and Hungary, now turned their attention towards Germany. Poland and Russia overcame their differences and signed a non-aggression treaty. France and the Soviet Union signed non-aggression and conciliation pacts. All of this took place shortly before Hitler became chancellor in 1933, evidence of the concern over the increasing power of Nazism in Germany. In the years that followed, however, Hitler managed to play some of these nations against one another, attract the sympathies of capitalists in the West with his vehement anti-communism, and secretly rebuild Germany's military might. The impact of Hitler's presence and politics was felt differently, and at different times, by each nation. It did not end their internal feuds or their struggles with economic and social problems. All would have to face the Nazi challenge and threat sooner or later.

Spain was one of the first nations to be affected by Hitler's Germany. In January 1933, the young Spanish Republic was still ruled by its first left-centre-liberal government, headed by Manuel Azaña. The elections to the Cortes in November of that year marked a turn towards the right-wing conservative-monarchical-Catholic camp. Another political crisis in 1935 strengthened this development and led to Spain's first contact with the Hitler regime regarding the purchase of arms. The Popular Front government that emerged from the February 1936 elections would represent just a short interlude before Germany's massive show of support for nationalist Spain in its uprising against the Republic. Indeed, Germany's Condor Legion, with its hundreds of warplanes and five thousand pilots and soldiers, would play a major role in the success of the forces commanded by Francisco Franco. For the Luftwaffe, the Nazi air force commanded by Hermann Goering, the Spanish Civil War served as an important training ground. On 26 April 1937, it deliberately bombed the civilian population of Guernica, the historic Basque capital. This air raid, which took place on a market day, lasted three hours and marked the first time that a civilian population in Europe was intentionally attacked by air; it left more than fifteen hundred dead and nearly nine hundred wounded.[1] The attack shocked the world's conscience, but reproaches from afar did not prevent the Nationalist victory proclaimed by Franco on 1 April 1939. The massive numbers of Italian and German troops soon departed Spanish soil, but Spain remained deeply indebted to Mussolini and Hitler and largely embraced their anti-democratic policies, which included repression of internal opposition.

The French debacle and surrender in the summer of 1940, along with the Blitz on London and the possibility of German victory over all of Europe, dramatically increased Spain's importance for the Nazis. With its control of Tangier and the southern coast of the western Mediterranean, Spain was in a position to close the sea to British navigation. Allowing the Wehrmacht to participate in conquering Gibraltar would have dealt the British one of the heaviest blows of the war. But Spain had been devastated by the civil war, and its people were starving. Britain and the United States were providing Spain with indispensable goods. All of this made Franco a very hesitant friend of Hitler and Mussolini. At the dramatic personal meeting between the Führer and the Caudillo at Hendaye on 23 October 1940 – their only meeting – Franco presented Hitler with a long list of material demands and an even more ambitious list of political conditions to which Germany would have to agree before Spain abandoned its declared neutrality. Franco fully believed that the Axis Powers would be victorious, but meanwhile, Spain's stance as a neutral (and later "non-belligerent") actor in the global conflict enabled him to stabilize his dominion over Spain and spare the Spaniards the consequences of any deviation from that position.

Hitler's Operation Barbarossa – the invasion of the Soviet Union – presented Spain with an opportunity to help destroy its arch-enemy, which it saw as the catalyst of the Spanish Civil War. By recruiting volunteers (all of them officially Falangists) for a Spanish Blue Division attached to the Wehrmacht in the east, Franco was able to avoid a declaration of war on the Soviet Union, now one of the Allies, and maintain Spain's non-belligerency.

During the last year and eight months of the Nazi era, as evidence mounted that Germany might be defeated in Russia, and with the breakaway of Italy from its alliance with Germany, Franco tried to distance Spain from Hitler. To survive after the war, it would have to curry favour with the victors. The Blue Division was dismantled at the end of 1943; half a year later, so was the Blue Legion, its much reduced successor. This period began with Franco restoring Spanish neutrality and retreating from "non-belligerency" and ended with his mythic transformation into the "saviour" of Sephardic Jewry.

Jews and Spaniards at Points of Convergence

During the twelve years and ninety-eight days of the Nazi era, Jewish and Spanish history intersected several times in important ways.

From their offices at the Spanish Embassy in Berlin and consulates throughout the Reich, Spanish diplomatic representatives had witnessed the systematic persecution and expulsion of the Jews from German society. In Geneva, the headquarters of the League of Nations, Jewish leaders of the Comité des Delegations Juives met the esteemed representatives of Spain, Luis de Zulueta and Salvador de Madariaga, and sought their help in rescuing the Jews of Upper Silesia from Nazi persecution. Meanwhile, German-Jewish refugees began to settle in Spain, significantly increasing the presence of Jews on Spanish soil. Under a different set of circumstances, Jewish communities in the Spanish protectorate in Morocco, with its predominantly Muslim population, provided a venue for yet another direct encounter between Spaniards and Jews. Opposition to the Olympic Games in Berlin in 1936 also brought Jews and Spaniards together.

The Spanish Civil War – the horrific clash between the two Spains – had a powerful impact on all of Europe as well as global implications. Many Jews joined the International Brigades, viewing their defence of the Republic as an opportunity to take up arms against Nazism and Fascism. When the war ended in defeat, Jews and Spaniards met on French soil in internment camps.

Another convergence of Jews and Spaniards related to the huge wave of Jews (and others) seeking transit visas through Spain on their way to Portugal and the New World. Here the Spaniards included the Franco regime's consuls, military personnel, and Seguridad officials (on consuls, see Lisbona, chapter 8; on Jewish refugees, see Calvet and Linhard, chapters 5 and 6.

From the summer of 1940 to mid-1941, Jews fleeing France without visas attempted to reach Portugal by crossing the Pyrenees on foot. Most of them were arrested, which led to another form of meeting between Jews and Spaniards. In the summer of 1942 and the following two years, up until the liberation of France, an additional wave of Jewish refugees reached Spain; this time they were seeking asylum, which broadened the range of interactions with Spaniards.

Efforts in 1942 to rescue some 4,000 Sephardic Jews in France, Greece, Romania, Bulgaria, and Hungary created a further occasion for Jewish–Spanish contact. Germany recognized these Jews as citizens or at least protégés of Spain and were willing to allow the Spanish government to take them in and thereby save their lives. The Spanish diplomats in these countries had met many of them in person, but for Franco and his government, the group was too large, and less than one quarter of them reached Spain safely.

During their march to the Eastern Front, tens of thousands of young Spaniards in Wehrmacht uniforms, members of the Blue Division, had encountered Jewish communities in eastern Poland and Byelorussia. Later, Spanish military hospitals were established in Vilnius and Riga, and thousands of Spaniards – medical personnel, convalescent soldiers, and others – found themselves in a close proximity to what remained of the ghettoized Jews in these cities (see Kovalev and Tejada López, chapters 23 and 24).

Mauthausen, the horrific labour and death camp in Austria, was another place where Spaniards and Jews encountered each other. Some seven to eight thousand Spanish Republicans were imprisoned in the camp in 1940 and 1941. Dutch and Czech Jews brought to the camp in 1941 and early 1942 were all killed before twelve thousand Jews were transferred there from Auschwitz in mid-1944. Tens of thousands of starving survivors from Auschwitz as well as from Hungary were deported to Mauthausen in 1945 prior to its surrender. Most of them were Jews, and very few survived. The intersection of these two tracks of history is immortalized at the site by two monuments, one Spanish and one Jewish, alongside several others (on monuments, see Calvo, chapter 11; on the legacies of Spaniards in Mauthausen, see Brenneis, chapter 14).

Jews and Spaniards found themselves at the confluence of Spanish and Jewish history at multiple points during the Nazi era, as this volume discusses in great detail. Three examples of these moments of convergence follow: the first explores the stance adopted by Jews and Spaniards against Nazi Germany's greatest feat of propaganda: the 1936 Olympic Games; the second looks at how Jews and Spaniards were thrown together by the vicissitudes of history in the same French concentration camps; and the third dwells on the encounter of Spaniards and Jews under Nazi rule.

The Nazi Olympic Games

The Berlin Olympic Games were born in Barcelona, yet Barcelona was at the forefront of the protest when they commenced in Berlin. In April 1931, the International Olympic Committee, comprised of delegates from all the national committees, met in Barcelona to decide where to hold the 11th Olympic Games. The candidates were Barcelona and Berlin. Because the vote took place just after the founding of the Spanish Republic, many of the committee members worried that the meeting would be marred by violence, so instead of appearing in person, they voted by post. When the votes were counted, Berlin had won.

In August 1932, at the 10th Olympic Games in Los Angeles, Berlin was officially declared the host of the 1936 Olympics. Less than six months later, the Nazis rose to power. Hitler was delighted with this inheritance from Weimar that had literally fallen in his lap, and the games were highlighted in Nazi propaganda plans as early as March 1933. When the democratic world realized that the Nazis had seized control of all state mechanisms and were brutally applying racial policies in every sphere of life, including sports, a loud clamour arose to move the

Olympics to a different venue. In 1933, such a move was still possible, but later the only option remained a boycott – that is, refusal to participate in the Nazi-organized event. The hundreds of athletes from all over the world who were in training for the Olympics would obviously be hurt by this, and political conservatives from various countries who were not averse to Nazi policies – a group prominently represented on the Olympic board – presented a solid front against it. Only one argument held the power to reverse the decision: that athletic achievement was the sole criterion for participation in the games, not race or political affiliation. Jewish organizations bent on stopping the games from opening in Berlin were well aware of this. For a variety of reasons, the United States became a leader in this battle.

The flag bearer for the struggle on the Jewish side was the American Jewish Congress (AJCongress), an umbrella organization dominated by Eastern European immigrants. Its campaign dovetailed with the anti-Nazi stance of Catholic organizations, which were motivated in part by the pagan character of Nazism and its tense relations with the Church, as well as with the views of many Protestant churches and the liberal press. On the eve of the World Olympic Committee meeting in Vienna in June 1933, the AJCongress asked America's three delegates "to take a firm stand against America's participation under the existing circumstances and conditions, 'inter alia' because it clashed with American ideals, standards of 'fair play' and traditional sponsorship of a 'sporting chance' for all."[2] In Vienna, however, the American delegates made do with hazy promises by the German delegates that all Olympic rules would be honoured and that German Jews would not be barred from competing on German teams. Upon their return to the United States, they declared the problem solved.

But the battle continued, and the AJCongress, together with other opponents of the Berlin Olympics, appealed to the Amateur Athletic Union (AAU), the organization in charge of authorizing the participation of amateur athletes in Olympic Games, when it met for its annual convention in November 1933. These same groups appealed to the members of the United States Olympic Association, which was convening at the same time. They tried to convince them to pass a resolution opposed to the attitude of the chairman, Avery Brundage, and his colleague General Charles Sherrill, who insisted on American participation. Sherrill even intimated that Jewish opposition was liable to increase antisemitism in the United States. Brundage, who had visited Germany in August 1933, was asked by the Olympic Association to go back and submit a new report on his findings. He did so, and his positive report led the association to accept the German invitation.

The next step was to appeal to the AAU, whose convention was scheduled for early December 1935. The Jews – the AJCongress, the Jewish War Veterans, and the Jewish Labor Committee – were not alone. The Catholic War Veterans, Catholic and Protestant periodicals, the Friends of Democracy, an organization of German Americans, and others all demanded that the AAU bar its members from going to Berlin. On 1 December, a week before the convention, the presidents of forty-one American universities from twenty-seven states called upon the Olympic Committee and the AAU to support an official boycott. The convention was asked to vote on a proposal declaring opposition to American participation in the Nazi Olympics. However, before the vote Avery Brundage announced that no matter what the outcome, the United States Olympic Committee would send a delegation to Berlin, even without the AAU's approval. In the end, the motion was defeated by only two votes.

Throughout this period, the Jewish organizations refrained from any contact or identification with Jewish socialist and communist circles in the United States and elsewhere. These groups were ideologically opposed to the Olympic Games as a symbol of competitive capitalism. In Spain, the Olympic Committee accepted the invitation to take part in the event, but the sports sections of the Spanish press do not reveal much evidence of preparations being made. Only in early February 1936, at the height of the country's game-changing election campaign – but with no definite connection – does an item appear about the government's decision to allocate 300,000 pesetas to support the Spanish Olympic team. Fierce left-wing opposition also surfaced at this time, as the Winter Games began.[3] A Spanish delegation to Berlin was not cancelled as a result of the electoral victory of the Popular Front, in the same way that the victory of a similar front in France headed by the Jewish statesman Leon Blum did not lead the French government to slash its Olympic funding. However, both administrations stood prepared to financially support an alternative sports competition in Barcelona in protest against the Nazi games, an initiative of the left-wing sports clubs in Catalonia.

The organizer was the Comité Catalán pro Deporte Popular in Barcelona, which invited six thousand athletes to take part, half of them from the provinces and cities of Spain and the rest from overseas, including fifteen hundred athletes from France. The French government provided generous funding for the event, and Spain, too, opened its coffers. One of the foreign clubs invited was the socialist Zionist sports club in Palestine, Hapoel. The invitation to Hapoel reached its headquarters in April 1936, while the country was in the throes of Arab attacks against the Jewish community and British Mandate authorities. Death notices were posted everywhere, Jewish refugees from around Jaffa filled schools and public institutions in Tel Aviv, and the Jewish population, only 384,000 strong, was struggling financially. The club needed 600 pounds sterling to send a delegation to Barcelona but could not come up with the money. On 6 June, however, the organizers notified Hapoel that it would receive a 400-pound subsidy, and preparations hastily began. A proclamation the athletes carried with them to the event, directed to the "Participants of the Anti-Nazi Olympic in Barcelona," traced the historic bonds between the Jewish people and Spain and declared: "We are happy for this privilege of renewing the relations between these two old and young peoples – the Hebrew people and the Spanish people."[4] The delegation consisted of twenty-four athletes and escorts, and their presence was not passed over in silence by the Spaniards who had suffered defeat in the February 1936 elections. "Olimpiada Judía Internacional" (The International Jewish Olympics), the right-wing press witheringly called the alternative games, citing the Jewishness of French premier Leon Blum and the participation of the Hapoel delegation.[5]

The games were scheduled to begin with a gala opening on Sunday, 19 July, at Montjuic Stadium, featuring a parade of the athletes and a gymnastics and folklore program. A chess match and a dance were planned for that evening. The closing was scheduled for 26 July. None of these events ever took place: On Friday and Saturday, 17 and 18 July, a military coup erupted in Spanish Morocco and other parts of the Republic. Barcelona turned into a battlefield, marking the onset of the civil war, which would rage for the next two years and eight and a half months.

Gurs and Other French Concentration Camps

Jews and Spaniards met on French soil as victims of French enmity. At the time, Jews in France were being victimized in the wake of the antisemitism that had been widespread in society since the nineteenth century, and that increased in the 1930s following the economic crisis, the influx of Jews from Eastern Europe, and the arrival of Jewish refugees from Germany. The Spaniards fell victim to the same animosity and overall suspicion of foreigners, with the right wing and Catholics targeting them for being "red," anti-religious, and burners of churches. The rise to power of Leon Blum's Popular Front, which supported (with reservations) the Spanish Republic, increased right-wing hatred of both Spaniards and Jews.

In January 1939, some 150,000 civilians – men, women, and children – crowded against the French border, along the Pyrenees. In February, they were joined by 250,000 soldiers. After some hesitation, the government of Edouard Daladier agreed to let them in but did not open shelters to house them. At the height of winter, they were sent to makeshift camps along the Mediterranean coast in St Cyprien, Argelés, and Rivesaltes near the district city of Perpignan. Those places became hellholes of suffering, and for quite a few, places of death. Some five thousand Spaniards, mainly women and children, were sent to Angoulême, in the Bordeaux region (on French camps, see the chapters by Dreyfus-Armand and Coale in this volume).

In March 1939, permanent camps were hastily erected at St Cyprien and Rivesaltes, which housed primarily women and children, as well as at Gurs. The builders were the refugees themselves, who were also the first detainees. In mid-June, after the work was complete, 162,932 people were interned at these locations. However, the policy of the French government was to encourage civilian refugees to return to Spain, and those whose suffering outweighed their fear of persecution in nationalist Spain began to head home. Others found low-paid jobs or joined the Compagnies de Travailleurs Étrangers, which employed them for public works for very paltry wages. Soldiers received coercive invitations to join the Foreign Legion. Immigration, especially to Latin America, was another option. The number of internees thus dropped quickly. By late July, only 95,336 Spaniards remained in detention, and by the end of the year, the number of Spanish refugees in all of France was 140,000, of whom 100,000 were ex-soldiers.[6]

When the Maginot Line collapsed, the French army retreated in panic, and France was divided into occupied and "free" zones – transformational events for France and the war. Tens of thousands of Spaniards flooded the roads or squatted in cities and towns without permits, living in fear of the Nazis and the Vichy authorities. Indeed, the French police arrested many of them and locked them up for short or long periods of time in various locations, including Gurs. Most of the 3,659 Spaniards interned at Gurs were released on some pretext, so that by the end of October 1940, only 1,570 remained.[7]

France's declaration of war on Nazi Germany on 3 September 1939 was a turning point for those who had fled Germany and found temporary refuge in France. All of them – persecuted opponents of the Nazi regime and Jews who had lost their German citizenship – were declared "enemy aliens," and the men were imprisoned in detention camps, some briefly and some for longer stints. The German invasion on 10 May aggravated their plight. All of the men and some of the women received an immediate summons and were taken into custody. Meanwhile, Jewish refugees who had found shelter in Belgium were arrested, packed into sealed freight trains, and deported to France. Their final stop was the St Cyprien detention camp, where they crossed paths with the Spaniards – a gloomy encounter indeed.

Rabbi Yehuda Ansbacher, who was on one of the trains and went on to play a central role in the life of the detainees, testified: "We saw the bones and skulls of the Spaniards who crossed the Pyrenees ... and were not welcomed by the French. They had been in the camp, and their remains were still there, near us." The presence of the dead Spaniards when the Jews first came to the camp was also noted by Dolly Steindling, a young Jewish refugee from Vienna who was on the train from Belgium. In his memoirs, he wrote: "When we arrived there was already a well-established cemetery." There were still a few thousand Spaniards living there, in rows of wooden barracks. The personal contact with Jews was random, but the harsh living conditions were the same for all: "The shacks were very primitive, the sand was everywhere and it was infested with millions of fleas," Rabbi Ansbacher recalled. Dolly Steindling wrote: "There were no beds and we had to sleep on the sand ... We were like sardines in a can, head to toe, but there was no other way." None of this deterred them from practising their religion: Rabbi Ansbacher served as the pillar of Jewish life in the camp. At the same time, Steindling and his colleagues, left-wing communist ideologues, served as paragons of cooperation and mutual aid in the most trying conditions. In this respect, they resembled the volunteers of the International Brigades and the groups of Spanish refugees detained with them at St Cyprien and later Gurs.[8]

Haim Ozerowitz-Raviv, who was eight years old when he and his mother were sent to the Rivesaltes camp for women and children, remembers his contact with Spanish children: "It was a very big camp," he recalled twenty-three years later, in 1963. "We were together with the Spaniards – Spanish exiles – and many Jews." At a certain point, he was transferred with his brother to "some children's camp not far away, where there were mainly Spanish children." During their six-week stay, they studied French and La Fontaine's fables together with the young Spaniards before returning to their mother at Rivsaltes. Soon after, he was sent to a Jewish school operated by Ouevre de Secours aux Enfants (OSE), a move that ultimately saved his life.[9] Aid organizations, both Jewish and non-Jewish, were active in the internment camps. In this regard, the Secours Swisse stood out, especially in Gurs, where the young representative, Elsbeth Kasser, received repeated and profuse thanks from camp residents.

The refugees from Germany who were declared enemy aliens were distributed among a number of camps, including Gurs. Hanna Schramm, a German Jew, was one of them. She was part of a group of forty women from different backgrounds but all sharing the label "enemy" and facing the same unknown fate. They arrived at Gurs on a hot evening in June. It was close to a year since the camp had opened and the barracks were in poor shape. They had been built in twelve blocks on both sides of a paved road 2 kilometres long; twenty-five to twenty-seven barracks per block with barbed wire between them. Sixty women and their children were crammed into each barrack, with sacks of straw for beds. The number of women continued to mount, reaching 9,283 on 23 June. After France surrendered, however, women with German and Austrian papers were no longer considered enemy aliens. An expedited release process also applied to those who could prove they had a guaranteed source of income and place to live. As a result, the proportion of Jewish women without citizenship steadily rose.

Among the Spanish detainees were 250 members of the "labour battalion," which was the most permanent feature of the camp. The labourers were in charge of all maintenance work and services. Unlike the others, they had passes that allowed them to move around freely. Each barrack had a small staff of these workers, who took care of routine services and repairs. In her memoirs, Hanna Schramm wrote about the great affection of the women in her barrack for Gustave, an International Brigade volunteer from Berlin, and Antonio, a Spaniard who had been an officer in the Spanish air force. As men and women were separated in the camp, the same was probably true for all the barracks and for all the Spaniards who came their way. This attraction led to close personal relationships with some of women detainees, and the fondness, lust, and love affairs would not be limited to Hanna Schramm's bunkmates. Administrative records for the camp show that thirty-nine babies were born there, nine of them from Spanish fathers and German, Polish, or Austrian mothers, who were probably Jewish.[10]

Meanwhile, the legal status of the Jews of "unoccupied" France took a sharp turn. On 3 October, the Statut des Juifs was published, which defined Jewishness as a race. The following day, 4 October, the district governors, the prefects, were authorized to lock up "foreigners of the Jewish race" in special camps or to deport them to designated residences in remote locations. In this way, the Jews were separated from the Spaniards and other foreigners. Indeed, the police began to stop people on the street if they had a foreign accent. The Statut des Juifs required Jews to complete questionnaires that made it easy to track down where they lived. For three years, from November 1940 onwards, 3,750 Jews were sent to Gurs using these methods.[11]

Two other incidents in October 1940 turned Gurs into an almost completely Jewish camp. On 23 October, the Vichy authorities were taken by surprise by the arrival of nine trains packed with Jews. These were the Jews of Baden and Saar-Platinat, whose Gauleiters had decided to make their districts "Judenrein." Suddenly, without prior warning, the Jews were ordered to leave their homes; each was permitted to take along one suitcase weighing no more than 50 kilograms. Adolf Eichmann was the organizer. At his trial in Jerusalem, he explained that in order to get around the clause in Marshal Pétain's surrender treaty prohibiting the Germans from deporting civilians into "free France" without the consent of his government, the transport was registered as sponsored by the Wehrmacht, which was not bound by this restriction. Beginning on the dark and rainy afternoon of 24 October, and continuing into the night, trucks pulled up at Gurs crammed with Jews, ranging from men over the age of eighty to women cradling babies in their arms. All were shaking with cold and fear as they underwent a laborious registration process. According to the camp index cards, 6,538 Jews were admitted at this time.[12] Before the German Jews had settled in, a ferocious storm in the vicinity of St Cyprien levelled the camp, and all the residents had to be evacuated. At the end of October, 3,870 men had been brought to Gurs. To make room for them, one thousand Spanish women and their children were moved to Rivesaltes. Jews made up the overwhelming majority of the newcomers. If there was any opportunity for them to meet the few Spanish inmates left in the camp, they would have encountered one of the three hundred Spaniards in the maintenance battalion who continued to work there.[13]

Most of the prisoners at Gurs and other camps, as well as the few who were permitted to move to designated residences, believed they would remain where they were until the end of the war. The Nazis, however had other plans. In the summer of 1942, the Final Solution reached France. On 18 July, Theodor Dannecker, Eichmann's representative, arrived in Gurs. Two days later, preparations began for the deportation of all the Jews to Drancy, and from there to the death camps in Eastern Europe. The first transport left Gurs on 6 August, followed by three more that month. Later transports emptied the camp of its Jewish residents, severing the link between living Jews and Spaniards.

In the camp cemetery, the link remained. A list of prisoners who died in the camp and were buried there from the day it opened reveals that the first five were Spaniards who died before the war broke out. Joseph Jung, born in Budapest, who died in June 1939, was apparently a combatant with the International Brigades. If he was Jewish, that would have made him the first Jew to be buried in this cemetery. Martha Karlebach-Mendel, a native of Frankfurt who died in June 1940, was certainly Jewish and probably one of the "enemy aliens" deported to Gurs after the defeat of the French army. Thereafter, Jewish and Spanish names alternate on the list. After the end of October 1940, Spanish names become increasingly rare and the names of Jews predominate.[14]

As the names intertwine on the list, the graveyard stands as a silent testament to the tragic encounter between Spaniards and Jews on French soil during the Nazi era.

Barbarossa, the Blue Division, and the Holocaust

When the German ambassador in Madrid informed the Spanish foreign minister, Ramón Serrano Suñer, about Operation Barbarossa, he was told that Spain was prepared to send units of volunteers to the Russian Front to fight against their common enemy. Hitler was pleased: he had hoped that Spain would officially join the war. Germany footed the entire bill for equipping and training the volunteers and paying their salaries and stipends to their families. Thus the Blue Division was born, named for the blue uniforms of the Falange, to which all the volunteers supposedly belonged. In practice, many of the soldiers in the first group of 18,000 volunteers were officers and commanders in the regular army.

By 23 July 1941, all of the division's soldiers had arrived at the Grafenwoehr training base in Bavaria and exchanged their Falange uniforms for the grey uniform of the German army. Small tags in the colours of the Spanish flag – red and gold – on their sleeves and helmets were the only clue that they were not German soldiers. Soon after, they stood in military formation and swore allegiance to the Führer of Germany – the commander-in-chief of the army in which they served. Basic training began immediately and lasted only a few weeks, as opposed to the standard three months, because the Spanish leadership and General Augustín Muños Grandes, commander of the division, feared that the battle would end before they reached the front, keeping them from realizing their glorious dream of taking part in a victory march through Moscow.

To their great surprise, the army high command decided there would be no transport to the battlefield: the division would march there on foot, a 1000 kilometre trek from the border of Eastern Prussia to Vitebsk, Byelorussia. The Spanish soldiers marched for forty-one days, from 29 August to 8 October, coinciding with the first stage of the mass murder of the Jews in Nazi-occupied Russia and the ghettoization of those who remained alive, although the Spaniards did not witness exterminations first-hand. This march through the valley of death of Polish, Lithuanian, and Byelorussian Jewry summoned up a powerful convergence of Jewish and Spanish history.

The Spanish volunteers' training in Germany had an ideological impact on them. Bolshevism was portrayed – as it was in Spain – as inspired and orchestrated by the Jews. This antisemitic motif merely reinforced the Satanic image of the Jews perpetuated in Catholic religion and culture. At the same time, it was quite likely that most of these soldiers had never met a flesh-and-blood Jew in their lives. A few of them wrote briefly about their encounters with Jews; still fewer published their writings upon their return to Spain or years later, as discussed by Macarena Tejada López later in this volume.

The first large Jewish community they reached was Grodno, a Polish city that had been occupied since 23 June. Some twenty-five thousand Jews were living there at the time, and it was a relatively calm period in the city's Holocaust history, just after a short spate of murders and "routine" decrees but before the brutal eviction of the Jews from their homes and deportation to two ghettos. The Jews stood out from the rest of the Polish and Russian population due to the white armbands emblazoned with a blue Star of David that they were forced to wear and the fact that they were forbidden to walk on the sidewalks. All Jewish males aged sixteen to sixty had to work for the Germans, and forty of them were sent to the camp of the Spanish soldiers as cleaners and maintenance workers. "Es la primera vez que he visto judíos ocupados en trabajos manuales" (It was the first time I had ever seen Jews doing manual labour), wrote one of the Spanish officers in his memoirs. "Ellos no estaban disgustados con los sentidos cristianos de nuestra gente, y por las mañanas se peleaban en la sinagoga para venir a 'servir a los españoles'" (They were not bothered by the Christian character of our men, and in the morning they fought in the synagogue over who would "serve the Spaniards").[15] He claimed that the Jews were happy to work at the Spanish camp because the Spaniards treated them well. Indeed, according to the sources at our disposal, many of the Blue Division soldiers violated the Wehrmacht's strict ban on socializing with the local populace, especially the Jews. Other memoirists echoed the hostile, antisemitic views of the Falange and the Franco administration. However, those recording the history of Jewish Grodno at the time were inclined to agree with the testimony of Spaniards like Jímenez Malo de Molina: "In total contrast to the Germans, the Spaniards showed compassion for the Jews during their short stay in Grodno," wrote a prominent Yad Vashem researcher.[16]

A handful of Blue Division soldiers knew Grodno a bit longer because they had arrived before the others, but all left on 4 September. Two days later, they camped at Lida, aghast at the horrific destruction of the city and its environs. On 8 September, they continued on to Vilnius. While the division as a whole did not enter the city, small, select groups did venture into what had been a vital hub of Eastern European Jewry. The commanding officers of the division, accompanied by a German liaison unit, reached Vilnius on Sunday, 7 September. It was the day after the Lithuanian police, on orders of the Nazis, had raided the homes of the Jews, who had been celebrating the Sabbath. They were dragged into two neighbouring ghettos meant to hold the forty thousand Jews who remained in the city. On that Sunday, clusters of sick and disabled Jews were still being carted into the ghettos. A handful of Spanish officers and soldiers were given a day off in Vilnius, and two of them recorded their impressions of the city. One wrote that he saw "a la pobre gente judía la veo circular con el estigma discriminador de una estrella" (the poor Jews walking around with a star as a tag of discrimination), and felt sorry for them.[17] The other, who spent a day in Vilnius on 12 September 1942, extolled the beauty of the city but did not say a word about the Jews. This was not so for Karl Jäger, commander of the German Security Police (SIPO) and Security Service (SD), who coordinated the genocide of the Jews of Lithuania. He kept a careful daily log of all the murders of Jews in the districts under his control. According to his report for 12 September 1941, "993 Jews, 1,670 Jewesses, 771 Jewish children, 3,334 (total)" were murdered on that day.[18]

From its camp in the Vilnius district, the Blue Division continued on its march towards Minsk. All along the way, the soldiers saw signs of the battle that had been fought along this route: burnt-out German and Russian tanks and endless crosses erected over the graves of the fallen. On 25 September, they reached Orsha, an important junction in eastern Byelorussia, and here they were in for a disappointment: the plan for them to join the German army group that was advancing towards Moscow had been called off, and the division had been reassigned to the army group besieging Leningrad. They were forced to retrace their steps and turn north, towards Vitebsk, which they reached in early October. Here, in the hometown of the famous Jewish painter Marc Chagall, the Spaniards in German uniform again touched base with the Holocaust history of the Jews of Russia. On the day the Blue Division was boarding the trains from Vitebsk for the front at Novgorod, the systematic murder began of sixteen thousand Jews who had been herded into a ghetto established on a bombed- and burned-out site that resembled a "wasteland of rubble and scorched iron." An eyewitness who survived described the scene: "For three days, they transported the Jews by truck to the banks of the Vitba river. Here they separated the babies and took them to another place. The adults were killed on the spot and dumped into the river."[19]

On 12 October 1941, the Spaniards were deployed along a 40 kilometre stretch at the centre of which lay the historic city of Novgorod. There were no Jews in this region, and the same was true for another part of the front where the division took up positions in the summer of 1942. Casualty figures from death, injury, or illness were extremely high, with the frigid Russian winters and harsh summers serving as a contributing factor. Militarily, the front was static. After the spring of 1942, reinforcements began to arrive from Spain. Over the next two years, until 12 October 1943, a total of forty-five thousand soldiers served in the Blue Division. To treat the large number of sick and wounded, Spanish hospitals had been established on the home front. After February 1942, Spanish hospitals operated in Vilnius and Riga, in addition to the hospital in Königsberg. Over time, thousands of soldiers were brought to the two hospitals within the German-administered Ostland Territory, ruled from Riga. In response to the heavy movement of soldiers between Ostland and Spain, a Spanish military police force was established – in full coordination, of course, with the German police. All these institutions operated in cities where thousands of Jews still lived, huddled in ghettos and utterly dependent for their lives on their usefulness to the Nazis as a source of manpower in factories and services. These circumstances created an opportunity for encounters of various kinds, direct and indirect, between Jews and Spaniards. Boris Kovalev expands in detail on these encounters in his chapter 23 of this volume.

In the second half of 1943, the paths of these two historical channels, Jewish and Spanish, diverged. On 21 June, Himmler ordered the immediate liquidation of all remaining ghettos and the murder of most of their inhabitants. The operation took place in stages, continuing through September and October. The Blue Division, which began to disband in October, had been completely dismantled by the end of the year. With the establishment of the twenty-three-hundred-man Legion of Spanish Volunteers, aka the Blue Legion, the official successor of the Blue Division, opportunities for the convergence of Jewish and Spanish history in the Soviet Union ended.

Jews and Spaniards in This Volume

It seems likely that when Spaniards and Jews met during the Nazi era, the fateful historic encounter between the two peoples on Spanish soil, which had ended in the expulsion of the Jews some 440 years earlier, lurked in the minds of many, if not most, on both sides. This traumatic memory remained etched in Jewish consciousness, leading to a tradition passed down from one generation to the next about an alleged ban declared on their ever returning to Spain. At the same time, many Spaniards continued to harbour a belief in the positive, purifying effect of the expulsion, and perhaps the gnawing suspicion that the "new Christians" and their descendants had toiled over the centuries to undermine the foundations of the Catholic faith. These negative thoughts had been compounded by the spread of modern antisemitic propaganda and incitement in Spain in the decades before the Nazi era. Add to this the efforts of official representatives of Nazi Germany to inculcate antisemitic race theory in Spain, which stoked religious hatred and the socio-economic myth that the media and the governments of the democracies were controlled by Jewish capital. These issues are discussed at length in the first chapters of this volume and arise throughout the rest.

In two of the three examples cited above – the anti-Nazi Olympics in Barcelona and the Jewish-Spanish encounter in French concentration camps – we are talking about the Republic of Spain. There is no question that from the moment the Republic was proclaimed in 1931, the vast majority of Jews pinned their hopes for historic normalization with Spain on this government, albeit sometimes for very different reasons. The Republic's unsuccessful war against the other Spain – the nationalist, Catholic Spain, backed by the Fascists and the Nazis – was seen as a stinging failure for the Jewish struggle against Hitler and Nazi Germany, which by January 1939 had been going on for six years. This volume devotes considerable space to the continuation of the Spanish Republicans' war on the Nazis within various French frameworks. A particularly large section is devoted to the harassment and persecution of those involved, as well as those singled out by Franco's Spain for special abuse. Particularly infamous in this context was Mauthausen, the concentration and torture camp near the city of Linz in Austria, which became a symbol of Republican suffering: of the many thousands of fighters against Franco and the Nazis sent there as part of the camp's early contingents of forced labourers, some survived to tell the tale.

Sovereign Spain in the second half of the Nazi era – that is, the six and a half years from January 1939 to 8–9 May 1945 – was Franco's Spain. The control of this regime over all parts of Spain, including Spanish Morocco and Tangier, its ideological and political kinship with the Axis powers Germany and Italy, its importance in the eyes of Germany, and its debt to Germany and Italy for helping it win the civil war, placed Spain in a special position in terms of potential for saving Jews. Indeed, many chapters of *Spain, the Second World War, and the Holocaust* explore these rescue possibilities from two sides of the coin: on the one hand, Spain provided – or denied – refuge to those who crossed the Pyrenees on foot from Nazi-occupied territory; and on the other, it allowed into the country some of those Jews whose lives Nazi Germany was willing to spare. The policy regarding illegal crossing of the border along the Pyrenees was the same for everyone – refugees from countries around the world, members of the anti-Nazi underground, Allied soldiers who had escaped German captivity, pilots whose planes had been shot down, and more. Jews accounted for only a moderate portion of these numbers. The Germans and the diplomatic representatives of the Allies both had critical interests at stake, and both stepped up their pressure on Spain accordingly at one time or another.

Spain's ability to rescue Jews by evacuating them from their home countries and bringing them to Spain was limited. It could only save those whom Germany had chosen not to kill – four thousand Jews at most – and who held Spanish papers attesting to their legal ties to Spain. The Germans refrained from killing them, fearing that Spain might give in to Allied pressure and start calling for their release after they had already been murdered. They therefore proposed repatriation to Spain. Several chapters of the volume address these issues as well as the tendentious propaganda of the post-war regime, which tried to pass itself off as "Quijote contra Hitler" (Don Quixote confronting Hitler) when in fact it had brought to Spain only about one quarter of the Jews the Germans were prepared to hand over.

Other chapters in this collection explore how the above issues are reflected in Spanish literature, theatre, film, and education. In the final analysis, what the general public and younger generations are taught about the Holocaust and the struggle against Nazism, and how this content is transmitted, is of utmost importance to all researchers and students of the dark period in modern history that was the Nazi era.

NOTES

1 Paul Preston cites 1,645 dead and 889 wounded in *Franco: Caudillo de España*, 276–7.
2 Gottlieb, "The American Controversy," 184–5, quoting the stenographic minutes of the Emergency Session in Washington, DC, on 20–2 May.
3 "La situación política," *La Libertad* (Madrid), 7 February 1936, 3; "Deportes," *Heraldo de Madrid*, 1 February 1936, 7.
4 Lavon – Labor Party Archive, Mercaz Hapoel, IV 208-1-767, meetings of 17 June, 27 June, and 11 July 1936; *Davar* (Worker's Union daily), 11 July 1936, 3.

5 *La Veu de Catalunya,* quoted in Colomé and Suerda, *Deporte y relaciones internacionales,* 14: https://ddd.uab.cat/pub/worpap/1995/hdl_2072_4865/WP020_spa.pdf.

6 Rubio, "Francia, La acogida," 92–104; idem, "Población española en Francia," 43–9.

7 Laharie, *Le camp de Gurs,* 138–43.

8 Rabbi Yehuda Ansbacher, interview with Haim Avni, 25 April 1960, 1–3, The Hebrew University of Jerusalem, Institute of Contemporary Jewry, OHD (1)1; Steindling, *Hitting Back,* 44–8.

9 Haim Ozerowitz-Raviv, interview with Haim Avni, 25 April 1963, OHD (In process of registration), 1–4.

10 Schramm, Vormeier, and Petit, *Vivre á Gurs,* 12–22, 28–33; Laharie, *Le camp de Gurs,* 26–34, 126 table 4; 180–1.

11 Ibid., 175–80.

12 Schramm, Vormeier, and Petit, *Vivre á Gurs,* 76–8.

13 Laharie, *Le camp de Gurs,* 167–8; 139 table 7.

14 Laharie lists 1,070 names: *Le camp de Gurs,* 371–9. The total number of those who died at Gurs was 1,037, of whom 820 or 79.1 per cent were German Jews, deported from Baden and Saar-Platinat. Ibid., 195.

15 Jímenez and Molina, *De España a Rusia,* 45.

16 Fatal-Kna'ani, "Grodno," 108.

17 Castañon, *Diario de una aventura,* 26–7.

18 Photocopy of the document, Levin, ed., and Pinkas Hakehillot, *Encyclopaedia of Jewish Communities,* vol. 8, 95. The actual total should be 3,434; the mistake is in the document.

19 P. Friedman, "Hashmadat Yehudei Vitebsk," 447, 451.

PART ONE

Legacies of Antisemitism in Spain

1 Hero and Monster: The Place of Jews in Spain's National Identity

MARTINA L. WEISZ AND RAANAN REIN

Ever since the Spanish Empire, the paradigm of "the Jew" has played a key role in the construction of Spanishness.[1] Imperial Spain saw itself as the legitimate heir of Judaism as God's chosen people. Religious fervour and persecution of heresy were expressions of this belief, and the "cleansing" of any Jewish presence from Hispanic lands was considered part of such a mission. After the expulsion of the Jews in 1492, the struggle to achieve "racial-spiritual" purity was waged through the Estatutos de Limpieza de Sangre (purity-of-blood statutes) and was a central element in consolidating Spanish nationalism.[2]

Yet at the same time, in a move both antagonistic and complementary, Jews and their descendants converted to Christianity have often evoked respect and admiration among local elites, to the point that "almost all aristocratic houses have kinship ties with former Jews."[3] Significantly, this inherently positive aspect of "the Jew" endows its otherness with a distinctive character when compared to the other two emblematic "others" of the Spaniard: the Muslim (incorrectly called "Moor") and the indigenous peoples of Latin America.[4]

We argue in this chapter that Jews had been placed at the very centre of Iberian Christian identity long before a Spanish national identity took shape. Located in the realm of myth, their ambiguous and caricature-like features have been discussed and assigned new meanings at various historical crossroads of the country. Being both hero and monster, the mythological Hebrew/Jew is often stripped of his more prosaic human features. Thus, to a certain extent, the actual, flesh-and-blood men and women who belong to the Jewish people continue to be, in Spain, invisible beings, doomed to inhabit the dark and desolate centre of an imaginary labyrinth.[5]

The Loss of an Empire and the Illusion of a Sephardic Hero

In the early nineteenth century, a series of independence wars in the Spanish colonies in the Americas led to dismemberment of the empire, which had been conquered "por la gracia de Dios" (by the grace of God). This process, which came to an end with Spain's defeat in the "Guerra de Cuba" (Cuban War) of 1898 (during which it lost Cuba, Puerto Rico, and the Philippines to the United States), plunged the country into a deep identity and cultural crisis.[6] Predictably, this suddenly imposed search for a collective identity brought on, in important intellectual circles, a revision of the place of Jews in the imperial project.

During the first half of the nineteenth century, Spain's Jewish past was a prominent issue in the internecine struggles between liberals and traditionalists. Liberal intellectuals like Adolfo de Castro y Rossi used the expulsion of the Jews as part of their core argument in denouncing the national decline brought about, in their view, by the historical collusion of the Church with the monarchy.[7] Meanwhile, the traditionalists had no qualms about asserting a close association between Francophile liberals and the hated Jews in order to consolidate the latter's demonization.[8]

By the end of the century, as Spain ceased to be a world power, liberal rethinking of the Jews' place in Spanish history would influence a growing number of intellectuals and even translate into practical terms: if their expulsion and persecution had contributed to national decline, then re-establishing ties with these "judíos de patria española" (Jews of a Spanish homeland) could help save the country from decline.[9] Thus in 1881, King Alfonso XII and his government made the momentous decision to offer asylum to Jews persecuted in Russia and the Balkans. Thirty years later (on 20 December 1924, to be precise), a Royal Decree signed by his successor Alfonso XIII during the rule of dictator Miguel Primo de Rivera would enable some Sephardim to become Spanish citizens.[10]

In the context of nineteenth-century political struggles, philosemitism had become a cultural code of liberalism.[11] At the same time, the establishment of the Spanish protectorate in Morocco in 1912 strengthened a right-wing philosephardic current that would put its stamp on the "Jewish question" in Spain. By philosephardism we are referring to the rhetoric of rehabilitating the Jewish presence in Medieval Spain and including Sephardic Jews as an integral part of the Spanish nation. This rhetoric often had an instrumental quality, in that different individuals and groups used Spain's Jewish past in order to advance various interests or justify certain policies, from colonial expansion in North Africa, through the promotion of commerce, to challenging Catholic hegemony in Spain. In this case, however, as during the "Guerra de África" (African War) of 1859–60, Jewish communities were seen as an important ally of the Spaniards in their struggle to hold on to their domains in Morocco. As an oppressed minority, they saw colonial penetration as a chance for liberation, and from the outset they contributed to the war effort of their ancestral homeland.

At a rational, ideological level, the defenders of the colonial undertaking in North Africa – known as the Africanistas – appealed to the myth of medieval coexistence on the Iberian Peninsula among the three monotheistic religions (Islam, Judaism, and Christianity) to justify their geopolitical aims. Spanish control over North Africa, they argued, would lead to a revival of this idyllic period. Additionally, in these efforts to justify the imposition of a common destiny, Africanista discourse held both Muslims and Moroccan Jews to be "hermanos de sangre" (blood brothers) of the Spaniard.[12] However, unlike with the Muslims, all of the descendants of the Jews expelled centuries earlier – both those living in the protectorate and those in the Balkans and the Middle East – were placed at the core of several large-scale projects aimed at restoring Spain's power beyond African horizons.

The clearest example of the complexities involved in including Sephardic Jews in the plans for a revival of imperial Spain is, probably, the case of Spanish fascist Ernesto Giménez Caballero. As had happened with the first great promoter of philosephardism, Dr Ángel Pulido, it was meeting in person the descendants of those who had been expelled that sparked Giménez Caballero's interest in the subject. In his case this happened in Morocco, where he arrived in 1921 as a conscripted soldier.

In this colonial context the Jews were the Spaniards' strategic allies, and as King Alfonso XIII put it to the representatives of the Jewish Hispano associations of Spanish Morocco, they were expected to promote "la obra de colonización y el enriquecimiento económico de la Zona" (the task of colonization and economic enrichment of the Zone).[13] Based on the work of Ángel Pulido and Américo Castro, Giménez Caballero transformed the Africanistas' interest and empathy regarding Sephardic Jews into a key element of their Spanish national and imperial rehabilitation project, defined as *Hispanismo* or *Hispanidad*.[14] Having emerged as a result of the "Desastre de 1898" (Disaster of 1898), and within the framework of the so-called regenerationist projects, these concepts sought to define a type of imperialism based not on controlling territory but rather on a shared language and culture.

Notwithstanding the spin the regenerationist intellectuals tried to put on it in the twentieth century, Spanish imperialism maintained important lines of continuity with the imperialist project launched four centuries earlier. As in the past, there was an attempt to spiritually legitimize the undertaking.[15] Until 1931, the year he completed his turn towards antisemitism, Giménez Caballero would strive to "prove" the alleged affinity between the Spanish people and the people who, according to the Bible, had been God's original chosen. Faithful to those Hispanic traditions that associate the spiritual with the "racial," he held that Spaniards must recognize certain positive aspects of Sephardic Jews, such as the "aristocracia de raza" (aristocracy of race), as a precondition for national regeneration. In his political project, the Jews were to play a crucial role in recovering for Spain its status as the "Israel Ibérico" (Iberian Israel), endowed with a divine mandate for imperial expansion.[16]

Sephardic Jews, whom Giménez Caballero considered "the most select part of the race," embodied all of the attributes that would be required to return to Spain its former splendour.[17] Located at the centre of the quest to decode his own identity, they returned to the Spaniard what he perceived as the best image of himself. Consciously or not, Giménez Caballero would allude to the classical labyrinth symbol in his short film *Judíos de la Patria Española* (Jews of the Spanish homeland, 1929):

> Giménez Caballero, filming himself, appears on the roof of the Madrid headquarters of the *Gaceta Literaria*. He slowly zooms in and the camera remains focused on his facial features for several seconds ... More than merely an act of reflexivity, it may be that the acute focus on his facial features, meant to frame the images of Sephardim in the film, represents a statement of his theories on racial mixing, one that engaged contemporary notions of Spanish racial hybridity ... and which suggests linkages between his own origins and Spain's Jewish past.[18]

The Civil War and the Second World War: The Prevalence of the Monster

The philosephardism of Giménez Caballero, which peaked during the second decade of the twentieth century, was not devoid of sporadic references that were clearly antisemitic in tone. When the Second Republic was established in April 1931, these initially marginal references became dominant. From then on, he made repeated use of the extensive rhetorical and ideological heritage of modern antisemitism to justify the struggle against a democracy that he believed to be debased by "el oro que presta el judío" (gold lent by the Jew).[19]

Far from being an isolated instance, the case of Giménez Caballero helps understand the historical processes that led, during the first two decades of the twentieth century, to a positive reassessment of the Sephardic legacy and to a strengthening of the ties with the descendants of those who had been expelled; but also to the reversal of this trend when the civil war broke out and Franco established a dictatorship.[20]

Indeed, although during the Second Republic prominent right-wing philosephardists like Giménez Caballero and Agustín de Foxá turned to antisemitism, the dominant trend during those years within the government was a continuation of the monarchy's philosephardic rhetoric. The Constitution of 1931 guaranteed freedom of religion, and a new law was drafted – for which regulations were never issued – granting citizenship to "personas de origen español que residan en el extranjero" (persons of Spanish origin residing abroad).[21] Also, even at a time of dire economic straits, the Republican government admitted between 1934 and 1936 about two thousand German Jews fleeing Nazism.[22]

After the Civil War broke out in 1936, imperial and national regeneration projects gradually lost their relevance. For both sides in the conflict, the priority became the fight against the monster-enemy. For the rebels this often took on the features of a caricature-like, evil Jew. Relying on the long tradition of conservative antisemitism, "enriched" by the modern form of antisemitism that had achieved a solid position early in the century in the rest of Europe, important Nationalist leaders such as Generals Queipo de Llano and Miguel Cabanellas and the intellectual Pío Baroja associated the Republican side with the evil mythological Jew (to whom, depending on circumstances, would be added Freemasons and "demás ralea" [other lowlifes]). This was a means to legitimize the insurrection and boost the morale of the rebel troops.[23]

General Francisco Franco, however, was careful not to make public statements that were clearly antisemitic, partly because of the criticism that antisemitic propaganda aroused abroad. However, the cohesive power of traditional Spanish anti-Judaism was too strong to abandon in the context of a war. On 31 December 1939, the Caudillo sent a "mensaje a la nación" (message to the nation) in which the role of the Jew as monster-enemy was openly declared:

> Ahora comprenderéis los motivos que han llevado a distintas naciones a combatir y alejar de sus actividades a aquellas razas en que la codicia y el interés es el estigma que les caracteriza, ya que su predominio en la sociedad es causa de perturbación y peligro para el logro de su destino histórico. Nosotros, que por la gracia de Dios y la clara visión de los Reyes Católicos, hace siglos que nos liberamos de tan pesada carga, no podemos

permanecer indiferentes ante esta nueva floración de espíritus codiciosos y egoístas tan apegados a los bienes terrenos que con más gusto sacrificarían sus hijos que sus turbios intereses.

Now you can understand the reasons that have led different nations to fight against and banish from their activities those races for which greed and financial gain are their characteristic stigma, since their predominance in society brings about disturbances and endangers the achievement of their historical destiny. We, who by the grace of God and the clear vision of the Catholic Monarchs, rid ourselves of this heavy burden centuries ago, cannot remain indifferent to this new blooming of greedy and selfish spirits, so attached to earthly goods that they would rather sacrifice their children than their shady interests.[24]

In Franco, secular Spanish antisemitism merged with the relatively recent Africanista philosephardism. The latter emerged with particular vigour shortly after the Second World War started, when the German invasion of France and the establishment in that country of the collaborationist Vichy regime was viewed by the Francoist regime as an opportunity for imperial expansion in North Africa at the expense of its weakened neighbour to the north.[25]

Clearly, Franco and his fellow Africanistas were aware of how contradictory their attitude was towards Jews. To fix the mess they resorted to distinguishing between Sephardim and Ashkenazis, attributing positive qualities to the former and only negative ones to the latter.[26] A particularly instructive example in this regard is *Raza* (Race), a film script published in 1942 and probably written by Franco between 1940 and 1941, in which he seeks to juxtapose his personal history with the national one.[27] Significantly, the dictator chose that vehicle for an explicit reference to the Hebrews, in order to present the heterodox theological argument that the Jews of Toledo "no sólo se negaron, sino que protestaron" (not only refused, but protested) against the murder of Jesus. Taking his argument even further, supposedly on the basis of the *Libros de sapientísimos varones* (Books of Very Wise Men), he also says that it was these same Sephardim who requested the patron saint of Spain, Santiago Matamoros, to come to the Iberian lands for the sacred purpose of preaching the Gospel. The reason for this exceptionality was, according to Franco, that these Jews had been "purified" by their contact with Spain – an argument already often made in philosephardic circles.[28] In this way the Generalísimo would, in a certain manner, renew and update the historical Hebrew/Jew antinomy by replacing it with the Sephardic/Ashkenazi antinomy. In labyrinthine terms, the

Sephardim would have – from his point of view – heroic qualities, while the monstrous predominated among the Ashkenazi.

During his almost forty years in power, Franco used this duality in a pragmatic and selective manner, one more proof of the gap between public discourse and social realities. As soon as it was established, his regime returned Jews and other non-Catholics to the legal condition that had been their lot before the Constitution of 1869 was enacted, thereby forbidding them from worshipping publicly *or* privately. Thus, even while philosephardic policies were being promoted in North Africa, Jewish cemeteries and synagogues were being shut on the peninsula in order to return to the Catholic Church the powers the Republic had taken from it. From then on and until the democratic transition took place, Jews living in Spain would be considered "tolerados" (tolerated).[29]

During the Holocaust, the Franco regime only reluctantly accepted the German proposal that Sephardic Jews be repatriated to Spain (the alternative being to let the Nazis exterminate them). Extremely demanding bureaucratic requirements were set, so that in the end, out of the tens of thousands of Sephardic Jews that Spain could have saved, it took in no more than eight hundred. Also, the regime allowed new groups of Jewish refugees to enter Spain only after those preceding them had exited, in order to preserve the "purity" of the national territory. Obviously, this meant that fewer Jews were able to escape the Nazis via Spain.[30] In the words of Spain's foreign minister, Francisco Gómez Jordana, in late 1943: "The possibility of bringing them [the Jews] in groups of about 100 people each was considered, and when one group had left Spain, passing through the country as light passes through glass, without leaving traces, a second group would be brought in and then moved on to enable others to come. This being the system, obviously we will under no circumstances allow these Jews to remain in Spain."[31] An official circular dated 5 May 1941 ordered the creation of a Jewish Archive with a list of all Jewish residents in the country (nationals and foreigners), along with their political affiliation, profession, and "nivel de peligrosidad" (level of dangerousness).[32] However, despite the regime's close political and ideological ties to the Axis forces, consolidated by the important contribution of Nazi Germany and Fascist Italy to the Nationalist victory during the Civil War, racial laws were never enacted in Spain. This is probably due to the regime's desire to maintain at least the appearance of official neutrality. Nevertheless, it is estimated that some thirty thousand Jews managed to escape Nazism by passing through Spain between 1940 and 1942 (See chapters 5, 6, and 20 for further discussion regarding the number of Jews who crossed into Spain during the Second World War). If one adds to this the hundreds of Jews saved on the brave personal initiative of some of the regime's diplomats, one may conclude that despite all, Spain was the saviour of many European Jews. (On the complexity of the view of Franco as "saviour" of European Jews, see Correa in this volume.)[33]

Fascist Defeat and the Need to Adapt to a New Era

After the Allied victory, anti-Jewish clichés became politically incorrect, and Franco's regime somewhat adapted to this international environment. The ban on non-Catholic worship slowly crumbled. In 1945 the Fuero de los españoles (one of the eight basic laws of Franco's regime) again allowed non-Catholics to worship in private, which meant that synagogues could reopen in Barcelona and Madrid.

This timid opening towards religious diversity prepared the ground for the arrival, during the second half of the 1950s, of a wave of Jews from the recently decolonized territories of French and Spanish Morocco, who feared the recently installed Muslim governments. Something similar happened a decade later, with the exodus of North African Jews triggered by the Six-Day War.[34]

However, in an early expression of the type of antisemitism that has become more widespread in the twenty-first century, deeply rooted antisemitic prejudices would resurface within the framework of a conflict of interests with the recently established State of Israel. In 1946 the UN General Assembly adopted, at the behest of the Mexican delegate, a condemnatory resolution against the Franco regime based on the fact that it had been established with the support of the Axis powers.[35] Immediately after the State of Israel was established, in 1948, the Spanish government mobilized influential Jews in Israel and in the diaspora, friends of the regime, to promote the establishment of formal diplomatic relations with the young state with the goal of improving its sagging international image. With memories still alive of Franco's sympathy for Nazism, and of the many Palestinian Jews who had joined the Republican side during the Civil War, Israel declined the offer – indeed, its UN delegation voted in 1949 and 1950 against lifting the sanctions against Spain.[36]

The media close to the regime responded to this affront with rabid antisemitism. At the same time, the Franco government combined barely veiled support for these anti-Jewish diatribes with a strong propaganda effort intended to exaggerate its efforts to save Jews during the Second World War. According to Álvarez Chillida, it is during those years that Franco "publica los textos más antijudíos de su vida" (publishes the most anti-Jewish texts of his life).[37] In these articles, published under the pseudonym Jakim Boor in the Falangist newspaper *Arriba*, Franco combined clichés typical of medieval antisemitism, such as the blood libel, with others stemming from the *Protocols of the Elders of Zion* in order to accuse Jews and Freemasons of complicity in a dark, worldwide conspiracy. However, even during this period of enthusiastic antisemitism, the dictator kept to the duality inherent in the Jew/Hebrew antinomy: "Pero judaísmo no quiere decir pueblo hebreo, sino esa minoría judía conspiradora que utiliza a la masonería como uno de sus instrumentos" (But Judaism does not mean Hebrew, but rather that conniving Jewish minority that uses Freemasonry as one of its instruments).[38] Álvarez Chillida, Javier Domínguez Arribas, and Mercedes Peñalba-Sotorrío explore aspects of Francoist antisemitic propaganda in chapters 2, 18, and 21 of this volume.

This ambiguous and even contradictory attitude would enable Franco to shift towards a progressive rapprochement with Jewish communities inside and outside Spain as part of an alternative strategy for legitimating his regime, without establishing full diplomatic relations with the State of Israel.[39] From the 1960s onward, this attitude marked a new era for a local Jewish community now succeeding, after a centuries-long absence, in re-creating itself on Spanish soil. On the eve of Rosh Hashanah in 1968, for the first time since 1350, a new synagogue was publicly and formally inaugurated on Spanish territory.[40]

The Return to Europe and the Incomplete Humanization of the Jew

The death of Francisco Franco in 1975, and the end of his dictatorial regime, eliminated what had been the greatest obstacle to admitting Spain into the nascent European institutions. However, it would take more than ten years after the democratic transition started for – finally – the much wished-for admission of Spain into the European Economic Community (EEC) to take place.

Spain's official "return" as a full member of the European concert of nations was received with great joy in the country, and not only because of the juicy profits it would bring. Indeed, admission to the EEC in 1986, and joining NATO that same year, solved to some extent the profound identity crisis into which the country had plunged since losing its colonial possessions in America. According to Fusi and Palafox,

> la importancia de ambas decisiones –Europa, OTAN– estaba en que España se definía, al fin, como un país occidental y europeo y en que, al hacerlo, recobraba el papel internacional que mejor parecía adecuarse con

> su historia, con su posición geográfica, con su significación cultural. [...]
> Con la entrada en Europa y en la OTAN, España resolvía un problèma –su
> papel en el mundo– pendiente desde que perdió su Imperio ultramarino,
> primero entre 1808 y 1826, y luego en 1898.

> the importance of both decisions – Europe, NATO – was that Spain finally
> defined itself as a Western and European country, and by doing so recov-
> ered the international role that seemed to best fit its history, its geograph-
> ical position and its cultural significance ... By joining Europe and NATO,
> Spain solved a problem – its role in the world – pending since it lost its
> overseas empire, first between 1808 and 1826, and then in 1898.[41]

Establishing full diplomatic relations between Spain and Israel was a
direct consequence of these events. This took place on 17 January 1986,
a few days after Spain joined the EEC. The lack of formal relations between the two countries was considered a serious anomaly by a Europe
that was still trying to assimilate the harsh lessons of the Holocaust.
The European Parliament had been exerting pressure since 1978 for
the "normalization" of ties between the then-aspiring member of the
European reconstruction and the Jewish State.[42] The Spanish rapprochement with the young state founded in 1948 was widely perceived as a
precondition for ensuring the country's credibility in Europe.

This important milestone contributed greatly to the normalization of "the Jew" in Spain. This process was further invigorated when
the democratic constitution of 1978 came into effect, affirming the
non-denominational nature of the Spanish state, and it became entrenched
during the 1990s. During that decade, a number of institutions flourished that significantly expanded the range of activities of local Jewish
life. Within a few years there emerged in Madrid the cultural and social
organization Hebraica (1993), the sports and cultural society Maccabi
(1995), and the Conservative synagogue Bet-El (1995). In Barcelona in
1992, the Reform congregation Comunitat Jueva Atid de Cataluny, the
cultural and social society Maccabi, and the social and cultural organization Asociación Hebraica de Catalunya all opened their doors.[43]

These communal institutions emerged in the context of the Fifth
Centennial of the "discovery of America," in 1992. The celebrations
held within this framework helped deepen the new appreciation for
religious pluralism that had begun in the aftermath of the Franco era;
they also marked a point of inflection in the reconciliation of the Spanish
people with their Jewish past. The most important symbolic gesture,
in this sense, was probably the visit paid by the King and Queen of
Spain to the Madrid synagogue on 31 March, exactly five hundred

years after the Catholic monarchs signed the Edict of Expulsion. To this unprecedented gesture were added cooperation agreements between the Spanish government and the Federation of Jewish Communities of Spain, and the launching of Sefarad '92, a special program aimed at "redescubrir la España judía" (rediscovering Jewish Spain). The magnitude of these events and of others with the same aims has led David Grebler, leader of the Jewish community and president of the Comisión Nacional Judía Sefarad '92, to proclaim the "completa normalización del elemento judío en la sociedad hispana" (complete normalization of the Jewish element in Spanish society).[44] This statement may be overly optimistic, but it must be noted that the celebrations of the "discovery" were followed by a gradual expansion of "Jewish" topics on offer on the local culture scene.[45] At the same time, there has been a growing interest in Spain in literature on Spanish Judaism.[46]

Early in the twenty-first century, the Spanish government took on a particularly active role in amplifying Jewish voices and memories. In October 2004 the Council of Ministers established the Fundación Pluralismo y Convivencia, dedicated to "promover la libertad religiosa a través de la cooperación con las confesiones minoritarias, especialmente aquellas con reconocimiento de Notorio arraigo en el Estado español" (promoting religious freedom through cooperation with minority religious denominations, especially those recognized as having clear and well-known roots in the Spanish state). It would "ser un espacio de investigación, debate y puesta en marcha de las políticas públicas en materia de libertad religiosa y de conciencia; todo ello orientado a la normalización del hecho religioso y a la creación de un adecuado marco de convivencia" (be a space for research, discussion and implementation of public policies in the field of freedom of religion and conscience; all of this aimed at normalizing religious practices and at creating an adequate framework for coexistence).[47] For the first time, the Spanish state was funding social and cultural projects organized by representative institutions of minority religious denominations. Two other important acts were, in 2005, the designating of 27 January (the anniversary of the liberation of the Auschwitz-Birkenau extermination camp) as the Day of Remembrance of the Holocaust and for the Prevention of Crimes against Humanity, and the opening in December 2006 of the Sefarad-Israel Centre.

By the year 2000, all of this had fostered a growing determination among the local Jewish community regarding their relations with society in general, and also with the Spanish government. But despite the interest these types of activities have stimulated among the general public, the media have shown "[un] desinterés absoluto por lo que ocurre en la comunidad judía de Madrid o en las comunidades judías españolas" (an absolute lack of interest in what happens in the Jewish community of Madrid, or in Jewish communities in Spain).[48] According to Uriel Macías, there are at least two possible reasons for this. One is simply "ignorancia, pereza mental, quizá no entender ciertas cosas" (ignorance, mental laziness, perhaps not understanding certain things). The other, spoken a bit sadly, is that after "tantos años de invisibilidad voluntaria, al final se olvidaron de que existimos" (many years of voluntary invisibility, they finally forgot we exist).[49]

This last argument casts some light on what is probably one of the more prominent traits among contemporary Spanish Jewry. It is a relatively small community, well integrated into society, whose members have achieved considerable success in the social, economic, and cultural fields. Nevertheless, it has been invisible, and to some extent it remains so.

The Return of the Hero? Economic Crisis and the Granting of Citizenship to Sephardic Jews

On 24 June 2015 the Spanish government enacted a law granting Spanish citizenship to some of the descendants of Jews expelled from Spain. This was not an unprecedented action: besides the decree of 1924 signed by Primo de Rivera, there was a subsection in the Ley de Extranjería (Aliens Act) of 1985 that reduced to two years the minimum requirement for residence in the country for Sephardim requesting citizenship.[50] However, it was an important symbolic gesture, the practical consequences of which are as yet uncertain.

The text of the act recognizes that Jews suffered iniquities on Spanish territory and seeks not only a "reunion" with them but also a more committed "reconciliation":

> Se antoja justo que semejante reconocimiento se nutra de los oportunos recursos jurídicos para facilitar la condición de españoles a quienes se resistieron, celosa y prodigiosamente, a dejar de serlo a pesar de las persecuciones y padecimientos que inicuamente sufrieron sus antepasados hasta su expulsión en 1492 de Castilla y Aragón y, poco tiempo después, en 1498, del reino de Navarra. La España de hoy, con la presente Ley, quiere dar un paso firme para lograr el reencuentro de la definitiva reconciliación con las comunidades sefardíes.

> It seems fair that such recognition should lean on the appropriate legal remedies in order to ease the way to becoming Spaniards for those who resisted, zealously and prodigiously, to cease being so – in spite of the

persecutions and sufferings wickedly visited on their ancestors until their expulsion in 1492 from Castille and Aragon and, shortly afterwards, in 1498, from the Kingdom of Navarre. The Spain of today, through this Act, wishes to take a firm step towards accomplishing its reunion and final reconciliation with Sephardic communities.[51]

This brief reference to the desire for reconciliation with Sephardic Jews is a novelty in the Spanish official lexicon, since, significantly, the historic visit of the King of Spain to the Madrid synagogue on 31 March 1992 was described by Spaniards as a "reunion," while Israeli officials insisted on referring to it as a "reconciliation." Obviously, unlike all the other rapprochement gestures made by the Spanish state since the transition to democracy, under this new law the state has assumed full responsibility for a series of historic injustices inflicted on Jews on Spanish soil, and a means of adequate reparation is being sought.[52]

There are, however, important similarities between the political context in which this legislation arose, and that which fostered the rise of philosephardism about a century ago. Although less drastically than during the "Disaster of 1898," Spain had since 2008 sunk into a deep economic and political crisis from which it hasn't fully recovered to this day. And even though the current political context does not allow speaking openly of the Jews as a possible lifeline when the status of Spain as an international power is being questioned, the symmetries between the two situations are plain to see.

In contemporary Spain, Sephardim are no longer seen as potential promoters of trade expansion in the Balkans or as strategic collaborators for colonial penetration into North Africa. However, both in the daily press and in government circles they are often perceived as having great influence on the government of the United States, in the world of finance, and in the mass media.[53] In fact, then–Minister of Justice and Foreign Affairs, Alberto Ruiz-Gallardón, who was a strong promoter of the citizenship act, made a special trip to the United States to present the project to the local Jewish community. It is noteworthy that the popular newspaper *El País* headlined the news of the trip: "El Gobierno vende en EEUU su gesto hacia los sefaradíes" (Government Sells in the US Its Gesture Towards Sephardim).[54]

At the same time, however, and in keeping with the long-established tradition that combines philosephardism with antisemitism, this important reparation is being made in the context of a sustained dissemination of antisemitic prejudices among the population in general.[55] As with the yin and yang of the Orient, the two seem to complement perfectly and thereby contribute to perpetuating an original myth.

NOTES

1 Fine, "El entrecruzamiento de lo hebreo."
2 Kaplan, "Jews and Judaism." The purity of blood statutes were in force from 1449 to 1860.
3 Qtd in Yovel, *The Other Within*, 63.
4 Rein and Weisz, "Ghosts of the Past."
5 Kerényi, *En el laberinto*; Santarcángeli, *El libro de los laberintos*.
6 Balfour, *The End of the Spanish Empire*; Shaw, *The Generation of 1898 in Spain*; Harrison and Hoyle, eds., *Spain's 1898 Crisis*.
7 Junco, *Mater dolorosa*, 402. See also Shinan, *Victims or Culprits*.
8 Álvarez Chillida, *El antisemitismo en España*, 112.
9 González, *El retorno de los judíos*, 96; idem, "El antisemitismo moderno llega a España: el Affaire Dreyfus," in Álvarez Chillida y Izquierdo Benito, eds., *El antisemitismo en España*, 165–80.
10 Rein, "Past Images, Cultural Codes."
11 On antisemitism as a cultural code in German history, see Volkov, *Germans, Jews, and Antisemites*, ch. 5.
12 Rohr, "'Spaniards of the Jewish Type,'" 62–4. See also Rohr in chapter 4 of this volume.
13 Qtd in ibid., 68.
14 Schammah Gesser, "La imagen de Sefarad y los judíos españoles."
15 Friedman, "Reconquering 'Sepharad,'" 44.
16 Schammah Gesser, "La imagen de Sefarad y los judíos españoles," 79–81.
17 Friedman, "Reconquering 'Sepharad,'" 44.
18 Ibid., 53.
19 Álvarez Chillida, *El antisemitismo en España*, 345–7 at 346.
20 In the early twentieth century, various institutions were established in order to strengthen Spain's ties to "its Jews," such as La Unión Hispano-Hebrea, established in 1910 under the sponsorship of King Alfonso XIII; the Hebrew Language and Literature Chair at Universidad Central de Madrid (1915); and the Casa Universal de los Sefaradíes in Madrid (1920). See Rein, *In the Shadow of the Holocaust*, 52–3.
21 Álvarez Chillida, "La eclosión del antisemitismo español," in Álvarez Chillida and Izquierdo Benito, eds, *El antisemitismo en España*, 182–3.
22 Jean-François Berdah, "España y los judíos en la primera mitad del siglo XX," in Joan i Tous and Nottebaum, eds., *El olivo y la espada*, 369.
23 Ibid., 370–2; Lisbona, *Retorno a Sefarad*, 63–4. See also Boris Kovalev's discussion of cartoonish images of Jews in the trench newsletter of the Blue Division, chapter 23 in this volume.
24 Quoted in Berdah, "España y los judíos," 371.

25 See S. Payne, *Franco and Hitler*.

26 Rohr, "'Spaniards of the Jewish Type,'" 72.

27 Vernon, "Re-Viewing the Spanish Civil War"; Higginbotham, *Spanish Film under Franco*, ch. 3.

28 Andrée Bachoud, "Franco y los judíos: filosefaradismo y antisemitismo," in Joan i Tous and Nottebaum, eds., *El olivo y la espada*, 383–5; Rohr, "'Spaniards of the Jewish Type,'" 66, 72.

29 Rein, "Una minoría tolerada"; Avni, "Los judíos en la España contemporánea," 149; Bachoud, "Franco y los judíos," 383.

30 On Spain and the saving of Jews during the Second World War, see Rother, *Franco y el Holocausto*; Avni, *Spain, the Jews, and Franco*; and chapters by Correa, Calvet, Lisbona, Linhard, Israel Garzón, and Fragkou in this volume.

31 Quoted in Rein, *In the Shadow of the Holocaust*, 42.

32 Rozenberg, *L'espagne contemporaine et la question juive*, 149.

33 For the initiatives of several Spanish diplomats to save Jews during the war, see Lisbona, *Más allá del deber*; and Lisbona's chapter 8 in this volume.

34 Rein and Weisz, "Ghosts of the Past," 109.

35 Lleonart Ansélem, "El ingreso de España en la ONU," 103–4.

36 Rein, *In the Shadow of the Holocaust*, 32–7.

37 Ibid., 38–44; and Álvarez Chillida, *El antisemitismo en España*, 425.

38 Cited in Bachoud, "Franco y los judíos," 389.

39 Setton and Rein, "La diplomacia franquista y los judíos."

40 Rein, *In the Shadow of the Holocaust*, 202–5.

41 Fusi and Palafox, *España: 1808–1996*, 392.

42 Setton, *Spanish–Israeli Relations*; Lisbona, "Presiones internas y externas," 128.

43 Rozenberg, *L'Espagne contemporaine et la question juive*, 217–18.

44 Lisbona, *Retorno a Sefarad*, 13, 349–70.

45 Rozenberg, *L'Espagne contemporaine et la question juive*, 273.

46 Flesler, Linhard, and Pérez Melgosa, "Introduction."

47 See the official site of the Fundación: http://www.pluralismoyconvivencia.es/quienes_somos/ (accessed 14 May 2014).

48 Interview with Uriel Macías, former Secretary-General of the Jewish community of Madrid (Madrid, 28 October 2010).

49 Ibid.

50 *Boletín Oficial del Estado* (BOE) 158/1985, 20824–20829.

51 BOE 151/2015, 52557.

52 Lisbona, *Retorno a Sefarad*, 362.

53 Ibid., 345, 351; Lassalle, "Paloma antisionista," 7; Parada, "Terrorismo contra Terrorismo"; Navarro-Valls, "Tribuna Libre," 4–5.

54 Gutiérrez Calvo and González, "El Gobierno vende en EE UU su gesto hacia los sefardíes," elpais.com (13 March 2014). http://politica.elpais.com/politica/2014/03/15/actualidad/1394895807_715302.html (accessed 28 July 2016).
55 According to a study conducted by the Pew Research Center in 2014, 18 per cent of Spaniards had an unfavourable opinion of Jews. See http://www.pewglobal.org/2014/05/12/chapter-4-views-of-roma-muslims-jews/ (accessed July 29 2016).

2 Antisemitism and Philosephardism in Spain, 1880–1945

GONZALO ÁLVAREZ CHILLIDA

Traditional Anti-Judaism, Liberal Revolution, and Antisemitism

In the popular culture of the diverse peoples of Spain, an exceedingly negative view of the "Jew" or of "the Jews" (always in generic terms) as exploiters, usurers, weasels, vengeance-seekers, hypocrites, deceivers, and traitors and as hostile to Christians ever since "they" killed Jesus has lingered well into the twentieth century. To a lesser degree, this view has endured until today, although this traditional prejudice has been eroded significantly in recent generations. It is an image analogous to the negative view of those disparagingly called "Moors," given that both Jews and "Moors" have comprised the "other" par excellence to the Christian "we" since as far back as the Middle Ages. Since the expulsions of the era of the Catholic Monarchs (Isabel and Fernando), a new ethnic identity has emerged from the "old Christian" we. At the time, this identity was referred to as traditional or pure-blooded (*castiza*), and it was held against the castes of the "new Christians," which is to say the descendants of Jews and Muslims. Despite having been baptized as Christians, the "Moorish" people were violently expelled from Spain at the beginning of the seventeenth century; meanwhile, the so-called *conversos* (converts; descendants of Jews) continued to be discriminated against by the statutes of purity of blood, surveilled and persecuted by the Inquisition, and scorned by their neighbours, who branded them as "Jews." After the liberal revolution, city-dwellers managed to erase their genealogical stigmas, even incorporating themselves into the former "old Christian" majority, with the important exception of the *chuetas* of Palma de Mallorca. Yet in many towns and villages the identity of the *converso* families, and the social discrimination and contempt they faced from their neighbours, lasted until the late twentieth century. In popular culture, anti-Jewish sayings alluded to these new Christian neighbours, sometimes explicitly (e.g., "Puerco en casa judía, hipocresía" [Pork in a Jewish home, hypocrisy]).[1]

Following the precedent set by a number of distinguished thinkers of the Enlightenment who fought the discrimination against the new Christians, the liberal revolution of the nineteenth century eliminated the twin pillars of *casticismo*: the Inquisition, and the purity-of-blood laws. During the reign of Isabel II a few small groups of Jews had settled on the peninsula, and the Glorious Revolution of 1868 established freedom of religion. During the Canovist Restoration, this tolerance was limited to the private worship of those of non-Catholic faith. Yet even under that regime, Jewish communities and their respective synagogues were founded in Seville in 1913, Madrid in 1917, and Barcelona in 1918. With the Second Republic in 1931, full freedom of religion was re-established.[2]

The fight against absolutism and inquisitorial "obscurantism" led quite a few liberal intellectuals to sympathize with the historically persecuted Jews and *conversos*. They began to rewrite the history of the Jews in Medieval Spain, integrating them into the Spanish national identity that these same liberals were endeavouring to construct. They highlighted Jewish and *converso* scholars and writers as wonders of Spanish national culture. Anti-liberal Catholic intellectuals and historians had justified the cruel measures against the people responsible for "deicide" with the customary arsenal of accusations and anti-Jewish legends from traditional literature (hatred towards Christians, treachery, usury, sacrilegious profanations, ritual infanticide, etc.). Confronted with such a viewpoint, progressive liberals presented Jews and *conversos* as innocent victims of the much-despised inquisitorial and absolutist intolerance, which had also battled against and persecuted liberals in the nineteenth century. A good example of this progressivism can be found in the *Historia de los judíos en España* (History of the Jews in Spain, 1847) by Cadiz native Adolfo de Castro (nonetheless, Castro later tended towards fundamentalist and anti-Jewish Catholicism). From their location between these two tendencies, the liberal-conservatives reclaimed the Medieval Jewish past as a part of Spanish national history. They rejected the cruel excesses of the fourteenth and fifteenth centuries, especially the pogroms, such as those of 1391, even while sharing many traditional anti-Jewish prejudices (including the accusation of deicide). They also tended to justify, albeit with some qualifiers, the decisions of the Catholic Monarchs. This was the tack taken by *Estudios históricos, políticos y literarios sobre los judíos de España* (Historical, Political, and Literary Studies on the Jews of Spain, 1848) by José Amador de los Ríos. Years later, the same author would expand this work (in a version less saturated with traditional Spanish prejudices) into three volumes: the *Historia social, política y religiosa de los judíos de España y Portugal* (Social, Political, and Religious History of the Jews of Spain and Portugal, 1875–6).[3]

When the modern antisemitic movement was organized in Europe in the last decades of the nineteenth century, its propaganda began to arrive in Spain, often through Barcelona, especially from the France of Drumont and the Dreyfus Affair. But this propaganda remained largely circumscribed to sectors of anti-liberal Catholicism, especially to those traditionalists and fundamentalists who were apologists for the era of the Inquisition. During those years, Pope Leo XIII launched an anti-Masonic crusade. Many of his supporters (in Spain and other countries) linked the Freemasons to the Jews through the myth of a global conspiracy to destroy Christian civilization and enslave its peoples though the hidden control of revolutionary movements, capitalist hegemony, and international politics. The attribution of Freemasonry to the development of a revolutionary Satanic conspiracy to destroy the altar and the throne emerged from the same thinking prevalent during the French Revolution. *Mémoires por servir à l'histoire du jacobinisme* (1797), by the abbé Augustin Barruel, was read widely by counter-revolutionaries across the continent, including in Spain, where the translation saw five reprints during the years of the war against Napoleon. Then, at the end of the nineteenth century, the myth of the Freemason conspiracy was reintroduced, the allegation being that the Jews were acting as the secret leaders of the order. Unscrupulous Catholic priests and propagandists dedicated themselves to spreading these new ideas throughout Spain (they even translated Drumont's *Jewish France*). They also applied these ideas to Spain, whose liberal revolution was viewed as the outcome of the sinister dealings of the sect and its patrons: the Jews, eternal enemies of the country until the Catholic Monarchs liberated it.[4]

Philosephardism

Yet liberal Judeofilia continued. Towards the end of the nineteenth century, at a time when European antisemitism was beginning to take hold, sympathies towards the Sephardim – the communities of descendants of those expelled from Spain in 1492 – began to develop. This current spread throughout the Mediterranean basin and into some Central European countries, especially among the Krausists of the Institución Libre de Enseñanza (Free Institute of Education). Above all, though, it was the trauma of the "Disaster of 98," with its consequent regenerationist fever, that allowed Doctor Ángel Pulido, liberal senator and old friend of the moderate Republican Emilio Castelar, a well-known Judeophile, to launch a successful campaign to spread the new philosephardism. Pulido and his many followers presented "españoles sin patria" (Spaniards without a homeland) as a topic that affected "intereses nacionales." He began his campaign with two books that bore precisely these titles: *Intereses nacionales. Los israelitas españoles y el idioma castellano* (National Interests: Spanish Hebrews and the Castilian language, 1904) and *Intereses de España. Españoles sin Patria y la Raza Sefardí* (Spanish Interests: Spaniards without a Homeland and the Sephardic Race, 1905). Philosephardism looked to renew Spain's global influence and impact through a reconciliation with the Hispano-American republics (an objective of the thriving Hispano-Americanist movement) and with the aforementioned Sephardic communities in North Africa, the Middle East, and the Balkans. This would entail cultural policies to strengthen their ties to the "Motherland." It also sought an economic policy that would greatly expand commercial trade with the vast Latin American republics. The nationalist map of the territories of the Spanish-speaking world, which various generations of Spaniards studied in Francoist textbooks, extended to the Philippines as well as to various locales marked by the Sephardic diaspora. If secular traditionalists and modern antisemites had imagined a sinister Jew, the Spanish Philosephardis, for their part, imagined a Spanish-speaking Sephardi, lover of his old homeland, preserver of Spanish culture and customs, and desirous of meeting the "España-Sefarad" again now that it had decided to open her arms to him. The rhetoric of this cliched image has remained to the present day, though even at the time of its appearance it was quite distant from reality.[5]

The philosephardic movement enjoyed support across almost the entire political spectrum, except among Catholic traditionalist and antisemitic minority circles, which obviously fought against it. It also enjoyed official support from the Restoration Regime (1874–1931), although in practice its political initiatives were largely limited to sentimental gestures of love for those "españoles sin patria." In 1924, dictator Primo de Rivera's government passed a decree that, in line with philosephardic thought, limited itself to offering full Spanish nationality to the few thousand Sephardim of the old Ottoman Empire who had enjoyed Spanish protégé status, which was no longer recognized in the new states that had followed that empire. The application of the decree imposed many obstacles, which explains why a large number of the hypothetical beneficiaries continued to obtain their passports in Spanish consulates without having been granted formal access to full nationality. The importance of this decree is discussed further in chapters by Correa, Calvet, Fragkou, and Lisbona in this volume dealing with Spanish involvement in – or neglect of – the rescue of European Jewry, Ashkenazi and Sephardic alike, during the Second World War.

Yet one must not forget that if Pulido was focused at the time on the Sephardim he had met while travelling through the Balkans, the communities from northern Morocco gained great notoriety when, beginning in 1909, Spain began to stake its claim there. Spain established a protectorate in Morocco in 1912, at a time of hard fighting against the Riffian people, who were leading an armed rebellion against the new colonialists (see Rohr on North Africa in this volume). In the bloody and costly Moroccan War, which lasted until 1927, the country's Jews, most of them Sephardim, strongly supported the Spaniards. They could communicate well with the invaders in Spanish, and this earned them sympathy, especially among the Africanist soldiers who governed the protectorate and did the fighting on the ground. One of those soldiers was General Franco.

Spain's residual antisemitism and active philosephardism, reinforced by the Moroccan War, explains why the famously spurious *Protocolos de los Sabios de Sión* (Protocols of the Elders of Zion), which spread throughout the continent immediately after the First World War, would not be published in Spain until the Second Republic was proclaimed. But everything thereafter would change dramatically.

The Second Republic

With the founding of the new democratic regime on 14 April 1931, the Liberal-Conservative right collapsed. The anti-Liberal Catholic right increasingly fought against the Republic. This group was comprised of the old traditionalists and fundamentalists, monarchists who had abandoned the cause of constitutionalism and were loyal to the ex-king Alfonso XIII, and the powerful Christian social movement united around Popular Action and the Spanish Confederation of Autonomous Rights (CEDA). CEDA defended a legal and electoral path to power, but it aimed to establish an authoritative and corporative regime, inspired by the Catholic dictatorships of António de Oliveira Salazar in Portugal and Engelbert Dollfuss in Austria. Its Catholic anti-Republicanism began to spread antisemitic ideas, even though there were almost no Jews in Spain. Those ideas would have made little sense had there not been a popular, abstract image of the Jew. By 1931, anti-liberal Catholicism, which had been antisemitic since Drumont's time, had spread to the point that it had become the dominant view among Spain's conservative classes. Before Primo de Rivera's dictatorship, those classes had accepted the liberal constitutionalism of the Restoration. The trauma of the dictator's fall in January 1930, and the much greater anguish caused by the fall of the monarch in April of the following year, does much to explain this drift towards authoritarianism (more or less radical according to the different stated political tendencies). Furthermore, the myth of a worldwide Jewish or Judeo-Masonic conspiracy perfectly encapsulated the cause of the catastrophe as experienced by the right with the coming of the Republic. It predicted that Spain was heading straight for communist revolution and the founding of a Satanic regime that would enslave the Christian people under the rule of the Jews, just as had happened in Russia. This myth also forged the disparate (indeed, opposing) forces of the 14 April revolution – from the Republican right to the socialists, communists, and anarchists – into a common enemy, since all of them were mere puppets of the Judeo-Masonic shadow forces that – just like the Bolsheviks in Russia in 1917 – would impose communist tyranny on Spain.[6]

From this perspective, the importance of the *Protocols of the Elders of Zion* is clear. That spurious document had by then been translated, published, and republished numerous times. Between 1932 and the beginning of the Civil War, it underwent twelve editions, half of them in the *Editorial Fax* version, thanks to Pablo Montesinos Espartero, Duke of la Victoria. That version, republished periodically even today, is seen as canonical in Spain. Among the publishing houses that released the *Protocols*, the prestigious M. Aguilar Press stands out.

Yet curiously, antisemitism proved much less significant among followers of Spain's rather small fascist party. Spanish fascism took hold under the umbrella of the Falange Española (Spanish Falange, FE), founded in October 1933 by José Antonio Primo de Rivera, son of the deceased dictator. The FE united the following February with Ramiro Ledesma Ramos and Onésimo Redondo's Juntas de Ofensiva Nacional-Sindicalista (Councils of the National Syndicalist Offensive; JONS), becoming the FE de las JONS. Redondo was a Catholic militant and a fervent antisemite. In his newspaper *Libertad* (Freedom), out of Valladolid, he published excerpts of the *Protocols* in 1932, then compiled them as a booklet two years later. However, the main leaders, Primo de Rivera and Ledesma Ramos, were not particularly interested in this cause. The governing bodies of Primo de Rivera's party applauded the National Socialism in power in Germany, including its antisemitism, but his principal model was Benito Mussolini's Italian Fascism, which at that point had not shown itself to be racist or antisemitic. Nonetheless, FE de las JONS was against Spain taking in German refugees of Jewish origin who were fleeing their country. With regard to Spanish policy, both leaders must have thought that antisemitism was a cause particular to reactionary Catholicism, which they aspired to overcome through devotion to the nation (Ledesma was even an atheist, not so Primo de Rivera). Only in 1935 did the party launch direct action against the new, discount SEPU (Sociedad Española de Precios Únicos) department stores, which had been opened by two German-Jewish refugees on Madrid's Gran Vía. They invaded these stores, destroyed their display windows, and discharged firearms on one occasion. The party leaders must have intuited that SEPU stores, with their low prices, created an opportunity to mobilize small merchants, who would have felt threatened by the new competition. The Falangist press stirred up the campaign, accusing SEPU of harming honourable Spanish merchants by selling stolen clothing.[7]

The Republicans in power expressed sympathy for the Sephardim, although once again with sentimental declarations and good intentions rather than with deeds. Article 23 of the constitution promised a law that would facilitate "la adquisición de la nacionalidad a las personas de origen español que residan en el extranjero" (the acquisition of citizenship to persons of Spanish origin who live abroad) – a promise that directly affected the Sephardim. But that law was never drawn up. In the League of Nations, Spain condemned the antisemitic persecution launched in 1933 by Nazi Germany, but in practice it refused to open its doors to refugees (except for announcing that it had offered Albert Einstein a professorship at the University of Madrid). In the end, only three thousand Jews in flight from the Nazis were able to enter the country during the Republican period. Ironically, in 1935 Spain's right-wing government solemnly celebrated in Córdoba the eighth centenary of the birth of Maimonides.[8]

Antisemitic Propaganda after the Civil War

When the Spanish Civil War broke out, monarchists, traditionalists, Catholics, and Falangists supported the soldiers who had risen up against the Popular Front government. After only a few weeks, Catholics took up arms, mobilized mainly in militias of traditionalist *requetés*. They instilled a religious fervour among the rebel soldiers, and the war came to be defined as a new crusade. The Falange embraced Catholicism as well, albeit without abandoning its totalitarian Fascist program. This variety of fascism came wrapped in antisemitism, which became a leitmotiv of rebel propaganda during the war and also of the Francoist regime during the Second World War. Here one must not forget that Franco won the war thanks to the military assistance that Hitler and Mussolini contributed from the beginning. Also, during the Second World War Franco aligned with the two leaders and offered help in a multitude of ways, though Spain remained officially non-belligerent. This stance was declared on the eve of the entrance of the Germans into Paris, on 13 June 1940, although it turned into a formal neutrality in the autumn of 1943, when Italy was already out of the battle and the Germans began their retreat in the east. Franco decided not to enter the war directly in 1940 when Hitler refused to allow Spain to annex French Morocco, which was what Franco most wanted (although he occupied Tangier the day after declaring non-belligerency).

Antisemitic propaganda from the anti-liberal right during the Republican period and the early years of Francoism had its roots, above all, in Catholic antisemitism, especially French antisemitism as expressed by figures like Monsignor Jouin and León de Poncins. The press also received antisemitic news and propaganda from Nazi Germany, which carried out a sweeping plan to influence the Spanish press. Even before the Civil War, under the Republic, the Germans had financed a few publications, the most important being Madrid's newspaper *Informaciones* (Information), directed by the Catholic journalist Juan Pujol. Pujol assembled a staff of ultra-right-wing collaborators who stood out for their virulent antisemitism. These men included César González Ruano, Alfredo Marqueríe, Vicente Gay, Luis Astrana Marín, Ernesto Giménez Caballero, Federico de Urrutia, and Francisco Ferrari Billoch. In those years, the propagandistic writings of the Catalan priest Juan Tusquets, including his collection of books titled *Las sectas* (The Sects), which during the Civil War became *Ediciones anti-sectarias* (Anti-sectarian Presses), also proved influential.[9]

The antisemitism of the era presented Spanish history largely as one long battle against Jewish enemies. That battle is what had justified the Expulsion of 1492 and the Inquisition's persecution of *conversos*. Republicans and revolutionaries were presented as the new enemy of Spain, who also needed to be persecuted and/or expelled. This new enemy was viewed as at the service of global Jewish powers that were driving the Spanish Republic and the country at large towards communism. During the Civil War, the Republican side was presented as openly communist, under the direct authority of Stalin's Soviet Union, which was the embodiment of Jewish tyranny over Christian peoples. No wonder the antisemitic general Queipo de Llano declared over the radio that the acronym USSR (URSS in Spanish) meant "Unión Rabínica de los Sabios de Sión" (Rabbinic Union of the Elders of Zion).[10] During the Republic, antisemitic propaganda had warned that the new regime was backing a Jewish invasion – by the Sephardim in 1931, and by German refugees in 1933. During the Civil War, many pointed to the large numbers of Jews in the International Brigades (which was in fact accurate – some seven thousand Brigadists were of Jewish origin).[11]

The Francoist regime was defined from the start as Catholic and Falangist. Until the Axis's defeat, "Falangist" clearly meant fascist and, above all, totalitarian (points cited by the Falange itself and established in official laws and discourses of the time). As previously noted, the Catholic Falange joined the antisemitic cause from the beginning. For example, the party newspaper *Arriba España* in Pamplona, directed by the "blue" priest Fermín Yzurdiaga, printed the following slogan in its first edition on 1 August 1936: "¡Camaradas! Tienes la obligación de perseguir al judaísmo, a la masonería, al marxismo y al separatismo!" (Comrades! You have the obligation to chase down Judaism, Freemasonry, Marxism, and separatism!).

Antisemitic propaganda spread during the first wave of Francoism in books (as in the aforementioned Anti-Sectarian Presses during the Civil War, and in *Ediciones Toledo* [Toledo Press] during the Second World War), in the press, in official speeches, in bishops' homilies, and in school textbooks, many of which repeated old anti-Jewish legends. Those legends, which included the ritual infanticides of Santo Dominguito del Val and Santo Niño de la Guardia, were what had justified the policies of the Catholic Monarchs. During the Second World War, the Jews were affirmed to be the hidden power that controlled the Allied governments, the Soviet Union, and the plutocratic democracies of the United States and Great Britain. The Spanish press reported on the anti-Jewish policies being implemented in Axis Europe in a neutral or complementary tone. Those policies included expropriations, exclusions, yellow stars, humiliations, and imprisonment in ghettos or in concentration camps. Obviously, the mass exterminations were not mentioned in the Spanish press (nor were they in Germany), but sometimes one could read disturbing statements, such as this one from the official Efe news agency in February 1943: "la guerra actual terminará con la destrucción del judaísmo" (the current war will end with the destruction of Judaism). Often, Franco himself took the time in some of his speeches to praise the wise expulsion of the Jews ordered by the Catholic Monarchs, who had saved the country from their pernicious influence, and to speak of the need for today's European countries to adopt anti-Jewish policies. The Catholic press echoed this position – for example, *Ecclesia,* an official organ of Catholic Action, declared in June 1943: "España resolvió el problema judío adelantándose en siglos y con cordura a las medidas profilácticas que hoy han tomado tantas naciones para librarse del elemento judaico, fermento tantas veces de descomposición nacional" (Spain sensibly solved the Jewish problem centuries ahead of time, advancing the prophylactic measures that today so many nations have taken to liberate themselves of the Jewish element, so often the ferment of national decomposition). The text subtly implied that such preventative measures were being avoided now with good reason. One year before, the same publication made this point even more clearly: "Podemos abrigar reservas sobre lo que hoy ha movido a los estados a precaverse de las influencias perturbadoras de los israelitas. Pero en cambio la actitud de España con los Reyes Católicos no tiene reservas pues supo fundamentar su repulsa a los judíos no en móviles de índole física, sino espiritual y económica" (We can have reservations about what has today motivated states to take precautions against the perturbing influences of the Jews. But, by contrast, one has no such reservations towards Spain's position during the time of the Catholic Monarchs because they found out how to base their condemnation of the Jews not in motives of a physical kind, but rather a spiritual and economic one). As we can see, the Spanish Church fully shared the antisemitism of the era, although it questioned Nazi racism and rejected treating baptized people in the same manner as the Jews (see Graciela Ben Dror's chapter 19). It is no surprise that the Vatican asked the Italian government of Badoglio in 1943 not to repeal the 1938 fascist antisemitic laws, but to reform them to exclude baptized persons and catechumens.[12]

Franco's Policy and the Jews

Curiously, in the Francoist camp, Franco himself stood out very little among antisemites and much less than other well-known military men, such as Gonzalo Queipo de Llano, Emilio Mola, and Luis Carrero Blanco, the dictator's personal adviser since 1941. In the 1920s Franco had demonstrated that his philosephardism in reference to the support the Jews of the protectorate had extended to the Spanish during the Moroccan War, especially in an article titled "Xauen la triste" ("Chaouen the Sad"). Some of the territory's wealthy Jews supported him in the 1936 revolt. And in his film script for *Raza* (Race), published in 1942 when the Axis had attained its maximum reach, and brought that same year to the big screen, the protagonist affirms in front of the synagogue of Santa María la Blanca in Toledo: "Judíos, moros y cristianos aquí estuvieron, y al contacto de España se purificaron" (Jews, Moors, and Christians were here, and through contact with Spain they were purified). It was necessary, then, to distinguish the Sephardim purified by

Spain from the rest of the Jews. During the Civil War, Franco had hardly mentioned the Jews, except in some of the orders he drafted for the front lines. The main enemies were communism, which had infiltrated the Popular Front and was driving the country towards revolution, which only the July military revolt had prevented, and Freemasonry, an obsession of Franco. Yet at the same time, he did not raise any obstacles to antisemitic propaganda. From the final days of the Civil War until 1943, he made many allusions to the "espíritu judaico" (Jewish spirit) that had to be eradicated (in his victory speech of 19 May 1939). Franco justified the European antisemitism of the time, from which Spain was free thanks to the Catholic Monarchs, who had liberated Spain in time from the "pesada carga" (heavy burden) of the Jews (end-of-year speech from 1939).[13] In a letter to Pius XII from 12 April 1943, Franco warned the pope of the manoeuvres "entre bastidores" (behind the scenes) of "la masonería internacional y el judaísmo" against "nuestra civilización católica" (among supporters of international Freemasonry and Judaism against our Catholic civilization).[14]

In any case, philosephardism did not completely disappear during the first years of the new regime. In 1940 the Consejo Superior de Investigaciones Científicas (Spanish National Research Council) founded the Arias Montano Institute, along with its Escuela de Estudios Hebraicos (School of Hebrew Studies), which published the journal *Sefarad* beginning in 1941. At the time, though, this official philosephardism remained restricted to the academic world.[15]

For forces on the right during the Republic, antisemitism functioned to (a) explain the new government's proclamation of 14 April 1931, (b) conflate all of the liberal and revolutionary forces, and (c) claim that the new Republican regime was headed towards communism, secretly and sinisterly driven by the Jews. During the war, these perceptions continued: it was claimed that communism and its terror had already become engrained, and the war was legitimized in terms of an apocalyptic battle between God and Satan, as represented in *El Poema de la Bestia y el Ángel* (The Poem of the Beast and the Angel, 1938) by José María Pemán.[16] Yet the enemies to be hunted down were not the Jews, but rather those who had supported the opposing side: socialists, communists, libertarians, Republicans, Basque or Catalan nationalists, and Freemasons. This, even though the large majority of the world's Jews sympathized with the Republican cause and several thousand participated in the International Brigades (a notable initial exception being the Revisionist Zionists of Palestine's *yishuv*, who initially sympathized with the rebels and, when faced with German intervention, declared themselves neutral).[17] Even small Jewish communities suffered under the new regime; many of their members were persecuted for their political militancy or their Masonic affiliations.

In Ceuta and Melilla, the leaders of Jewish communities supported the rebel soldiers from the beginning. Despite this, in Melilla several hundred Jews were detained over a four-month period and the synagogues were closed for six months. Beatings, insults, brief detentions, and economic extortion by way of fines and patriotic contributions abounded, especially early in the Civil War and at some points during the Second World War. After the American landing in the French zone of North Africa in November 1942, there were again massive round-ups of Jews, especially in occupied Tangier, which ended the following May with the liberation of the prisoners. Yet on a list of 750 people executed or assassinated in the entire territory during those years, there are only eighteen typically Jewish surnames, and almost all of these people were Republican or leftist militants. It does not seem that Jewish status was an aggravating factor, given that at a November 1936 war council in Ceuta against eleven leftists, the sole person of Jewish origin (an anarchist) was not among the four executed.[18] The Jewish community in Seville suffered harassment and economic extortion at the hands of Queipo de Llano, and it seems that almost all of its members eventually emigrated. In Zaragoza, three Jewish vendors were executed and a fourth had his wares confiscated and had to go into hiding for a time. His oldest son, however, a militant belonging to the Federación Universitaria Escolar (University Students Federation; FUE), managed to avoid the fate of his fellow salesmen by agreeing to be baptized Catholic. In Granada, the wife of a university professor who was executed managed to save her life through baptism as well; she was German of Jewish origin.[19]

In the Republican zone, the Jewish community of Madrid stopped functioning during the Civil War, but the two Barcelona communities continued their activities until the end of the war. In both cities, many Jews fled the conflict. When the Francoists entered Barcelona, the two Jewish communities dissolved and their synagogues were looted. After the Civil War, all Jewish organizations (and, in general, non-Catholic ones) were prohibited, except in Ceuta and Melilla. No other type of marriage existed apart from religious marriage until 1941. In that year, civil marriage was reinstated for those who could demonstrate with documentation that they were not baptized (something that no Jew dared to do for several years). That same year, police were ordered to create a record of all of the country's Jews because of their supposed threat (see the discussion of the "Archivo Judaico" in Israel Garzón's chapter 3). A number of Jews suffered imprisonment or persecution as Masonic or Republican militants. Many who lacked Spanish citizenship were offered the opportunity to leave the country in order to be released from jail. Baptism generally was a good way to be granted clemency. In fact, a large proportion of families underwent baptism in order to free themselves from the hostile environment in which they lived. And it seems that almost all of the Agudad Ahim community in Barcelona – Sephardic sellers of old clothing who worked near the San Antonio market – were expelled from the country. They were forbidden to stay in business and disappeared from the municipal census. Stateless Jews with years of residence in the country were also expelled in no small numbers.[20]

After the summer of 1940, the Franco government was faced with Jews who wanted to flee Axis Europe through Spain, and with the more than four thousand continental Jews (most of them residents of France, and quite a few of Greece) who held a Spanish passport.[21] As Josep Calvet explains in chapter 5, thousands of the former were rejected or sent back across the Pyrenees. When Germany urged the repatriation to Spain of the latter, almost half were abandoned, their Spanish citizenship unrecognized on some formal pretext. Those who did manage to enter Spain were later expelled to French Morocco, despite their fully recognized Spanish citizenship. This topic is more fully explored by Isabelle Rohr in her contribution to this volume.

It seems that what motivated Franco when he implemented his policy vis-à-vis the Holocaust was not personal antagonism towards Sephardim. Ever since his war years in Morocco, he had viewed Sephardim as having been purified by the sublime Spanish culture. In his estimation, the Spanish-descended Jews ought to be studied by scholars. He believed that Jews should be tolerated in their land, Morocco (which here included Ceuta and Melilla). But Franco had also won the war in the name of Eternal Catholic Spain, which had been forged by the Catholic Monarchs, who had imposed religious unity in the country and built their imperial glory. Without explicitly saying it, the Spanish dictator tried to reinstate the 1492 Edict of Expulsion during those first years: there should be no Jews in Spain. From this came the closing of the synagogues, the prohibition of all Jewish life, and an open invitation to Jews who chose baptism in order to escape the prevalent hostility. The same policy served for the Jews who were fleeing the continent during the Second World War, as discussed at length by Josep Calvet in this volume. Jewish refugees could pass through the Pyrenees, as the majority did, and leave Spain through the Portuguese border, having been sustained by international Jewish organizations during their stay (in Spanish detention camps, usually). Even so, no small number were sent back to the border. Because the expulsion of those who held a Spanish passport was more complicated, Franco personally decided to stave off the Germans and look for a place that would temporarily take in these Jews, since they would have to leave the country eventually anyway because the regime did not allow Jewish refugees to settle in Spain. On 28 December 1943 the foreign minister, General Francisco Gómez Jordana, explained in a letter to General Carlos Asensio that he had had to discharge from the Army a handful of young Sephardic Spaniards who had been repatriated from France, in order to be able to deport them with their families, since "el Caudillo" wanted everyone to pass "por nuestro país como la luz por el cristal" (through our country like light through a crystal).[22] Facing an uphill battle to achieve this, the regime chose to abandon a large portion of those affected. On occasion, they attempted to use the refugee evacuation operation as a front to deport Jews who had been settled in the country for decades. It seems that they managed this with the Barcelona second-hand clothing vendors and with a few others. And persecuted Jewish Freemasons were encouraged to avoid prison by leaving the country. After the defeat of the Axis, the Franco regime put a damper on antisemitic propaganda and applied its Sephardic policies to improve Spain's foreign image, especially in the United States (see chapter 20 in this volume by Pedro Correa). The new historical era ushered in by the end of the war would bring new complications and mindsets to Spain in regard to the Jewish people.

NOTES

1 Christiane Stallaert, "La cuestión conversa y la limpieza de sangre a la luz de las conceptualizaciones antropológicas actuales sobre la etnicidad," in Joan i Tous and Nottebaum, eds, *El olivo y la espada*, 1–27; Álvarez Chillida, "El antisemitismo en España," 197–220. See also three overviews that cover a large part of the topic of this study: Álvarez Chillida, *El antisemitismo en España*; Rozenberg, *L'Espagne contemporaine et la question juive*; and Rohr, *La derecha española y los judíos*.
2 On these communities: Lisbona, *Retorno a Sefarad*; Israel Garzón and Macías Kapón, *La comunidad judía de Madrid*; Berthelot, *Memorias judías*; Berthelot, *Cien años de presencia judía*; Ojeda Mata, *Identidades ambivalentes*.
3 Shinan, *Victims or Culprits*; idem, "Ingratitud y fanatismo"; Lacave, "Los estudios hebraicos en España," in Macías, Moreno Koch, and Izquierdo Benito, eds, *Los judíos en la España contemporánea*.
4 González García, *El retorno de los judíos*, 129–74; Álvarez Chillida, *El antisemitismo en España*, 171–207.

 5 Touboul Tardieu, *Séphardisme et hispanité*; Aliberti, *Sefarad une communauté imaginée*.

 6 Manfred Böcker, *Antisemitismus ohne Juden*, 301–50; Álvarez Chillida, *El antisemitismo en España*, 171–207.

 7 Rodríguez Jiménez, "El discurso antisemita en el fascismo español"; Isidro González García, *Los judíos*, 271–3.

 8 González García, *Los judíos*; Aliberti, *Sefarad une communauté imaginée*, 85–96.

 9 Domínguez Arribas, *El enemigo judeo-masónico*; Böcker, *Antisemitismus ohne Juden*.

10 The citation of Queipo de Llano in Cruz, "¡Luzbel vuelve al mundo!," 300.

11 Lustiger, *¡Shalom libertad!*

12 Ben Dror, *La Iglesia católica ante el Holocausto*; Álvarez Chillida, *El antisemitismo*, 351–64, 381–94. The petition to Badoglio in Miccoli, *I dilemi e i silenzi di Pio XII*, 401–2.

13 "Xauen la triste," in Franco Bahamonde, *Papeles de la guerra de Marruecos*, 181–99. Jaime de Andrade [Franco's pseudonym], *Raza*, 87; *ABC*, 20 May 1939, 20–1; *Arriba*, 2 January 1940, 3; Domínguez Arribas, *El enemigo*, 84–97. On the help of the wealthy Jews from Morocco, see Blin, "Franco et les juifs du Maroc," 33–57; and Lisbona, *Retorno*, 68–70.

14 Rother, *Franco y el Holocausto*, 73.

15 Lacave, "Los estudios hebraicos," 118–19.

16 Álvarez Chillida, *José María Pemán*, 357–66.

17 Isidro González García, *Los judíos y la Guerra Civil española*. Regarding revisionist Zionism, see Rein, *Franco, Israel y los judíos*, 104–5, 110.

18 Martín Corrales, "Represión contra cristianos, moros y judíos." Regarding the lists, see Sánchez Montoya, *Ceuta y el norte de África*, 511–20; and Moga Romero, *Las heridas de la historia*, 281–300.

19 Lisbona, *Retorno*, 63–8; Álvarez Chillida, "Zaragoza en la guerra civil"; Granada, in Ojeda Mata, *Identidades ambivalentes*, 167–8.

20 Ojeda Mata, *Identidades*, 166–215; Israel Garzón, "El Archivo Judaico del franquismo"; Lion Lewin, "Madrid, años cuarenta."

21 Avni, *España, Franco y los judíos*; Marquina and Ospina, *España y los judíos en el siglo XX*, 145–232; Rother, *Franco y el Holocausto*; Calvet, *Las montañas de la libertad*. For testimonies of those who took part, see Alexy, *La mezuzá en los pies de la Virgen*; Garzón y Baer, eds, *España y el Holocausto*; and Berthelot, *Memorias judías*.

22 Marquina y Ospina, *España y los judíos*, 198.

PART TWO

Spain and the Fates of Jewish Communities

3 Spain and the Jews during the Holocaust

JACOBO ISRAEL GARZÓN

To be able to determine what Spain's position was towards the Jews during the Holocaust, it is necessary to differentiate between the treatment given to the four sectors of the Jewish population residing in or with connections to the country: Jews living on the Iberian Peninsula; Jews from the zone of Spanish influence in Morocco; European Jewish refugees who arrived legally or illegally; and Sephardic Spanish nationals in zones occupied by the Nazis. Franco's policy during the years of the Holocaust would prove different for each of these Jewish populations and can be summarized as follows:

- Pressure on Jews living on the Iberian Peninsula, not recognizing their religious rights or those of association.
- Neutrality towards Jews of the Moroccan Protectorate.
- Limited generosity in the provision of transit visas to refugees in the country, as long as the Jews passed through the country and did not remain there.
- Non-recognition of the citizenship rights of Spanish Sephardim abroad.

Treatment of the Jews from the Peninsula's Interior

Numerous Jews were exiled after the defeat of the Republic, among them Margarita Nelken and her sister Magda Donato, together with their mother Juana Mansberger; Máximo José Kahn; Max Aub; Alfredo Bauer and Gisela, his wife, together with their children; Menahem Coriat; Mauricio Amster; Enrique Hauser; Mariano Rawicz; and others.[1]

Other Jews who remained in Spain experienced various difficulties: José Bleiberg, one of the founders of the Madrid community, committed suicide, and his son, Germán, poet and scholar, was condemned in a summary trial to twelve years of prison, of which he served four; Moisés Benhamú, councilman in Ceuta, was taken prisoner and executed by Falangists in 1937. The regime, besides outlawing communities and synagogues, arresting Jews for their Republicanism or their association with Freemasons, limiting their access to work (much like they did to other religious minorities such as the Evangelicals), and pressuring them to convert, opted to file police reports on members of the Jewish population not because the persons were suspected of any social or political crime, but rather based on a supposed danger they posed. The Sephardic population was particularly monitored.

After the fall of Barcelona in January of 1939, the synagogue and community centre on Provenza Street was looted and the president of that community, Edmundo Graembaum, was detained for being a high-level Freemason. In addition, the *jazan* Bechor Isaac Nahum, also a Freemason, was sentenced to thirty years and one day; he was saved from prison only by his Turkish nationality, but with the obligation to report to the police station daily.[2]

In April of 1939, a commission comprised of Jacques Danon, community vice-president, Marcel Calef, secretary, and Samuel Maytek appeared in the civil government office asking to see the governor, González Oliveras, to obtain permission to reopen the synagogue and the community centre. After waiting three hours they were not attended to; that same month the synagogue and the community building were officially closed.[3] Their documents were confiscated and sent to the Salamanca Archive, where they remained until they were transferred to the Generalitat of Catalonia decades later.

The German embassy and consulates in Spain attempted to create an archive of the Jews in Spain as well as of the commercial and industrial businesses owned by Jews. To that end, they asked for the cooperation of the Spanish police. Several of these petitions[4] and the responses by Spanish police are available in archives.

Many Jews who lived in Spain did not have Spanish citizenship, and this often served as the pretext for their expulsion, especially for the poorest Jews. Furthermore, their Judaism increased the defencelessness of those deported. This was the case with the Seror family: Marcos was the first of the family to arrive in Madrid from Tangier in 1922. He later brought over his brother Rafael and subsequently the remaining members of the family, who settled in Madrid without any problems. Marcos was the manager of Wagon Lits in Granada, and his sister Alegría worked in SEPU (Sociedad española de precios únicos), the major department store at the time. After the war, Rafael, his sisters

Cota, Esther, and Sarah, and his mother, Simy, found themselves forced to leave the country.[5]

New laws established exclusively Catholic religious marriage and birth registry with baptismal certificates. However, in March of 1941 a procedure was established for civil marriage between partners who could present documentary proof that they had not been baptized.[6] For this reason, there were a few Jews who converted, such as Alegría Seror, whose marriage at the beginning of the war to Antonio García Millares was declared null in November of 1939:

> [Alegría]... se vio en estado de concubinato al acabar la guerra y declararse nulo su matrimonio.... hubo de firmar [el documento de apostasía] para poder bautizarse, ... finalmente [realizar] la boda religiosa.... De no haber hecho esto... tendría que haber dejado el país como el resto de la familia. Los hijos, por supuesto, fueron bautizados.

> [Alegría] ... found herself in a state of concubinage upon the war's end and her marriage declared null ... She had to sign [the document of apostasy] to be able to be baptized ... finally [to be able to have] the religious wedding ... In case she had not done this ... she would have to have left the country like the rest of her family. Her children, of course, were baptized.[7]

A certificate of baptism and good conduct granted by the parish was required in order to gain access to a position as a civil servant. Pressure on non-Catholics increased the number of conversions, as was the case with twenty of twenty-five Jewish families of German origin who lived in Madrid.[8] On 22 July 1939, the German Embassy in Madrid alerted the Spanish foreign ministry to impede their naturalization, noting that "en muchos casos tratan de conseguir esa naturalización abrazando la religión católica, para poder desorientar de ese modo a las autoridades españolas"[9] (in many cases they try to get that naturalization embracing the Catholic religion, in order to be able to mislead Spanish authorities by doing so).

In this context, it seems paradoxical that in 1940 the regime approved the creation of the Arias Montanos Institute for Jewish and Near East Studies, which began to publish the journal *Sefarad* the following year.

Memo no. 11 of the Dirección General de Seguridad (General Directorate of Security), dated 5 May 1941 and currently held at the Archivo Histórico Nacional (National Historic Archive, AHN), addressed the civil governors of the Spanish provinces.[10] Previously unknown to scholars, this memo asked for individual reports on "los israelitas, nacionales y extranjeros avecindados en esa provincial" (the

Hebrews, both nationals and foreigners residing in that province) to be sent indicating "filiación personal y político-social, medios de vida, actividades comerciales, situación actual, grado de peligrosidad, conceptuación policial" (personal and socio-political affiliation, livelihood, commercial activities, current situation, degree of danger, police assessment).[11]

The preamble of the memo specifies:

> la necesidad de conocer de modo concreto y terminante los lugares y personas que, en un momento dado, pudieran ser obstáculo o medio de actuación contrario a los postulados que informan al Nuevo Estado, requiere se preste atención especial a los judíos residentes en nuestra Patria, recogiendo, en debida forma, cuantos detalles y antecedentes permitan determinar la ideología de cada uno de ellos y sus posibilidades de acción, dentro y fuera del territorio nacional.[12]

> The need to know concretely and conclusively the places and people who, at some given time, could be an obstacle or means of action contrary to the postulates that inform the New State, requires that special attention be paid to Jewish residents of our nation, duly collecting as many details and as much history to permit a determination of the ideology of each one of them and their likelihood of taking action, in and out of national territory.

As the memo continues, Francoist philosephardism is called into question:

> las personas objeto de la medida que le encomiendo han de ser principalmente aquellas de origen español designadas con el nombre de sefarditas, puesto que por su adaptación al ambiente y similitud con nuestro temperamento poseen mayores garantías de ocultar su origen y hasta pasar desapercibidas sin posibilidad alguna de coartar el alcance de fáciles manejos perturbadores.[13]

> The persons targeted by the measures that I entrust to you must be principally those of Spanish origin with Sephardic names, given that they possess greater guarantees of hiding their origin – due to their adaptation to the environment and the similarities to our temperament – and even passing undetected without any possibility of limiting the reach of their disturbing dealings.

The memo considers to be true

que podrá llegar a determinarse la personalidad de los judíos españoles existentes en esa provincia, aunque aparentemente surjan señaladas dificultades, como la de no haber mantenido una relación y vida social en sus peculiares comunidades israelitas, sinagogas y colegios especiales (salvo lugares como Barcelona, Baleares y Marruecos), que pudieran aportar datos concretos de su número y alcance, individual y colectivamente considerados.[14]

that the identity of Spanish Jews living in that province could be determined, although apparently certain difficulties may emerge, like that of not having had a relationship and social life in their peculiar Israelite communities, synagogues, and special schools (save for places like Barcelona, the Balearic Islands, and Morocco), that could provide concrete data of their number and reach, individually and collectively speaking.

The memo concludes by soliciting a general impression of the significance of Jewish activities in the province, as well as details on the institutions, and urges expediency in fulfilment of the task.

Police records of a certain vintage that could be of historical importance have been progressively incorporated into the AHN. Unfortunately, the Archivo Judaico (Jewish Archive) has disappeared, and remnants of it must be sought among the nearly hundred thousand extant personal files in the AHN. Furthermore, as the records have been passed along to the Archivo Central de la Policía (Central Police Archive), not all are present; many of them remain in provincial archives, and more than a few have been lost.

We do not know when this record-keeping on Jews was suspended or if there were instructions to end it. Police documents from 1957 refer to the Archivo Judaico. One file notes that a Jewish citizen requested the cancellation of unfavourable records:

en el año 1938 se practicó informe en el que *se le consideraba peligroso por su origen israelita* ... estuvo afiliado a la FUE y a la Juventud de Izquierda Republicana, actuó en favor del Frente Popular, del que era simpatizante, por cuyo motivo, *además del racial*, se le consideró enemigo de la Causa Nacional. (emphasis added)

In the year 1938 reports were filed in which he *was considered dangerous due to his Hebrew origin* ... He was affiliated with the FUE and the Republican Leftist Youth, he acted in favor of the Popular Front, of which he was a sympathizer, for which reason, *aside from the racial one*, he was considered an enemy of the National Cause.[15]

One comes away with the impression that the Archivo Central Judaico, which was held under the División de Investigación Social,[16] was not transferred intact. However, provincial ones were, for which reason there exists the possibility that the archive was eliminated at the end of the Francoist period, or that it could still at some point resurface.

In the extant files, it was impossible to find the documents for well-known Jews, such as Ignacio Bauer, Germán Bleiberg, and the Lawenda family, whose name is on the first Jewish prayer house that was opened in Madrid after the Civil War. Regarding those that still exist, some details about how these documents were interpreted can be found in certain files referring to Jews. For instance, a report from the Chief Commissary of the 2nd Section to the Chief Commissary of the 1st Section of the Comisaría General Político-Social, dated Madrid 30 June 1944, explains regarding the file of María Sinaí León, daughter of a past president of the Agudat Ahim society:

> nacida el 16 de septiembre de 1920 en Barcelona, hija de Mauricio y Susana, dedicada a sus labores, soltera, vecina de Barcelona y con domicilio en la calle de Borrell 58, 2°- 2ª. Carece de nacionalidad y no se le conoce filiación política ni haber desempeñado cargos políticos o de secta. Vive a expensas de su padre, Mauricio Sinaí Cario, y le fue concedida autorización de residencia... Se le supone la peligrosidad propia de la raza judía a que pertenece (sefardita).[17]

> Born on 16 September 1920 in Barcelona, daughter of Mauricio and Susana, dedicated to her work, single, Barcelona resident with domicile at 58 Borell Street, 2°–2ª. Lacks citizenship, and political affiliation and any political or religious positions unknown. Lives off of her father, Mauricio Sinaí Cario, and was granted residency authorization ... Assumed to be dangerous, as is inherent to the Jewish race to which she pertains (Sephardic).

Despite all the challenges, groups of Jews – striving to preserve their identity – met in private homes to pray and to celebrate holidays, notwithstanding the ban on meetings (which affected all Spaniards). These people also helped refugees, visiting them in jails and in camps and bringing them wool socks, shoes, clothes, and so on.

It is necessary to underscore the danger the Archivo Judaico could have represented for the Jewish community, when we consider that in May 1941 it appeared likely that Spain would be pulled into the Second World War.

Treatment of Jews of the Protectorate and of Sovereign Territories of North Africa

During the Holocaust, Spain held two sovereign territories – Ceuta and Melilla – in North Africa, as well as the Spanish Protectorate in Morocco, which ceased to be under Spanish rule in 1956. Alleging security needs, Spain occupied the International Zone of Tangier for years, only leaving at the end of the Second World War. During this period, they controlled an area in which some thirty thousand Jews lived, principally in the cities of Tangier, Tetuán, Larache, Alcázarquivir, Arcila, Ceuta, and Melilla, as well as smaller towns.

Jews living in the protectorate had been allies of the Spanish, whom they had seen as liberators, faced as they were with legal inferiority as well as scorn from non-Jews. From the beginning, Spain saw the Jews as allies – even more so during the Rif War. The Franco regime did not establish laws of racial discrimination like those Mussolini had put into effect in Italy.

Jews in Morocco's zone of Spanish influence were not allied with the winning side in the Civil War, nor were the governing parties of the new regime allied with the Jews. Some historians have focused on the help extended by certain Jews on the Francoist side of the Civil War, although anyone familiar with the situation knows these were isolated cases.[18] The new regime and the Jews coexisted without particular amity and with some practical, though not legal, limitations. Discrimination towards North African Jews during this period was uncommon. No legislation of which we know targeted Jews as such,[19] although there were numerous financial levies, and the Jewish community centre in Melilla and the "casino israelita" (Israeli social club) in Tetuán were both confiscated by the regime.

Complaints by the Spanish consulates in Rabat and Casablanca regarding the anti-Jewish measures applied by the French Protectorate against those coming from the Spanish Protectorate are documented.[20] Those measures included the French rejection of the Spanish passports of Jewish citizens born in Morocco and in the sovereign territories. No strong reaction to these measures was noted. A Jewish citizen born in Melilla, Isaac Tapiero Melul, saw his Spanish passport rejected on the pretext that "si la Ley española considera a aquél como español, la de Marruecos francés lo tiene por israelita marroquí de derecho común" (if Spanish law considers that man a Spaniard, French Moroccan law takes him for a common law Moroccan Hebrew). In addition, the Resident General of France in Morocco criticized the delivery of an identity certificate to a native of the Spanish Protectorate, Alberto

Levy.[21] Jews did not suffer racial laws in the Spanish protectorate in Morocco like those that existed in the French Protectorate, although they did have to live with the antisemitism and Fascist radicalism that inspired the new regime.[22]

Treatment of Jewish Refugees from Nazi Europe

Spain had stopped serving as a country of refuge after the Civil War, and most Jews, both Spanish and foreign, went about leaving the country. The new refugees from Nazism did not find it easy to seek asylum in Spain, given the ideology of the victors in the Civil War, nor did they see the country as a transit route. All of this changed starting in the spring of 1940: on 10 May, the Germans invaded the Netherlands; on 24 May, Belgium surrendered; and on 22 June, so did France. For thousands of refugees from all over Europe, Jews and non-Jews, Spain was the main path to freedom (see the chapters in this volume by Lisbona, Avni, and Calvet). During the first weeks, the Spanish government granted transit visas liberally to refugees holding an immigration visa for Portugal, although they tried to block the entry of those considered enemies of the regime. The border was closed for a few weeks and opened again on 4 December 1940 through Cerbère, which saw twenty-five persons per day. Initially, it was enough to have a Spanish *and* a Portuguese transit visa, but soon an exit visa from the Vichy authorities was also required. Later, transit visas were centralized in Madrid, which meant that individual consulates could no longer provide them. The requirements grew increasingly strict, and they could not be met by many. Walter Benjamin, the great German-Jewish philosopher, turned back at the Spanish border and in dread of returning to France, committed suicide in Portbou.

Until October 1941, Germans still allowed Jews to leave the Reich and the Western countries it had occupied. However, Germans had been preparing the Final Solution since June 1941. In October, the Nazis decided to exterminate Europe's Jews; in July 1942, the Vichy regime voided the exit visas of French and foreign Jews and committed itself to extraditing foreign Jews to Germany. This impeded the procurement of Spanish visas and thereby ended the legal exodus to Spain. Early research by Haim Avni calculated that by the summer of 1942, some thirty thousand Jews had travelled through Spain; recent research by Josep Calvet estimates half that number.[23]

Thus deportations to Eastern European concentration camps began for foreign Jews in Holland, Belgium, and France, at a volume and with a violence that shocked many. Elsewhere, the Allies landed in North

Africa and the Germans invaded the south of France, forcing the Vichy regime to disband its military units. The commanders of the French fleet anchored in Toulon decided to sink their own ships instead of handing them over to the Germans.

All of these events generated an illegal exodus of Jewish and non-Jewish refugees to France.[24] The former were fleeing deportation, the latter – young politicians and military commanders – planned to join the Free French in North Africa. According to a report from the American Joint Distribution Committee (the Joint; JDC), in October 1942, three hundred Jewish and non-Jewish refugees were being held up in transit, of whom 250 were allowed to stay in Madrid, Barcelona, Vigo, and Bilbao. Legal refugees in transit were monitored until they exited the country, and when this exit could not take place or they had come in illegally, they were jailed in the internment camps at Figueras, Nanclares de Oca, or Miranda de Ebro. Until 1942, Jewish charities could not offer direct assistance to refugees. For a short time, authorities permitted American Red Cross services, which distributed food, clothing, and medicine to the Spanish people and also to the refugees. Two Americans, the wives of Ambassador Weddell and Military Attaché Stephens, used their diplomatic immunity to help refugees in Miranda de Ebro. The Joint helped refugees until 1942 through its unofficial representatives: in Barcelona, the Norddeutscher Lloyd of Bremen, and in Madrid, the doorman of a hotel, Moisés Eizen. Both offered help to those who reached out to them.

The new US ambassador, Carlton J.H. Hayes, tried to arrange matters so that Jewish charities could work openly on Spanish territory. When Spanish authorities denied this request, the Portuguese Cruz Vermelha (Red Cross) stepped in. Through this agency's intervention, a young Jewish Portuguese man, Samuel Sequerra, arrived in Barcelona to help Jewish refugees. Sequerra first set up his office in the Bristol Hotel; he later moved it to 28 Paseo de Gracia. The authorities at first mistrusted Sequerra, and he was harassed on various occasions by police and Falangists, but they changed their position as the Nazis began to lose the war.

Stateless Jewish refugees suffered more than those who had a consulate to approach for advice. Some refugees were deported *because* they were Jewish, even though the Franco regime had not signed any agreement to this end, as Vichy France had. One of the most dramatic cases is that of Jenny Kehr, who received a deportation order from Spain for being a Jew. She was first sent to the camp at Miranda de Ebro (a strange occurrence, given that this camp was only for men); then she was sent back, and the civil governor of Lérida issued a deportation order for the sole reason that she was Jewish. He pointly wrote: "se ha dispuesto su expulsión del mismo [territorio nacional] por ser judía" (her deportation from this place [national territory] has been arranged because she is a Jew). At the women's jail where she was sent the day before her deportation, Jenny Kehr – whose story is also addressed by Calvet and Linhard in this volume – committed suicide.[25]

León Hoffman, a refugee, was turned over to German authorities by order of the General Director of Security on 27 March 1943. An exit slip from the Madrid prison from 4 March 1943 contains a note that he was not to be admitted to the San Sebastian jail and was instead to be turned over to the German consulate.[26] There is also a petition from the German consulate to the Civil Governor of Guipúzcoa on 4 May 1943 for Hoffman to be granted an exit visa on that same letter and be handed over to Delegate Denker in order to be taken to Hendaye.

The case of Jankiel Rosenwald offers proof of instructions against Jewish refugees from the General Director of Security. The civil governor of Lérida, Juan Antonio Cremades Royo, sent the following to the Chief of Police in the town of Les on the border between Lérida and France:

> Por ser orden terminante de la superioridad que no se admitan los judíos en territorio nacional y los que se encuentren sean obligados inmediatamente a repasar la frontera se servirá ordenar la expulsión del detenido en la cárcel de Viella Jankiel Rozenwald y me dará cuenta de haberlo efectuado para hacerlo yo a la Dirección General de Seguridad.[27]

> Due to the injunction from the authorities that Jews shall not be admitted to national territory and that those found shall be obliged to immediately cross the border, this will serve to order the expulsion of the detained party currently held in the prison of Viella, Jankiel Rozenwald, and to give me an account of having done so, in order that I may report this to the General Directorate of Security.

Albert Blumel, ex-chief of Léon Blum's cabinet, director of the French Socialist Party, and head of the Popular Front government in 1936 and 1937, arrived in Spain with his wife and child, all with badly frostbitten feet. The family was taken to Portugal, where they were detained and turned over to Spanish police, who in turn transferred them to the border at Le Perthus.[28]

In October 1942, while the Spanish authorities were deporting some new arrivals to France, the Vichy ambassador Pietri asked foreign minister Jordana and governing minister Blas Pérez not to send back any more refugees. Men of military age were to be held at Miranda de Ebro to await subsequent decisions. Career military personnel would be gathered at a military base and given fair treatment, and civil refugees would remain free if they provided proof that someone could take care of them or that they had independent means.

As Josep Calvet notes in this volume, hundreds of refugees crossed the border, which was closed on the French side, every day by way of often snowy trails. Terrified and frozen, they were treated like normal prisoners and generally held at the Miranda de Ebro camp (the fifteen hundred internees in October 1942 had grown to thirty-five hundred by December of that year). In January 1943, the authorities began to turn over some of the detainees to their home countries' consulates, for consular sections in occupied countries had begun to operate again. Sequerra arranged permission for Jewish women and children imprisoned in Catalonia to stay in their obligatory residence at a summer colony, and they went to hotels in Caldas de Malavella.

The Germans tried to force the Spanish authorities to close the border, and in March 1943, it was indeed closed. However, the Spanish government reopened it in April, for the war's tide was turning in favour of the Allies and the Spanish government now faced a strong reaction from the United States and Great Britain. The relative liberality in the handover of refugees to consulates and charitable organizations – among them the Mission Française, which was beginning to represent the interests of the Free French in North Africa – reduced the number of internees at Miranda de Ebro through the month of May, down to some twelve hundred. Charities and the French mission tried to evacuate refugees to North Africa, first through Portugal and later through Málaga.

The stateless persons were supported by the Joint through Samuel Sequerra and his brother Joel. Finally, from 1943 onwards, the Franco regime permitted the JDC to open a representative office in Madrid, and David Blickenstaff became the official JDC representative there. American charities were now allowed to work in Spain on behalf of these stateless people under the umbrella of American Relief Organizations (ARO), which was funded largely by the Joint.

In April 1943, the Bermuda Conference was held in order to accelerate the evacuation of the refugees. In August, Blickenstaff arranged for most of the stateless refugees from Miranda de Ebro to live in supervised freedom in Madrid and Barcelona until they left Spain, economically aided by his organization. The Jewish agency and the Zionist agency also sent workers to Spain. Near the end of 1943, Rafael Spanien arrived in Spain, where he counted some twenty-one hundred Jewish refugees, of whom twelve hundred were stateless. Only in 1944 were some able to arrive at the Lyautey camp, in Fedala, Morocco.

In August 1944, France was liberated and the wave of refugees came to a halt. Between the summer 1942 and August of 1944, some seventy-five hundred Jews had passed through Spain. Calculating from the beginning of the war, this meant that between twenty-three and thirty-seven thousand Jews passed through Spain.[29] Testimonies exist from refugees from this time.[30]

Treatment of Sephardic Jews of Spanish Nationality in Nazi Europe

Starting in last third of the nineteenth century, Spanish authorities had been extending protection to Sephardim in the Ottoman Empire and other regions. After the Treaty of Lausanne, which brought an end to the protection system, the Spanish government opened a naturalization process, better known as the Primo de Rivera Decree, for "antiguos protegidos españoles" (Sephardim made protégés in 1924), in the words of that decree. Some were admitted; others were admitted but their nationalization was not completed due to administrative issues; still others were refused but held on to their former protection documents.

In areas of Nazi control, the Sephardic population holding full Spanish citizenship was composed of 303 persons in Bulgaria, between three and five hundred in France,[31] 830 in Greece, forty-five in Italy, and 110 in Romania, apart from those residing in Austria, Belgium, and Holland. According to José Antonio Lisbona, the total number was nearly two thousand.[32]

Two thousand Sephardim (with full Spanish nationality or simply protégés) were registered at the Spanish Consulate in Paris, as indicated by a document sent in November 1940 to the Spanish foreign ministry by the French ambassador, Lequerica.[33] Around this time, the Germans and the French occupation authorities had promulgated strict legislation regarding Jews and businesses. When the consul Bernardo Rolland asked what action his office should take, Spanish authorities responded that it should "únicamente darse por enterado de estas medidas y en último caso no poner inconvenientes a su ejecución conservando una actitud pasiva" (only acknowledge that they are privy to these measures and in the worst case not put roadblocks to their execution, maintaining a passive attitude).[34]

To the despair of Spanish Sephardim, the Spanish government decided to act flexibly towards the Germans and to freeze the assets of Spanish Sephardim in Spanish banks. Spanish authorities rejected a May 1941 petition from the Paris Association Culturelle Sepharadite asking for the return to Spain of descendants of deported Jews.[35] In September of the same year, a commission of Spanish Sephardim made up of Nicolás and Enrique Saporta Beja, Alberto Nehu Carasso, Ricardo Sadace Bitti, and Edgardo Hassid Fernández held a meeting with Ramón Serrano Suñer in Madrid and told him of the situation of the Spanish Sephardic colony in occupied France, but achieved nothing.[36] In the fall, the authorities detained numerous Jews in Paris, among them a number of Spaniards, and Consul Rolland's efforts failed to free them. The German policy of Jewish extermination was gradually becoming stricter. Sustained help for Spanish Jews was not clearly established in Spain, even though Rolland helped bring many to Spain.[37]

As discussed at length in Lisbona's chapter in this volume, the petitions of the consuls in Paris (Rolland, Fiscowich) and in Athens (Gasset, Radigales), and of the embassies in Bucharest (Rojas, Barzanallana) and in Sofia (Palencia),[38] along with letters to General Franco himself from a group of Spanish Jews in Paris and others to the Spanish Chamber of Commerce, could do little.[39] Other consuls, including the ones in Milan (Martínez, Merello, Canthal), managed to protect their Spanish Sephardim, telling them to come to Spain with the given documentation but to register as Catholics at the border.

In April 1943 the Spanish authorities changed their position on not allowing Spanish Jews to enter Spain, coinciding with the Bermuda Conference.[40] They decided that Spain would grant visas, since they had negotiated entries by blocs with Blickenstaff. The ARO financed the stay and the departure as if they were in transit despite having Spanish nationality. In May 1943, a few dozen Spanish Jews entered from Belgium and France by way of the border at Irún. On 10 August, a larger group made up of eighty Spanish Jews arrived; they were confined in different cities: Zaragoza, Logroño, Burgos, Toledo, and Granada. In October 1943, another group of forty-five coming from the south of France arrived, entering through Cerbère.

Police records on the twenty-three Sephardim held in Zaragoza between September and December 1943 – a number of them belonged to the Benveniste and Rossanes families, although there was also one Elías Canetti Rossanes – indicate that they were speaking with other French constituents and with workers and soldiers "desplegando gran propaganda en contra de los países totalitarios, por lo que sería conveniente tomar alguna medida" (unveiling major propaganda against the totalitarian countries, for which it would be useful to take measures).[41] Neither the ARO nor the Joint managed to secure asylum for them until the French mission began sending them from Málaga to Morocco by boat, a process that started in 1943 with those who had arrived through August.

Once there was a system in place to send Spanish Jewish refugees out of the country, the transit of another group of Spanish Jews from Salónica began. As Maria Fragkou describes in this volume, these Jews had been in the Bergen-Belsen concentration camp and their destination would be either Spain or Auschwitz. Thus 365 Spanish Jews arrived in Portbou in February 1944 en route to Palestine and Africa, many of them from the Gattegno, Saporta, Benveniste, Francis, Hassid, and Israel families, among others.[42] It appears that this group was sent off in June to Casablanca and sent on by the English to Israel in November 1944.[43] A second group of 155 Greek Spanish Jews that had been taken prisoner after arriving at Bergen-Belsen on 14 April 1944 did not come to Spain because negotiations with Spanish authorities lasted longer than the end of the war.[44]

Taking into account the 195 Spanish Sephardim who had arrived from France, the 365 Greek Sephardim coming from Bergen-Belsen, and the two hundred Sephardim who may have arrived individually in the country, the number of Spanish Sephardim saved was around eight hundred. Only a small number of Spanish protégés and citizens were saved, and those who were saved benefited from transit operations, not from repatriation and asylum.

This rescue of Jewish co-nationals was delayed because the Spanish authorities did not want their country's Jewish population to increase. This idea is reinforced when we take into account that at the end of the war the government dictated memos no. 2083 and 2088, which nullified any documentation previously provided to Spanish Jews. These memos indicated that one should "evitar, en lo possible, la entrada y permanencia en España de aquellos sefarditas cuya residencia anterior fuera en el extranjero" (it was to be avoided, to every extent possible, the entrance and stay in Spain of those Sephardim whose previous residence had been abroad) and that only the most limited groups with full Spanish documentation would be given "facilidades posibles para su repatriación a los domicilios de origen" (possible assistance for their repatriation to their residence of origin).[45]

General Assessment

At the end of the Second World War, in order to prevent an economic blockade, the regime ordered its embassies and Ignacio Bauer, Africanist and ex-president of the Jewish community in Madrid, to move closer to the American Jewish Community and the Israeli state in order to convince them of the *"immense"* labour of rescue and aid Franco provided to the Jews during the war years. In 1950, Israel voted against the cancellation of a diplomatic blockade against Spain that the United Nations had implemented in 1946. In the face of Israel's no vote, Bauer would write that "se ha cometido una gran injusticia inútil, pero confío en que no habrá perjuicio para los sefarditas, amantes como siempre de Sefarad y dispuestos también a demostrarlo" (a great useless injustice has been committed, but I trust that there will be no harm towards the Sephardim, lovers as always of Sepharad and inclined to demonstrate it).[46]

This disinformation campaign, complete with ad hoc diplomatic documents, has confused the work of certain diplomats with official regime policy and overlooked the internal antisemitism of the regime. This misinformation campaign was accepted more wholeheartedly after the Franco regime became an ally of the United States and inasmuch as the regime softened its pressure on the country's religious minorities. So it is not easy to evaluate the "help" Franco offered the Jews, because this purported aid was imbued with the tricks of its own lights and shadows (see Correa, chapter 20).

But other shadows exist as well: if the responsible parties of the ARO and of the Joint had found exit visas for refugees more quickly, it would have been possible to save more Jews in Spain. As it was, they crossed through the country "como la luz por el cristal" (like light through a crystal), as Spanish foreign minister Jordana stated, leaving no trace ("sin dejar rastro") and never finding asylum in Spain.[47] This was the limit of the Franco regime.

NOTES

1 Israel Garzón, "El exilio republicano," 49–50.
2 Cullá i Clará, "Crónica de un reencuentro," 225.
3 See Lisbona, *Retorno a Sefarad*.
4 Archivo Histórico Nacional (National Historic Archive, AHN): Notes from the German Consulate in San Sebastián to the Chief Inspector of Investigation and Surveillance of the same city asking whether Pablo Zenzer's company Herederos is of Jewish origin (15 May 39); the same applies to the companies J.G. Girod S.A., José M. Maquibar, Juan Mojedano, and Emilio Ciordia (20 November 39); response from the Chief Commissary from San Sebastián to the German Consulate in the same city regarding the Jewish origin of Adolfo and Ernesto Pfeifer (12 August 39).
5 See García Seror, *Los Seror en España*, 79.
6 A question that was usually subject to the goodwill of the civil servant on shift.
7 García Seror, *Los Seror en España*, 88–9.

8 See Avni, *España, Franco y los judíos*, 65.

9 Salinas, *España, los sefarditas y el Tercer Reich*, 31.

10 I originally documented this memo in Israel Garzón, "El Archivo Judaico del franquismo."

11 AHN, 36145. In carrying out this research, I had the support of the Lead Inspector of the Historical Archive Technical Group of the Central Police Archive, Miguel Ángel Camino, to whom the General Secretary of the Ministry of the Interior, Rafael Ramos Gil, introduced me. Carmen Alonso, head of the Contemporary Collection of the AHN, also aided me.

12 Ibid.

13 Ibid.

14 Ibid.

15 Police document from 17 January 1957 and the Decree of the Archivo Central from 18 February 1957 in Jaime Cohen Loya's file.

16 In the document for the cancellation of unfavourable records of Jaime Cohen Loya, native of Tangier and resident of Ceuta, the Ministerio de la Gobernación wrote on 5 January 1957 to the Comisario Jefe of the aforementioned division, saying that "existiendo una tarjeta en este Archivo Central en la que dice tiene antecedents en el archivo judaico de esa División, ruego a V. I. me remita cuantos existan a su nombre para resolver tal petición." (given that there exists a card in the Central Archive in which it says that he has records in the Jewish archive of that Division, I beg you to please send me everything that exists in his name to fulfil this request).

17 A photocopy of the record can be viewed in Israel Garzón, "El Archivo Judaico del franquismo," 60.

18 These cases include some bankers and suppliers for the Spanish Army, in addition to some who tried to make a living as police informants.

19 Nevertheless, numerous Jews suffered because of their sympathies for the Republic or because of their membership in Masonic lodges.

20 A Jew with the last name Cohen, Spanish national and owner of seventy shares of Galeries Lafayette, was forced to sell his stock to another person of the Aryan race.

21 Salinas, *España, los sefarditas y el Tercer Reich*, 53–7, 84–5.

22 Isabelle Rohr further details the relationship between the Jews of North Africa and the Franco regime during the Second World War in chapter 4 of this volume.

23 Various testimonies from the refugees of period are collected in Israel Garzón and Baer, eds, *España y el Holocausto*.

24 Fittko, *Mi travesía de los Pirineos*, includes testimonies of non-Jewish refugees who crossed clandestinely.

25 Sala Rosé, *La penúltima frontera*.

26 AHN; Israel Garzón, "El Archivo Judaico del franquismo," 60n4.

27 Calvet, *Huyendo del Holocausto*, 83.

28 Téllez Solá, *La red de evasión*, 212.

29 The former figure is cited by Rother, *Franco y el Holocausto*, 409; the latter, by Avni, *España, Franco y los judíos*, 89, 123. See the introduction to this volume as well as chapter 5 by Josep Calvet and chapter 8 by José Antonio Lisbona regarding the discrepancies among statistics related to the numbers of Jews who crossed into Spain to escape Nazi persecution.

30 See Yessica San Román, "La experiencia española," in Israel Garzón and Baer, eds, *España y el Holocausto*, 2007.

31 Added to an additional 1,500 to 2,000 Spanish Sephardic *protégés* without full nationality.

32 Lisbona, *Más allá del deber*, 43.

33 Salinas, *España, los sefarditas*, 47.

34 Ibid., 46.

35 Ibid., 61–2.

36 Ibid., 68.

37 He told some to not make known their Jewishness when they arrived in Spain.

38 Palencia was moved from his position because he adopted two Jewish boys whose father had been unjustly hanged.

39 Papo, *En attendant l'aurore*; Lévy, ed., *Les Cahiers Séphardis*.

40 They would be given a transit visa if they had a prearranged host in a foreign country. Regarding this see Salinas, *España, los sefarditas*, 99–102.

41 AHN, 53553.

42 AHN, 657.

43 Evelyne Grand, *Le deuxième groupe. Les juifs espagnols internés au camp de Bergen Belsen 14 Avril 1944-9 Avril 1945* (Jerusalem: EMN, 1994), 19.

44 Grand, *Le deuxième groupe*, 19. See also Salinas, *España, los sefarditas*.

45 Lisbona, *Retorno a Sefarad*, 124.

46 Letter from Bauer to Sánchez Bella, President of the Hispanic Cultural Institute, AMAEC (Archivo General del Ministerio de Asuntos Exteriores y de Cooperación), num. 2328/35.

47 Letter from Francisco Gómez Jordana to Carlos Asensio, Minister of the Armada, 28 December 1943, AMAE (Archivo del Ministerio de Asuntos Exteriores), leg R. 1.372, n2.

4 The Franco Regime and the Jews of North Africa during the Second World War

ISABELLE ROHR

Recent historiography has paid growing attention to the attitude of the Franco regime towards the Jews during the Second World War, but this research has focused mainly on the dictatorship's antisemitism and its response to the Holocaust in Europe. Spain's policies towards the Jews of Spanish Morocco and its Jewish citizens living in French Morocco have largely remained ignored. This lacuna is partly due to the fact that primary sources are rare and scattered. This chapter examines the dictatorship's motivations for reviving philosephardism – the turn-of-the-century movement that sought to foster a rapprochement between Spaniards and Sephardic Jews – and for posing as defenders of the Spanish Jews living in French Morocco.

Spain's campaign in Morocco in 1859–60 sparked an interest in the Jewish population of North Africa. Upon capturing Tetuán in February 1860, the Spanish troops discovered that the six thousand Jews living there were descendants of the exiles of 1492 and spoke a Judeo-Spanish dialect known as Haketia, which incorporated Hebrew and Arabic words. Muslim pillagers had entered the Jewish quarter and sacked all the houses upon the approach of the Spanish troops. On the entrance of the Spaniards, the Jews came out in the streets and welcomed them with cries of "¡Bienvenidos!" (Welcome) and "¡Viva la Reina!" (Long Live the Queen).[1]

The situation of the Jews improved considerably under Spanish occupation as relief funds, food, and clothing were distributed to destitute Jews. In addition, thanks to their linguistic skills, Jewish traders played a prominent role in provisioning the Spanish army. The Spanish occupation brought an economic boom to the Jewish community.[2]

Spain became increasingly involved in northern Morocco in the following decades. Colonial expansion in Morocco was seen as compensation for the loss of Cuba and the Philippines. In an era when a nation's prestige depended on its colonial possessions, Spanish politicians believed that Morocco was essential to Spain's international status. However, Spain's imperial ambitions were frustrated by the Treaty of Fez of 30 March 1912, which gave it a protectorate consisting of a coastal strip of 20,000 square kilometres that represented one fifth of Morocco. The mountainous terrain given to Spain was resistant to military conquest; it was also inhabited by Berber tribes who had a reputation for being uncontrollable. France, by contrast, had given itself the most fertile and peaceful area of Morocco.[3] Adding to Spanish resentment was the fact that Spanish Morocco did not include Tangier, the largest and most important city in northwestern Morocco, which had a natural relationship with the other regions of the Spanish Protectorate.[4] An international conference, which met in 1923, internationalized the port of Tangier. Tangier's executive organ was the Control Commission, whose chairmanship was supposed to rotate among the various nations who were members of the commission. But in practice, a French official headed the commission for fifteen years, a development that reflected France's supremacy in Morocco.[5]

A neocolonial lobby composed of businessmen, journalists, and politicians and including well-known figures such as the regenerationist social thinker Joaquín Costa and the premier, Count Romanones, campaigned for the "peaceful penetration" of Spanish capitalism in Morocco to counter French influence. Among the various groups making up this lobby were the philosephardites, who hoped the promotion of commercial and cultural ties with Morocco's Jews would facilitate Spain's colonial penetration of Morocco. The movement's most prominent champion, Ángel Pulido y Fernández, had ardently defended the clause in the 1869 Constitution granting religious freedom. (For more on Pulido and his association with philosephardism, see chapter 2 in this volume.) Pulido believed that reconciliation with the Sephardim would promote the nation's economic regeneration by opening new markets for Spain, given that Spain had owed its dominance in the Middle Ages to the financial acumen and hard work of the Jews and that their expulsion had crippled Spain's industry and commerce.[6]

Stressing the importance of the Jews of Morocco, Pulido had written: "Ningún pueblo puede ni debe interesar tanto a España, en la actualidad, como Marruecos, y ninguna grey sefardita, entre todas las repartidas por el mundo, debe atraer tanto su atención ni merecer sus solicitudes, como la cuantiosa que vive en este descompuesto Imperio" (No other nation can or should interest Spain as much as Morocco and of all the Sephardic congregations scattered throughout the world, none should attract our attention or should deserve our solicitude as much as the large one that lives in this decomposed Empire).[7]

It was in the mercantile elite of these Jewish communities that the philosephardites were interested. With their linguistic skills – many of them were bilingual or trilingual – the wealthier Jews of Morocco served as intermediaries between the Muslims and the outside world. They held a monopoly over the textile trade and the production and distribution of jewellery.[8]

The philosephardic movement also had a political side. Its proponents, who were persuaded that the Jewish elites of North Africa had promoted France's colonial expansion in the region, campaigned to have Jews switch their allegiance and facilitate Spain's penetration of Morocco. The French had indeed won support among the Jews through the work of the Alliance Israélite Universelle (AIU), which had founded French-speaking schools for Jews throughout the Mediterranean. By 1912, the AIU had twenty-seven schools in Morocco, including five in the Spanish Protectorate.[9] The language of instruction was French, and the AIU teachers used French methods; this led the graduates to identify culturally with France, a matter of concern to the philosephardites. In *Los Hebreos en Marruecos* (The Jews in Morocco), published in 1919, Manuel Ortega, the editor of the philosephardic organ *La Revista de la Raza* and a collaborator of Pulido, argued that Spain could improve its situation in Morocco if it implemented a policy similar to that of France. Emulating the Crémieux Decree, which had extended French citizenship to the Algerian Jews, he declared that Spain should grant Spanish nationality to the Moroccan Jews. The Spanish authorities of northern Morocco should set up Spanish schools and require the schools of the AIU to teach in Spanish rather than in French. Spain should also establish registry offices for the Sephardic Jews in the main cities of the protectorate: Tetuán, Larache, Elksar, Chauen, and Arcila. Finally, the Spanish government should promote trade by having Spanish businessmen visit Morocco and Jewish businessmen come to Spain.[10]

The philosephardites' desire to use the Jews of Morocco to promote Spain's economic and cultural expansion led to the founding of Hispano-Jewish associations in Tetuán, Larache, Arzila, Ceuta, and Melilla between 1912 and 1914. Hispano-Jewish associations were also set up in Tangier's international zone and in the cities of Fez, Saffi, and Mazagan, which were in French Morocco. The goal of the associations was to foster ties between representatives of Spain and the Jews of Morocco and to develop Spain's trade relations with Morocco. The philosephardites also hoped the associations would propagate love for Spain and Spanish culture among the Jews of Morocco, thereby boosting Spain's prestige and moral authority. In Morocco, board members of the associations belonged to the economic elite of the Jewish communities, an indication that philosephardism focused mainly on the wealthiest and most influential sectors of these communities.[11]

The philosephardic movement saw its high point in December 1924, when the Primo de Rivera dictatorship promulgated a Royal Decree that granted Spanish citizenship to a number of Sephardic Jews. The decree was prompted by the abolition of the system of capitulations in the aftermath of the First World War, which had allowed some residents in the Ottoman Empire to enjoy extraterritorial rights and protection by a foreign power. Among the people affected by this abolition were a number of Sephardic Jews who had been Spanish protégés in the Ottoman Empire and as such had enjoyed full protection from the Spanish consulates. They had found themselves without legal status or protection in countries that were prey to nationalist policies (see Lisbona, chapter 8 in this volume). The military dictatorship of General Primo de Rivera seized the opportunity to expand Spain's influence over the Sephardic Jews, enacting the Royal Decree, which granted full citizenship to individuals of Spanish origin who had enjoyed the protection of Spain's diplomatic agents. The decree also affected countries such as Morocco, where the regime of capitulations did not exist but where a number of Sephardic Jews were Spanish protégés. Many Sephardim, however, convinced that they were already Spaniards, passed on the opportunity to obtain full citizenship. Others did not benefit from the decree because the Spanish government required many documents that they did not always possess and because the procedure was quite arduous. As a result, very few Sephardic Jews in Spanish Morocco obtained citizenship through the decree. After the enactment of the 1924 decree, the philosephardites continued to call for the government to grant Spanish citizenship to all Jews of the protectorate, to no avail (see chapter 2 of this volume).[12]

Philosephardism experienced its heyday in the first two decades of the twentieth century and did not disappear completely. Interest in the Jews of Morocco continued after the founding of the Second Republic in 1931 and the coming to power of a Socialist-Republican coalition. In May 1931, the foreign minister, Alejandro Lerroux, announced that the Spanish government was considering the question of naturalization of all the Jews of Spanish Morocco, though nothing came of this. In December 1932, Fernando de los Ríos, the education minister, offered to grant a subsidy of 57,000 pesetas to the rabbinical schools of Tangier. The proposal was attacked by the anti-Republican right, which rejected philosephardism on the basis that Jews, the traditional enemies of Catholic Spain, were scheming with the Freemasons and the communists to bring down Spain.

The generals who staged an uprising against the Republic on 17 July 1936 echoed these arguments, characterizing their rebellion as a religious crusade against a "Jewish-Masonic-Bolshevist" conspiracy. For the next two and a half years, the Jews of Spanish Morocco found themselves in a precarious position as the rebels drew on antagonism between the Muslims and the Jews to mobilize Moroccan mercenaries to fight the Republicans. The Jews were now portrayed as "representatives of Red Spain" who would violate harems and burn mosques in the event of a Republican victory.[13] This antisemitic campaign was accompanied by economic extortion. When the rebellion broke out, fascist youths victimized the Jews by boycotting their businesses and confiscating their properties on the grounds that they were sympathetic to the Republican government. In Tetuán, the fascist-inspired Falangists decided on their own authority to establish their headquarters in the house of a Jewish notable. In the same vein, the military authorities fined Jews large sums of money as a means to finance the war effort. Jews were also forced to hand over their merchandise, including foodstuffs, jewellery, and gold. Those who refused to do so were subject to arbitrary arrests, compelled to drink castor oil, or had their estates confiscated. Albert Saguès, the director of the AIU in Tangier, noted that the Moroccan Jews were unwillingly financing the Nationalist war effort.[14]

Some members of the Jewish mercantile elite, however, did back the Nationalists willingly. At the onset of the Spanish Civil War the high commissioner, Juan Beigbeder, struck a deal with Jacob Benmaman, the agent in Tetuán of the Banque Hassan of Tangier, who offered to finance the rebellion. As a result of his assistance, Benmaman gained the favour of the Spanish authorities, which he used on his co-religionists' behalf. Republican newspapers did not fail to note the hypocrisy of the insurgents, who claimed that the rebellion was a crusade against the Jewish-Masonic conspiracy yet were financed by a Jewish bank.[15]

Although the Franco regime had been helped to power by Nazi Germany and Fascist Italy and loudly expressed antisemitic views, the outbreak of the Second World War did not alter the status of the Jews of the Spanish Protectorate. No antisemitic legislation was enacted despite the repeated requests of the German consul in Tetuán.[16] On the contrary, the eruption of the conflict was accompanied by a spurt of imperial ambitions, which led to the revival of philosephardism. Setting their sights on Gibraltar as well as Tangier, French Morocco, and northwestern Algeria, the Francoists did not attempt to conceal that imperial expansion in North Africa would come at the expense of France and Great Britain. On 18 July 1940, Franco himself proclaimed the mission of empire in his annual speech to celebrate the start of the

Nationalist uprising. "It is necessary" he declared, "to make a nation, to forge an empire. To do that our first task must be to strengthen the unity of Spain. There remains a duty and mission the command of Gibraltar, African expansion and the permanence of the policy of unity."[17] At the time of this speech the first step towards the building of a new empire had in fact already been taken. A month earlier, on the morning of 14 June 1940, when Italy had just joined the war and France seemed defeated, Spanish military forces had entered the international zone of Tangier. Spanish officials contended that the sole object of Spain's move was to ensure the strict neutrality of the zone and that there would be no interference with the existing international civil administration of the town and district.[18]

When the Spaniards occupied Tangier, the Jewish community there had between twelve and fourteen thousand Jews. As the Franco regime consolidated its position in Tangier it abrogated the Dahir of February 1925 concerning the structure of the Jewish council and institutions. All communal projects now came under Spanish supervision. The community leaders, who had previously been elected by that community, were now appointed by Spain and had to be either Spanish or Moroccan citizens.[19] The Spanish occupation adversely affected the Jewish lower middle classes; the Spanish authorities imposed heavy taxes on their businesses and often refused them new licences.[20]

Tangier's Jewish elite, by contrast, which had developed some ties with the Francoists during the Civil War, continued to enjoy a privileged place. They maintained a large share of the import and export market for eggs, hides, and manufactured goods, and they still controlled the banking sector. The Franco regime believed that the wealthier Moroccan Jews, with their considerable economic power, could serve Spain's imperial ambitions. On that account, the Spaniards went out of their way to persuade the affluent Jews in the protectorate that their interests and those of Spain coincided.[21] One gesture of friendship, albeit an incongruous one, was the awarding of the Cross of Isabella the Catholic to the president of the rabbinic tribunal of Tetuán in January 1940.[22]

Colonel Tomás García Figueras, who was first the secretary-general of General Carlos Asensio Cabanillas, then the high commissioner for the Spanish zone of Morocco, and still later the delegate for educational culture, exemplified the regime's efforts to combine Germanophilia and philosephardism. He had been the *interventor* (administrator) of the district of Larache during the Civil War and held considerable power in the zone. Although he was a friend of Ramón Serrano Suñer and was regarded by the British consul general in Tangier as "thoroughly pro-German," he was also eager to promote Spain's ties to the Moroccan

Jews. During the Civil War he objected to the antisemitic campaign in Larache, and after Franco's victory he deplored the fact that Spain had abandoned the Jews of the protectorate by failing to counteract French influence as promoted by the AIU schools.[23] A Francophobe and staunch Africanista, he drew a distinction between the Jews of Spanish Morocco and their co-religionists. Thus, in 1939 he wrote:

> La escasa población israelita de nuestro Protectorado, que se purifica en el ambiente de la España Nacional, se muestra cada día más separada de los métodos y de los designios del judaísmo universal, que lo hacen, a tan justo título, enemigo de la civilización del mundo. [...] [V]iven esas poblaciones, colaborando con su esfuerzo al triunfo de nuestra Causa [...].

> The small Jewish population of our protectorate, which was purified by its contact with Spain, has proved to be unconnected to the methods and designs of universal Judaism, which, with good reason, is [viewed as] the enemy of civilization ... Through its efforts this population lives collaborating to the triumph of our cause.[24]

García Figueras's position was echoed in the Spanish press. In 1941, *El Mundo* noted that the Moroccan Jews did "not serve the aims of International Judaism" and that "they had not infiltrated the state's administrative apparatus, nor invaded the liberal professions."[25]

Central to Spain's philosephardic policy was the desire to reduce the influence of the French over the Jews of the protectorate. The Spanish authorities tried to minimize the role of the AIU, which they regarded as the instrument of France's influence over the Jews of the protectorate.[26] In November 1939 the director of the school in El Ksar wrote to the director in Paris: "The Spanish authorities do not like us. They tolerate us. They are convinced that we are here in the service of France and that we disseminate French propaganda in our schools."[27]

Although they did not close the AIU schools, the Spaniards encouraged the Jewish children of the zone to attend the tuition-free Hebreo-Español (Jewish Spanish) schools instead. But their efforts were to no avail, and the AIU school remained more popular with the Jews of northern Morocco than the Spanish institutions.[28]

An important fulcrum of Spain's philosephardic policy was the defence of the rights of Spanish-Jewish nationals in French Morocco who were affected by the antisemitic legislation of the Vichy regime. On 3 October 1940, the Vichy government published the first Statut des Juifs (Jewish Statute), which forbade Jews to hold any post in the public service, the officer corps of the armed forces, teaching, journalism, the theatre, radio, or cinema.[29] The law, introduced in French Morocco through the Dahir of 31 October 1940, affected the two thousand Spanish Jews living in the French protectorate.[30] The reaction of the Spanish diplomats to the Dahir must be understood in the context of Spain's efforts to squeeze out concessions from France in Morocco. In their campaign for imperial expansion, the Francoists were using demographic arguments, pointing out that many Spaniards lived in French North Africa.[31]

On 31 July 1941, the Spanish Consul in Casablanca reported that the French authorities were refusing to recognize the naturalizations of the Spanish Jews on the grounds that they had not been obtained with the consent of the Sultan, as stipulated in the agreement signed at the Madrid Conference of 1880. This meant, in practice, that the Spanish Jews living in French Morocco were set to lose their citizenship and would be subjected to the antisemitic legislation. These Spanish Jews were persecuted, the Spanish consul in Casablanca, Jaime Jorro, believed, not because they were Jews but because they were Spaniards who, as such, constituted "un factor no desdeñable de penetración económica" (a factor of economic penetration) in the French zone. Anticipating the impending enactment of further antisemitic decrees, Jorro asked the foreign ministry for instructions.[32]

Six days later, on 5 August 1941, another Dahir was issued to introduce Vichy's second Statut des Juifs of 2 June 1941. This decree enlarged the list of occupations prohibited to the Jews to include moneylending and real estate brokering. It also required all Jews in the French protectorate to register themselves and their occupations and to declare their property to the authorities.

On 22 September, Jorro sent a telegram to the foreign ministry asking whether the Spanish Jews could be exempted from the census. "Considero," he wrote, "que desde un punto de vista español no parece posible aceptar la formula francesa y abandonar consecuentemente un importante factor de penetración política y económica" (I believe that from a Spanish point of view, it is not possible to accept France's policy and to abandon an important factor of political and economic penetration).[33]

Jorro's dispatches indicated that the Spaniards' objection to the imposition of antisemitic legislation on their citizens arose from the need to protect their economic position and their prestige in the French zone rather than from ethical concerns. Explicit in all Spanish representatives' reports was a belief in the enduring economic and political power of the Jews and a desire to harness it to Spain's advantage. Thus, on 8 October 1941, the Spanish High Commissioner in Morocco, Luis Orgaz, wrote a report to the foreign ministry in which he made the following suggestion: "Wouldn't this be the best occasion to exploit in the neighboring protectorate a matter, which could have so much political and economic significance for us since the Jews might seek refuge in our protectorate and bring their capital with them?"[34]

The opportunism of the Spanish representatives was not lost on the French. "Jorro is above all interested in protecting the properties of the Jews," wrote the resident-general in French Morocco, General Charles Noguès, in a report to the French foreign minister, Admiral François Darlan, on 4 December 1941. The Spaniards' policy, Noguès added, had a double aim: to create a minority problem by increasing the number of Spanish nationals in French Morocco, and to enhance Spain's economic position there. Spain's overall aspiration was to substantiate her claims in Morocco.[35] Noguès feared that Spain's actions could threaten France's authority in French Morocco.[36]

As the French administration in Morocco continued to refuse to acknowledge Spanish naturalizations, Lequerica brought the issue to the attention of Vichy in February 1942, to no avail.[37] Faced with the resoluteness of the French government, Lequerica came up with an original idea: Spain could retaliate by adopting hostile measures against the French Jews living in Tangier and the Spanish Protectorate.[38] But Lequerica's malicious proposal, reflecting Francoist hostility to non-Spanish Jews, was not implemented, and the issue of Spanish naturalizations remained a thorn in Franco-Spanish relations in Morocco until the Allied landing of November 1942.

Lequerica's suggestion was not all that surprising, given that Spain's "benevolent" policies towards the Jews were directed solely at Spanish nationals living in the French and Spanish protectorates. The Franco regime's indifference to the fate of other Jews living under its control in Morocco is revealed in its position towards the two thousand Jewish refugees of Tangier. Since the latter could not really serve Spain's imperial ambitions, they were barely tolerated. Half of the refugees were Sephardim, mostly from the Dodecanese Islands; the remainder had come from Poland, Italy, Germany, and Austria.[39] They had arrived in Tangier in the late 1930s.[40] In May 1940, one month before the Spanish occupation, the Legislative Assembly of the International Zone of Tangier had passed a law prohibiting the admission of more refugees.[41]

The doors of Tangier remained officially shut after its incorporation into the Spanish Protectorate of Morocco in June 1940; except for American citizens and British subjects, no one was to enter the city unless he or she had been granted a special authorization from the foreign ministry in Madrid.[42] As late as March 1944, the US representative in Tangier noted that "the Spanish occupying authorities in Tangier do not encourage or cooperate in any way either to permit the entry of refugees or succor those who are here." The Spanish High Commissioner in Morocco, Luis Orgaz, opposed Jewish immigration to Morocco over concerns that it might trigger the opposition of the Muslim population.[43] More generally, Spain's policies in Tangier were in line with the Spanish government's refusal to allow Jewish refugees to settle in Spain on the grounds that along with the Bolsheviks and the Freemasons they had fomented the Spanish Civil War and were the enemies of Franco's Spain. (For more on Spain's policies towards Jewish refugees see chapters 3, 5, 7, 8 and 20 in this volume.)[44]

A number of refugees saw their condition deteriorate after Spain occupied Tangier. Among them was Jakub Reiner, who noted in his letter to Ignacy Schwarzbart: "When the Spanish authorities took over the administration in Tangier, the situation changed drastically. Life got much tougher."[45] The growth of German influence in the Tangier zone reflected the Franco regime's pro-Axis leanings.[46] In March 1941, Germany was permitted to set up a consulate general in the Mendoub's palace, which became the Third Reich's espionage base in North Africa. In May 1941, Spanish authorities required all citizens of German-occupied countries to obtain German permits before they could leave Tangier.[47] In August 1942 a group of refugees wrote to the Joint Distribution Committee in New York to complain about the Germans' increasing influence over the Spaniards. They reported being harassed by the Spanish police, who asked them when they intended to leave Tangier. As the majority of refugees did not have visas to another destination, they said they would depart Tangier at the end of the war. The Spanish police informed them that if they did not leave Tangier within four months they would be given "board and lodging free of charge in some brand new concentration camp."[48]

The situation of the Jews in the Spanish Protectorate deteriorated as the tide of the war turned in favour of the Allies. Operation Torch, on 8 November 1942, put an end to the dictatorship's imperial ambitions as the Allied forces landed precisely on the territories in French Morocco and Algeria that Spain had coveted. In Spanish Morocco and Tangier, Operation Torch led to a tightening of Hispano-German relations. The appointment of the Germanophile General Juan Yagüe as commander of the Spanish forces in Melilla facilitated the rapprochement.[49] According to the British Consul General in Melilla, Gore Edwards, the hostility of Spanish officials was such that Melilla had to be considered "enemy territory."[50] The situation was no better in Tangier. There too the Spanish authorities were upset that Spain's chance of taking over

French Morocco had vanished. They were also concerned about possible Anglo-American incursions into Spanish Morocco.

Suspicion abounded that the Jews of Spanish Morocco were harbouring pro-Allied sentiments, and the Spaniards put many of them under surveillance.[51] In May 1942, the security apparatus, the Dirección General de la Seguridad, charged that the Jews of Tangier were volunteering to fight with the Allied forces and were working for the British intelligence service.[52] Oddly enough, even the Jews who had supported the Nationalists during the Civil War were now believed to be at the service of the Allies. The Hassan family, for instance, whose bank had funded the Francoist uprising, was suspected of financing the French war effort, disseminating pro-Allied propaganda among Muslims, and plotting with the English and American diplomatic representatives to re-establish the international status of Tangier. In June 1942, the Spanish police in Tetuán considered expelling Augusto and Joe Hassan but realized that it was impossible because the former was the Portuguese Consul in Tangier and the latter the Portuguese Vice-Consul in Larache.[53]

Jewish refugees were especially targeted. In mid-December 1942, after Spanish authorities raided a synagogue during services, fifty-five Jews were apprehended and incarcerated without evidence for trial on charges of "communist" activities. Five Hungarian refugees were ordered expelled.[54] In the winter and spring of 1942–3, the Spanish authorities ordered all stateless Jews and all Jews who had arrived in Tangier over the past five years to register themselves with the Spanish authorities. The injunction caused panic among the Jewish refugees as rumours abounded that registration would be followed by deportation.[55] But in the end, these threats did not materialize and most refugees were able to leave Tangier for Canada, the United States, and Palestine at the end of the war.

The Spaniards also kept an eye on the situation in French Morocco. Spanish newspapers, which in the first years of the war had denounced the anti-Jewish legislation enacted in the French Protectorate on the grounds that the Moroccan Jews had no part in the "Jewish conspiracy," now decried the fact that along with the Freemasons, the Jews of Morocco and Algeria were recovering their rights. In January 1943, *El Español* charged that there were 170,000 more Jews in Algeria than in 1940, "swarming in big businesses," and that 45 per cent of the leather industry was in the hands of the "undesirable race," though in fact the situation of the Jews in Algiers remained precarious.[56]

Wary of the Committee of National Liberation, formed by General Charles de Gaulle and General Henri Giraud in the spring of 1943 in Algiers, Francoists claimed that it was in the hands of a Jewish-Bolshevik conspiracy whose ultimate aim was to transform French North Africa into a Soviet Republic.[57] The Spanish press saw evidence of Jewish influence on the Gaullist administration in the reintroduction of the Crémieux Decree, which gave rights of citizenship to Algerian Jews and had been suspended by the Vichy regime. *El Mundo*, for instance, wrote in December 1943 that "El restablecimiento del decreto era obligado en atención a la significación política de los grupos que trabajan mas activamente cerca del General de Gaulle" (the reestablishment of the decree was logical in view of the political significance of the groups which most actively support General de Gaulle).[58] Clearly, the myth of the Judeo-Masonic conspiracy was still alive, and to it were tied the Free French and the United States, whose landings in North Africa had thwarted Spain's colonial ambitions.

The Franco regime's attitude towards the Jews of Morocco during the Second World War was determined by its colonization project. The dictatorship's desire to expand its empire in North Africa led it to rekindle philosephardism. The turning of the war's tide in favour of the Allies put an end to Spain's imperial ambitions, sweeping with it the Francoists' pretensions to defend the interests of the Spanish Jews living in French Morocco. The opportunistic nature of the regime's philosephardism was further revealed during the conflict as the dictatorship opposed proposals from Spanish diplomats serving in France and the Balkans to transfer the Spanish Jews whose lives were in danger to Spain. The Franco regime remained determined to prevent the Sephardic Jews from settling after the Second World War. Madrid published two decrees on 24 July and on 10 October 1945, confirming that anyone who had not received citizenship by means of the Primo de Rivera decree of December 1924 or who was not listed in the citizens' register could not be considered a citizen of Spain.

NOTES

1 *Jewish Chronicle* (24 February 1860), qtd in Joseph Jacob Lichtenstein, "The Reaction of West European Jewry," 35.
2 Bautista Vilar, "L'Ouverture à l'Occident," 99–100.
3 On Spain's policy in Morocco see Balfour, *The End of the Spanish Empire*.
4 Pennell, *Morocco since 1830*, 166.
5 Halstead and Halstead. "Aborted Imperialism."
6 Pulido, *Españoles sin patria*, 529–30.
7 Ibid., 480.
8 Driessen, *On the Spanish Moroccan Frontier*, 93–4.

9   Laskier, *The Alliance Israélite Universelle*, 93.

10   Ortega, *Los hebreos en Marruecos*, 343–5.

11   Rohr, "'Spaniards of the Jewish Type.'"

12   Ibid.

13   Archives of the Alliance Israélite Universelle, Paris (AAIU), IV.C.II, "Dépêche de Toulouse" (11 August 1937).

14   AAIU, IV.C.II, Letter from Albert Saguès (27 October 1937).

15   Rohr, *The Spanish Right and the Jews*, 89.

16   Archives of the Ministère des Affaires Étrangères Français (MAEF), Nantes, France, Protectorat Maroc, Direction Intérieure – questions Juives, note au sujet de la situation des israélites au Maroc (6 August 1945).

17   Hoare, *Ambassador on Special Mission*, 48.

18   Public Record Office, Kew London, UK (PRO) FO 371/26960 C4225, summary for 1940 of political events in Spanish zone of Morocco, prepared by Mr Monypenny (17 March 1941).

19   Laskier, *The Alliance Israélite Universelle*, 70.

20   Ibid.

21   MAEF (Paris), *Série Guerre 1939–1945*, Vichy. Sous-série: Maroc, No. 32, bulletin de renseignements No 5 Casablanca (17 January 1942).

22   *L'Univers Israelite*, 12–19 January 1940.

23   Tomás Garciá Figueras, *Lineas generales de la obra de educación y cultura que se desarrolla en nuestra zona de protectorado en Marruecos*, unpublished manuscript, Biblioteca Nacional, Madrid, Colección Garciá Figueras. (1940) p. 22, quoted by Geoffrey Jensen, "Toward the 'Moral Conquest' of Morocco," 223.

24   García Figueras, *Marruecos*, 298.

25   Abitbol, *The Jews of North Africa*, 79, quoting *El Mundo*, 20 June 1941.

26   MAEF (Nantes) Protectorat Maroc, Direction Intérieure – questions Juives, box 2, note au sujet de la situation des israélites au Maroc, 6 August 1945.

27   AAIU, Maroc XI E 178, letter from Mr Almaleh to the AIU in Paris, 29 November 1939.

28   MAEF (Nantes) Protectorat Maroc, Direction Intérieure, note au sujet de la situation des israélites au Maroc, 6 August 1945.

29   Zucotti, *The Holocaust, the French, and the Jews*, 58.

30   Archives of the Ministerio de Asuntos Exteriores y Cooperación, Madrid, Spain (MAEC) R1716/1, note enclosed to the letter of Luis Orgaz, 31 October 1941.

31   Bosch and Nerín, *El imperio que nunca existío*, 56–7.

32   MAEC R1716/1, letter from Jorro, Spanish Consul in Casablanca to the Foreign Ministry, 31 July 1941.

33   MAEC R1716/2, telegram from Jorro to the Foreign Ministry, 22 September 1941.

34 MAEC R1716/1, letter from Luis Orgaz to the Foreign Ministy, 31 October 1941.

35 MAEF (Paris) Série Guerre 1939–1945, Vichy. Sous-série: Maroc. vol. 39, letter from Noguès to Darlan, 4 December 1941, and note from Rabat, 17 September 1941.

36 MAEF (Paris) Série Guerre 1939–1945, Vichy, Sous-série: Maroc, vol. 39, letter from Noguès to Darlan, 11 February 1942.

37 MAEF (Paris) Série Guerre 1939–1945, Vichy, Sous-série: Maroc, vol. 32, bulletin de Renseignements No. 5, 17 January 1942.

38 MAEC R1716/2, letter from Lequerica, 16 September 1942.

39 US National Archives and Records Administration (NARA), RG 59, General Records of the Department of State 881.5011/1 (1940–1944), census International Zone of Tangier, 7 May 1942; Laskier, *North African Jewry*, 68.

40 Blandin, "La Population de Tanger en 1940," 115.

41 Archives from the American Jewish Joint Distribution Committee (JDC), collection 1933/1944 file #1045 (Tangiers, General 1940–1944), report from the Jewish Community of Tangier to the War Refugee Board, 24 February 1944.

42 JDC, collection 1933/1944 file #1045, report from the Jewish Community of Tangier to the War Refugee Board, 24 February 1944.

43 MAEC, R1716/3, letter from Orgaz to the Spanish prime minister, Francisco Gómez y Jordana, 10 January 1944.

44 On the antisemitism of the Franco regime and its reluctance to allow Jewish refugees to settle in Spain, see Marquina and Ospina, *España y los judíos en el siglo XX*; Rother, *Franco y el Holocausto*; and Rohr, *The Spanish Right and the Jews*.

45 Yad Vashem Archives, Archive of Dr I. Schwarzbart, letter from Jakub Reiner, 22 March 1943. The translation from Polish is by Maya Zawistowska.

46 On Spain's aid to the Axis powers, see Preston, *Franco. A Biography*, chs 14–19.

47 Stuart, *The International City of Tangier*, 145

48 JDC collection 1933/1944 file #1045, letter from Jewish refugees to JDC New York, 2 August 1942.

49 Preston, *Franco*, 478.

50 PRO/FO 371/34779 C477, letter from S.R. Gore Edwards to Gascoigne, 17 December 1942.

51 This file can be seen at the Archivo General de la Administracion, Alcalá de Henares, Spain (AGA), Sección Africa, M-2646. The Jews were not the only ones to be put under surveillance; some Spaniards, suspected of being "Reds," and a number of Muslims were also closely watched.

52   AGA, Sección Africa, M-242, letter from the delegation of native affairs to the information service, Tetuán, 1 May 1940, and letter from the Dirección General de Seguridad in Madrid, 4 July 1942.
53   AGA, Sección Africa, M-2644, Note from the Chief of Police of Tangier, 5 December 1942.
54   *Jewish Chronicle*, 11 December 1943, and *American Jewish Yearbook 1943*, 296.
55   *Jewish Chronicle*, 9 April 1943.
56   Vichy sympathizers continued to dominate the administration in Algeria after the US landings, and the situation of the Jews did not improve until June 1943. See Laskier, *North African Jewry*, 71.
57   Olascoaga, *El Norte de Africa*, 3, 5.
58   *El Mundo*, 19 December 1943.

5 Spain, Refuge for Jews Fleeing Nazism during the Second World War

JOSEP CALVET

During the Second World War, Spain became a refuge for thousands of Jews fleeing persecution in the countries controlled by the Third Reich. Jews born in Poland, Germany, Austria, Russia, Belgium, the Netherlands, and France arrived on the Iberian Peninsula during those years. While the Franco regime would falsify the degree to which Spain had played the role of a "land of salvation," it is at the same time true that Spain had taken in hundreds of Jews who chose to flee Germany after Adolf Hitler's rise to power in 1933. Their experiences were varied, but many ended tragically, largely due to the military uprising that became the Spanish Civil War (1936–9)[1] and the subsequently declared antisemitism of the regime installed in the country and led by General Francisco Franco. After the Civil War, Nationalist propaganda continued to fuel the notion that a supposed coalition between Jews, Freemasons, and Marxists embodied a united "anti-Spain," a threat to Franco's regime that must be fought. Jewish residents in the country faced persecution. In 1940, Hebrew rituals such as circumcisions, weddings, and funerals were forbidden. Furthermore, by decree, Jewish institutions were dissolved, Catholicism was imposed on Jewish schoolchildren in public schools, and Jews could not pray in synagogues (see the chapter by Ben Dror in this volume). Consequently, many Jews converted to Christianity out of fear.[2]

Spain, Portugal, Sweden, and Switzerland declared neutrality during the Second World War, and people fleeing Nazi persecution escaped to those countries. Spain and Portugal quickly became important havens due to their maritime connections with the American continent. Spain officially maintained a position of "non-belligerency" (later, "neutrality") despite its ideological similarity to German Nazism and the pre-existing close relations between the two countries. These dynamics impacted the Spanish government's policies, which were characterized by contradictory and inconsistent approaches towards the largely

Ashkenazi Jewish refugees arriving over the Pyrenees. During those six years, Spain went from tolerating those who passed through its territories with a passport and visa to relocate to a third country, to expelling the recently arrived and turning them over to the French and German authorities of the occupation, and finally to allowing them to stay in the country until they acquired documentation to emigrate to America or Palestine, then still a British Protectorate.[3] In this final case, Spain's primary interest was that they leave the country as soon as possible.

After September 1939, those fleeing Nazi persecution began to appear at the customs posts along the French-Spanish border. As Spain tightened the requirements for entering the country and stopped issuing visas, those who were trying to escape had no other option than to sneak into the country across the Pyrenees, which constituted the border between France (as well as the Principality of Andorra) and the Iberian Peninsula. The trails over the Pyrenees thus became paths of hope and liberty for thousands of people seeking to escape death.

Not all the refugees who arrived on the Iberian Peninsula were Jewish. It is estimated that around eighty thousand people passed through Spain between 1939 and 1945. Besides Jews, they included French resistance fighters, politicians from countries occupied by Nazi Germany, soldiers demobilized from those same countries, and military allies. Young French men fled out of patriotism, with the goal of enlisting in the army that General de Gaulle was organizing in North Africa and, after 1943, avoiding the Service du travail obligatoire (STO), which would have compelled them to work for the German war effort. Politicians from occupied countries (Belgium, Poland, the Netherlands) were trying to reach the United Kingdom, where their respective governments-in-exile had been established. And finally, there were Allied soldiers and pilots (North American and British) who had been defeated or shot down and were trying to return to England in order to rejoin the fighting.[4]

Jewish Refugees Arrive in Spain

The flight of the Jews had distinct phases that coincided with the war's events and, especially, with the persecution to which they were subjected in France, a country where thousands from German-occupied countries had taken refuge. The first wave of refugees took place between 1939 and 1940. Initially, most of these refugees were Poles, but after the German occupation of Belgium, the Netherlands, and France (June 1940), the exodus from those countries notably increased. The arrival of the German army in Paris and the drawing of the demarcation line that divided the country into two zones – one occupied by the Nazis, the other remaining under control of the French, presided over by

Marshall Pétain – marked an uptick in escapes. A third phase – the most intense one – took place between July and November of 1942. During those months, the Vichy government became directly involved in the persecution of Jews, culminating in the Vel'd'Hiv round-up in Paris on 16 and 17 July, which saw almost thirteen thousand arrests, followed by executions on 26 August that affected more than six thousand foreign Jews residing in the southern departments of the country. The occupation of Free France on 11 November 1942 saw a spike in the number of refugees-in-hiding there who fled. During 1943, the situation stabilized and the intensity of escapes lessened. The final phase took place from the beginning of 1944 until August of that same year, when the Allies liberated the south of France. After the Italian surrender in September 1943 and the conquest of the territory to the east of the Rhône by the German army, many children and young people who were hiding in that zone moved to Spain when they found it impossible to enter Swiss territory.

Notwithstanding certain reports written by diverse entities and documented historical studies that reveal higher figures (see José Antonio Lisbona's chapter 8 in this volume),[5] recent research conducted in the Spanish archives suggests that fifteen thousand Jews were able to save themselves by passing through Spain.[6] The places of passage varied according to the regulations established at any given moment by the Spanish government. Until the middle of 1940, the refugees appeared at customs posts with the required documentation: a valid passport, an exit visa from France, entrance and transit visas for Spain, and tickets to embark on a ship from a Spanish or Portuguese port. The Spanish authorities gave these persons five days to leave the country.

The situation became complicated in the summer of 1940 when, in response to German pressure, Spain reduced the number of entrance visas it would provide. At the same time, it made a pact with the Vichy government to expel all the refugees it detained within 5 kilometres of the border. These expulsions were indiscriminately applied; there were no set criteria for them. Jewish refugees' fear that they would be turned over to the French police – or, beginning in November of 1942, to German guards – drove some to suicide or self-harm. Strange circumstances contributed to the death in Portbou on 26 September 1940 of the German philosopher Walter Benjamin. Recent investigations have revealed other cases of suicide that had been forgotten for decades. The researcher Rosa Sala has delved into the history and tragic end of the German Jenny Kehr Lazarus, who died in the women's prison in Barcelona in 1942.[7] In June of 1944, various groups of Jews were detained in the province of Huesca and were handed over to German surveillance forces. They were later deported to the Dachau concentration camp.[8] This act represents once instance of Spain's apparent collaboration in the Holocaust. Complications with regard to accessing Spanish police and military archives make it difficult to quantify and analyse the total number of people turned away at the Spanish–French border and returned to France.

The clandestine routes across the Pyrenees followed mountain trails, some of them rising to nearly three thousand metres. There were many access points – two hundred have been recorded just in the Catalan Pyrenees. Simply reaching a crossing point involved a long and arduous journey. Those who were fleeing had to walk for many days through brutal weather, especially in the winter, when the snow was often deep. Consider also their minimal physical preparation and deficient equipment; most of the refugees were wearing urban clothing inappropriate for mountain treks. Some died from accidents; others arrived in Spain only after having suffered fractures, frostbite, or symptoms of physical exhaustion that required hospitalization. Clearly, these flights were epic – even dramatic – acts, and the surveillance in France, especially after the country came under German rule, contributed yet another element of danger. German forces had secured the Pyrenees to prevent escapes, and as part of that effort they had sent Austrian alpine units and dogs trained to follow people's scents. An arrest could mean immediate deportation to an extermination camp.[9]

To minimize risk and ensure the success of the expeditions, resisters organized escape networks whose task was to guide fugitives from anywhere in Europe to the Iberian Peninsula. These networks were initially composed of members of the Allied secret services, who worked to rescue soldiers, politicians, and young men of military age. At the far end of these networks, exiled Spaniards, opponents of General Franco's regime (communists, anarchists, Basque and Catalan Nationalists), and those knowledgeable about the mountain trails into Spain all cooperated. These people helped the Allied forces, confident that their victory would mean the fall of Francoism.[10] These same networks helped Jewish refugees. Others worked exclusively to save Jews; for example, the North American journalist Varian Fry oversaw an escape network from Marseille.[11] As the war ground on, other networks were created under the leadership of the Armée Juive, a resistance group founded in Toulouse in 1942, and the Œuvre de secours aux enfants (OSE), which organized the well-known "Réseau Garel." Both organizations were able to evacuate hundreds of adolescents and children from France. During the German occupation of France, the OSE's actions proved crucial for the survival of children who were hiding in castles and other internment centres.[12]

The refugees counted on the solidarity of their neighbours in border towns on both sides of the French-Spanish border. These people were prepared to help by hiding them in their barns and providing them with food and shelter. In France, some of these saviours have been recognized by the Israeli government as "Righteous Among the Nations," a title that honours non-Jews who helped Jews escape persecution. The Principality of Andorra became the epicentre of some escape networks because of its unique political status and the presence of many guides, as well as hotels where refugees could rest before embarking on the final stretch of the route to Barcelona.[13]

Some refugees were able to cross the Iberian Peninsula and reach Portugal without being captured, but most were detained. Spanish police guarded all the routes out of Andorra and France. The detainees were accused of clandestinely crossing the border and, in some cases, of monetary contraband for bringing foreign money and jewels into the country. As the months passed, the initial bureaucratic improvisation gave way to rigid rules that defined how the authorities were to act with each detainee, depending on age and nationality.

On being captured, the detainees began a long journey through various prison centres. Initially, they would be sent to small cells located in the towns where they had been arrested. They would then be transferred to jails in the capitals of the border provinces (Guipúzcoa, Navarra, Huesca, Lleida, and Girona). Men between the ages of eighteen and forty were then placed under military jurisdiction; they were considered prisoners of war and could be interned in the concentration camp Miranda de Ebro (Burgos), which had survived the end of the Spanish Civil War. It is calculated that in its ten years of existence (1937–47), some sixty thousand political prisoners – including Republicans, members of the International Brigades, foreigners arrested for illegal border crossings, and German border guards – passed through that camp.[14]

Women experienced different treatment depending on the province in which they were detained. In Girona, it was customary for them to be interned in the women's prisons and their children in the provincial orphanage; they would be reunited later in the seaside town of Caldes de Malavella. In Huesca, the detention centre was a prison that had been established in the convent Capuchinas de Barbastro. In Lleida, where there was no women's prison, they were released. Some were occasionally moved to the Provincial Women's Prison in Barcelona or to the Ventas Prison in Madrid. On their release, they would wait for their husbands to be released so that together they could complete the paperwork that would allow them to leave Spain. The defenceless situation in which these people found themselves – they were in an unfamiliar country, unable to speak the language, and usually without economic resources – made decisive and coordinated action necessary to help them.

Aid to Refugees

Beginning in 1940, two organizations dedicated to facilitating the emigration of European Jews – the HICEM and the American Joint Distribution Committee (JDC)[15] – tried and failed to set up offices in Spain. However, they continued to aid refugees from their respective offices in Marseille and Lisbon. Despite their resources, these groups were able to exert only a minor influence as they were working from a distance and going up against the colossal bureaucracy of the Spanish administration. Given these barriers, they sought sympathetic helpers in Spain. The JDC secured the services of a Jew based in Barcelona named Oberlander, who carried out their work, albeit his efforts were severely restricted due to a lack of resources. Luis Stern, a prominent member of the Jewish community of Barcelona (Comunidad Israelita de Barcelona), was also involved in a decisive way. Stern received and secretly sheltered many families and helped others acquire documentation to legally enter Spain or to leave the country.[16]

In this harsh environment for aid workers, some diplomatic representatives of the Allies, especially those from Poland, Belgium, the Netherlands, the United States, and Great Britain, took it upon themselves to aid the Jewish refugees.[17] The British Embassy played an important role, attending to all – without differentiating nationality or origin – who asked for help. The Belgian and Polish representatives took care of their compatriots. The consular representatives stationed in Barcelona who were responsible for the Catalan Pyrenees – the zone through which the largest number of Jews crossed – played an important role. The Spanish Red Cross played a minor part, ceding a leading role to the International Red Cross, which took charge of the refugees who were considered to be stateless – a category that encompassed, among others, the Germans and Austrians who had been stripped of their nationality under the Nazi racial laws.

This fragile organization was overwhelmed as persecutions increased in Nazi-occupied France and Jews took refuge in Spain. During 1941, many obstacles arose that did not have an answer or solution. In the first place, families were separated. Men, women, and children were imprisoned in different centres. The most serious situation was the one facing the men in the Miranda de Ebro concentration camp, who were ill housed and poorly fed and whose release was repeatedly delayed. Also, the process of leaving Spain was far from simple for it required refugees to obtain, besides a Spanish exit visa, an entrance visa for the destination country and tickets for the sea journey. At that time, ships to America – the preferred destination for the refugees on the Iberian

Peninsula – left only infrequently, which meant that a huge number of refugees accumulated in Spain.

Samuel Sequerra and the American Joint Distribution Committee

The JDC was able to establish itself in Spain at the end of 1941. (See also Maria Fragkou's chapter 7 in this volume, which deals in part with "the Joint.")[18] It did so with two basic objectives: to resolve the cases of the prisoners in Miranda de Ebro, and to organize the growing numbers of refugees in Barcelona who had crossed the Pyrenees. Samuel Sequerra, born in Faro (Portugal), knew about the problem first-hand, as several months earlier he had travelled to Spain to resolve a conflict in which a boat had been detained in Cádiz that was supposed to bring refugees to America.

Initially, the Spanish authorities maintained a rejectionist attitude towards Sequerra and his activities, such that he was forced to begin his work under the umbrella of the Portuguese Red Cross. Little by little, his situation improved and he was able set up an office in the Bristol Hotel, where eighteen people worked literally around the clock to help the Jews who, by different routes, had arrived in Catalonia. Their primary tasks were to gather records from groups arriving from the Pyrenees, to negotiate with the civil governments of the border provinces to prevent their imprisonment, to organize medical and economic attention for those who were brought to Barcelona, to fill out the paperwork for their emigration, and to search for disappeared family members.

To attend to so many people, they used a large number of hotels and boarding houses as well as rented rooms in private apartments. The JDC always covered the costs in full. The refugees were required to periodically appear before the police to pass through the established checkpoints. The rest of the time they spent in the city as free citizens, regaining their physical strength, participating in leisure activities, establishing contact with family members, and preparing their departure from Europe. The complexities of organizing their departure meant that their stays would last for months.

The year 1944 saw an increase in arrivals of young Zionists and orphaned children. Many of them had entered through Andorra. The orphans were children whose parents had been deported and who had been rescued from internment camps by Jewish social organizations. These children received special attention: a house in a residential neighbourhood of Barcelona had been rented for them, and Laura Margolis, social assistant of the JDC, who had arrived from the United States for this express purpose, selected its personnel. Its direction was entrusted to Fagia Rabinovitch, who had arrived in Spain illegally, accompanied by her husband, in 1943. In Barcelona, these children and adolescents went to school while they prepared for their departure for the United States or Palestine.

Sequerra opened a JDC delegation in the city of Lleida in order to be closer to the Pyrenees. Finally, his paperwork was successful, and the refugees were housed in hotels in the Pyrenees and immediately moved to other hotel establishments in Lleida and Girona to be brought as quickly as possible to the city of Barcelona. Most of the time, Sequerra was able to prevent the refugees' imprisonment. The JDC's work aroused suspicions among those sectors of the Spanish regime that were closest to the Nazis. In August of 1942, the police searched the rooms that Sequerra occupied in the Bristol Hotel. Two years later, on 18 July 1944, a group of Falangists invaded those same rooms and inflicted significant damage.

From Madrid, David Blickenstaff, representative of the American Friends Service Committee (AFSC), who worked out of an office within the United States Embassy, was in permanent contact with Sequerra. His basic mission was to arrange liberations from the Miranda de Ebro concentration camp and to coordinate the stay in the Spanish capital of refugees who had entered through the provinces of Guipúzcoa, Navarra, or Huesca. The JDC assumed two thirds of the expenses that arose when completing their paperwork. Blickenstaff organized the departure of some of the children who were in Barcelona with their families. The AFSC's work in the name of the American government and in conjunction with Eleanor Roosevelt, the president's wife, facilitated the provision of visas for these children. In many cases, their parents remained in Spain until they acquired their visas months later. Meanwhile, their children waited for them in the United States, protected by relatives or humanitarian organizations.

The process of leaving Spain was organized, initially, by the embassies or by the Red Cross, but when the JDC assumed its place in Barcelona, it took over these procedures. The departures were made from Portuguese (Lisbon) or Spanish (Vigo and Cádiz) ports. The destination for all the refugees tended to be North America (the United States and Canada) or Palestine. In 1944, Sequerra organized two major voyages to Haifa. These ships left from Lisbon and stopped in Cádiz to pick up those who had arrived from Barcelona. Franco had not authorized the departure of these convoys from Barcelona.

In February of 1944, Sequerra and his team aided the 365 Sephardic Jews of Spanish nationality, all of them from Thessaloniki (Greece), who had arrived at the border train station of Portbou from the Bergen-Belsen concentration camp. Their liberation had been authorized by the German government. As had happened with the Jews of

Ashkenazi origin, the Spanish government had authorized their stay on the condition that they leave the country immediately. After spending a few weeks in Barcelona, they were taken to Cádiz, where they left for Morocco. There they settled in the Fadhala refugee camp. Months later, most of them left for Palestine. Maria Fragkou writes about this contingent of Sephardic Jews in chapter 7 of this volume.

**Pursued and Saved: The Memory of the Passage
of Jewish Refugees over the Pyrenees**

Today, the memory of the passage of Jewish refugees through Spain and the importance of the Pyrenees in this historic episode generates notable interest, both in the field of historical investigation and in that of public memory and pedagogical dissemination. Beyond the history books and exhibits that recount the arrival of the refugees, the government of Lleida has promoted the project "Perseguits i salvats" ("Pursued and Saved"). In that territory, bordering France and Andorra, some four thousand Jews were saved.

This emerging project aims to be an exercise in historical memory and focuses on preserving patrimonial roots. In this sense, it highlights the value of these spaces and of the cross-border trails as cultural itineraries, memorials, and works that communicate their roles as places of escape for people who were persecuted and hunted during Nazism. At the same time, it elevates the values of aid and solidarity that the inhabitants of the Lleida Pyrenees showed towards these people. The project's most prominent acts include the marking of five routes used by the Jews who were trying to escape Nazi-occupied Europe and converting the old Sort prison into a museum,[19] a memorial to the presence of these refugees in Spain.[20] The aim, then, is to recognize the acts of humanity and solidarity those living in the Lleida Pyrenees showed towards the fugitives and their plight.

NOTES

1 Valentín, *Voces caídas del cielo.*
2 Rother, *Spanien und der Holocaust;* Israel Garzón, "El Archivo Judaico del franquismo."
3 Josep Calvet, "Spain and Jewish Refugees during World War II," in Guttstadt et al., *Bystanders, Rescuers or Perpetrators?*, 113–22.
4 See this global study about the refugees who arrived in Spain during the Second World War: Calvet, *Las montañas de la libertad.*
5 Avni, *España, Franco y los judíos,* 89.

6 Calvet, *Huyendo del Holocausto*, 277. These data and statistics are derived from my analysis of diverse Spanish archives: the archival holdings of the governments of Girona and Lleida (Arxiu Històric de Girona and Arxiu Històric de Lleida), as well as those of the Ministerios de Asuntos Exteriores (Archivo General de la Administración) and the army (Archivos Generales Militares de Ávila and Guadalajara). My research is also based on an analysis of documentation held by the American Jewish Joint Distribution Committee, which operated in Barcelona and whose archives are held at the committee's headquarters in New York. Its archives contain references to Jews detained in Spain as well as to Jews who managed to cross the Iberian peninsula both legally and clandestinely.

7 Sala Rose, *La penúltima frontera*, 210–23; Calvet, *Huyendo del Holocausto*, 64–5.

8 Calvet, *Las montañas de la libertad*, 95.

9 Eychenne, *Pyrénées de la liberté*, 86–7.

10 On evasion networks, see Calvet, Annie Rieu, and Riudor, *La Bataille des Pyrénées*.

11 Marino, *A Quiet American*; Isenberg, *A Hero of Our Own*.

12 Hazan and Klarsfeld, *Le sauvetage des enfants juifs*.

13 On the role of the Principality of Andorra, see Benet, *Passeurs, Fugitifs et Espions*; Viadiu, *Andorra*.

14 On the concentration camp Miranda de Ebro, see Fernández López, *Historia del campo de concentración*.

15 Bauer, *American Jewry and the Holocaust*. HICEM was an organization established in 1927 whose goal was to help European Jews emigrate. It was formed with the merger of three Jewish migration associations: HIAS (Hebrew Immigrant Aid Society), based in New York; ICA (Jewish Colonization Association), based in Paris but registered as a British charitable society; and Emigdirect, based in Berlin. The name HICEM was an acronym of HIAS, ICA, and Emigdirect.

16 Calvet, ed., *Barcelona, refugi de jueus*, 81.

17 Calvet, "Història del Consolat Honorari."

18 Calvet, *Huyendo del Holocausto*, 245–64.

19 www.camidelallibertat.cat

20 The project can be followed through this Web page: www.perseguitsisalvats. cat/en. The accompanying documentary, "Perseguits i salvats," prod. La Xarxa de Comunicació Local and Diputació de Lleida, 2017, illustrates the plight of these refugees and their importance to the country's historical memory.

6 Routes of the Renowned and the Nameless: Clandestine Border-Crossing at the Pyrenees, 1939–1945

TABEA ALEXA LINHARD

Anne Frank in Spain

In twenty-first-century Spain, just like nearly everywhere else in the world, Anne Frank is a familiar figure. Her diary is widely read and taught in schools; in 2008 a musical, titled *Ana Frank. Un canto a la vida* (Anne Frank: A Song to Life), was staged at Madrid's Teatro Calderón for four months.[1] That same year, Encarnació Martorell, known as the "Catalan Anne Frank" published *Amb ulls de nena* (With a Girl's Eyes), a book based on the diary she had kept during the Spanish Civil War.[2] As Salvador Domènech i Domènech notes in the introduction to *Amb ulls de nena*, Martorell wrote her diary six years before Anne Frank did, between 1936 and 1939. Even though Martorell chronicled her experiences during the Spanish Civil War for reasons that perhaps were not that different from Anne Frank's, her book appeared roughly fifty years after Anne Frank's diary did in Spain.[3] Domènech i Domènech points out that had the Republic not been defeated, Martorell's testimony would have been known much earlier.[4] Yet it is hard to ascertain whether the book *Amb ulls de nena* (not to be confused with the actual diary Martorell wrote) would even exist without the prior publication of Anne Frank's diary, a text that in many ways has become a template for young women's wartime chronicles around the world.[5]

Anne Frank also is present in public areas in Spain: Madrid has its Calle Ana Frank, and in Barcelona's Plaça d'Anna Frank one can find a sculpture that (different from the abstract Anne Frank memorial unveiled in 1998 in Girona on the fiftieth anniversary of the diaries' publication) shows a young girl lost in thought, holding a diary with one hand and a pen with the other. However, passers-by need to look up in order to see the statue reclining on a canopy affixed to the roof of a local cultural centre. Given the name of the square, those who see the statue will immediately recognize the most renowned refugee, the most renowned victim, and the most renowned writer of the Holocaust.

A more interesting consideration here is whether that process of recognition also involves reflection on the links between memories of the Spanish Civil War and memories of the Holocaust. From the Plaça d'Anna Frank it takes only a few minutes to reach yet another sculpture – Xavier Medina-Campeny's rendition of Colometa, the protagonist of Mercè Rodereda's *La Plaça del Diamant* (*The Time of the Doves*), a compelling account of life in Barcelona before, during, and after the Spanish Civil War. This monument has been raised on the actual Plaça del Diamant, suggesting perhaps that the sculpture representing Colometa and the sculpture representing Anne (Anna?) belong not only in the same neighbourhood but also to a shared memory. The proximity of the sculptures proves that the multidirectional connections (to use Michael Rothberg's term) between the memory of the Spanish Civil War and that of the Holocaust are a visible and even palpable reality. Multidirectional memory makes it possible to recognize the ways in which remembrances (and also forgettings) of different events relate to one another, invigorating a deeper and more nuanced understanding of our relationship with the past.[6]

Not only Anne Frank but also other victims of the Holocaust are commemorated in public venues in Spain: in 2016, the municipal government of Navàs (Barcelona) installed seven "Stolpersteine" (stumbling stones), "the biggest decentralized monument in the world," in order to commemorate local men who died at the concentration camps of Mauthausen and Gusen.[7] *Stolpersteine* were also placed at various locations in Catalonia in 2018 in remembrance of Republican deportees, including Neus Català, born in Els Guiamets and deported to Ravensbrück after being imprisoned for participating in the French resistance (see Gina Herrmann's chapter 12 in this volume). Unlike the *Stolpersteine*, which commemorate individuals who once lived in the locations where the stumbling stones are placed, the Anne Frank monuments in Girona and Barcelona are nowhere near where the young diarist ever lived. Yet the connection between Anne Frank and Spain persists, not only because of the well-known diaries but also because Anne Frank's fate is tied to Pieter Kohnstam's. Pieter, seven years younger than Anne, entered Spain clandestinely with his father, Hans Kohnstam, in 1943. In *A Chance to Live*, a book based on Hans's account of the family's escape from occupied Europe, Pieter Kohnstam explains that like the Frank family, the Kohnstam family had left Germany shortly after Hitler was named chancellor.[8] In Amsterdam, the two families happened to live on the same street, Merwedeplein. Anne often played with and also watched Pieter before the Nazi invasion forced the Frank family to relocate to a secret annex in Amsterdam, and the

Kohnstam family to leave the country. The Kohnstams' perilous journey to Spain was a crucial segment of their escape route, which eventually led to Argentina. It is along these escape and exile routes for refugees, today commemorated with various memorials and signposts along the border between Spain and France, that the multidirectional connections between the memory of the Spanish Civil War and the memory of the Holocaust materialize in remarkable ways.

In 2018, a trek across the Pyrenees may not immediately bring to mind the plight of refugees, as today clandestine border crossings take place on the Mediterranean coast, at the limits of the Schengen zone, or at recently fortified border fences. Josep Calvet writes (see chapter 5 in this volume) that between 1939 and 1945 the escape routes across the Pyrenees, both out of and into Spain, were where refugees from Spain and from Nazi-occupied Europe ended up sharing an uncertain fate. Countless Spanish refugees fled north after the Republic had been defeated, and before these refugees' tracks vanished from the trails that took them across the mountains, another group of desperate people on the move used the same ones: Jews fleeing occupied Europe, among them the Kohnstams, and also Walter Benjamin, Jenny Kehr, and Henny Seidemann.

The rules at the Spanish/French border changed quickly and erratically, depending on Spanish, French, and German regulations. Legal entry into Spain was an option for at least some refugees until 1942, but most of them entered Spain clandestinely. The secret and often treacherous paths across the Pyrenees came to serve as crossroads where the Spanish Civil War, the Second World War, and the Holocaust all met. Not all of those who crossed the border in either direction, legally or clandestinely, were as fortunate as the Kohnstams – admittedly, "fortunate" may not be the most appropriate term to describe the experience of a family forced to flee, to hide, and to cross borders at great risk. A look at escape and exile routes leading out of and into Spain shows that those refugees heading north shared many of the experiences of displacement with those fleeing south.[9] Yet studying the plight of refugees, both north- and south-bound in the 1930s and 1940s, is as timely as it is problematic, especially considering current figures about forced displacements around the world.

Escape and Exile Routes

The escape routes into exile from the Spanish Civil War and the Second World War are extraordinarily revealing with regard to connections between the legacies of European imperialism and colonialism, the Second World War, and the Holocaust. Sometimes en route to exile or in the places where refugees settled, the (mainly European) exiles encountered, questioned, accommodated, and at times even supported the racial and social hierarchies that had arisen from earlier imperialist endeavours in Africa and Latin America.

German writer Anna Seghers's long itinerary from France to Mexico comes to mind here.[10] On the deck of the ship that was carrying her and her family from Martinique to the Dominican Republic, she watched two Spanish women, refugees like her, "probably as exhausted as I was," talking to two black sailors from the Caribbean. She offers this insight: "As I was listening, without understanding a whole lot, the size and violence of the past Spanish colonial power became clear to me, the breadth of the 'Conquista,' of the Spanish colonization, that explain why here, the most distant point on earth I have ever reached, part of the population spoke Spanish."[11]

Seghers only became aware years later that Dominican dictator Rafael Leónidas Trujillo, who made possible the relocation of Jewish exiles in the settlement of Sosúa, was responsible for the massacre of the local Haitian population in 1937. Marion Kaplan has studied the history of the Sosúa settlement in further detail, and her research has uncovered the contradictory circumstances Jewish refugees faced in the Caribbean nation. The disturbing fact that Trujillo, who was responsible for the violent and racially motivated deaths of Haitians in 1937, had become a rescuer of exiled European Jews certainly was on the minds of the Sosúa refugee community, as one of its members recalls: "The person who wanted to help us was not a humanist. But did we have a choice? Hitler, the German racist persecuted us and wanted to murder us. Trujillo, the Dominican racist, saved our lives. [We] were in the awkward position of having to be thankful to a murderer."[12]

These words may echo, to a certain extent, the contradictory sentiments and narratives that surface when one takes into account that another dictator, Francisco Franco, also appears to have saved Jewish lives. Yet considering Trujillo and Franco to be Holocaust "rescuers" is problematic, not only because the myth of the Francoist salvation of European Jewry has largely been debunked (see Fragkou, Lisbona, and Correa – chapters 7, 8, and 20, respectively), but also because these two very different instances of rescue need to be understood within larger geopolitical and historical circumstances that made the (rather limited) protection and rescue of Jews in the Dominican Republic and in Spain politically convenient for the dictators.

The reflections of some of the refugees prove revealing with regard to racial hierarchies that remain unquestioned and that are indeed sometimes buttressed in their writings. Photographer Germaine Krull, who, like Anna Seghers, reached the Americas aboard the ship *Paul Lemerle*, was shocked when she realized that European refugees were being guarded by black troops: "Not only are we under the control of Vichy and the boot of the Gestapo, but besides, we whites are now being guarded by Negroes."[13] As Eric Jennings observes, "Krull's racial hierarchies added to her sense of humiliation rather than leading her to reflect on the nature of Nazi or Vichy racism."[14]

The multiple places, borders, and checkpoints that those fleeing racism and fascism in Europe crossed also revealed different yet related forms of racism that the refugees sometimes recognized, sometimes ignored, and sometimes even endorsed. It is in these places that the knotted memories of Spain's war and the Holocaust intersect and where it becomes clear that these "noeds de mémoire" (to borrow another expression from Michael Rothberg) need to be understood in relation to the legacies of European imperialism and colonialism.[15]

However important and revealing the study of escape and exile routes may be, it also is a deeply flawed endeavour. When we study the lived experiences of those who were saved, the fates of those who could not acquire a *sauf-conduit* or a visa, those who lacked the money to pay bribes or purchase their ocean passage, those whom the rescue networks did not reach – in short, all of those who were not saved – should also be part of the conversation. The fact that twenty to thirty thousand refugees crossed into Spain reminds us that there were others who could not do so, who were detained at the border or sent back, or who simply could not make it as far south as the Pyrenees.[16]

Moreover, accounts of escape and exile often appear most vividly in the works of prominent intellectuals and writers, whose experiences tend to overshadow those of ordinary people. Rescue efforts, such as those spearheaded by Varian Fry, were aimed specifically at endangered artists and intellectuals, not at the entire population at risk. Fry, the leader of the Emergency Rescue Committee, helped around two thousand refugees (mainly Jews and anti-fascists) flee occupied France. Hannah Arendt, Marc Chagall, and Max Ernst were among the refugees Fry assisted. Fry is also credited with helping many others, among them Leon and Alma Feuchtwanger, to cross the border between France and Spain clandestinely.

Walter Benjamin, who took his own life in Portbou after the Spanish authorities informed him he would be returned to France, is perhaps the most renowned member of the community to which nobody wanted to belong. As Deborah Dwork and Robert Jan van Pelt point out, "Benjamin died alone and afraid in a strange town, sharing the fate of many unknown refugees who succumbed during their flight or exile."[17] The historians here conjure up the inscription on a glass panel that is part of Dani Karavan's memorial "Passages," in Portbou, a monument that, while certainly invested in the memory of unknown refugees, is intended mainly as tribute to a famous philosopher. The text on the glass panel, taken from Benjamin's own writing, reads: "It is more arduous to honor the memory of the nameless than that of the renowned. Historical construction is dedicated to the memory of the nameless."

"Passages" has become one of the most recognizable and widely discussed memorials in a geography of remembrance that spans the Spanish Civil War, the Second World War, and the Holocaust. A lesser-known (but equally stirring) site of remembrance can be found in the small town of Sort, in the province of Lleida, where the town's prison has been turned into a small museum and memorial. As Josep Calvet explains in his 2008 book *Las montañas de la libertad*, around 2,660 refugees, most of them Jewish, who had crossed into Spain clandestinely, were incarcerated in the town prison.[18] For some of them, the nights they spent in the Sort prison represented the last uncertain moments along their paths to safety and freedom; for others, the Sort prison became yet another link in a chain of incarcerations.

The Nameless

Benjamin was not, of course, the only refugee who died trying to cross the border (though he may be the most famous one). Jenny Kehr, who like Walter Benjamin committed suicide, comes to mind as well. Kehr hanged herself on 12 December 1942, in a cell (or, possibly, a shower stall) at Les Corts prison in Barcelona; the prison reports state that she took her own life because she was "cansada de vivir" (tired of living).[19]

As Rosa Sala Rose narrates in *La penúltima frontera. Fugitivos del nazismo en España*, Jenny Kehr and her elderly mother were deported to the internment camp in Gurs (France) in 1940. Kehr's mother died shortly after arriving in the camp. Two years later, those who were still alive in the camp were about to be deported to the east, and at this point Kehr managed to escape, travelled south, and crossed the Pyrenees, as Benjamin had tried to do two years earlier, on foot. It is likely that she crossed through Andorra. She was arrested, however, on 8 October, in Coll de Nargó, a small town in the province of Lleida, together with her fiancé Max Regensburger, whom she had met in Gurs. Juan Antonio Cremades Royo, the civil governor of the province, ordered that Kehr and Regensburger be sent to the Miranda de Ebro concentration camp in Aragón. But it turned out that the camp was for male prisoners only, so Kehr was instead transferred to a prison in Logroño, then back to Lleida, "como cabeza de ganado" (like cattle).[20]

In a letter that Cremades Royo wrote to the civil governor of Girona, the former referred to her as the "extranjera hebrea JENNY SARA KEHR" (the Jewish foreigner Jenny Sara Kehr) and stated that because she was Jewish and because she had entered Spain illegally, she was to be deported to France.[21] In 1942, Francoist Spain was openly sympathetic to the Axis; officially, though, it was non-belligerent, and there were no antisemitic laws in Spain that would have made the arrest or deportation of Jews mandatory. Yet Spanish policies vis-à-vis the Jews were not based on anything remotely close to a non-refoulement principle. A version of history in which Francoist Spain became a safe haven for Jews had begun circulating even before the war was over; stories like Jenny Kehr's and Walter Benjamin's undermine that narrative.

Kehr's unfortunate encounter with Cremades Royo led to her death. When the civil governor declared that Kehr was to be deported because she was Jewish, he was not following a specific policy. Yet nobody challenged him, so his written order sealed her fate. The rugged terrain and the climate further complicated Kehr's situation, delaying her deportation to France. Since the winter of 1942 was particularly harsh, with snow blanketing the mountain passes, Kehr was sent first to Figueres. It is not clear when she found out that she was to be deported; possibly it was on 30 November 1942, when Cremades Royo signed the order, or on 10 December, when she left Logroño. Because of inclement weather, the train journey was interrupted, forcing her to spend the night in the Les Corts women's prison in Barcelona. The following day, she was to be sent to Figueres, where refoulement to France awaited her. On the night of 10–11 December, Kehr hanged herself in the Les Corts prison in Barcelona. Rosa Mateu Segalés, who at the time was imprisoned at Les Corts, remembers a woman referred to only as "la polaca" who was brought to the prison late on a winter's night. Enriqueta Borrás, Mateu Segalés's daughter, recalls that her mother was asked to fetch "la polaca" early the next morning. She found her body hanging from her belt in the shower. While Borrás does not mention the name Jenny Kehr, it is likely that she was indeed the woman the other prisoners called "la polaca."[22]

The story does not quite end here, as on 27 December, Cremades Royo established a new norm for the refugees who had reached the province of Lleida: family members should no longer be separated from one another, and they were to stay in hotels, not prisons or concentration camps. For Jenny Kehr, of course, it was too late. Marianne and Ursula Kehr, her daughters, who had left Germany with the *Kindertransport* and eventually settled in the United States, published an obituary for their mother on 7 May 1943: "We have only now received the news that our dear mother, Ms. Jenny Kehr, née Lazarus, has left us in Spain on 11 December. Those who knew her will know how much we lost."[23] Marianne and Ursula's loss therefore must be part of a discussion of transit and exile in Spain, including when we consider stories with more fortuitous outcomes, such as that of Henny Seidemann.

Unlike Walter Benjamin and Jenny Kehr, Seidemann crossed the border twice and both times was able to continue her journey to Barcelona. Also differentiating her story from Benjamin's, from Kehr's, and from the Kohnstams' is that Seidemann's entry into Spain was authorized – she had arrived there *before* the Spanish Civil War broke out.[24] Born in Berlin in 1922, Seidemann and her recently divorced mother fled Nazi Germany via Genoa, reaching Barcelona in 1935. There they joined Henny's uncle, who had been working in the Catalan capital. Being "official" residents of Barcelona, the Seidemanns had to register with the German consulate. When the Civil War broke out, the consulate ordered Henny Seidemann, still a teenager, to return to the now increasingly hostile country of her birth (the Nuremberg Laws had been passed three years before Henny's forced return). When she arrived in Munich, the Gestapo detained her, accusing her of being a spy. For roughly eighteen months, Seidemann, whose mother was still living in Spain, was confined to a Jewish children's home in Munich. The situation for Jews in Germany was becoming increasingly dangerous, so in 1938, while Spain was still at war, Henny Seidemann returned to Spain.

Crossing checkpoints and borders in Europe was now far more complicated and dangerous than it had been the first time Henny and her mother left Germany. Henny Seidemann's second escape route took her not to Italy but to Switzerland, where she was detained for six weeks. Her passport was now marked with a "J" and listed her name as Henny *Sara* Seidemann – not unlike Jenny *Sara* Kehr, whose identification as a Jewish foreigner sealed her fate, even though Spain, unlike Italy and France, had never passed racial laws.[25] Seidemann did not have the required French transit visa, so she was trapped in Zürich until a prominent Swiss family was able to procure that document for her. Yet even with the visa, her return to Spain was not exactly a smooth ride. The French visa was valid for only twenty-four hours, and the ride to Cerbère took up most of the allotted time. Seidemann remembers being deathly afraid of controls on the train. The relief she felt on reaching Cerbère was short-lived, for the station was the target of an air raid that coincided with her arrival: "Suddenly I heard a strange sound, 'ssss,' 'ssss.' I thought, what could that be? Back then I knew nothing about air raids. I was scared to death."[26] Yet Seidemann also remembers, quite fondly, that the other travellers were able to comfort her, and even shared their food with her in a shelter while they waited for the raid to end. Eventually Seidemann made it to Portbou, the same town where Benjamin would take his own life two years later.

As the war continued, Seidemann and her now remarried mother were able to scrape out a living in the same city that Jenny Kehr committed suicide. Two years before Kehr's death, the Nazi occupation of several European countries led to the displacement, deportation, and deaths of millions. Among them were Anne Frank and her sister Margot, who died in Bergen-Belsen in 1945; the Kohnstam family, forced to flee Amsterdam in 1942; and a young boy, referred to only as "Armand" in Seidemann's memoir. Seidemann explains that after she and her mother had become aware that displaced Jewish families from Belgium and the Netherlands were crossing the Pyrenees on foot, they contacted the bishop of Tortosa to offer assistance to displaced children. That is how Armand ended up living with Henny and her mother in Barcelona for two years. Armand eventually left for England and later was able to join the surviving members of his family in the United States. Seidemann only mentions Armand briefly in her memoir; his story barely takes up three paragraphs. It is unclear how he was first separated from his family. Stories like Jenny Kehr's and the Kohnstams' reveal the chaotic and unpredictable circumstances at the border that easily led to family members being separated from one another. In that sense, Pieter Kohnstam, who may have been the same as age Armand when he entered Spain clandestinely, indeed was more fortunate, for he never was alone during the arduous escape from Amsterdam to Barcelona.

As mentioned earlier, the Kohnstams and the Franks were not just of the same German-Jewish background; they were also neighbours during their exile in Amsterdam. Otto Frank had offered Hans Kohnstam the option of sharing their hiding place on Prinsengracht 263, but the latter decided that the better option for him, his wife Ruth, and their son Pieter was to leave the Netherlands and travel south. Like so many other narratives of escape and exile, the Kohnstams' is one of near misses. Fleeing occupied Europe, especially after 1942, was possible only with help from relief networks and clandestine operators, and (in Spain) with the complicity of certain elected officials and church authorities who were willing to circumvent rules and regulations to ensure safe passage for refugees.

The map on the cover of Pieter Kohnstam's *A Chance to Live* depicts the family's journey from Amsterdam to Barcelona via Maastricht, Antwerp, Lille, Paris, Chateauroux, Lyon, Gurs (where, among others, Jenny Kehr, Walter Benjamin's sister Dora, and Hannah Arendt were imprisoned), Perpignan, and from there to Barcelona. Missing from that cover is Figueres, the city where Ruth Kohnstam, Pieter's mother and Hans's wife, was jailed for nearly three months. The fact that the account is based on Hans's memories, not Ruth's, may explain why Figueres is left off the cover map. Being separated from a family member was a tragic and all too common aspect of clandestine border crossings into Spain: Jenny Kehr was not simply "tired of living" in the prison cell in Barcelona, she was also, to use Dwork's and von Pelt's description of Benjamin's death, "alone and afraid in a strange town."

The Kohnstams departed Amsterdam in July 1942, just a few days after the Frank family left their home on Merwedeplein Straat. Like Anne's older sister Margot, Hans Kohnstam had received his deportation orders. While one family went into hiding, another family left the country. The Kohnstams' journey across the Netherlands, Belgium, and France was filled with hardship and uncertainty. The farther south they went, the more Spanish refugees they encountered. Kohnstam remembers Perpignan being overrun with refugees.

Unlike other refugees who were trying to enter Spain clandestinely, the Kohnstams decided against crossing the Pyrenees on foot. At this point (early 1943), the controls at the border represented a clearer danger than jumping from one moving train onto another – which is how Pieter and Hans managed to enter Spanish territory. A number of individuals and organizations, among them several lawyers, the French Repair and Maintenance Workers Union, and veterans of the Spanish Civil War, assisted the Kohnstams. Father and son managed to overcome all the risks and eventually reach Barcelona.

Ruth Kohnstam endured a more arduous journey. She was caught trying to cross the border and taken to the women's prison in Figueres. Ruth was imprisoned not because she was Jewish but because she had crossed the Spanish border illegally. It is worth noting here that Jewish refugees often had become stateless by 1943 and therefore were unable to secure documents or visas that would have made an authorized entry possible. Clandestine border crossing was the only choice for most of them.

Waiting, with increasing anxiety, for Ruth to be released, Hans and Pieter managed to survive in Barcelona, possibly crossing paths with Henny Seidemann and her family, or at least with other Jewish refugees in the city, who, like the Kohnstams, were trying to get help from the American Jewish Joint Distribution Committee (JDC), which had established an office in Barcelona. Besides fearing for his wife, Hans was well aware that his and his son's circumstances in Barcelona could change at any moment. Thus, even though the narrative of

Spain as a safe haven during the Second World War continues to circulate, Hans Kohnstam could not have been alone in fearing the threat of arrest or deportation while living in Barcelona: "Although we were guests in a supposedly neutral country, we had to remain vigilant. We frequently saw what I assumed were members of the Gestapo on the streets – suspicious looking men in black overcoats and fedora hats – who made me wary."[27] Ruth, however, underwent a far more harrowing ordeal, which she shared with her husband shortly after their reunion in Barcelona.

The conditions at the overcrowded prison in Figueres were dire, and Ruth witnessed verbal, physical, and sexual assaults. Ruth befriended members of the French resistance and a Polish refugee who, like Walter Benjamin and Jenny Kehr, had crossed the Pyrenees on foot. Shortly before her death, the Polish woman entrusted Ruth with a message and a map for the Allies; she was able to deliver both to the British chargé d'affaires. The diplomat subsequently negotiated Ruth's liberation.

In July of 1943 the now reunited family immigrated to Argentina; a year later, Ruth and Hans divorced. Ruth died in 1995, more than a decade before Pieter published the book based on his father's account of the family's escape from Europe to Latin America. Ruth's actual experience in the prison in Figueres therefore reaches readers via various layers of memory and representation. The implication here is not that her husband and her son misrepresented her ordeal, but rather that Ruth's story, like Jenny Kehr's, Armand's, and even Walter Benjamin's, reaches contemporary audiences in fragments and through the accounts of others.

The fates of these individuals may corroborate that "it is more arduous to honor the memory of the nameless than that of the renowned," as the inscription on Karavan's "Passages" states. Yet most chronicles of escape and transit, even of the "renowned," tend to be contradictory and incomplete. Moreover, given that their names are known, the memories of Ruth Kohnstam, of Jenny Kehr, and of young Armand technically do not count among the nameless. Yet honouring their memory is an arduous task, for it is difficult to evaluate its impact. Henny Seidemann's and Pieter Kohnstam's books are self-published, with very limited circulation. The accounts that Seidemann and Kohnstam themselves were able to write and the accounts of the deaths of Benjamin and Kehr that the refugees, for obvious reasons, could not tell in their own voices represent only a limited sample of the lives forever marked by crossing the Pyrenees during the Second World War, and therefore only a small part of the intricately knotted memories of the Spanish Civil War and the Holocaust.

NOTES

1 The musical was staged between February and July 2008. The play ended
   abruptly and earlier than expected, not because of controversy over its
   form and content, but rather because the production company had not
   paid its rent to the theatre. While the show had the backing of the Anne
   Frank Foundation in Amsterdam, the Anne Frank Fonds in Basel did not
   support it. As Paul Cahill explores in chapter 30 of this volume, Frank has
   become a subject of poetic inquiry in contemporary Spanish verse as well.
2 "El diario de la 'Anna Frank' catalana narra los sufrimientos de la
   retaguardia de la Guerra Civil," *El País*, 20 September 2008; Doncel and
   Gambín, "El dietario de una niña de guerra," *La Vanguardia*, 23 April 2011.
3 *Las habitaciones de atrás*, with a translation by María Isabel Iglesias,
   appeared in 1955, with Editorial Garbo.
4 Salvador Domènech i Domènech, "Encarnació Martorell i Gil," in
   Martorell i Gil, *Con ojos de niña*, 26.
5 There is young Zlata Filipović, the "Anne Frank of Sarajevo"; the
   physician Đặng Thùy Trâm, the "Anne Frank of Vietnam"; Hélène Berr,
   the "Anne Frank of France"; Bophana, the "Anne Frank of Cambodia";
   Hadiya, the "Anne Frank of Iraq"; and Nina Lugovskaya, the "Anne
   Frank of Russia." See Shandler and Kirshenblatt-Gimblett, *Anne Frank
   Unbound*, 13.
6 Rothberg, *Multidirectional Memory*.
7 In 1996, German artist Günter Demnig created the *Stolpersteine* in order to
   commemorate the victims of the Holocaust with plaques placed outside
   their homes (or where their homes once stood). These plaques provided
   information about the individuals who lived in the homes, the date of
   their deportation, and, if available, their date of death. Cook and Van
   Riemsdijk, "Agents of Memorialization." On the *Stolpersteine* in Catalonia,
   see "Projecte Stolpersteine a Navàs."
8 Kohnstam, *A Chance to Live*.
9 Dwork and van Pelt, *Flight from the Reich*, 23.
10 Anna Seghers (1900–1983) was forced to leave Germany in 1933, first settled
   in Paris, then fled to Mexico in 1941. She returned to Germany after the
   war and became one of the GDR's most prominent writers. Before crossing
   the Atlantic, Seghers visited Spain in 1937 in order to attend the Second
   International Writers Congress for the Defense of Culture, where she met
   many Spanish intellectuals and writers. Edward Barsky's Joint Anti-Fascist
   Rescue Committee, initially created in order to support Spanish Republican
   refugees, helped Seghers finance her family's journey from France to Mexico.
11 Seghers, *Briefe an Leser*, 67–8. Unless otherwise noted, all translations are
   mine.

12 M. Kaplan, *Dominican Haven*, 27.

13 Germaine Krull, "Camp de concentration à la Martinique," Germaine Krull archives. Estate Germaine Krull, Folkwang Museum, Essen, qtd in Jennings, "'The Best Avenue of Escape,'" 43.

14 Ibid., 43.

15 "Knotted Memories" is taken from Rothberg, "Introduction."

16 See chapters 5 and 8 by Calvet and Lisbona in this volume, as well as this volume's introduction on the subject of numbers of refugees, Jews and non-Jews, who crossed Spanish territory during the Second World War.

17 Dwork and van Pelt, *Flight from the Reich*, xv.

18 Calvet, *Las montañas de la libertad*, 164.

19 Sala Rose, *La penúltima frontera*, 220.

20 Ibid., 214.

21 Ibid., 215.

22 "Libro de altas y bajas. Libros de filiaciones," *Memoria de Les Corts*. Preso de Dones, 7, http://www.presodelescorts.org/sites/default/files/LlibresAltesBaixes.LlibresDeFiliacions.pdf (accessed 26 June 2018).

23 *Aufbau* 9, no. 19 (7 May 1943), 21.

24 Seidemann, *Berlin–Barcelona–München*.

25 At this point the Nazi government required that Jewish men and women whose first names were of "non-Jewish" origin add "Sara" or "Israel" to their given names.

26 Seidemann, *Berlin–Barcelona–München*, 35.

27 Kohnstam, *A Chance to Live*, 99.

7 Spanish Jews in Bergen-Belsen Camp, 1943–1944: Primary Evidence of Spanish Diplomacy

MARIA FRAGKOU

Before the Holocaust, Thessaloniki (Salónica), Greece, was home to the world's most prosperous Sephardic Jewish community.[1] Some Greek Sephardic Jews who could trace their ancestors to the Iberian Peninsula had been given the opportunity to acquire Spanish citizenship.[2] The Germans occupied Thessaloniki on 9 April 1941 and immediately took possession of Jewish homes and plundered Sephardic libraries that housed significant cultural treasures. The violent persecution of the Jews began in the summer of 1942.

In early February 1943, SS special units arrived in Thessaloniki to enforce the Nuremberg laws. Their task was to put the "Final Solution" into practice. By the beginning of 1943, the Greek Jews of Thessaloniki were living in ghettos, and the German authorities subjected them to many other restrictions and humiliations. They were arrested, and after a brief time at the Baron Hirsch camp, they were deported to Auschwitz.[3] By the spring of 1943, Thessaloniki had been emptied of Jews and declared "judenrein." Both diplomatic archives and oral testimony by Jews during the post-war years provide evidence of the efforts on the part of some Spanish diplomats to convince the Germans to respect the Spanish citizenship of Spanish Jews by exempting them from anti-Jewish measures and persecution. The Spanish consulate in Greece intervened in order to guarantee protection for those Jews who were Spanish citizens.[4]

The radicalization of antisemitism in Greece occurred in 1942; the hysterical tone of the German policy of persecuting Jews reached its height in 1943. Jews with Spanish citizenship were included in the arbitrary detentions and deportations. On 2 August 1943, a train carrying 366 Spanish Jews left Thessaloniki. Until that date, the Spanish consulate had not been informed of the facts of the round-up and displacement.[5] At the same time, the Spanish consular office in Athens, headed by

Sebastián Romero Radigales, asked foreign minister Francisco Gómez Jordana to ensure the immediate return of people who would not be able to bear the punishments of the camp: the elderly, women, children, and those with health problems (see José Antonio Lisbona, chapter 8 in this volume, on Radigales and other Spanish diplomats who aided in the rescue of Jews). The transport of Spanish Jews from Thessaloniki to Germany took nearly six days,[6] although there are witnesses who speak of a longer journey.[7] The displacement of the Spanish Jews is mentioned in archival sources as the result of Spain's refusal to accept them in its own territory.[8] A group of seventy-four Greek Jews also left with the transport of Spanish Jews.[9] Available evidence shows that by the summer of 1943, the consulate was aware that several Spanish Jews had managed to escape.[10] Since the summer of 1942, many Spanish Jews, as well as Greek Jews, had been able to escape to the Italian-occupied zone in Athens, a much safer area. Athens offered possible asylum for Jews fleeing German persecution; those who escaped from Thessaloniki to Athens hid in the homes of Christian friends until the end of the war.

Approximately ten to fourteen days after the detention of 366 Thessaloniki Spanish Jews in July of 1943, all of the Spanish Jews were sent to the Bergen-Belsen concentration camp and jailed in the so-called neutral camp, for prisoners who were citizens of neutral countries. The conditions were less harsh than those faced by other prisoners.[11] Even so, there was a complete lack of hygiene in the quarters, and many fell ill due to overcrowding. The meals were meagre, and hunger was a major threat. Witnesses recall this scarcity as more terrible than the fear of death.[12]

In response to the displacement of the Spanish community, Spanish Ambassador Ginés Vidal was obliged to explain in a report to Jordana why Spain should approve repatriation. Most importantly, there existed the possibility that the Spanish Jews would be sent to Poland, which would make their return impossible.[13] If we examine this information from the perspective of the Spanish government, we arrive at the following conclusion: the Spanish government was, in fact, openly fearful that those returning from the camp might be used for propaganda, possibly by the Allies in Germany.[14] The multiple negative effects of this propaganda could include the political weakening of Spain or the growth of anti-Spanish sentiment.

Support for Spanish Jews was Spanish government policy almost from the beginning, but that policy gradually shifted as the war went on and the issue took on unprecedented importance for Spain's diplomatic relations. Madrid had no choice but to concern itself with the Sephardic community in Greece, and this turned out to be a complex and daunting task. The Spanish government declared its intention to bring the Spanish Jews to Spain; however, Francisco Franco, Francisco Gómez Jordana, and José María Doussinague were not in favour of granting them permanent residence in Spain.[15] It was clear that the Spanish government had begun, through its conversations with Berlin, to establish its own strategy for ensuring the survival of the Spanish Jews. The diplomats' evident interest in seeing a successful resolution to the situation prefigures the later efforts of members of the Spanish government, who sought ways to more effectively counter pressures from the Allies. We shall examine these pressures in the next section.

The Final Solution in Athens and the Detention of Spanish Jews

In August of 1943, the Spanish consul Sebastián Romero Radigales attempted to protect the Spanish Jews living in Athens from forced labour and displacement. On 8 September 1943, after Italy surrendered to the Allies, the Germans occupied Athens. That same month, the Rosenberg committee, responsible for the enforcement of race laws, arrived in Athens and took preliminary measures against Greek Jews, whose deportation was all but certain. The Spanish consulate was informed that foreign Jews would be deported under the responsibility of their countries of citizenship.[16] The Spanish consul had communicated to the foreign affairs ministry its demand that the Spanish Jews in Athens be repatriated. That ministry decided not to accede to the consul's demand.[17] Spanish diplomatic protection had proved to be exceptionally effective in Greece, but it was only a unilateral solution. There was no bidirectional communication between the consulate and the foreign affairs ministry.

The Spanish consul had made enormous efforts to organize the safe transport of Spanish Jews to Spain, in accordance with its strategy during the war and its hope of reaching a diplomatic solution to the situation.[18] Spain's offer of territorial asylum would restore the uneasy security the Spanish Jews experienced in Greece. The petition made by the Spanish consulate apparently sought to prevent displacement, forced labour, and persecution. Radigales stated, "Por supuesto, saben la tragedia que esto significaría. La comunidad está aterrorizada y es rehén de la angustia mientras espera la respuesta que se de a mi solicitud" (Of course, you know what a tragedy this would be. The community is terrified and is in the grip of great anxiety as it awaits an answer to my request).[19]

A confidential report from the German Embassy stated that, in the negotiations carried out from 1942 to February 1943, the Spanish government repeatedly emphasized that it was not concerned about the Spanish Jews and only much later (in the winter of 1943) approved their return in general terms. The deadlines agreed upon for this repatriation passed without a declaration of intentions on the part of the Spanish authorities. The approval of the return of the Spanish Jews was later modified so that each case would require individual authorization by officials in Madrid. As a consequence, the transfer of the Spanish Jews from Thessaloniki was delayed for months, with the result that those Jews were taken to a special concentration camp, Bergen-Belsen.[20]

In the spring of 1944, the Germans in Athens began to implement a harsher policy towards the Jews. Later, Hauptsturmführer Dieter Wisliceny arrived in Athens with detailed plans for destroying the city's Jewish community.[21] Jews, Greeks, and foreigners were detained by German police on the night of 24 March 1944.[22] These unexpected nocturnal detentions were carried out in such a way that no one could escape. Many Christian Greeks and several organizations attempted to help the Jews by finding hideouts for them. Some Jews in Athens joined resistance organizations.[23] The detentions in Athens, which had been carefully planned, followed the same pattern as had been employed in Thessaloniki. In many cases, married couples in which one member was not Jewish were not detained.[24]

The Spanish Jews were taken to the Haidari concentration camp, 6 kilometres from the centre of Athens, where the Spanish consul was permitted to visit them.[25] The number of Spanish Jews captured rose to 180 persons; sixty were still at large.[26] Many attempted to hide, but most turned themselves over to the German authorities. Indeed, those who asked the Spanish consul what they should do were advised to turn themselves in, given that if they hid, they would be lumped together with the Greek Jews and would be given the same treatment if arrested. If they turned themselves in, however, they would be guaranteed transfer to Spain within a reasonable time.

Those detained in Athens and in various other parts of Greece (Thessaloniki, Epirus, Corfu), and Jews of different nationalities – Spanish (180 persons), Portuguese (nineteen), French, Italian, and Greek – were all taken to Athens and, on the night of 1 April, driven in secured vehicles to the Rouf railway station. There they were loaded into thirty-seven packed train cars in groups of eighty to one hundred to be sent north.[27] The train cars were sealed, and employees placed boards and barbed wire over the small windows. People were piled on top of one another; pregnant women, children, persons with disabilities, and seniors were all crying out for help. In other cars, just as full, were the Spanish Jews.[28] The windows of these cars were not sealed, and the Germans allowed the consul to provide them with foodstuffs.[29] After an exhausting and miserable journey, the Spanish and Portuguese Jews arrived at the Bergen-Belsen camp.[30]

The German foreign affairs ministry later reported to the Spanish Embassy in Berlin that the Spanish Jews were not in fact being sent to Portbou, but rather to a concentration camp in Germany.[31] This deceit on the part of the Germans was likely a common tactic; in this case, it seems that the Germans had convinced the Spanish consul that the Jews would be sent to Spain in order to enlist the consul's help in getting them out of Athens. In April of 1944, after some delay, the foreign ministry pushed through an urgent authorization for the transport of a group of four hundred Spanish Jews from Athens, from Greece to Turkey and thence to Palestine. Following the Athens deportations, several Spanish citizens who were in hiding in the city were identified by German police and sent to the Haidari concentration camp, to be freed only after the Spanish consulate had repeatedly intervened.[32]

When the Spanish Jews from Athens arrived at Bergen-Belsen, they found the Greek Jews from Thessaloniki already there. They learned, moreover, that other Jews from Thessaloniki, those with Spanish citizenship, had been there but had left three months earlier, although no one knew exactly where they had been sent.[33] They remained in the camp with their families for one year, living in large wooden barracks, the women separated from the men. Among those brought to Bergen-Belsen were Polish Jews (who were citizens of South American countries), as well as Jews from Hungary, the Netherlands, France, Argentina, Romania, Yugoslavia, and Turkey. The German authorities did not require the Spanish Jews to engage in forced labour, but as was the case in all camps, the prisoners suffered from illness, malnutrition, and beatings.

Materials in the foreign ministry archives in Madrid provide valuable information regarding the protection of property belonging to Spanish Jews in Athens. In July of 1944, the Spanish consul named a committee to help with the task of collecting, storing, and documenting property that the deported Spanish Jews had left behind in Athens.[34] Using the network of Spanish volunteers who had stayed on in Athens, the committee stored furniture, valuables, and other property. The consulate's intervention sought mainly to avoid confiscations[35] by the Greek authorities and, later, to offer practical aid in solving problems surrounding the recovery of property.

The displacement of the Spanish Jews, and more specifically their unknown destination, as well as new political commitments taken on mainly in Madrid, led to Spain's diplomatic contacts with the Allies. At the same time, the case of Greece was influenced by the important but relatively "silent" presence of humanitarian groups and their various actions on behalf of the Spanish Jews.[36] The intervention of the

American Joint Distribution Committee (JDC) would help in the successful completion of the rescue mission (see Calvet, Rohr, Lisbona, and Correa in this volume on the Joint). Indeed, in May of 1944, the Lisbon chapter of the JDC, in a letter to the New York chapter, emphasized the dire situation of Athens's Spanish Jews, and the organization recommended that they be returned to Spain or taken out of the country by way of Turkey and Palestine.[37]

From the Bergen-Belsen Camp to Spain

The Spanish Jews remained in the Bergen-Belsen camp until 7 February 1944. Then, under American diplomatic pressure, they were transferred to Spain in two groups.[38] Spain received the Spanish Jews, agreeing to house them, but without offering them any economic assistance or direct support. In this way, Spain could neutralize any anti-Spain political campaign that might seek to accuse the country of having adopted racist policies.[39] The route passed through Hanover, Frankfurt, Salzburg, Mulhouse, Dijon, Lyon, Perpignan, and Portbou, with Barcelona as the final destination. For the first group, the journey from Germany to the Spanish border lasted six days. Between 10 and 13 February, 365 Spanish Jews from Bergen-Belsen were allowed entry at Portbou, and it was assumed that when they left Spain, efforts would continue on behalf of other Spanish citizens. Portbou became a symbol of freedom.

The commander of the German police, who accompanied the mission, returned their certificates of nationality to the refugees. The Spanish Ambassador in Berlin, Ginés Vidal, travelled to the Spanish border at Portbou to witness the entry into Spain of the 365 Spanish Jews and to give them their passports. On a special train, the group from Thessaloniki left Bergen-Belsen for Portbou; they were divided into two groups to facilitate the repatriation process. The first group, consisting of 182 people, arrived in Quimper, France, on 8 February and remained there until 10 February, later crossing the Spanish border at Portbou. The second group, consisting of 183 people, left Bergen-Belsen on 7 February. The mission arrived in Spain on 13 February and proceeded to Barcelona the next day.[40]

The voyage was to have lasted four days, and rations were provided accordingly, but by the time they had reached Quimper, food was in short supply. The German authorities were unable to provide anything, first because there was no food, and second because the village was small and they were unable to source what would be needed for such a large group.[41] Among other problems the group faced was the delay in the approval for their exit from France. Thus, the group was forced to remain at the station, unable to leave the train, until 10 February. On 11 February, after being approved to leave France, 172 members of the mission left on a train to Barcelona.[42] Before their entry into Spain, the members of this group found themselves without money, without any luggage, and in a deplorable situation; many of them were ill.[43] Three members of the mission had been unable to continue because they had to remain at the station hospital.

The second mission, made up of 183 people, made the journey without incident, except for a day's delay due to bombings in the area around Frankfurt. The group left Germany on 7 February and arrived in Spain on 13 February, making a single stop in Quimper, where the police conducted a border check. This time there was no food shortage, as rations were supplied by social aid. On 14 February, the day after their arrival in Spain, the group headed for Barcelona in three cars that were added to the train.

At the Spanish border they were greeted by Spanish authorities and a representative of the American JDC, Samuel Sequerra.[44] The Spanish government was entirely responsible for the six-month delay in the group's arrival in Spain. German authorities were not responsible for the protracted process; indeed, the Germans had asked the Spanish government to speed up the paperwork.[45] The Spanish government considered itself responsible only for the entry permits and had tasked the American JDC with clearing the remaining bureaucratic hurdles, even though those hurdles involved Spanish citizens.

Spanish authorities had insisted that the refugees be sent to the ports of Cadiz and Málaga and from there to a camp in northern Africa.[46] When, on 10 and 13 February, 365 Spanish citizens arrived in Spain, Spanish authorities took on the responsibility of housing them temporarily in Barcelona.[47] The diplomatic status of the Spanish Jews had been designated as "special," similar to that of other war refugees.[48] The Franco government had not agreed to permanent residence for the Spanish Jews, but decided they would be allowed to remain in the country temporarily. The Spanish government argued that this was necessary in order to make room for other Spanish deportees who were expected to be set free. This policy reduced the number of Jews who entered Spain during the war. It could be argued that the policy had two consequences for the Spanish Jews. The first was of a legal nature: the rights of the Spanish Jews were structurally different from those of other Spaniards. The second consequence proved purely political, in that the policy was linked to the fear of the communist threat, as well as to the conspiracy between Jews and Freemasons that all Jews represented.

Special Diplomacy and Organization of Rescue and Recovery Missions by the American Joint Distribution Committee

The War Refugee Board (WRB) was founded by the American government in 1944 as an integral part of the war effort against the Germans and with the goal of saving the greatest possible number of people belonging to defenceless persecuted groups.[49] Responding to an urgent request from the WRB representative, the interior minister in Madrid assured the JDC representative, David Blickenstaff,[50] that residence permits and immigration visas would be granted to all refugees who arrived in Spain. In accordance with a diplomatic agreement between Spain and the United States, the groups of Spanish Jews would be accepted in Spain.[51] The Spanish government finally agreed to an increase in entry and transit visas, and in general to cooperate with US diplomatic missions aimed at rescuing groups of Jews. In the winter of 1944, American diplomats cited the "Jewish question" as a factor in Spain's foreign policy.[52] American diplomacy had already used threats of boycott, and of famine by economic blockade, as well as extortion and psychological warfare, to bend Spanish foreign policy to its will.[53] By every indication, these relations were complex and shifting throughout the war and point to the effective coordination between different government services and humanitarian organizations. These organizations, in turn, sought to support collective action on the part of government officials, diplomats, and volunteers of various stripes, who undertook a wide range of actions in an effort to overcome the deficiencies of anaemic Spanish institutions. The Spanish government, for its part, sought guarantees and set forth requirements to be met prior to the 1944 repatriation:

a) All expenses resulting from the Spanish Jews' time in Spain, as well as the costs of documentation and travel to their final destinations, were to be the sole responsibility of the Jewish organizations that had promised the Spanish government their assistance in facilitating these actions.[54]
b) The American JDC and the American Friends Service Committee would make all arrangements necessary for acquiring Spanish visas for the foreign countries they considered of interest. Also, these American agencies would take on the costs of visas for the final destinations.[55]

Within a short time, American diplomacy had successfully exerted its influence despite opposition from the Spanish foreign ministry.

Pressure came from all sides of the rescue program for Spain to offer refuge to the 155 Spanish Jews from Athens still at Bergen-Belsen and whose entry into Spain had been agreed upon by the Spanish government and German authorities. The transfer of this group to Spanish territory would depend, however, on military developments. The US government urged the Spanish government to use all means at its disposal to facilitate the group's arrival in Spain.[56] If their transfer to Spain proved impossible, the Spanish government was to take the measures necessary for the group's temporary entry into Switzerland until such time as a more permanent solution could be found. The group's entry into Switzerland represented a viable option, given that the Swiss government already viewed that proposal favourably.[57] The months that followed were particularly significant for the process of repatriating the Spanish Jews; their exit from Switzerland was blocked by German authorities.[58] The US embassy clung to the humanitarian nature of the matter and thought that the Spanish embassy in Bern should communicate with the Swiss government.[59] Exerting strong diplomatic pressure, a report from the US Embassy, dated 24 October 1944, sought the Spanish government's intervention on behalf of those 155 Spanish citizens. The diplomatic missions focused on the measures to be adopted and led to two successive actions. The first was the mobilization of the Spanish Ambassador in Berlin, Ginés Vidal, who worked with the German government to arrange the group's release and its entry into Switzerland.[60] The second was a detailed study of the specific requirements of such a plan, which emphasized the role of the American JDC. Specifically, JDC representative Sally Mayer, from Sankt Gallen (Switzerland), made the necessary agreements with the Swiss government to ensure appropriate care for this group during their stay in Switzerland.[61]

After the repatriation of the two groups of Thessaloniki Spanish Jews from Bergen-Belsen to Spain, once on Spanish territory, the liberated Spanish Jews were taken to Barcelona, where they received housing at five different hotels. They remained in the city for four months. The JDC attended to the growing needs of the Spanish refugees, offering them services, food, money for transportation, and so on. As we learn in the especially vivid oral testimonies of those who were children at the time, for many of them Spain represented a return to "normal life," and their personal memories are closely tied to Spain during that period. These testimonies underscore the facts by offering a richer, more complex view of the past. The personal memories often focus on the hospitality, the care, and the hot meals they received after the scarcity they had experienced in the camp.[62] But soon, a new disappointment

came: the arrival of these Spanish citizens spurred the government ultimately to deny their permanent settlement in Spain.[63]

Shortly after the repatriation of the Spanish Jews, vice-consul
Salomón Ezratty and José María Doussinague (Director General of
Foreign Policy) attempted to resolve the group's various problems.[64]
After four months in the country, 1,100 refugees left Spain. In April
1944, the two groups of Spanish Jews from Thessaloniki, as well as
other Jews, boarded two ships sailing to Palestine under the supervision of the Jewish Agency.[65] As stated in an AJCD document concerning this group of refugees, Spanish and French authorities had agreed
to allow their transfer to North Africa.[66] On 15 June 1944, the Spanish
Jews left Barcelona, headed by way of Madrid to the Port of Cádiz,
where they would board an American ship that would take them to
Morocco.[67] Their destination was the UNRRA camp "Mariscal Lyautey"
near Casablanca, controlled by the US government. The group was
moved from Spain to North Africa to the Fadhala refugee camp, near
Casablanca.[68] This is confirmed in a report by the American official M.
Beckelman, head of the UNRRA mission.[69] As director of the camp,
Beckelman did everything possible to ensure good conditions – both
materially and in terms of morale – for the group's arrival and stay. The
result was a pleasant environment with the possibility of school for the
children and work in the camp or in the city for the adults. The adults
received training in various skills to facilitate their reintegration into
the workforce; they also participated in artistic activities.[70]

The Spanish Jews had to remain at the camp until such time as they
could return to Greece or, if they wished, immigrate to Palestine.[71] In
addition to the Spanish Jews living at the camp, there were also Spanish
Communists, who had been persecuted by the Franco regime. Three
months later, the Spanish Jews were transported to Gaza in Palestine.
Soon, other refugees from Europe would arrive at the Egyptian camp.
This time, the Spanish Jews were taken to Algeria, with liberated Italy
as their final destination. In Port Said, British soldiers greeted them and
guided them to the UNRRA camp near Gaza.[72] After a period of isolation in the difficult conditions imposed by the British army, they settled
in Tel Aviv.[73] Most of them returned to Greece[74] on 7 August 1945.[75]

The British Army liberated Bergen-Belsen on 15 April 1945. By the
spring of 1945, only the Spanish Jews from Athens (155 persons) were
left at Bergen-Belsen, as the Spanish Jews from Thessaloniki (365 persons) had been repatriated to Spain. During the evacuation of the camp,
the Germans placed the Spanish Jews – along with Dutch, Hungarian,
Polish, Belgian, and Czechoslovakian internees – aboard a train, which
was freed by US troops between Magdeburg and Stendahl. Chaos

prevailed during the early days of the liberation following Germany's defeat, with hundreds of thousands of refugees wandering from place to place throughout Europe. The Spanish Jews who had been taken to Bergen-Belsen faced difficulties returning to their homeland after the war.

As recent history indicates, the Spanish government attempted to balance political pressures, ideological commitments, and diplomatic requests with regard to its citizens residing in Greece. Antisemitic ideas prevailed at the expense of aid and acceptance. As one studies the history of the Second World War – the tensions between aspirations and expectations, between aid and indifference, between neutral countries and the Allies, between political vision and self-interest – the contradictions of politics patently reveal themselves. The Spanish government of that period was not in a position to address the issue of the Spanish Jews with a generous policy.[76] Nevertheless, Spain did contribute to rescue operations in spite of strong disagreements over its strategy. That strategy followed government objectives that changed according to historical, political, and diplomatic circumstances. All of this causes us to reflect, productively and critically, upon how the history of Spanish Jews in Greece exposes the pain and the loss experienced even by those Jews who had the good fortune of being citizens of a neutral country.

NOTES

1 Mazower, *Salonica, City of Ghosts.*
2 In the late nineteenth century and into the twentieth, the predominance of a liberal political agenda in Madrid, with a broadening of civil liberties, revived Spanish interest in the eastern Sephardic communities. In Europe as a whole, the Sephardic campaign, begun in 1904, had as its objective the granting of Spanish citizenship to the Sephardim, in the name of a supposed reconciliation with the past. Spanish senator Ángel Fernández Pulido was the first to emphasize the urgent need to protect the interests of Spain in the eastern Mediterranean. This agenda linked the protection of Spanish interests in the East with the preservation of the Sephardic language and culture. The objective was to conserve Spanish influence and to prevent the Jewish element from being absorbed by the Greek state. Historically, politically, and juridically, the Spanish government favoured recognition of Spanish citizenship for Jews of Spanish origin, for their descendants, and for all persons belonging to families of Spanish origin. Those interested in pursuing citizenship were to present an application and the necessary documents to the Spanish Consulate in Thessaloniki.

The program began in 1913, after the Balkan Wars ended, with the first registrations of Sephardim by the consulate. The granting of Spanish citizenship continued in 1916, with 190 to 298 families, in accordance with Miguel Primo de Rivera's Real Decreto, and in 1930 with the bilateral agreement, with 144 families. See Morcillo Rosillo, "La diplomacia española." See also Alcheh Saporta, *Los españoles sin patria de Salónica.*

3 For the extermination of Jews in Greece, see Mazower, *Inside Hitler's Greece*; Bowman, *The Agony of Greek Jews.*

4 Archives of the Ministry of Foreign Affairs and Cooperation, Madrid (AMAE), R 1716, Dispatch from the Spanish Ambassador in Berlin, Ginés Vidal, to the Minister of Foreign Affairs, Francisco Gómez Jordana, Berlin, 18 June 1943. For oral testimonies referring to Spanish consular protection, see Paul V. Galvin Library, Illinois Institute of Technology (PVGL IIT), Testimony of Jacob Button, Spools 9–25, Paris, 5 August 1946.

5 AMAE, R 1716, Dispatch from the Spanish Consul General in Athens, Sebastián de Romero Radigales, to the Minister of Foreign Affairs, Jordana, Athens, 8 August 1943.

6 Testimony of Isy Revah, Thessaloniki, 2007.

7 eSefarad Noticias del Mundo Sefaradí, Testimony of Isaac Revah, Madrid, 28 January 2011.

8 AMAE, R 1716, Dispatch from the Spanish Ambassador in Berlin, Vidal, to the Minister of Foreign Affairs, Jordana, Berlin, 20 August 1943.

9 AMAE, R 1716, Dispatch from Spanish Consul General in Athens, Radigales, to the Minister of Foreign Affairs, Jordana, Athens, 8 August 1943.

10 AMAE, R 1716, Dispatch from Spanish Consul General in Athens, Radigales, to the Spanish Ambassador in Berlin, Vidal, Athens, 13 August 1943.

11 Centro Sefarad – Israel (CSI), Testimony of Isaac Revah, Madrid, 27 January 2014.

12 PVGL IIT, Testimony of Nechama Epstein-Kozlowski, Spools 9–95, 9–96, 9–104A, Tradate, Italy, 31 August 1946.

13 AMAE, R 1716, Dispatch from the Spanish Ambassador in Berlin, Vidal, to the Minister of Foreign Affairs, Jordana, Berlin, 13 August 1943.

14 Ibid.

15 AMAE, R 1716, Dispatch from the Minister of Foreign Affairs Jordana, to Spanish Consul General in Athens, Radigales, San Sebastian, 20 August 1943.

16 AMAE, R 1716, Dispatch from Spanish Consul General in Athens, Radigales, to the Minister de Foreign Affairs, Jordana, Athens, September 1943.

17 Ibid.

18 Ibid.

19 Ibid.

20 AMAE, R 1716, Dispatch from the German Ambassador in Spain to the Ministry of Foreign Affairs, Jordana, Madrid, 18 January 1944.

21 Alois Brunner and Dieter Wisliceny were leaders of Eichmann's *Sonderkommando*; they arrived in Thessaloniki on 6 February 1943. Brunner and Wisliceny applied the Nuremberg laws, which were aimed at the destruction of Jewish communities, first in Thessaloniki in the spring of 1943, and later in Athens in the spring of 1944.

22 AMAE, R 1716, Dispatch from the Spanish Consul General in Athens, Radigales, to the Minister of Foreign Affairs, Jordana, Athens, 26 March 1944.

23 For scholarship on the history of resistance in Greece, see Novitch, *Le passage des barbares*; Eudes, *Les kapetanios*; Bowman, *Jewish Resistance in Wartime Greece*.

24 AMAE, R 1716, Dispatch from the Spanish Consul General in Athens, Radigales, to the Minister of Foreign Affairs, Jordana, Athens, 26 March 1944.

25 Ibid.

26 Ibid.

27 Hellenic Ministry of Foreign Affairs (MFA), 5/3, Administration of Special Services of War, Office II, A, Information, Athens, May 1944.

28 Ibid.

29 Ibid.

30 PVGL IIT, Testimony of Nino Barzilai, Spools 9–21B, Paris, 4 August 1946.

31 AMAE, R 1716, Dispatch from the Spanish Ambassador in Berlin, Vidal, to the Minister of Foreign Affairs, Jordana, Berlin, 9 April 1944.

32 AMAE, R 1716, Dispatch from the Spanish Consul General in Athens, Radigales, to the Minister of Foreign Affairs, Jordana, Berlin, 15 July 1944.

33 PVGL IIT, Testimony of Jacob Button, Spools 9–25, Paris, 5 August 1946.

34 AMAE, R 1716, Dispatch from the Spanish Consul General in Athens, Radigales, to the Minister of Foreign Affairs, Jordana, Berlin, 15 July 1944.

35 Ibid.

36 American Jewish Joint Distribution Committee (JDC), folder Sephardim 1943–1948, Document no. 1013, from JDC Lisbon, Robert Pilpel, to JDC New York, Lisbon, 11 May 1944.

37 JDC, folder Sephardim, 1943–1948, Document no. LJ 852, from Representation in Spain of American Relief Organizations, David Blickenstaff, to JDC Lisbon, Joseph Schwartz, Madrid, 14 April 1944.

38 JDC, folder Sephardim, 1943–1948, Document no. 901, from JDC Lisbon, Schwartz, to JDC New York, Lisbon, 25 March 1944.

39 AMAE, R 1704, file 4, telegram no. 13, from the Minister of Foreign Affairs, Jordana, to all Chiefs for the Mission in America, Madrid, 19 February 1944.

40 AMAE, R 1716, Dispatch from the Spanish Ambassador in Berlin, Vidal, to the Minister of Foreign Affairs, Jordana, Berlin, 29 February 1944.

41 AMAE, R 1716, Dispatch from the Spanish Ambassador in Berlin, Vidal, to the Minister of Foreign Affairs, Jordana, Berlin, 18 January 1944.

42 AMAE, R 1716, Dispatch from the Spanish Ambassador in Berlin, Vidal, to the Minister of Foreign Affairs, Jordana, Berlin, 29 February 1944.

43 JDC, folder Sephardim, 1943–1948, Document no. 1299, from JDC Lisbon, Schwartz, to JDC New York, Moses Leavitt, Lisbon, 19 February 1944.

44 JDC, folder Sephardim, 1943–1948, Document no. 1306, from JDC Lisbon, Schwartz, to JDC New York, Leavitt, Lisbon, 21 February, 1944.

45 Morcillo Rosillo, "Spain and Sephardim of Thessaloniki," 193.

46 JDC, folder Sephardim, 1943–1948, Document no. 827, from JDC Lisbon, Schwartz, to JDC New York, Leavitt, Lisbon, 22 February 1944.

47 AMAE, R 1716, Communication from the Office of Foreign Policy, P. Pons, Madrid, 20 May 1944.

48 JDC, folder Sephardim, 1943–1948, Document no. 1283, from JDC Lisbon, Schwartz, to JDC New York, Leavitt, Lisbon, 15 February 1944.

49 JDC, folder Reports, 1945, Executive Order no. 9417, White House, Franklin D. Roosevelt, Washington, 22 January 1944.

50 JDC, folder Sephardim, 1943–1948, Document, from J.C. Hyman, to World Jewish Congress, Rabbi Maurice L. Perlzweig, 4 February 1944.

51 JDC, folder Sephardim, 1943–1948, Document no. 1162, from Ministry of Foreign Affairs, General Department of Foreign Politics – Europe, General Director of Foreign Politics German Baraibar, to JDC Spain, Blickenstaff, Madrid, 16 August 1943.

52 JDC, folder Sephardim, 1943–1948, Document, from World Jewish Congress, Perlzweig, to JDC New York, Hyman, New York, 11 February 1944. See also JDC, folder Sephardim, 1943–1948, Document no. 1283, from Hyman, to World Jewish Congress, Perlzweig, 14 February 1944.

53 Ruhl, *Franco, Falange y III Reich*, 239–49; García Pérez, *Franquismo y Tercer Reich*, 438–73.

54 JDC, folder Sephardim, 1943–1948, Document no. 1202, from Ministry of Foreign Affairs, General Department of Foreign Politics – Europe, General Director of Foreign Politics Baraibar, to JDC Spain, Blickenstaff, Madrid, 25 August 1943.

55 JDC, folder Sephardim, 1943–1948, Document no. 1202, from Ministry of Foreign Affairs, General Department of Foreign Politics – Europe, General Director of Foreign Politics Baraibar, to JDC Spain, Blickenstaff, Madrid, 25 August 1943.

56 AMAE, R 1716, Memorandum from the U.S. Ambassador in Madrid to the Minister of Foreign Affairs, José Félix de Lequerica, Madrid, 25 September 1944.

57 Ibid.
58 AMAE, R 1716, Memorandum from the US Ambassador in Madrid to the Minister of Foreign Affairs, Lequerica, Madrid, 15 November 1944.
59 Ibid.
60 JDC, folder Sephardim, 1943–1948, Document no. 154B, from War Refugee Board, J.W. Pehle, to JDC New York, Leavitt, Washington, 24 October 1944.
61 AMAE, R 1716, letter from the director American Jewish Joint Distribution Committee in Spain, Blickenstaff, to the sub-secretary of the Ministry of Foreign Affairs, Cristóbal del Castillo, Madrid, 4 November 1944.
62 eSefarad, Testimony of Isaac Revah, Madrid, 28 January 2011.
63 Ibid.
64 AMAE, R 1716, letter from the Spanish Vice-consul in Thessaloniki, Salomón Ezratty, to the Spanish Consul General in Athens, Radigales, Barcelona, 20 February 1944.
65 JDC, folder JDC Lisbon 1944–1945, Document, from American Consulate General of Istanbul, Mordecai Kessler, to JDC Lisbon, Robert Pilpel, Istanbul, 20 October 1944.
66 JDC, folder Sephardim, 1943–1948, Document no. 9564, from JDC Lisbon, Schwartz, to JDC New York, Leavitt, Lisbon, 20 April 1944.
67 Novitch, *Le passage des barbares*, 34.
68 AMAE, R 1716, Letter from the Representative in Spain of American Relief Organizations, Blickenstaff, to the sub-secretary of the Ministry of Foreign Affairs, Castillo, Madrid, 4 November 1944.
69 JDC, folder Morocco: M. Beckelman UNRRA Casablanca 1945, Document, from Representation in Spain of American Relief Organizations, Blickenstaff, to JDC Lisbonne, Schwartz, Madrid, 15 December 1944.
70 eSefarad, Testimony of Isaac Revah, Madrid, 28 January 2011.
71 AMAE, R 1716, Letter from the Representative in Spain of American Relief Organizations, Blickenstaff, to the sub-secretary of Foreign Affairs, Castillo, Madrid, 4 November 1944.
72 JDC, folder Morocco: M. Beckelman UNRRA Casablanca 1945, Document, from Representation in Spain of American Relief Organizations, Blickenstaff, to JDC Lisbon, Madrid, 15 December 1944.
73 eSefarad, Testimony of Isaac Revah, Madrid, 28 January 2011.
74 Benroubi, *Life Is Sweet and Bitter*, 176–96.
75 Molho and Nehama, *In Memoriam*, 124.
76 About the Spanish policy and Spanish Jews see Avni, *Spain, the Jews, and Franco*; Rother "Spanish Attempts to Rescue Jews from the Holocaust"; Lisbona, *Más allá del deber*.

8 Beyond Duty: The Spanish Foreign Service's Humanitarian Response to the Holocaust

JOSÉ ANTONIO LISBONA

During the Second World War, a group of diplomats and Spanish foreign service officials were assigned to posts in the Europe of the Holocaust. With their humanitarian response, they were able to save around eight thousand Jews from deportation and likely extermination.[1]

The individual interventions of these diplomats went beyond the simple fulfilment of ethical or professional duty. Defying Nazi brutality, they broadly interpreted the instructions they received from Madrid and on their own initiative issued protective documents, liberated detainees, secured hiding places, facilitated escapes, and organized repatriations. These men were motivated by different goals. Some extended protection to Jews as a matter of legal principle – they were defending fellow nationals – or even as an expression of patriotism. For others, their work as protectors was an extension of their deeply held beliefs, be they Christian or simply humanistic. For many, their work reflected their sympathy for the Sephardic world, to which they had grown close over the course of past diplomatic assignments.

Most of these men kept their actions secret and never spoke of the good deeds they performed. Their silence, even within their families – who would learn about their actions many years later – proved inherent to their mission. Consuls general, ministers, chancellors, vice-consuls, chargés d'affaires, and attachés worked with modesty and discretion to protect those Spanish Sephardim who had been safeguarded by Primo de Rivera's 1924 decree.

Philosephardism and the 1924 Decree

At the beginning of the twentieth century, Spanish public opinion began to shift towards sympathy for Jews, especially Sephardim. As a result of this "rediscovery," a campaign in their favour slowly took root (see Weisz and Rein, Álvarez Chillida, and Rohr, in chapters 1, 2, and 4, respectively, in this volume). Even so, the softening of government policy towards Jews remained little more than symbolic until Spain began to debate laws that would offer naturalization for Sephardim.

After the First World War, the Lausanne Treaty of 24 July 1923 declared the end of the system of "Capitulationes," under which foreign powers extended protection to certain residents of Turkey. As the Ottoman Empire crumbled, and new nations were born in the Balkans and the Arab world,[2] the Eastern Sephardic colonies found themselves in desperate straits, without rights or protections in countries that now were enacting strict nationalist policies. To address this issue, General Primo de Rivera's Directorio Militar tabled the Royal Decree of 20 December 1924, which granted Spanish citizenship to the "antiguos protegidos españoles o descendientes de estos" (former Spanish protégés or the descendants thereof).[3]

This decree offered all protégés (protected persons) an opportunity to legalize their Spanish nationality. Yet the law was little publicized, and its impact was less than had been anticipated – scarcely four thousand Sephardim exercised their new right.[4] Many of them assumed there was no need for them to act, believing it sufficient to hold a Spanish passport, even if their names were not included in the Civil Registry or on consular lists. During the Second World War, the decree would create the legal basis for offering consular defence to those Sephardim who had protected themselves by obtaining Spanish nationality. Furthermore, it would serve as the key instrument for Spanish diplomats to wield when protecting the lives of Jews during the Holocaust. As it turned out, the Germans did not question the validity of the Spanish Jews' nationality, nor did they raise legal obstacles to those "saved" by the 1924 decree.

The diplomats and foreign service officers who aided Jews fleeing Nazi persecution had to work both with and against the shifting and complicated policies of the Franco regime with regard to entry visas, residence status, and rules about repatriation (topics discussed at length by Israel Garzón, Calvet, Fragkou, and Correa in chapters 3, 5, 7 and 20 in this volume).[5] Let us now examine the actions taken by some Spanish diplomats and foreign service officers to help Jews faced with deportation and extermination.

HUNGARY

Miguel Ángel de Muguiro y Muguiro, Minister (Budapest 1938–1944): An Ongoing Condemnation

Miguel Ángel de Muguiro (1880–1954) arrived at his post in Budapest on 15 May 1938 with thirty-one years of diplomatic service behind him. Upon his arrival, the new minister in Budapest expressed open criticism towards the Magyar government's antisemitism. Between 1938 and 1944 he sent more than twenty communiqués to Madrid solely to denounce the racial decrees against the approximately 825,000 Jews residing in Hungary and annexed territories. As he exhaustively detailed, these decrees included a prohibition on any public activity (which implied the dismissal of all Jewish functionaries of the state), the obligation to wear badges and yellow stars, the declaration of all their possessions (which, like their businesses, were frequently subject to looting), forced participation in work battalions, and a travel ban (which prevented evacuation). On 22 May 1944, Muguiro dispatched a letter to Madrid signed by "un húngaro Cristiano" (a Christian Hungarian). It denounced the victims' cruel treatment, the looting of their properties, and their transfer in closed cattle cars to Poland, probably to exterminate them.[6]

In the wake of the Nazi invasion, and aware of how little time he had, Muguiro embarked on a rescue mission. Between the end of May and the middle of June 1944, he granted Spanish visas to five hundred Hungarian children, between five and fifteen years old, and seventy adults who would accompany them to Tangier. His goal was save them from a death he believed to be certain. Nonetheless, despite the authorizations to exit the country that he and the Red Cross had obtained, the Reich ultimately denied the Hungarians' transit. Protected from Nazi brutality by the Spanish Legation, these Jews would remain safe in refugee camps under the care of the International Red Cross.[7]

Ángel Sanz Briz, Chargé d'Affaires (Budapest, 1942–1944): The Miraculous Multiplication of the Sephardim

Today the most recognized and celebrated of the Spanish diplomats involved in the rescue of Jews is Ángel Sanz Briz, the subject of recent books, films, and a TV series.[8] In May 1942, Sanz Briz (1910–1980) arrived in Hungary as the first secretary of the Spanish Legation at the age of thirty-two. Midway through June 1944, after Minister Muguiro left Budapest, he took over as chargé d'affaires.

Alongside Muguiro, Sanz Briz witnessed the racial escalation in Hungary, which began with the propagation of antisemitic legislation, followed by, in the summer, the deportation and extermination of half a million Jews. On 24 June he sent a detailed thirty-page report about Auschwitz to the foreign ministry, which included an account of mass murder in gas chambers provided by two escapees.[9] The response of the ministry was complete silence.

In October 1944, Regent Horthy was overthrown and Ferenc Szálasi's pro-Nazi Arrow Cross took power. Faced with the prevailing terror,

156 José Antonio Lisbona

Sanz Briz decided on his own, without permission from Madrid, to rent houses to shelter the Jews under his protection. There would come to be eight *casas protegidas* (protected houses) under the Spanish flag in the International Ghetto. In addition, twenty-five refugees were sheltered in the Széchenyi Villa in Buda, thirty in the Podmanski house, and sixty in the legation building itself. As well, Spain harboured some five hundred children in three Red Cross Hospices, while one hundred Jews resided in other "safe" places, such as hospitals, maternity wards, and asylums. The façades of many of these buildings were marked with signs that declared them to be an "Anejo a la Legación de España. Edificio extraterritorial" (Annex of the Spanish Legation: Extraterritorial Building).[10]

Sanz Briz did not limit himself to sheltering Jews in the *casas protegidas*; taking advantage of the confusion in the city, he also provided documents called *cartas de protección* (letters of protection). When the massive persecution of Jews began in Budapest, Sanz Briz determined it necessary to offer Spanish documentation to those who were targeted. He obtained Madrid's authorization to issue protection documents based on the 1924 decree. He developed a plan whereby he would grant ordinary passports to Hungarian Sephardim and provisional ones for Jews with relatives or "contacts" in Spain. Eventually, almost all of those who sought help at the legation received *cartas de protección* – most of them with false information, but all otherwise "official" – in the name of the Spanish state.

Once Sanz Briz received the Hungarians' consent to issue up to three hundred letters of safe conduct to Jews of Sephardic origin, he ingeniously converted those three hundred individuals into three hundred families; those three hundred in turn indefinitely multiplied via the simple procedure of not issuing documents or passports with a number over three hundred. Instead of the initial three hundred, he authorized 45 ordinary passports, 235 provisional (many of these including various members of the same family and thus including 352 people), and 1,898 letters of protection. The number of people saved was even higher, for one must also add the five hundred children under Spanish custody, several hundred provisional Paraguayan passports, and another group of seven hundred persons.[11] It is calculated that in total, Sanz Briz managed to save some five thousand people.

In mid-November 1944 the diplomat, now willing to risk not only his post and his career, but also his life, personally confronted Nazi officials to liberate several Jewish protégés from the death march columns heading for Germany.[12] On 18 October 1966, Yad Vashem recognized Ángel Sanz Briz as Righteous Among the Nations.[13]

ROMANIA

José Rojas Moreno, Conde de Casa Rojas, Minister (Bucharest, 1940–1943): Simply, Spaniards

The Count of Casa Rojas (1893–1973) arrived in Bucharest at the beginning of December 1940 after twenty-five years as a diplomat. But it would not be in Romania where José Rojas first took up the defence of his Jewish compatriots. In 1938, in response to the Italian government's decree to expel foreign Jews, Rojas – as Head of the Europe Section – ordered the embassy in Rome to grant passports to all Jewish citizens, given that "no estableciéndose discriminación en nuestra legislación, ni por razón de religión, ni por razón de raza, solo hay españoles de una categoría" (there is no discrimination established in our legislation on motives of religion or motives of race; there is only one type of Spaniard).[14]

In Bucharest, between 1940 and November 1943, thanks to his decisive intervention and his friendships with members of the government (principally, with Prime Minister [Conducător] Antonescu), Casa Rojas prevented the enactment of antisemitic laws towards 110 Jewish Spaniards. With some setbacks, their factories remained open and their urban properties respected; their automobiles and their radios were not confiscated, and they even found exemption from a special tax imposed on Jewish residents.[15]

In April 1941, Casa Rojas arranged for an expulsion order to be revoked for twenty-four Spaniards of Jewish background – some Catholic – and extracted the formal promise that in the future no Spaniard would be deported from Romania.[16]

On his own initiative, in February 1942, Casa Rojas advised Spanish naturalized citizens of Jewish origin not to register themselves with the Romanian census of Jews. He also signed and distributed certificates from the Spanish Legation, which were to be placed on the doors of their homes, and which declared, in Spanish, Romanian, and German, that these residents were under Spanish protection.[17]

Starting in April 1941, Casa Rojas continuously invoked the 31 March 1934 Exchange of Spanish-Romanian notes in the presence of the Conducător so that the most favoured nation clause would be applied regarding the right of Jews to reside in the country. In this way, the Jews would be able to keep their professional identity cards and continue their industrial and commercial activities.[18]

After Casa Rojas complained about it, in August 1942 Antonescu ordered the National Center of Romanianization to nullify the order to confiscate Hispanic properties. The Spaniards were thus made equal to the Germans, Italians, and Swiss.[19]

For Casas Rojas the Spanish Sephardim who resided in Romania were simply compatriots. In his verbal notes to the Romanian government and in his interviews with Antonescu, he usually spoke of "súbditos españoles" (Spanish subjects) or of his "connacionales" (fellow citizens), without mentioning their Jewishness.

Despite his effective protection, the Sephardic community faced certain further persecution in Romania, so Casa Rojas set out to repatriate them, given their desperate situation. On 26 September 1941, he demanded Madrid's consent to issue visas, without waiting for prior approval or confirmation from the administration. Finally, in May 1943, the foreign ministry authorized him to facilitate travel if circumstances required, while underscoring that each case should be examined individually – which was against Rojas's wishes. On 8 June, now that the increasingly dangerous circumstances required action, he mailed a list with the names of 110 Spanish Sephardic subjects residing in Romania to Madrid and the Spanish embassy in Berlin. He secured the necessary evacuation permits for them.[20]

Manuel Gómez-Barzanallana y García, Minister (Bucharest, 1943–1945): A Personal Commitment

When he arrived on 27 October 1943 at his post in Romania, Manuel Gómez Barzanallana y García (1876–1964) was almost sixty-eight years old. He hoped to retire in the Bucharest Legation after a diplomatic career spanning forty-five years.

The Spanish community in Bucharest was in great peril due to heavy American bombing and the stunning Russian advance. In mid-April 1944 the new minister supported their desire to repatriate. He set out to obtain for them the all-important transit visas through Germany or alternatively through Turkey. Unsuccessful in Bucharest, he asked José Rojas y Moreno – then head of the Ankara Mission – for the necessary documentation for the sixty-eight Spanish Jews still in Romania. In spite of his efforts, the Turkish and British governments wanted nothing to do with the matter.[21]

On 1 May 1944, Madrid asked whether those who sought repatriation "son propiamente españoles o son sefarditas" (are Spaniards, strictly speaking, or Sephardim). Barzanallana responded that, except for four families, the rest were Sephardic Spanish nationals. Of those, fifty wanted to go to Spain (in reality, there were sixty-eight). He added that their entrance already would have been authorized in 1940, given that they were on the list of 110 Jews that Casas Rojas had sent to Madrid and

Berlin. Days later, Barzanallana added to his initial testimony, reporting that some six Jews were actually Catholic and another three or four had decided to convert. He also sent two lists of "sefarditas con pasaporte español que habitan en Bucarest y desean repatriarse" (Sephardim with a Spanish passport who live in Bucharest and wish to repatriate).[22]

On 8 May, Barzanallana received a secret telegram from the foreign minister, Francisco Gómez Jordana, ordering passports to be granted only to the twenty-six Spanish Jews who were Catholic or who could possibly convert. Barzanallana disregarded the instructions and safeguarded the evacuation of the entire community.[23]

Even after Berlin rejected the granting of transit visas that would have allowed Jews to cross Germany, Barzanallana did not give up. Instead, he pressed the matter with the German ambassador in Bucharest, reminding him of the precedent set by the evacuation of the Romanian Jews living in France: the Reich had authorized their passage through Germany.[24]

On 28 July 1944, thanks to his incessant efforts alongside his German colleague, Baron von Killinger, Barzanallana acquired the aforementioned stamp for all of his "compatriots" who wished to go to Spain, Sephardim or not. Barzanallana himself proposed the plan, and subsequently received the dual approval of the German Legation in Bucharest and the Berlin government. The arrangement held that Germany would stamp the transit visas for Spanish subjects residing in Romania who wished to go to Spain "siempre que lleven consignados en sus pasaportes el 'visto bueno' de Barzanallana como 'garantía ideológica de sus respectivos titulares'" (as long as they carry written confirmation in their passports of Barzanallana's "seal of approval" as an "ideological guarantee of their respective holders").[25]

Finally, in July 1944, the Spanish foreign ministry accepted that Barzanallana's "Spaniards" – Jews who had converted to Catholicism, Jews who were willing to convert, simply Jews, and even those whom Madrid initially did not authorize – could come to their homeland, even though "en su día hayan de seguir viaje saliendo de España" (at an appropriate time they have to continue their voyage out of Spain).[26]

GREECE[27]

Eduardo Gasset y Diez de Ulzurrun, Consul and Chargé d'affaires (Athens and Sofia, 1941–1944): A Confidential Mission

Eduardo Gasset (1907–1996) was assigned to the Athens Legation on 15 April 1941 to replace the ailing José María Doussinague. Getting ahead of the "negro futuro que pronto llegará" (dark future that will soon arrive), Gasset asked Madrid – unsuccessfully – to repatriate the Spanish Sephardim in Salonika and for food to alleviate the widespread famine in Greece.[28]

Between July 1942 and March 1943, he dedicated himself to obtaining freedom for the detainees and to ending the seizure of their property.[29] He was able to arrange for two Spanish Jewish women to be excluded provisionally from deportation: Dudan Revah (a widow with a paralytic son), and Lina Capuano (who had two minor children and was alone after her husband's deportation).[30]

Towards the end of March 1943, Altenburg, the German Minister-at-Large, expressed to Gasset that according to reports from Berlin, Madrid wanted nothing to do with its Jewish subjects in Salonika. These Jews would be deported to Poland along with the rest. Distressed, Gasset replied that since he had not received orders to the contrary, he would continue offering them support. Gasset lacked direct communication with Madrid and had to send his telegrams through Reich channels. Georg Vogel, Altenberg's adviser, tipped off Gasset that those channels had "neutralized" the content of his messages asking for instructions.[31]

To circumvent Nazi control of his communications, Gasset secretly employed a merchant marine captain as an undercover diplomatic courier. He sent him to the Spanish Legation in Sofia with the confidential mission to send two encoded telegrams to the foreign ministry. The first one, intended only as a feint, merely repeated the one that had already been intercepted. Hours later, the second telegram informed Minister Jordana that half of Salonika's Jews had already been deported and that Spanish Jews would be the next group to face deportation. He pointed to Italy's decision to protect its subjects, and he forwarded a communiqué dated May 1941 from Doussinague, his old boss in Athens, which insisted that Jews of Spanish nationality be defended and protected as if they were non-Jewish Spaniards.[32]

Gasset received no reply. Then on 3 May, Berlin communicated to the embassy in Greece that Spain had expressed its willingness to repatriate its Jewish compatriots. Twenty days later, believing he had achieved his goal, Gasset left Athens for his new assignment with the Sofia Legation in Bulgaria. Nonetheless, in August the Spanish Jews in Athens were deported to Bergen-Belsen. Their lives were ultimately saved when they were evacuated in February 1944.[33]

According to communications from the Nazis on 22 June 1943, the secret telegrams he was sending to Madrid demonstrated "el gran interés de Eduardo Gasset por la suerte de los judíos" (the great interest Gasset held in the fate of the Jews), highlighting as well his close contact with the "conocido enemigo alemán, Doussinague" (well-known German enemy, Doussinague).[34]

Gasset took the post of chargé d'affaires in Sofia, Bulgaria, on 25 August. Thanks to his intercession on behalf of his Jewish fellow citizens, at least five families were saved from the enforcement of antisemitic legislation.[35] On 30 October 1943, Gasset left Bulgaria just after freeing the legation's ambassador, the Spanish Sephardi Santiago Béjar.[36]

Sebastián Romero Radigales, Consul General (Athens, 1943–1945):
Stop Deportations

A devout Catholic, Romero Radigales (1884–1970) took the post of Spanish consul in Athens on 9 April 1942, just as the Germans declared that the Salonikan Jews were to be deported. Facing this dramatic situation, he worked ceaselessly to persuade Madrid to repatriate its Sephardic citizens.

Despite receiving his ministry's refusal and express instructions to maintain "una actitud pasiva y no desarrollar iniciativas personales" (a passive attitude and not to develop private initiatives), Radigales established contacts with other foreign diplomats who were working to prevent deportations. His efforts failed to halt the transport of 367 Spanish Jews from Salonika to Bergen-Belsen at the beginning of August 1943. Nonetheless, he repeatedly intervened to ensure "good treatment" during their transport and their time in the concentration camp and, later, to arrange for their evacuation to Spain.[37]

Previously – in concert with the Italian consul, but behind the backs of the Germans and without Madrid's authorization – Radigales had helped 150 Spanish Sephardim from Salonika to flee Athens in an Italian military train.[38] Furthermore, as a result of his mediation, the Italians extended their protection to a few dozen Spanish Jews with Italian or Greek spouses.[39]

When German troops occupied Greece's capital on 9 September 1943, Radigales immediately alerted his superiors that Athens's Spanish Jews would undoubtedly meet as tragic an end as their Salonikan brothers and sisters. Thus he pled for their urgent repatriation to Spain, expressing his personal anguish.[40] In the meantime, his incessant efforts to convince his ministry to reach an accord with the German government paid off: six and a half months after their deportation from Salonika, the 365 persons who had survived their internment in Bergen-Belsen were freed and sent to Spain in February 1944.

The joy caused by this repatriation would not last long. Because Radigales did not have Madrid's approval to stop it, on 2 April 1944 the

Nazis deported another group: 155 Sephardic Jews detained in Athens and confined in the Haidari camp. As proof of his Christian charity, Radigales and his wife – Elena Cutava Anino, of Greek origin – visited them repeatedly to alleviate their suffering. They also brought them a truckload of provisions and personal requests. The consul petitioned the Germans not to send the elderly, the infirm, and children on the cruel journey, but his pleas would be disregarded.[41]

Between July and September 1944, Radigales provided help and protection on his own accord to a group of some eighty Jews (Spanish and Greek) who had escaped deportation by hiding in Athens. Without notifying Madrid, he offered shelter to some of them in a hotel near the legation, which he was able to endow with extraterritoriality. His wife Elena gave refuge for a few weeks in her own house to Ino Gattegno's aged father, later arranging asylum for him[42] thanks to Priest Typaldos, himself responsible – in his role as a functionary of the Spanish Embassy in Greece – for the remarkable rescue of Jewish children in Athens.[43]

On 26 February 2014, Yad Vashem recognized Sebastián Romero Radigales as Righteous Among the Nations.[44]

BULGARIA

Julio Palencia y Álvarez-Tubau, Minister (Sofia, 1940–1943):
"The Friend of the Jews"

On arriving in Sofia as a minister in November 1940, Julio Palencia (1884–1952) faced the proclamation of racial laws that gravely harmed the interests of Jews of Spanish nationality. He protested repeatedly – verbally and in writing – directly to the president of the Council of Ministers. He spoke against the application of these ordinances, which the Bulgarian government enforced arbitrarily against the Jews without distinction based on nationality.[45]

Palencia repeatedly tried to convince the Bulgarian authorities that their antisemitic measures were illegal and Spanish authorities that they had a duty to protect their Jewish subjects. The Bulgarians' measures ranged from confiscating Jewish goods and property, to prohibiting their use of public services and requiring them to do forced labour, to confining them in designated neighbourhoods and districts. Furthermore, Jews could not visit cafés, restaurants, cinemas, or theatres, nor could they walk through gardens and parks.[46] Palencia's desperate pleas managed to get at least eighty-one Spanish Jews exempted from some of these rulings.[47]

In successive reports to his ministry, Palencia described the horrors confronting Sofia's Jews; he likened their situation to that of "rebaños de ganado destinados al matadero" (herds of cattle headed for the slaughterhouse) or "esclavos de África" (African slaves).[48] Anguished Sephardim besieged the legation; some even committed suicide. This dramatic situation prompted the diplomat on 14 September 1942 to urgently request that Madrid grant visas for the four hundred Jewish citizens wishing to go to Spain. The repatriation would eventually be unnecessary thanks to Bulgarian popular opposition to the deportations.[49]

Palencia came to be called "the friend of the Jews," and the Bulgarian government responded by launching a smear campaign against him. The secret service permanently monitored his wife because of her Greek origin.[50] The tactics used against him intensified with the May 1943 detention of the legation's chancellor, the Spanish Sephardi Santiago Béjar, who was first accused of espionage and then of smuggling.[51]

Furthermore, Palencia vociferously opposed the execution of the Sephardi León Arié, even confronting local authorities about it. When Arié was finally hanged, Palencia adopted his two children, Claudia and Renato. He also granted Arié's widow status as a member of his family. After forging this relationship, he issued the family diplomatic passports and sheltered them in the legation. After a few days, when Bulgarian pressure became threatening, he sent the three to Bucharest, entrusting them to his friend and colleague Casa Rojas. These initiatives infuriated the Sofia government, which viewed these actions as a serious affront and as an "acto de intromisión en los asuntos de Estado" (act of meddling in the state's affairs). For this reason, on 24 June 1943, Palencia was declared persona non grata, obliged to abandon his post and leave the country on a strict deadline.[52]

FRANCE

Eduardo Propper y de Callejón, First Secretary (Bordeaux, 1940): Granting Visas in Transit

Eduardo Propper y de Callejón (1895–1972) was the son of Max Propper, a Jew from Bohemia, and Juana de Callejón, a Spanish Catholic. He began his diplomatic career after the First World War, with initial appointments to Brussels, Lisbon, and Vienna, where he met his future wife, Hélène Fould-Springe. Fould-Springe, born to a famous Franco-Austrian Jewish family (her sister Liliane was married to Baron

Elie de Rothschild), would convert to Catholicism before their wedding in December 1929.

In April 1939, at the age of forty-four, Propper was appointed First Secretary of the Spanish Embassy in Paris. Later, from the Spanish Consulate in Bordeaux, he showed his humanitarianism in the face of the rapid German advance and the signing of the armistice. In June 1940, thousands of refugees of all nationalities, many of them Jewish, desperately rushed the doors of the consulate to request transit visas to Spain and then Portugal in order to reach safety.

On the way to Vichy, where the French government had been re-established, a retinue of the Spanish Embassy directed by Ambassador José Félix de Lequerica arrived in Bordeaux. With the ambassador's consent and in the absence of the principal consul, Propper, helped by fellow diplomat Eduardo Casuso, remained in the consulate to attend to the great influx of visa petitions over a period of only eight days (18–26 June).[53]

The Spanish foreign ministry's May 1940 memo no. 152 stated that foreigners' entry into Spain was to be restricted as much as possible. Those visas were to be given out only in the most urgent circumstances, for a clear reason and with prior notice. Propper, ignoring this imperative to consult with Madrid, decided to grant those visas for a four-day limited period, which was enough time for the refugees to cross Spain and reach Portugal.

Because the consulate's registry books have disappeared, the exact number of visas that Propper managed to issue remains unknown. The known performance of other Spanish consulates on the same dates suggests that he granted between fifteen hundred and two thousand visas. Hendaye and Bayonne granted two thousand each, primarily for Jews. Also, it is known that Aristedes de Sousa Mendes, the Portuguese consul in Bordeaux, distributed 1,574 visas between 15 and 22 June.[54]

Six months after he signed the visas that allowed Jews to transit through Spain, Spanish foreign minister Ramón Serrano Suñer dismissed Propper from his French posting and transferred him immediately to a consular position in Larache, in Morocco. Before he left, President Pétain awarded him the Legion of Honour Cross for his work that culminated in the French-German armistice. Nonetheless, Serrano Suñer seemed incensed with the diplomat and penned a note in his own handwriting that the decoration was due to "los servicios prestados a la judería francesa" (services rendered to the French Jewry).[55]

On 6 August 2007, Yad Vashem recognized Propper as Righteous Among the Nations.[56]

Bernardo Rolland y de Miota, Consul General (Paris, 1939–1943):
Individual Repatriations

When Bernardo Rolland (1890–1976) arrived in Paris as Consul General
in March 1939, he had already held diplomatic posts for twenty-seven
years. In October 1940, Rolland opposed adherence to the German military administration's antisemitic ordinances for Spanish citizens of
Jewish origin. Without instructions from his ministry, he told the French
and Nazi authorities that since no legislation in Spain established racial
differences, the application of those ordinances to his compatriots was
unacceptable, even in the case of Jews. Furthermore, he pointed out
that those ordinances contradicted stipulations that had been in effect
since the signing of the 1862 Hispano-French Consular Convention. On
his own initiative, he handed out to his Jewish subjects certificates of
protection that he had signed that permitted them to be partly excluded
from the Statut des Juifs's racial laws. The Spanish foreign minister,
Serrano Suñer, condemned this conduct.[57]

One initiative discreetly developed by Rolland entailed the individual repatriation of a number of Jews via personal authorizations.
Between 1 June 1940 and 1 April 1943, he granted entry visas to Spain
to twenty Sephardic citizens and to some twenty-seven protégés even
though they were not listed in the consul's registry of citizens. By
February 1943, according to a list of members of the Official Chamber of
Commerce of Spain in Paris, 126 Jewish compatriots had already been
repatriated to national territory. He sometimes executed this quiet act
through a surprising channel: namely, the weekly trains leaving France
that transported Spanish citizens who wished to return to their homeland. The consul used these trains to carry a few Sephardim in wagons
reserved for the Falange.[58]

Together with four Spanish Jews, Rolland also established an office
that served as a link between Paris's Spanish Sephardic community
and the consulate to authorize certificates of nationality and passports
for the protégés, thus disobeying his superiors.[59]

With regard to the confiscation of Jewish property, with great zeal
and by intervening personally with the occupying German authorities,
in September 1941, Rolland arranged privileged treatment for Spanish
Jews: their bank accounts would be unblocked; they would be able to
use and save the money generated by the forced liquidation of their
property; exclusively Spanish administrators would be named for their
properties; and management of those properties would be centralized
in the Bank of Spain in Paris.[60]

Rolland's interventions with the French and Germans secured the liberation of fourteen Spanish Jews, detained in the 20 August 1941 raid, from the Drancy camp on 3 April 1942.[61] Less well known are the abetting relations that Rolland established with the Spanish Catholic Mission of Paris to procure false certificates of baptism and marriage with which to convert some Jewish compatriots to "Catholics."[62]

In May and November 1942, the German occupation authorities expressed their wish that Rolland be relieved of his post in France "por haber protegido mucho a los judíos de París" (for having protected many of the Jews of Paris). Ambassador Lequerica communicated the Nazis' displeasure to Madrid, but the foreign ministry opposed ordering his return, despite a Falange report in France that accused him of being a "conspirador, promonárquico y antifalangista" (conspirer, pro-monarchist, and anti-Falangist). On 15 April 1943, Rolland left Paris after being named Head of Personnel of Spanish Diplomacy.[63]

Alfonso Fiscowich y Gullón, Consul General (Paris, 1943–1944):
In Favour of the Protégés

On 1 May 1943, Alfonso Fiscowich (1884–1972) became head of the General Consulate in Paris. Before his arrival, he had learned about the "Jewish question" in Tunisia, then a French protectorate. Without great difficulty, he had defended the 134 Spanish Jews listed at the consulate from a series of antisemitic laws that were less robust than those applied in Vichy.[64]

Now in France, Fiscowich continued the repatriation work begun by Rolland. Between three and five hundred Jews were properly registered there, as Madrid required. As for the rest of the Jews, government guidelines excluded them from protection and repatriation, which left them at risk of deportation since the Nazis viewed them as stateless. Fiscowich decided to involve himself on behalf of those who held citizenship but were not registered, as well as those who had not taken advantage of the 1924 decree but nevertheless held Spanish identity documents.[65] Fiscowich was aware that if they were treated as nationals, these Jews would have the right to the documentation necessary for their survival and repatriation.

Something surprising happened between 5 May and 27 June 1943: Fiscowich received instructions from the Spanish Embassy in Berlin to provide entry visas to all protégés to date, even those who lacked the requisites. Astonished by this order, the diplomat arranged for the protégés to come to the consulate to acquire the necessary entry visa stamps and to request German letters of safe conduct at a later time. Some 143 protégés came to request evacuation.[66]

Then foreign minister Jordana telegraphed on 27 June to prohibit this action, claiming that Fiscowich had not followed previous orders and demanding that he "atenerse estrictamente a sus instrucciones, sin modificarlas ni discutirlas" (strictly abide by his instructions, without modifying them or debating them). Censuring Fiscowich's humanitarian actions, Madrid, communicating via telegram, retracted earlier statements. The diplomat thus found himself forced to stop the preparations for repatriation, and even though the passport and departure applications had already been handed over to the German Consul General in Paris, he had to rescind the visas he had already authorized. Nevertheless, throughout those two months he continued to hand out identity documents to many protégés. With these documents, they would later be able to demonstrate their link to Spain. The consul's personal concern for the protégés continued throughout his term of office.[67]

In August 1943, Ruth and Marcelo Canetti joined a group of seventy-nine Sephardim to be repatriated to Spain with Spanish documentation even though they had acquired French citizenship years before. In another case in October 1942, after great effort, he secured the liberation of Elisa Carasso Modiano, whose husband had died while interned in Drancy,.[68]

As a result of Fiscowich's repeated warnings that many Spanish Sephardim faced detention, Madrid changed its policy. In this regard, in October 1943 Fiscowich broached the possibility that Spanish Jews in Paris might leave for a third country; if they did not do so, they would be deported to Central European concentration camps. On 20 November – after some detentions had already occurred – he asked the foreign ministry to reconsider granting entry visas or at least to try to get Germany to agree to a special ruling for his Jewish compatriots. Finally, on 1 December 1943, Jordana gave the green light and ordered Fiscowich to request their freedom after the distraught consul informed Madrid of the arrest of fifty Spanish Jews. On 25 February 1944, Fiscowich obtained the liberation of twenty-three of the detainees in the Drancy camp.[69]

Alejandro Pons Bofill, Honorary Vice-Consul (Nice, 1939–1944): Fallen in the Act of Service

In December 1942, Alejandro Pons (1896–1944) recommended that Spanish Jews not go to the French prefecture to have their identity documents and ration cards stamped with the J for *juif*. He wrote to the prefect that in Spain there was no distinction based on race and that all citizens had the same rights. At the same time, he issued certificates affirming that the bearer was a Spanish national and thus covered by the Hispano-French Convention of 1862, then in force. He would hand out these certificates – without the knowledge of the consul in Marseille – until the German occupation in September 1943.[70]

Pons made numerous submissions to the General Commission on Jewish Questions of Vichy France defending the goods and properties of Spanish Jews, including Samuel Frances, Adolfo Gruenebaum, and Laura Hass de Saporta. He deftly prevented hasty liquidations of assets. Despite the prefecture's reluctance, he succeeded in getting Spanish administrators to replace the French administrators put in place by the Vichy government. When the homes of Spanish Jews were looted, Pons lodged various protests with the commander of the Nazi police and posted a Special Certificate of Property of Spaniards on the doors of Jewish homes and property.[71]

Pons's most laudable humanitarian action remains his vigorous fight for the liberation of Jews detained by the Gestapo, among them Max Feinstein Berlowitz and his wife (in October 1943) and Alberto Cohen Hassan (in December 1943). With hard work, he also succeeded in liberating Enrique Madany and his wife Lubov in April 1944. After Pons interceded, the Republican ex-representative María Lejárraga García, wife of the writer Gregorio Martínez Sierra, took in Madany's six-year-old daughter Lucia during their detention.[72]

As the raids on Jews became more frequent, the diplomat advised the Spanish Jewish community to take advantage of the agreement with Berlin to repatriate to Spain. By means of a collective passport, he arranged for the departure of fifteen adults, five children, and one baby in October 1943. Given that inclusion in the repatriation lists favoured the liberation of deportees in French concentration camps, among the thirty-nine registered in March 1944, he added twelve detained in Drancy, arranging for seven of them to be freed. Later, from the 22 April 1944 convoy, another two prisoners were repatriated.[73]

But the case in which Pons involved himself most tenaciously was the liberation of Pedro Rosanes and his wife Elena Pisanty, detained in Nice in October 1943 and transferred to Drancy, from where they were deported to Auschwitz. Unaware of their tragic fate, he had included them on the group passport to be repatriated in July 1944. Meanwhile, he personally took custody of their daughter Elisa, a minor, whom he sheltered first in his own home and later in the homes of some Sephardic Spaniards. He also filed three separate complaints about their detention and the plundering of their property. He himself placed the Consular Certificate of Property of Spaniards on their door.[74]

Alejandro Pons died on 26 May 1944 near the Sant-Laurent-du-Var station. As he travelled by train from his residence in Cannes to the consulate in Nice, he fell victim to an Allied aerial attack.

Antonio Zuloaga Dethomas, Press Attaché (Paris-Vichy-Algiers, 1939–1944): Help with Escape

A native of Bordeaux, Antonio Zuloaga (1906–1981) was the son of the renowned painter Ignacio Zuloaga and the Frenchwoman Valentine Dethomas. He belonged to a family of politicians and bankers with valuable friendships in Paris's cosmopolitan society (for instance, Marshall Pétain and Pierre Laval), which would benefit him in his diplomatic activities. From November 1939 to the end of 1942, he served as a press attaché in the Spanish Embassy in Paris and Vichy. Afterwards, and until the end of 1944, he served as attaché in the consulate in Algiers with the French Committee of National Liberation.[75]

Recruited in Paris by Albert Naud, in September 1940 Zuloaga began clandestine work with the Musée de l'Homme resistance network. A year later, in Vichy, he met Suzy Borel, French diplomat and wife of prime-minister-to-be Georges Bidault. As a prominent agent in various resistance networks, such as Combat, NAP, and Martial-Armand, Borel had taken on the *nom de guerre* "The Queen." Exploiting his diplomatic status and taking advantage of regular journeys between Paris and Vichy, Zuloaga worked discreetly on behalf of persecuted persons. He collaborated with Borel and her network "Escape" to help resistance members and prominent French Jews flee to Spain.[76]

Among the latter, Zuloaga helped the Jewish leader René Mayer, who managed to arrive in Barcelona in January 1943 after several attempts. Once there, Mayer reunited with his son Antoine, who had crossed the border with two companions, all under false Canadian names. René Mayer established a close friendship with Zuloaga and became a prominent politician: minister for several terms, French prime minister in 1953, and, two years later, president of the High Authority of the European Coal and Steel Community (CECA).[77]

Zuloaga's intervention proved essential in the multiple operations to get Baron Rothschild's descendants – including his two children James and Philippe, Philippe's wife Claude, and their two daughters – to Spain.[78] (Rothschild was an old friend of Zuloaga and Valentine, Zuloaga's mother.)

All this underground activity did not go undetected by the director of the Falange stationed at the Paris consulate, who began to suspect that Zuloaga had been involved in the escape of prominent Jews. Facing possible exposure to the Germans, Antonio left the embassy at the end of 1942; soon after, he was transferred to Algiers.[79]

In Algiers, a number of Sephardim with Spanish passports boarded repatriation ships thanks to Zuloaga's friendships among supporters of Generals Giraud and De Gaulle. Organized by the French Committee of National Liberation, the ships headed for North Africa.[80]

GERMANY

José Ruiz Santaella and Carmen Schrader, Agriculture Attaché (Berlin, 1942–1944): Hiding in the Shadows

José Ruiz Santaella (1904–1997) completed his degree in agricultural engineering in Madrid in 1931 and three years later his doctorate at the University of Halle-Wittenberg, Germany. There he made the acquaintance of Waltraud Schrader Angelstein (1913–2013), born to a Protestant family from Saxony. In 1936, they married after she adopted the Catholic faith, took on Spanish nationality, and changed her name to Carmen.

Because Santaella had studied in Germany, spoke the language perfectly, and had German family by marriage, he was named the new agricultural attaché in the Spanish Embassy in Berlin on 28 December 1942, later transferring to Diedersdorf.

From April to September 1944, Santaella and Schrader, under privileged diplomatic cover, managed to hide three Jewish women in their house as domestic workers under false identities.[81] The first one, Gertrud Neumann, had miraculously escaped deportation by jumping from a truck headed to an extermination camp. Since February 1943, she had been surviving secretly as an Aryan person, working as a seamstress several days a week in the Santaellas' Berlin home. After recognizing their deep humanitarian sentiments, Neumann anxiously confessed her Jewish origins to them. The couple employed her full-time and urged her to live with them so that they could provide her with consistent protection. Later, when Neumann heard that Carmen required a caregiver for her four children, she hazarded to recommend Ruth Arndt, the daughter of her doctor, a prominent Jewish psychiatrist whose family lived in hiding.[82] In April 1944, the Santaellas hired the young Ruth; a short while later they also took in her mother, Lina, as the house cook. For his part, the father, Dr Arthur Arndt, found refuge in the basement of a former patient. Santaella personally delivered food to Arndt's hiding place.[83] To avoid raising suspicions among the house's other employees – including a girl who was a member of the Hitler Youth – the Arndt family changed their identity. The mother and daughter, meanwhile, working together in the house, kept their relationship secret.[84]

Faced with the Allied advance and continuous bombardments in Berlin, on 15 September 1944 Ruiz Santaella was sent to the nearby Spanish Legation in Bern. From Switzerland, Santaella continued to take care of the Arndt family throughout the war, sending them ration cards and packets of food via Max Köhler, one of the Spanish Embassy's local functionaries.[85]

On 13 October 1988, Yad Vashem declared the Santaellas Righteous Among the Nations.[86]

ITALY

Luis Martínez Merello y del Pozo, Consul General (Milan 1937–1942): Anticipating the End

In October 1937, in the middle of the Spanish Civil War, Luis Martínez Merello (1892–1958) was named Consul General in Milan, where he would remain for five years and seven months. As of September 1938, foreign Jews – among them, Spanish Jews – who had arrived in Italy after 1 January 1919 were required to leave the country within six months. This decree and later ones passed by the Italian government were on paper even more drastic than Germany's. At the time these racist laws were passed, some forty-five Sephardim of Spanish nationality resided in the country, almost all of them in Milan.[87]

Nonetheless, these regulations concerning the "defence of the race" did not impact Spanish Jews until the spring of 1940. Until that time, Martínez Merello was able to obtain authorization for nineteen families to continue living in Milan. The other three concessions stemmed from marriages to persons of the Aryan race. There would be only one case of expulsion: that of Arturo Semo.[88]

In March 1940, Martínez Merello protested before Milan's local authorities against a decision by the General Administration of Demography and Race to deport five Jewish Spaniards from the country: the Isaac brothers, Jaime Coir, and Elio Meir Nacmias and his wife. After obtaining an extension, he stated: "Para nosotros, los hebreos inscritos en el Consulado son tan españoles como los nacidos en la península y en tal forma les protegen nuestras leyes nacionales y, por tanto, los convenios internacionales hechos a base de reciprocidad" (For us, the Jews registered in the Consulate are as Spanish as those born in the Peninsula and, as such, they are protected by our national laws and therefore international agreements made based on reciprocity). Although the authorities refused to void the expulsion orders, the consul general succeeded in preventing them from being carried out.[89]

In May 1942 the situation worsened: one thousand foreign Jews were detained in Italian concentration camps. The following month, a new decree established obligatory work service for Jews. At this, Martínez Merello made known to the Milan prefect that he assumed that this decree would not be applied to Spaniards. He supported his argument with the Consular Agreement between Spain and Italy, in force since 21 July 1867. In particular, he interceded on behalf of Elkan Papo y Levi. With Martínez Merello's intervention, Papo y Levi obtained an exemption from the work battalions.[90]

At that time, some Spanish Jews were summoned to the prefecture's Foreigner's Office, where they were notified of their obligation to present documents (distributed to their homes) regarding their status and race to the local police. The consul advised all of his "connacionales de raza hebrea" (fellow citizens of the Jewish race) not to offer any such information to the authorities.[91]

Martínez Merello wielded his influence again in the case of Lina Aftalion, the widow of a Spanish Sephardi named Bensasson. After her application for permanent residency had been denied, she had been informed that she would be deported from Italy. The consul's intervention guaranteed that she could remain in Milan, along with her daughter, who was gravely ill and married to an Italian.[92]

Because of the surge in antisemitic acts, Martínez Merello decided of his own accord to encourage his Jewish fellow citizens to leave for Spain while they still could. At the end of September 1942, he personally provided passports and visas to various families in the Spanish community, including the families of José Papo and Rafael Nacmias, which allowed them to settle in Barcelona. Between 1939 and 1944, of the forty Spanish Jews living in Milan, twenty-eight moved to Barcelona and ten to Switzerland.[93]

Fernando Canthal y Girón, Consul General (Milan, 1943–1945):
The Double Play between Mussolini and the Partigiani

Fernando Canthal (1896–1964) arrived in Milan in July 1943, leaving a previous post at the Swiss Legation. While still in Bern, he had looked after some of the Jews who had escaped by crossing the border from Italy. As soon as Canthal took office, the Spanish community revealed its need for his protection. After his predecessor Martínez Merello's departure, the Milan prefecture followed orders from the General Administration of Demography and Race and issued notices to incorporate six Jews of Spanish nationality – José Benarroyo, Jorge and Olga Nacmias, Orefice and Mauricio Barcilon, and Mariana Lalet Esinzia – into a work battalion.[94]

The decision was revoked as a result of two complaints, one by the Spanish Embassy in Rome to the Italian foreign ministry and another by the new consul to local authorities. In February 1944, Fernando Canthal granted passports and organized the repatriation to Barcelona of one of the six, José Benarroyo, along with five family members.[95]

On 23 September 1943, Benito Mussolini became head of the Republic of Salò (Italian Social Republic), a Nazi puppet state in the north of Italy. Once Milan became the capital of the Republic of Salò, the Spanish consulate gained diplomatic importance. Madrid did not officially recognize the new state but did ask the consul to use the political benefits he was granted, maintaining at the same time a reserved, courteous attitude. Thus, in the complex circumstances that ensued from the German occupation and intensifying Jewish persecution, the diplomat did everything possible with regard to protecting and repatriating Spaniards of the Jewish race who still resided in and around Milan.[96]

In October 1943, authorities detained Mario Covo Mair, a Spanish Jew with an Aryan wife. Canthal managed to have Covo Mair released because of his good relationship with the German Consul General, who even apologized for his detention.[97]

In the face of Salò's fascist authorities and German occupiers, Canthal bravely named the young Spanish Jew Isù Elias Borni, a long-time resident of Milan, as vice-consul in January 1944. Furthermore, Canthal sheltered his parents, Gisela Borni and Santiago Elias, as refugees.[98] Santiago had been Spain's vice-consul in Sofia for many years.

Canthal also negotiated with and protested to the area's German High Commissioner, Gauleiter Friedrich Rainer, in order to protect Spanish Jews' houses, furniture, and properties in Fiume. Elkan Papo's case stands out. Papo would be repatriated to Spain in February 1944 on a special train that the Consul General in Geneva had organized for the Spanish community. On this same train, Canthal evacuated two other Milanese Jews, Haim Papo and Jorge Nacmias Sonsino. Canthal had previously arranged Nacmias Sonsino's liberation and later transfer to Milan. In Milan, Nacmias Sonsino received a regular passport that enabled him to evacuate.

After his brother Jorge's capture, José Nacmias fled Milan and secretly crossed the Italo-Swiss border, without time to pick up the passport with the visa that Canthal had prepared for him. Fortunately, at the Bern Legation, Nacmias was able to show the certificate of nationality that he had been given in October 1943, testifying that he was a Spanish citizen and entitled to consular protection. For this reason, Nacmias was also repatriated.[99]

During the Republic of Salò's twenty-month existence, Fernando Canthal conspired to get Il Duce's attention. In the last months of his life, Mussolini even tried to get Canthal to negotiate – either his surrender or part of his family's flight through Spain – with British diplomats in Bern.[100]

The consul also took advantage of his good relationship with the *partigiani* to help Jews get to Switzerland through the mountains or to hide in country houses in Brianza or Lecco. The *partigiani* expressed gratitude to Canthal for his help in recruiting various young Spanish workers (who had fled Germany) for the Lorenzini Brigade, associated with the Christian Democratic Party.[101]

The Fates of Jews Who Received Protection

What happened to the Jews who received diplomatic protection? This depended on the country and on the nature of the Spanish diplomatic protection received.

For those who lived in France, the most obvious route of departure (facilitated by the diplomats) was through Spanish territory. Jews crossed individually between 1940 and 1944, and after 31 March 1943 others made it across the border with the help of repatriation organizations officially constituted by Spanish authorities to aid specifically Sephardic Jews who held Spanish nationality. In Romania and Bulgaria, Sephardic Jews with Spanish nationality were able to stay in their countries, protected "in situ" due to the intervention of Spanish diplomats in Bucharest and Sofia. In Italy, primarily in Milan, Sephardic Jews with Spanish nationality and diplomatic protections initially (until September 1942) remained in their country. Between September 1942 and February 1944, families were "repatriated" to Spain, many in Barcelona. A small number escaped by crossing clandestinely across the Italian–Swiss border, most of them after April 1944. Bulgaria, whose government collaborated with Nazi Germany, occupied Macedonia, where Sephardic Jews barely escaped deportation to Treblinka. These Jews were able to remain in their country, primarily in Skopje and Monastir (Bitola).

As we have seen, the case of those Jews "saved" in Greece is the most complex. As Maria Fragkou details in chapter 7 of this volume, two groups faced different destinies. In Salonika, most of the Sephardic Jews holding Spanish nationality and diplomatic protections were abandoned by Madrid at the beginning of August 1943 and transported to Bergen-Belsen. Earlier, a group of 150 Jews, with the aid of Spanish diplomats, had been able to escape to Athens. Meanwhile, the larger group managed to be transferred out of Bergen-Belsen through the intervention of officials in Madrid and repatriated to Spain. They settled in different cities, but mainly in Málaga, and later departed for Morocco. After the Holocaust many of these Jews would go to Palestine; or they would return to Salonika, which would never again be a major centre of Jewish life.

On 2 April 1944 the Nazis deported Greek Jews with Spanish nationality from Athens to Bergen-Belsen. A group of Jews, some Spanish but also some Greek, managed to hide and escape this deportation thanks to Spanish diplomats in Athens. Those who were deported, despite the dogged efforts of Radigales, only found freedom when British forces liberated Bergen-Belsen on 13 April 1945. Many of this group went then to Belgium or returned to Athens.

Conclusion: More Could Have Been Done

At the end of the Second World War the Franco regime orchestrated a vast propaganda campaign directed at presenting Spain to the international community as a protector of all Sephardim – indeed, of all Jews, not just those with Spanish citizenship. To that end, the government "mythologized" its humanitarian attitude and appropriated as its own the rescue work that a group of foreign service officials had conducted individually and privately (Pedro Correa writes about this myth in chapter 20 in this volume). For the benefit of Spain and Francisco Franco, the regime claimed all the credit for these actions. Along the way, it wilfully omitted any mention of the disinterested intervention these diplomats carried out, beyond simply noting that they had complied with ethical or professional duty.

Clearly, Spain did not exhaust all the possibilities at hand for helping Jews; if it had wanted, it could have done much more. Just as clearly, the regime was not the guardian of the Jews' safety as it so much liked to claim after the war. Luckily for many Jews, however, some Spanish diplomats and other foreign service officials took strong, decisive, and proactive personal positions in the interest of saving of thousands of Jews from deportation and extermination in countries occupied by the Nazis.

NOTES

1 This chapter is based on extensive research previously published as Lisbona, *Más allá del deber*, 2015.
2 Centro de Información Administrativa de la Presidencia del Gobierno, "España y los sefardíes. Nota sobre concesión de nacionalidad española a los judíos sefarditas," in *Actas del I Simposio de Estudios Sefardíes* (Madrid: Instituto Arias Montano-CSIC, 1970), 581–611.
3 Royal Decree Statement, 20 December 1924. Foreign Affairs Ministry Archive (Madrid), from here on referred to by the Spanish acronym AMAE (Archivo Ministerio Asuntos Exteriores) Leg. R. 7330. Ex. 122. "Real

Decreto concediendo plazo hasta el 31 de diciembre de 1930 para facilitar la naturalización de individuos de origen español," 20 December 1924. Fondo Ministerio de la Presidencia del Gobierno, Serie Leyes y Decretos originales Leg. 21, Doc. N° 157, Archivo General de la Administración (Alcalá de Henares), from here on referred to as AGA 51/10376.

4 Lisbona, *Retorno a Sefarad*, 21.

5 See also Lisbona, "Se pudo hacer mucho más"; Avni, *España, Franco y los judíos*; Rother, *Franco y el Holocausto*.

6 Communiqué no. 98, "Sobre trato cruel a los judíos en Hungria," 22 May 1944, Diplomatic Information Office Archive (Madrid), hereafter referred to by the Spanish acronym AOID (Archivo Oficina Información Diplomática).

7 González-Arnao Conde-Luque, "Los héroes de Budapest." Note from the Chief of the Overseas and Asia Section to the Chief of European Policy, 13 June 1944. In the margins, there appears a handwritten annotation that says: "Alemania se negó a permitir la salida después de hechas las gestiones por nosotros" (Germany denied exit after the paperwork done by us), AOID.

8 See, for instance, *El ángel de Budapest* (The Angel of Budapest 2011), a television miniseries directed by Luis Oliveros, and the documentary *La encrucijada de Sanz Briz* (The Crossroads of Sanz Briz, 2015), directed by José Alejandro González.

9 Communiqué no. 160, "R/informe s/. trato a los judíos en los campos de concentración alemanes," and attached in French "Rapports sur les les camps de travail" de Birkenau et d'Auschwitz," 26 August 1944. AMAE. Leg. R. 1716. Ex. 5 (AGA 82/5247).

10 Francisco Boves, "La valija de un diplomático," interview with Ángel Sanz Briz, *Heraldo de Aragón*, 12 June 1949, 5. Report from Giorgio Perlasca sent to Ministry of Foreign Affairs, 13 October 1945, 35. AMAE. Leg. R. 6362. Ex.48. (AGA 82/6362).

11 Lisbona, *Más allá del deber*, 91–2.

12 Encoded telegram no. 171, 17 November 1944. AMAE. Leg. R. 1071. Ex. 47 (AGA 82/3662).

13 Document from Sanz Briz in Yad Vashem Archives (YVA), M.31 121/331.

14 Report "Expedición de pasaportes para venir a España a sefarditas expulsados de Italia," 13 October 1938. AMAE Leg. R. 1716. Ex. 3 (AGA 82/5246).

15 Communiqué no. 396/41, "Situación de los españoles sefarditas y defensa de los mismos," 14 October 1941. Order no. 11908 from the Romanian Ministry of the Interior, 29 July 1941. Notes from Rojas for Antonescu, 23 September and 14 October 1941. Verbal note no. 75213, 13 October 1941. AMAE Leg. R. 1343. Ex. 207 (AGA 82/4327).

16 Communiqué no. 114/2, "Expulsión significativa de españoles sefardi-
   tas del territorio rumano," 27 March 1941. AMAE. Leg. R. 1261. Ex. 102.
   (AGA 82/4132). Communiqué no. 124/41, "Expulsión de españoles de
   Rumanía," 2 April 1941. Text no. 3621 c.c./941 from the Office of the
   Council of Ministers of Romania, 29 March 1941. Text from the Secretary
   General of the Interior Ministry, 1 April 1941. AMAE. Leg. 1261. Ex. 102
   (AGA 82/4132).
17 Communiqué no. 62/41, "Gestiones para excluir a la colonia española del
   censo obligatorio para personas de origen judío," 10 February 1942. Note
   from Rojas, 9 February 1942. AMAE. Leg. R. 1343. Ex. 207 (AGA 82/4327).
   "Nota sobre la conversación del 14 de febrero de 1942 de D.M. Antonescu,
   Vicepresidente del Consejo, y el Sr. Ministro de España, en la Presidencia
   del Consejo de Ministros" United States Holocaust Memorial Museum,
   Romania Foreign Affairs Ministry Archive RG 25006M.
18 Lisbona, *Más allá del deber*, 149–50.
19 Communiqué no. 392/41, "Exención de ciertos extranjeros en la aplicación
   de leyes dictadas contra judíos," 10 August 1942. *Monitor Oficial de
   Rumanía*, first part, no. 182, 7 August 71942, 6631. AMAE. Leg. R. 1343.
   Ex. 207 (AGA 82/4327). Communiqué no. 345/41, "Gestiones para
   asegurar la libre disponibilidad de los bienes pertenecientes a españoles
   en Rumanía"), 7 July 1942. AMAE. Leg. R. 2156. Ex. 27. (AGA 82/6337).
20 Lisbona, *Más allá del deber*, 151–2.
21 Ibid., 155, 167–8.
22 "Lista de sefarditas con pasaporte español que habitan en Bucarest y
   desean repatriarse" AMAE. Leg. 2303. Ex. 10 (AGA 82/6684).
23 Encoded telegram no. 36, 8 May 1944. AMAE. Leg. R. 1549. Ex. 13
   (AGA/4875).
24 Encoded telegram no. 85, 1 June 1944. AMAE. Leg. R. 1549. Ex. 14
   (AGA/4875).
25 Encoded telegram no. 98, 28 July 1944. AMAE. Leg. R. 1293. Ex. 4
   (AGA/4157).
26 Note from Doussinague, 6 July 1944. AMAE. Leg. R. 1716. Ex. 5
   (AGA 82/5247).
27 See Maria Fragkou's chapter 7 in this volume expressly regarding diplomatic interventions on behalf of the Sephardic Jews in Greece.
28 Lisbona, *Más allá del deber*, 180–1.
29 Telegram from 18 September 1942. AMAE. Leg. R. 1717. Ex. 1. Gasset's
   testimony, 28 September 1971, AOID.
30 Communiqué no. 3, 13 May 1943. Communiqué no. 33, 13 May 1943.
   AMAE. Leg. R. 2154. Ex. 1 (AGA 82/6333). Communiqué no. 12,
   "Solicitud de visado para Sra. Revah e hijo," 9 June 1943. AMAE.
   Leg. R. 1716. Ex. 3 (AGA 82/5246).

31 Lisbona, *Más allá del deber*, 184–6.

32 Encoded telegrams nos. 21 and 22, 6 April 1943. AMAE. Leg. R. 1548. Ex. 4 (AGA 82/4873).

33 Lisbona, *Más allá del deber*, 187–8.

34 Letter from the *Oberführer* Walter Schellenberg, 22 June 1943, NG-5352. Dublon-Knebel, *German Foreign Office Documents*, 165–7 and 407–8. YVA, AAJM 3123, 2218, K-213095.

35 Notebook of "Intercessions," n/c 1070: Arav (20405); n/c 1302, Graciani (10856); n/c 1502, Benaroyo (19034); n/c 2883, Tabah (76827); n/c 4826, Israel. Paul Duroni's record is in the Bulgarian Central State Archives (CSA) Sofia, units 133 and 176.

36 Lisbona, *Más allá del deber*, 189.

37 Ibid., 200–1.

38 Communiqué no. 38, "Deportación de los españoles de Salónica," AMAE. Leg. R. 1716. Ex. 5 (AGA 82/5247 (593–2)).

39 Letter from Romero Radigales to Doussinague, 31 July 1943. AMAE. Leg. R. 1716. Ex. 3 (AGA 82/5246 (571–2)).

40 Letter from Romero Radigales, 18 October 1943. Letter from the Spanish community's committee in Athens. AMAE. Leg. R. 1716. Ex. 4 (AGA 82/5246 (593–1)).

41 Lisbona, *Más allá del deber*, 202–4.

42 Communiqué no. 58, "Situación de los españoles sefarditas," from Romero Radigales to the Minister, 3 September 1944. AMAE. Leg. R. 1716. Ex. 5 (AGA 82/5247 (593–1)). Transcription of Federico Ysart's interview of Ino Gattegno in Grecia, 1973. AOID.

43 For more on the life-saving work of Father Ireneo Typaldos, chancellor of the General Consulate of Spain in Athens, recognized by Yad Vashem as Righteous Among the Nations, see Lisbona, *Más allá del deber*, 213–24.

44 Document from Romero Radigales in Yad Vashem. YVA.M.31.2.1270.

45 Lisbona, *Más allá del deber*, 234–6.

46 Communiqués no. 270, "Nuevas disposiciones antisemitas," 19 September 1942, and no. 314, "Aplicación de la Ley antisemita," 30 September 1942. AMAE. Leg. R. 2153. Ex. 43 (AGA 82/6332).

47 Paperwork filed by Palencia in the folder titled "Intercesiones." CSA, Collection 190, Leg. 3. Unit 133.

48 Communiqué no. 207, 27 May 1943. AMAE. Leg. R. 2153. Ex. 43 (AGA 82/6332).

49 Communiqué no. 258, 14 September 1943. AMAE. Leg. R. 2153. Ex. 43 (AGA 82/6332).

50 File Commission, Report from 26 February 1941, CSA, collection 5, file 3, unit 1569, 8.

51 Lisbona, *Más allá del deber*, 241–3.

52 Ibid., 243–7.

53 *New York Times*, 21 June 1940, 14. Albert Rèche, "Juin 40 à Bordeaux" in
    Sud-Ouest, 12–15 June 1990. Police report on the protection of the Spanish
    Consulate in Bordeaux, June 1940. Archives Municipales de Bordeaux
    (Bordeaux), AMB 320 I 171 and AMB 420 I 10. Draft of a text from
    Propper regarding events that occurred between Paris and Bordeaux in
    June 1940, doc. 3, 9–11. YVA.M.31.10867/13252. Communiqué no. 944,
    "Comportamiento del personal de la Embajada," 7 August 1940. AMAE.
    PG. 88. Ex. 21857 (1).

54 Lisbona, *Más allá del deber*, 269–71.

55 Telegram no. 61, 3 February 1941. Communiqué no. 23, 28 February 1941.
    Communiqué no. 112, "Concesión Legión de Honor al Secretario Sr.
    Propper-Castellón," 26 February 1941, and Ramón Serrano Suñer's hand-
    written draft for the official text of communiqué no. 6, 14 March 1941).
    Communiqué no. 6, Note, AMAE. PG. 88. Ex. 21857 (1).

56 Propper's file in Yad Vashem, YVA.M.31.10867/13252.

57 Communiqué no. 880, "Texto ordenanza contra empresas judías,"
    24 October 1940, AMAE. Leg. R. 1716. Ex. 2 (AGA 82/5246). Certificate
    granted to Benveniste Covo, 28 October 1940, Centre de Documentation
    Juive Contemporaine (Paris), CDJC XXXVI-92ª. Certificate issued
    to Alberto Naar in Cohen, "Españoles sin patria," 216. Telegrams
    no. 330, 7 June 1941, and no. 408, 27 June 1941. AMAE. Leg. 1716. Ex. 1
    (AGA 82/5246).

58 Lisbona, *Más allá del deber*, 284–5.

59 Blint, *Franco et les juifs*, 226, 294–5.

60 Memoria: "El problema de los 'Sefarditas' españoles en Francia,"
    14 October 1941. AMAE. Leg. R. 1716. Ex. 6 and 7 (AGA 82/5248).

61 File presented by Alain de Toledo to Yad Vashem for the granting of the
    title Righteous Among the Nations, page 13 (Bilan du Consul general
    Bernardo Rolland [21 mars 1939/20 février 1943]).

62 Alain de Toledo's testimony to the author in May 2012 in Paris. Blint,
    Franco et les juifs, 296–7.

63 Lisbona, *Más allá del deber*, 292–4.

64 Communiqué n° 23, Fiscowisch to the minister, July 3, 1941.
    Communiqué I F-72, August 9, 1941. AMAE. Leg. R. 1716. Ex. 2 (AGA
    82/5246).

65 Lisbona, *Más allá del deber*, 304–6.

66 Communiqué no. 37, 13 May 1943. AGA 54/11329. Communiqué no. 372,
    15 May 1943. AMAE. Leg. R. 1716. Ex. 2 (AGA 82/5246). Telegram no. 22,
    25 June 1943. AMAE. Leg. R. 1180. Ex. 6 (AGA 82/3955).

67 Lisbona, *Más allá del deber*, 306–7.

68 Ibid., 307–8. Communiqué no. 626, 27 October 1943, AGA 54/4473.

69 Lisbona, *Más allá del deber*, 308–10.

70 Communiqués no. 1341 and 1342, both from 23 December 1942, AGA 54/11329 and AGA 54/4473. Certificate template, 1943. AGA 54/4860.

71 Lisbona, *Más allá del deber*, 318–20.

72 Ibid., 322–3.

73 List from "Passeport Colletif Espagnol," and second list communiqué no. 12, "Repatriación sefarditas españoles," 7 October 1943. Comminqué no. 12, "S/entrada España sefarditas españoles en cumplimiento," Memo no. 3, 2 February 1944, and attached "Lista de sefarditas que deseando reintegrar la patria se especifica la documentación que presentan." AGA 54/11371. Communiqué no. 9, 23 January 1945. AMAE. Leg. R. 1716. Ex. 6. Rother, *Franco y el Holocausto*, 286–91; 320–3.

74 Lisbona, *Más allá del deber*, 324–8.

75 AMAE Leg. PG. 366. Ex. 25668.

76 Lisbona, *Más allá del deber*, 340–2.

77 Ibid., 342–8.

78 Ibid., 348–53.

79 Ibid., 354–5.

80 Ibid., 355–6.

81 *The Encyclopedia of the Righteous Among the Nations*, 513. Lovenheim, *Survival in the Shadows*, 132, 226–7.

82 USC Shoah Foundation, Ruth Gumpel's testimony (Ruth Arndt). 1997. Code: 31226. Fragments 19–23, 30, and 53–4. Paldiel, *Diplomat Heroes of the Holocaust*, 17–18. Ruth and Bruno Gumpel's testimonies, 30 November 1987, 16 May 1988, and 2 August 1989. Letter from Paldiel to Ruth Gumpel, 25 October 1988. YVA M.31 3984/5505.

83 Lovenheim, *Survival in the Shadows*, 34–135.

84 USC Shoah Foundation, Ruth Gumpel testimony. Paldiel, *Diplomat Heroes of the Holocaust*, 17–18.

85 Lovenheim, *Survival in the Shadows*, 135. Ruiz Díaz, "Un Olivo en Yad Vashem"; Planelles, "Ayudar a las sombras."

86 File of José Ruiz and Carmen Schrader in Yad Vashem, YVA M.31 3984/5505.

87 I. Papo, *Viaje en el ocaso de una cultura ibérica*, 191.

88 "Lista de sefarditas (cabezas de familia) residentes en la jurisdicción del Consulado en Milán" 4 March 1940. AGA 54/12191.

89 Communiqué no. 36, 4 March 1940, and communiqué no. 25, 9 March 1940. AGA 54/12191.

90 Lisbona, *Más allá del deber*, 396–7.

91 Communiqué no. 18, 5 June 1942. Communiqué no. 92, "Aplicación trabajo obligatorio a israelitas españoles," 5 June 1942. AMAE. Leg. R. 2154. Ex. 14 (AGA 82/6333).

92 Communiqué no. 153 from Martínez-Merello for the ambassador in Rome, 7 September 1940. Letter from General Director of Security for the Ambassador of Spain, 14 September 1940. AGA 54/12191.
93 Lisbona, *Más allá del deber*, 397–9.
94 Communiqué in Milan, 3 July 1943, in which there is a copy of the official letter no. 85 from the Spanish Embassy in Rome dated 30 June 1943. AGA 54/12192.
95 Communiqué no. 85, 30 June 1943. Communiqué no. 37, 2 July 1943. Communiqué no. 36, 26 June 1943. Official letter no. 31498 regarding "Hebreo José Benarroyo Gheron= Subdito spanolo," 19 July 1943. Communiqué no. 40, 21 July 1943. Letter from Isidoro Benarroyo, Communiqué no. 67, 18 June 1940. AGA 54/12192.
96 Lisbona, *Más allá del deber*, 405–6.
97 Letter from Canthal, 27 October 1943. Communiqué no. 49, 6 November 1943. AMAE. Leg. R. 2193. Ex. 25. Communiqué no. 165, 17 November 1943. AGA 54/12192.
98 Communiqué no. 1, 8 January 1944. AGA 54/12192.
99 Lisbona, *Más allá del deber*, 407–9.
100 Ibid., 409–10.
101 Communiqué no. 149, 18 February 1948. AMAE. PG. 293. Ex. 24283. Communiqué no. 24, 6 May 1945. AMAE. Leg. R. 1466. Ex. 23. AGA 82/4663.

PART THREE

Spanish Exiles in France

9 Spanish Republicans Exiled in France during the Second World War: War and Resistance

GENEVIÈVE DREYFUS-ARMAND

In May 1940 Germany invaded France, and within a month it had occupied the northern and western parts of the country. France was now ruled by an antisemitic nationalistic puppet government, the "Vichy regime," which collaborated with the Germans. While the supposed "French state" established itself in the city of Vichy, little by little those who rejected both the Nazi occupation and German order started to organize resistance.

Many Spanish Republicans had been in exile in France since the beginning of 1939. Many of them participated in the Second World War on the side of the Allies and of the resistance against Nazism. In this way, they carried on the fight against fascism that had begun in Spain. Spanish exiles organized clandestine networks across the Pyrenees, ran underground presses and published secret tracts, joined French Resistance movements, and created, in southern France, an autonomous guerrilla movement. Under close surveillance by the Vichy regime headed by Marshal Pétain (who had been the first French Ambassador in Madrid after the Francoist victory), and hunted by the German occupiers as well as by Francoist agents, the Spanish Republicans faced significant repression and surveillance. Several thousand of them were deported to Nazi concentration camps in the east; indeed, Spanish Republicans constituted the first deported group from France – their deportation to the Mauthausen camp began in August 1940.

Thus, many Spanish Republicans exiled in France fought for the liberation of a country that had not received them very well. Setting aside their often inhumane reception after the *Retirada* (Retreat), many exiled Spaniards participated in the defence and the liberation of France. They fought for a country that was not their own; they did it because they were continuing the fight against Nazism and for freedom and because they hoped to free Spain after liberating France.

This page of twentieth-century history – the role played by the Spanish Republicans exiled in France, and their long fight to liberate the country that had exiled them – remains little known in both Spain and France, yet it touches on the people of both countries.

The Spanish Exile in France

To better understand the role Spanish exiles played during the Second World War, it is necessary to remember the significance of their presence in France when that war began. After 1936, the year the Spanish Civil War began, as fronts shifted and the Nationalists advanced, Spanish refugees began to cross into France. In 1939, at the end of the war, around half a million Spaniards fled to France ahead of advancing Francoist troops in Catalonia. However, the mass exodus known as the *Retirada* began in late January of 1939,[1] specifically on 26 January, when Barcelona was taken by Franco's troops and the Republicans thought that all was lost. Hundreds of thousands of refugees fled on foot across the Pyrenees and over the French border in harsh winter conditions. The French government opened the border to civilians on 28 January and a few days later to soldiers as well.

When they arrived together, family members were separated. Women and children were usually taken to shelters in the interior of the country. Men of military age, and sometimes also women and children, were interned in camps by the French authorities, who distrusted these refugees and were overwhelmed by their sheer numbers. The Spanish would be the first foreigners subject to a decree (of 12 November 1938) for the administrative internment of "unwanted foreigners."[2]

A large number of camps – referred to as "concentration camps" during the First World War, but also understood as internment camps – were opened for the hundreds of thousands of refugees.[3] Many refugees would stay in these camps throughout the war, with other "unwanted foreigners" replacing the Spaniards who had managed to leave them. The main camps were located in the following departments: Eastern Pyrenees (Argelès-sur-Mer, Saint-Cyprien, Le Barcarès), Ariège (Le Vernet), Hérault (Agde), Aude (Bram), Tarn-et-Garonne (Septfonds), and Lower Pyrenees (Gurs).[4] In 1939, many Spaniards returned to Spain, compelled to do so by the French authorities, who were trying to bring an end to the refugee problem. Some Spaniards immigrated to other countries, particularly Latin America. By the end of 1939, between 150,000 and 200,000 refugees remained in France.[5]

As the Second World War began, the participation of Spaniards in the liberation of France took three different forms: some were incorporated into Companies of Foreign Workers, later called "Groups of Foreign Workers" under the Vichy government; others enlisted in the Foreign Legion or in volunteer regiments; and still others joined the Resistance. This chapter thus has three parts: the participation of Spaniards in the defence of France; their activities in the Resistance; and the long silence about those activities.[6]

Spanish Participation in the Defence of France

The Spaniards first participated in the war on the side of the French through Compagnies de Travailleurs Étrangers (Companies of Foreign Workers, Compañías de trabajadores extranjeros, CTEs), which were created by decree on 12 April 1939. Largely a response to the influx of Spanish Republicans, this decree set out the obligations of foreigners considered to be refugees or stateless. Spanish men between twenty and forty-eight years old were obligated to provide peacetime services that equalled in duration the military service required of the French men (see Robert S. Coale, chapter 10 in this volume).

In the late spring of 1939, a number of companies were formed simultaneously within the internment camps. The Spaniards represented a large majority of the foreign workers assigned to these militarized units, which answered to the war ministry. For those who could not, or did not want to, return to Spain, the only alternatives were to remain in the internment camps or work abroad. Not counting those Spaniards who had been directly recruited to work in industry or agriculture, around fifty to sixty thousand refugees were incorporated into these units, most of which were assigned to help strengthen France's border defences. Many of them were sent up to the Maginot Line or to the Italian border.

During the German offensive of May–June 1940, many of these CTEs were transferred to combat zones, where Spaniards paid a heavy toll in dead and wounded. Spaniards taken prisoner by the Germans were deported to Reich territory, to concentration camps, primarily Mauthausen near Linz in Austria. These deportations began during the first days of August 1940. Thus, the first deportees from French territory were Spanish Republicans. At Mauthausen (the central camp and annexes like Gusen), they were made to work in granite quarries. Some seventy-two hundred Spanish Republicans were sent to Mauthausen, and close to five thousand perished there. They faced the animus of their own country's leader, Francisco Franco, who had disavowed them. At the same time, the Nazis wanted to take revenge on the Spanish anti-Francoists against whom they had fought in the Spanish Civil War.

(See Brenneis, chapter 14 of this volume, for more on the legacy of the Spaniards in Mauthausen.)

After the armistice between France and Germany, on 27 September 1940 the Vichy government created other entities, which this time answered to the Ministry of Industrial Production. These entities were for foreigners aged eighteen to fifty-five, who were "in overabundance in the national economy." The Grupos de trabajadores extranjeros (Groups of Foreign Workers, GTEs) were chiefly made up of Spaniards: in August 1943, of a total of thirty-seven thousand workers, thirty-one thousand were Spanish. When the Germans began to recruit manpower wherever they could find it in order to construct coastal fortifications and submarine pens on the Atlantic and Mediterranean coasts, and for work in Germany itself, they found that the GTEs comprised an ideal labour reserve. More than twenty thousand Spaniards were recruited by the Todt organization between 1942 and 1944, and around forty thousand were sent to Germany. In 1942, when German labour requisitions truly began, French prefects did not hesitate to turn to the GTEs in response to the German demand for labourers.

Moreover, at the insistence of the authorities, and for the sake of leaving the internment camps in southern France, many refugees enlisted in the Foreign Legion for a five-year period or in the Marching Regiments of Foreign Volunteers (Regimientos de marcha de voluntarios extranjeros, RMVEs) for the duration of the war. They thought that the moment had come to settle accounts with the Nazis who had helped the Nationalists entrench themselves in Spain. These were the only possible ways for Spaniards to enlist in the military, given that the French Army, eager to preserve its relationship with the Franco government, did not want to form regular Spanish units, as the Poles and Czechs had done. Between six and seven thousand Spaniards enlisted, though many of the more politicized Spaniards opposed enlistment in the Legion as a matter of principle. Including CTE workers who fell in combat, around five thousand Spaniards died fighting for the French, not counting those killed during the Narvik expedition in Norway in April–May 1940.[7]

The Spaniards of the Foreign Legion fought in Norway, North and East Africa, Palestine, Italy, and later in Alsace and Germany, helping liberate many of these places from the Nazis.[8] Many Spaniards who had been part of the Cuerpo franco de África (African Free Corps) joined General Leclerc's Segunda División blindada (Second Armored Division, 2ª DB). In one company, "La Nueve" (The Nine), Spaniards predominated, including Republican army officers. This company provided a vanguard for the Second Armored Division when it entered

Paris on 24 August 1944. The first armoured vehicles that arrived in Paris that day were named *Madrid, Guernica, Teruel, Guadalajara,* and *Don Quijote.* In short, Spaniards were a vital part of the French army. With their bravery, the Spanish Republicans often inspired the admiration of their comrades in arms. (For more on La Nueve, see Coale's chapter in this volume.)

Exiles in the Resistance

Spanish Republicans also combated Nazism by joining the French Resistance, determined to continue the fight they had begun in Spain. In this regard, they contributed their practical experience in armed conflict, particularly guerrilla warfare. The Spanish Resistance in France took three main forms: the creation of escape networks, participation in resistance movements, and the formation of an autonomous armed movement.

During the occupation of France, the vast majority of refugees focused on day-to-day survival. But many Spaniards, those who refused to work for Germany and who wanted to continue the fight against fascism, felt compelled to resist the Nazis. Stunned by the Republican defeat in Spain, disillusioned by the cold welcome they had encountered in France, the "country of human rights," and worn down by conditions in the detention camps, Spanish refugees remained disoriented for many months after the Second World War broke out. Their political organizations had broken down as a result of the vicissitudes of exile and severe inter- and intra-party discord inherited from the Civil War. Socialists and anarchists were divided, and the Spanish and French Communist Parties had both been banned under the German-Soviet Nonaggression Pact of August 1939. Furthermore, during the global conflict, as a result of the departure of many leaders for England or Latin America, the political centre of gravity of the Republican exile shifted to London or Mexico (or to Moscow in the case of the communists).[9]

From the beginning of the occupation of France, Spanish refugees were at the very centre of the exclusion policy established by the Vichy regime, which created a special bureau to keep watch over them. The Germans asked the bureau for regular reports on those they called the "Rotspanier" (Red Spaniards). The Spanish Embassy provided that bureau with reports on the Republicans and tried to arrange extraditions. These controls greatly diminished the manoeuvring room for Spanish exiles. Nevertheless, at the beginning of 1941, the Spanish began disseminating clandestine propaganda in order to raise the anti-fascist consciousness of their compatriots and to encourage them to fight.

Among these secret publications, *Reconquista de España* (Reconquest of Spain) stands out. It was first published as a Communist Party bulletin, and its title alone indicated a plan of action: the objective continued to be Spain.

Coordinating with the Allied secret services, Spaniards also helped operate secret transit networks across the Pyrenees. In most cases, these relied on connections with Spain that were already being used by Republican political organizations in exile (Calvet and Linhard describe these crossings in chapters 5 and 6 of this volume). These escape networks were organized mainly by the militants of the Confederación nacional del trabajo (National Confederation of Labor, CNT), anarcho-syndicalist militants, and the Partido obrero de unificación marxista (Workers' Party of Marxist Unification, POUM), a Marxist movement strongly opposed to Stalinism. The Allied secret services contacted these militants to help Allied pilots, resistance fighters, and Jews flee from France to England. The oldest and most famous network was organized by the anarchist militant Francisco Ponzán, alias François Vidal. Ponzán, former head of a branch of the Republicans' Servicio de información especial periférica (Special Peripheral Information Service, SIEP), was placed in charge by the libertarian movement of helping anarchist militants escape with their lives from Francoist concentration camps. His network collaborated with the British and French secret services, collecting intelligence (passed on to the British) and organizing crossings of the Franco-Spanish border for hundreds of pilots, Jews, and resistance fighters. (On women in the Ponzán network, see Gina Herrmann, chapter 12 of this volume.) Taken prisoner in 1943, Ponzán was murdered by the Germans on the eve of the liberation of Toulouse, in August 1944.

Another escape network through the Pyrenees in which Spanish exiles played an important role was the "Martin group" of the Vic organization, headed by the Catalan Josep Rovira, former director of POUM and commander on the Aragonese Front during the Spanish Civil War. Rovira, working alongside the commander, "Vic" (René Jeanson), secured safe passage into Spain for downed airmen, parachutists, resisters, and numerous political agents fleeing Nazi-occupied territory. During his exile in France, despite the danger he faced, Rovira made a clandestine journey back into Francoist Barcelona in February 1944 to look for Vic, who had gone missing while on his own secret mission to Spain, where he had hoped to establish a northbound Spain–France escape route. Meanwhile, the Basque government-in-exile had placed its secret services at the disposal of the Allies. The head of that service was executed in Madrid in May 1943.

After transit networks through the Pyrenees had been organized, and while the Resistance was publishing and distributing clandestine tracts, armed conflict began in German-occupied France. In Paris, in the summer of 1941, communist organizations launched an urban guerrilla movement in which exiled Spaniards took part. The Spanish Communist Party was able to reorganize thanks to the French party, through the former directors of the International Brigades, especially Lise Ricol and her husband Artur London. The Miret Musté brothers, Josep and Conrado, militants belonging to the Partido socialista unificado de Cataluña (Unified Socialist Party of Catalonia; PSUC), played a role in this armed conflict; one died in Mauthausen, the other from torture during his detention by the Gestapo.

Towards the end of 1942, the Spanish Resistance entered a new period. The Partido comunista de España (PCE) became its driving political and military force. In the spring of 1942, the PCE established a military formation with the same name as the unit that had helped defend Madrid during the civil war – the 14th Corps of the Cuerpo de Guerrilleros españoles (Spanish Guerrillas). At the same time, the PCE launched a unified political movement, the Unión Nacional Española (National Spanish Union, UNE), following the example of the national fronts created by other communist parties after the invasion of the Soviet Union. The UNE was a broad alliance that brought together not only communists but also Spaniards of other political perspectives – socialists, republicans, anarchists. The fragmentation of the politically exiled organizations and the silence of their leaders had led some militants to unite with the only organized group engaged in armed conflict against Nazism. However, the PCE would remain the only *political* force within this alliance.

The armed Spanish Resistance was organized in a way that closely reflected the refugees' situation. The guerrilla groups arose directly from the protection or resistance nodes that had been developed around GTE worksites, especially in the places most conducive to secret activities because of their wild surroundings, such as logging regions in the Pyrenees, dam construction projects in the Massif Central, and mining enclaves. In many forest regions, for example, the Spaniards were employed in the making of charcoal, which was especially valuable at the time due to the scarcity of other fuels. In these places, they served as screens for guerrilla groups. Furthermore, the *maquis*, an organizational form inherited from the Spanish Civil War, enabled them to avoid repression, to resist the occupier, and to prepare exiles for the "reconquest" of Spain to the greatest extent possible.

The 14th Corps of Spanish Guerrillas was an autonomous armed movement, with actual military leaders, and was independent of other movements of the French Resistance. This group started small, with only a few units in 1942, before expanding greatly in 1943. The first guerrilla groups were formed in the Ariège, Aude, Tarn, Haute-Garonne, Aveyron, Cantal, and Haute-Savoie departments. Later on, groups were formed in many other departments. They carried out various types of sabotage: attacking German detachments, helping prisoners escape, and taking part in protection operations closely linked to actual combat.

At the beginning of 1944, the military leaders of the 14th Corps controlled Spanish units in thirty-one departments in the southern zone. On 6 June 1944, the day of the Normandy landing, the corps numbered around ten thousand men throughout France. These guerrillas, experienced and brave soldiers, helped pursue German and Vichy forces in some regions and gained the respect of many Resistance leaders, from Serge Ravanel, head of the Toulouse region resistance, to Commander "Aube," the future General Bigeard.

The Spaniards held on to their independence within the Resistance. In October 1943, the 14th Corps of Guerrillas was officially integrated into the Francs-Tireurs et Partisans (FTP) of the Mano de Obra Inmigrada (Immigrant Workforce, MOI), an organization comprised of immigrants from diverse backgrounds. This change, though, was largely symbolic. In the spring of 1944, Spaniards began preparing to operate on the other side of the Pyrenees. The UNE reorganized its armed wing and formed the Agrupación de Guerrilleros españoles (Group of Spanish Guerrillas), with Luis Fernández in charge. The movement maintained close ties to other resistance groups, which were included under the umbrella of the Forces Françaises de l'Intérieur (French Forces of the Interior, FFI), the unified organization of the French Resistance. However, the guerrillas represented themselves directly before the FFI staff and not through the intermediary FTP-MOI. The UNE would play a vital role in the politics of the Spanish exile community during the long years of underground resistance, but not without first engaging in heated confrontations with the other political forces within that community after the war.

One of the Spanish *maquis*[10] that did not depend on the UNE was the group from the l'Aigle Dam in the Cantal. It was made up of anarchists. Spaniards also participated in French Resistance movements, often alongside other foreigners. Such collaboration was most common in departments beyond the meridional regions, where Spaniards tended to operate in larger numbers. In the Charente and Charente-Maritime departments, where refugees had suffered more than most at the beginning of the German occupation (more than nine hundred civilians, men, women, and children, were deported from Angoulême to Mauthausen), the Spaniards contacted the FTP group and organized acts of sabotage against the Nazis. In various departments, such as the Eure, the Nièvre, and the Yonne, and in regions such as the Pays de Loire, the Franche-Comté, and the Jura, Spaniards united with French groups, especially with the FTP. In Brittany, Pedro Flores, also an FFI captain, led the Rennes group. Flores was executed by the Germans in June 1944.

In the southeast, some Spaniards participated in French groups for strictly local reasons (i.e., because their first contacts had been established with the French Resistance), or for political reasons (i.e., to evade UNE hegemony). This may have been the case for socialists or anarchists. This occurred, for example, in the departments of Lot and Aveyron. In Decazeville in the latter department, it seems that the partition occurred cleanly: communist sympathizers united with the UNE, while the non-communists committed themselves directly to the French movements. Several UNE leaders abandoned that group to join French movements. These include the socialist Julio Carrasco – alias Commandant "Renard" – and some of his comrades after an altercation with the communist Tomás Guerrero ("Camilo"), chief of the 35th Brigade of Gers. Spanish participation in the French Resistance movements is, to this day, poorly known in many departments. It was likely within the fold of French groups that many of the civil war refugees first encountered the "old immigration" Spaniards – for example, in the city of Saint-Denis, where the oldest Spanish colony in the region of Paris had been established.

During the summer of 1944, Spaniards played an important role in the battles to liberate French territory. The guerrillas played an active role in liberating many departments of the Midi, a liberation that was exclusively the work of the Resistance. Many Spaniards participated in the battles to free the Gers (in l'Île-Jourdain), the Gard (the Battle of La Madeleine, near Anduze), the Hérault (in Montpellier), the Tarn (in Albi, Carmaux, and Castres), the Aveyron (Rodez), the Dordogne (Périgueux and Bergerac), and the Eastern Pyrenees (Prades, Céret, and Perpignan). It was in the Ariège that guerrillas played the most important role. They fought in battles around Foix and Pamiers, in the Prayols ambush, and in the Castelnau-Durban battles, and they liberated the principal city of the department – French *maquis* arrived *after* the liberation of Foix. Some Spaniards also took part in battles carried out by the larger *maquis*, for example, in the Vercors (between Isère and Drôme), on the Glières plateau, in Haute-Savoie (where an "Ebro section" had been formed), and in Mont-Mouchet. The war continued for many of them on the "forgotten fronts," which is to say near Lorient, Royan, Le Verdon, and Pointe-de-Grave, in which the Basque battalion Guernika and a battalion called Libertad (Freedom), which was non-Communist and predominantly anarchist and socialist, participated.

Throughout this period of the liberation, the primary goal continued to be Spain, since the Spanish Republicans were convinced that the fall of Hitler and Mussolini would lead to Franco's fall as well. The Spaniards harboured no doubts that the battle in France against fascism should continue in Spain. This explains their desperate attempt to invade the Aran Valley in the fall of 1944. The operation began on 19 October, led by Vicente López Tovar, head of a division of guerrillas, who was personally reticent towards these orders, which came from Communist Party leaders. López Tovar mobilized around four thousand men, who entered the Aran Valley in different groups. The lack of communication between the groups, the speedy arrival of Francoist troops, which had been alerted many days before, and lack of support from the local people compelled the guerrillas to retreat in disorder after a few days. The Second World War was not over, and none of the Allies – who had not been consulted before the operation – wanted to open a new front in the Pyrenees.

Like the CTE members arrested in 1940 (the "blue triangles"), the Spaniards who fought against the Nazi occupation (the "red triangles") were deported. The number of Republicans deported for their involvement in the Resistance is difficult to estimate since they were spread across different camps, especially Buchenwald (where Jorge Semprún ended up), Bergen-Belsen, Dachau, Flossenbürg, and Auschwitz. In Mauthausen, where they arrived in large numbers, the Spaniards could coalesce as a group, as the CNT militant José Ester Borrás, a resistance fighter in the Ponzán network, has explained.[11]

Because of their association with the Resistance, many women were deported, especially to Ravensbrück. They included Alfonsina Bueno Ester, the wife of José Ester Borrás and a member of the escape network directed by Ponzán; and Neus Català, a young Communist militant from a Dordogne-based FTP-MOI *maquis*. History is indebted to Neus Català for her writings, in which she rescued her female colleagues from oblivion. These women were even more forgotten than male Spanish resistance fighters, as discussed at length by Herrmann in this volume. Yet they played an indispensable role in the regions in which they were located. They covered long distances on foot, by bicycle, or by train in order to carry out their essential mission as liaisons. Their role demanded great secrecy: they transmitted instructions to scattered groups of resistance fighters; they secured relationships with *maquis*; they carried mail, materials, money, false documentation, and very often, weapons. Women helped to distribute secret press publications and to organize escape networks across the Pyrenees. Pilar Ponzán, Francisco Ponzán's sister, was one of these women. Women resisters often had children whom they had to leave behind when they were arrested or deported. Memories of these children haunted them inside the concentration camp: infants whose baby carriages had served to carry weapons, children helping their mothers during clandestine missions (as in the case of Alfonsina Bueno), children placed with social services at the time of their arrest, adult children arrested while working with the Resistance. Many of these women's companions were arrested, tortured, executed, or deported, such as Català's first husband, who perished in a Nazi camp. The Spanish women who participated in the Resistance are the forgotten women among the forgotten people of this period's history, although recent scholarly and popular attention to the life of Neus Català has gone some distance in correcting this injustice of memory.[12]

The Prolonged Oblivion of the Spanish Resistance

Despite recent research,[13] the participation of Spanish Republicans in the battles of the Second World War on the side of the democracies, and particularly in the French Resistance against the Nazi occupier, remains a little-known fact, long forgotten or ignored by historians and largely absent to this day from the French and Spanish collective memories.

The reasons for this "historical oblivion" are varied. In France, this forgetting stems from the way in which the history of those years of war was written: the dominant memories of the postwar era – the Gaullist memory and the Communist memory – ignored the participation of foreigners in the Resistance. They have instead offered the image of a broad national consensus against the Nazi occupier, behind a charismatic boss or a vanguard party. Only in recent decades, starting in the early 1990s, has French historiography begun to take an interest in foreign participation in the Resistance. The mechanisms of this concealment are unique in the case of the Spaniards. France was the country where the Spanish Civil War most reverberated and where the strongest passions arose. That civil war was an integral part of internal political debates in France. And after the Second World War, the "Cold War" led to normalized relations with Francoist Spain and thus to the burying of the role that Spanish Republicans played in the resistance.[14]

Moreover, Francoist Spain was committed to the Axis countries and could not and did not want to defend the resistance work of their opponents. When the Cold War started, Franco, who had been condemned by the United Nations, returned little by little to the concert of nations. In November 1950, the UN General Assembly cancelled the December 1946 resolution against Franco, and member countries re-established relations with Spain (in the case of France, this took place in 1951). Francoist Spain also joined UNESCO in 1952 and the UN in 1955. As a result, the role played by the adversaries of the Franco regime in the fight against Nazism fell into oblivion.

Nonetheless, in France, some monuments commemorate the role of the Spaniards, such as those in Morette in Haute-Savoie and in Annecy, where a monument has been raised in memory of the Spanish combatants who died for the cause of freedom. In the military cemetery reserved for those from the Glières *maquis*, there is an "Ebro Section" for Spanish Republicans. In 1994, on the fiftieth anniversary of France's liberation, the Spaniards' role was not clearly acknowledged; however, a ceremony for that purpose was conducted on 21 October 1994 in Prayols in the Ariège, presided over by the president of France and the prime minister of Spain at the time, François Mitterrand and Felipe González.

In the twenty-first century, official recognition of the Spaniards' role during the Second World War has grown. On 26 October 2002, a plaque commemorating the founding of the 14th Corps of Guerrillas was installed in the port of Py in Ariège. The ceremony was conducted in the presence of civil and military authorities, national and regional French authorities, and representatives of French and Spanish associations of former soldiers. Today in France, both researchers and descendants of exiles are calling loudly for a better understanding of this page of history.

In August 2004, the role of Spanish Republicans in the liberation of Paris finally enjoyed an homage in the French capital. Commemorative headstones were placed on the route in Paris that had been followed by Spaniards from La Nueve, who led the way into the French capital on 24 August 1944. But it was only in August 2014 that a president of the French Republic offered a public tribute to those Spaniards, most of whom had been anarchists. In 2015, the mayor of Paris, Anne Hidalgo (herself of Spanish Republican stock), unveiled the Garden of the Combatants of the Nine, near the Paris city hall. (On commemoration and the Mauthausen monument, see Juan M. Calvo Gascón's chapter 11 in this volume.)

Spaniards' participation in the Resistance against the Nazi occupier was considerable. Of course, this participation was the work of a minority, as in the French case, but it is highly significant not only because of the number of participants but also because of the diversity of its activities. Spanish participation in the French Resistance would always be understood as a continuation of the battle they had carried out (and would have to continue for decades) in Spain. Spanish Republicans were convinced that the fall of Hitler and Mussolini would lead to the fall of Franco. For that reason, their objective was to carry the battle against fascism across the Pyrenees. But the Cold War consolidated Franco's position, and the exiles had to wait more than thirty years to return to their country. Meanwhile, their participation in the liberation of France had disappeared from the collective memories of both peoples. In the case of the Spanish Republicans, the French philosopher Paul Ricoeur's words in his book *Memory, History, Forgetting* are very much on point: "Memory can only be happy if it is fair."

NOTES

1 Javier Rubio, *La emigración de la Guerra Civil de 1936–1939. Historia del éxodo que se produce con el fin de la República Española* (Madrid: Editorial San Martín, 1977).
2 Journal officiel. Lois et décrets, 13 November 1938, pp. 12,920–3.
3 The term "concentration camp" was always utilized in the administrative documents of the time. France's interior minister said: "The Argelès-sur-Mer camp will not be a penitentiary place, but a concentration camp. It is not the same thing." After the terrible experience of the Nazi camps – well known by numerous Spanish Republicans – the term used by survivors was always "concentration camps." Even when they were not camps where death was planned as in the Nazi camps, the descendants of the Spanish exile still use that same expression today to talk about French camps. But to avoid confusion, French historians often use the more generic expression "internment camps" for the French camps of this period. See Peschanski, *Les camps français d'internement*; and Dreyfus-Armand, "Les mots de la souffrance."
4 Dreyfus-Armand and Temime, *Les camps sur la plage*.
5 Dreyfus-Armand, *L'Exil des républicains espagnols en France*, 453, 475.
6 Dreyfus-Armand, "Les républicains espagnols."
7 The Norway Campaign was the first land battle between the Allies and the German army during the Second World War. Nazi Germany occupied Norway to ensure the provision of Swedish iron, which crossed through the ports of that country, particularly Narvik.

8 Crémieux-Brilhac, "L'engagement militaire des Italiens et des Espagnols," 586–90.
9 Dreyfus-Armand, *El exilio de los republicanos españoles en Francia.*
10 "Maquis" refers to groups of resistance fighters and also to the places where they hid from the Nazi occupiers in order to organize the underground fight against them. The place was generally in an isolated, forest area, often in the mountains.
11 Dreyfus-Armand and Martinez-Maler, *L'Espagne, passion française. 1936–1975.*
12 On 4 October 2019, a Paris street was named in honour of Neus Català.
13 See previously cited works by Dreyfus-Armand; Gildea, *Fighters in the Shadows.*
14 Robin, *Résonances françaises de la guerre d'Espagne.*

10 From Internees to Liberators: Spanish Republican Exiles in France, 1939–1945

ROBERT S. COALE

As analysed in the previous chapter, the defeat of the Spanish Republic in 1939 led to the exodus of hundreds of thousands of Spanish Loyalists into France. Many eventually returned to Spain, and others made their way to exile in countries around the globe, but more than one hundred thousand others had nowhere else to go. Once the Second World War broke out, the anti-fascist ideal pushed many of these refugees to take up arms again, and they served in many capacities, from sailors in the Merchant Marine, to privates in the French Foreign Legion and the British Army, and as agents in the Special Operations Executive or the French Underground. They fought on battlefields from the Eastern Front to North Africa and Narvik, and from Dunkirk to the D-Day invasion of Normandy.

In recent years the participation of Spanish Republican exiles in one of the most celebrated French army units of the Second World War, the French Second Armored Division, more commonly known as the Leclerc Division, has received much attention in both the press and institutional circles. The fact that the vanguard of Allied troops to enter Paris on the evening of 24 August 1944 under the command of Captain Raymond Dronne included Spanish anti-fascists has been reported widely in the Spanish and French press since the sixtieth-anniversary celebrations of the liberation in 2004.[1] More recently, in 2015, the city of Paris, under Mayor Anne Hidalgo, has renamed the municipal gardens next to the Hôtel de Ville "Jardins des Combattants de la Nueve" in honour of those men, soldiers of the 9th Company of the Régiment de Marche du Tchad. Following the lead of Paris, a small garden on the outskirts of Madrid was also named in their honour in 2017.[2]

The Spanish Loyalists who integrated the Leclerc Division in 1943 had endured the shifting policies of successive French governments concerning refugees. As detailed in the previous chapter, these programs included the hastily organized internment camps of 1939, the Compagnies des Travailleurs Étrangers (CTEs) and their Vichy government avatar, the Groupements des Travailleurs Étrangers (GTEs), and, of course, the option of the French Foreign Legion. The Allied invasion of North Africa in November 1942 brought about changes in the opportunities afforded to exiles. Many anti-fascists, of Spanish or Central European origin, and Frenchmen who refused to serve in units with former Vichy officers chose to fight in the ranks of the motley Corps franc d'Afrique, where they saw considerable action under British command during the Tunisian campaign of 1943. These men subsequently found their way into the Régiment de March du Tchad, the infantry backbone of the Leclerc Division. That any number of these men managed to survive through internment, service in the French Foreign Legion, and forced labour camps followed by the 1943 campaign in North Africa and that of France in 1944–5, to end up on 5 May 1945 as victors in the Nazi stronghold of Berchtesgaden was an enormous feat of resistance as well as proof of a stalwart commitment to an ideal.

One of the approximately five hundred Spaniards who, when given the opportunity, followed the call of General de Gaulle and ended up in the Leclerc Division, was Lucas Camons Portillo of Santander. He served from 1943 to 1945 as a sergeant in La Nueve, the 9th Company of the Third Battalion of the Régiment de Marche du Tchad. The middle of three brothers from a militant socialist family, he and his siblings had served in the Republican Army in Spain and escaped to French territory at the close of the conflict in early 1939. In this chapter, the parallel experiences of Lucas Camons's brothers will serve to illustrate the experience of Spanish anti-fascists who fought in France in regular French army units, notably in the Leclerc Division. The travails of Eduardo (born in Madrid, 1900), Lucas (born in Santander, 1913), and Félix (born in Santander, 1917) illustrate three of the paths that choice or fate left to Spanish exiles in France from 1939 to 1945. Their different war experiences can be interpreted as paradigms of the fortune suffered by many of their fellow countrymen.

When the Spanish Republican army collapsed in March of 1939, Lucas Camons Portillo was serving in the Central zone. As a lieutenant in a transportation unit, he had a car at his disposal, and with several comrades, he managed to drive to Alicante in time to board the *Stanbrook* and escape before that port city fell. During the period of quarantine the French authorities imposed on the refugees in the port of Oran, Lucas Camons began to record his experiences in a diary. By early May, the refugees had been disembarked and men of military age were sent to camp Morand in the hinterland of French Algeria. After one month of internment Camons wrote of the general morale of the internees:

> Los días pasan y nuestro porvenir era el campo de Moran con alambradas por todos los lados y Senegaleses que aullaban más que hablaban, [...] Todo el mundo se dedicaba a mandar cartas a los organismos políticos y a las entidades de ayuda, yo no me preocupaba de nada, pues creía que todo era mentira, pues los que estaban fuera se dedicarían a preocuparse de ellos mismos y de los que se encontraban en los campos nadie se preocuparía, así que yo no quería molestarme y menos en mandar medias afiliaciones que no sabía a qué manos podían caer: El tiempo pasaba y nosotros marchábamos en peores condiciones.

> The days go by and our future in Camp Moran, with barbed wire enclosures all around and Senegalese soldiers who howl more than speak ... Everyone set about writing letters to all the political organizations and relief agencies. Personally I did not worry about such things because I thought it was all a pack of lies: those who were on the outside would take care of themselves first, and no one would care about those of us in the camps. So I didn't want to worry and even less to join organizations half-heartedly as you couldn't know in whose hands the information would fall. As time went by we suffered ever-worsening conditions.[3]

Due to his geographical location when the Spanish Republican resistance crumbled, Lucas Camons had been able to escape to North Africa, but that was not the case for his brothers. In February, Eduardo and Felix had retreated from Catalonia with the remnants of the Loyalist army and hundreds of thousands of civilians, into France as part of the *Retirada*. The two brothers had served in the same regiment in Santander and were both stationed in Barcelona from 1937 to 1939, but it is unclear whether they crossed the border together, for they ended up in different camps. In April of 1939, one Eduardo Camon [*sic*] wrote to the authorities of the Pyrenees-Orientales requesting permission for his brother Felix to be allowed to join him in the Combe-aux-Loups camp near Angoulême.[4] For whatever reason, the request was apparently not granted, and this relatively minor detail may very well have saved Felix Camons Portillo's life.

Compagnies de Travailleurs Étrangers

By the spring of 1939, it was obvious to the French authorities that, regardless of those who had accepted the conditions for returning to

Francoist Spain, and despite the departure of thousands of refugees to Latin America, large numbers of exiles were going to remain in France. Javier Rubio estimates that by December of 1939 there were still 140,000 exiles in France, and of these approximately 100,000 were ex-combatants.[5] In an attempt to address the persistent refugée crisis, the French authorities created the Compagnies des Travailleurs Étrangers (Foreign Labor Companies, CTEs) with two goals in mind: to control the population, and to put idle hands to work as the drums of war sounded ever louder.[6] (Dreyfus-Armand discusses the formation and composition of the CTEs at length in chapter 9). By October 1939 there were approximately fifty-five thousand Spanish refugees serving in 227 CTEs in Metropolitan France.[7]

Following the success in mainland France, the 8e Régiment de Travailleurs Étrangers was set up in North Africa in December 1939, and Lucas Camons was assigned as cadre to one of its companies. After his initial exhilaration at the prospect of leaving the internment camp and the relatively easy work requirements of the first few weeks, reality set in. In April 1940, Lucas Camons left a blunt description of the CTE in which he had been enrolled. Describing the extreme labour conditions during the construction of the Trans-Saharan railway across the desert, he writes:

El clima y el trabajo eran insoportables, pues los hombres caían sin fuerzas y muertos y enfermos, en el tiempo de 15 días hubo 50 por cien de enfermos y un cinco por cien de muertos, a consecuencia de esto empezaron las protestas y la dejación al trabajo. Como esto se extendía en todas las compañías no se pudo solucionar nada, pues a las protestas nadie nos escuchaba y lo único que sacamos fue que nos llevaran a compañías disciplinarias. Esto era un crimen que se cometía con nosotros. En alrededor de unos cuatro días se llevaron más de mil españoles. [...] Se pudo sacar la protesta y los crímenes que hacían con nosotros al exterior, pero nadie se preocupaba de nuestros problemas, pues la vida de nueve mil españoles no valía gran cosa. Nos encontramos solos y sin consuelo de nadie.

The climate and the work were unbearable. Men fell exhausted, ill or died. In two weeks 50 percent of the Spaniards were ill and 5 percent had died. Due to this we began to protest and to stop working. The protests spread to other companies but there was no solution in sight, because no one was about to listen to us. The only tangible result of our actions was to be sent off to the disciplinary company. This was a crime in itself. In about four days one thousand Spaniards were sent there.... Nevertheless, we were successful in spreading the word outside the camps concerning the conditions and crimes that were committed against us, but no one worried about our problems. The lives of nine thousand Spaniards [were] not worth much. We found ourselves alone and without consolation.[8]

The French Foreign Legion

From the moment they arrived in France, except for returning to Spain or immigrating to another country, joining the French Foreign Legion was one of the most direct methods of eluding internment. However, the veterans of the Spanish Republican Army generally disdained the Legion as little more than mercenaries or misfits and outlaws seeking to distance themselves from a blemished past. Lucas Camons's description of the visit of a recruiting officer to Camp Moran in Algeria in early September of 1939 evokes the dilemma with which refugees were confronted. According to the former transportation lieutenant, the officer's pitch:

cayó por unos bien y por otros mal, pero el resultado de todo que se apuntaron para la Legión, yo no lo hice, pues no creía el momento todavía, pero tampoco yo criticaba o lo veía mal el que estos compañeros solucionaran su situación de esta forma. Al fin y al cabo lo hacían por una causa más, para combatir a sus enemigos como eran Alemania e Italia, no para darle un golpe de más al capital como algunos les decían.

made a favorable impression on some and an unfavorable one on others with the result that some enlisted. I did not because I didn't consider the time had come but neither did I criticize the comrades who enrolled because each individual had to resolve his personal situation as best he could. In any case, they were choosing to fight our enemies – Germany and Italy – and not to help Capitalism as some protested.[9]

By the end of 1939, the harsh conditions of internment had convinced approximately three thousand Spaniards to enlist in the army. This number was 27.7 per cent of all legionnaire recruits for that year.[10] Prior to the outbreak of the Second World War, the minimum enlistment into that most notorious of units had been five years. Once the war began, however, the situation changed significantly. Parallel to the traditional Foreign Legion battalions, so-called Régiments de Marche de Volontairs Étrangers (Foreign Volunteer Regiments, RMVEs) had been created in which enlistments were offered for the duration of the war. In the fall of 1939, many Spanish Loyalists who had felt misgivings about joining the Foreign Legion now signed on. As they saw it, France had declared war on their common enemies and any way, shape, or form they could take up arms was acceptable. By early 1940 another three thousand Spaniards had joined the RMVEs.[11] The seemingly minor detail concerning the type of enlistment would have serious consequences for many Spaniards after the armistice of June 1940.

Although in September of 1939 Lucas Camons was not prepared to join the Legion (see above), the extreme labour conditions along the Trans-Saharan railway and the threat of a transfer to the disciplinary company compelled him to change his mind and enlist in early May 1940. Although the discipline and the training were severe, his interpretation of his new situation was probably shared by many Loyalist veterans at the time: "La compañía de Instrucción es muy fuerte pero se puede llevar cuando se come bien y la libertad no falta" (Basic training is very harsh, but you can withstand it when there is plenty to eat and you have your freedom).[12]

By all accounts, by virtue of the solidarity they showed among themselves, the influx of Spanish Loyalist veterans altered the atmosphere in some Legion units.[13] It is true that the Spanish veterans of a popular army who had fought for an ideal had little in common with the officers, non-commissioned officers, and old rank-and-file legionnaires. Nevertheless, both time and rapidly developing events would change the opinion of the Legion cadres, who eventually learned to appreciate the soldierly qualities of the Spanish veterans.[14]

When the German army launched its blitzkrieg attack on the Western Front in May 1940, Spanish volunteers were on the front lines, both in Legion regiments and in the *régiments de marche*. As a rule, they acquitted themselves honourably, most notably the 11th and 12th Legion regiments, which suffered heavy casualties during the Battle of France. Of the three RMVEs formed in the south in 1939–40 – the 21st, 22nd, and 23rd RMVEs – the 22nd served with the most distinction in the campaign of June 1940 despite staggering losses and was awarded the Croix de Guerre *avec palme*.[15]

One other French Foreign Legion unit deserves special mention: the 13th Demi-Brigade, which took part in the Allied expedition to Narvik, Norway, in April of 1940 and included approximately five hundred former Spanish Loyalists in its ranks.[16] In the midst of its victorious Scandinavian campaign, it was recalled to France to stem the German advance. Arriving too late to affect the outcome, it ended up in England in June, where the rank and file were given the choice of joining Gaullist forces or returning home to defeat. Many of these Spanish legionnaires chose to remain in England and became some of the first to join the ranks of the Free French. The 13th Demi-Brigade remained a bulwark Gaullist unit for the entire war.[17]

The Spanish legionnaires were not the only Loyalists caught in the German attack, nor were they the most numerous. By virtue of the location of the military installations on which they were labouring, many of the men enrolled in the CTEs found themselves on the battlefield. In many cases, the cohesiveness of the companies vanished and it was each man for himself. Some banded together and took up arms, others escaped to the south, and still others were captured by the advancing invaders. The latter, taken in French army uniforms, were at first treated as prisoners of war and sent to Stalags. Later on, however, they were separated from their French comrades and found themselves in Nazi concentration camps, most notably Mauthausen.[18] Approximately two thirds of the eighty-seven hundred Spanish prisoners who eventually found themselves in German concentration camps perished before the liberation in 1945. (For more on Spaniards in Mauthausen and other Nazi camps, see chapters 11, 14, 15 and 17 in this volume.)[19]

Many of the Foreign Legion recruits who had been sent to North Africa for training, and those like Lucas Camons, who were already in the area when they joined the Legion, did not take part in the Battle of France. After the armistice of June 1940, the German military demanded that the Vichy regime reduce the size of its standing army. In order to comply, and to rid themselves of soldiers who were ideologically opposed to the new regime under Pétain, the French authorities discharged the foreigners who had opted for an enlistment in the Régiments de Marche des Volontaires Étrangers for the duration and sent them to GTEs. This was a new twist on the CTEs, which had existed from 1939 to 1940. The living and labour conditions for these groups were even more severe than those prior to the war. According to one witness, "The men had all the disadvantages of being soldiers and none of the advantages. They wore soldier's uniforms, but they were treated as if they were men condemned to hard labor."[20] Lucas Camons was discharged in this fashion in October 1940 and found himself returned to the same area he had left in May. He was to spend the next two years in a narrow strip of desert along the Moroccan–Algerian border between Aïn Séfra, Colomb-Béchar, and Kenadza.

Only two months prior to his discharge from the RMVE, and unbeknownst to Lucas Camons at the time, his eldest brother, Eduardo, was deported from France. As mentioned earlier, in April of 1940 Eduardo was interned in the Combe-aux-Loups camp outside of Angoulême. These refugees were later transferred to the newer Camp des Alliers, from which 927 were deported directly from the occupied zone of France to the Nazi camp of Mauthausen, where they arrived on 24 August 1940.[21] Of the 430 men and adolescent boys who were detained in the camp, almost 90 per cent perished, a much higher rate than that of all Spanish Republican internees in Nazi Germany.[22] Eduardo Camons Portillo endured the camps for fifteen months. In January 1941 he was transferred from Mauthausen to the Gusen subcamp and from there to Hartheim, where he was gassed on 19 December 1941.[23] Lucas and Felix Camons did not learn of the murder of their eldest brother until August 1945. One can safely suppose that had Felix Camons been granted permission to join Eduardo in the Cambe-aux-Loups camp in the spring of 1940, he probably would have been deported in the same convoy that left Angoulême in August 1940, which was, in fact, the first deportation of civilians of any nationality or creed from occupied France directly to Nazi Germany.

The Leclerc Division

Back in North Africa, discharge into the GTEs generally concerned those who had enlisted for the duration and not for the standard five years. Accordingly, other Spaniards remained in the Legion ranks enduring the rigours of the French army under the Vichy regime. Operation Torch, the Anglo-American invasion of North Africa and the subsequent rallying of the French army to the Allied cause, changed the situation somewhat, but not completely. From late 1942 to mid-1943, a number of legionnaires carried out what were jokingly referred to as "spontaneous transfers," that is, desertions from the Foreign Legion to the unyieldingly anti-fascist Corps franc d'Afrique (CFA), which had gained a solid reputation in the Tunisian campaign of 1943. This unit later provided, wittingly or not, the bulk of the infantry for the Division Leclerc. Two veterans, Luis Royo and Manuel Fernández Arias, narrated their "transfers" to the Leclerc Division. Royo served in the Legion in North Africa from 1939 to 1943, when he was able to desert to the CFA. From there, he joined the French Second Armored Division, where he served in the 9th Company under the assumed name of Escudero until September 1944, when he was wounded in the Battle of Chatel-sur-Moselle. Fernández Arias fought in the ranks of the Legion throughout the Tunisian campaign of 1943, when he was wounded. He, too, "transferred" himself to the CFA. He later made his way into the Leclerc Division, where he served in the heavy weapons company of the 3rd Battalion of the RMT under the name of Belmonte until he was wounded outside of Sées, Normandy, in August 1944.[24] These cases, and many others too numerous to mention here, illustrate a curious relationship within the regular French army. Two units, the French Foreign Legion, including the Régiments de Marche des

Volontaires Étrangers, and the French Second Armored Division, took in the majority of Spanish Republicans who chose to serve in French regular army formations. In fact, a majority of the men who served in the Leclerc Division passed through the ranks of the Foreign Legion at one point or another during their exile in France.

Lucas Camons Portillo also joined the Leclerc Division via the Corps franc d'Afrique. Unlike many of his comrades, since he was not a deserter from the Legion, he enlisted in the CFA under his real name. As mentioned above, he was in Kenadza enrolled in a GTE when the Anglo-American invasion of North Africa took place in early November of 1942. Taking advantage of the confusion the invasion caused, he escaped from his labour camp and joined the Allies. Trained as a mechanic, he rapidly found work in Oran with the Americans assembling military equipment as it was unloaded from Liberty ships. Notwithstanding his valuable job, and after savouring some seven months of freedom as a civilian contractor, in July 1943 he decided to once again take up arms and join Spanish comrades who were serving with the Free French.

After training in North Africa with new American equipment, the French Second Armored Division was sent to England for further exercises prior to its commitment to the liberation of France as part of General Patton's Third Army. The vast majority of Spaniards in the division served in the four companies of the 3rd Battalion of the Regiment de Marche du Tchad. As such, they participated in several key battles: the Falaise Gap, the liberation of Paris, the Lorraine campaign, the liberation of Strasbourg, the Battle of the Colmar Pocket, and the mad rush in April–May 1945 to Berchtesgaden, Austria, including the Battle of Inzell.

Certainly the most famous episode involving the Leclerc Division, one that had great political as well as military importance, was the liberation of Paris in August 1944. As mentioned earlier, in recent years much has been said of the Spanish Loyalists who entered Paris on the evening of 24 August 1944. In fact, besides the three platoons of the 9th Company, which were manned mainly by Spaniards, French soldiers were present in Captain Dronne's column. The reduced platoon of Sherman tanks and a platoon of combat engineers had no Spanish Loyalists in their ranks, a detail that has been systematically omitted by amateur historians and Spanish journalists. But perhaps the most curious detail of the mission was not the nationalities of its soldiers, but rather that it was accomplished under extreme circumstances without firing a shot.

Another detail that is ignored by recent accounts of the Spanish participation in the Leclerc Division is that in addition to being the first into Paris, elements of that same company were also the *last*. When Captain Dronne was hastily organizing his column to enter Paris on the afternoon of 24 August, he was unable to include his first platoon, which was engaged in combat around the Croix de Berny. It subsequently remained in the suburbs until the following morning, when it was ordered to join the divisional column into Paris. Thus, in addition to being the first into Paris, the Spanish of the 9th Company curiously were also the last of the Leclerc Division to enter the capital, a position that paradoxically turned out to be more dangerous than that of their comrades the night before. Lucas Camons was a squad leader in the first platoon, and he describes his entry into Paris on the morning of 25 August 1944 as one of the most wonderful experiences of his life. He also contrasts the few days' rest the division received as very different from the reception they had gotten as refugees just five years earlier:

> A las 9 de la mañana; al entrar en París yo fui cortado por una resistencia alemana. Pudimos abrir paso y unirnos nuevamente a la columna. Pocas calles después parecía que se había acabado la guerra pues todo el pueblo nos recibía con las manos abiertas. Esto fue una cosa emocionante, pues yo no había visto en mi vida una cosa tan fantástica. Los coches blindados y los tanques parecían tranvías pues todo el mundo se subía a ellos como si fuéramos dioses. En todos los lados que parábamos éramos asaltados por las mujeres y nos besaban por todo nuestros trajes guarros que traíamos. Era una emoción para nosotros, pues yo toda mi vida me recordaré de esta entrada triunfal en París.[...] Pasamos unos buenos días en París, pues por todas las partes que pasabamos éramos aclamados y no nos dejaban pagar nada. El mundo nos felicitaba y nos abría todas la puertas. Ya no eran los momentos del 39 y 40 que nos consideraban como *pauvres malheureux*.

At nine in the morning, upon entering Paris my squad was separated from the column by German resistance. After fighting through it, a few blocks further on, it seemed like the war had ended. Everyone was welcoming us with open arms. It was an emotional moment. I had never seen such a fantastic scene in my life. The halftracks and tanks looked like streetcars as everyone was climbing all over them reaching up to us as if we were gods. Everywhere we stopped we were swamped by women who kissed us despite our dirty faces and uniforms. It was very emotional for us. As long as I live I will always remember our triumphant entry into Paris ... We spent a few happy days in Paris. Everywhere we went we were welcomed and we weren't allowed to pay for anything as we were congratulated by everyone. All doors were open to us. It was no longer 1939 and 1940 when we were thought of as wretched souls.[25]

The entry into Paris and the ten-day rest period in the capital were episodes long remembered by the men who experienced them, but the campaign to liberate France was far from over in August 1944. The Leclerc Division had many months of hard campaigning ahead of it, and the path from Paris to Berchtesgaden is dotted with the tombs of Spanish Loyalist volunteers.

All through the war, Lucas Camons noted in his diary entries the names of most of the Spanish comrades who were wounded or killed and how their loss was felt by those who remained. Nevertheless, perhaps even more telling than combat episodes or casualties are the political observations that pepper his diary. His anti-fascist commitment was constant, and in several passages he goes beyond describing daily events to include reflections on the broader implications of the war and the future downfall of Franco. For example, at the close of the war, elements of the Leclerc Division participated in the conquest of Berchtesgaden, one of the cradles of Nazism. How ironic that a very few of the soldiers who entered the town in early May 1945 were men who had been fighting Fascism since 1936. With the German Army on the point of total surrender, Camons wrote:

A la caída de la tarde llegamos a Bertsdiesgaden lo cual enlazamos con la fuerza Americana y tomamos la villa.[...] Cayó la villa donde Hitler tenía el cuartel general. Por fin fueron los Españoles quien[es] llegaron a la casa de Hitler y pudieron demostrar a todo el mundo [los que] perdieron la guerra en España llegaron triunfante al corazón de Alemania y tomaron parte en dar la muerte al Ejército Fascista que tanto peligro era para las democracias y que se prepara par dar lo merecido a Franco y su cuadrilla. En Berchtesgaden se puede ver el ejército poderoso Alemán en la más humilde derrota. Sus Generales y Coroneles, hasta el último soldado habían dejado de ser los soldados más orgullosos del mundo, como ellos se creían con su política de engaño y miseria.

At the end of the day we arrived in Berchtesgaden, linked up with the American forces and took the town. Thus the town where Hitler had his general headquarters fell. At last, we were the Spanish who got to Hitler's house and were able to show the world that those who lost the War in Spain were conquerors in the heart of Germany and took part in the death stroke against the Fascist Armies which were such a danger to the democracies and we are preparing ourselves to give Franco and his gang what they deserve. In Berchtesgaden one can see the once powerful German Army in the most humiliating defeat. Its generals, and colonels down to the lowliest private are no longer the proudest soldiers in the world like they thought they were with their policy of trickery and misery.[26]

These few lines of his personal diary illustrate what must have been the mindset not only of the Spanish in the Leclerc Division, but also that of many, if not all, of the men who volunteered to continue the fight in uniform under the banner of France. For his services in the liberation of France Lucas Camons was awarded the Médaille Militaire (France's highest honour for combat experience), three Croix de Guerre, and, in 1989, the Legion of Honour. The Camons Portillo family, to some extent, exemplifies the sacrifices of Spanish exiles in France. From death in Mauthausen for the eldest brother, to victory over Nazi Germany as a non-commissioned officer in the Leclerc Division for another, and merely surviving the war years in southern France as a farmhand for the youngest of the three.

All things told, it is perhaps not completely fortuitous that Spanish Loyalists found their place in the Leclerc Division, as it was truly a unique French outfit. Its Free French origins were key elements in the Gaullist narration of the Second World War, which portrays a country that never gave up the fight against Nazism and fascism, a discourse that rang true to Spanish exiles from its earliest calls for resistance.

An intensely anti-fascist *esprit de corps* was maintained in "La Nueve" throughout the war, which was felt even by the young Frenchmen who, over the course of the campaign to liberate France, took the places of the fallen Spanish comrades. It is interesting to note that compared to the several thousand Spaniards who had served in the French Foreign Legion, the five hundred Spaniards of the Leclerc Division are praised to a greater degree. One explanation may be the strong Free French identity of the Regiment de Marche du Tchad as opposed to the general image of the Foreign Legion. Nevertheless, in both military units the Spanish volunteers were considered "French" soldiers, because they wore French uniforms and served under the French *tricolour*. Notwithstanding military discipline, compared to that of the Foreign Legion, the more lax regimen within the French Second Armored Division born of its unique Free French origins allowed the Spanish contingent ways to express itself and to maintain its identity. These possibilities ranged from the names with which some vehicles were baptized – *Tunisie 43, L'Ebre, Madrid, Teruel, Guadalajara, Don Quichotte* – to the daily use of the Spanish language in the ranks and the occasional display of miniature *tricolor* Spanish Republican flags. In this way, these volunteers managed to assert a direct connection between their service in the Leclerc Division and the struggle that many had begun in 1936. Lucas Camons reflects this relationship in his diary, especially in its rare politically motivated passages and persistent expression of a truly anti-fascist identity.

Conclusion

Spanish Loyalist participation in the Second World War was significant and diverse. There were anti-fascist Spaniards on all fronts in France and also beyond, from Norway to Stalingrad and back. They unanimously viewed the Second World War as a continuation of the Spanish Civil War. Numbers are inherently difficult to establish, for these nationless men and women did not participate under their own flag but rather were incorporated into armies of many nationalities. Despite their numbers and their presence on many fronts, the Nazis killed more Spanish Republicans in Mauthausen than were lost in combat operations in the Legion and the Leclerc Division. The Camons Portillo family was on both fronts, and possibly more. Family accounts state that Felix Camons, the youngest sibling, managed to survive the war working on a farm in the Aveyron department of southern France and may have collaborated with the local resistance movement. In 1945, the brothers got word of each other: Lucas Camons invited his younger brother to move in with him and his new family while they awaited the downfall of the Franco regime before presumably returning to Santander. They ended up sharing a home for the next fifty-odd years.

In 1984, forty years after he wrote his last entry in his war journal, Lucas Camons Portillo, a married family man with three daughters and several grandchildren, reopened his elementary school copybook to jot down his thoughts with an unsteady hand. He was evidently tired of waiting for public recognition of the efforts of Spanish Loyalists in the victory over fascism, and he desperately wished their fight not to be forgotten:

> A los 50 años de la muerte de muchos Españoles en los Campos de Exterminación Alemanes, por los asesinos SS, solo las familias y compañeros, tienen recuerdo de sus caras medio llenas de sangre. Estos compañeros murieron por la libertad en España. Entre estos compañeros había de todas las ideales libres y democráticos que defendían la República.
>
> El pueblo Español no debe olvidar estos caídos por la tortura Fascista y de acuerdo con la Falange de los Españoles de Franco y las milicias Francesas, las SS y la Gestapo. Honor para los Republicanos Españoles.

Fifty years after the death of many Spaniards, in the Nazi extermination camps, at the hands of the SS assassins, only the family and comrades of the dead remember their faces half covered in blood. These comrades died for freedom in Spain. They were of all political persuasions of those who defended the Spanish Republic. The Spanish people should not forget those who fell at the hands of fascist torture. At the hands of Franco's Falange, the French Militia, the SS and the Gestapo. Honor to the Spanish Loyalists.[27]

It is evident by this and other passages from his journal that Lucas Camons had come to accept the fact that the Western democracies had allowed Franco to continue to control Spain after the Second World War. For geopolitical reasons, a cruel dictator was permitted to rule Spain for forty years and to die in his sleep an old man. What Camons urged democratic Spain of 1995 to do was to remember the sacrifices of a previous generation that had lived under a short period of democracy and then had suffered considerably. The Spanish Republicans who were exiled to France in 1939 and who took up arms in units of the French army to fight to victory in 1945 exemplify one of the facets of the anti-fascist fight of that generation.

NOTES

1   Artero Rueda and Larrea, "Españoles en París, 60 años después."
2   Laura Galaup and Marcos Servera, "El Ayuntamiento de Madrid homenajea a los republicanos que liberaron París del nazismo," *El diario*, 20 April 2017.
3   Camons Portillo, "Diario de mi vida," 7 May 1939. Author's collection and translation.
4   Armengou and Belis, *El convoy de los 927*, 69.
5   Rubio, "Población española en Francia," 44.
6   Dreyfus-Armand, *L'Exil des républicains espagnols en France*, 107.
7   Gaida, *Camps de travail sous Vichy*, 59.
8   Camons Portillo, "Diario," 9 April 1940.
9   Ibid., 10 September 1939.
10   Porch, *The French Foreign Legion*, 448.
11   Ibid., 448.
12   Camons Portillo, "Diario," 7 May 1940.
13   Porch, *The French Foreign Legion*, 448–51.
14   Printer, "Spanish Soldiers in France", 488.
15   Porch, *The French Foreign Legion*, 463.
16   Gaspar Celaya, *La guerra continúa*, 216–23.
17   Crémieux-Brilhac, *La France Libre*, 655.
18   Bermejo, *Francisco Boix, el fotógrafo de Mauthausen*, 50–5.
19   Bermejo and Checa, *Libro Memorial: Españoles deportados a los campos nazis*, 21.

20 Printer, "Spanish Soldiers in France", 488.
21 Bermejo and Checa, *Libro Memorial*, 18–19.
22 The women and younger children on the convoy were deported to Spain.
    Ibid.
23 Ibid., 414.
24 Luis Royo Ibáñez and Manuel Fernández Arias, interview with the author,
    Cachan, France, 5 July 2001.
25 Camons Portillo, "Diario," 25 August 1944.
26 Ibid., 4 May 1945.
27 Ibid., [circa 1984].

11 The Stateless Monument: Memory of the Spanish Republicans Who Died in Mauthausen

JUAN M. CALVO GASCÓN

Ever since the UN General Assembly declared 27 January as International Holocaust Remembrance Day, various ceremonies organized in Spain have recognized the Spanish victims deported to Nazi camps as one of the groups politically pursued by the Third Reich during the Second World War.[1] Additionally, some regional governments have organized acts of tribute and recognition in which survivors and victims' family members are present – for example, the Catalan Generalitat (October 2005) and the Aragonese government (May 2010). Throughout the country, local governments have organized and promoted various events to commemorate Holocaust Remembrance Day, and most of them specifically acknowledge Spanish victims. At the local level, some of these events are responses to demands made by family members or by associations that work to preserve the memory of the Republican deportation – for example, the Amical de Mauthausen. (See Brenneis, Toran, and Coale on Mauthausen in this volume.)

These initiatives, all of which are valuable, make even clearer how the Spanish state has failed to recover the memory of the anti-Franco fighters who opposed the *coup d'état* that triggered the Spanish Civil War in July 1936. Among the first European anti-fascist fighters, Republican exiles who had been forced to seek refuge in France in 1939 after their defeat in Spain were deported from there to Nazi camps. Since the re-establishment of democracy following the death of dictator Francisco Franco in 1975, no Spanish government has instituted policies or programs to officially clarify the Franco government's involvement in the deportation of thousands of Republicans to Nazi territory following the defeat of France in the spring of 1940. They have never been legally recognized as victims of Nazism. According to recent news reports, however, Spain's Ministry of Justice has announced an effort to legally recognize the Spaniards who were killed in Nazi camps via the publication of their names in the *Boletín de Estado* (State Bulletin, BOE). Nevertheless, as of this writing, it is unclear whether this measure will be accompanied by other official directives to recognize the sacrifice of the Republican victims of the deportation.[2]

During the annual tribute to those imprisoned in the camp in Mauthausen (Austria), national delegations remember their deportees. In what is essentially an extended process of converting the space into a memorial, these tributes take place at the monuments that have been constructed in honour of the victims.[3] Many of these delegations pay homage to the Spanish Republicans by visiting the monument that represents their martyrdom. The monument's erection in 1962 was a milestone in the international recognition of the Spanish victims. The process that led to its creation is significant in explaining some of the characteristics unique to the Spanish collective deported to Mauthausen, a collective whose institutional orphanhood remains despite the intervening decades.

The Deportation of Spanish Republicans[4]

Early in 1939, following their defeat in the Spanish Civil War, around half a million people crossed the French border. As we have seen in the chapter by Dreyfus-Armand in this volume, several thousand were imprisoned in camps the French government had improvised in southern France. The refugees' stay in those camps was difficult, especially in the mid-winter. They felt pressure to return to Spain as they attempted to appease a sector of the French public that held a hostile view of the exiles of the *Retirada*.

With the mobilization of French forces in September 1939, after the declaration of war against Germany, the French government decided to exploit the refugees as a workforce. The French created the Compañías de Trabajadores Extranjeros (Companies of Foreign Workers, CTEs), along the lines of military units. Some fifty thousand Spaniards enlisted; another eight thousand opted to enlist in the Regimientos de Marcha (Marching Battalions) or in the Legión Extranjera (Foreign Legion). In May 1940, Germany invaded France, and in the ensuing confusion, the CTEs were dispersed. Within a few weeks, the Germans had triumphed over France, and on 14 June, they entered Paris. Some five thousand Republicans, members of the CTEs and the Regimientos de Marcha, died during the invasion, and another ten thousand fell into German hands and were taken to Frontstalags and Stalags as prisoners of war.

In the armistice signed between France and Germany, the Spaniards were not recognized as combatants by the Vichy government, leaving them at the mercy of the Reich security police. They were first placed in the Stalags, and because of their status as anti-Franco fighters (or "Spanish Reds"), they were declared political enemies of the Reich. They were deported in August 1940 to the Mauthausen camp, where eventually some seven thousand Spanish Republicans would be sent. As foreign civilians without a state that would recognize them, they were declared stateless and were forced to wear a blue triangle with an "S" at its centre, which paradoxically identified them by nationality as "Spanier."

Meanwhile, in occupied France between 1942 and 1944, another sixty thousand Republicans served as forced labour for the Nazis. Many of those who faltered at their work or who were discovered carrying out sabotage, engaging in political activities, or attempting to escape ended up being deported to Germany. The collaborationist authorities of the "free zone" formed the Grupos de Trabajadores Extranjeros (Groups of Foreign Workers, GTEs) and forced thousands of Spanish refugees to join them. These groups sparked the emerging clandestine resistance. Others were able to avoid these forced enlistments and secretly looked for means to participate in armed resistance against the Nazis. Those who fell into the Gestapo's hands risked being executed, imprisoned, or sent into forced labour. After the D-Day landings in Normandy in June 1944, the Germans emptied the prisons in France and deported the occupants to camps in the Reich. As a result, another twenty-five hundred men and women, classified as resistance fighters, must be added to the number of Republicans deported to Mauthausen and other camps between 1940 and 1942.[5]

When the first Republicans arrived, the Mauthausen camp was still under construction. They were sent to work in the quarry, on the paving of the Appellplatz, or on the construction of the camp walls. Most of them died in Gusen, part of the Mauthausen camp system a few kilometres away, where they laboured in hellish conditions: punishing physical effort combined with freezing winter temperatures, illnesses, torture, accidents, and lack of food led to their deaths. Some were murdered outright. Of the Spaniards sent to Mauthausen as their first destination, some four thousand died in Gusen and another 456 were murdered in the gas chambers of Hartheim Castle; the rest, totalling 4,738, died in the central camp or in one of its work *Kommandos* in the vicinity.

The Spaniards were exploited and murdered in various *Kommandos* throughout the Reich territory, but Gusen would prove to be the most murderous of the camps. Sixty-five per cent of the total number of Spanish Republican deportees died during their imprisonment in the Mauthausen concentration camp system.

Reclaiming Dignity with French Friends

After the liberation of Mauthausen on 5 May 1945, the French survivors were repatriated. The paperwork requesting protection for the Spanish Republicans who had remained in the camp without knowing where to go was successful, and they were accepted back into France, the country from which they had been deported. As the Franco dictatorship strengthened, they – like many other Republicans – would have to become accustomed to a long exile. For the most part, they settled in France. Franco and his government – collectively responsible for the deportation of the Republicans – did nothing to recognize the sacrifice of the Spanish victims of Nazism. The few who returned to Spain during this period had to live with the memory of their experience in the German camps in isolation and silence.

The Spanish survivors faced a difficult integration into French society, and they created unique organizations that reflected the existing political contradictions among the Republican exiles. (See Dreyfus-Armand and Herrmann, chapters 9 and 12 in this volume.)[6] Given their strong links with the French in the camp, many Spaniards connected with the Amicale de Mauthausen, an association created by French survivors in the summer of 1945.[7] That organization's *Bulletin*, which began to publish activities, testimonies, and minutes from official meetings, and which advocated for the Spaniards' rights, remains the primary source of information about the construction of the monument to the Spanish Republicans in the Mauthausen camp.

In the spring of 1948, the Amicale announced a proposal to build a monument at the Mauthausen camp that would preserve the memory of the French who died there. It would be financed by the group's members; initial contributions were publicized through the mailing list.[8] The Amicale recognized Emile Valley, in particular, for successfully completing the project.[9] The first stone was placed on 8 May 1949, during the commemoration of the liberation. On 22 September, the monument was unveiled, with various survivors and numerous civil and military authorities from France, Great Britain, the Soviet Union, and Austria in attendance. It was located on the outskirts of the camp itself, close to the road that led to the quarry. That same year, the Amicale placed commemorative plaques at various *Kommandos* outside the camp: at Melk, Ebensee, and Gusen.

During this time, the bonds between the French and Spanish deportees were strengthening, a relationship reflected in the *Bulletin*: in April 1955, a notice to Spanish comrades was included, in Spanish, providing the Spanish deportees with instructions on how to solicit "el certificado de refugiado" (refugee certification). The same *Bulletin* included an invitation for a Spanish delegation to participate in the commemoration activities planned for the coming year and thereby pay tribute to the memory of the Spaniards who died in Mauthausen.[10] A couple of months later, this attitude of solidarity was reflected in an announcement in the *Bulletin*:

> Sería conveniente que los españoles, antiguos deportados del campo de Mauthausen, formasen parte de la Amical de dicho campo. Esto les permitiría de mantener un contacto entre ellos y el recibir el boletín que les daría a conocer todos sus derechos.
>
> Este año, a través de la Amical, los españoles han tenido la posibilidad de obtener una ayuda, distribuida por el Comité de Ayuda a los Refugiados.
>
> Insistimos acerca de todos los españoles miembros de la Amical a fin de que establezcan contacto con todos los aislados y les inviten a agruparse en el seno de la Amical.

> It would be advisable for the Spaniards – former deportees to the Mauthausen camp – to join the Amicale of said camp. This would allow them to maintain contact among themselves and to receive the Bulletin that keeps them informed of their rights.
>
> This year, through the Amicale, Spaniards have had the opportunity to obtain aid distributed by the Refugee Aid Committee. To the Spanish members of the Amicale, we ask that you establish contact with all those who are isolated and that you invite them to come together under the auspices of the Amicale.[11]

The *Bulletin* also published information it had gathered on Spaniards who died in Mauthausen, communicated the death of survivors, helped locate acquaintances, and aided with searches for housing or work: all evidence of the strengthening connection between the Spanish survivors of Mauthausen and the Parisian Amicale. When the German indemnities were established, the Amicale advised "a los antiguos deportados de origen español dirigirse al servicio jurídico de la Amical[...] que les dará todas las indicaciones" (the former deportees of Spanish origin to approach the Amicale's legal services ... who will give you instructions) and who would put their paperwork in order.[12] The popularity of this service exceeded expectations: the Amicale decided that José Rodés Bley[13] would take care of the corresponding demands from family members in Spain as director of "un servicio especial" (a special service) alongside the Amicale's legal team.[14]

At its April 1957 conference, the Amicale discussed the progress of the monument they were planning to construct in the Parisian Père Lachaise cemetery by presenting the mock-up, which suggested "la escalera de la muerte de la cantera de Mauthausen" (the staircase of death of the Mauthausen quarry), according to Gerard Choain, the project's sculptor.[15] Also, for the first time a Spanish survivor, Josep Borrás Lluch, would form part of the Administrative Committee of the Amicale, to look out for the interests of the Spanish survivors and the family members of the victims.[16]

The Survivors' Promise: To Honour the Victims' Memory

The monument to the French deportees was inaugurated in May 1958 with full honours before a contingent of international delegations and representatives of the Spanish survivors who had helped finance the monument.[17] This event marked the beginning of the debates surrounding the possibility of erecting another monument that would memorialize the Spaniards. At the Amicale meeting on 12 October, the Spanish representative requested that the *livre d'or* (visitor's book) that would be placed on the recently inaugurated monument include the names of Spanish victims because "fueron arrestados en Francia, viven actualmente en Francia y la consideran como su segunda patria" (they were arrested in France, they currently live in France, and they consider it to be their second home). In his response, Valley suggested that it would be better to erect a "un monumento en su memoria" (monument in their memory) in the same cemetery once the German indemnities had been carried out. Those present at the meeting concluded that the most appropriate thing to do would be to install a plaque with the following text: "A los 8.000 camaradas republicanos españoles, arrestados en suelo francés, muertos en el campo de Mauthausen y comandos" (To the 8,000 Republican Spanish comrades, arrested on French territory, who died in the Mauthausen camp and work units).[18]

Disagreements emerged at the headquarters of the Amicale, and these led to a meeting on 8 March 1959 presided over by Pierre Mabile, with Spanish survivors and Borrás in attendance.[19] Valley began the session by acknowledging the fraternal nature of the two groups of deportees, noting that the Spaniards had been forced to remain as refugees in exile in France. He spoke about indemnities and questions surrounding the French government's recognition of their deportation. One of the Spaniards present expressed his opposition to the new monument: he had helped finance the Père Lachaise monument and confirmed that the Spaniards were not mentioned on it. Valley responded that the

Amicale had not considered it opportune to mention the Spaniards on the monument, as it could have offended the deportees of other nationalities who had also settled in France. He instead suggested that the organization begin fundraising to create a monument in memory of all the Spanish Republicans who had died in concentration camps. The monument would perpetuate their memory better than a simple plaque or their names on the *livre d'or* on the French monument. He added that the Amicale would make financial contributions and proposed "la erección de una estela en el campo de Mauthausen, en memoria de los españoles muertos" (the erection of a stele [stone slab] in the Mauthausen Camp, in memory of the Spanish dead). The Spanish survivors in attendance were happy with these proposals and agreed to approve the construction of both monuments, one in Père Lachaise and another in Mauthausen; to ask all of the Spanish deportees to join the Amicale; to organize their own pilgrimage to Mauthausen; and to meet once a year to form a commission responsible for collecting funds for the erection of both monuments.[20]

The commission's work moved along quickly, and in October it announced its decision to build another monument:

> [D]ebemos elevar un monumento en memoria de nuestros camaradas Españoles que recordará su sacrificio y coraje, nosotros lo haremos, no solamente en homenaje a los camaradas muertos en Mauthausen sino también en memoria de todos los Republicanos Españoles, muertos en los diferentes campos de concentración.
>
> Lanzamos una suscripción, que permitirá llevar a cabo esta obra, nosotros queremos dar las gracias a nuestros camaradas Españoles que habiendo cobrado del gobierno alemán su indemnización por privación de libertad, nos han enviado su óbolo, nosotros contamos que todos seguirán este ejemplo a fin que el monumento que se elevará en el Cementerio -Pere Lachaise- sea digno del coraje de los Republicanos Españoles muertos en los campos de concentración y que recuerde su sacrificio.[21]

We should raise a monument in memory of our Spanish comrades that will record their sacrifice and courage. We will do it, not just in tribute to our comrades who died in Mauthausen but also in memory of all the Spanish Republicans who died in different concentration camps.

We are launching a fundraiser that will allow us to accomplish this work. We want to thank our Spanish comrades who, having charged the German government with indemnity for denying their liberty, have sent us their small contributions. We hope that everyone will follow this example with the goal of building this monument in the Père Lachaise

Cemetery that will be worthy of the Spanish Republicans who died in the
concentration camps and that will memorialize their sacrifice.

In this announcement of the fundraiser, French members were urged to
participate, just like the Spaniards had done with the French monument.
The Amicale made the first contribution of 200,000 francs; this was followed by Emile Valley's contribution of 10,000 francs and by thirty-eight
donations from other Republican survivors, for a total of 450,000 francs.

In October 1959, several Republican survivors were invited to discuss the monument.[22] Valley participated to demonstrate that the fundraising had begun, and said he believed it would be easy enough to
raise the necessary funds. Borrás reminded those in attendance that it
was ultimately impossible to include the names of the Spaniards on the
French monument or to place a plaque on it in their honour, as had been
discussed at the meeting of 8 March. One of the people present, Félix
Murcia García, indicated that most of the compatriots with whom he
was in contact thought it would be better to erect the monument in the
camp itself.[23] Casimir Climent i Sarrió[24] expressed his agreement but
added that perhaps diplomatic difficulties would emerge if the monument was built in Mauthausen; he suggested that the Spanish survivors
and the families of those who had died as a result of the deportation should be consulted to decide on the proposals: a monument in
Mauthausen, in the Père Lachaise cemetery, or in both places.

The majority opted for the monument to be in Mauthausen, but Félix
Murcia proposed that a plaque in memory of the Spaniards who had
been deported to other camps be included. Valley declared that he
did not think there would be any problem building the monument in
Mauthausen and added that the Amicale would take care of the request
to the Austrian government.

It was not clear where the monument would be located. The general agreement at the October meeting to place the monument in
Mauthausen carried a great deal of weight, but on the other hand,
the idea of constructing a monument for *all* the Spanish deportees
in the Père Lachaise cemetery seemed better able to accomplish the
Spaniards' objectives. The public visited the cemetery regularly, and it
could accommodate meetings of international delegations. Everything
was discussed at a new meeting on 12 December among Spanish representatives and Valley, and they agreed to launch the fundraiser to
erect "Un Monument à la Mémoire des Republicains Espagnols morts
dans les camps de concentration" (A Monument to the Memory of the
Spanish Republicans who died in the concentration camps), setting the
location decision aside so as to focus on "la importancia de los fondos

recogidos" (the importance of collecting funds). It was also decided that a commission, formed of five or six Spaniards residing in the Paris region, would be in charge of organizing the whole process. Among the commission's many actions, Féliz Murcia's call for all Spaniards to collaborate in the monument's financing is particularly significant:

> Prácticamente para los muertos de 16 naciones, representando el total de detenidos, varios monumentos, estelas, han sido construidos, unos magníficos, otras más modestas, pero todos ellos son destinados a la misma causa, inmortalizar la memoria de quienes fueron exterminados para que la historia y las generaciones futuras jamás olviden los crímenes y las atrocidades cometidos en aquel lugar. Entre estas 16 naciones sólo los españoles siguen sin figurar.

> In reality, for the dead of sixteen nations, representing the total detainees, various monuments and steles have been constructed, some of which are magnificent, some more modest, but all of them are there for the same reason: to immortalize the memory of those who were exterminated so that history and future generations will never forget the crimes and atrocities committed in that place. Among the sixteen nations, only the Spanish continue to be absent.[25]

In the meeting of the Administrative Committee in January 1960, the treasurer announced that they had collected 1,256,500 francs and Valley commented that "harían falta seis millones para hacer el monumento a los españoles en el cementerio de Père-Lachaise por lo que posiblemente se verían obligados a ergirlo en Mauthausen" (it would take another six million to construct the monument for the Spaniards in the Père Lachaise cemetery, which is why they might be forced to erect it in Mauthausen).[26] The economic argument was, in the end, decisive in swaying the Spanish survivors. The proposals were disseminated and a campaign was organized to explain the project and raise funds. Contributions arrived, in many cases accompanied by personal notes expressing gratitude for the initiative and the donor's commitment to fund the monument. From October 1959 to July 1962 more than 1,052 contributions came in, totalling 96,893 francs.[27] Most of the contributions came from the Spanish survivors themselves, although French deportees, the Spanish Federation of Deportees, the García Lorca Republican Circle in Brussels, and International Brigade veterans from Austria also made donations. As will be discussed below, 28,628 francs from the Contencioso Mauthausen (Mauthausen Litigation) were also added to the total. [28]

A "Stateless" Monument in the Spaniards' Camp

Gérard Choain was asked to present the project to the commission at a meeting called by the Amicale and not "por cualquier otra asociación española" (by any other Spanish association), making it clear that the Amicale assumed full responsibility for the coordination of the entire process. Sebastián Mena defended this position, reminding the group that they been arrested in France, had died as French, and, as such, "seremos nosotros quienes erigiremos el monumento" (we will be the ones who construct the monument).[29] The definitive selection was soon made: the monument would be constructed in the Mauthausen camp, "un monumento digno de su sacrificio, que perpetuará su recuerdo y mostrará a todos que los republicanos españoles fueron las primeras víctimas de los nazis y pagaron un gran tributo a la causa de la Libertad" (a monument worthy of their sacrifice that will perpetuate their memory and will show everyone that the Spanish Republicans were the first victims of the Nazis and they paid a great price to the cause of Liberty).[30] Once the Amicale approved the plans, it was considered appropriate to celebrate the act of placing the first stone in May 1961 and to save the inauguration for the following year.

The project moved forward, the funds were consolidated, and deadlines were set, but permission from the Austrian government for the erecting of the monument did not arrive. The Amicale pressured the Ministry of Former Combatants to intervene before the Ministry of the Interior of Austria, reminding them again of the specific journey of the Spaniards, their deportation from France, their current situation, and the recognition of their rights.[31] At the beginning of March, Valley himself announced that he would be leaving for Vienna to meet with the interior minister to try to smooth over the situation,[32] a decision supported by members of the commission a few weeks later when they launched a call among the Spaniards to participate in the placement of the first stone, planned for the following 14 May.[33]

The Amicale's response to the needs of the Republican deportees and of the family members of those who had died in the camps, together with the necessary coordination of the "monumento a los españoles" (Monument to the Spaniards), was reason enough for the meeting held in Paris on 6 and 7 May 1961 to increase the Spanish presence on the Administrative Board.[34] From that moment on, Sebastián Mena, Félix Murcia, Baltasar Nebot Pujol, and Tomás Martín Pascual played an important role in coordinating and disseminating the project.[35]

The ceremonial placing of the first stone was conducted during the anniversary of the liberation of the camp, with some thirty Spanish survivors present. Félix Murcia addressed those in attendance, explaining the value of the friendship that had united them in the camps, the sacrifice of the Spanish deportees, and the significance of the ceremony: "La primera piedra de este monumento representa en la historia de la humanidad un periodo de devastación y de crímenes nazis, de dominación del mundo en nombre de una *raza superior'*" (The first stone of this monument represents to the history of humanity a period of devastation and Nazi crimes, of world domination in the name of a *superior race*). He finished his address by acknowledging the authorization that the Amicale had received from the Austrian government, "en particular a su secretario general, nuestro camarada Emile Valley" (in particular, the General Secretary, our comrade Emile Valley), and by thanking all those who were financially supporting the monument. Sebastián Mena added similar sentiments when he addressed those present in the name of their compatriots.[36]

The site in the camp chosen for the monument was on the grounds assigned to the French. The Austrian government had to give prior authorization for this because no space had been allotted for the Spaniards.[37] Valley informed the board, which met on 5 November, that the final cost would be about 80,000 new francs; he described the monument's characteristics and announced a special pilgrimage for its inauguration on 6 May of the following year.[38]

The mock-up was presented in the sculptor's studio on 17 December to a group of Spanish deportees accompanied by various members of the Amicale. They finalized the details and the design was approved. They decided to create a postcard with a drawing of the design and a photograph of the image to distribute among the survivors as an acknowledgment of their fundraising efforts.

The "Mauthausen Litigation" had been organized in 1957 when deportees were faced with egregious legal fees charged by some of the lawyers representing them in their claims before the German government. Valley himself took on the responsibility of navigating the German bureaucracy for the compensation owed the Spanish deportees. Through this process, the Amicale was able to gather a small fund, a percentage of the claims paid to the Spanish litigants, to cover the difference in the cost of the monument when not enough money was raised by popular subscription, as promised.[39]

Over the following months the call went out repeatedly for participation in the pilgrimage being organized. There was also ongoing correspondence with Spanish survivors and family members of victims. The Amicale received many letters from former deportees thanking it for including them in the project and from others explaining their absence from the inauguration ceremony, but in all of these missives it was clear

11.1 Front of Amicale postcard (Amical de Mauthausen collection).

De 1940 à 1945, des milliers de républicains espagnols furent déportés dans les camps d'extermination nazis, parce qu'ils n'avaient pas abandonné leur lutte pour la liberté.

En hommage à leur sacrifice et pour perpétuer leur mémoire, un monument sera érigé au Camp de Mauthausen.

Dans ce camp et ses kommandos, 7.000 déportés espagnols trouvèrent la mort, après avoir connu la faim, le froid, les coups et les tortures.

Il sera l'hommage de leurs familles, de leurs amis, de leurs camarades rescapés.

L'AMICALE FRANÇAISE
DE MAUTHAUSEN.

De 1940 a 1945, millares de republicanos españoles fueron deportados a los campos de exterminación nazis, porque no habían abandonado su lucha por la libertad.

Como homenaje a su sacrificio y para perpetuar su memoria, un monumento será erigido en el Campo de Mauthausen.

En ese campo y en sus « kommandos », 7.000 deportados españoles hallaron la muerte, después de haber padecido hambre y frío, golpes y torturas.

El Monumento sera el homenaje de sus familias y amigos, de sus camaradas sobrevivientes.

*LA AMICAL FRANCESA
DE MAUTHAUSEN.*

PRIX DE LA CARTE : 1 NF

11.2 Reverse side of Amicale postcard (Amical de Mauthausen collection).

that they were happy there would be a monument to honour the memory of their comrades who had died in Mauthausen.

After final logistical issues with the Austrian government were overcome,[40] the moment arrived to leave for Mauthausen for the ceremonies to commemorate the liberation of the camp. Some two hundred Spanish survivors left Paris on the afternoon of 3 May 1962, travelling with the Amicale's delegation and hoisting the Spanish Republican flag that would fly, from that moment on, at the monument they were about to inaugurate. After visiting Ebensee, Hartheim, and Gusen, on 6 May they arrived at Mauthausen. The delegation visited the camp, and after holding a ceremony at the French monument, they headed for the monument they were going to inaugurate.

A special edition of the *Bulletin* dedicated to the event detailed the ceremony.[41]

The monument was covered by a sheet with the colours of the Republican flag (red, yellow, and purple) and was surrounded by Spanish (Republican), French, Belgian, Italian, Czech, and Austrian flags. Valley, accompanied by Paulino García,[42] uncovered the sculpture: on a granite base, the monument rose four metres high and ten metres long, and consisted of five vertical granite columns. The central image, sculpted from bronze, is of Mother Liberty supporting her injured son. The other four columns have engraved plates, each one reading "Homenaje a 7.000 Republicanos Españoles muertos por la libertad" (In homage to 7,000 Spanish Republicans who died for freedom) in German, Spanish, French, and Russian.

An orchestra played the hymn of the Spanish Republic, then made way for the emotional words of Valley, followed by those of Ramón Bargueño Gómez, who represented the Spaniards;[43] Arthur London,[44] on behalf of the Czech volunteers; Heinrich Durmayer,[45] on behalf of the Austrian volunteers; and, interpreting in German, Luis García Manzano,[46] all representing the International Brigades. The various national delegations lined up and placed their wreaths, which, along with others offered by many of the attendees, covered the monument. The ceremony served as a recognition of the deported Spaniards, of their martyrdom in the camp, of their fighting spirit for being the first anti-fascist combatants as well as the ones who had maintained the anti-fascist spirit for the longest time, and of the international brotherhood forged behind those walls of humiliation and death during the almost five years their imprisonment lasted.

The monument to the Spanish Republicans deported to the Mauthausen camp was the first to be constructed in their memory. The previous aspiration of inaugurating another monument in

Nous avons édité ce Bulletin spécial à l'occasion de l'inauguration du Monument élevé au camp à la mémoire des 7.000 Républicains Espagnols.

Ce numéro spécial doit être un témoignage de l'action que nous menons pour que nos frères ne soient pas oubliés et que leur sacrifice ne soit pas vain.

Nous espérons que dans un avenir proche ce sera à Madrid que nous irons pour inaugurer un Monument à la mémoire de tous ceux qui tombèrent pour la liberté.

Publicamos este Boletin especial con motivo de la inauguración del Monumento erigido en el campo de Mauthausen en memoria de los 7.000 Républicanos españoles.

Este número especial, debe ser testigo de la acción que llevamos a cabo para que nuestros hermanos no sean olvidados y que su sacrificio no haya sido en vano.

Esperamos que un futuro, no muy lejano sera en Madrid a donde iremos para inaugurar otro monumento a la memoria de todos los que cayeron por la libertad.   *Le Secrétaire Général :*

11.3 Cover of special edition of *Amicale de Mauthausen* (Paris) newsletter for the inauguration of the Spanish monument, 1962 (Amical de Mauthausen collection).

11.4 Monument to Spanish Republicans in Mauthausen (Amical de Mauthausen collection).

Madrid lay far off; decades would have to pass before the history of the Spanish deportees became known in their own country. That same year, in Barcelona, with the help of the French Amicale, a group of survivors founded the Amical de Mauthausen y de otros campos y de todas las víctimas del nazismo de España (Association of Mauthausen and Other Camps and All of the Victims of Nazism in Spain). It was legalized in 1978, three years after the death of the dictator.[47] In 1965, a large delegation from the Spanish Amical travelled to Mauthausen for the first time, together with the French Amicale. Ever since, the two associations have met their moral obligation to honour the victims of Nazi barbarism before the monument to the Republican deportees, who for so many years were "stateless" in that they could not count on the support of an official Spanish organization. The monument was erected on land given over to the French, but the Spaniards were responsible for financing the project, for the most

11.5 Members of the Spanish delegation in front of the Spanish Republican monument in Mauthausen, 1975 (Amical de Mauthausen collection).

11.6 Groups paying homage in front of the Spanish Republican monument in Mauthausen, 2016 (Amical de Mauthausen collection).

part through direct contributions from victims. As such, the Spanish deportees and their heirs will continue to be the sole "owners" of the monument in perpetuity.

NOTES

1 During the 42nd plenary session on 1 November 2005, Resolution 60/7, "Holocaust Remembrance," was approved. It set the date and established principles for the Prevention of Crimes Against Humanity. Visit http://www.un.org/es/holocaustremembrance/res607.shtml; http://www.un.org/en/holocaustremembrance/docs/res607.shtml.
2 Ana Rodrigo, "España rescata del olvido seis décadas después a los 4.435 de Mauthausen," *EFE*, 19 May 2019.
3 To learn more about the process of this conversion, see https://www.mauthausen-memorial.org/es.
4 Summary of the "Informe de la Amical de Mauthausen y otros campos y de todas las víctimas del Nazismo de España," sent to the special rapporteur for information on the truth, justice, and reparation of the UN, Barcelona, 5 May 2014.
5 According to the Spanish Amical de Mauthausen, 6,980 Republicans were deported to Mauthausen, 532 to Buchenwald, 530 to Dachau, 389 to Neuengamme, 104 to Sachsenhausen, ninety-eight to Ravensbruck (female resistance), and lesser numbers to the Channel Islands, Natzweiler-Struthof, and Auschwitz, for a total of 9,000 deportees.
6 To learn more about these two issues, see Constante, *Tras Mauthausen*, 28–30; and Toran, *Joan de Diego*, 199–212. The first, written by a Spanish survivor of Mauthausen, is a collection of his experiences after being freed. The second is a biographical study of Joan de Diego, a Republican deportee who, from his position in the camp offices, provided important assistance to the Spaniards.
7 The complete collection of the *Bulletin d'information de l'Amicale de Mauthausen affiliée à a la F.N.D.I.R.P.* is available under the tab "A la memoire des déportes de Mauthausen morts pour la paix et la liberté." Visit http://www.campmauthausen.org. Hereafter it will be referred to as *Bulletin*.
8 *Bulletin* no. 11, April 1948.
9 Valley (1910–1999), born in Anglefort, France, was a member of the French Resistance who, after being detained by the Germans, was moved around to different prisons. He was deported to Mauthausen (as number 60652) on 25 March 1944. After the liberation, he helped found the Amicale and

was a prominent activist to secure the rights and memory of the deported. He was the General Secretary of the Amicale and a friend to the Spanish Republican deportees, for whom he advocated. He was an Official of the Legion of Honour and received a Resistance Medal.

10 *Bulletin* no. 42, April 1955.

11 To avoid confusion with the Spanish Amical de Mauthausen, we will refer to the French "Amicale" in this and subsequent translations. *Bulletin* no. 46, July 1955.

12 *Bulletin* no. 57, March 1957, no. 59, April 1957, and no. 61, August 1957.

13 Rodés Bley (1895–1968) was born in Lleida. A cobbler by trade, he was a public commissioner during the Spanish Civil War. While in exile in France, he was arrested in Montauban in February 1941 by the collaborationist French police. He was sentenced to fifteen years of forced labour. From the Central de Eysses, he was deported to Dachau (number 73950) on 20 June 1944. He was liberated in April 1945, and settled in Paris, where he died in August 1968.

14 *Bulletin* no. 66, December 1957.

15 Choain (1912–1988) was born in Lille (France). He was a sculptor, and after the Second World War, during which he was wounded and made a prisoner, he created numerous monuments and memorials to the victims. In 1974 he received the Legion of Honour. See *Bulletin* no. 172, September 1974.

16 Borrás Lluch (1917–1997) was born in Barcelona. An exiled Republican, he was deported to Mauthausen (number 3776) on 23 July 1941. He was subsequently transferred to Styer, where he worked as an interpreter. After the liberation, he settled in France, where he actively participated in the Amicale. He later published the book *Históire de Mauthausen. Les cinq années de deportation des républicains espagnols.*

17 *Bulletin* no. 71, June 1958.

18 *Bulletin* no. 73, November 1958. The figures for Republican deportations (totals and deaths) have been recalculated in recent decades. At the time, the figures used were approximations made by the survivors.

19 Mabile (1900–1966) was born in Paris. A resistance fighter, he was deported to Sarrebruck Neu Bremm on 20 September 1943 as "NN" (*Nacht und Nebel* or "Night and Fog"). A few weeks later he was transferred to Mauthausen (number 37790), where he was freed in May 1945. He served as the vice-president of the Administrative Board of the Amicale for many years until his death.

20 *Bulletin* no. 75, March 1959; and *Bulletin* no. 76, April 1959.

21 *Bulletin* no. 79, October 1959; capitalization in the original.

22 *Bulletin* no. 80, November 1959. Josep Ester refused to be present.

23 Born in Piqueras (Guadalajara), Murcia García (1917–1983) fought
in defence of the Spanish Republic and was forced into exile in 1939.
Detained by the Germans, he was interned in Stalag XI-A, from which
he was deported to Mauthausen (number 3963) on 26 April 1941. He was
later sent to different external work units. Following the camp's liberation,
he lived in the French town of Besançon until his death.

24 Climent i Sarrió (1910–1978) was born in Valencia. A Republican
combatant, he exiled himself to France. He was detained while in a CTE
and interned in Stalag XI-B; from there, he was deported to Mauthausen
(number 4540) on 25 November 1940 and assigned to the camp quarry. He
was later transferred to the Gestapo offices, where he worked as an interpreter. Following the camp's liberation, he settled in Paris, where he died
in October 1978.

25 *Bulletin* no. 81, January 1960.

26 *Bulletin* no. 82, March 1960.

27 After this point the donations were calculated in new francs to take into
account the contributions made after the change in French currency in
January 1960.

28 In later *Bulletins* (from no. 81 to no. 101), sixteen lists were published that
provided, in detail, the names of donors, their places of residence, and the
amounts given.

29 Mena (1909–2006) was born in Guadalajara, Spain. A farmer, he was a
Republican combatant. He was arrested in France in the spring of 1940
and deported to Mauthausen (number 4317) in September 1940, where
he was assigned to various external Kommandos. After the liberation,
he settled in France. He later returned to Spain and lived in the province of Alicante. He was an active participant in the Spanish Amical de
Mauthausen.

30 *Bulletin* no. 86, October 1960.

31 *Bulletin* no. 88, December 1960.

32 Constante, *Tras Mauthausen*, 150.

33 *Bulletin* no. 91, April 1961.

34 *Bulletin* no. 93, June 1961.

35 Nebot Pujol (1913–1993) was born in Lleida. He exiled to France and
was deported to Mauthausen (number 3780) on 25 January 1941. After
the liberation, he moved to Béziers. He was an active member of the
entities that defended the rights of the deportees and their families,
for which the French government named him a Chevalier de l'ordre
national du Mérite (Knight of the National Order of Merit). He died
in Béziers on 29 October 1993. Martín Pascual (1912–1972) was born in
Madrid. He fought in defence of the Spanish Republic, which led to his
exile to France. He was a part of a CTE in Carcassone. As a Resistance

member beginning in 1942, he was detained by the Gestapo in January 1944 and deported to Mauthausen (number 60252) on 25 March 1944. He was part of the clandestine Comité Nacional Español (Spanish National Committee) and, after the camp's liberation, moved to Carcassone, where he lived until his death.

36 *Bulletin* no. 93, July 1961.

37 Constante, *Tras Mauthausen*, 151–2.

38 *Bulletin* no. 96, December 1961.

39 *Bulletin* no. 92, June 1961.

40 Constante, *Tras Mauthausen*, 157.

41 *Bulletin* special edition, August 1962. Its forty pages cover in detail the journey, the meaning of the monument, and the development of the ceremony.

42 García (1909–1988) was born in Jadraque (Guadalajara). A Spanish Republican refugee and member of the 28th CTE, he was arrested by the Germans and sent to Mauthausen (number 3214) on 3 November 1941. After the camp's liberation, he moved to Perpignan. He died on 4 July 1988 in an automobile accident while travelling to Spain.

43 Bargueño Gómez (1919–2003) was born in Toledo. A Republican combatant, he was arrested by the Nazis and deported to Mauthausen (number 3183) on 3 November 1941. He worked in the camp's armoury, was later sent to the Steyr Kommando, and was then returned to the central camp, where he was known as "Mermelada." Repatriated to France, he moved to the town of Villejuif.

44 London (1915–1986) was born in Ostrava (Czechoslovakia). He was an International Brigadist during the Spanish Civil War and a resistance fighter against the Nazis in France, where he was arrested by the Germans. A prisoner in various German prisons, he was deported to Sarrebruck Neue Bremm on 29 February 1944, and one month later to Mauthausen, where he was a member of the International Committee. He was liberated by the Red Cross on 24 April 1945. He was married to Lise Ricol (Fredo Ricol's sister), who had been deported to Ravensbruck. After the war, he held various positions in the Czechoslovakian government. He then settled in Paris, where he died on 7 November 1986.

45 Durmayer (1905–2000) was born in Vienna. He was a lawyer and International Brigadist who fought in Spain in defence of the Spanish Republic. He was deported to Mauthausen, where he was a member of the International Committee in charge of the camp, negotiating the situation with the Viennese police after the SS fled. He represented Austria in the International Committee of Mauthausen, on which he served as General Secretary for many years.

46 Manzano (1922–1999) was born in Madrid. From Stalag XII-B he was sent
    to Mauthausen (number 4817) on 19 December 1941, where he worked in
    the quarry. He was liberated in May 1945. Known in camp as "Luisín,"
    he participated in the clandestine resistance organization and was one
    of the founders of the string band organized by a group of Spaniards.
    Repatriated to France, he settled in Perpignan. He actively participated
    in the defence of the rights of the deported Republicans. He was made a
    Knight of the Legion of Honour.
47 To learn about the founding and the history of the Spanish Amical,
    see Toran, *Amical de Mauthausen*. Also visit http://www.amical-
    mauthausen.org.

PART FOUR

Spanish Republicans in Nazi Camps

12 Spanish and Catalan Women in Ravensbrück

GINA HERRMANN

On 14 April 1945, the day the US 2nd Infantry Division arrived at the HASAG Leipzig-Schöenfeld slave labour camp, where ammunitions were manufactured, the Spanish inmate Mercedes Núñez Targa (1911–1986) had been slated for transport to the gas chamber. She was ill with scarlet fever and had barely survived the horror-filled journey from her capture as a member of the French Resistance to deportation to the Ravensbrück concentration camp for women. By 1944 Ravensbrück had become a crucial collection and transit point for female forced labour, with some 50 per cent of the prisoners taken for slave labour to one of its more than two hundred subcamps. Like thousands of able-bodied women originally detained in Ravensbrück, Núñez Targa faced a second transport, along with seven of her Spanish women comrades, to the *Kommando* HASAG, where the women fabricated shells, primarily for shoulder-fired launchers.[1] By January of 1945, at this one factory complex alone, more than five thousand women of many nationalities had performed slave labour, suffering through interrogations, overcrowding, and lack of sleep, nutrition, and hygiene. Women who became severely ill or unable to work faced selection for extermination. Long roll calls and punishments hastened illness and exhaustion. Although fewer than twenty women survivors of the Spanish deportation have left testimonial accounts, this sample suggests that the story of Spanish women in the Nazi camp system was largely one about slave labour and about the methods women employed, in difficult circumstances, to continue their anti-fascist resistance by any means available. Forced labour was the principal category of experience for Spanish political detainees transported to Nazi camps, men and women alike. For Spanish women prisoners, slave labour took place in subcamps designed for women, where so much of the mistreatment entailed trying to weaken or terrorize women through gendered abuse as well as violent rituals that sought to break down female identities.

Núñez Targa's route to Ravensbrück began in 1931 with the declaration of Spain's Second Republic. Mobilized in youth organizations along with hundreds of thousands of women who supported the Republic, Núñez Targa eventually headed the Spanish Communist Party in her native region of Galicia. After the defeat of the Republic in 1939, she was arrested by the Francoist police. Released from the infamous Ventas prison three years later on a clerical error, she fled to France, where she joined a Spanish unit of the French Resistance in Carcassonne, serving as a clandestine agent (under the alias of Paquita Colomer) providing false papers for the underground.[2] Captured in 1944 by the Gestapo, Núñez Targa was deported along with other women prisoners to Ravensbrück. Like thousands of Spaniards and Catalans liberated from Nazi camps, she remained in exile in France, unable to return to her Spanish homeland, where Franco would remain in power until 1975. Núñez Targa's experiences exemplify the five-decades-long, transnational anti-fascist commitments of Spanish left-wing women, perhaps two to three hundred of whom found themselves in the very abyss of fascist punishment, the Nazi *Lager*.

What is meant by anti-fascist resistance in the testimonies of Spanish women? How did women political deportees understand it as both disposition and action? Deportation to concentration camps and to forced labour details drastically changed and limited the expression and belligerent action of anti-fascist resistance. Robert Gildea has recently defined a kind of resistance "minimum," a concept that is useful here in trying to account for how Spanish women deportees viewed their own position. Describing the French case – to which the Spanish women belonged, yet which they also exceeded – he writes that resistance "meant refusing to accept the French bid for armistice and the German occupation, and a willingness to do something about it that broke rules and courted risk." Resistance with a capital R entailed "providing intelligence for the Allies, escorting downed airmen to safety, spreading propaganda against the Germans or Vichy, sabotage, and in the last instance, armed struggle."[3] (For more on the Spanish presence in the French Resistance, see chapter 9 in this volume.) This second definition, which emphasizes physicality and risk, is the one in which Spanish communist and anarchist women locate their own experience. The concept of "anti-fascism" embraced by Spanish women deportees extended across Europe but pointed always back to Spain and to the ultimate goal of freeing the peninsula from the talons of the dictator Francisco Franco. Spanish resisters saw themselves as part of a global movement for class and racial justice, sought to defend the humanistic values born from the Enlightenment, and devoted themselves wholeheartedly to an anti-Nazi, anti-Franco struggle against "fascist" savagery.

Taking these observations as its point of departure, this chapter has two primary aims. The first is to provide the reasons why and the conditions under which Spanish women political prisoners were deported to Ravensbrück and its *Aussenkommandos* (external labour details). The second is to describe two connected modes of resistance to Nazi oppression – sexual and labour – both of which the women cast as logical and necessary continuations of earlier anti-fascist work. Spanish women conjured the mental will to hold on psychologically in the face of sexualized violence. When faced with degrading treatment aimed at diminishing their sense of womanhood, prisoners sought methods to maintain their dignity and will to survive – as individual women but also as part of a politically bonded, gendered anti-fascist group. Solidarity among women, especially in cohesive national groups of communists, also facilitated acts of sabotage when women were transferred to branch camps for the manufacture of armaments. Slave labour offered one vehicle for extending tangible, pride-conferring anti-fascist resistance activities in which women had long been involved during the 1930s and 1940s. By resisting forced labour, these Spanish and Catalan women survivors expressed the integrity of their agency and preserved a self-conception of communist valour that could not be compromised by the hardships they suffered as captives. This chapter also considers how Spanish and Catalan women attempted to find their place in the context of other national, primarily communist groups of prisoners.

Ravensbrück: Gateway to Slave Labour

Spanish Republican women who fled Franco's Spain in 1939 and also women who belonged to previous waves of economic immigration to France became involved in resistance activities after the Nazi occupation in 1940, usually through Spanish-led resistance units in southern France. Captured by the Vichy police or the Gestapo, the women faced detention and often torture in French prisons alongside their French women comrades. Most French women were deported to Ravensbrück in 1944, as the resistance became a mass movement. Among the eight thousand French women packed into overcrowded trains destined for Germany were perhaps two to three hundred Spanish women. Seventy thousand women political prisoners of diverse nationalities passed through Ravensbrück over the course of the war.

Built in 1938, Ravensbrück was the largest concentration camp for women in the German Reich. The camp was first envisioned as a place to isolate and reform "asocials" – alcoholics, vagrants, and social deviants – and eventually held inmates from more than thirty countries. The representation from Spain was tiny. SS authorities interned political prisoners, Roma and Sinti, Jews, Jehovah's Witnesses, and women categorized as "criminals," "work-shy," and "race defilers." Survivors describe feeling terrified and disoriented upon their arrival, during which they were assigned a number and a coloured triangle to be sewn onto their clothes. The intake rituals entailed undressing, the shearing of hair, unhygienic genital probing, and inspection of teeth and muscle mass. Women at Ravensbrück and its subcamps were forced to endure scarcity and subjugation, and they died from various causes, including disease and executions by hanging, gas, or shooting. SS doctors carried out medical experiments on women's bodies, including sterilizations, amputations, and the treating of wounds with various chemical substances. Today is it estimated that thirty thousand women were murdered in Ravensbrück and its satellite camps.[4] On 30 April 1945, when the Red Army reached the camp, from which the SS had fled, there were few women left. Some had already been rescued, many had been transferred to other camps, and still others had been sent on death marches. Many had left on their own, seeking help from civilians in the countryside.

The experience at KL Ravensbrück for many political prisoners was short-lived, for after a few weeks or months, most entered a slave labour force that might include heavy outdoor work, mobile construction brigades, salvage operations after bombings, textile manufacture, or building V-2 rocket parts for the Siemens Electric Company in a plant adjacent to Ravensbrück. As noted above, thousands of women, the Spanish women among them, were transferred to satellite camps, mainly for war material production. Many women were employed in departments that finished and inspected ammunition parts. Threats of hanging, beating, or gassing weighed on prisoners who were tempted to interrupt production. Some women operated state-of-the-art machines that were susceptible to damage, making it possible, at least in theory, for prisoners to sabotage them. Precautions against sabotage were thus a top priority at the factories, as well as for the SS, who repeatedly vowed to execute any prisoner implicated in such acts.[5] Especially for political prisoners who had experience in anti-fascist resistance work, sabotage represented a means to exercise ideological resistance to Nazi terror. There were four possible ways to carry it out: reduce output, introduce defects, go on strike, and – when factories were in locales where partisans were nearby – steal production for the resistance. For example, women could manipulate the precision threading of shells, thus ruining the efficacy of the anti-aircraft projectiles they filled on assembly lines. Spanish women report that they would loosen the screws of winches to stop their operation or fill boxes of shells with water or snow so that they would be unusable. Besides disrupting manufacturing, acts of resistance included launching hunger strikes and refusing to take part in a bonus system offered by the SS, which women saw as a threat to their solidarity.[6] Whenever possible, national groups stuck together and provided their own members with sustenance and moral care. In this regard, the Spanish women – because of their small numbers – were at a distinct disadvantage, and were often integrated into the "camp families" formed among the French women.

Researchers have been unable to determine the exact number of Spanish women detained in Nazi camps. The census maintained online by Amical de Ravensbrück currently stands at 119 entries for women sent to Ravensbrück, while the database of Amical de Mauthausen lists 277 documented cases of Spanish women deported to all Nazi camps.[7] Historians working from the Ravensbrück archive (Archiv der Mahn- und Gedenkstätte Ravensbrück) estimate that the camp and its satellites held 170 Spanish women deportees. About many of these women there is scant information. Some listings, based on the testimonial accounts of comrades, are as meagre as a nickname, for example, "Felisa, La Gitana, desparecida en Ravensbrück" (Felisa, the gypsy, disappeared in Ravensbrück). Most women were captured as resisters, "politicals," or "reds." Spanish women were active in the resistance throughout France, but the majority operated in the south and southeast, as was true of the Spanish presence in the resistance generally. The registers show that Spanish women were transported to Ravensbrück in 1944 mainly from large French prisons or from rail transit points at Compiègne, Bordeaux, Paris Gare de l'Est, or Romainville.

For a number of reasons, we know little about the Spanish women at Ravensbrück. First, we are dealing with a very small number, about whom historians and other survivors cared rather little if at all. Second, the Nazis destroyed almost all of the camp's records, and registers of Spanish women would have disappeared along with the others. However, the latter is not a sufficient explanation, given that historians have been able to create histories of many national groups. A more telling factor is that in Spain, throughout the Franco dictatorship and into the 1980s, narratives of persecution and Nazi camps were rare and difficult to tell. It is also hard to determine their numbers because of the circumstances in which Spanish women were deported. After the fall of the Spanish Republic, hundreds of thousands of Spanish nationals fled to France, where they were held in harsh and sometimes lethal detention camps in the south. Many then were transferred from those camps into forced labour battalions or into domestic work. Others found their way into units – some French, some Spanish, some mixed – of the French Resistance. It was through the resistance that Spanish and Catalan women were captured, along with their French comrades (and often with French *noms de guerre*). Labelled as French or possessing French papers, many women may well have perished or been murdered without having had their Spanish identities registered. Other women after liberation never bothered to correct the record or to share their testimonies. Moreover, the frequent self-censorship of Spanish women with regard to their lives during the Second World War and their exile in France reflects the extraordinarily difficult conditions under which Spanish women strove to survive over decades.

Reintegration after the experience of the concentration camp was complicated by the prolonged isolation of Spanish women, who remained linguistically, economically, and culturally in a continued exile and on the margins of French society; and who were also spiritually focused on the devastating reality that Franco remained in power back home. In the immediate post-war years, in French narratives about the occupation that cast the country as a nation of *resistantes*, many groups that had played crucial roles in the Resistance were erased from public memory: women in general as well as international immigrant members of the resistance, including anti-fascists from Spain, members of the International Brigades, economic immigrants from central and eastern Europe, Jewish refugees, and British operatives.[8] The rivalry for "ownership" of the French Resistance submerged not only Spanish and Catalan men but also Spanish and Catalan *women*. With France offering no nationally sanctioned venues for them to express their experiences in the resistance or deportation, Spanish women largely remained silent.[9] Most of the survivors were working-class women who did not feel entitled to a valued war story. They did not wear the halo of resistance that many French deportees later donned in the heroicization of the French struggle against the occupation, and because Spanish women at Ravensbrück were "encuadrados en la organización clandestina francesa" (incorporated into the French clandestine organization), when French women began staking claims for recognition as resisters and camp survivors, Spanish women yet again found their experiences framed by the French war stories.[10] Still another explanation for the erasure of Spanish women from the history of Ravensbrück brings us to the Cold War exclusion of many victim groups from the commemorative practices and historical narratives that upheld the heroism of especially East German communist women at the expense of a more plural representation of the camps' diverse inmate populations.

Finally, various women refused to give their testimonies for the same reasons many survivors remained silent: they could not plumb the depths of the tragedy, the dread horrors, the agonies of guilt, the abiding internalized shame, the stain of the continual humiliation and highly gendered degradation under captivity by the Nazis.[11] In the face of the extermination of millions, for survivors to write or talk about themselves ran the risk of seeming self-interested or vulgar. After 1945, millions of lives felt themselves to be unrepresentable.[12] Spanish women consistently employ the leitmotif of their unique, vanguard Spanish anti-fascism as the key to their determination to resist, and to their will to solidarity under conditions that sought to destroy mutual support. Beyond their value as records of participation in the resistance and the deportation, these testimonies capture some of the rare instances in which Spaniards were direct witnesses to the Holocaust, for the Ravensbrück inmates describe the torment and murder of Jews and Roma – mothers and children – with whom they briefly crossed paths in the camp at Fürstenberg.

If the census of Spanish female deportation is sparse, the testimonial record is rich. It is also confined primarily to three sources: (1) Montserrat Roig's (1946–1991) *sui generis* and groundbreaking book of the history and memories of Catalan deportees, *Els catalans als camps nazis* (Catalans in the Nazi Camps, 1977); (2) Neus Català's (1915–2019), *De la Resistencia y la deportación. 50 testimonios de mujeres españolas* (On the Resistance and the Deportation: Fifty Testimonies of Spanish Women, 1984), a collection of testimonies of Spanish women *resistantes* and survivors of Ravensbrück; and (3) Mercedes Núñez Targa's (1911–1986) memoir of her work in the French Resistance and her deportation to Ravensbrück, *El carretó dels gossos. Una catalana a Ravensbruck* (The Dog Catcher Wagon: A Catalan Woman in Ravensbrück).[13] These books offer sixteen, including those of Català and Núñez Targa, autobiographical accounts of Spanish women deported to Ravensbrück and other camps. Two further testimonies were collected respectively by Eduardo Pons Prades and another by Benito Bermejo and Sandra Checa, both reproduced in *Memorial de las españolas deportadas a Ravensbrück* (Memorial to the Spanish women deported to Ravensbrück, 2012).[14] In 2018, Amalia Rosado Orquín published the oral history of another survivor, *Virtudes Cuevas: una superviviente del campo de concentración alemán de Ravensbrück* (Virtudes Cuevas: A Survivor of the German Concentration Camp of Ravensbrück), with a prologue by Baltazár Garzón.[15]

Thus the testimonial record consists of the accounts of the following women:

1 Mercedes Núñez Targa, *El carretó dels gossos*; in Spanish, *Destinada al crematorio* (Destined for the Crematorium)
2 Neus Català, *De la resistencia y la deportación*, which contains the oral testimonies of women nos. 3–16 below
3 Secundina Barceló
4 Mercedes Bernal
5 Carme Buatell
6 Alfonsina Bueno Ester
7 Lola Casadellà
8 María Ferrer
9 Antonia Frexedes
10 Felicitat Gasa
11 Sabina González
12 Mónica Jené
13 Constanza Martínez Prieto
14 Rita Pérez
15 Conchita Ramos
16 Elisa Ruiz
17 Ángeles Álvarez (Bermejo and Checa)
18 Ángeles Martínez (Pons Prades)
19 Virtudes Cuevas (Rosado Orquín)

Like Núñez Targa, Neus Català lived through many of the most dangerous and iconic moments of the Spanish Civil War, the resistance, and the deportation. Català was born and raised in Els Guiamets, a Catalan village in the Priorat wine region. She became active as a militant in the Juventudes Socialistas Unificadas. At sixteen, she entered nursing school, studies that would eventually lead to her lifelong profession as a nurse. At the end of the Spanish Civil War, she led a group of orphan children across the border into France, where she worked to find them appropriate shelter and helped many of them find their families. Neus re-established her family life in the Dordogne and married a French anarchist, Albert Roger. Together they started a farm that served as a safe house for the *maquis* of Turnac, folded into the Franc-tireurs et Partisans. Català has described her responsibilities in the clandestine movement, driving home the point that she and other women did not simply act as "auxiliaries" but fulfilled crucial roles, such as carrying materials and documents across regions, helping plan acts of sabotage, vetting potential members of the *maquis*, fabricating explosives, creating false identity papers, and helping people evade deportation and obligatory forced labour in Germany through the Service du travail obligatoire.

By November 1943, Neus and her French husband Albert Roger understood that someone had betrayed them and that their farm was "quemado" (i.e., its cover was blown). Half an hour before they were to leave, they found themselves surrounded and trapped by armed SS. Neus was eventually incarcerated at Limoges, where her interrogators broke her jaw in a torture chamber that – she was certain – she would never leave alive. In the Limoges prison, Neus met a young French re-sister named Thérèse Menot (Tití), with whom she established a rela-tionship difficult to quantify. Tití and Neus would remain together as a kind of protective mother-daughter couple throughout their deporta-tion, their experiences in the main camp, and later as slave labourers at Holýšov in Czechoslovakia.

As a prelude to the German camps, Català, Tití, and thousands of other prisoners were transferred to Compiègne. That would be the last place Neus saw her husband Albert alive. Finally, in the winter of 1944, she faced deportation to the concentration camp of Ravensbrück along with women from many other nationalities (French, Czech, Polish) in the "convoy of 27,000" (that number referring to the registration num-bers of the women being sent to Ravensbrück). On 7 February 1944 the train reached Fürstenberg, a verdant spa town in the present-day prov-ince of Brandenburg, Germany. Survivors have repeatedly commented on the cruel disjuncture between the charm of the village and the hell of the KL. During her intake, Neus was selected as "fit for work" and as-signed to barrack 22, in which some five hundred women fought for air and space. Among the useless labour details described by Ravensbrück survivors, women were forced to dig up and move loads of earth from one place to another and to expand the frozen Lake Schwedt, removing the mud from the bottom with bare hands. Hunger and disease carried off many women.

After a month at Ravensbrück, Català was transferred again, this time to Holýšov (Holleischen), a *Kommando* attached administratively to the Flossenbürg camp in the Czech Sudeten region, where she was put to work in a metalworks facility from 8 March 1944 until 8 May 1945.[16] Here Català formed a new camp "family," with her "daughter" Tití but also with another Spaniard and a Hungarian woman. There was no critical mass of Spanish or French women with whom she could form a national unit.[17] At Holleischen, prisoners made anti-aircraft shells in a factory day and night, driven by violence and starvation to manufac-ture ten thousand units per day. The survivors of this *Kommando* later reported with great pride the extent and success of their acts of sabotage that interfered with production, significantly reducing the number of usable shells produced at the camp. The women resisted the murderous labour conditions also by staging a hunger strike and refusing the SS offer of wages. When the war was virtually lost for the Germans, the prisoners waited for death either from disease or starvation or at the hands of the Germans, who had ringed the site with explosives, intending to blow it up, thus killing all the remaining prisoner-workers before the Allied forces arrived. Czech and Polish partisan units freed the camp in early May 1945, liberating about seven hundred women, shortly before the Americans arrived.[18]

Liberation brought its own difficulties. Català, physically and mentally battered, found her way back to Sarlat, France, in May 1945, reuniting with family members, with whom she found it impossible to communicate the depths of her suffering. Her husband Albert Roger had died of exhaustion in Bergen-Belsen. The recipient of numerous awards and honours, Català has become, especially in 2015, the year of her hundredth birthday, Catalonia's symbol of the woman of the Spanish Republic, the heroic Spanish resister in France, and the Catalan deportation experience. Català died on 13 April 2019 in an assisted living facility only a few hundred yards from the house where she had been born 103 years earlier in the Priorat.

In her study of Spain's other well-known woman resister, Núñez Targa, Maureen Tobin Stanley has described the remarkable scope of Spanish women's anti-fascism:

> If we simply look at the case of Mercè Núñez Targa who went from being Nobel Laureate Pablo Neruda's secretary and administrator within the communist party, to being incarcerated at the Ventas women's prison, to crossing the Pyrenees only to be interned in a refugee camp, to then land at the Nazi concentration camp at Ravensbrück, we see that within less than a decade, Targa's situation went from political prisoner in what had been her homeland, to an undesired countryless woman in a land riddled with its own anti-Hispanic sentiments soon to be occupied by an unparalleled Fascist force, to a human being that Nazism tried to reduce to nothing but a number.[19]

In their respective works, Català and Targa interrogate gender as a fundamental category for interpreting the Nazi camps: How did French and Spanish women organize among themselves and with other national groups of political prisoners in their efforts to blunt the impact of violence and corporeal degradation? How did bonding *between women* help them resist the annihilationist efforts of the camp guards and other authorities?[20] These questions are addressed by the women's accounts of the camps, and their testimonies are rich in insights. The following pages focus on the most salient thematic trends in the testimonial corpus: the experience and memory of (a) sexualized violence against women, and (b) how sabotage served identity-conferring functions, then and now. Anecdotes offered here will illustrate how women both resisted and were psychically mutilated by sadistic attacks on their individual sense of gendered personhood and on the ideologically bonded group.[21]

Spanish Women Remember Sexualized Violence

Ravensbrück was known as the "hell for women," where women suffered sexualized violence in complex ways. Among many women survivors, the internalized values associated with stories of hope and triumph over evil have often displaced accounts of coerced sexual abuse including forced nudity, sterilizations, abortion, and the recruitment of inmates to serve as sex workers in KL brothels.[22] Spanish women were not exempt from sexualized rituals of shaming, including stripping in front of guards, being made to stand naked in assemblies, the shaving of body hair, penetrative public and unhygienic gynecological exams, and medical experiments. Spanish and Catalan women drew on an array of psychological and physical resources to resist internalizing the gendered self-loathing the Nazis sought to instil in them.

Mercedes Núñez Targa would recall that of all the accumulating horrors of the camp, nothing diminished her core sense of self more than the long hours at roll call. For some women, it was the violation and injection of chemicals into the genitals that most degraded them (see Bueno Ester in Català). For Núñez Targa, however, the incurable wound of incarceration occurred during the *Appel*: "La herida que todos los deportados heredamos de los campos y arrastramos de por vida. No os lo cuento por daros lástima. Os lo cuento para que podáis comprender qué profunda herida, como la señal de un hierro ardiente, ha dejado el *Appel* en nosotras" (The wound that all of us deportees have inherited from the camps and that we drag with us our entire lives. I'm not telling you this to make you feel pity. I'm telling you so that you can understand how profound this wound is, like an iron brand, that the *Appel* left burned into us).[23] Núñez Targa calls the *Appel* a method of sexualized torture and describes her strategy for combating the Nazi endeavour to dehumanize her as a woman:

Appel! Appel![...] Ni el hambre, ni los azotes, ni la perpetua amenaza de la cámara de gas te llegan tan al fondo del alma como aquella humillación profunda de verte obligada a ordenar a tus propios músculos una inmovilidad de piedra, a imprimir en el rostro la impasibilidad, a no estremecerte ni siquiera cuando el zurriagazo cae en la carne martirizada de una compañera, amiga, hermana. Te sientes vencida, cobarde, como si de golpe te hubieran arrebatado tu dignidad de combatiente, sientes asco y vergüenza de ti misma[...] Grupos de SS seguidos de perros vagan por allí: pistola en mano. Personalmente no tengo ninguna vergüenza en verme desnuda en su presencia, como si fuese un perro más o una piedra. A base de verlos un día y un otro ladrando insultos y clavando azotes como verdaderas bestias, *termino por excluirlos de la comunidad humana. Para mí son bípedos y basta.* (emphasis added)

Appel! Appel! ... Not the hunger or the blows, nor the perpetual threat of the gas chamber reaches as deeply into the soul as that profound humiliation at seeing yourself forced to tell your muscles to stay still as stone, to stamp on your face a look of total impassivity, to not shiver or shake not even when the whip falls on the martyred flesh of your comrade, friend, sister. You feel defeated, cowardly, as if suddenly they have stripped you of your dignity as a combatant, you feel disgust and shame at yourself ... Groups of SS with their dogs guard the perimeter: pistol in hand. Personally, I have no shame in finding myself naked in their presence, as if I were another dog or a stone. After seeing them day after day barking insults and nailing punches like true beasts, *I end up exiling them from the human race. For me they are mere two-footed animals and nothing more.* (emphasis added)[24]

Targa's only possibility for resistance remains in her mind: she banishes her captors from the human family, so that they are mere animals on two legs, and in this way she reclaims her personhood, in her proud, naked, flagellated immobility. Women relied on remarkable powers of psychic resistance to gendered violence in a realm of terror in which luck, innate fortitude, and psychological resilience varied among victims.

Neus Català was a tenacious woman of remarkable toughness and intelligence. In her testimony, readers find very few instances in which she admits feeling spiritually annihilated.[25] There are times, however, when the sadism towards the sexual and reproductive female body proves nearly too much to bear. Beaten for retching when she is forced to put on the used, pus-encrusted underwear of another, perhaps murdered prisoner, Neus nearly breaks her oath to never weep in front of the guards.[26] Earlier, the "vaginal control" had reinforced Català's outrage at the assaults on the prisoners' femininity: "Un nuevo viaje a la enfermería para el control vaginal en condiciones tan vergonzosas como humillantes. Con el mismo instrumento, y sin desinfectar, sacaban muestras de todas. ¡Qué asco y qué miedo! Esto era una tortura suplementaria impuesta a nuestra condición de mujer; todas salíamos con rabia, y cabizbajas" (Another trip to the infirmary for the "vaginal control" under such shameful and humiliating conditions. With the same instrument and without disinfecting between women, they take samples from each of us. How disgusting and terrifying! This was an extra torture imposed on us due to our condition as women; we filed out enraged, and with our heads hanging.).[27] Like Núñez Targa, Català combats the assault on her intimate body by imagining the German enemy as mere un-human organism, nothing more than "escoria moral, tubos digestivos para cumplir una misión bestial" (moral scum, digestive tubes merely to fulfil a bestial mission.).[28]

If resistance to sexualized violence could reside only in the mind, forced labour offered means to respond to the Nazi onslaught in concrete ways. Upon surveying the factory at Holleischen, Català recalls: "se nos plantó el caso de conciencia más grave de nuestra vida ... en el mismo instante vimos la forma de continuar la Resistencia: no producir y sabotear por todos los medios el armamento nazi." (the situation in the factory forced us to confront the most serious crisis of conscience of our lives ... at that very instant we saw how we could continue the Resistance: by failing to produce and by sabotaging, through any means possible, the Nazi war materiel). [29] Being able to continue resistance work through physical labour gave Spanish women the chance to assert their anti-fascist credentials.

Slave Labour Sabotage

Núñez Targa's memoir and the oral histories collected by Català do not veer from the "hinge" themes that typically reveal themselves in communist concentrationary literature. Those themes include arrest and interrogation; transport; arrival; acts of cruelty; acts of kindness; perceptions of their captors; cultural, ethnic, national, linguistic, ideological, and socio-economic diversity in the camp; solidarity and resistance; a welcoming of death; assisting the dying; hunger; a gallery of characters, including the still open wound of the memory of Jewish women and children; the narration of "near misses" (e.g., "how I nearly met my end in the gas chamber"); liberation; and, lastly, the biological reality of femaleness and the long-term psychological and corporeal impact of captivity. That said, it is remarkable that Targa's memoir and the testimonial speakers in the Català collection favour descriptions of acts of sabotage as the signal activity through which they could continue to resist fascism. This makes sense for two reasons, one temporal, the other ideological. As we have noted, most of these women's time was spent not at the main camp but in factories or in labour details under severe conditions. Survivors show excellent recall of the specifics of the manufacturing processes, the long hours spent toiling, often nearly starving, at risk of beatings, and with work sessions bracketed by long and sometimes lethal roll calls. The attention in the testimonies paid to labour also meets an abiding communist imperative to highlight acts of resistance during incarceration. The sabotage storyline not only speaks to the "facts on the ground" but also pulls this tiny Spanish camp population into a larger community of communist women bold enough to try to cripple the production of fascist munitions. Two anecdotes stand for many and illustrate in predictable but also moving ways how the sabotage plotline fostered a sense of transnational communist belonging and at the same time served to distinguish specifically Spanish and Catalan courage.

Núñez Targa recounts – in the heroic tones prevalent in many survivor testimonies – how she formed part of a group of, by her count, six thousand women incorporated into the factory work squads at the HASAG-Leipzig plant, where they were assigned to fabricate shells. Felicja Karay, also imprisoned there, writes that women had to learn to become "in a matter of days, a skilled worker who could operate a complicated machine." Most women manufactured light ammunition, work that involved cleaning, polishing, and moving heavy shells. The output expected of the female labour force was constantly "being raised, and the assembly-line work demanded intense concentration."[30]

Núñez Targa recalls that she was one of eight Spanish women, friends, who formed a close surrogate family who felt that "desorganizar la industria de guerra representa ganar una batalla importante" (to disorganize [i.e., sabotage] the German war industry signified winning an important battle).[31] Manufacturing sabotage and other forms of labour disruption also counted as an important *gendered* performance of resistance. Various narrative strategies show how – even when faced with language barriers – women managed to get their overseers or fellow inmates to understand that they were not "common" prisoners (prostitutes) but committed anti-fascists. Sabotage storylines constituted one such performance. To be observed in acts of subterfuge provided evidence of political acts as the reason for incarceration in the first place as well as of the collective fortitude of the women captives. In a letter, Núñez Targa explains: "Puesto que los castigos, (palizas, etc.) jamás nos los imponían en la fábrica sino más tarde en el campo, decidimos arriesgarnos a una acción de cara a reivindicar nuestra condición de presas políticas frente a los obreros alemanes, a quienes habían dicho que éramos ladronas, prostitutas, etc, a las que reeducaban por el trabajo y con las que no debían hablar en absoluto, cosa tampoco fácil a causa del idioma" (Given that the punishments [beatings and so forth] were never given in the factory itself, but rather later in the camp, we decided to take the risk to undertake an action with the intention of vindicating, in front of the German workers, our condition as political prisoners. The Germans said we were prostitutes and thieves who were being re-educated through labour and with whom they should not communicate under any conditions – something not easy anyway given our language barriers.).[32] Núñez Targa found an opportunity to exteriorize her gendered political credentials during an episode in which she realized that a young blond German worker who oversaw the assembly line was paying particularly close attention to her movements. She was concerned that he might have observed how she was manipulating a mechanical file in order to drill oval, as opposed to round, holes in the shells. To be caught trying to undermine the production line could mean lashes, punches, or death by hanging or gas. Worried that the German might be on to her, Núñez Targa worked slowly but without any obvious attempt to interrupt production. At the same time, she was giddy at the success of her own mechanical ingenuity, and she continued to drill what would be junk shells. At one point, the German approached her and gestured to the red triangle that marked her uniform, which did not bear a letter to indicate her nationality. She replied that she was Spanish. He responded in German: "Spanisches? Franco oder Pasionaria?" She confided: "Pasionaria." "Communist?," he asked. And they exchanged a small smile of complicity.[33] Some days later, Núñez Targa's system of defects had worked so unintentionally well that the machine's axle broke. She froze with terror. When the *Obermeister* verbally attacked her, the German communist came to her defence. Never did the German worker and the Catalan woman ever communicate directly about the incident: it was all glances and a silent mutual understanding based on the exchange of two nouns: "Communist," "Pasionaria." At the end of the incident, Núñez Targa's relief was palpable, but her greatest feeling was the joy at having found a "comrade" in Hitler's Germany. The powers of solidarity – communicated through the "purity" of the Spanish Republican example of self-sacrifice and camaraderie represented by the symbol of Dolores Ibárruri, Pasionaria (the leader of the Spanish Communists and embodiment of anti-fascism)[34] – stand as the climax of this long section devoted to sabotage. Pasionaria in the *Lager* rises up between comrades who do not share a language but who can evoke her as a surreptitiously exchanged code word, a life-saving, female-protection-conferring signal among slaves. Pasionaria moreover serves to associate Núñez Targa with an unimpeachable model of female anti-fascist action, thus leaving no room for the German worker to mistake Núñez Targa and her cohort for "common" women prisoners.

In Català's collection, as in the Núñez Targa memoir, significant narrative space is devoted to describing acts of armament sabotage.[35] In Català's own testimony the narrative slows, fashioned with pleasure around the details of describing the mechanics of sabotage. In the novelized version of her life story, *Cenizas en el cielo* (*Ciel del plom* / Ashes in the Sky, 2012), Català details how she and her Spanish and French comrades slackened the production of anti-aircraft shells by decelerating the rate of work and through the discovery that adding anything at all – in particular, saliva, spit – to the gunpowder would render the shells ineffective. With delight at their cunning and their success – "¡cómo nos entusiasma!" (how this thrilled us!) – women stole tiny drops of oil from other machines and mixed that with the powder as well. These techniques "y la manipulación de las máquinas bajamos la producción de 10000 a 5000, a veces 6000 para disimular, y nos bautizan con el nombre de 'Comando de las holgazanas.' ¡Qué honor tan grande ese menosprecio!" (and the manipulation of the machines brought production down from ten thousand to five thousand or sometimes six thousand so as not to draw too much attention, and so they baptized us the Lazy Woman Kommando! What a great honour this insult!).[36] Small details in the passages devoted to labour sabotage coalesce around the theme of Spanish protagonism in these efforts. For example, Català claims that it was she and Blanca Ferón, another Spanish deportee, who first proclaimed, among the entire multi-national inmate group, the necessity of sabotaging the armaments built to kill their male comrades on the battlefield.[37]

Català, again like Núñez Targa, turns the story of her and her comrades' acts of sabotage into an opportunity to bring forward the exemplary character of *Spanish* resistance and heroics. Català writes: "Aunque el hambre retorciera nuestros estómagos no éramos capaces de quitarnos una brizna de pan, pero para la lucha éramos unas perfectas ladronas; sabotear, sabotear, sabotear" (although hunger twisted our stomachs we were unable to steal bread from one another. But for the struggle against our captors we were perfect thieves: sabotear, sabotear, sabotear!).[38] Subversion, treachery, vandalism was the order of the day. She continues, signalling the sacrifices of Spanish women:

Si nos sorprendían seríamos acusadas del más alto crimen de traición: tortura y ahoracada de pies y manos y colgada en un gancho de carnicero por debajo de las mandíbulas, muerte lenta y atroz, pues no desangrabas. Lo mejor que podías hacer era moverte todo lo que podías para que el gancho subiera sin parar hasta encontrar el cerebro. Así fueron ejecutadas Mimi de Pau, su cuñada Elena, Françoise de Paris y una soviética por sabotaje, en el campo central de Flossenbürg ... Mimí, madre joven de dos niños, tuvo el heroísmo de hacer la Resistencia. Me acordaré siempre con nostalgia y ternura de las fugaces conversaciones de algún domingo por la tarde con ella. De los labios de esa mujer frágil, de ojos bellos en una cara de muñeca brotaban palabras de sentimientos profundos: "Verdad que no he sido mala madre? Es que yo no me sentía madre solamente de mis hijos, sino de todos los niños del mundo."

If we were caught in the act, we would be accused of high treason: tortured and hanged by feet and hands, hung up on meat hooks under the chin, a slow and atrocious death, because you didn't bleed to death, the best you could do would be to try to adjust yourself so that the hook would penetrate your brain. This is how Mimí de Pau, her sister-in-law Elena, Francoise from Paris, and a Soviet woman were executed, for sabotage, in the central camp of Flossenbürg. Mimí de Pau was Spanish ... Mimí, the young mother of two, was heroic enough to do the resistance. I will always remember with nostalgia and tenderness the fleeting conversations we had on Sunday afternoons. From the lips of this fragile woman, with beautiful eyes, in her doll-like face, would burst forth profound feelings: "Have I really been a bad mother? It's that I feel that I was not simply the mother of my own children but the mother of the whole world."[39]

The passage continues with Català's displeasure that the early French account of women in the camps, *Les françaises à Ravensbrück* (1965), does not identify Mimí as Spanish but lists her as a Frenchwoman. Surprisingly, anger at the misidentification of the Spanish Mimí as a Frenchwoman appears in other testimonies collected in Català's book. We can note in this memory a number of elements that echo the Núñez Targa episode in which dangerous acts of sabotage conjoin with a figure of communist maternal self-sacrifice in order to distinguish a specifically *Spanish* solidarity and valour. First, the portrayal of a Mimí whose purported understanding of her own maternity maps onto the Pasionaria character: the long-suffering mother of her own biological children whose wholesale internalization of communist belief renders her mother to all. Resistance is thus feminized. Second, we can observe how the "Frenchification" of Mimí stands in for a pervasive

French erasure of Spanish and communist experience that began with the Republican exile, extended through to the French Resistance, and was heightened and prolonged at Ravensbrück and its subcamps. Let it be known, avers Neus Català, that the *worst*, that is, a prolonged and sadistic murder at the hands of the Nazis, happened to Spanish women too.[40] We count among the martyrs and the heroes, her testimony asserts. Núñez Targa and Català use narratives of *Spanish* acts of sabotage in order to strike against the hegemony of French ascendancy in the discourse of the post-war at the same time that their stories of resistance work under Nazi captivity further their reputation as anti-fascist fighters.

Conclusion

In her book on the hidden social dimensions of prisoner society in concentration camps, sociologist Maja Suderland describes how even in the topsy-turvy world of the camps, prisoners "used every available means in their steadfast attempt to restore a certain degree of 'rightness' within it."[41] The possibilities for expressing one's sociality were violently constrained. Yet still, Suderland argues, cultural activities, many of which the Ravensbrück political prisoners recall in their memoirs – such as singing, performing plays, sharing recipes, and marking national holidays and rituals – could help prisoners briefly reclaim their human dignity and suppress the "'odors of death.'"[42] The Spanish and Catalan testimonial record is replete with memories of small acts of cultural expression that afforded the prisoners individual and collective reminders of their humanity. Català and her camp "sisters" used small amounts of warmed paint to make figurines, while Núñez Targa and her campmates pinned tiny, clandestinely sewn Spanish Republican flags to their uniforms. Although Suderland does not discuss forced labour, it is easy to see that the expressions of agency enacted by Spanish women, including munitions production sabotage, hunger strikes, and refusal to accept pay for slave labour, constituted self-determined actions that validated a self of sense and purpose rooted in anti-fascist resistance.

Many subcamps of Ravensbrück were largely monosexual female spaces. Within them there was limited potential for opposition to degradation, starvation, and torture. Nevertheless, what opposition could be made was meaningful, and stories can be told about that resistance. In such spaces, the Spanish women cast themselves as actors whose credentials as Spanish anti-fascists attempted to break national and gendered hierarchies. It is this memory of resistance against deathly odds that Spanish women ultimately put forward as their portrait of their descent into the *Lager*. By shining the spotlight on *manual* labour-oriented manifestations of antifascist resistance, women produced self-portraits of courage and initiative that kept faith with the long communist tradition of the workplace and the body in-and-at work as a site of pride, strife, and contestation.

NOTES

1 Hugo-Schneider-Aktiengesellschaft (HASAG) was a large armament production company that produced the Panzerfaust anti-tank weapon. On its corporate structure and utility to the Nazi regime, see Karay, *Hasag-Leipzig Slave Labour Camp for Women*; see also Karay, "Women in Forced Labor Camps." Núñez Targa – also enslaved at HASAG Leipzig – described fabricating "obuses" (shells). Karay (2002) is more specific and describes the manufacture of shoulder missile ammunition (26).
2 ITS (International Tracing Service) documents list her resistance alias Francisca (Paquita) Puig née Colomer. Under that name, she arrived at Ravensbrück on 23 June 1944; on 21 July, she was transferred to "commando de Leipzig-Schönefeld au camp de concentration Buchenwald."
3 Gildea, *Fighters in the Shadows*, 5.
4 The most authoritative study on Ravensbrück remains Strebel, *Das KZ Ravensbrück*. See also Helm, *Ravensbrück*. On slave labour, see Wagner, "Work and Extermination"; Buggeln, *Slave Labor*; Allen, *The Business of Genocide. United States Holocaust Memorial Museum Encyclopedia*, vol. 1, contains entries on all the slave labour camps to which Spanish women were deported.
5 Buggeln, *Slave Labor*, 118.
6 Andrieu, "Réflexions sur la Résistance," 3; Reboul, "La Résistance dans les camps."
7 http://www.amicalravensbruck.org; http://www.amical-mauthausen.org.
8 Gildea speaks of "resistance in France," as opposed to "The French Resistance," in his effort to elevate the profiles of these various groups (including women and Spaniards). See Wieviorka, *Histoire de la Résistance*.
9 While recent historical studies (Gildea, Dreyfus-Armand) have corrected the record, attending to the struggle's Spanish and international dimensions as well as to the centrality of women, scholarly work remains to be done on how the gender and international pieces of the puzzle connect. See Dreyfus-Armand, *L'exil des républicains espagnols en France*. On resistance in Spain, see Yusta Rodrigo, «Rebeldía individual.»
10 Hoyo, *Memorial de las españolas*, 77.
11 Roig, *Els catalans als camps nazis*. Roig describes the women's reluctance to offer testimony: "Ha sido difícil conseguir que muchas deportadas

prestasen su testimonio para este libro. La Historia ha dado pruebas más que suficientes de hasta qué punto ha sido importante la participación de la mujer en toda clase de resistencias y de combates por la libertad y, a la vez, de que un extraño PUDOR hace que ella misma silencie sus gestas en épocas de paz," (It has been difficult to get women deportees to contribute their testimonies for this book. History has provided enough examples of just how important these women have been to many forms of resistance and struggles for liberty. But at the same time there is a strange reluctance or shyness in times of peace that makes the women silence their own heroic deeds; 65).

12 Caplan, "Gender and the Concentration Camps," 94.

13 Here I am citing Català, *De la resistencia y la deportación*. Also key are these biographies of Català: Belenguer Mercadé, *Neus Català*; the novelized autobiography by Martí and Català, *Un cel de plom*; and Trallero, *Neus Català*. The memoirs of Núñez Targa have appeared in various editions in both Spanish and Catalan; the Nazi camp memoirs first appeared as Núñez Targa, *El carretó dels gossos*. The most authoritative of these editions is the recent Spanish book, edited by her son, Pablo Iglesias Núñez: *El valor de la memoria*. All citations are from this volume. This 2016 edition contains two books: her choral, collective memoir of the women's prison of Ventas, *Cárcel de Ventas* (Paris: Éditions de la Librairie du Globe, 1967), the very first memoir published by a former political prisoner of the infamous Madrid jail, and the memoir of Ravensbrück.

14 Although there are extant only eighteen *autobiographical* accounts, *Memorial de las españolas deportadas a Ravensbrück* contains many more biographical sketches of the Spanish deportees, pieced together from various sources, including the most complete census of Spanish deportees: Bermejo and Checa, *Libro memorial*. See also the Fondation pour la mémoire, *Le Livre-Mémorial*.

15 Rosado Orquín and Garzón, *Virtudes Cuevas: una superviviente del campo de concentración alemán de Ravensbrück*.

16 On the sub-camps, see USHMM's *Encyclopedia of Camps and Ghettos*, vol 1. Entry on Holleischen-Holýšov, 614–16; under Buchenwald, Leipzig-Schönefeld (HASAG) (women), 378; and on Ravensbrück Main camp and sub-camp system, 1187–92.

17 According to the census, de Hoyo, ed., *Memorial*, only four Spanish women were transferred to Holleischen: Català, Adrianne Calderón, Dolors Casadellà, and Blanca Ferón. The French communist resister Catherine Roux published her memoirs of Ravensbrück and Holleischen in *Triangle rouge*, in which episodes align closely with those recounted by the Spanish women. The *Memorial* shows at least eight Spanish women sent to one of the HASAG sites near Leipzig, including Núñez Targa.

18 For a summary of the metalworks and of the conditions there, visit and
search http://www.warrelics.eu/forum/content/

19 Tobin Stanley, "Mujeres silenciosas," 136.

20 On the creation of non-biological family groups, see Milton, "Women and
the Holocaust." See also Eschebach, ed., *Homophobie und Devianz*.

21 Political prisoners from many countries tell the same kinds of anecdotes,
with similar narrative structures. See *The Ravensbrück Women's Concentration Camp*.

22 Sommer, *Das KZ-Bordell*.

23 Núñez Targa, *El valor de la memoria*, 170.

24 Ibid., 171–2.

25 One merit of Martí's novelized biography – based on extensive interviews
with Català – is the attention paid to a variety of experiences in the camp
and the levels of emotional response accorded to them. Català's own testimony does not contain the same depth and variety of expression.

26 Martí and Herrera, *Cenizas en el cielo: la vida de Neus Català*, 202.

27 Cited from https://www.amicalravensbruck.org. See also Català, *De la
Resistencia*, 61.

28 Ibid.

29 Ibid., 67

30 Karay, *Hasag-Leipzig*, 287.

31 Núñez Targa, *El valor de la memoria*, 189.

32 Núñez Targa, "1982. Una carta," (letter reproduced in Galician newspaper), http://www.buscameenelciclodelavida.com/2016/05/una-carta-de-
mercedes-nunez-targa.html.

33 Núñez Targa, *El valor de la memoria*, 190–1.

34 On La Pasionaria as the embodiment of "the nobility and pathos of the
Spanish people and their cause," see Kirschenbaum, "Exile, Gender, and
Communist Self-Fashioning," 568, 575.

35 On labour, consult the testimonies of Soledad Alcón, Carmen Buatell,
Mónica Jené, Constanza Martínez Prieto, Mercedes Bernal, and Lola Casadellà in Català, *De la resistencia*.

36 Martí and Herrera, *Cenizas en el cielo*, 171.

37 Ibid., 169.

38 Català, *De la Resistencia*, 67.

39 Ibid., 67.

40 The story of Mimí appears in the testimonies of other Spanish women and
is recounted in detail in the Martí-Català novel, 205.

41 Suderland, *Inside Concentration Camps*, 5.

42 Ibid., 110.

13 Between Compiègne and Neuengamme: Testimony and Trauma of Spanish Prisoners in German Concentration Camps

ANDREA HEPWORTH

That Spaniards from France were deported to the Nazi concentration camp of Neuengamme is not widely known. In this chapter, the journey and experience of Spanish prisoners at Neuengamme will be traced mainly through an analysis of the testimony of José López, one of the few survivors of the camp. I will also explore the long-term manifestations of trauma brought about as a result of the imprisonment of Spaniards at Neuengamme.

The segregation of Spanish Republicans – exiled to France and imprisoned in French camps, as detailed in Dreyfus-Armand's chapter 9 in this volume – from French combatants and their subsequent deportation by the Nazis must be understood in the context of the Francoist repression in Spain. The systematic use of terror and violence against the Other, the "reds," the "anti-Spain," formed an essential part of the Franco regime. After Franco's victory, about twenty thousand more Republicans were killed and many others died of malnutrition and disease in overfilled prisons, work battalions, and concentration camps in Spain; a system of forced labour was developed in Francoist Spain from 1937 onwards. In the same year, the Inspección de Campos de Concentración de Prisioneros (ICCP) was established, which was even in name reminiscent of Nazi Germany's Inspectorate of the Concentration Camps, established in 1934.[1] Francoist Spain's disownment of the exiled Republicans and lack of interest in their repatriation left them in the Nazi system; only a few prominent prisoners were handed over to Spain and subsequently executed, such as the last president of the Generalitat, Lluís Companys i Jover.[2] It has long been speculated that the visit of Ramón Serrano Suñer, Franco's interior minister, to Berlin in September 1940 was connected to the deportation of Spanish Republicans to Nazi concentration camps,[3] and recently a paper trail has emerged corroborating the Franco government's involvement.[4]

This is further supported by the existence of a Gestapo circular dated 25 September 1940, the month of Serrano Suñer's visit, stating that Spanish Republicans and other nationals who had belonged to the International Brigades were not to be treated as prisoners of war, but instead sent to concentration camps.[5]

Compiègne

After late 1941, Spanish Republicans were mainly arrested as members of the French Resistance – it is estimated that about ten thousand Spaniards actively participated[6] – and deported to German concentration camps via transit camps such as Compiègne.[7] Several of these transit camps, in which thousands of prisoners were gathered before they were sent on to Nazi concentration and extermination camps, were located in Western Europe: Drancy and Compiègne in France, Mechelen in Belgium, Vught and Westerbork in the Netherlands. The former Royallieu military base in Compiègne, 87 kilometres from Paris, was officially renamed Frontstalag 122 by the occupying German authorities. It held political prisoners, foreigners, and Jews. An estimated fifty thousand of the fifty-four thousand interned at Compiègne between June 1941 and August 1944 were deported,[8] and between 1943 and 1944, 1,090 of those deportees were of Spanish nationality.[9] One of the many Spaniards on a deadly days-long cattle car transport from Compiègne was Catalan resistance fighter Neus Català, who was sent to the women's concentration camp of Ravensbrück.[10] Another was author Jorge Semprún: in his case the transport was destined for Buchenwald.[11] (See Herrmann's chapter 12 for Neus Català's trajectory; Soledad Fox Maura's chapter 16 for Jorge Semprún.) These transports, during which many died, also went to the concentration camp of Neuengamme, near the city of Hamburg in northern Germany.

The Concentration Camp of Neuengamme

The first Spaniards arrived in Neuengamme in 1941–2 and were, like Semprún, exiled Republicans who had been in the French Resistance when captured by the Nazis.[12] Resistance fighters also arrived on later transports. One of these was José Ros, who had grown up in France and joined the resistance in the Jura Mountains, having become the head of the secret military force in that area in 1943. Ros was arrested in April 1944 and sent via various prisons to Compiègne and then on to Neuengamme, where he arrived on 24 May 1944.[13] His was the biggest transport of Spanish prisoners from Compiègne, consisting of

315 Spaniards out of an estimated two thousand total prisoners. The second-largest group arrived on 18 July of the same year – twenty-seven of about 1,500 prisoners.[14] In total, an estimated 750 Spaniards were incarcerated in Neuengamme, of whom only about twenty survived.[15]

Neuengamme had been established in 1938 as a satellite of the Sachsenhausen concentration camp and was converted into an independent camp in June 1940; by the end of 1944 it was comprised of eighty-five subcamps.[16] The location of the subcamps was linked to industrial and commercial interests; the main camp at Neuengamme included a brick factory intended to help in the redevelopment of nearby Hamburg. After 1942, Walther-Werke, the Carl Jastram Motorenfabrik, and Deutsche Meß-Apparate GmbH established plants at the camp crucial to the German defence industry. Until the late 1930s, most of the Neuengamme prisoners were of German nationality, among them political prisoners and criminals. After 1940, Spaniards and prisoners from Nazi-occupied territories formed the majority, including about 11,500 French prisoners. Even though Neuengamme was a slave labour camp and not an extermination camp, between fifty-five and fifty-six thousand prisoners died during its operation, which amounts to almost half of the estimated 106,000 prisoners who had been incarcerated there during its existence.[17]

Neuengamme was the largest concentration camp in northwestern Germany, yet it was largely forgotten after 1945. The material legacy of suffering at Neuengamme, including the records kept at the camp, was destroyed by the Nazis during evacuations. The only surviving documents – books containing death registers, and laboratory records from the infirmary – had been hidden by prisoners during the destruction. The cleaned-up site of the camp remained a relatively obscure topic in public discourse and certainly did not form a focal point of the post-war "media blitz."[18] Moreover, the empty and well-preserved camp of Neuengamme was almost immediately reused by the British forces, not only as a displaced persons camp and an internment camp for German prisoners of war, SS, and Nazi officials, but also – from 1948 until 2006 – by the city of Hamburg as a prison facility.[19] The memorial reckoning with Neuengamme was focused mainly on utilitarian considerations and the repression of the camp's dark past until the early 1980s; today, the site of the Neuengamme Memorial covers nearly the entire former camp. Between 1991 and 1994, the Neuengamme Memorial conducted an Oral History Project, in which 265 former prisoners there were interviewed about their life stories; one of these was the Spanish survivor José López.[20]

Testimony of José López

Born in 1921 in Catalonia, José López and his family were economic migrants who moved to Bessèges, France, in 1925. Although many of the Spanish prisoners who arrived in May 1944 in Neuengamme were resistance fighters, López was not. He was one of the civilians arrested and deported as a means of repression, carried out by the German authorities in France from 1942 onwards.[21] López described his arrest as a result of his Spanish citizenship: he had not complied with the conscription order he received in 1942 from Francoist Spain and was consequently considered a deserter by the regime. After the Spanish vice-consul hinted to him that failure to comply with the military conscription could have significant negative consequences for him despite his French residence permit, López moved to southwestern France, where he worked as a woodcutter. Through his association with Spanish co-workers who were *maquis* resistance fighters, López was arrested with them on 12 April 1944. The Spaniards were incarcerated in Bordeaux and then transferred to Compiègne and later to Nazi concentration camps.[22] López was convinced he would have been freed had he been a French citizen; his observation is certainly congruent with newly emerging documentary evidence.

Thus López was arrested by the German occupying forces in April 1944 and arrived from Compiègne by train in Neuengamme on 24 May 1944. He remembered the cramped conditions of the boxcar, how between eighty and 110 prisoners were packed tightly into cattle cars, into which usually about eight horses would fit.[23] Sleep was not to be had; although everyone was exhausted, if one person were to lie down, others would lie on top of him due to the lack of space and prisoners could suffocate. The rations for deportees consisted of a 300–400 gram chunk of bread and a tiny piece of sausage for a journey that could last between three and five days, sometimes longer.[24] To prevent escape, the prisoners in López's group were told that up to three hundred would be crammed into their wagon should anyone attempt to flee, which would have meant certain death. On arrival in Weimar, it was discovered that Buchenwald, the original terminus of the journey, was overcrowded. After spending a night in the train without water or additional food, the prisoners were transported to Hamburg and then Neuengamme. Semprún described his own, similar train trip to Buchenwald as an advancing "hacia nuestros inmóviles cadáveres futuros" (towards the motionless corpses we were destined to be).[25] Some, in particular older prisoners, did not survive the journey; others lost their minds, reported López.[26]

The testimonial accounts of these lethal cattle car trips to concentration and extermination camps have become powerful representations of the Holocaust in the public imaginary and are mainly viewed as a prelude to the prolonged death experience at the camps. However, the train trips themselves, as becomes evident in López's account, were traumatic enough to induce post-traumatic stress disorder and psychoses in and of themselves. Consequently, this step of the deportation process, in between the phases of apprehension, sorting, identification, and concentration in camps, needs to be classified as a separate element, in Raul Hilberg's estimation.[27] The cramped conditions of the inescapable space of the wagons, the smells, the tactile sensations, as well as the sense of uncertainty all contributed to a particular type of "transport shame" and trauma.[28] This was then followed by a process of depersonalization upon arrival at Neuengamme: all personal belongings were taken, all hair shorn off, and a prison number was assigned to which one was required to respond at the daily roll call.[29] Some of the personal belongings of the prisoners can still be found at the archive of ITS Bad Arolsen: there are watches, wallets, keys, pens, and rings – material witnesses to the dehumanization of the prisoners.[30] Documents show, for example, that López's white chain-strap watch, his wallet with twenty-three photos, and a key were held at the archive until June 2018.[31] Records also indicate that he turned twenty-three on the day of his arrival in Neuengamme; his profession was noted as hairdresser, and his name is given as "Jose Lopez" and "Jose Lopez Gabarron" on different documents.[32]

Though López did not belong to the resistance, his Neuengamme prisoner card classified him as a political prisoner,[33] and so did his badge, which consisted of a red triangle inscribed with an "S" for Spain.[34] The various categorization systems through badges and marks on the prisoners' clothing served more as tools of humiliation, dissociation, and discrimination than as means of bureaucratic classification, although the colour of the badges could have a profound impact on the prisoners' treatment in the camps.[35] Upon arrival in Neuengamme, López described how the prisoners' clothes were swapped for different civilian clothing, ill-fitting and marked on the back. However, he also saw some prisoners with striped prison garments,[36] the "zebra-uniform."[37] The mixing of civilian clothing with the camp "uniforms" was a sign of severe overcrowding, as was the use of one bed for three prisoners.[38] The purpose of the camps was not only the "elimination of every trace of potential opposition to Nazi rule," and to serve as a training ground in brutality for the SS, but also the economic exploitation of forced labour, which was particularly brutal in Neuengamme.[39]

In 1944, when López and the other 314 Spaniards arrived in Neuengamme, most concentration camp prisoners were interned in subcamps, which were established near important armament production sites.[40] The number of Neuengamme's subcamps rose from four to seventy in 1944, when the availability of new civil foreign labourers dropped and concentration camp prisoners became the "last available labour reserve."[41] López spent about ten days in the main camp before he and about two thousand others were sent to the subcamp of Braunschweig, an important locus of Nazi armament production. In Braunschweig, striped prison garments were allocated to the prisoners, the scarce food was distributed inside the barracks, and prisoners gathered by nationalities; hence López joined the "Spanish tables." Friendships developed mainly through common nationality; however, some of the prisoners had also belonged to the same resistance networks.[42]

After a short stay in Braunschweig, López was transferred to the Reichswerke Hermann Göring, a factory that primarily produced ammunition for the Wehrmacht. Here, twelve hours a day, López manufactured bombs and grenades, which were then transferred for further processing to a different warehouse where Jewish prisoners worked. The only breaks were when the Allies bombed the factory, events that terrified the *Kapos*; in contrast, according to López, the prisoners "feared neither the bombs, nor death anymore."[43] This lack of fear evokes Primo Levi's description of the *Muselmänner*, whom "one hesitates to call ... living: one hesitates to call their death death, in the face of which they have no fear, as they are too tired to understand."[44] However, when López was not only beaten unconscious but also threatened with execution after he committed a serious mistake at the factory, he suggested that he spent "eight very uncomfortable days" awaiting his fate (the time frame for executions after an act of sabotage was eight days, which means that López's actions may have been intentional).[45] Apathy and stoicism in the face of death, then, had not entirely become part of his emotional and spiritual make-up. Moreover, López's other comments exhibit a profound desire to return to his family, which, he recounted, instilled in him the will to survive.[46] In November 1944, López returned to the block for the sick in Neuengamme with a purulent ear infection. At the end of March 1945 he was transferred to the subcamp of Kaltenkirchen, where prisoners worked on the expansion of a Luftwaffe airfield.[47]

Throughout his time as a forced labourer in the Neuengamme subcamps of Braunschweig, Kaltenkirchen, and Wöbbelin, López witnessed several murders and acts of torture; he also had to endure severe beatings himself. Conditions in the subcamps were often even more horrific than in the main camp. What is more, a fellow prisoner, Jerzy Budkiewicz, stated that the fate of the "Rotspanier," the "red" Spanish political prisoners, was particularly dire due to their general lack of knowledge of the German language, severe hunger – their food rations were systematically stolen – and the adverse weather conditions, to which they were not accustomed.[48]

On 17 April 1945, all remaining prisoners of the subcamp of Kaltenkirchen were transferred to Wöbbelin, a subcamp established in February 1945 to accommodate prisoners evacuated from other concentration camps on account of the advancing Allied forces. Wöbbelin was severely overcrowded, with very little water and food; disease was rampant, and extermination was conducted "by deliberate negligence."[49] Budkiewicz observed that prisoners "died like flies ... [d]ead bodies were lying on plank beds next to the living for days on end"; hunger and misery seemed interminable; there were even cases of cannibalism.[50] When the US Army liberated Wöbbelin on 2 May 1945, they found the bodies of about one thousand prisoners.[51] Among the survivors was a severely emaciated and ill López, weighing only thirty-eight kilos. He was first transferred to a hospital, then quickly transported back to France to be reunited with his family.

Return from the Camps

The Spanish deportees returned deeply marked by their experience. Eduardo Pons Prades, a Spanish historian who fought in the French Resistance, observed that those who did come back from the camps in the summer of 1945 were not, and would never be again, the same people as before their detention.[52] For many concentration camp survivors of different nationalities, there was no return to their previous lives; many had become displaced persons, their communities, families, and homes having been obliterated or dispossessed. Similarly, for most of the Spanish Republicans, a return to Spain was impossible. Hopes that the Allies would remove Franco's regime were not fulfilled, and many Spaniards remained in exile in France. Pons Prades vividly recounts the deep disillusionment experienced by Spanish exiles when it became clear that the Allies would not overthrow Franco's regime after the war. He recalls the desperation of a survivor of a Neuengamme subcamp on the Channel Islands, Catalan resistance fighter and former president of the Comité Catalán de Ayuda a Euskadi, Joaquín Cid, who stayed in exile in France until his death, as did many other survivors.[53]

Although France granted official refugee status to Spanish Republicans in March 1945, many survivors encountered negative reactions to their presence on French soil after their return from the camps: Català's "fiesta del milagro" (celebration of her miracle of survival) in returning to France – she had been interned at Ravensbrück – was severely tarnished by verbal abuse from representatives of the French Red Cross greeting her convoy.[54] Joan Mestres, a Catalan survivor of Sachsenhausen, remarked that although his Spanish nationality did not play a role when he joined the French Resistance, it was the first question asked of him after his return.[55] Not many questions were asked of the survivors; there was a "pervasive immediate postwar unwillingness to hear the accounts of returning deportees."[56] Return to Spain was an option for few; many of those who did return had to endure interrogations, discrimination, and prison in Spain, where the ambiguously worded 1939 Law of Political Responsibilities, in force until 1963, could cover many different acts or even "non-acts," when defined as "serious passivity."[57] Survivors as well as released prisoners in Spain faced a society in which they were unable to share their experiences due to others' fear that they would be identified as political activists just by listening, which could have serious repercussions.[58] An agenda of "repressive erasure"[59] or *damnatio memoriae* was directed against the memory of the defeated, which resulted in a silenced society in Spain, where the political memory of the Franco regime was uncontested.

Between Testimony and Silence

The notion that the Holocaust was shrouded in silence and that Jewish survivor stories in particular were eschewed or suppressed directly after the Second World War has been challenged in recent years by Holocaust scholars whose research has uncovered a vast diversity of responses to the Holocaust in the 1940s and 1950s.[60] In Spain, the fate and existence of Spanish Republican deportees to Nazi concentration camps was kept in complete silence in the post-war years. Until 1968, the Spanish government did not officially acknowledge Spanish deaths in the camps; it did not release death certificates from the camps until 1974.[61] Testimonies of survivors published before the Spanish transition did exist but were scarce.[62] In 1977, Montserrat Roig's foundational study on Catalans in Nazi concentration camps brought the topic to wider public awareness and helped break the silence about the deportations. (See Rosa Toran's chapter 17 in this volume on the importance of Roig's *Els catalans als camps nazis*.)[63]

The ways in which Spanish survivors attempted to cope with their ordeal varied. Semprún, for example, stayed silent for many years about his experience; after his return, he needed to choose between "la escritura o la vida" (writing or life).[64] "Liturgical" silence such as Semprún's arises in order to enable "those experiencing loss to engage with their grief in their own time and their own ways."[65] Although most of the physical wounds inflicted on the deportees disappeared, the mental consequences of the trauma of the concentration camps did not. Suicides were common among survivors, even years after their return.[66] Similarly, Neuengamme survivor López suffered from depression and harboured suicidal thoughts for years.[67] Moreover, he never talked about his internment in Neuengamme with his children or grandchildren and very rarely with his wife; nor did he want to go into specific details of cruelties in his testimony. Nearly fifty years after his liberation, he still had recurring nightmares about his experience.[68]

López suggested that his silence was rooted in the fear of not being believed, of being accused of being mad – or a liar.[69] To be able to narrate traumatic experiences, to give testimony about them, there needs to be an empathetic audience – an Other willing to listen, which survivors such as López lacked in the early post-war years both in Francoist Spain and in France. According to psychoanalyst and Holocaust survivor Dori Laub, in order to heal from trauma, the survivor must articulate the traumatic experiences in order to integrate these into their autobiography and eventually move beyond them.[70] These historical traumatic events need to be worked through rather than "acted out" (what historian Dominick LaCapra defines as "emotionally repeating a still-present past").[71] The recurring nightmares experienced by survivors such as López are evidence of "acting out." They point to a lack of closure of the traumatic event; an event that "has no ending ... and ... as far as its survivors are concerned ... continues into the present and is current in every respect."[72] It took López nearly fifty years to unlock his internal library of suffering and give testimony about his experience at Neuengamme, roughly coinciding with the "memory boom" Spain has experienced since the 1990s in regard to its traumatic twentieth-century history. The silence about and obliteration of the traces of Spain's past have prevented the healing of its society from trauma for a long time. Hence a working through of traumatic experiences is essential not only for individuals but also for societies as a whole.

Knowledge of Imprisonment of Spaniards in Neuengamme

The fact that Spaniards were imprisoned in the concentration camp of Neuengamme has not received much public attention. Because a greater number of Spaniards were imprisoned in the Mauthausen concentration camp, the tragic Spanish connection to that camp is much better known (see chapters 11, 14, and 15). Other reasons for the relative obscurity of Neuengamme in this context include the incorrect classification of Spanish prisoners as French upon their arrival from Compiègne (a misclassification that also characterized the registration of Spanish Republican women at Ravensbrück; see Herrmann in chapter 12).[73] The main factor, however, that hinders research about these Spanish inmate populations is the destruction of the internal documents at the camp and the low number of Spanish survivors from Neuengamme. In the "Cap Arcona catastrophe" of May 1945, the ships *Deutschland, Cap Arcona, Thielbek,* and *Athen,* which held thousands of Neuengamme concentration camp prisoners, were attacked by British forces, and around sixty-four hundred prisoners died.[74] Paul Weißmann, a member of the International Brigades who had been on board the *Thielbek,* testified that he was the only survivor of the Spanish contingent.[75] The records at Neuengamme, however, only register the place of death of one of the Spanish prisoners as "Cap Arcona"; many others are marked as "disappeared," hence the place of death is unknown.

Stanley Cohen suggests that for "the collective … 'coming to terms with the past' is to know (and admit to knowing) exactly what happened."[76] Placing the stories, voices, and memories of the few Spanish survivors of the Neuengamme concentration camp in the wider context of the political violence of war, exile, deportation, and repression that many Spaniards had to endure before, during, and in the aftermath of the Spanish Civil War, the Second World War, and the Franco dictatorship is a necessary step towards an inclusive post-violence society.

NOTES

1 Rodrigo, "Exploitation," 557.
2 S. Payne, *The Franco Regime,* 223.
3 Roig, *Noche y niebla,* 25–7.
4 Hernández de Miguel, *Los últimos españoles de Mauthausen,* 187–201; 225–40; Preston, *The Spanish Holocaust,* 515–16.
5 Bermejo and Checa, *Libro memorial,* 19; Bermejo, "Los republicanos españoles," 163–6.
6 S. Serrano, *Maquis,* 129.
7 Ruppert, "Spanier in deutschen Konzentrationslagern," 6–7.
8 Poznanski, *Jews in France during World War II,* 224.
9 Bermejo and Checa, *Libro memorial,* 20.
10 Català, *De la resistencia y la deportación,* 25; Bermejo and Checa, *Libro memorial,* 332.

11   Pike, *Spaniards in the Holocaust*, 322.

12   Bermejo and Checa, *Libro memorial*, 13–15. At least one Spanish prisoner, Facunde Sagera Saezy, prisoner number 03104, is supposed to have arrived in Neuengamme earlier, on 19 November 1940: "Auswertung der Häftlingsdatenbank nach Haftgruppen – Spanier," 2003, Ng. 2.6.1.4, Archive KZ Neuengamme, Hamburg, Germany; "Datenbank Auszug Spanier mit Doubletten," 2007, Archive KZ Neuengamme, Hamburg, Germany. Nevertheless, a prisoner with a very similar name and the same date of birth – Facundo Saez-Sagera – was registered with prisoner number 31064 and appears under that number in Bermejo and Checas's list as Facundo Sáez Izaguirre, having arrived in Neuengamme in May 1944, which casts doubt on the earlier date; Bermejo and Checa, *Libro memorial*, 32, 456. Spelling errors, inconsistencies, and omission of the second surname of Spanish prisoners in the Nazi system makes reaching a definitive identification particularly challenging.

13   KZ Gedenkstätte Neuengamme, *Lebensläufe: Lebensgeschichtliche Interviews mit Überlebenden des KZ Neuengamme: Ein Archiv-Findbuch*, (Hamburg: KZ Gedenkstätte Neuengamme, 1994), 247–9; Bermejo and Checa, *Libro memorial*, 55. Ros's first name is listed as Joseph in Neuengamme's archive and as José in Checa and Bermejo's work – the Spanish version is likely the correct one. Both studies list the same prisoner number, 31218.

14   KZ Gedenkstätte Neuengamme – 2007, Offenes Archiv, "Spanische Häftlinge und Spanienkämpfer im KZ – Offenes Archiv," accessed 1 August 2015, accessed 6 May 2019, http://media.offenes-archiv.de/ha2_2_5_5_thm_2363.pdf, 10; http://media.offenes-archiv.de/spanischehaeftlinge.pdf, 10; "Auswertung der Häftlingsdatenbank nach Haftgruppen – Spanier." The lists in Bermejo and Checa's *Libro memorial* show three Spanish prisoners arriving from Compiègne on 25 January 1943; three on 31 January 1944; fourteen on 7 June 1944; twenty-three on 18 July 1944; two on 31 July 1944; three from Fort Hatry-Belfort on 31 August 1944; two without date or transfer camp; and the rest arriving from Compiègne on 24 May 1944.

15   Claudia Römer, "También hubieron españoles en Neuengamme," 1989, Folder Thematische Sammlung KZ Neuengamme Hauptlager, Häftlingsgruppen Spanien, Claudia Römer, Archive KZ Neuengamme, Hamburg, Germany.

16   Buggeln, *Arbeit und Gewalt*, 1–2.

17   Kaienburg, "Funktionswandel des KZ-Kosmos?," 260.

18   Marcuse, "The Afterlife of the Camps," 202.

19   Garbe, "Ein schwieriges Erbe," 115–17.

20   The interview with José López was conducted in French and German by Jens Michelsen and translator Karin Höpp on 29 May 1993 in Bessèges, France; the transcript is housed at the Neuengamme Archive. The main

exhibition, "Traces of History," at the memorial camp also features a combined section on foreign prisoners from France and Spain.

21 Bermejo and Checa, *Libro memorial*, 16.

22 José López, "Gespräch mit José López am 29. Mai 1993 in Bessèges, Frankreich," 1993, Folder KZ Gedenkstätte Neuengamme Archiv, Häftlingsberichte, Oral History Project, 1549, Archive KZ Neuengamme, Hamburg, Germany, 30–2. All translations are my own unless otherwise stated. López, "Gespräch," 17–29.

23 López, "Gespräch," 17–29.

24 Ibid., 29. Trains could stop anywhere for days – Josep Ambròs's trip from Compiègne to the final destination took seventeen days, and only one third survived. Roig, *Noche y niebla*, 45.

25 Semprún, *El largo viaje*, 2.

26 López, "Gespräch," 31–2.

27 Hilberg, *The Destruction of the European Jews*, 53, 116, 278.

28 Gigliotti, *The Train Journey*, vol. 13, 21.

29 López, "Gespräch," 33–5.

30 Schönemann and Möller, "Der Bestand der Effekten," 251–2.

31 Jose Lopez, prisoner number 30590, case 2, bundle 63, envelope 19, 1.1.30.2/3458696, Archive ITS Bad Arolsen, Germany. López's personal belongings were returned to "family members (or other entitled persons) of the original owners" on 21 June 2018 following the ITS's #StolenMemory campaign. ITS Bad Arolsen – Digital Collections Online. "Lopez, Jose," https://digitalcollections.its-arolsen.org/01020903/name/view/193053, accessed 20 February 2019.

32 Jose Lopez, prisoner number 30590, Häftlingskarte, 1.1.30.6/3627854, Archive ITS Bad Arolsen, Germany; Jose Lopez Gabarron, prisoner number 30590, Effektenliste, Documents 108009887–96, Archive ITS Bad Arolsen, Germany.

33 Lopez, Häftlingskarte.

34 López, "Gespräch," 44. In most concentration camps, Spaniards wore the red triangle; however, Spanish prisoners at Mauthausen were assigned the blue triangle of the stateless inscribed with the letter S.

35 Wachsmann, *KL*, 119.

36 López, "Gespräch," 34.

37 Wachsmann, *KL*, 119, 313, 480.

38 López, "Gespräch," 35.

39 Kogon, *The Theory and Practice of Hell*, 20–2.

40 Buggeln, *Arbeit und Gewalt*, 57–8.

41 Buggeln, "Building to Death," 614.

42 López, "Gespräch," 37–44.

43 Ibid.," 46.

44 Levi, *The Drowned and the Saved*, 82.
45 On the similar slave labour conditions for Spanish Republican women in sub-camps, see Herrmann, chapter 12 of this volume.
46 López, "Gespräch," 47–8.
47 KZ Gedenkstätte Neuengamme, *Lebensläufe*, 145.
48 Jerzy Budkiewicz, "Häftlingsbericht162, 1964," Folder Thematische Sammlung KZ Neuengamme Archiv, Häftlingsberichte 154–75. Archive KZ Neuengamme, Hamburg, Germany.
49 Buggeln, *Arbeit und Gewalt*, 277.
50 Budkiewicz, "Häftlingsbericht 162, 1964."
51 Megargee, *Encyclopedia of Camps and Ghettos*, 1185.
52 Pons Prades, *Morir por la libertad*, 15.
53 Ibid., 175–80.
54 Català, *De la resistencia*, 66.
55 Roig, *Noche y niebla*, 337.
56 Ferrán and Herrmann, *A Critical Companion*, 11.
57 Preston, *The Spanish Holocaust*, 503. For example, the brother of Ravensbrück survivor Neus Català, who had first joined the French resistance and then the guerrillas in Spain, was condemned to thirty years and a day in prison in Spain after his death sentence was commuted, Català, *De la resistencia*, 67.
58 Gómez Bravo, *El exilio interior*, 218–19.
59 Connerton, "Seven Types of Forgetting," 60.
60 See, for example, Cesarani and Sundquist, eds, *After the Holocaust*.
61 Roig, *Noche y niebla*, 344.
62 Joaquim Amat-Piniella (see Marta Marín-Dominè's chapter 15 in this volume) and Amadeo Sinca Vendrell were the first of the Mauthausen survivors whose testimony (or, in Amat-Piniella's case, fictionalized account thereof) was published. Sinca Vendrell's report was published in 1946 in Spanish in France with a limited edition of 1,500, and much later in Spain as *Lo que Dante no pudo imaginar*. Amat-Piniella wrote *K.L. Reich* in 1946, but it was only published in the 1960s. Other early reports published in France include Manuel Razola and Mariano Constante, *Triangle bleu*. Letters by Pere Vives i Clavé about his experience of deportation to Mauthausen were published posthumously in 1972: *Cartes des dels camps de concentració*. See also Brenneis, "Carlos Rodríguez del Risco," for discussion of an early testimony of a pro-Franco Mauthausen survivor. See also Brenneis's chapter 14 in this volume for additional discussion of these early Mauthausen survivor publications.
63 Roig, *Els catalans als camps nazis*.
64 Semprún, *La escritura o la vida*, 211. Ferrán and Herrmann point to an exception to his early silence in their introduction to *A Critical Companion*, 10–11.

65 Winter, "Thinking about Silence," 4.
66 Pons Prades, *Morir por la libertad*, 15–16.
67 KZ Gedenkstätte Neuengamme, *Lebensläufe*, 145.
68 López, "Gespräch," 3–5.
69 Ibid., 5.
70 Laub, "Bearing Witness or the Vicissitudes of Listening," in Felman and Laub, *Testimony*, 57–66.
71 LaCapra, *Representing the Holocaust*, xii.
72 Laub, "Bearing Witness," 69.
73 There were many discrepancies; one of these was regarding aforementioned José Ros. He wore a red badge with an "F" but was listed as a Spaniard in Neuengamme's register. KZ Gedenkstätte Neuengamme, *Lebensläufe. Lebensgeschichtliche Interviews mit Überlebenden des KZ Neuengamme. Ein Archiv-Findbuch*, (Hamburg: KZ-Gedenkstätte Neuengamme, 1994), 246–9; "Datenbank Auszug Spanier mit Doubletten."
74 Orth, "Die nationalsozialistischen Konzentrationslager," 60.
75 Paul Weißmann, "Häftlingsbericht 1130, 1958," Folder Thematische Sammlung KZ Neuengamme Archiv, Häftlingsberichte 1115–48. Archive KZ Neuengamme, Hamburg, Germany.
76 S. Cohen, *States of Denial*, 222.

14 Spain's Mauthausen: Narratives of the Nazi Deportation of Spanish Republicans, 1946–2018

SARA J. BRENNEIS

Hundreds of thousands of Spaniards streamed over the border into France as the Spanish Civil War drew to a close in 1939. Their trajectories in exile – from the French internment camps, through coerced service in the Compagnies de Travailleurs Étrangers (CTEs) and the French Army – have been detailed in chapters 9 and 10 in this volume.[1] Germany breached the Maginot Line in May of 1940. The Spaniards in the CTEs and the French military units were now inexorably involved in the Second World War. Captured by the Nazis, they would first be sent to German POW camps (Stalags) throughout Germany. Miguel Serra i Grabolosa, who was sent to Stalag XVII-B in Krems-Gneixendorf, expressed the feelings of many of the Spanish deportees when he remembered that "el tracte dels soldats de la Werhmacht, que ens vigilaven [en el Stalag], no tenia res a veure amb la crueltat que després trobaríem en els SS del camp de Mauthausen" (the treatment by the Werhmacht soldiers, who guarded us [in the Stalag], had nothing to do with the cruelty that we would later encounter with the SS in the Mauthausen camp).[2] These Spaniards waited in the German POW camps while the Nazi authorities made repeated contact with Spanish bureaucrats in an effort to decide what to do with them.

Although Spain has never officially acknowledged its role, Franco's government was complicit in the deportation of Spanish nationals from French internment and German POW camps to Nazi concentration camps.[3] The Germans sent communiqués to members of the Spanish diplomatic corps in Germany as well as to the Franco government – in particular to the office of Ramón Serrano Suñer, who was Franco's foreign minister and brother-in-law – throughout 1940, asking for guidance on how to proceed with the Spaniards they were holding. These were roundly ignored. Serrano Suñer met with Hitler in September 1940. While the minister was still in Berlin, the Gestapo released an order mandating the forced imprisonment of the *Rotspanienkämpfer*, the Spanish "reds" who had fought for the Republic and were in German POW camps: that Serrano Suñer was involved in this order is now widely accepted by historians.[4] This edict formalized an arrangement between the Spanish government and Hitler that was in fact already in effect: the first convoy of Spaniards was deported to Mauthausen on 6 August 1940.

These some four hundred Spanish deportees were herded onto cattle cars at Stalag VII-A in Moosburg, Germany, and sent to the small town of Mauthausen in Upper Austria.[5] Located about 25 kilometres east of Hitler's childhood home of Linz, Mauthausen was renowned for its granite quarries and natural beauty. With Hitler's annexation of Austria in 1938, Mauthausen became the site of that country's first Nazi concentration camp, built as a granite fortress atop a hill overlooking the Danube. The Spaniards who were offloaded at the Mauthausen train station and forced to march the 4 kilometres to the concentration camp, like Joan de Diego, a Catalan man on that first convoy, remembered that "no teníamos ni idea absoluta de aquello" (we had absolutely no idea what it all was).[6] Although Spaniards were sent to concentration camps throughout the Nazi empire, as Gina Herrmann and Andrea Hepworth document in chapters 12 and 13 in this volume, it was Mauthausen that saw the largest contingent of Spanish Republican deportees. Over the next five years, around seventy-two hundred Spaniards were deported to Mauthausen.[7] The majority had been captured by the Wehrmacht as prisoners of war when Germany invaded France in 1940. Although some were civilians – like the well-known 927 Spaniards on a convoy from Angoulême – most had been active in the CTEs, the Foreign Legion, or the Régiments de Marche. The other significant group of Spaniards had been detained in France in 1942 mainly for their clandestine activities related to the French Resistance and deported to the camp in various transports.[8] Only 30 per cent of all the Spaniards deported to Mauthausen – around twenty-two hundred – survived.[9]

Formally classified as a Category III Nazi concentration camp, Mauthausen was not an extermination camp. It was a slave labour camp that confined primarily male international political prisoners, and as the years passed it would receive additional transports of Jews and women. Most if not all of the Jews who arrived in Mauthausen were exterminated upon arrival.[10] The non-Jewish political prisoners for the most part were not gassed; they were, however, treated with murderous cruelty: regularly starved, worked, shot, frozen, and beaten to death by the SS.[11] The Spaniards who arrived in 1940 and 1941 were particular targets. Given their experience in the building trades, they were often tasked with cutting and hauling stone in the Mauthausen quarry and with constructing the main camp. During these years, the Spanish deportees occupied the lowest rung on the Mauthausen camp hierarchy, and they died at an alarming rate.[12]

By 1942, however, the fortunes of the Spaniards had begun to turn. Now camp veterans, they had worked their way up the Mauthausen ladder into positions of relative safety. Although Spaniards continued to perish in Mauthausen -- particularly in the subcamp of Gusen – throughout the camp's years of existence, many obtained privileged positions in the Mauthausen offices, the kitchens, the garages, the barbershop, and other semi-protected spaces. Others became *Kapos* who oversaw their fellow prisoners, affording them protection but also putting themselves in a position to collaborate with the Nazis in the torment of their countrymen. Communists who had been active during the Spanish Civil War and the French Resistance managed to form a clandestine organization inside Mauthausen that functioned to protect and feed fellow Spaniards, while also working to undermine or gather information on the Nazis' activities and the war's progress. Thus the Spaniards inside Mauthausen arguably distinguished themselves from their fellow prisoners during the latter half of their imprisonment, and as a result, their experience of Mauthausen, the concentration camp system, and the policies and practices of the Nazis was unique.

The 5th of May 1945 marked the beginning of a new phase for Spanish perceptions of the camp: just as it ceased operations as a Nazi concentration camp, Mauthausen began its role as a touchstone in Spain's collective memory. The camp has held a place in Spain's national imagination virtually since that liberation day. Over the past eighty years, Spanish survivors, family members, and interested outsiders have created a substantial body of narrative that captures the camp through a Spanish lens. One of the most striking aspects of this diverse corpus is how it grapples with the Spanish experience of Mauthausen as juxtaposed with the Holocaust: some authors stridently defend the use of the term to describe the Spaniards' ordeal; many others tell of a different, deadlier Mauthausen, the one to which Jews were subjected.

From Carlos Rodríguez del Risco's earliest serialized memoir, "Yo he estado en Mauthausen" (I Was in Mauthausen, 1946) to Carlos Hernández de Miguel's social media narrative "@deportado4443" (2015), the Spanish image of Mauthausen has claimed a stake in the country's canon of narrative representations of the Nazi era. These varied texts – encompassing fiction, memoir, graphic novel, drama, film, and historiography – were released mainly in Spain, even during the most repressive years of the Franco dictatorship.[13] Although they have had varying impacts on audiences inside the country, almost none of them have found international acclaim. These representations trace the country's evolving awareness of the deportation of Spanish Republicans to Nazi camps. The narratives were published during four distinct periods and reflect the limitations and concerns of each era: dictatorship (1946–60s), transition (1970s), early to mid-democracy (1980–2012), and contemporary (2008–18). Dictatorship-era survivor narratives such as Rodríguez del Risco's serialized articles and Joaquim Amat-Piniella's novel *K.L. Reich* (1963) overcame strict censorship policies to introduce a public that was almost wholly ignorant of this history to the Spanish presence in the camp. Transition-era texts such as Montserrat Roig's historiography *Els catalans als camps nazis* (Catalans in the Nazi Camps, 1977), considered the foundational oral history of the Spanish deportation, and Mariano Constante's popular memoirs began to paint a clearer picture of the Spanish experience, albeit in a subjective way. A host of memoirs by Mauthausen survivors were published beginning in the early democratic period in Spain through the second decade of the 2000s, communicating an urgency to record survivors' life narratives before they disappeared. Finally, contemporary narrative approximations written by family members or non-survivors, such as Hernández de Miguel's Twitter narrative and Mariano Llorente and Laila Ripoll's play *El triángulo azul* (The Blue Triangle, 2014), also explored by Marilén Loyola in chapter 27 of this volume, have raised the story of the Spaniards in Mauthausen to a new mainstream legitimacy, now without the input or participation of survivors. Spain's Mauthausen has gone through a multi-decade process of transformation that continues to impact the country's historical imagination.[14]

Mauthausen Narratives During the Franco Dictatorship (1946–1960s)

Only two Mauthausen survivors were able to publish versions of their experiences in Spain while Franco was in power, in two strikingly different venues: Carlos Rodríguez del Risco, in his serialized memoir "Yo he estado en Mauthausen," and Joaquim Amat-Piniella, whose novel *K.L. Reich* was based on his ordeal.

Rodríguez del Risco was deported to Mauthausen from Stalag XI-B in Fallingbostel on 9 August 1940. He would be assigned to the Steyr *Kommando* and transferred to the Gusen II satellite camp, where he lived to see liberation day.[15] Less than a year later, his thirty-four-part serialized memoir appeared in the Falange newspaper *Arriba* under the headline "Yo he estado en Mauthausen: *Carlos R. del Risco relata en exclusiva para "Arriba" sus siete años de aventura en el exilio*" (I Was in Mauthausen: *Carlos R. del Risco relates exclusively for "Arriba" his seven years of adventure in exile*; emphasis in the original). This extensive account of Rodríguez del Risco's experience as a refugee in the French camps, fighting on the front lines against the Nazis, his capture in a German Stalag, his deportation to Mauthausen, and his daily encounters and travails inside the camp was the first Spanish Mauthausen narrative to be published inside Spain. Its author and provenance were shrouded in mystery. Rodríguez del Risco was an anti-fascist combatant yet at the same time a Nazi apologist, a victim of the abuses of the SS and witness of the Holocaust while also an antisemite who applauded Spain's return to "peace" under Franco.

In articles published between 20 April and 1 June 1946, Rodríguez del Risco spared no detail of the cruelty of his captors, yet he absolved the Nazis of the most egregious crimes: "el mayor número [de muertes] haya que cargarlos a los jefes de barraca, cabos y enchufados; presos todos ellos como sus víctimas, pero inducidos por las S.S. con métodos más o menos violentos" (the largest number [of deaths] must be attributed to the barrack bosses, the *Kapos* and the well-positioned; prisoners who were all like their victims, but who were induced by the SS with more or less violent methods).[16] He admitted that the Jews had been singled out for the deadliest violence but betrayed his antisemitism by writing, "es preciso reconocer que todos los israelitas que pasaron por Mauthausen confirmaron la tesis de que 'los judíos son una raza deleznable.'" (one must recognize that all of the Israelites who passed through Mauthausen confirmed the thesis that "the Jews are a despicable race").[17] And he had only kind words for Hitler, calling him a "true patriot" who "siente la necesidad imperiosa de trabajar por el resurgimiento de su país ... elevando a la nación muy por encima de aquellos que la humillaron con la victoria militar" (feels the pressing need to work for the resurgence of his country ... elevating the nation well above those who humiliated it with military victories).[18] Yet Rodríguez del Risco also painted an accurate picture of the Spanish experience of the camp, from his day-to-day privations with the Steyr *Kommando*, to the twenty-five lashes meted out by the SS for seemingly innocuous infractions, to the convoys of Russians and Yugoslavs who were treated with supreme inhumanity. These contradictions would have made Rodríguez del Risco's pioneering narrative of the Spanish deportation to Mauthausen the single most contentious account to emerge from this historical episode, had it not been entirely relegated to obscurity.

A series of bureaucratic manouevres allowed Rodríguez del Risco to return unharmed to his homeland after the war's end, despite having left as a vanquished enemy. The author is not mentioned by any of his fellow survivors in eight successive decades of Mauthausen narratives, a marginalization that suggests how "Yo he estado en Mauthausen" was able to navigate Franco's iron-fisted press censorship regarding the presence of Spaniards in Nazi camps.[19] Rodríguez del Risco seemingly collaborated with his pro-Franco editor at *Arriba*, narrating in this series of articles his gradual conversion from Republican fighter to Hitler apologist. He mused over this process:

> Podría encontrar todavía divergencia de conceptos entre el actual Régimen y mi antiguo modo de pensar; pudiera sentirme monárquico o republicano, e incluso notar – que no lo noto – algún ligero resquemor hacia la figura humilde y buena, cristiana y española del Generalísimo.

> I would still be able to find a conceptual divergence between the Regime today and my old way of thinking; I would have been able to see myself as a monarchist or a Republican, and even note – which I do not – some light resentment toward the humble and good, Christian and Spanish figure of the Generalísimo [Franco].[20]

This lack of rancour towards the dictator set Rodríguez del Risco apart from his contemporaries in Mauthausen, aligning him instead with the regime and with contemporary Holocaust trivializers. Even so, the author's series is the foundational Spanish Mauthausen narrative, roundly ignored in light of better-known memoirs of the Third Reich.[21]

The first recognized narrative to emerge from the Spanish ordeal in Mauthausen, however, was Joaquim Amat-Piniella's novel, *K.L. Reich*.[22] Amat-Piniella survived four and a half years in the Nazi camp, and he began writing a draft of what would become Spain's touchstone novel of the deportation just months after his liberation. He published fragments in two Catalan magazines in 1945 and 1947 in France and Spain, but the full volume would not see the light of day until 1963.[23] Writing in Catalan, Amat-Piniella acquiesced to a number of substantive changes and published the Castilian translation first in order to be able to release the book under Franco's stringent censorship laws. Nevertheless, *K.L. Reich* was a revelation: it painted a portrait of Mauthausen (unnamed in the text, but nevertheless identifiable) that left no stone unturned. From the lowest of the *Muselmann* prisoners – the walking dead – to the cruel *Kapos* and the German high command, Amat-Piniella explored the relations between national groups, among individual prisoners, and between the prisoners and the Nazis in harrowing detail. (See chapter 15 in this volume for Marta Marín-Dòmine's critical reading of the novel.)

Emili, *K.L. Reich*'s protagonist and a foil for the author, becomes disillusioned with the Spanish clandestine organization when he realizes it is infected with the same kind of corruption he has witnessed outside the camp's walls: "La gent és apàtica i egoista. Ningú no creu que valgui la pena d'intentar res" (People are apathetic and selfish. No one thinks it's worth the effort to try).[24] Yet Emili also recognizes that the Spaniards' efforts at resistance and survival set them apart from the Jews who are being exterminated en masse in the camp. Witnessing the atrocities perpetrated against Jews as they are beaten and killed almost immediately after passing through the gates produces in Emili an unsettling sensation: "Un món d'espectres es movia sota els seus ulls closos, enmig d'un silenci més punyent que els udols de terror d'una estona abans" (A world of spectres shifted behind his closed eyes through a silence even more shrill than the howls of terror a little while before).[25]

One of the most sublime qualities of *K.L. Reich* is Amat-Piniella's ability to capture the conflicting emotions produced by the camp's central events, as experienced by individual prisoners from Viçent, a Catalan man who dies as a direct result of his insatiable hunger, to Hans Gupper, the camp's second-in-command Nazi officer, who is sympathetic to the Spaniards while having "adquirit l'aurèola dels herois a força de matar jueus i comunistes" (acquired his hero's laurels through the murder of Jews and communists).[26] As the first Mauthausen survivor fiction published in Spain, *K.L. Reich* quietly joined other seminal Holocaust narratives, yet it has never been recognized as a canonical work of Second World War fiction. The novel remains an underappreciated window into the ordeal of Spanish political prisoners caught in the Nazi concentrationary machine who witnessed the suffering of Jews in the Holocaust.

Mauthausen Comes to Light during the Spanish Transition (1970s)

By the 1970s, Spaniards would begin to conceptualize the Spanish experience of Mauthausen thanks to a series of publications that sparked audiences' interest. The highly visible Spanish Mauthausen ex-deportee Mariano Constante, safely in exile in France, published three increasingly melodramatic accounts of his survival throughout the decade.[27] In *Los años rojos* (The Red Years, 1974), *Yo fui ordenanza de los SS* (I Was an Orderly for the SS, 1976), and *Triángulo azul* (Blue triangle, 1979), Constante spun subjective tales of his imprisonment, his central role with the communists in the Spanish clandestine resistance organization inside the camp, his privileged role as an SS orderly, and his continuing postwar efforts to preserve the legacy of the Spanish Republicans in the camp.[28] Each memoir tells a slightly different version of the same story of fortitude, solidarity, and resistance, and this burnished Constante's reputation as the decade wore on. However,

Constante's quest to position himself as *über*-survivor rankled his fellow Mauthausen ex-deportees, who called him out for his questionable facts and rose-coloured narratives. Though romanticized, his accounts began a process of placing the stories of the Spanish deportees in the public eye – a process that would take on new life at the turn of the twentieth century.

But it was Montserrat Roig's oral history of the Catalans in Mauthausen and other Nazi camps, published originally in Catalan as *Els catalans als camps nazis* (Catalans in the Nazi camps) in 1977 and in a Castilian translation a year later, that had the greatest impact on narratives of the Spanish deportation. As Rosa Toran also relates in chapter 17, Roig was inspired to dig into the topic in part by the 1972 publication of Pere Vives i Clavé's slim volume of letters, *Cartes des dels camps de concentració* (Letters from the Concentration Camps).[29] Published posthumously, Vives's volume collected the sensitive intellectual's missives to his family from his increasingly dire surroundings in a series of French internment camps and a German Stalag. But on arriving in Mauthausen, he fell silent. He was killed by lethal injection in Mauthausen on 31 October 1941, months after his deportation to the camp. His experience inspired not only many of his compatriots – including Amat-Piniella, who dedicated *K.L. Reich* to his close friend – but also Roig, a non-survivor and journalist who was motivated by Vives's moving account to delve into the unknown story of the deportees.

The result was a massive tome of unparalleled historical significance. Over the course of five years of research, Roig sought out and interviewed scores of Spanish and Catalan concentration camp survivors, collecting and curating their fragile memories. She provided necessary historical context while also stamping the book with her distinct defence of the people she called, intimately, "els nostres deportats." Roig's voice joined the voices of "her deportees," adding editorial commentary that defended the subjectivity of the survivors' accounts and in no uncertain terms laid the blame for their ordeal and death at the hands of Franco himself. In her homage to the Catalans in Nazi camps, the author privileged the words of the individuals, allowing their perspectives to rise to the surface. They discussed matters both seemingly banal – the daily filth, the starvation rations, the favourite abuses of the SS – and momentous – the public hanging of the attempted escapee Hans Bonarewitz, the gradual Spanish infiltration of the Gestapo's inner offices, and the camp's chaotic liberation.

With an appendix that revealed, for the first time, the names and identifying information of thousands of Catalans who entered the camps, *Els catalans als camps nazis* became a point of reference for every successive historiographic narrative of the Spanish deportation. Many Spanish families were only able to confirm what they had long suspected about the fate of their loved ones who disappeared over the border in 1939 by scouring Roig's volume decades later. Roig was criticized for limiting her work to Catalan survivors and for aligning herself with the communists; nevertheless, her work provided a staggering amount of detail that has been corroborated by historians of the Spanish deportation in the interim.[30] In the introduction, Roig described the moment when she realized that the Holocaust resonated in Spain:

Aleshores vaig adonar-me que el nazisme no era per a nosaltres només cosa de les pel·lícules o dels llibres d'història, no altres només la 'qüestió jueva' o la resistència als països ocupats durant la guerra, el nazisme havia perseguit gent de casa nostra, gent que parlava la meva llengua.

It was then that I realized that for us Nazism wasn't just a thing from movies and history books, nothing more than the "Jewish question" or the resistance in the occupied countries during the war, rather Nazism had persecuted our people, people who spoke my language.[31]

With *Els catalans als camps nazis*, Roig made the story of the Spanish deportation to Nazi camps relevant to a generation of Spaniards coming of age in a newly post-dictatorial Spain who were only vaguely aware of their traumatic past.[32]

Mauthuasen Life Narratives during the Democratic Period (1980–2012)

The 1980s and early 1990s in Spain saw a relative lull in Spanish Mauthausen narratives, plausibly because of the country's tumultuous transition from dictatorship to democracy. Antonio Sinca Vendrell's personalized historiography *Lo que Dante no pudo imaginar* (What Dante Could Not Imagine, 1980) inaugurated the decade.[33] Chronicling the author's arrival with the first transport of Spaniards deported to Mauthausen and his survival until liberation day, Sinca Vendrell's account was the first non-fiction book about Mauthausen published by a Spanish survivor. The author combined historical information about Mauthausen with florid prose describing his passage through the camp, giving the work its title: "Mi impresión era tan intensa que el interior del campo me lo imaginaba como si fuese el infierno de Dante" (My impression was so intense that I imagined the interior of the camp as if it were Dante's inferno).[34] Sinca Vendrell paved the way for the dozens of Spanish Mauthausen survivor memoirs published in the 1990s and the first decade of the 2000s: he reflected on history as he lived it, suffering in the French internment camps, finding solidarity among the Spaniards in Mauthausen, and being transferred to the even more horrific surroundings of the Gusen subcamp. He aimed to leave a record of his – and his compatriots' – unimaginable ordeal, which he illustrated with his first-hand account of men being drowned in the Gusen showers: "Hago esta narración y afirmo haberlo presenciado. Durante este martirio escuché dos veces la voz de dos españoles que decían: '¡Muchachos, tened suerte ...! Aguantad y cuando regreséis a nuestro país, haced que el mundo sepa cómo se moría en Gusen'" (I create this narration and affirm having lived it. Twice during this martyrdom I heard the voice of two Spaniards who said: "Guys, good luck ...! Resist and when you return to our country, make sure the world knows how people died in Gusen").[35]

Lo que Dante no pudo imaginar captured the spirit and subjectivity of a host of Spanish life narratives that emerged years later. These memoirs almost invariably followed a particular equation: each was a first-person account of a Spanish Mauthausen survivor that focused primarily on his years in the camp, displayed the literary idiosyncrasies of a non-professional author, were often written with the aid of an editor (usually a relative of the author), and were released to little fanfare and with a limited distribution by a small regional press in Spain. The more than two dozen Mauthausen life narratives published in Spain between 1995 and 2012 are visceral introductions to Spaniards' daily existence in Mauthausen, as experienced by men who were often afforded some kind of privilege to enable them to survive. They are subjective and detailed memoirs that delve into details such as the regimented process of first entering the camp – warnings from camp veterans, stripping naked, shaving, showers, barrack assignment – the starvation rations,[36] the brutal conditions in Gusen, and the names of friends and relations who didn't survive to liberation day.

The Spanish Mauthausen memoirists, writing at a time when European nations had begun to systematically address their role in the Holocaust, often examined the differences between the Spaniards and the Jews in the camp. Lope Massaguer was conscious that "[s]er *Rotspanier* [rojo español] en Mauthausen era estar dispuesto a los más atroces castigos, ser *Juden* [judío] era todavía peor, significaba la peor de las muertes" (to be *Rotspanier* [a Spanish Red] in Mauthausen was to be prepared for the most atrocious punishments, to be *Juden* [Jewish] was even worse, it meant the worst of deaths),[37] while Antonio García Barón knew that "[l]os judíos nunca duraban con vida más de un mes" (the Jews never lasted more than a month alive).[38] Because Raimundo Suñer worked in the SS garages, he was a witness to the journeys of the "coche fantasma" that gassed prisoners. Suñer described cleaning out the "ghost car" after it had served its mortal purpose: "Dentro encontraba señales de las personas: vello, sangre, trozos de ropa y hasta sesos" (Inside I found signs of people: hair, blood, pieces of clothing and even brains).[39] These men were witnesses to the Holocaust who also had a personal experience of Mauthausen, one that had been ignored by their government, their countrymen, and the world. They felt a sense of urgency to communicate what they had experienced there, including as much historical background as they could to corroborate their stories. As José de Dios Amill wrote in 1995:

> Sobre el holocausto nazi hay un sinfín de libros que describen la persecución del mundo hebreo pero se ha escrito muy poco, y gran parte del mundo lo ignora, sobre los millones de personas no judías que también perecieron en los campos de concentración.

> There are innumerable books about the Nazi Holocaust that describe the persecution of the Jewish world but very little has been written – and much of the world ignores it – about the millions of non-Jewish people who also perished in the concentration camps.[40]

These Spanish and Catalan Mauthausen memoirs were a last plea from the survivors themselves to remember their ordeal for posterity.

Contemporary Mauthausen Representations (2008–18)

As the number of Mauthausen survivors has dwindled over the last ten years, the task of representing the Spanish experience of the camp has fallen to a new generation of writers. While they can be criticized for banalizing their historical source material and profiting from the Spanish public's renewed interest in its past, they all expose new audiences to the fact of the deportation of Spaniards to Nazi concentration camps. Unlike with previous representations, however, the focus remains firmly on the Spaniards: these texts tend not to broach the presence of Jews in Mauthausen. Thus they have allowed Spanish Mauthausen representations to drift further away from the genre of Holocaust narrative and closer to a particularly Spanish resurrection of the collective memory of the Second World War.

Joanna Melenchón i Xamena's 2008 novel *Mauthausen, des de l'oblit* (Mauthausen, from Oblivion) was the first attempt to fictionalize the story of the Spaniards in Mauthausen by a second-generation survivor.[41] The author is a niece of Rafel Xamena, who died in Gusen in 1942.[42] She composed her novel as a metatextual Mauthausen memoir in the vein of what Marianne Hirsch has termed post-memorial accounts of second-generation Holocaust survivors.[43] Melenchón i Xamena displays the process of identifying, investigating, and rejoining Rafel's story to the historical record of Mauthausen survivors. However, the novel focuses more on the narrator's quest to understand her family and herself than on a detailed retelling of a Mauthausen victim's experience. In this regard, her novel reflects Spain's present-day mission to find and reassemble the pieces of its collective memory. The book was published a year after the passage of Spain's Law of Historical Memory, which attempted to regulate how the country was to interact with the scars of the Spanish Civil War and the Franco dictatorship. The law mentioned the Spanish deportation to Nazi camps only in passing, and in that regard, this novel demonstrates the reverberations of a national effort to recuperate Spain's historical memory at a grassroots level.

Carlos Hernández de Miguel, the nephew of a Spanish Mauthausen survivor, has also ridden a wave of interest in the country's historical memory via his Twitter account "@deportado4443."[44] This narrative serialized Antonio Hernández's imprisonment in and liberation from Mauthausen in 140 character bursts. In another post-memorial effort, Hernández de Miguel adopted the voice of his uncle, resurrecting a Mauthausen survivor through the dynamic interactions possible on social media. Over the course of five months during 2015, the author posted short missives that sought to capture the incredulity, pain, and joy of a Spanish Mauthausen prisoner. The immediacy of these messages seemingly sent from inside Mauthausen's walls some seventy years earlier placed the reader – Twitter followers around the world – in Antonio's shoes. Indeed, these observers were able to interact apocryphally with Antonio by sending messages, re-emitting, and showing their approval of individual tweets. Hernández de Miguel fictionalized his uncle's ordeal by inserting historical context and interactions with other prisoners and Nazis into his narrative, as well as images and video that would only be available decades later. In this sense, "@deportado4443" risks conflating an imagined autobiography with the actual accounts of Spanish deportees to Mauthausen published since 1945. Via the self-aware Antonio, Hernández de Miguel curated the Spanish experience of Mauthausen for a generation that had a limited knowledge of the Spanish deportation. Writing messages such as "Otro día en la cantera. Si sigo con vida es porque realizo un trabajo especializado y no cargo piedras casi nunca. Pero, ¡han muerto tantos!"

284   Sara J. Brenneis

(Another day in the quarry. If I continue alive it is because I perform specialized work and I hardly ever haul stone. But, so many have died!) gives some sense of the violence of the Nazis while also acknowledging the privilege that allowed many Spaniards to survive Mauthausen.[45] Ultimately, to tell a story of the Spanish experience of Mauthausen for the digital age, Hernández de Miguel took advantage of the flexibility of social media while returning to the classic serialized adventure story pioneered by Rodríguez del Risco. Even after the narrative of Antonio Hernández's imprisonment concluded, the "@deportado4443" Twitter account has remained active: as of this writing, Hernández de Miguel's reincarnation of his uncle – who died in 1992 – continues to weigh in on the ever-unfolding memory debates in Spain.

El violinista de Mauthausen (The violinist of Mauthausen, 2009) by Andres Pérez Domínguez, *Lo que esconde tu nombre* (*The Scent of Lemon Leaves*, 2010) by Clara Sánchez, and *Prisionero en Mauthausen* (Prisoner in Mauthausen, 2011) by Toni Carbos and Javier Cosnava collectively represent the turn towards mass media that narratives of the Spanish deportation to Mauthausen have taken in the first decade of the 2000s.[46] These publications have banalized Mauthausen for the purposes of entertainment, but they have also brought the historical fact of the deportation to new audiences. They fictionalize and sensationalize historical events in an effort to elicit adventure and melodrama out of the suffering and death of the Spanish deportees. *El violinista de Mauthausen* focuses on a love triangle set during and just after the Second World War: one of the characters, Ruben, is a Spaniard imprisoned in Mauthausen. Through Ruben, the author delves into the dynamics of the Spaniards there, describing the camp and the violence of the SS. One German bystander serves as the voice of the reader's conscience when he imagines: "nadie quiere saber la verdad, por qué desaparece la gente y ya no se la vuelve a ver nunca más, qué sucede en los sitios adonde se los llevan" (no one wanted to know the truth, why people disappear and are never seen again, what happens in the places they are taken).[47] Pérez Domínguez's novel imagines these inner workings of the camp as part of a larger drama of human suffering.

Sánchez's novel was inspired by the communities of Nazis who fled to Spain and lived in hiding during the postwar period (David Messenger writes about these Nazi cells in chapter 26, while Stacy N. Beckwith writes more on Clara Sánchez's novel in chapter 29 of this volume). In the novel, former SS come into direct contact with their former Spanish Mauthausen prisoners in a town in Alicante.[48] Sánchez provides a window inside Mauthausen through the perspective of two ex-deportees who become "Nazi hunters," seeking justice for thousands of Spanish victims. The novel also tackles the complicated memory of Spanish Mauthausen survivors, as one ex-deportee recalls:

No nos sentíamos como héroes, sino más bien como unos apestados. Éramos víctimas, y nadie quiere a las víctimas ni a los perdedores. Otros no tuvieron más remedio que callar y sufrir el miedo, la vergüenza y la culpa de los supervivientes, pero nosotros nos convertimos en cazadores ...

We didn't feel like heroes. Plague-ridden, more like it. We were victims – and nobody wants victims or losers. Others had no alternative but to keep quiet and suffer the fear, shame and guilt of survivors, but we became hunters ...[49]

The tale of victims of Nazi atrocities hunting down their torturers glorifies what has in reality been an uphill battle for recognition and justice for ex-deportees inside Spain.

Prisionero en Mauthausen takes an even more vivid approach to reimagining the ordeal of the Spaniards in Mauthausen via a graphic novel. Through the sensationalized story of Juan Placambó, a Spanish Mauthausen prisoner who becomes a *Kapo* tasked with victimizing his own countrymen and spying for the Nazis, the authors portray Mauthausen as a sordid space of violence and treason among the Spaniards. The genre of graphic novel lends itself to glorified violence: in one frame, we see an SS dog rip the arm off an agonizing prisoner while two SS laugh.

All three of these novels treat the years of imprisonment and death of Spaniards in Mauthausen as background for dramatic tales of mystery and violence. While they tap into historical fact – describing, for instance, the Mauthausen quarry as a site of Spanish victimization and incorporating actual figures such as the camp commander Franz Zeireis into their narratives – a historically accurate depiction of the Spaniards in Mauthausen remains firmly secondary to the plotting in these novels. They straddle the line between exploiting and exposing the Spanish experience in Mauthausen for a popular audience.

Llorente and Ripoll's 2014 musical drama, *El triángulo azul*,[50] imagines perhaps the most noted accomplishment of the Spanish prisoners of Mauthausen: Francesc Boix and Antoni García's secret preservation of photographic evidence of Nazi violence.[51] The authors of this dramatic representation of the Spanish deportation to Mauthausen return to a literary recourse last seen in Amat-Piniella's novel: a top-down examination of the universe of the camp, from high-ranking Nazi officers to the most expendable of prisoners. In a departure from the many contemporary Spanish Mauthausen representations that filter the story through the perspective of a Spanish prisoner, the playwrights ask the audience to empathize with the guilt and grief of an individual Nazi officer, Paul Ricken. The play's outline is rooted in historical fact: Ricken was the SS officer who oversaw the Mauthausen laboratory where Boix and García worked and where Boix masterminded the smuggling out of damning photographic evidence that he later presented at the Nuremberg trials.[52] In the play's closing moments, Ricken describes how the photographs of Mauthausen that "Paco" spirited out of the camp with the help of young Spanish prisoners incriminated the Nazis: "Gracias a esos negativos que los españoles sacaron del campo se pudo demostrar nuestra culpabilidad" (It is thanks to those negatives that the Spaniards took out of the camp that our guilt was able to be demonstrated).[53] Ricken insists, however, that he and his fellow Nazis will not suffer retribution for the Holocaust in general: "Y aun así no pagaré, no pagaremos" (Even so I won't pay, we won't pay).[54]

One Spaniard tells Ricken that the legacy of the Nazis will fade to black, while their victims will be afforded a rekindled future: "Para ustedes la noche. Para nosotros, el día" (For you the night. For us, the day).[55] These references to light and dark bring the metaphor of photography to bear on the fine line between good and evil encountered within the perverse morality of a Nazi concentration camp. As depicted in *El triángulo azul*, the Spaniards in Mauthausen – and indeed some of the Nazis as well – were neither heroes nor villains, but rather complex individuals victimized by the Nazis who lived and died responding in a variety of ways to the endless violence in the camp. Llorente and Ripoll do not shy away from the discomfort, humour, humanity, and sadism that are integral not only to the original experience of the Spaniards in Mauthausen but also to the collective memory that seeks to reinvigorate their ordeal for new generations of Spaniards.

A recent addition to the body of post-memorial Mauthausen narrative returns to the genre of the graphic novel. *El fotógrafo de Mauthausen* (The Mauthausen Photographer, 2018) depicts Francesc Boix from his entry into Mauthausen in 1941 to his testimony at Nuremberg in 1946. Originally published in France, this visual rendering of Mauthausen strives to remain faithful to the underlying legacy of the Spaniards in the camp, fortified by the inclusion of drawings that reproduce the photos Boix helped save and bring to international attention. However, the graphic novel is also shaded by melodrama and comic book depictions of Nazi violence. It folds in a number of spurious episodes – Boix attacking Ricken, a scenario that would have resulted in the immediate elimination of Boix, had it actually occurred – that sensationalize Boix, in particular, as an untouchable superhero. Nevertheless, *El fotógrafo de Mauthausen* has had an influence beyond the page. Its particular combination of pictorial accuracy and counterfactual heroism is also captured in the first cinematic portrayal of Boix and the Spaniards in Mauthausen: the identically-named *El fotógrafo de Mauthausen*, directed by Mar Targarona and released the same year.[56] By eschewing historical rigour in favour of audacity and suspense, the graphic novel and major motion picture anticipate future Mauthausen representations that aim to mould a narrative arc out of the raw material of the Spaniards who were imprisoned and died in Mauthausen.

As a whole, the Mauthausen narratives published in Spain from 1946 to 2018 constitute an interdependent body of texts that draw from survivors' memories and historical volumes in an attempt to represent the horror of life and death as a political prisoner in a Nazi concentration camp during the Second World War. Over the decades, these texts have deepened the public's understanding of the Nazi deportation of Spanish Republicans and have begun to add this historical moment to the country's collective memory movement, which at one time had been largely restricted to recuperating the Spanish Civil War and the Franco dictatorship. As Mauthausen survivors disappear, however, some contemporary narratives risk dehistoricizing the ordeal of the Spaniards in the interest of appealing to mass audiences. Nevertheless, these representations of the Spaniards in Mauthausen implicitly argue for the relevance of this non-Jewish population of concentration camp prisoners to Spain's involvement in the Second World War and the Holocaust. In these narratives, the breadth of humanity and human suffering is on display. By their mere presence, they ask readers to – at the very least – remember the Spaniards who suffered and died at the hands of the Nazis.

NOTES

1 Along with Geneviève Dreyfus-Armand and Robert Coale's authoritative accounts in this volume, see Soo, *The Routes to Exile.*
2 Roig, *Els catalans als camps nazis*, 182. Unless otherwise indicated, all translations are my own.
3 See Fonseca, "La deuda de España." Juan M. Calvo Gascón and Rosa Toran also discuss aspects of this complicity in chapters 11 and 17, respectively, in this volume.
4 Bermejo and Checa, *Libro memorial*, 19.
5 Many of the Spanish nationals deported to Mauthausen were Catalan, a fact reflected in the higher ratio of Catalan survivors who would subsequently write about their experiences.

6 Joan de Diego, interview by Mercedes Vilanova (Vienna: Archiv der KZ-Gedenkstätte Mauthausen [AMM], 2002), OH/ZP1/178.

7 Casimir Climent i Sarrió, a Spaniard who worked as a clerk in the Politische Abteilung, the Gestapo's branch office in Mauthausen, counted 7,187 Spaniards who entered the camp in "Ya es hora ..." Hans Marsálek, an Austrian Mauthausen prisoner and, like Climent, a camp clerk, arrived at 7,189 Spaniards deported to Mauthausen in *Die Geschichte des Konzentrationlagers Mauthausen*, 237.

8 Bermejo and Checa, *Libro memorial*, 16–17.

9 Climent counted 2,183 who were liberated and 4,765 who were killed: "Ya es hora ..." Marsálek calculated 2,187 Spanish survivors: *Die Geschichte des Konzentrationlagers Mauthausen*, 161.

10 Daniel Goldhagen records, for instance, that between November 1942 and December 1943, the death rate for the Jews who arrived at Mauthausen was 100 per cent: *Hitler's Willing Executioners*, 312. Mauthausen had a gas chamber, but the Nazis also gassed Mauthausen prisoners at nearby Hartheim Castle.

11 Approximately five hundred Spanish prisoners were gassed at Hartheim Castle. Roig, *Els catalans*, 200.

12 Some 6,690 Spaniards entered Mauthausen between 1940 and 1941 (94.9 per cent of the total number of Spaniards who would eventually arrive in the camp); by the winter of 1942, only three thousand were still alive. Toran, *Vida i mort*, 165.

13 A number were published first in France, then republished in Spain.

14 See also Brenneis, *Spaniards in Mauthausen*.

15 Bermejo and Checa, *Libro memorial*, 299.

16 Rodríguez del Risco, "Yo he estado en Mauthausen," 3.

17 Ibid., 8 May 1946, 4.

18 Ibid., 7 May 1946, 4.

19 See Brenneis, "Carlos Rodríguez del Risco."

20 Rodríguez del Risco, "Yo he estado en Mauthausen," 3 June 1946, 3.

21 Well-known early international Holocaust survivor narratives such as Antelme, *L'espèce humaine*, Lengyel, *Souvenirs de l'au-delà*, Levi, *Se questo è un uomo*, Rousset, *L'univers concentrationnaire*, and Szpilman, *Śmierć miasta*, are Rodríguez del Risco's contemporaries.

22 The Catalan author Mercè Rodoreda published "Nit i boira," a short story based on Mauthausen, in Mexico in 1947. The story was not widely known, however, until it was published in Spain in 1978. See Brenneis, "Moral Ambiguity in Mauthausen."

23 Amat-Piniella published "La fam" in *Per Catalunya* in Nice in 1945 and "Eutanàsia" in *Antologia dels fets* in Barcelona in 1947.

24 Amat-Piniella, *K.L. Reich: novella* (1963), 127; in English, *K.L. Reich* (2014), 106.

25 Amat-Piniella, *K.L. Reich:* (1963), 144; in English, *K.L. Reich* (2014), 123.
26 Amat-Piniella, *K.L. Reich* (1963), 51–2; in English, *K.L. Reich* (2014), 39. The character of Hans Gupper is based on Georg Bachmayer, the Nazi captain under Franz Ziereis from March 1940 until Mauthausen's liberation. Bachmayer poisoned himself, his wife, and his children as the US Army approached the camp in 1945.
27 Two of these volumes were originally published in France, then translated for a Spanish audience: Constante, *Les années rouges*; Razola and Constante, *Triangle bleu.*
28 Constante, *Los años rojos*; idem, *Yo fui ordenanza de los SS*; Razola and Constante, *Triángulo azul.*
29 Vives i Clavé, *Cartes des dels camps de concentració.*
30 See Bermejo, *El fotògraf de l'horror*; Bermejo and Checa, *Libro memorial*; Pike, *Spaniards in the Holocaust.*
31 Roig, *Els catalans*, 13.
32 Roig also wove the story of the Catalans in Nazi camps into her fictional work of the era. See Brenneis, *Genre Fusion*, 52–69.
33 Sinca Vendrell, *Lo que Dante no pudo imaginar*. Sinca Vendrell's volume was first published by a small press in France, in 1946, within months of Rodríguez del Risco's articles. The author sought a publisher in Spain for decades from his exile in France.
34 Sinca Vendrell, *Lo que Dante no pudo imaginar*, 88.
35 Ibid., 114–15.
36 Calcerrada Guijarro and Pavón Mariblanca, *Republicanos españoles en Mauthausen-Gusen*, 140.
37 Massaguer and García-Maroto, *Mauthausen, fin de trayecto*, 151.
38 Leguineche, *El precio del paraíso*, 112.
39 Suñer Aguas, *De Calaceite a Mauthausen*, 250.
40 Dios Amill, *La verdad sobre Mauthausen*, 59.
41 Melenchón i Xamena, *Mauthausen, des de l'oblit.*
42 Both in the novel and in actuality, Rafel Xamena's (or Chamena's) death in Mauthausen was recorded in Roig's *Els catalans als camps nazis*, 703.
43 See Hirsch, *Generation of Postmemory.*
44 Hernández de Miguel collected and published this narrative as Hernández de Miguel and Ensis, *Deportado 4443: Sus tuits ilustrados.*
45 Carlos Hernández de Miguel, "Otro día en la cantera," ed. @deportado4443 (2015), Tweet.
46 Pérez Domínguez, *El violinista de Mauthausen*; Sánchez, *Lo que esconde tu nombre*; idem, *The Scent of Lemon Leaves*; Carbos and Cosnava, *Prisionero en Mauthausen.*
47 Pérez Domínguez, *El violinista de Mauthausen*, 354.

48 In giving one of the Mauthausen survivors an apocryphal concentration-camp tattoo (the Nazis tattooed prisoners only at the Auschwitz complex), Sánchez demonstrates how Spanish writers often borrow from Holocaust tropes in order to suggest equations between genocidal and political victims of the Reich, and thus also wades into a process of Holocaust dehistoricization or popularization common in many contemporary Holocaust novels. Sánchez, *Lo que esconde tu nombre*, 247.
49 Ibid., 11; idem, *The Scent of Lemon Leaves*, 3.
50 Llorente and Ripoll, *El triángulo azul*.
51 See Bermejo, *El fotògraf de l'horror*; Pike, *Spaniards in the Holocaust*. Chapters 15, 17, 27, and 28 in this volume also discuss aspects of Boix's story.
52 Ricken's suicide at the end of the play, however, is pure fiction. Ricken died in Düsseldorf in 1964 (Rubio, Colombo, and Landa, *El fotógrafo de Mauthausen*, 140).
53 Llorente and Ripoll, *El triángulo azul*, 123.
54 Ibid., 124.
55 Ibid.
56 Llorenç Soler's *Francesc Boix: un fotógrafo en el infierno* (2000) was the first documentary film to recover Boix's legacy. See Brenneis, *Spaniards in Mauthausen*, 210–13 as well as Isabel Estada's chapter 28 in this volume.

15 Joaquim Amat-Piniella's Novel *K.L. Reich*: The Gaze of the Political Deportee

MARTA MARÍN-DÒMINE

It could be argued that the novel *K.L. Reich* (1963) by Catalan author Joaquim Amat-Piniella holds a rather symbolic place within the Spanish as well as Catalan narrative discourse constructed around concentration camps, and more specifically around the camp of Mauthausen. The extra-literary information that surrounds the reception of *K.L. Reich* makes it suited for a particular case study. Factors such as the difficulty the author found in first publishing the novel, the two versions of it in circulation since 2000, and the place it occupies in the cultural imaginary as the result of being the first Catalan novel about the experience of Spaniards deported to Mauthausen all contribute to a certain mythification. So *K.L. Reich* has not yet been the object of a critical approach unbound from the repetitive commonplaces used to describe the novel.

Joaquim Amat-Piniella was born in 1913 in Manresa, a village not far from Barcelona. In his early twenties he became very active in the cultural and political milieu of that village. In 1936, when the Spanish Civil War broke out, he volunteered for the Republican anti-fascist army, in which he fought until the end of the war. After the fall of Barcelona to Franco's army in February 1939, he sought refuge in France, crossing the border in July 1939. Like many, he found himself in one of the makeshift internment camps set up by the French government in the southeast of the country, and he was sent to the Companies of Foreign Workers to carry out various military tasks after the Second World War began. He was captured by the Germans and deported to Mauthausen in January 1941. (The common trajectories of exiled Spaniards in France is detailed in chapters by Dreyfus-Armand and Coale in this volume; their deportation to Mauthausen in the chapter by Brenneis.) After the camp was liberated in May 1945, he found refuge in Andorra, where he began writing the first draft of *K.L. Reich* in Catalan. He continued to work on it upon his return to Catalonia in 1946 and did not consider the novel finished until 1955, as can be attested by his correspondence with Catalan poet Agustí Bartra, who was exiled in Mexico at that time.[1]

K.L. Reich is a fictionalized account of the experience of Amat-Piniella in Mauthausen. The novel focuses on a group of Spaniards: Emili is the main character; Francesc is his best friend and a key character in building Emili's testimonial role, as we will see. Alongside these two protagonists a set of secondary characters unfold, among whom Rubio, a leader of the communist clandestine organization, and August, the anarchist leader, stand out. *K.L. Reich* is highly referential, and this has invited some critics and scholars to read it as a historical document.[2] It has to be pointed out, however, that half of the novel is devoted to the conflict between Rubio and August as a means to represent the opposite ideological positions taken by communists and anarchists, a tension already present at the time of the Spanish Republic and during the Civil War. These disputes have often been overlooked in the Spanish and Catalan critical reception of the novel.

K.L. Reich was not published until 1963, first in its Castilian translation and some months later in its original Catalan. The novel had been rejected twice by Spanish censors. During the many years that Amat-Piniella polished the text he had excluded from it four long fragments, which he kept in a folder, now available in the Municipal Archives of Manresa. In 2001, the year marking the entrance of both Spain and Catalonia to the process of recovering the memory of a long-silenced past, *K.L. Reich* became the object of a new Catalan edition, described by its editor, David Serrano, in the introductory pages, as the "uncensored" original text. This apparently "complete" text claimed to return the original four fragments that the author himself had excised from the manuscript. This rather strategic twist, if we look at it from a commercial perspective, contributed to the belief that the "new" version of *K.L. Reich* was authoritative – that it had saved the "original" from oblivion.[3]

The beginning of the twenty-first century was marked in Spain by an eruption of information about the Nazi camps, most specifically about Mauthausen. Yet the recuperation of this previously ignored history was made without attention to the variations within the concentration camp system. As a result, concentration camps and extermination camps are often treated as interchangeable, with Mauthausen presented as an "extermination" camp, although it was not categorized as such by the Nazis. So it is no surprise that for the general public, the extermination of the European Jews is often equated with deportation of politicals.[4] Some of the literary particulars of *K.L. Reich* can contribute to the study of an epistemology of the political deportation in Nazi camps, towards the development of a methodology for differentiating the testimonial literature of the political deportation from that of the Holocaust and other cultural and ethnic genocides.[5]

Images for a Frozen Vision

The earliest photographs of the "liberation"[6] of the camps were probably the first objects to offer the world a glimpse of what life and above all death had been like in Nazi camps. All of the liberation forces had military or professional photographers and filmmakers who documented the moment they first entered the camps and the chaotic days that followed. These images, especially the ones taken in Bergen-Belsen, Dachau, and Buchenwald, helped shape how the Nazi camps were represented to the point that today they are often wrongly presumed to be images that represent the camps as they were while still functioning.

These images have circulated largely without captions or with misleading information. For their viewers, these photographs and short sequences of film have come to represent the iconography of the "the Nazi horror" even though they are far from capable of showing what life in the camps had been like prior to liberation; that aspect will remain forever off-screen, symbolically inscribed in the encounter between two perspectives: that of the astonished survivor, and that of the incredulous liberator.[7]

The filmmakers and photographers who first entered the camps were aware of how impossible it was to portray the "inside" of the camps; their goal was to make the world if not understand, then at least know. Looking became a way to try to understand. The US army, for instance, forced the civilian populations living near the camps to look at the piles of corpses found in them. The intention was to compel the neighbouring populations to accept what some individuals among them might have been tempted to negate, to ignore, or even to countenance.

In conjunction with this will to match the vision with the truth, in some camps such as Mauthausen, the survivors, fully aware of the exceptionality of their experience, decided to re-enact some key moments of the liberation. In 1945, this sense of vision had an unprecedented prominence. For some readers and viewers, looking at the "pain of others" would have further consequences for their own being in the world.[8] In this sense, the French art historian Georges Didi-Huberman states the crucial role of the gaze in our understanding of the Nazi camps: "Our knowledge of the camps was above all and even before the publication of the first great stories from survivors and those of the first historical analysis, a visual knowledge, journalistically, military and politically filtered, of the camps viewed under the state of destruction performed by the Nazis and as they were found when the allies opened them."[9] Moreover, the corpus of photographs taken inside the Nazi camps during the time they were functioning – with the known exception of four photographs taken clandestinely in Birkenau by the *Sonderkommando* – is the result of the SS's point of view, and therefore in contrast to the general public's perception, these images represent a framing from which the perspective of the victim is excluded.[10]

The photographic corpus of Mauthausen is often referred to in the Hispanic peninsular context as the "photographs of Francesc Boix." This significant series of negatives, saved through the mediation of some Spaniards, including Francesc Boix himself, are comprised mainly of a batch of photographs taken by the SS or by some unknown assistants. The exceptions are the photographs that depict scenes of the liberation of the camp and the days after, which were taken by Boix. (For more on Boix, see chapters 14, 17, 27, and 28 in this volume.) The official photographs can be divided into various series according to their function. When it comes to depicting prisoners, they are taken from a point of view that justifies the prisoners' "less than human" condition and consequently their deportation. Most of the detainees entered the camp after a long journey and under extremely harsh conditions. However, none of these photographs were taken to convey a sense of pity. They stressed facial features, the rags the detainees were wearing, the dirt, all seeming to point to the "barbaric" nature of the detainees. It is precisely because of the nature of these photographs that the opening of the exhibit *La part visible des camps* (The Visible Part of the Camps) stirred so much controversy among some survivors of Mauthausen. Daniel Simon, president of the French Amicale de Mauthausen, commented on his apprehension as follows:

> The doubt, perhaps the deafening anxiety of the survivors of Mauthausen, is that we do not know to what extent photography attests to the everyday life that was theirs – and in any way, symmetrically, that of the executioners when we see their complacent self-portraits ... In the end, we are invited not only to see the image along its textual and narrative apparatus but to measure "the visible part of the camps."[11]

Simon's argument reflects the fact that the experience of life and death in Nazi camps belongs to the affective register, for which there are no visible records. At the same time, words might become both a tool for treating the effects of trauma as well as one means for making visible, if only through fragments, what is left out of the field of vision. The title of the exhibit points to the fact that there is so much that is invisible and that will always remain so. The word, therefore, can be taken as a way to treat this invisibility.

In the preface to *K.L. Reich*, Amat-Piniella justified the use of "fiction" as a way to better access the "inner truth" of those who experienced the camps.[12] The narrative underscores the importance of the act of looking, both in the construction of testimony and in the negative drive that requires an ethical response on the part of the subject as well as the reader.

Looking from Inside the Camp

K.L. Reich is built from the author's experience of four years of survival in Mauthausen and some of its satellite camps. The book recounts, through an omniscient narrator, the experience of a group of Spaniards, with the focus on the main character, Emili, as the author's alter ego. The novel depicts a kaleidoscope of situations and characters, some of whom are based on real people who either played a role in organizing the clandestine political resistance of the camp or managed to remain in the memory of many survivors due to their unethical or conflicted behaviour. Although focused on the experience of Spanish deportees, *K.L. Reich* also documents other relevant events that took place in Mauthausen between 1941 and 1945: the executions of political deportees, the gathering of naked deportees in the "plaza of the garages," and the brutal treatment of Jews and specific groups of other political deportees such as Russians. In most of these descriptions, Amat-Piniella applies a microscopic view as if trying to ensure that no detail escapes his field of vision; this close perspective somehow duplicates that of Amat-Piniella himself, who was extremely near-sighted and whose condition had been a source of suffering in Mauthausen.[13] The narrative of *K.L. Reich* relies on multiple perspectives, from panoramas to close-ups. Amat-Piniella's call to fiction might be taken, then, as the text's effort to access what remained invisible even to the deportee.

Parallel to this descriptive vision, *K.L. Reich*'s narrative constructs other modalities of looking that might well be taken as attempts to construct an epistemology of the political deportation based on the use of the eye: observing in order to be able to document, to later narrate, and thereby turn the narration into a testimonial. *K.L. Reich* starts in *media res*, reinforcing as it were the inexplicable fate of the detainees along with their ignorance about the camp. The sequence begins with the physical description of the discomfort and harsh weather conditions experienced by a group of frightened Spaniards coming from an unnamed prisoner-of-war camp. The scene signals a transition from the known world – even if in this case it was the world of war, from which one could nevertheless extract some meaning – to the unknown. It is at this point that Emili first sees the bodies of the emaciated and ghost-like deportees who have long been in the camp. The presence of these bodies announces the future that awaits Emili and his comrades.[14] This awareness works as an inflexion right at the start of the narration, since it announces the gradual disappearance of the individual from the outside world. Soon after, as required by camp protocol, the newly arrived prisoners are stripped of any symbolic elements (photographs, rings, watches, notebooks) that constitute their identity and the last bridge that links them to the outside world. Uniforms are provided randomly; numbers are given to substitute for names. This succumbing from the personal and intimate to the undifferentiated opens a new dimension of experience in which the image of the other indicates the potential destruction of the self. It is the "point zero" of the experience of survival for a political deportee in a Nazi concentration camp.

From this moment on the deportee must adjust his eyes to images of destruction and violence: life and death will soon lose their symbolic meanings. The consequence is a fall into an emotional state close to numbness. Jean Cayrol refers to this state as "the hypnosis of concentration camps."[15] Only in retrospect will words rescue the subject from this blocked vision by helping him regain his link to society and the symbolic tissue that allows for recognition.

Yet this hypnotic vision spares the deportee from the constant emotional confrontation with daily death and horror, circumstances expressed in *K.L. Reich* by the suggestion one character utters to Emili: "Se t'han de fer durícies als ulls —li digué uncompany—; és la vista la que treballa" (You get calluses on the eyes ... It's the eyes that do the real work).[16] Parallel to this unreactive vision, *K.L. Reich* displays another point of view that concerns the narrative itself as "observed" by the omniscient narrative voice while describing situations and spaces otherwise hidden to most of the deportees. Most notorious is the description of the murder of Francesc at the *Isoleirun* (isolation unit), when he is injected with phenol, a method employed in Mauthausen to get rid of those deemed incurable, and the incursion of a group of deportees – among them Emili – into the crematorium. This sequence also attests to the existence of a gas chamber in Mauthausen, a subject that entered public debate in France during the 1960s.[17]

The third modality of vision concerns the act of seeing in order to remember. This modality is appropriated by Emili just after the death of Francesc. Emili's activation of the act of seeing emerges as a consequence of his desire to fulfil Francesc's will: "Recorda-te'n. . . de tot això. . . quan s'acabi la guerra. ¡Recorda't de mi! És tan trist no deixar cap memòria, cap rastre. . ." (Remember ... remember all of this ... when the war is over. Remember me! It's so sad to leave no memory, no trace ...)[18] Observing, from this moment on, becomes an act of resistance for Emili, prefiguring his status as witness and thus making possible the character's transition from object to agent. With this transformation the narration itself becomes a piece of meta-literature that testifies to Emili's place as future narrator and of *K.L. Reich* as the product of Emili's act of resistance. This process signifies not only the act of becoming an active witness in the service of transmission, but also the ethical choice – common in testimonial texts – of becoming a witness for the dead. This sort of "narrative-to-come," existing as a seed in Emili's act of observing in order to be able to document and narrate, parallels the reassuring role that literature played among deportees. To recite a poem into the ear of a comrade, to read or write away from the eye of the *Kapo*, were gestures through which the deportee had a chance to reaffirm his belonging to world outside, his or her will to survive in order to be able to narrate,[19] the same way as dreaming – that is, narrating one's own desires to oneself – was also a way to defy destiny, as Jean Cayrol has written.[20] In *K.L. Reich* the narrative voice attests to this defiance:

> Les mantes escampades per damunt d'aquell empedrat d'homes capiculats uniformaven el pis i li donaven l'aparença d'una catifa immensa on hi hagués hagut dues-centes decapitacions. I tanmateix, era l'hora del somni, el moment de les evasions cap a mons millors on els camps de concentració eren ignorats; era l'instant curt, l'únic de tots que ho era, per als qui tenien la sort de poder dormir.

> The blankets scattered over that floor paved with men lying side by side and head to toe, made a uniform pattern, and gave the appearance of a huge carpet decorated with two hundred decapitations. Nevertheless, this was the time for dreams, a moment of escape to better worlds where concentration camps were unknown; it was brief, but unlike any other in the day for those lucky enough to be able to drop off to sleep.[21]

Like the dream, the narration frames the experience within a place and a time through which the subject, in this case Emili, and subsequently the omniscient narrator, can have a feeling of mastering his own time. However, following Cayrol's reflections, while dreams might have been a way to free oneself from the oppression of the camp, the detainees were also avid consumers of images: those that were created by themselves or by the sudden perception of the beauty of the landscape in stark contrast with the camp. But the eye of the deportee, as numb as it might be, reacts too to the stimuli that emanate from the scenes of horror. In *K.L. Reich* this factor is courageously acknowledged to indicate the fascination of both the characters and by extension the reader in watching the "pain of others."

The narrative treatment of this attraction is mediated through the construction of one of the novel's most disturbing scenes. Francesc has been assigned to a new job that relieves him of the hardship of working in one of the external *Kommandos*. The simple task of filling up a bucket of water gives him a drunken feeling of freedom. He falls prey to a scene that captivates his gaze: an SS officer beating a Jew. Moments later, the officer discovers Francesc watching the scene, and from that moment on Francesc becomes the new object of enjoyment, for the SS will force him to torment the Jew. Francesc refuses to comply, a negation that will lead to his death.[22]

The scene thus develops through two steps in which the vision is the articulation point: first, watching the other suffering, and second, being watched by the executioner, which determines Francesc's change of position, from agent to object. The refusal to inflict more pain on the Jew – the paradigmatic victim of the camp – introduces the ethical dimension needed to place a limit on the scopic drive and thereby humanize the victim.

K.L. Reich thus signals the reader's own attraction to violence and hence to the ethical gesture of Francesc, who refuses to carry out the command of the SS. This points to the need to block our own voyeurism when confronted with the representation of the horror. *K.L. Reich*, besides offering a testimonial novel of the Spanish experience of the concentration camps, as such can also be interpreted as adding to the epistemology of mapping the political deportation to Nazi camps, offering the modalities of seeing and looking inside the camp as key critical elements of this work of fiction.

NOTES

1 Archives of Bages, Manresa, Catalonia.
2 See for instance the introduction by Ignacio Martínez de Pisón to the latest Castilian edition of *K.L. Reich* (Madrid: Libros del Asteroide, 2014).
3 For further details on the vicissitudes of the publication of *K.L. Reich*, see Marta Marín-Dòmine, introduction to the English translation of Amat-Piniella, *K.L. Reich*, trans. Robert Finley and Marta Marín-Dòmine (Waterloo: Wilfrid Laurier Press, 2014), vii–xxii. This English translation

will be referenced throughout the article. References to the original version of the novel in Catalan will cite *K.L. Reich* (Barcelona: Club Editor, 2013). See also Pérez Vidal, "Censura y oídos sordos."

4 For a detailed analysis see Baer, *Holocausto*.

5 Other than the assimilation of the the Holocaust with the political deportation, some other beliefs remain crystallized and have not yet been the object of criticism: treating Mauthausen as an extermination camp and the resort to a heroic narrative to explain the Spanish deportation are the most salient elements of an acritical literary approach.

6 In this chapter I use the common terms "liberation" and "liberators" while acknowledging a recent perspective in French academia that has questioned this usage given that the survivors were hardly liberated of anything, and that in any case, a more appropriate term could be the "opening" of the camps.

7 This encounter has been textualized in works such as Delbo, *Auschwitz et après, II,* 174; Levi, *Si c'est un homme,* 162–86; Semprún, *L'écriture ou la vie,* 258–61; and Phillips, *The Nature of Blood,* 12–13.

8 I borrow the expression from Susan Sontag's essay *Regarding the Pain of Others.* It is also Sontag who describes the impression that photographs of Bergen-Belsen and Dachau left on her: "One's first encounter with the photographic inventory of ultimate horror is a kind of revelation, the prototypically modern revelation: a negative epiphany. For me, it was photographs of Bergen-Belsen and Dachau which I came across by chance in a bookstore in Santa Monica in July 1945. Nothing I have seen – in photographs or in real life – ever cut me as sharply, deeply, instantaneously." Sontag, *On Photography,* 19. The impact of the encounter with the images of the camps has also being incorporated into films such as *Marianne and Juliane* (1981) by Margarethe von Trotta.

9 Didi-Huberman, « Ouvrir les camps, fermer les yeux », 1017. My translation.

10 For a critical reception of the visual history of the camps see Didi-Huberman, "Ouvrir les camps"; and Van Vree, "Indigestible Images." A detailed analysis of the visual corpus of the camps should depart from a methodology that considers the nature of the concentration camp, the chronology, the themes and subthemes represented, and the purpose behind the act of photographing. However, the photographs ordered by the SS were taken mainly for the following purposes: to classify prisoners, to record the process of camp construction, to show the German population how "comfortable" the camps were (e.g., in the case of Theresienstadt), or as souvenirs (e.g., the portraits taken of SS officers at Auschwitz-Birkenau).

11 Simon, *K.L.-Mauthausen,* 67–8. My translation. *La part visible des camps* is an itinerant exhibit composed of some hundreds of photographs taken by the

SS in Mauthausen. The exhibit was part of the events organized in France in 2005 to commemorate the sixtieth anniversary of the liberation.

12 Amat-Piniella, *K.L. Reich*, 6; Catalan edition, 9.

13 This detail was revealed by his son, Marcel Amat, in a conversation with the author.

14 Amat-Piniella, *K.L. Reich,* 20; Catalan edition, 23.

15 Cayrol, *Lazare parmi nous*, 17.

16 Amat-Piniella, *K.L. Reich*, 145; Catalan edition, 197.

17 In 1968, the historian Olga Wormser-Migot stated in her PhD dissertation that the existence of gas chambers in the camps located in the West such as Mauthausen and Ravensbrück was part of a legend. It took the work of survivor Pierre-Serge Choumoff to disprove Wormser-Migot's assertion. See Choumoff, *Les assassinats nationaux-socialistes*.

18 Amat-Piniella, *K.L. Reich*, 129; Catalan edition, 174.

19 Writing and drawing clandestinely was highly risky for deportees. Regarding the Spanish deportees, we know some of the clandestine drawings made by José Cabrero Arnal, who managed to survive by drawing pornography for the amusement of some SS officers. The character of Emili is loosely based on him. For samples of work made in the camp and inspired by the life there, see the exhibit *En los campos nazis*, organized by the Centro Documental de la Memoria Histórica in 2010 (http://www.culturaydeporte.gob.es/cultura-mecd/areas-cultura/archivos/novedades/en-los-campos-nazis-supervivencia-testimonio-y-arte-de-los-republicanos-espanoles.html). For more detailed information about the creativity of victims of Nazism in prisons, camps, and ghettos see Borwicz, *Écrits des condamnés à mort*.

20 Cayrol, "Les rêves concentrationnaires." My translation.

21 Amat-Piniella, *K.L. Reich*, 27; Catalan edition, 37.

22 Amat-Piniella, *K.L. Reich*, 93–7; Catalan edition, 129–33.

16 Jorge Semprún and the Holocaust

SOLEDAD FOX MAURA

Jorge Semprún (1923–2011) was born in Madrid, where he and his siblings led a comfortable upper-middle-class life until the outbreak of the Spanish Civil War in July 1936. Soon after the military coup and the ensuing violence, Semprún's Republican family fled to France, where they led a peripatetic existence as exiles until they settled in Paris in 1939.

In exile, Semprún adapted to Parisian life as best he could. He became fluent in French while continuing his studies. By 1939, the Spanish war had ended with Franco's victory and the defeat of the Republic and the Second World War was beginning. By then he had been taken under the wing of a wealthy Catholic mentor, Edouard-Auguste Frick. He was a brilliant philosophy student and was preparing for graduate studies when the Germans occupied France. In June 1941 he obtained his *baccalauréat* degree and was awarded the second prize of the *concours general* in philosophy, but several factors would pull him away from his education towards an active role in the Second World War. The primary cause was that, despite his stellar performance, his mentor decided to cut him off. As Semprún tells it, this dismissal left him newly orphaned and desperate: "After completing my studies in Philosophy, with my baccalaureate degree in hand, and the multiple lessons learned from Edouard-Auguste F., I was flung out into the world."[1] Frick's timing could not have been worse. France was under siege, and on 14 June 1940 the Germans occupied Paris. In November, Semprún took part in demonstrations at the Place de l'Étoile. These were some of the first student-organized resistance activities, and they resulted in numerous arrests and injuries as well as the closing of the Université de Paris.[2] By then he felt himself a true Parisian and was a regular at the Café Flore and other Saint-Germain-de-Près haunts. The Flore, made famous by its clients

Simone de Beauvoir and Jean-Paul Sartre, was also the only well-heated café during the occupation:[3]

> Flore was a symbolic spot, and a regular meeting place for Philosophy students from Henri IV and Louis-le-Grand, and for those of us in preparatory classes for hypokhâgne and khâgne. It was this atmosphere that made me a lifelong fan of the Rive Gauche. When we were seventeen years old, that was where we spent our days, before the Resistance drew most of the people in my entourage into real military and militant action.[4]

Semprún was swept up by the anti-German sentiments around him. He was recruited to join the Jean-Marie Action Resistance network, a group headed by Maurice Buckmaster of the British Special Operation Services. He was arrested by the Gestapo on 8 October 1943 and held at the Maison d'Arret in Auxerre. His crime was being a member of the French Resistance *maquis* "Tabou" unit. He was twenty years old on the day of his arrest, and turned twenty-one on 10 December 1943 in prison in France. In January of 1944 he was deported to Buchenwald.

Semprún remained a prisoner until the camp's liberation in April 1945. While in Buchenwald, he worked in the office of Labor Statistics, which was run by communists. He had been educated by a German governesses as a child in Madrid, and his bilingualism made him an asset to the camp underground. He was the only comrade able to translate the Nazi press into Spanish. After his release from the camp, he returned to Paris, where he remained an active militant, first within the French Communist Party and later within the Partido comunista de España (Spanish Communist Party, PCE). During the 1950s he rose through the ranks of the PCE and worked as a clandestine agent. Under various aliases, he made frequent illegal recruiting and intelligence trips to Franco Spain. He eventually became a key member of the PCE Executive Committee and the only party leader "on the ground" in Spain. As such, his perspective on day-to-day Spanish life under Franco and his vision for strategies of resistance and change often conflicted with those of other party leaders, especially Santiago Carrillo and Dolores Ibárruri, who had not set foot in Spain since 1939. As tensions within the party mounted, he began to write – in French – about his experiences in Buchenwald. Soon after, he broke all ties with the PCE and fulfilled his lifelong dream of being an author.[5]

After the publication of his first novel, *The Long Voyage*, in 1963, Semprún became one of the best-known Spanish survivors of a Nazi camp. Over the years he wrote a dozen more autobiographical works and became an iconic figure, especially in France, Germany, Spain, and Israel.

He is recognized today as one of Europe's leading intellectuals and political figures from the last century and the beginning of this one and as an eloquent and prolific witness to the horrors of the Second World War.

In 1997, he was awarded the Jerusalem Prize for his expression of "freedom of the individual in society." It is significant that in his work he shows such a feeling of connection to Jewish victims of Nazism. As the product of a Spanish family in early-twentieth-century Spain, Semprún's childhood world was hermetically Catholic. Before his deportation to Buchenwald, he had encountered few Jews, only a classmate or two at the Lycée Henri IV in Paris. His father, José María Semprún Gurrea, was a devout Catholic, and the family's life as refugees in France depended almost entirely on people involved in the Catholic organization Esprit. There was a small but active Jewish community in early-twentieth-century Madrid, but there was scant Jewish presence in Spanish popular culture, save antisemitic cartoons. In short, in his youth Semprún had few if any positive Jewish references.

Through his role as a witness, survivor, and public intellectual, Semprún forged an international reputation as a moral authority, as someone who knew both fascism and communism from the inside and who wrote extensively about the violent crises of the twentieth century. By mining his own memories and imagination, he became a major contributor to the collective battle against forgetting the Holocaust. Thanks to his oeuvre and his political activities, he was named Spain's Minister of Culture under Felipe González, a position he held from 1988 to 1991.

Georges, as Semprún was known in France, also wrote the Oscar-nominated screenplay for Constantin Costa-Gavras's political thriller Z. Yves Montand played Semprún in the latter's autobiographical film *La Guerre est finie*, directed by Alain Resnais. Semprún was a tailor-made hero for postwar and Cold War Paris: a man of action and thought, as much at ease with false passports and double-bottomed suitcases from his clandestine work in Francoist Spain in the 1950s and 1960s as he was in the cafés of the Parisian boulevards, Les Deux Magots and the Flore. He wrote in French and lived in Paris, but he was Spanish. His point of view was unique. Despite his Catholic background and his exciting and chameleonic life in the movie world and Spanish politics, for decades he was known primarily as a voice of the Holocaust, and it is within the canon of Holocaust studies that his work is most valued today. He often claimed that he was neither Spanish nor French, but "un deporté de Buchenwald."

Semprún has been considered an "honorary Jew," and his books have a place within the Holocaust canon, yet it is important to note how different his circumstances were – before, during, and after

Buchenwald – from those of Jewish prisoners, as well as from those of other Spanish Republican deportees. These differences shape the question of how his work relates to the bigger picture of literature written by Jewish survivors, including authors such as Primo Levi, Elie Wiesel, and Imre Kertész. Though he carefully pointed out that he did not share the experience of Jews persecuted by the Nazis, his work clearly draws from iconic references to the Holocaust.

Semprún's extensive oeuvre is largely autobiographical, yet the fact that it draws inspiration from his experiences should not lead us to assume it gives us a complete or historical picture of his life. On the contrary, he was outspoken about his right as an author to blend fiction and fact, and we can be sure that he freely embroidered, invented, and omitted. His narratives move between historical fact and literary self-fashioning. Semprún's literary voice is seductive, and it is tempting to believe everything he writes. Yet he was a natural at subterfuge and self-censorship: his versions of events often give the impression of being personal and intimate, but time and again they add fictional elements and omit key facts. What he relates in his body of work cannot be taken as pure historical fact, nor as pure fiction. His works are a mix of experiences dressed in the guise of literature, fiction conflated with memories.

Semprún has sometimes been misclassified as a testimonial author, because his work often mimics testimony, but what he in fact writes is sophisticated autobiographical fiction full of literary touches akin to the picaresque. As a *pícaro*, Semprún as protagonist/narrator/author embraced a deeply Spanish genre of grifters and storytellers. Like his literary ancestor, Lazarillo de Tormes, he recounts his life selectively and artfully, adding and subtracting elements to gain sympathy and admiration from his reader. Picaresque heroes are orphaned at a young age and compelled to seek protection from a succession of cruel masters, often venerated clerical figures who introduce them to the sordid and secret underbelly of society. *Pícaros'* lives are episodic, random, and devoid of any of the coherent structure of the grand epic until they have the opportunity to tell their own story and rebrand their lives as meaningful and respectable. The most important lesson the picaresque hero learns from his hypocritical masters is the art of self-defence through concealment. Through clever self-fashioning and the retelling of his own suffering and travails, he acquires the social status that has always eluded him. Semprún acknowledged and defended his use of fictional devices: "Ever since *Le grand voyage*, I've always used fiction, sometimes as a shortcut, sometimes to take things up a notch, and other times because there was simply no alternative."[6]

In fact, he thought fiction was more powerful than history as a medium to communicate atrocities. In her interview with Semprún, Lilah Azem Zanganeh writes:

> Semprún allows that testimony is vital to historians, but he notes that testimony, too, is not always precisely reliable, and that historians, alas, are never quite as effective as novelists at conveying the essence of experience. "Horror is so repetitive," he says, "and without literary elaboration, one simply cannot be heard or understood." Hence, he argues, "The only way to make horror palpable is to construct a fictional body of work."[7]

Semprún elaborated on this potentially thorny issue and staked his claim that fiction was not the best, but the *only* way to represent the Nazi camps:

> I will always defend the legitimacy of literary fiction in expounding historical truth. In the case of deportation, both Jewish and non-Jewish, it is simply not possible to tell, or write, the truth. The truth we experienced is not credible, and this is a fact the Nazis relied upon in terms of their own legacy, for future generations. If we tell the raw, naked truth, no one will believe us ... It needed to acquire a human shape, an actual form. This is where literature begins: narration, artifice, art – what Primo Levi calls a "filtered truth." And I believe ardently that real memory, not historical and documentary memory but living memory, will be perpetuated only through literature. Because literature alone is capable of reinventing and regenerating truth.[8]

We could say that the studies of Semprún's work and life, including this one, are doing exactly what he hoped: using his own literature as a springboard to perpetuate the memory of the Nazi camps, and more generally of twentieth-century Europe's violent crises. It is important, though, to keep in mind broader questions about his approach to a "filtered truth."

Semprún made things up, yet his status as a witness blurred the line between his narratives and history. The converse is also true: he was a witness, yet he made things up. Shouldn't we have some respect for his claims about the power of invention? After all, it isn't easy to tell a good story. Because he based his literary career on the crafty intermingling of fact and fiction, contextualizing certain aspects of his oeuvre within its historical and literary background allows for a more nuanced understanding of his novels and enables readers to further appreciate his artistic flourishes and separate them from some of his actual experiences. Understanding how he recast his time in the camp helps pinpoint themes and issues that run through his work and trace how he forged his public persona as a writer.

From his very first book, *The Long Voyage*, we see him echoing his literary idols (Malraux, Hemingway), and we catch a glimpse of the burgeoning screenwriter he would become. His dialogues are taut and tough – à la Humphrey Bogart in *Casablanca* – and his scenes are blatantly literary and cinematic. He proudly flaunts his romanesque imagination and his international literary and philosophical references. He wrote at length about his time in Buchenwald in four of his major books: *The Long Voyage*, *What a Beautiful Sunday!*, *Le Mort qu'il faut*, and *Literature or Life*. He only fully recounted the torture he underwent in the prison in Auxerre, where he was held before his deportation, in the posthumous *Exercises de Survie*;[9] it took him nearly seventy years to do so. In *The Long Voyage*, he doesn't tell that story. He focuses, as the title suggests, primarily on the harrowing journey to Buchenwald from France in a cattle car in this first, groundbreaking camp novel. His only comments about his imprisonment in France are the following: "I've told myself I would write the story of the Auxerre Prison. A very simple story: the exercise period, that long conversation, in short snatches, each one of us on our own side of the bars ... And now I have a chance to write that story, and I can't. The time isn't right, my subject is this voyage."[10]

His only consolation, as his character says in *The Long Voyage*, was that it had been his decision to join the French Resistance. As a philosophy student, he prided himself on his ability to reason. Exerting his own will and his lucidity, he had chosen his path. He was not a victim, like the poor persecuted Jews, but a fighter: "I've been free to go where I had to go, and I had to get on this train, since I had to do the things which led me to this train. I was free, completely free, to get on this train, and I put that freedom to good use."[11]

The Long Voyage, in all its Hemingway-esque coolness, is Semprún's brilliant exercise in refashioning himself as a reluctant hero, the man of action and words he had always wanted to be and about whom Malraux had written so beautifully. Semprún strove to stand out amidst the deportees, he did not want to be a young *goy* who had been caught in the wrong place at the wrong time waving guns around and getting himself arrested by the Gestapo. He also establishes himself as a witness, and he does not want our pity. He saves his readers' emotions for the Jews. One scene in particular describes in harrowing terms a group of fifteen small Jewish children being pursued by the SS and their dogs. The children run as fast as they can, but they are quickly caught and beaten to death by the laughing officers. This scene in itself automatically puts the novel in the "Holocaust literature" category. It reads like an artfully rendered memory, yet other elements in Semprun's work remind us that we are in the hands of a novelist, not a testimonial writer.

For example, Semprún mentions the gate at Buchenwald repeatedly in *The Long Voyage* – indeed, there is a crescendo of references until the camp's liberation, when the inscription is finally revealed and emblazoned on the page in capital letters: "I show my pass to the American sentinel and glance up at the inscription, in large, wrought iron letters, set above the bars. ARBEIT MACHT FREI. Freedom Through Work. It's a fine paternalistic maxim, it's for our own good that we've been imprisoned here, it's through forced labor that they have taught us the meaning of freedom."[12]

The gate proved of paramount importance to Jorge Semprún's camp narrative, but the strange thing is that *Arbeit Macht Frei* was not in fact the inscription over the gates of Buchenwald. It was the inscription placed over the gates of Auschwitz. The gates of Buchenwald were inscribed with the words: *Jedem das Seine*, roughly translated as "to each his own" or "everyone gets what they deserve."

It is hard to imagine that Semprún would have fumbled something as historically significant as the inscription on the gate of Buchenwald, so we must look to other factors for this fictional inscription, for his borrowing of an inscription from the gate of another, much more famous camp. By the time Semprún started writing about his camp experiences in 1960–62, Primo Levi and Elie Wiesel had made the Auschwitz gates unforgettable in their respective novels *Se questo è un uomo* (Italian edition published in 1947, English translation in 1959, German and French editions in 1961); and *Night* (published in English in 1960, and first published in French as *La Nuit* in 1958). Levi mentions the inscription above the Auschwitz gates three times in *Se questo è un uomo*. At the end of the second chapter, "The Thaw," the camp is in the first chaotic stage of liberation, and the inscription suddenly seems miraculously declawed: "[F]or the last time there filed before my eyes the huts where I had suffered and matured, the roll-call square where the gallows and the gigantic Christmas tree still towered side by side, and the gate to slavery, on which one could still read the three, now hollow, words of derision: '*Arbeit Macht Frei*,' 'Work Gives Freedom.'"[13] The same words are prominently featured in Wiesel's *Night*: "But no sooner had we taken a few steps than we saw the barbed wire of another camp. This one had an iron gate with the overhead inscription: ARBEIT MACHT FREI. Work makes you free. Auschwitz."[14]

Alain Resnais's 1955 short film *Nuit et Brouillard* (Night and Fog) became the first movie to use footage and archival materials from concentration camps. Resnais received numerous accolades for the project;

Francois Truffaut called it the best movie ever made. In the film, which was broadcast on French television and watched in homes throughout the country just ten years after the end of the occupation and the war, one of the most unforgettable images is of prisoners entering through the gates of Auschwitz, under the sinister words *Arbeit Macht Frei*.

Either Semprún never saw the inscription at Buchenwald, or he deliberately chose *Arbeit Macht Frei* because it already had a resonance in the discourse of Holocaust culture, thanks to Levi, Wiesel, and Resnais.

It makes sense that Semprún, launching his career as a writer rather late in life – he was forty when *The Long Voyage* was published – would want to associate himself with the most successful representations of the Holocaust that had come out to date. Semprún inscribed himself on the canon of Holocaust literature, not deportation literature, by associating himself with the most famous Nazi camp gate inscription, not the inscription of his own camp. And he referred to Buchenwald as a death camp. Though thousands of prisoners died in Buchenwald, it was not a death camp like Auschwitz. It is perhaps in these distinctions that his conflation of literature, life, and memory becomes most fraught.

Sixteen years after *The Long Voyage*, Semprún published *What a Beautiful Sunday!* (1980), his second major novel/memoir about Buchenwald. In this book, the inscription on the gates appears again, but stands corrected. There is no reference to the misquoted inscription so prominently cited in *The Long Voyage*.

The question of the inscription over the gate at Buchenwald is just one specific example of the issues related to memory, poetic licence, and intertextuality surrounding the often contradictory work of Semprún. If our narrator/author comes full circle swapping one inscription – so physical, and unmistakable in its wrought-iron existence – for another, how are we to trust him on other matters? Was he, perhaps, simply catching up with himself and history, reflecting other works of camp literature that he read and assimilated as the genre developed over the decades?

Though "camp memoirs" are often grouped loosely into one category, the camp experience of a political prisoner and member of the communist underground resistance was a very different experience from that of other inmates, particularly Jewish prisoners, who were segregated in the "Small Camp" in Buchenwald. Wiesel, who survived this Small Camp as a boy, where his father died, found the distinction worth highlighting in one of his memoirs: "Many years later Jorge Semprún and I were exchanging memories of Buchenwald. He had been in the main camp. Working in the Shreistube, the office, he did not endure the hunger and cold. He knew the Small Camp at a distance. The fate of the Jews was unlike that of the non-Jews. We were in the same place, and yet."[15]

Semprún's success as a non-Jewish witness to history is valuable for a number of reasons. He undoubtedly brought the history of the Jews in Nazi camps to non-Jewish readers who otherwise might not have been drawn to this subject. Bruno Chaouat, who has examined numerous examples of Semprún's representation of Jews, contends that Semprún was rather uniquely able to grasp the dialectic between philosemitism and antisemitism, and that he neither celebrates nor resents what has been portrayed by others as Jewish "passivity."[16] Chaouat generally praises Semprún's capacity for dialectical thought and his transmission of testimony. Yet he doesn't shy from raising questions posed by Semprún's portrayal of Jewish identity, such as his portrait of the Russian Jew Edward Kusnetzov in *What a Beautiful Sunday!* Kusnetzov is, according to Semprún, Jewish despite himself, because – unlike other passive Jews – he chooses to be. Chaouat asks: "Why does Semprún consider that Kuznetsov is Jewish against at least a part of himself, while at the same time showcasing his Jewishness as an example of authentic Jewish identity – a chosen, willed, Jewish identity? These are hermeneutic problems that I cannot resolve but that need to be highlighted."[17]

When Semprún returned to Paris for good in 1991, after leaving his post as Minister of Culture in Spain, he produced a memoir that would become his most successful book ever, *L'écriture ou la vie*.[18] He was seventy-one years old when it came out.

In this work, he turns the subject of Nazi camps into a surprisingly appealing terrain. He employs frank and direct first-person narration and a wry tone. The chapters are broken up into manageable, self-standing segments and are characteristically sprinkled with famous names – Louis Armstrong, Pablo Picasso, Thomas Mann. He talks about jazz, cigarettes, poetry, and Smith & Wesson. The memoir is a celebration of life and culture and an ode to the twentieth century, apparently free of bitterness or resentment. In the category of Nazi camp memoirs, *Literature or Life* stands out as a non-threatening book. The tragic death of a Jewish prisoner is checked by the glory of fraternal bonds and the beauty of the Kaddish; the alienation Semprún felt on reaching a repatriation centre in Ettersburg after the liberation of Buchenwald is converted into joy and desire as the narrator dances with a girl listening to "The Sunny Side of the Street." There is not much reckoning with the Germans, nor is there criticism of the French and their murky collaboration with the Nazis.

When the book came out, France and Germany celebrated Semprún as hero, witness, media phenomenon, and a long-lost seventy-one-year-old son. They showered him with a steady stream of adoration and admiration he would enjoy for the rest of his life. There are dozens of newspaper and magazine headlines about Semprún from this period. In interviews he is asked almost exclusively about Buchenwald and about the possibility of forgiveness. He became an expert who was consulted about German camps, and he offered answers about evil, the Nazis, and the future. He became the man of the hour, a star witness to German atrocities, and he topped the bestseller lists.

In a 1986 talk titled "Stalinism and Fascism,"[19] Semprún revisited the liberation scene he witnessed at Buchenwald in April 1945, a moment he had written about so many times. This version focuses on Goethe's oak and on the possibility of hope, exemplified by rebirth:

> I would like to indulge in an evocation, a personal souvenir. At the end of April 1945 I spent my last afternoon in Ettersburg and my last hours in Buchenwald before returning to Paris. The repatriation trucks were part of a French Repatriation Mission, though I would not be returning to my homeland. In any case, I took advantage of those last moments in Buchenwald to say my farewell to Goethe's tree. The beech tree, which the Nazis had preserved when they razed the forest to build the first barracks of the camp, was located on an esplanade between the kitchen and the warehouse. A year before, in the summer of 1944 when the American air force had bombed the installations, a phosphorous bomb had hit Goethe's beech. But on that day, my last afternoon, Spring had returned announcing the end of a World War. Some branches of the burned out tree were turning green again.[20]

It was this ability to portray Buchenwald as a locus of hope and new life that gave Jorge Semprún a particular literary and moral success in the new European scene of the late 1980s, 1990s, and early 2000s. Did Goethe's tree really spring new green branches after being destroyed by the incendiary bomb? Perhaps the easiest answer is one Semprún became fond of saying about his work in general, quoting Boris Vian, "Everything is true because I made it all up."

Semprún became an unlikely star of Holocaust literature, and his key works about Buchenwald are indeed worth reading. They reveal a great deal about Semprún himself, the experience of deportation, Buchenwald, and the literary contexts he wrote about over the decades. But the man behind these books was not simply "un deporté de Buchenwald." This kind of statement made him an icon in postwar Europe, yet he was so much more than a deportee. He really was a Zelig-like figure, and his camp experiences were just one part of the bigger picture. As Ruth Weiss has written, "All 'literature of the Holocaust' is shaped by a particular culture, however complicated it may be by the author's crisis of identity."[21] In Semprún's case, there were many particular cultures – Spanish (by origin), German (by education), and French (by adoption), Communist, Catholic – that shaped his specific background and his voice vis-à-vis the Holocaust. Jorge Semprún was a chameleonic and complicated person, and a familiarity with his biography is indispensable for reading his autobiographical works about Buchenwald and relating them to the larger field of Holocaust studies. Since his death in 2011, many significant studies of his work have been published in English, which has helped make his work available to more comparative and international perspectives.[22]

NOTES

1 Louis-Panné, *Jorge Semprún*, 34. My translation.
2 Ibid.
3 Semprún, *Le langage est ma patrie*, 60. My translation.
4 Ibid., 61.
5 Fernando Claudín and Javier Pradera were his allies in dissidence. For more on their break with the PCE, see: Nieto, *La aventura comunista*; Preston, *The Last Stalinist*; Juliá, *Camarada Javier Pradera*.
6 Preliminary interview in Semprún, *Le mort qu'il faut*, 12.
7 Semprún, "Interview by Lila Azam Zanganeh."
8 Ibid.
9 See the following works by Semprún: *Le grand voyage*; *The Long Voyage*; *Quel beau dimanche!*; *What a Beautiful Sunday!*; *Le mort qu'il faut*; *L'écriture ou la vie*; *Literature or Life,*); *Exercises de Survie*.
10 Semprún, *The Long Voyage*, 47.
11 Ibid., 21.
12 Ibid., 167.
13 Primo Levi, *If This Is a Man*, 193.
14 Wiesel, *Night*, 40.
15 Wiesel, *All Rivers Run to the Sea*, 93.
16 Chaouat, "Jorge Semprún's Remembrance." See also Ursula Tidd's *Jorge Semprún*, where she offers an excellent treatment of the "Jew as other [who] hence occupies multiple 'situations' in Semprún's" writings. Tidd analyses Semprún's encounters with the Jews of Czestochowa: the Jewish intellectual Kuznetsov, but also the fifteen Jewish children among the bodies of Polish Jewish prisoners at Buchenwald (see Emmanuel Bouju on Semprún's writings about these children in Ferrán and Herrmann, *A Critical Companion*). Tidd also explores the important passage in which

Semprún encounters a Jewish woman survivor of Auschwitz on his way to Montparnasse station, and later imagines meeting her again, at which time she accusingly tells him that unlike the political deportees, who received some help during their persecution by the Nazis, no one ever helped her, because she was a Jew (135–7).

17 Ibid., 36.

18 See chapter 3 of Fox, *Ida y vuelta,* for further analysis of his representations of the camp experience.

19 In the French version of collected essays in which this appears, the title is "L'arbre de Goethe." In Semprún, *Une tombe au creux des nuages.*

20 Semprún, "Estalinismo y Fascismo," 24.

21 Weiss, "*Shoah, Khurbn,* Holocaust," 197.

22 The most complete bibliography of works published through 2014 is in Ferrán and Herrmann, *A Critical Companion;* see also Ferrán and Herrmann's introduction to that volume for a comprehensive introduction to Semprún's body of work.

17 Montserrat Roig and Her Contribution to the Memory of the Republican Deportation

ROSA TORAN

A Short Life, a Long Legacy

Montserrat Roig died on 10 November 1991 at the age of forty-five.[1] She was renowned in many respects: she wrote novels, one-act and full-length plays, essays, and biographies; she was also a prolific journalist who often led seminars and collaborated with newspapers.[2] She was never lacking for work with Televisión Española (Spanish National Television, TVE) – though not without certain difficulties due to political conflicts – and she conducted forty-nine interviews for the series "Personatges" (1977–8), "Clar i català" (1981), "Los padres de nuestros padres" (1983), and "Búscate la vida" (1986–7). Her complete body of work includes some forty-five different titles, for which she deservedly received many awards.

In the context of her multifaceted legacy, Roig's involvement in what has been called Spain's Political Transition is particularly relevant to this volume. At the end of the 1960s, cultural and university circles produced movements that fought the grey panorama of the dictatorship, which bragged about its "Twenty-Five Years of Peace" and economic development yet firmly maintained its repressive impulse against any dissidence. Roig studied philosophy and literature at the University of Barcelona during the late dictatorship. The university openly challenged Franco through its students, the children of the bourgeoisie who, for better or worse, had been moulded by a regime that had been in place since 1939. The regime's repressive attacks directly affected Roig, but she did not falter in her determination to participate in public acts that took on the ignominious dictatorship. Notably, she protested the "proceso de Burgos" (Burgos trial), which sought six death penalties for ETA members, by occupying the Montserrat Monastery on 12 December 1970 with three hundred other intellectuals. Her political militancy, which began during her university years, reached its fullest expression in her activities with the Partit Socialista Unificat de Catalunya (Unified Socialist Party of Catalonia, PSUC), the anti-Francoist party par excellence, even though she was never inclined to strictly follow party lines.

The dictatorship attacked not only members of the political opposition but also supporters of the Spanish Republic, Catalanists, and feminists. These three vectors of resistance informed Roig's life's work. She translated works into Catalan, wrote in Catalan, and advocated for expanded publishing opportunities in Catalan, all while also publishing in Castilian. Cosmopolitanism was a mark of her identity, as demonstrated by her trips and stays abroad in Italy, France, England, the United States, Cuba, the Soviet Union, and Hungary. Without a doubt, Montserrat was a feminist. She distanced herself from Simone-de-Beauvoirist orthodoxy and focused on the daily experiences of women: in her novels she observed and depicted women of different generations as well as the struggles of working-class women in the 1970s and 1980s.

Roig embodies a particular moment of political engagement, yet she continues to be an esteemed reference for women journalists of newer generations.[3]

Preparation, Development, and Repercussions of *Els catalans als camps nazis* (Catalans in the Nazi Camps)[4]

After the war and the victory over fascism, European leaders, organizations, and governments constructed the memory of the deportation to Nazi camps. These various entities were tasked with maintaining the memory and defending the dignity of the deported, and along the way they had to grapple with elaborations of and modifications and substitutions to this collective memory in response to changing political interests and circumstances.

None of this happened in Spain. The Civil War (1936–9) launched an anti-fascist movement trained on the Franco regime, which had come to power with the help of Italy and Germany. That regime impeded the legalization of associations that would maintain an anti-fascist memory; it also denied victims of fascism the right to memory and even to their own existence. All of this meant that Spain was kept on the sidelines of the political and ideological debates that took place in Europe and of an entire literary and historiographic tradition that forms part of twentieth-century culture.[5]

As Juan M. Calvo Gascón describes in chapter 11 in this volume, anti-fascist Republican deportees were ignored by their own country and condemned to exile. Most of the survivors set down roots outside Spain and offered their support under other flags, waiting for the fall of the regime. In 1947, it became clear that the regime would endure, which left many in despair as they awaited the dictator's death.

Montserrat Roig herself admitted she was ignorant of her own history as a result of the Republic's defeat. She belonged to the generation born after the war: the deportation of almost ten thousand Spaniards to the Reich's camps was hidden from them for various reasons. The terrible images of the camps, and the persecution and extermination of the Jews (and, to a lesser extent, the French Resistance), were not unfamiliar, for they formed part of the culture in certain circles. But few people knew the torment that Joaquim Amat-Piniella, deported to Mauthausen, had experienced until they read his work *K.L. Reich*, published in a censored edition in 1963 (See chapters 14 and 15 in this volume).[6]

Montserrat Roig's yearning to understand what had happened led her to read *Cartes des d'un camp de concentració* (Letters from a Concentration Camp) by Pere Vives i Clavé,[7] which recounts the infamous French camps that held Republican refugees. It also includes a prologue by Agustí Bartra, who suffered the same fate as Vives in France. Vives, who also wrote a letter after he had been taken prisoner by the Germans, would be murdered in Mauthausen in 1941; one year later, his friend Bartra was able to leave for South America, saving himself from deportation. It was through that reading and the discovery of a man whose life she described as having been a great defeat that Roig came to write her first article in a long series on the subject of the deportation. (Sara J. Brenneis discusses Roig and her exposure to this early deportation text in chapter 14 in this volume.) Perhaps she did not know how far-reaching or impactful her interest in the topic would turn out to be.

Roig began reading Amat-Piniella's unique work, and that ignited her desire to meet him in person. This meeting took place during the launch in Barcelona of *Los SS tienen la palabra* (The SS Have the Floor), by Vicenzo Pappalettera, ex-deportee to Mauthausen, and his nephew Luigi.[8] At this point in 1972 the survivors who had met up in Spain had been struggling for a decade to organize to defend their moral and material rights against the regime's repeated negations. As it turned out, the dictatorship could not prevent them from strengthening their bonds, impede them from their work locating widows and orphans, or block them from sharing their experiences in the clandestine circles to which Montserrat Roig also belonged. Roig's friendships with Amat-Piniella, Ferran Planes, and Joan Pagès, a seemingly bulletproof fighter whose imprisonment in Franco's prisons had not weakened his determination to give life and light to the former deportees, were not coincidental.[9]

Her critical journalism soon appeared in a long interview published in the magazine *Triunfo*: "Una generación romántica. Españoles en los campos nazis" (A Romantic Generation: Spaniards in Nazi Camps).[10] This collaborative piece combined the words of the survivors with an homage to all of those who, like Vives, were murdered and "a los que aún vivos no han visto realizadas sus ilusiones y sus esperanzas" (to those still alive who have not yet realized their hopes and dreams). Stunning and emblematic photographs by Pilar Aymerich showing the faces of Planes, Pagès, and Amat-Piniella illustrated the article.

The editor and anti-Francoist cultural activist Josep Benet saw in Roig someone who could bring to light ignored and hidden episodes from Spain's history. For some time, he had considered creating a general work on the deportation, but he recognized the impossibility of starting the project because he lacked a passport, which he would need in order to travel to France and meet those survivors of the deportation who were still in exile. Montserrat Roig seemed to be the ideal person for the job, in that she had demonstrated her sensitivity and was known for the quality of her prose. Benet responded to Roig's initial hesitations – related to the workload, her other commitments, and how she would fund the research – by convincing her that it would be a short-term investigation, lasting about three months. Roig continued to feel uneasy about the project, but Benet was always at the ready with arguments to convince her. He also arranged for no-strings-attached funding from Josep Andreu Abelló. Above all, he pointed out to her that "ella con todas las cosas que había hecho, tenía la suerte de no estar encarcelada, como lo estaban otros, en cuyo caso su situación económica sería peor" (with everything she had done, she had the fortune of not being in prison, where many others were, in which case her economic situation would be much worse).[11] In October 1973, she began to work on the book, as she explained to a friend in Bristol: "M'he portat força feina: periodisme que m'ha quedat pendent, la novel·la i un projecte que em va oferir Josep Benet. No se si te'n vaig parlar. És tracta d'un llibre sobre els exdeportats catalans. Pot ser interessant" (I've brought quite a lot of work: unfinished journalism, a novel, and a project that Josep Benet offered me. I don't know if I told you about it. It's a book on Catalan ex-deportees. It might be interesting).[12]

The first step was to immerse herself in background reading. The well-known works in Spain on the topic had not been written by historians, but rather by journalists or other key players and survivors of the camps. These included *Le grand voyage* (*The Long Voyage*) by Jorge Semprún,[13] *Españoles en el Tercer Reich* (Spaniards in the Third Reich) by Javier Alfaya,[14] *Los olvidados* (The Forgotten) by Antonio Vilanova,[15]

Triangle Bleu. Les républicains espagnols à Mauthausen (Blue Triangle: Spanish Republicans in Mauthausen) by Manuel Razola and Mariano Constante,[16] and *Les 186 marchés* (The 186 Steps) by Christian Bernadac,[17] as well as general works on exile that dealt with the world of the concentration camps, such as Miguel Ángel's *Los guerrilleros españoles en Francia, 1940, 1945*[18] (The Spanish Guerrilla Fighters in France) and Federica Montseny's *Pasión y muerte de los españoles en Francia*[19] (Passion and Death of the Spaniards in France). A number of singular works were published in the years immediately following the death of the dictator, including Mariano Constante's early memoirs. Several former deportees attended the launch for his *Los años rojos. Españoles en los campos nazis*[20] (The Red Years: Spaniards in the Nazi Camps), including Josep Sugranyes, Amadeo López Arias, Salvador Figueres, and Joan Pagès, who introduced Constante to Roig. The year 1975 marked the thirtieth anniversary of the liberation of the camps, a moment when Constante became a key figure among the survivors of the deportation as a result of his body of work. He wrote a long article titled "Mauthausen. Españoles en los campos nazis"[21] (Mauthausen: Spaniards in the Nazi camps) and the book *Yo fui ordenanza de los SS*[22] (I Was an Orderly for the SS), following them up with interviews and reporting with other ex-deportees in the Spanish media. (See chapter 14 in this volume for more on Roig, Constante, and early Spanish survivor narratives.)[23]

It was a time of openness towards the topic of deportation; much of the media made space to disseminate it.[24] The Amical de Mauthausen y otros campos (The Association of Mauthausen and Other Camps) was finally openly acknowledged and became active in conferences and in screenings of the documentary *Nuit et brouillard* (*Night and Fog*) by Alain Resnais, in tandem with the campaign for its own legalization as an organization. Notable figures supported the Amical's push for legalization, including Cassià Maria Just, Antoni Tàpies, Raimon, Josep Trueta, Joaquín Ruiz Giménez, and Lluis Maria Xirinachs. But the death of the dictator did not fully erase all previous obstacles and prohibitions, as the prolific and well-known Constante discovered when he was banned from TVE on three different occasions.

Montserrat Roig was still studying the history of the deportation when she conducted a long interview with Amat-Piniella in the summer of 1973. She made contact with deportees residing in Paris at the same time, travelling there in February of 1974. One of her first conversations was with a survivor from Buchenwald, Jorge Semprún; that ended up being such a disappointing experience that she did not include his testimony in her book. (For more on Semprún and his body of work, see chapter 16 in this volume.)[25] Her relationship with Casimir

Climent, on the other hand, did yield results. Through the correspondence they maintained, Roig was able to interview him, as well as gain access to Josep Ester and Josep Bailina, once she overcame their initial hesitation. The gender and political contexts of their reluctance cannot be ignored: these men were all members of the Federación Española de Deportados e Internados Políticos (Spanish Federation of Deportees and Political Prisoners, FEDIP) and were struggling with political disagreements in their ranks. As such, exile circles reflected the aftermath of the divisions between communists, on the one side, and socialists and anarchists, on the other – divisions that had been acute since the Spanish Civil War and that had heightened since the Cold War. Beyond the FEDIP, a significant number of Spanish Republicans were members of the French Amicale de Mauthausen, even among the organization's governing body. The FEDIP and the French Amicale represented an active drive to preserve the accumulated memories of militants, those in hiding, and others who were still afraid.

The former deportees opened their doors and hearts to Montserrat Roig, who was close to the PSUC but was unknown to these individual men and women. As a result of her working relationships with former deportees, Roig's task as an oral historian took on emotional overtones; meanwhile she also had to contend with the potential repercussions in Spain. Once she entered the lives of the survivors, she tended to remain close to them until her death. Her project entailed interviews and correspondence with people who carried a heavy physical and emotional burden – what they themselves called "síndrome de los campos" (camp syndrome) – and whose personal and collective experiences had been erased from Spain's history. Neus Català, whose testimony about the deportation of women to Ravensbrück proved indispensable to the project, dared to speak about things that even her family did not know. (See chapter 12 in this volume for Gina Herrmann's discussion of Neus Català's experiences in the French Resistance and Ravensbrück.) Every trip from Bristol to Paris brought Roig new contacts, and she formed particularly intimate friendships with Lise Ricol and Artur London, as well as Miquel Serra Grabulosa from the PSUC. Roig maintained correspondence with Serra until his death in 1989, mutually committed as they were to changing the world and debating the possibility of Eurocommunism.[26]

It was not easy to contact all the deportees who resided in Spain, even those who had become politically active. Two ex-deportees asked to maintain their anonymity. One of them revealed, at the end of his life, the reasons for his fear. Edmón Gimeno Font, deported to Buchenwald, Dora, and Bergen-Belsen,[27] could not forget his humiliation when, upon his return to Spain, his father was arrested. Remembering the pain of watching the lines of Jewish children arriving in Bergen-Belsen – an image from which he had never recovered – Gimeno recalled a colleague's response: "pero eran judíos" (But they were Jews). The dictatorship was a radical and incurable evil for many.

Each witness recounted his or her experience in a different way, and as a consequence, the transmittal of their testimonies was a deeply complicated task. Roig was not spared these conflicts, as evident in the account of Joan Bisbal's unfortunate death. In a skirmish between deportees – anarchists and communists – searching for SS guards the night after Mauthausen's liberation, the two groups did not recognize each other and fired blindly, killing Bisbal. The version that circulated for years was that Bisbal died during a heroic confrontation with the SS. Even Constante, in "Mauthausen. Españoles en los campos nazis," praised Bisbal in a photo caption: "Montero y Perlado, velando a José Bisbal, muerto en los combates por la liberación del campo" (Montero and Perlado, watching over José Bisbal, who died in the struggle for the liberation of the camp). It was a pious lie, according to some who knew the facts. Eusebi Pérez Martín, in his frequent trips to Barcelona from Venezuela, tirelessly demanded that Roig include in her book a page that he himself wrote with the details of what had happened. The author had her concerns when presented with two contradictory versions.[28] In the end, she opted for the story that denied Bisbal's glorious death, as told by third parties who, significantly, were not identified by their last names.[29] Other accounts were equally difficult to confront, including those of the few Spanish *Kapos* who had behaved violently against their comrades, and that of the Valencian César Orquín, who led a *Kommando* and either saved lives or condemned people to death, depending on whom one spoke to.

The volume concludes with a series of appendices, which provide documentary and photographic evidence in support of the testimonies besides adding nuance to Roig's account of the deportation. One appendix lists the names and details the trajectories of individuals from Catalonia from the moment of their arrest in the Stalags or German prisoner-of-war camps to their deaths in the Mauthausen complex and its *Kommandos*. The list is a reorganization of one of the seven original lists that three Republicans – Joan de Diego, Josep Bailina, and Casmir Climent, all of whom occupied administrative positions in the camp – clandestinely maintained. In large part thanks to this work, the information about Mauthausen is exceptionally precise in contrast to that of other camps. Roig was, however, unable to count on up-to-date data, which explains why she lists only twenty-seven

Republicans in Ravensbrück – a number that is significantly lower than the 150 or so who are registered today[30] – and why she notes that the leader of the Republican government, Francisco Largo Caballero, was in Mauthausen, when in fact he was deported to Sachsenhausen.

The photographic corpus published with the book is even more exceptional. It is composed of previously published images; photos from negatives that deportees stole from the photo lab where Antonio García, José Cereceda, and Francesc Boix worked; and images that Boix made following the liberation. The contribution from what has incorrectly been called "the Boix archives" is significant.[31] Roig learned of its history from an article in memory of Francesc Boix, "Historia de unas fotos" (History of Some Photos), written by Luisín[32] for *Le patriote Résistant* in April 1975, but to her surprise she discovered that an important part of the archive was in the hands of the ex-deportee Joaquín López Raimundo, who had kept it since Boix's death in 1951. His brother, Gregorio López Raimundo, facilitated the delivery of a suitcase with the photo collection in Joaquín's possession and approximately thirteen hundred negatives to Barcelona in order to illustrate the book. Pilar Aymerich, one of Roig's good friends, played an important role in this story of an archive with international significance as she tirelessly worked to develop and print the images. Roig's generosity allowed her to donate this important photographic legacy to the Amical de Mauthausen.[33] Through expositions and audiovisual materials, the photographic archive has become a testimonial database for the Republican deportation. However, there was yet another important legacy in the suitcase: Boix's negatives from his time in Paris, Algeria, and Czechoslovakia following his liberation, which reveal the movements of the anti-Francoist opposition in exile and were unveiled in a 2015 exhibition.[34] For more on Boix, see chapters 14, 15, 27, and 28 in this volume.

But Montserrat Roig's big question – To what extent was the Spanish government responsible for the deportation of its country men and women to the camps? – was left unanswered. All of those who were interviewed accused Ramón Serrano Suñer, Franco's brother-in-law and the Spanish foreign minister in September 1940, of being responsible for their harrowing experiences in the camps.[35] Roig met with him in 1977 with the help of Rafael Borràs, an editor from Planeta Press, while Borràs was preparing the publication of Serrano's memoirs.[36] However, she did not elicit from Serrano Suñer anything but vague responses about facts already known, including the liberation of two prisoners from Mauthausen that Serrano Suñer had mediated, the existence of the infamous Angoulême convoy in which entire families were sent to Mauthausen in August 1940, and the correspondence that arrived in Spain from the camp stamped "Censura gubernativa" (government-censored) during a brief period starting in November 1942.[37] These historical fragments were all proof that the Franco regime was aware of the deportation of Spanish Republicans to Nazi camps – and in particular that there were Spaniards held in Mauthausen – but Serrano Suñer did not go so far as to claim responsibility for these deportations. The Nazi-phile Serrano, despite insisting that it was he who had ensured that Spain did not enter the Second World War, represents yet another example of the "falsificadores de la historia" (falsifiers of history), given his refusal to acknowledge the Franco regime's share of responsibility for the deportation and death of Spanish nationals in the camps.

As her work progressed and she began to grasp the magnitude of her project, Roig continued to push back the submission date. Contributions from former deportees were continuing to arrive – twenty-seven from Mauthausen, three from Buchenwald, four from Dachau, two from Sachsenhausen, four from Ravensbrück, one from Aurigny, and one from the *blockhaus* of Epperlecques – along with completed questionnaires from those survivors she could not interview in person. She enlisted her mother, Albina Francitorra, to help transcribe recordings and notes. Benet hoped to publish the work on the thirtieth anniversary of the end of the Second World War, but he ended up postponing it until the manuscript was ready for publication.[38] It was finally submitted in October of 1976, after three years of what was supposed to have been a three-month investigation. On 20 April 1977, the book was launched at the Barcelona Atheneum before a large audience, with Artur London, Joan Serra, and Casimir Climent in seats of honour. A few days later, on 6 May, the Amical de Mauthausen bestowed on Roig the title of Honorary Member. *Els catalans als camps nazis* was reviewed in the press, alongside interviews with former deportees. Roig also received many letters from family members with further details about facts addressed in the book.

Roig was awarded the Critica Serra d'Or Prize in 1978 and soon embarked on the Castilian translation, titled *Noche y niebla. Los catalanes en los campos nazis*. The translation was presented to a large public audience at the Antonio Machado bookstore in Madrid on 14 March 1979. The location, an emblematic centre of anti-Francoism since its foundation in 1971, symbolized a new push for the dissemination of the subject of the deportation in the Spanish press.

Roig had achieved something she certainly had not anticipated when she embarked on the project: making public the names of the Catalan deportees, men and women connected to their land who suffered exile, persecution, slavery, and death because they had defended the legitimate government of the Second Republic. Long-buried truths continued to emerge from orphans, parents, and widows, leaving a mark – especially on Catalan society – unlike that of any previous work of history. The book remains authoritative to this day because of its abundance of information and its place in the difficult process of rescuing the memory of those who were ignored and vilified by the Franco regime.

An assessment of *Els catalans als camps nazis* would be incomplete without considering the influence it had on the public through a varied catalogue of interviews with Roig, articles, and additional books by historians and journalists. Roig had achieved her desire to combat forgetting. A new moment was dawning, with a democratic constitution in the making; a chorus of voices of victims of repression, ex-political prisoners, and ex-deportees; and – lest we forget – the indignant far right crying out for "Ni amnistía ni perdón" and "Rojos a Moscú" (Neither amnesty nor forgiveness; Reds to Moscow). Montserrat approached her work through her staunch anti-fascist commitment. Ex-Nazi leaders such as the French antisemite Louis Darquier de Pellepoix lived a golden retirement in Spain. In response to the inflammatory statements from Darquier that "En Auschwitz sólo se mataron piojos" (In Auschwitz they only killed lice),[39] Roig published the article "El nazi y los piojos" (The Nazi and the Lice).[40]

The history of Mauthausen was becoming familiar in Spain; Roig had brought an end to its forty-year absence from Spanish public discourse. Exiles, the defeated, and the ex-deportees ceased to be timeless and landless abstractions; Spain's cultural reconstruction was giving them life. Articles and interviews with ex-deportees abounded in 1978,[41] but not without denialist rejoinders revelling in the "myth of six million,"[42] and the lies of executioners like León Degrelle, whom Roig reproached in her article "El buen nazi" (The Good Nazi).[43]

Along the way, Roig became friends with the deportees, her affective ties severed only with the premature death of some of them. The first was Joaquim Amat-Piniella (1974), followed by Joan Pagès (1978), neither of whom lived to witness the culmination of the process that finally brought about the legalization of the Amical de Mauthausen and initiated the organization's international reach. On 2 February 1978, King Juan Carlos I, while making an official trade visit to Austria,[44] sent the Chief of Protocol of the Royal Palace to place a wreath on the Mauthausen memorial to the Spanish Republicans. Five days later the Amical was legalized: a confluence of events with singular political significance, given the press's response and the monarch's gift, in his role of king to all Spaniards.

The International Mauthausen Committee met in Barcelona from 20 to 22 April 1979. Fifty-four representatives from eighteen countries and more than eight hundred ex-deportees and family members from across

Europe were able to fraternize with the deportees from Spain and show the world the role they played in the anti-fascist struggle, an event that Roig also chronicled.[45] It was the same year that many television viewers closely followed the American miniseries "Holocaust." The deportees capitalized on the popularity of that miniseries to emphasize their marginalization and remind the world that the Jews were not the only people murdered by the Nazis. Roig took part in the controversy in two articles that called attention to the deportees' situation – they had been ostracized and condemned to exile over the course of three decades.[46]

One of the interviews Montserrat Roig conducted for the TVE series "Los padres de nuestros padres" (Our Fathers' Fathers) was with "Joan de Diego, ex recluso de un campo de concentración, entre el sufrimiento y la esperanza" (Joan de Diego, Ex-Prisoner in a concentration camp, between suffering and hope), televised on 24 March 1984. Filmed in Paris on the banks of the Seine, in the Amicale de Mauthausen headquarters on Saint Germain Boulevard, in the Père Lachaise cemetery, in front of the monument constructed for the Spanish victims of Nazism, and around the Pompidou Centre, it wrapped up in the television studios. Roig would have been pleased that her interview subject, Joan de Diego, soon after his return to Barcelona, was at the centre of the ceremony of homage the Amical dedicated to her on the tenth anniversary of her death on 6 November 2011, in the Palau de la Música Catalana.

Over the course of her life, Montserrat Roig demonstrated her unwavering commitment to the fight against forgetting through her collaboration with the Amical de Mauthausen y otros campos and her persistent denouncement of denialism and neo-Nazism. She remained in a continuous state of alert. Her landmark work, *Els catalans als camps nazis*, had been the fruit of an intellectual apprenticeship and a great emotional responsibility that shaped her moral attitude and defence of the undeniable values of liberty and equality. In her articles, she demanded vigilance and attention, because she knew what would plague us if we did not respond to the most minor humiliation or discrimination. For Roig, moral conviction was meaningless without an active response.[47]

In her literary trajectory, *Els catalans als camps nazis* occupies a privileged position, not only because of its narrative ingenuity, or because it brought to light a subject that had been taboo under Franco, but also because of its impact related to historical circumstances that may now seem remote.[48] Our family members and neighbours in Catalonia testified to Nazi barbarism; the book documented the dictator's responsibility for so many thousands of dead, condemned to oblivion in spite of their identity as men and women who played a central role in twentieth-century European and world history.

Seventy-five years after the liberation of the camps, forty-five after the end of the Franco dictatorship, twenty-nine since Montserrat Roig's death, when most of the protagonists have died, when public discourse has proliferated significantly, and when young people have the means to re-create both the recent and the more distant past, there is now an avalanche of information far beyond that which our author had access to. The questions that Roig could now ask are perhaps the same ones she asked throughout her whole life: Why does a better understanding of the barbarism of the past ultimately fail to serve as a vaccine for the present? How can we confront the present knowing that people, under certain circumstances, can turn to evil? Surely, Roig would still be investigating the past and its referents with an eye towards recognizing the victims of our time.

NOTES

1 See Garcia's recent biography, *Con otros ojos*.
2 Such as *Tele/eXprés*, *Triunfo*, *Destino*, *El periódico de Cataluña*, *Avui*, and *El Mundo*.
3 The commemorative ceremonies that took place on the twenty-fifth anniversary of her death were promoted by the Asociación de Mujeres Periodistas, affiliated with the Colegio de Periodistas de Barcelona, following a commission created for this end, in which diverse associations participated, including the Amical de Mauthausen y otros campos. See chapter 11 in this volume for more on the Amical.
4 The research for this chapter has been carried out largely through the collections of the Historical Archive of the Amical de Mauthausen as well as the Montserrat Roig Foundation in the Catalan National Archives (ANC).
5 See Toran, "Entorn de la deportació (I)"; and "Entorn de la deportació als camps nazis (II)."
6 Amat-Piniella, *K.L. Reich*.
7 Vives i Clavé, *Cartes des d'un camp de concentració*.
8 Pappalettera and Pappalettera, *Los SS tienen la palabra*.
9 On the trajectory of the Amical de Mauthausen y otros campos in times of secrecy and legalization, see Toran, *Amical de Mauthausen*.
10 No. 532, 9 December 1972.
11 Interview with Josep Benet, Barcelona, 27 November 2001.
12 Amat, *El llarg procés*, 319.
13 Semprún, *Le grand voyage*.
14 Alfaya, *Españoles en el Tercer Reich*.
15 Vilanova, *Los olvidados*.

16 Razola and Constante, *Triangle Bleu*. Translated into Castilian in 1979 by Peninsula and republished by Amical de Mauthausen, Barcelona, 2008.

17 Bernadac, *Les 186 marchés*.

18 Ángel, *Los guerrilleros españoles en Francia*.

19 Montseny, *Pasión y muerte*.

20 Constante, *Los años rojos*. Following this work, he published an interview with Roig in *Tele/eXpres*, 21 November 1974.

21 *Triunfo*, nos. 641–2, 18 January 1975.

22 Constante, *Yo fui ordenanza de los SS*.

23 See: Martí Gómez "Un catalán recuerda ..."; Quintà, "Joan Pages, un català a Mauthausen"; Alemany, "Martorellencs als camps d'extermini de Hitler"; Hormigón, "Sachsenhausen."

24 See Monegal, "Mariano Constante"; Lladó, "Combatiente a los dicisiete años"; Blanco, "Mariano Constante"; Medina, "El nazismo, escarmiento para la historia"; *Mundo Diario*, 26 November 1976; Monegal, "Noche y niebla en Mauthausen."

25 Roig's encounter with Semprún resulted in an interview published as "Jorge Semprún, en un vaivén," *Triunfo*, no. 570, 1 September 1973, 32–5. Roig did not elaborate on her decision to exclude Semprún from *Els catalans als camps nazis*.

26 Testimony from Nathalie Serra Miralles, 15 June 2016.

27 Gimeno Font's memoirs were not published until 2007, with the title *Buchenwald, Dora, Bergen-Belsen, vivències de un deportat* (Barcelona: Amical de Mauthausen, 2007).

28 Letter to Joaquim Sempere. ANC.

29 Roig, *Els catalans als camps nazis*, 345–6. The citations throughout the essay correspond to the work in Catalan, in that the translation to Castilian under the title *Noche y niebla. Catalanes en los campos nazis*, (Barcelona: Ed. Península, 1978) does not include either the first section or the appendices. According to Josep Benet, in Madrid the editors initially proposed including the list of Spanish deportees, but the undertaking was not viable given the length of the list.

30 A number of contemporary databases are maintained by various collectives, including the Amical de Mauthausen y otros campos / Memorial Democràtic / Universidad Pompeu Fabra database and a database of Spanish deportees sponsored by Spain's Ministerio de Cultura.

31 The removal of the negatives from the camp involved a collective operation; the images taken prior to liberation were authored by the SS.

32 Luís García Monzano.

33 The photographic archive is currently housed for safe-keeping and preservation at the Museo de Historia de Cataluña. For the analysis and reproduction of a good part of the archive, see Toran and Sala, *Crónica gráfica*.

34 "Francesc Boix. Més enllà de Mauthausen," produced by the Museu d'Història de Catalunya and commissioned by Rosa Toran, June 2015.

35 A detailed explanation of her contact with Serrano appears in Gatell, "Después de la derrota vino el exterminio."

36 Serrano Suñer, *Entre el silencio y la propaganda*. Montserrat Roig was familiar with his previous work: Serrano Suñer, *Entre Hendaya y Gibraltar*.

37 Various studies have reproduced documents that prove the Franco regime's complicity in the deportation. See Toran, *Vida i mort*, 94–9.

38 Published by Edicions 62, *Els catalans als camps nazis* was meant to be published by Edicions Catalanes in Paris, which was founded in 1969 to document Catalan national history, financed by Banca Catalana and Jordi Pujol. Benet directed the publication from Barcelona, while Albert Manent operated as the assistant director; in Paris the book was shepherded by Romà Planas and Àngel Castanyer, two militants from the Moviment Socialista de Catalunya (Catalan Socialist Movement or MSC).

39 *Mundo Diario*, 31 October 1978.

40 *Por Favor*, 11 November 1978.

41 "Mauthausen se acerca a España"; Francesc Valls, "Mal en Mauthausen"; Carrasco, "Españoles en Mauthausen"; X.V., "Un català te el fitxer official dels presos"; Escudero and Pagés Moret, "Mauthausen es la historia trágica"; Escudero, "Amadeo López Arias"; Escudero, "Paco Boix"; Pere Ferreres, "El deporte dribló a la muerte en Mauthausen"; Constante, "Historia de una vergüenza"; J. Pujiula, "Olotins i el III Reich"; "Climen (sic) contable en Mauthausen."

42 Pons Rovira, "En defensa del nacionalsocialismo."

43 *El Periódico*, 6 February 1988.

44 The possible purchase of combat cars in a factory in Linz, Austria.

45 *El Periódico*, 22 April 1979.

46 "La verdad de 'Holocausto'"; "Sobre 'Holocausto.'"

47 Ten years after her death, between tributes, a selection of her journalistic work dealing with the deportation and written from 1972 until two days before her death was published as *La lluita contra l'oblit*.

48 The author of this chapter has repeatedly insisted on situating Montserrat Roig in the privileged position on the subject of the deportation that she deserves. See recently published articles by her such as "Record, homenatge i compromís. A Montserrat Roig"; "Montserrat Roig, una lección de libertad"; "Montserrat Roig, una dona per a la historia"; "Montserrat Roig i la fidelitat de la memòria"; and "Mauthausen: emoció i reflexió. En homenatge a Montserrat Roig."

PART FIVE

Propaganda

18 Francoist Antisemitic Propaganda, 1939–1945

JAVIER DOMÍNGUEZ ARRIBAS

According to fairly widespread belief, antisemitism was foreign to Spain during the Second World War – at most, limited to an anecdotal phenomenon that emerged from a few fanatics who were on the periphery of the system and influenced by Nazi Germany. This idea, not uncommon among historians, can be attributed to three factors. The first is the small size of the peninsular Jewish community in 1939 – probably fewer than one thousand people – as if antisemitism required the presence of Jews to develop. The second factor is the absence of systematically discriminatory measures against them, at least relative to the European context (in spite of initiatives such as the "Archivo Judaico" of 1941; see the chapter by Jacobo Israel Garzón in this volume). The third is the ambiguity of Francoist authorities with respect to Nazi antisemitic persecution, which has allowed a veritable white legend to develop regarding Franco's role in the Holocaust.[1]

But these incidents do not take into account the violence and the ubiquity of antisemitic propaganda distributed in Spain during those years. Even though this propaganda enacted an antisemitism more of word rather than of deed – in comparison with the situation in Hitler's Europe – generations of Spaniards have experienced it, and it has contributed to shaping their perception of the world. Through diverse methods, the Francoist propaganda apparatus spread a highly negative image of Jews and denounced their supposed schemes against Spain, often placing them in a conspiratorial alliance with Freemasons, according to an old, counter-revolutionary tradition. These factors allow one to speak of an authentic Judeo-Masonic myth.

Francoist antisemitic propaganda underwent a clear evolution. Its apogee – in terms of quality and quantity – was reached during the Civil War (1936–9), perhaps due to a greater need to mobilize against the enemy and a less-centralized propaganda apparatus. During the first half of Second World War (1939–42), when an Axis victory seemed inevitable, anti-Jewish propaganda continued to be both violent and common in Spain. During the second half of the war (1942–5), as the Allies advanced, the Francoist authorities cut back on their antisemitic references. Finally, after the fall of the Third Reich and the "discovery" of the Holocaust (1945), antisemitic topics were almost abandoned in Francoist propaganda.

This chapter will focus mainly on the Second World War years and will present a panorama of the antisemitic propaganda spread by Francoist authorities, which is to say the official propaganda. To begin, we will observe specific conditions that influenced the propaganda. The bulk of the chapter will then turn to the diverse propagandistic media employed for the transmission of these discourses (leaflets, books, pamphlets, newspapers). However, this chapter pays special attention to the press, which, compared with the other propaganda media, leaves more of a paper trail, allowing one to grasp the timeline of this phenomenon.[2]

Preconditions

Various factors influenced Francoist antisemitic propaganda: first, the pre-existing discourse that had grouped together Freemasons and Jews for decades; second, the official propaganda organizations that spread said discourse starting with the 1939 Francoist victory; and third, the figure of the dictator himself and his opinion of the Jews.

The Judeo-Masonic Myth

The themes present in Francoist antisemitic propaganda had been passed down from a long tradition with many offshoots. The first was secular Christian anti-Judaism, which with its proto-racist purity-of-blood doctrine had marked the modern Hispanic age. The second was anti-Freemasonism, which had developed in parallel with Freemasonry since its inception at the beginning of the eighteenth century. Anti-Freemasonism grew especially after the French Revolution, with works such as Augustin Barruel's *Mémoires pour servir à l'histoire du jacobinisme* (Memoirs Illustrating the History of Jacobinism). From the beginning of the nineteenth century, these two branches began to intertwine. Those who were considered old and new enemies of Christianity – Jews and Freemasons, respectively – came to be included by their enemies in the bosom of the same conspiratorial alliance, which resulted in a Judeo-Masonic myth. Various authors, particularly French and Catholic ones, strengthened the myth throughout the nineteenth century, and even more after Leo XIII's call to expose Freemasonry in the encyclical *Humanum genus* (The Human Race, 1884). From then on, anti-Masonic campaigns in the Catholic world, including in Spain, were often accompanied by antisemitic arguments. During the interwar years, the same myth encompassed an anti-Bolshevik thread and was propelled thanks to the global spread of the *Protocols of the Elders of Zion*, an antisemitic forgery with anti-Masonic elements, as underscored by its editors.[3]

During the Second Republic (1931–6), the *Protocols* became quite influential in Spain. A similar phenomenon occurred with the work of two French authors, Ernest Jouin and Léon de Poncins – both Catholic traditionalists – who denounced the dealings of Freemasons and Jews.[4] Within the framework of the Republican regime, right-wing groups, especially Carlists, but also Alphonsine monarchists, Catholics, and in lesser measure Falangists because of their greater secularization, used these antisemitic – and anti–Judeo-Masonic – arguments as a political weapon.[5]

These right-wing movements are precisely the ones that supported the July 1936 military revolt and constituted the Franco regime. Now from a position of power, they continued to spread the same antisemitic theory throughout the entire Civil War (1936–9), but with much greater intensity than before because they could count on the propaganda services of the nascent Francoist state. This situation continued throughout the Second World War. At the same time, the Freemasons suffered systematic persecution by the regime, in contrast to the Jews.

The Organization of Propaganda in Francoist Spain (1939–1945)

Another contributing factor relates to the propaganda services that spread these ideas. Over the course of the Second World War the Caudillo left the control of propaganda to the Falangists – one faction in the Francoist conglomerate in addition to the Alphonsine monarchists, the Carlists, and the Catholics. However, two very distinct stages of this become clear: before and after May 1941. Before that date, these propaganda services depended on the Ministerio de la Gobernación (interior ministry) and were in the hands of a group of quite radical and relatively autonomous Falangist intellectuals, such as Dionisio Ridruejo and Antonio Tovar. During the second stage, after May 1941, the organizations in charge of spreading the regime's ideas came to be the official responsibility of the party (Falange Española Tradicionalista [Traditionalist Spanish Falange], FET), but the Falangists that predominated in these organizations were much more submissive to Franco as well as more religious than the earlier group.

This transformation involved a change of name for the bodies responsible for propaganda. The Dirección General de Propaganda (General Directorate of Propaganda) and the Dirección General de Prensa (General Directorate of the Press), which had been subordinated to the Subsecretaría de Prensa y Propaganda (Under-Secretary of Press and Propaganda), became Delegaciones Nacionales (National Delegations) in 1941, subordinate to the Vicesecretaría de Educación Popular (Vice-Secretary of Popular Education). Afterwards, in July 1945, following the defeat of the Axis in Europe, Franco transferred responsibility for the press and propaganda from the Falangists to the Ministerio de Educación Nacional (Ministry of National Education), which was controlled at the time by Catholics.[6] Together with the propaganda created by these Spanish services, the propaganda that stemmed from Nazi Germany's intervention must also be taken into account. (This is examined in detail in chapters 23 and 24 in this volume.)

Franco's Position and His Contribution to Antisemitic Propaganda

The dictator's personal opinion of Jews constituted a final key condition for antisemitic propaganda. While the other component of the Judeo-Masonic pairing inspired an obsessive hatred in him – greater even than what he professed of communism – Judaism does not seem to have worried him excessively, which perhaps complicates any interpretation of his position. Various scholars have applied terms such as ambivalence, ambiguity, and even incoherence to Franco's position.[7] On the one hand, there is no doubt that Franco expressed himself in a philosephardic manner in two of his texts, written fifteen years apart. In the first, published in the *Revista de Tropas Coloniales* (Journal of Colonial Troops) and titled "Xauen, la triste" (Chaouen, the Sad, 1926), Franco spoke respectfully of the Jewish community from this city in the Moroccan Protectorate. He underscored its links to Spain and the Jewish community's use of Spanish there, probably in order to criticize a retreat that Primo de Rivera had ordered.[8] The second text was written in the time period that concerns us (specifically, the winter of 1940–1), when Hitler controlled Europe. It is an excerpt from *Raza* (Race), his now well-known film script signed with a pseudonym, in which many of Franco's thoughts are rather faithfully synthesized over the course of various autobiographical episodes. The story's protagonist, José Churruca, an alter ego of Franco, contradicts his mother and his sister when, in a dialogue about Spanish Jews, he upholds that "Judíos, moros y cristianos aquí estuvieron y al contacto con España se purificaron" (Jews, Moors, and Christians were here and through contact with Spain they were purified). He even implicitly absolves them of deicide, affirming that when they were asked to give their assent to kill Jesus, "los judíos españoles no sólo lo negaron, sino que protestaron" (Spanish Jews not only refused, they also protested).[9] This philosephardic position – not philosemitic – probably emerged from Franco's years in Morocco, thanks to the cordial treatment he received there from some Jewish families who helped him in the context of the colonial war. (Moroccan Jews supported the Spanish army, as Isabelle Rohr details in chapter 4 in this volume.) It is improbable that the possibility – impossible to confirm or refute – that Franco descended from *conversos* greatly influenced his attitudes.[10]

At the same time as he made these nods to philosephardism, Franco employed antisemitic themes at various times with a propagandistic intent, while barely associating them with anti-Masonic themes, an association common to the propaganda of the time. During the Civil War, Franco did this in one isolated case: in February 1937 he composed two handwritten but unsigned orders for newspapers in which he linked the French government with the Jews, although he wrote one in the voice of the Muslims of the protectorate.[11] That did not keep Franco from making, around the same time, declarations favouring religious tolerance when he addressed foreign correspondents.[12]

During the Second World War, the Caudillo resorted more and more to anti-Jewish themes or elements in his speeches; they appeared in at least seven between September 1939 and July 1943. In some, he used the adjective "judaico" (Judaic) to denigrate ideas, for instance "prejuicios judaicoliberales" (Liberal-Judaic prejudices). Others allude to the Jews as a "raza maldita" (cursed race), and in at least three speeches he applauded the 1492 Expulsion as a precursor to other contemporary antisemitic measures, which allowed him to link the anti-Jewish policies of the Spanish past to those of the European present. On 17 July 1940, he affirmed that the Expulsion was not "más que un acto racista como los de hoy" (more than a racist act like those of today), conducted against "una raza extraña adueñada de un pueblo y esclava de los bienes materiales" (a strange race that seized a people and was a slave to material goods).[13] However, these antisemitic allusions do not seem especially virulent if we view them in the context of the propaganda aimed at Spaniards during those years, and furthermore, they are contemporaneous to the *Raza* excerpt that was favourable to Sephardis. It seems reasonable to think that Franco's antisemitic rhetoric during the war was adopted in imitation of the hegemonic Nazi context, an explanation that will not always hold true in other realms of anti-Jewish propaganda in Spain, as we will see.[14]

Curiously, Franco expressed himself in an especially antisemitic way – although a bit confusingly – a few years after the end of the Second World War, when antisemitism was no longer the norm in official propaganda. In a series of articles written by the dictator under the pseudonym "Jakin Boor" for the *Arriba* newspaper, which were first and foremost anti-Masonic, nine (published between 1949 and 1950) point to the links between Freemasonry and Judaism. Several of them attack the "fanáticos deicidas" (deicidic fanatics) with the traditional Hispanic anti-Jewish arguments, including references to ritual crimes. Boor affirms that the Jews are "un pueblo enquistado en la sociedad en que vive" (a people deeply embedded in the society in which they live) at the same time that he carries out quite awkward attempts to downplay that violence: "Pero judaísmo no quiere decir pueblo hebreo, sino esa minoría judía conspiradora que utiliza a la masonería como uno de sus instrumentos" (Yet Judaism does not mean the Hebrew people, rather that conspiring Jewish minority that uses Freemasonry as one of their instruments).[15] This kind of writing can be viewed as a reaction, meant for internal use, to the hostility of the Israeli delegate to the UN towards the Francoist dictatorship. The Caudillo was perhaps the only one who could go against the official position of his own regime, which highlighted the support Spain supposedly lent the Jews persecuted during the Holocaust.[16]

Propagandistic Media

From the time of the Civil War, various media were put to use in order to transmit a negative image of Jews, and this continued during the Second World War. We examined one of those media – the dictator's speeches – in the previous section. There are also antisemitic elements in the fictional films *¡A mí la Legión!* (Follow the Legion, 1942) and *La torre de los siete jorobados* (The Tower of the Seven Hunchbacks, 1944), as well as in the documentary film *La División Azul* (The Blue Division, 1942).[17] Although the first two cannot be considered official propaganda, they at least enjoyed the authorization of Francoist authorities, since they had passed censorship. Radio, meanwhile, joined newspapers in certain official propaganda campaigns in which the invocation of the Judeo-Masonic enemy was essential. These campaigns will be examined in the section on the press.

Print propagandistic media, such as posters and leaflets, also contributed to the stigmatization of Jews. Although in the former the antisemitic content would never be of much importance, one can find a caricature-like Jewish character on a wall-mounted newspaper of the unified party or FET (1944), next to a text that designated other enemies:

"Masones, judíos, incendiarios, asesinos" (Freemasons, Jews, incendiaries, assassins).[18] We find similar caricatures in official propagandistic brochures and in the press.

As for political leaflets, it seems that antisemitic themes decreased in comparison to the time of the Civil War, when thousands dropped from airplanes and passed out through other means to the Republican combatants denounced the Judeo-Masonic control of "Red" Spain. After 1939, leaflets financed by the German Embassy linked Judaism to the Allies: "son los mismos JUDÍOS los que ordenan y mandan en Rusia, Inglaterra y Estados Unidos" (The same Jews are in charge and give orders in Russia, England, and the United States), one said. But, once again, this was not official Francoist propaganda, although the regime's authorities approved it.[19] However, another political leaflet did come from the Spanish propaganda services: fifteen thousand copies were distributed in Madrid in February 1942. It said the following:

> Español:
> Los agentes secretos al servicio de la Masonería internacional pretenden una vez más separar a los españoles en su fervoroso amor a ESPAÑA para entregarse a los enemigos seculares de la PATRIA.
> Si oyes en algún sitio que alguien habla mal de la FALANGE es que está al servicio de la plutocracia judía.
> Si oyes en alguna parte que alguien mancha el honor del EJÉRCITO es que está al servicio de la vesania bolchevique.
> ¡ARRIBA ESPAÑA! ¡VIVA EL EJÉRCITO ESPAÑOL!

> Spaniard:
> The secret agents at the service of international Freemasonry are once again trying to separate Spaniards in their fervent love for Spain in order to hand themselves over to the secular enemies of the Homeland.
> If you hear somewhere anyone who is speaking badly of the Falange, it is because they are serving the Jewish plutocracy.
> If you hear somewhere anyone who stains the Army's honor, it is because they are serving the Bolshevik fury.
> Long live Spain! Long live the Spanish army!

Once again, the propaganda warned of different enemies of Spain – among them the "plutocracia judía" – within the framework of a campaign aimed at promoting harmony between the Falange and the army at a moment of great tension between the two. Another element of this campaign that called citizens to unite against a common enemy was a poster of which ten thousand copies had been printed, titled "Maniobras masónicas" (Masonic manoeuvres). It did not explicitly mention Jews, but it contained the stereotypical representation of a Freemason capitalist (top hat, cigar, carpenter's square, compass) with a slightly hooked nose and hands. In the end, the figure of the Judeo-Masonic enemy was essential in this campaign, which had been conceived by the Falangist Federico de Urrutia, the provincial officer of propaganda in Madrid.[20]

Books and Pamphlets: The Case of Ediciones Toledo (Toledo Presses)

During the Second World War, quite a few books and pamphlets circulated that revealed the machinations of the Jews, often in alliance with Freemasons. Some of these were works by independent authors, such as Juan Segura Nieto with his *¡Alerta! ... Francmasonería y Judaísmo* (Alert! ... Freemasonry and Judaism, 1940). Other times, one can detect the direct intervention of Nazi Germany. This is the case with Ediciones Rubiños (Rubiños Presses), which, at the beginning of the war, published various books that defended the thesis of a Jewish conspiracy, such as *El problema judío* (The Jewish Problem), by the Mexican Alfonso Castro, and *Cuando Inglaterra quedó sola ...* (When England Was Left Alone ...), by José Joaquín Estrada.[21] The aforementioned Federico de Urrutia, an important Falangist author, also had German support. In *La paz que quiere Hitler* (The Peace That Hitler Wants, 1939) he presented Germany as the victim of an attack by Jews and Freemasons, while in *Por qué la Falange es católica* (Why the Falange Is Catholic, 1942) it was Spain confronting the same enemies. This last pamphlet was published by the official press of the Vicesecretaría de Educación Popular.[22]

The works mentioned above, and other propagandistic media, contributed to an increasingly hegemonic anti-Jewish discourse, independent of its origin. Nonetheless, the works that directly proceeded from the regime's propaganda, such as Urrutia's last book, are especially interesting. In this regard, the best example of the spread of antisemitic – and anti-Masonic – discourse at the beginning of the 1940s was a series of books and pamphlets printed under the rubric of Ediciones Toledo (Toledo Presses). In spite of the name, it was not a real publishing house but rather a collection created by the propaganda apparatus to disguise the official origins of a number of its publications. It was conceived in March 1941 by the Falangist writer Darío Fernández Flórez, head of the Sección de Ediciones de la Dirección General de Propaganda (Editorial Section of the General Directorate of Propaganda), later the Delegación Nacional (National Delegation), a department overseeing the publication of books and pamphlets. Throughout almost the entire existence of Ediciones Toledo, these propaganda services ultimately depended on Falangists faithful to Franco above all else.

Various texts by Fernández Flórez allow one to understand his intentions in creating Ediciones Toledo and to characterize the collection: he wanted it to be a series of quick propaganda booklets with a "theatrical" not to mention sensationalist flavour aimed at the common reader, all the while "evitando su apariencia gubernativa" (avoiding its governmental appearance). There were two reasons to hide the booklets' origins: to increase their persuasiveness "entre un público muy popular que acaso rechazara publicaciones descaradamente oficiales" (among a very common public that would perhaps reject blatantly official publications); and because the booklets' tone was not respectable enough ("plebeyo" and "estridente" [plebeian and strident] in the words of Fernández Flórez) for a clearly official collection.[23] The distribution of the booklets was especially cautious. Some copies were sold at very low prices, after intense publicity campaigns in the press and on the radio, ordered by the same propaganda services that had published them. Other copies of the same booklets were meticulously handed out for free, in places such as libraries, hospitals, barracks, and prisons, with the objective of reaching "personas poco compenetradas con nuestro Movimiento" (persons who don't sympathize with our Movement), according to the text by a provincial propaganda delegation. This system of distribution, together with generous print runs (from five to twenty-five thousand copies) made the reach of Ediciones Toledo volumes quite extensive.[24]

Seven of the eight Ediciones Toledo volumes that have been located – dated between 1941 and 1943 – contain antisemitic elements of varying significance. In three of them there are simple allusions. One describes Anthony Eden's politics as "judaicomasónica" (Judeo-Masonic); another alludes at various points to the power of "banqueros judíos" (Jewish bankers); a third, titled *¡Camarada: He aquí el enemigo!* (Comrade: This Is the Enemy!) and signed by the ever-present Federico de Urrutia, positions the "masones emboscados" (ambushed Freemasons) among Spain's enemies, who want to sell the country to the "judería de Ginebra" (Genevan Jewry). This last booklet's cover features a character resonant of antisemitic iconography.[25]

In three other volumes, the anti-Judeo-Masonic elements prove more central. This is the case with the first in the collection, an anonymous booklet titled *La masonería en acción* (Freemasonry in Action), of which two editions came out in 1941 and 1942, for a total of thirty-thousand copies, and which highlights the relationship between Freemasonry, Judaism, and communism. According to the anonymous author, Freemasonry fell under the "suprema dirección judía" (supreme Jewish leadership), and Judaism had played a key role in all revolutionary movements; this included support for the "Reds" in Spain.

The caricature on the cover affirmed the relationship: two orthodox Jews dressed with the Masonic apron (Figure 18.1).[26]

Another anonymous booklet titled *La masonería femenina* (Women's Freemasonry, 1942) widely denounced "los oscuros designios judío-masónicos" (the dark Judeo-Masonic plans) against the Christian family.[27] There are also numerous antisemitic references in the booklet *Andanzas del bulo* (Rumour's Adventures, 1942), signed by Francisco Ferrari Billoch and printed in a run of fifteen thousand. The author attempted to fight rumours, viewing them as one of the lodge's weapons against Spain, and he approved "la expulsión del pernicioso pueblo judío" (the expulsion of the pernicious Jewish people) in 1492. The booklet was widely distributed, sometimes in places where gossip could be spread, such as hotels and hair salons, all of this part of an official campaign against rumours.[28]

Ediciones Toledo reached its antisemitic height – and one of the most aggressive manifestations of Francoist antisemitic propaganda as a whole – with the anonymous booklet titled *La garra del capitalismo judío* (The Claw of Jewish Capitalism, 1943). Citing Henry Ford's *The International Jew* and *Protocols of the Elders of Zion*, the booklet insisted that the Jews controlled Great Britain and the United States. In particular, it attributed the cause of the war and related economic difficulties to "las altas finanzas de Israel" (Israel's high finance). Hoarders and black marketeers were thus accomplices of "judaísmo internacional, que quiere exasperar a las masas con el hambre" (international Judaism, which wants to exasperate the masses with hunger). The booklet, in an edition of decent quality, was illustrated with surrealist-inspired allegories that represented the specific evils it denounced. Among these, there was one on Judaism that contained Masonic symbols (Figure 18.2). Initially, the distribution of the more than twenty thousand copies was planned within the framework of another official campaign, this time against hoarding.[29]

An analysis of Ediciones Toledo's documentation shows that the author of *La garra del capitalismo judío* and of two other anonymous booklets with significant antisemitic content was Francisco Ferrari Billoch (1901–1958), who had signed *Andanzas del bulo*, a fourth pamphlet with the same slant. In two of those booklets – *La masonería en acción* and *La masonería femenina* – one can find Ferrari's self-plagiarism and even some plagiarism from Léon de Poncins's *Les forces secrètes de la Révolution* (The Secret Forces of the Revolution). Ferrari was a Catholic and monarchist journalist from Mallorca known for his denunciation of Freemasonry, always in relation to Judaism, in various works and especially in *La masonería al desnudo* (Freemasonry Exposed, 1936).[30] When

18.1 Cover of *La masonería en acción*, Madrid, Ediciones Toledo, 1941
(Collection of the Biblioteca Nacional de España).

18.2 Plate from *La garra del capitalismo judío*, Madrid, Ediciones Toledo, 1943 (Collection of the Biblioteca Nacional de España).

he began to collaborate with Ediciones Toledo in 1941, he had already published at least eight books at the service of the Francoist cause containing anti-Jewish references. His qualities as an anti-Masonic expert led him to participate in the persecution of Freemasonry in Mallorca at the beginning of the Civil War, before it was discovered that he himself had belonged to a Masonic Lodge at the beginning of the 1930s, in the Republican era. His Masonic affiliation led him to be sentenced in 1942 to twelve years in prison, of which he served two and a half in the Burgos penitentiary despite the services he had rendered to the regime and despite the fact that he had become the main anti-Judeo-Masonic propagandist of the Second World War era in Spain.[31]

Press

Newspapers functioned as the primary channel for Francoist antisemitic propaganda. Although the survival of different political sensibilities – primarily Catholic, monarchic, or Falangist – had been tolerated among the papers that supported the 1936 revolt, they became subject to growing control. This converted the press into a propaganda medium at the service of the state, even more if possible during the Second World War. This was achievable thanks to the vigilant surveillance that journalists faced, rigid prior censorship, and above all a system of *consignas* (orders). Said orders were instructions sent daily to newspapers by the propaganda services, in which the topics that should be included or avoided and how this was to be done were indicated, sometimes giving very specific details. In this way, different campaigns could be launched that, one way or another, resorted to antisemitic theses often accompanied by anti-Masonic arguments, as we have seen with other means of propaganda. It is also possible to find countless attacks on Jews that did not form part of organized campaigns but that had been authorized by the censors. That is to say, antisemitic arguments that appeared in the Francoist press enjoyed the endorsement of the new authorities, even when it was not these same authorities that had put them in circulation. This system, and more concretely, the use of orders, resulted in an increasingly uniform press, including in relation to the representation of Jews.[32]

This treatment of Jews from the Francoist press evolved between 1939 and 1945. In the months immediately preceding the Second World War, no organized press campaign that centres on the anti-Judeo-Masonic thesis can be found; but there are countless antisemitic references that appear in periodicals of different orientations. The association between Judaism and Marxism, and not just with Freemasonry, is common during those months. This identification between different enemies of the new Spain extended on occasion to France, and above all to the Anglo-Saxon powers, with the goal of discrediting them in the eyes of Spaniards. This is clearly detectable in Falangist newspapers during the month of May 1939, perhaps due to an order from the press services. For instance, attacks on Anthony Eden with antisemitic arguments were not uncommon, along with references to the "yugo judío" (Jewish yoke) suppressing the United States.[33] Furthermore, during the spring and summer the press reported, without criticism, on the antisemitic measures taken in different parts of Europe, such as Hungary, Slovakia, and Bohemia and Moravia. Often these were justified as defensive reactions against the Jewish threat. Along these lines, it is likely that around the middle of August the press services ordered that these Jewish people be presented as enemies of peace, given that many newspapers treated the topic in a similar fashion on the same dates. "El belicismo judaico no logrará desencadenar la guerra" (Judaic warmongering will not be able to set off war), a Catholic daily in Valladolid proclaimed.[34]

The start of the war in September 1939 had various simultaneous effects on the Spanish press. Newspapers continued to show great sympathy for Nazi Germany; however, they decreased their attacks on France, Great Britain, and the Soviet Union of the kind that identified those countries with Judaism – attacks that previously had been very common. This was due to the Spanish declaration of neutrality and the German-Soviet Non-Aggression Pact, which moderated the Francoist Anti-Bolshevik propaganda. This does not mean, though, that the Spanish press's antisemitic commentary itself disappeared; it continued in various newspapers throughout the first months of the war. And when those same newspapers informed readers about the measures taken against Jews in different countries across Europe, from Italy to Lithuania, they praised them or at the very least omitted all criticism.[35] Antisemitic commentaries during these months were apparently motivated by international events and less linked to anti-Masonic allusions than before.

At the end of February 1940, a significant anti-Masonic press campaign was launched after the passing of the Ley de Represión de la Masonería y del Comunismo (Law of Repression of Freemasonry and of Communism). Although Jews were not mentioned in the first orders the campaign gave, various newspapers published an identical text titled "Los masones y los judíos son los culpables de la guerra" (The Freemasons and the Jews are to Blame for the War); according to the subtitle, "hicieron fracasar la política de paz de Mussolini y Hitler" (they made Hitler and Mussolini's peace policy fail). This uniformity suggests that the press services had demanded the publication of this text within the framework of the anti-Masonic campaign that was already under way. Also within the framework of this campaign and of similar ones that would follow, Falangist and Catholic newspapers introduced Freemasonry as an instrument or ally of Judaism.[36]

After the French defeat in June 1940 and the declaration of "non-belligerency" whereby Spain abandoned its neutrality, support for the Axis in the Spanish press began to intensify.[37] Beginning in the summer and for the rest of the year, countless articles identified defeated democratic France with Judaism and in lesser measure with Freemasonry, attacking all three. The monarchist newspaper *ABC* suggested that "el siniestro tinglado del judaísmo y de la masonería" (the sinister mess of Judaism and Freemasonry) had been defeated, while the Falangist *Arriba* spoke scornfully of the "banqueros judíos" (Jewish bankers) fleeing France. The antisemitic measures taken by the Vichy government, the German occupier, and other countries – Romania, Bulgaria – were widely approved by newspapers of all persuasions amid reports of "la tiranía judaico-masónica" (the Judeo-Masonic tyranny).[38] *Arriba* and *ABC*, through their Paris correspondents Bartolomé Calderón and Mariano Daranas respectively, were especially excoriating towards French Jews. Both defended the fiercest antisemitic measures; Daranas declared that "en concepto de parásitos no hay quien gane a los individuos de origen judío" (as parasites, there are none that surpass individuals of Jewish origin).[39]

During 1941, a new tendency emerged in the Spanish press. Frequent articles highlighted the links between the Anglo-Saxon powers and Freemasonry and especially Judaism. This stance had appeared in newspapers ever since the Civil War without interruption, but the systematic treatment during 1941 (primarily in the FET newspapers) suggests an intervention of the press services. The Falangists who controlled those services, fervent supporters of the Axis, attempted to discredit not only the United States and Great Britain but also their Spanish supporters. Examples of this identification – including antisemitic stereotypes – can be found in the March editions of *Arriba* and in various articles that attribute the black market to Judeo-Masonic dealings. León's Falangist newspaper declared: "La masonería, instrumento del judaísmo apátrida para sus fines de dominar la economía del mundo, tiene en Londres y Washington sus núcleos inspiradores" (Freemasonry, an instrument of stateless Judaism for their goal of dominating the global economy, has its inspirational core in London and in Washington). According to the same newspaper, "las logias y el sanedrín en concubinato nos quieren reducir a la desesperanza" (lodges and Sanhedrin in concubinage want to reduce us to hopelessness).[40] Antisemitic arguments continued to predominate in the attacks against Anglo-Saxons, but – surprisingly – not so much in those aimed at the Soviets, even after the launch of the

Eastern offensive, in which a corps of Spanish volunteers, the Blue Division, participated. (See chapters 23 and 24 by Boris Kovalev and Macarena Tejada López in this volume.)[41]

In 1942 the attacks in the press against the Anglo-Saxons diminished, doubtlessly for diplomatic convenience. But attacks aimed at Jews continued, and these appeared in relation to a multitude of topics, independent of the newspaper's orientation.[42] The desire to please the German Embassy (and avoid its complaints) drove those in charge of the Spanish press to prohibit praise for Jewish German-language writers, even if that praise was strictly literary. In February, the following order was given:

> Queda prohibido terminantemente cualquier artículo o comentario elogioso acerca de la personalidad del escritor judío Stefan Sweig [*sic*], suicidado en Brasil. Únicamente se permitirán los trabajos que critiquen con dureza la vida y la obra de este escritor que ha pervertido tantas conciencias.

> Any article or commentary praising the figure of the Jewish writer Stefan Sweig [*sic*], who died by suicide in Brazil, is strictly prohibited. Only those works that strongly critique the life and the work of this writer, who has perverted so many consciences, will be permitted.

Some months later, the list expanded to encompass other authors viewed as "especialmente indeseables" (especially undesirable) by the German Cultural Attaché, Wilhelm Petersen. The National Delegate of the Press, Juan Aparicio, then prohibited in newspapers "toda clase de comentarios y propaganda de publicaciones de los judíos alemanes Franz Werfel, Jacob Wassermann, Emil Ludwig y Stefan Zweig" (all manner of commentaries and propaganda about publications by the German Jews Franz Werfel, Jacob Wassermann, Emil Ludwig and Stefan Zweig).[43] Other instructions sent to the press in the first months of 1942 contained antisemitic allusions. In March, one recalled the "garras judeo-masónicas" (Judeo-Masonic claws) that had gripped Spain before the new regime took power. In May, another ordered the publication of two similar blurbs inspired by a speech during which Franco justified the 1492 Expulsion. "Los judíos traicionaban a España" (The Jews betrayed Spain), one alleged, while the other praised the "política totalitaria y racista" (totalitarian and racist policy) of the Catholic Monarchs. Also during 1942, anti-Jewish commentaries proliferated in articles that referred to current racist measures, especially after antisemitic persecution intensified in France in the spring and summer. From Paris, Mariano Daranas praised the Vel d'Hiv roundup, and antisemitic allusions were daily fare in Juan Pedro Luna's articles for *Arriba*.[44]

But at the end of 1942, with the possibility growing of an Allied victory, the Francoist regime began to distance itself from the Axis. In November, the press was ordered to "apaciguar prudentemente las pasiones encendidas por la guerra" (prudently dampen the passions lit by the war) – in other words, to provide more balanced international news. This meant toning down past enthusiasm for the Axis. As a result of this order, in 1943, antisemitic references in the press, especially in the non-Falangist press, diminished, and the press was increasingly free of anti-Masonic allusions." In *ABC*, for instance, antisemitic invectives were now rarely encountered unless they were part of speeches made by foreign figures.[45]

But this prudent position, defended by Jordana, the foreign minister, was sometimes resisted by the Falangists who controlled the press and propaganda. This explains why, in 1943, the FET newspapers were less reticent than others about publishing antisemitic commentaries, since at the end of the day they answered directly to the official press services. It also explains why, despite the general trend, some official orders continued to demand the publication of this type of commentary. Thus in April 1943, newspapers were required to publish a text that listed the shared enemies of the new Spain and the Axis as "judíos, masones, demócratas, liberales, comunistas y anarquistas" (Jews, Freemasons, democrats, liberals, communists, and anarchists).[46] For the rest of 1943, it was not uncommon for antisemitic references to appear in newspapers when some press services' orders referred to Freemasonry, even if Judaism was not explicitly mentioned in those orders.[47]

A new Falangist weekly, *El Español* (The Spaniard), helped dampen the growing tendency towards moderation. It was a subsidiary publication of the National Delegation of the Press. Taking a sensationalist approach, it continued to run on its front pages articles about the machinations of Jews and Freemasons abroad, pointing to the "perfil judaico" (Judaic profile) of the Rothschilds and the "invasión judeomasónica" (Judeo-Masonic invasion) of Algeria. After the summer of 1943 and the fall of Mussolini, this publication seemed to deal a little less with the Jews in an international context, although it still published articles that resurrected hoary antisemitic tropes. One of these was titled "El 'super-gobierno' judío, al descubierto" (The Jewish "super-government," revealed), referring to the B'nai B'rith, while in another the revelation was equally striking: "Se dice que el Talmud ha sido falsificado. Traducciones especiales para los no judíos" (Talmud said to be falsified. Special translations for non-Jews).[48] These articles, and those that addressed Freemasonry, were illustrated with characters with hooked noses and greedily grasping hands, among other conventions of antisemitic iconography (Figure 18.3). Antisemitic caricatures also appear in the Blue Division's field newspaper, as discussed in chapter 23 by Boris Kovalev.

18.3. Caricature published in *El Español*. Article by Jules Carpentier, "Se dice que el Talmud ha sido falsificado," *El Español*, Madrid, 27 November 1943, p. 13 (Collection of the Biblioteca Nacional de España).

In October 1943, Spain ended its period of "non-belligerency" and returned to neutrality. At the end of the same year, Falangist newspapers adopted a policy of moderation with regard to the Jews that the rest of the press had been following since the end of 1942, and antisemitic allusions became increasingly rare for the first time since Franco came to power. In this context, references to the key part played by Jews in the French Resistance, present in newspapers at the beginning of 1944, or the praise of Hitler after his suicide in the Catholic daily *Ya*, were more the exception than the rule.[49]

Conclusion

The Falangists who controlled the regime's propaganda apparatus made abundant use of themes provided by the Spanish anti-Jewish tradition, remodelling them and spreading them through diverse means. As they transmitted these themes for propagandistic ends, the Falangists relied on the personal involvement of the Caudillo, although he seemed not to have been especially hostile towards the Jews and even less – contrarily – towards Sephardis because of their links with Spain. It can be said that Franco's attitude towards the Jews was neither so negative as to favour systematic persecution (as occurred with the Freemasons), nor so positive as to impede antisemitic propaganda or to allow persecuted Sephardis to settle on the peninsula.

At this point, it would be useful to examine the degree of Nazi influence in Francoist antisemitic propaganda. There is no doubt that the international context affected the propaganda carried out in Spain. Hitler Germany's influence is also indisputable. Yet this does not explain the collective wave of anti-Jewish propaganda seen during the first years of Francoism. Nazi influence does seem to have determined the timeline of the phenomenon; thus, there was a particular "antisemitic inflation" during the first half of the war, especially detectable in Franco's declarations and in newspapers.

Yet at other times the influence of the Third Reich is more uncertain. There remains no doubt that Spanish Fascists – Falangists – were enthusiastic philo-Nazis who sometimes collaborated in the distribution of German propaganda. However, if they played an important role in the spread of antisemitic themes, that can be explained by their control of the propaganda apparatus rather than by a particular aversion to the Jews or by the systematic transmission of slogans from Berlin. In fact, antisemitism had never been an essential element of Falangist ideology; it occupied a less important role for them than for other factions within the Francoist bloc. Furthermore, the antisemitic violence of the official propaganda was greater at the beginning of the Civil War, between 1936 and 1938, when it was not yet in the hands of Falangists.[50] And from an ideological point of view, the anti-Judaism being spread in Spain did not have Nazi origins. In Falangist propaganda such as Ediciones Toledo (and in Franco's occasional antisemitic attacks), what clearly predominated were topics in the Christian anti-Jewish tradition, well-rooted in Spain for decades, and not some newly imported racial theory. So one must not exaggerate the weight of Nazi influence, since that would lead to underestimating the relevance of internal factors, such as those mentioned.[51]

In a country with an insignificant Jewish population, one must underscore the utilitarian nature of antisemitic propaganda. Whether or not the disseminators of these discourses believed what they were saying – one sometimes doubts their conviction – there is no doubt they performed very different functions. To begin, one could speak of an explicative function, where antisemitic discourse was used to simplistically explain complex phenomena such as hunger, economic hard times, rumours, and even the world war, attributing these to the scheming of Jews and their allies. Pamphlets such as *Andanzas del bulo* and *La garra del capitalismo judío* went in this direction. One can also point to a legitimizing function of the regime and the measures it took: the 1936 revolt and the system that it had brought into being were characterized as nothing more than a healthy Spain rising against the dictatorship of Jews and Freemasons that had dominated during the Second Republic. These arguments continued to be present in various propagandistic media during the Second World War. Furthermore, some pamphlets from Ediciones Toledo justified specific measures taken by the regime. One can also detect a cohesive function: in a framework of profound differences and even tensions among the components of the Francoist conglomerate (tensions that were especially serious between 1941 and 1942), it could be useful to invoke a common Judeo-Masonic enemy against which they needed to close ranks, for example in the 1942 campaign for unity between the army and the Falange. Moreover, by means of a substitutive function, such attacks could be focused on Jews, alone or together with Freemasons, at a moment when it was not advisable to direct them at the regime's real enemies, which is to say the "Reds," foreign or domestic. This occurred in the press in the context of the German-Soviet Non-Aggression Pact, when anti-Bolshevik propaganda lost some steam, but it also can be observed in pamphlets from Ediciones Toledo, in which anti-communist discourse was not the most appropriate means for attracting popular sectors that might have sympathized with leftists. Neither was it wise to attack the *moros*

(Moors), even though they stood as the traditional enemies of the Christian Spain that Franco was defending, given that Moroccan troops had contributed heavily to the rebel victory in the Civil War. The Jews, meanwhile, functioned as the other hereditary enemy onto whom all invectives could fall.

In sum, if official Francoist propaganda launched a considerable effort to present the Jews as one of the primary evils confronting Spain, often in alliance with Freemasons, it was because multiple benefits could be obtained from that imaginary enemy.

NOTES

 1 Pedro Correa Martín-Arroyo discusses the Franco myth in chapter 20 of
    this volume. An overview of contemporary Spanish antisemitism can be
    found in Álvarez Chillida, *El antisemitismo en España*. On the Jewish Archive,
    see ibid., 402–3 and also Jacobo Israel Garzón's chapter 3 in this volume.
    Álvarez Chillida estimates the number of Jews who remained in 1939 in the
    only two peninsular cities with notable Hebrew communities: twenty-five
    families in Madrid and some five hundred individuals in Barcelona (402).
    The situation was different in the African territories, where the Jewish
    presence was larger. See also Álvarez Chillida's chapter 2 in this volume.
 2 This chapter synthesizes the results of research that can be consulted
    in the following Spanish and French publications: Domínguez Arribas,
    El enemigo judeo-masónico, and *L'ennemi judéo-maçonnique*.
 3 On the *Protocols*, see Taguieff (dir.), *Les Protocoles des Sages de Sion*.
    A general overview of the topic in Goldschläger and Lemaire, *Le complot
    judéo-maçonnique*; another is Domínguez Arribas, *El enemigo*, ch. 1. On
    Spain, see Álvarez Chillida, *El antisemitismo en España* and chapter 2 in this
    volume.
 4 See Jouin, ed., *Los peligros judío-masónicos*; Poncins, *Las fuerzas secretas*.
 5 On the Second Republic, see Álvarez Chillida, *El antisemitismo en España*,
    ch. 10.
 6 See Domínguez Arribas, *El enemigo*, 519–22; and Bermejo,
    "La Vicesecretaría de Educación Popular," 73–96. For an extensive discus-
    sion of the regime's relationship with the Catholic Church during the war,
    see Graciela Ben Dror's chapter 19 in this volume.
 7 See, for example, Bachoud, *Franco ou la réussite*, 242.
 8 Franco Bahamonde, *Papeles de la guerra de Marruecos*, 191–2.
 9 Jaime de Andrade (pseud., Francisco Franco), *Raza*, 76–7.
10 See Figueras i Vallès, *Las raíces judías de Franco*. On dealings with Jewish
    families, see Blin, *Franco et les Juifs*, vol. 1, 95–100, 116–18; vol. 2, 236, 275.

11 Archivo General Militar (Ávila), Cuartel General del Generalísimo, 5/284/20.

12 Lisbona, *Retorno a Sefarad*, 67–8.

13 *Arriba*, Madrid, 18 July 1940, 11; 18 July 1941, 16; Álvarez Chillida, *El antisemitismo en España*, 398.

14 The British Embassy in Madrid had already highlighted the German influence on Franco's antisemitic declarations. See Lisbona, *Retorno a Sefarad*, 109.

15 The articles were compiled in a book: J. Boor (pseud.), *Masonería*, 52, 96, 221 (citations).

16 See, for example, the pamphlet *L'Espagne et les Juifs*.

17 España, "Antisemitismo en el cine español"; Alegre Calero, "Las imágenes de la División Azul," 71–2.

18 *Aldea. Hoja para la formación nacional-sindicalista de la juventud rural*, April 1944, in Carulla and Carulla, *La guerra civil en 2000 carteles*, vol. 2, 573.

19 Leaflets reproduced by Schulze Schneider, "La cooperación de la Alemania nazi," 1183–5.

20 Archivo General de la Administración, Alcalá de Henares, Culture Section (AGA, C.), 21/39 and 119.

21 Segura Nieto, *¡Alerta! ... Francmasonería y Judaísmo*; Castro, *El problema judío*; Estrada, *Cuando Inglaterra quedó sola ...*

22 Urrutia, *La paz que quiere Hitler*; *Por qué la Falange es católica*.

23 AGA, C., 21/67, 23 January 1942; 21/109, 16 January 1942; 21/70, 15 March 1941; 21/43, 19 December 1941; 21/39, 8 May 1942.

24 AGA, C., 21/67–69. Quote on 21/68.

25 Baeza Mancebo, *La hora de Gibraltar*, 205; Giménez Caballero, *¡Despierta Inglaterra!*, 20, 28; Urrutia, *¡Camarada: He aquí el enemigo!*, 32.

26 *La masonería en acción*, 43; AGA, C., 21/67, 110.

27 *La masonería femenina*, 10. Five thousand copies were made. AGA, C., 21/38, 68 and 69.

28 Ferrari Billoch, *Andanzas del bulo*, 21 and 45; AGA, C., 21/68, 110.

29 *La garra del capitalismo judío*, 26; AGA, C., 21/76, 109, 146.

30 Ferrari Billoch, *La masonería al desnudo*, 3rd ed.

31 Centro Documental de la Memoria Histórica, Salamanca (CDMH), B 115/10 and TERMC 242/42 (Ferrari Billoch's records). See Domínguez Arribas, *El enemigo*, ch. 6. A preliminary version of this chapter in Domínguez Arribas, "La propaganda anti-judeo-masónica," 1165–94; republished in *Hibris*, n. 65–6, September–December 2011, 17–41.

32 See, for example, Sinova, *La censura de prensa*.

33 See *Arriba*, Madrid, 3 May 1939, 7; 10 May 1939, 7; 15 May 1939, 3; 21 May 1939, 8; 25 May 1939, 1; 30 July 1939, 1; *ABC*, Madrid, 17 June 1939, 6; Lazo, *La Iglesia, la Falange y el fascismo*, 2nd ed., 214.

34 *Diario Regional*, Valladolid, 18 August 1939, 1, cited by Pérez López,
    "Prensa, poder político y religión," 265. See also *Arriba*, Madrid, 4 May
    1939, 8; Lazo, *La Iglesia, la Falange y el fascismo*, 184, 187; *Amanecer*,
    Zaragoza, 17 August 1939, 3, in Morales Ruiz, *El discurso antimasónico*, 355.

35 See references cited by Lazo, *La Iglesia, la Falange y el fascismo*, 184, 186, 188,
    205, 207, 211, 214–16; *Arriba*, Madrid, 12 October 1939, 8; 3 November 1939,
    1. See also Sinova, *La censura de prensa*, 221–2, which mentions the orders
    that asked to show a "strict neutrality" at that time.

36 See *Arriba*, Madrid, 28 February 1940, 1; *Amanecer*, Zaragoza, 25 February
    1940, 1, in Morales Ruiz, *El discurso antimasónico*, 356–7; as well as the
    references cited by Martín de la Guardia, Pelaz López, and Pérez López,
    "Prensa y masonería en Castilla," in Ferrer Benimeli (co-ord.), *Masonería y
    periodismo*, 295–322, esp. 299.

37 See Lazo, *La Iglesia, la Falange y el fascismo*, 216; and Ros Agudo, *La guerra
    secreta de Franco*, 277.

38 *ABC*, Madrid, 22 June 1940, 3; *Arriba*, Madrid, 22 June 1940; 25 June
    1940, 1, 6; 27 June 1940, 4; 28 June 1940, 3; Martín de la Guardia et al.,
    "Prensa y masonería en Castilla," 298–300, 304; Lazo, *La Iglesia, la Falange y
    el fascismo*, 185, 250–1, 262.

39 *ABC*, Sevilla, 4 July 1940, in Lazo, *La Iglesia, la Falange y el fascismo*, 187–8;
    Arriba, Madrid, 1 October 1940, 8; 15 October 1940, 5; 20 October 1940, 8.

40 See *Arriba*, Madrid, 20 March 1941, 4; 25 March 1941, 4; 27 March 1941, 4;
    29 March, 1; 2 April 1941, 5; *Proa*, León, 15 June 1941, clipping in CDMH,
    A/291/1.

41 The National Delegation of the Press ordered the publication of an edi-
    torial on those dates that mentioned the "virus demoliberal, judío y
    masónico" (Jewish, Masonic, and Demo-Liberal virus) that had afflicted
    both Germany and Spain. See *Arriba*, Madrid, 24 June 1941, 1, 3.

42 See Ros Agudo, *La guerra secreta de Franco*, 283–4. Examples in Lazo,
    La Iglesia, la Falange y el fascismo, 198, 208.

43 AGA, C., 21/76, 25 February 1942; 21/219, 4 November 1942.

44 *ABC*, Madrid, 23 May 1942, 6; 21 July 1942, 8; *Arriba*, Madrid, 20 August
    1942, 6; 22 August 1942, 6; 25 August 1942, 5. The last orders mentioned in
    AGA, C., 21/76, 2 and 3 March 1942, and 21/77, 30 May 1942.

45 See, for example, *ABC*, Madrid, 6 March 1943, 8; and Blin, *Franco et les
    Juifs*, vol. 1, 216. The November order in Río Cisneros, *Viraje político
    español*, 130–1.

46 Lazo, *La Iglesia, la Falange y el fascismo*, 216–17, 284. See the aforementioned
    back and forth in Ros Agudo, *La guerra secreta de Franco*, 285–6.

47 See, for example *El Diario Vasco*, San Sebastián, 6 October [1943], clipping
    in AGA, C., 21/903.

48 *El Español*, Madrid, 14 November 1942, 13; 2 January 1943, 1, 13; 9 January 1943, 1, 12; 25 September 1943, 1, 10; 27 November 1943, 1, 13, among others.

49 See *La Voz de España*, San Sebastián, 6 January 1944, 4; 27 February 1944, 4; 3 March 1944, 5; *ABC*, Madrid, 19 February 1944, 13; 16 March 1944, 21; 9 May 1944, 27–8; *Ya*, Madrid, 2 May 1945, the latter cited by Álvarez Chillida, *El antisemitismo en España*, 414.

50 See Domínguez Arribas, *El enemigo*, ch. 3.

51 Mercedes Peñalba-Sotorrío explores the phenomenon of German propaganda in Spain during the war in greater detail in chapter 21 of this volume.

19 The Catholic Church and the Jews in Franco's Spain during the Holocaust, 1939–1945

GRACIELA BEN DROR

The establishment of General Francisco Franco's government in April 1939 worsened conditions for non-Catholic minorities in Spain, who faced exclusion from social and political life when Catholicism was reinstated as the state religion and freedom of worship was abolished.[1] The Church had supported Nationalist Spain during the Civil War, for which it received compensation in both the religious and social sectors. Once Franco consolidated his government, liberal and secular reforms were quickly reversed throughout the country. A series of laws revoked Republican legislation. In terms of education, the numerous decrees and laws enacted beginning in 1936 – in the Nationalist-controlled regions – re-established the obligatory teaching of the Catholic religion in schools. The state reallocated funds for all Catholic institutions, and the Church obtained the right to supervise the entire educational system after the Republic's defeat. The 1 March 1940 law against Freemasons and Communists decreed the illegality of both. Through state assets, the Church re-established its own structure of educational, social, cultural, and moral control.[2]

Jewish and Protestant communities lost their legitimacy as a social presence. The opening towards religious plurality, initiated in Spain with the 1869 constitution, came to an abrupt end with the Nationalist victory. From the beginning of the Franco regime, the government adopted a series of measures to limit and reduce Jewish activities. Between March and October of 1940, Jewish weddings and burials were prohibited, as were circumcisions. Newborns could not be recorded in the Civil Registry without being baptized; Jewish children who wanted to attend school had to take catechism classes. In Barcelona, a Jewish cemetery was destroyed. All Jewish institutions were closed, which compelled Spanish Jews to return to a state of semi-hiding.[3]

Spanish Catholic Action Youth

Catholic doctrine repudiated racism, and followers were repeatedly reminded of this in the Spanish Catholic media. But this repudiation did not signify a parallel repudiation of antisemitism. After the Germans invaded Poland, the youth of Catholic Action repudiated racism in general, but did not understand that their antisemitic messages would constitute a logical rejection of their anti-racist position. Judaism was seen as an integral part of the communist world. This type of thinking seems to have had its roots in Acción Católica (Catholic Action), initiated by the leaders themselves. The president of the youth branch of Catholic Action, Manuel Aparici, in a speech to Italian Catholic Action youth about cooperation between young Spaniards and Italians, argued in December 1939, four months after the Second World War began, that Judaism and paganism were Christ's two enemies:

> Jóvenes italianos de Acción Católica!
>
> Vosotros y nosotros en unidad de fin estamos, como en otros tiempos, señalados por el dedo de Dios para hundir de un modo definitivo en este mundo moderno, ebrio de concupiscencias, a los dos enemigos de Cristo: judaismo y paganismo. Judaísmo representado por leyendas de igualdades comunistas, destructoras de la civilización cristiana; paganismo representado por apariencias de culturas nacionales en que el Dios que nos dijo la unidad y la caridad de los hombres se ciñe a fronteras geográficas y raciales.

> Italian Youth of the Catholic Action! You and we, finally united as we are, as we were in other times, chosen by the finger of God to definitively bury in our modern world, drunk on lust, Christ's two enemies: Judaism and Paganism. Judaism, represented by legends of Communist equality, destroyers of Christian civilization; Paganism, represented by appearances of national cultures, in which the God who taught us about unity and charity of men, is reduced to geographic and racial borders.[4]

These positions underwent no modification once news began to arrive of the suffering of Jews following the Nazi German conquest of Poland. Catholic journalists did not condemn antisemitism after the war broke out; indeed, they justified and praised the founding of nationalist fascist and antisemitic organizations in Europe, such as the Iron Guard in Romania. That organization's leader, Corneliu Codreanu, constantly emphasized his Catholicism, and this legitimized him in the eyes of Spanish Catholics, who did not view his antisemitism as a reason to object to him in any way. According to the Catholic Action youth, the Iron Guard existed for the purpose of combating the corrupt current of Jewish immigration and its doctrine was based on the authority of God and Jesus Christ. Catholics could not approve of the violence carried out by the Iron Guard, yet a justification for their actions did exist. According to the Catholic magazine *Misión*, given that Romania's current constitution permitted total freedom of expression and association, "podían en Rumania propagarse las ideas disolventes más extremadas y el elemento semita desplegar sus actividades con holgura que jamás fue permitida a la Guardia de Hierro" (in Romania one could spread the most extreme ... ideas and the Semitic element could carry out their activities to an extent that was never permitted with the Iron Guard.)[5]

Another accusation against Jews arose in relation to Jewish influence in the North American film industry. Part of the Spanish Catholic press expressed its fear that the Jews would take over communications – above all, film, which was in the hands of "judaizantes empresas yanquis" (Jewish Yankee businesses) – thereby enabling them to intervene in the ideological struggle that now consumed the world. According to them, Yankee cinema was attacking the totalitarian countries. An example was *Confessions of a Nazi Spy*, an anti-Nazi Hollywood movie that provoked protests in Germany in 1939. The Catholic magazine *Misión* was not pro-Nazi but it did support Germany in the sense that it defended those who had supported the Nationalist cause. Furthermore, the Nazis offered an excellent example of how to eliminate Jewish influence in literature and the press, both of which were associated with Jewish leadership. *Misión* took an anti-racist position, yet in its desire to defend Germany, which it perceived as an ally and protector against a common enemy – the Communists – it lauded the fact that in Germany "el gran número de escritores judíos que llenaban editoriales y revistas ha desaparecido" (the large number of Jewish writers who filled the presses and magazines have disappeared).[6]

News of persecutions in Europe had started to filter out. The Catholic press reported that Jews in Nazi-occupied zones had been forbidden to participate in any form of publishing. The expulsion of the Jews, as a solution to preventing their evils, continued to be a topic of reference whenever the Jewish question raised its ugly head. Given that any attempt to integrate the Jews was bound to fail, "la única política posible era la expulsión" (the only possible policy was expulsion).[7]

Moreover, the members of Spanish Catholic Action, paraphrasing the well-known antisemitic Argentine priest Julio Meinvielle, argued that history revolved around an ongoing apocalyptic three-way struggle between paganism, Judaism, and Christianity. Judaism and its anti-Christian inclinations were manifest in the present day's chaos and in communism; paganism had appeared in Germany; and Portugal and Spain represented the Christian countries. According to Meinvielle, in the end the Christian Cross would triumph over the Gammadion Cross (the swastika), but before that happened the pagan nations would destroy communism, after which they would change their spots and be transformed by Christianity.[8] Meinvielle was a notable antisemitic theologian, and his influence stretched to Spain. Similar views were to be found in the writings of Hugo Wast, a Catholic layman of great influence in the Argentine Church. His book *Kahal-Oro*, practically a plagiarism of *The Protocols of the Elders of Zion*, also found an audience in Spain.[9]

The Jesuits, *Razón y Fe*, and the Jews

In Spain in the 1930s and 1940s, the Jesuits published a journal of the highest intellectual level, *Razón y Fe* (Reason and Faith), which concerned itself primarily with philosophy and theology. In its pages, references to politics were only indirect; its official position was anti-racist, anti-liberal, anti-parliamentary, and anti-communist. The Jesuits based their texts on ecclesiastic documents with philosophical and theological themes, including those related to Spanish and universal Catholicism.[10]

A prominent feature of the journal was its anti-racist and anti-Nazi stance, notable within the framework of Spanish Catholicism. That stance had emerged before the Second World War and would persist throughout it, notwithstanding the journal's enthusiastic support of Germany and Nationalist Spain: *Razón y Fe* stuck to its own theological and ideological tendencies. The Franco government enforced strict censorship, but with a focus on daily journalism; in that climate, the Jesuits enjoyed relative independence.[11]

In an article published in *Razón y Fe* in mid-1939, E. Fernández Almuzara tried to defend the Jews by critiquing Henry Ford's *The International Jew*, stressing that Jews could not be responsible for all the world's evils. In this defence, the author argued that viewing the Jew as a sort of demonic Prometheus or a terrible Pandora's box from whom, like a pestilent cesspool, all human misfortune comes, was both unjust and untruthful. He contended that Ford's book, which had become fashionable in Spain, was "cerradamente antisemita, basado *en Los Protocolos de los sabios de Sión*, cuya autenticidad histórica no puede defenderse en sana crítica" (covertly antisemitic, based on *The Protocols of the Elders of Zion*, whose historical authenticity cannot be defended by moral criticism). Yet he also admitted that

> [p]or perversa que juzguemos la raza judía no iremos hasta afirmar que es esencialmente mala. Hay, sin duda judíos malos, y hasta si se quiere, concedamos que sean los más numerosos. Pero mientras haya alguno, o algunos, que sean buenos, será injusto condenarlos a todos por igual y medirlos con el mismo rasero.

> as perverse as we judge the Jewish race to be, we will not go so far as to confirm it is essentially evil. There are, without a doubt, bad Jews, and even, if you will, we concede that they are the most numerous. But while there are some that are good, it will be unjust to condemn them all the same and to judge them on the same scale.[12]

The *converso* Jew could not, according to this conception, be an evil man. The author argued that the ideal example was that of the Catholic monarchs Fernando and Isabel, who "no alimentaron hacia los judíos odio de casta. Hubo entonces y después muchos israelitas que, asimilados por España alcanzaron altos puestos, dentro de ella, en las armas, en las letras y en la política" (did not even show class hatred to the Jews. Then and later there were many Israelites who, assimilated into Spain, reached high posts within the country, in the military, in literature, and in politics). Yet even within this firm anti-racist position and criticism of Ford's book, Fernández Almuzara's writing contained underlying anti-semitic arguments. In a subtle criticism of the Jesuits, Ford had accused them of being "instrumentos de los judíos" (instruments of the Jews). To refute this accusation, Fernández Almuzara employed antisemitic tropes common during the period:

> La habilidad de los judíos es sin duda, muy grande para introducirse en los círculos políticos y, valiéndose de aventureros, espías y secretos agentes, manejar la diplomacia a su antojo ... Tal vez la masonería es un disfraz del judaísmo. Pero que la Compañía de Jesús sea una potencia subterránea al servicio de la sinagoga, no se puede creer.

> The ability of the Jews is, without a doubt, strong enough for them to be able to enter political spheres and, making use of adventurers, spies, and secret agents, manipulating diplomacy to their liking ... Perhaps Freemasonry is a mask of Judaism. But the idea that the Society of Jesus is an underground power servicing the synagogue, is not believable.

Moreover, the author argued that "fuera de esto, nadie ignora ya que uno de los impedimentos para ser jesuíta es la falta de limpieza de sangre" (beyond this, no one can ignore that one of the barriers to being a Jesuit is the lack of blood purity). In his defence of the Jews on the one hand, and of Jesuits on the other, the author resorted to deeply rooted antisemitic arguments originating in the pervasive modern European antisemitism. From there, Almuzara was able to recommend Ford's book as worth reading: "Con todo, nada de esto destruye el mérito de la obra de Ford, que cuando no nos enseña nos deleita, y que puede servirnos de excelente ayuda para la mejor comprensión de uno de los problemas que más apasiona hoy a las gentes" (In the end, none of this undermines the merits of Ford's work, as when it does not teach us, it delights us, and it can be an excellent way to help us better understand one of the problems that concerns people today).[13]

If it is true that the Jesuits adhered to this anti-racist position along with the only viable Catholic position regarding the Jewish problem, they were not the only ones, for it was also the official position of the Catholic Church. For the Jesuits, much as it was expressed in *Razón y Fe*, "el racismo constituía un error moderno que quebrantaba la solidaridad de la especie humana mediante el mito de la raza" (racism constituted a modern error that broke the solidarity of the human species by means of the myth of race). Thus they rejected the content of *Mein Kampf* as well as *The Myth of the Twentieth Century* by Alfred Rosenberg. The Jesuits also prominently concerned themselves with the issue of euthanasia in Germany after the practice was repudiated by the German bishopric. They condemned euthanasia as irrational, unjust, and condemnable; they also criticized those who, based on eugenics, resorted to the law to restrict marriages between certain people.[14]

The Jesuit journal adopted a somewhat patronizing tone when referring to, for example, Native Americans, even while rejecting all racism and reaffirming the "doctrina de igualdad substancial" (doctrine of substantial equality) among all men. Regarding these peoples, they commented that "[p]recisamente porque su inferioridad civil, cultural, racial y religiosa saltaba a los ojos" (precisely because their civil, cultural, racial, and religious inferiority jumped out), the Spaniards helped them, unlike in the present day, which saw discussions of sharp differences between races as well as a fixation on "grupos superiores e inferiores" (superior and inferior groups), in the course of which "todos los derechos fundamentales" (all fundamental rights) were taken away from the latter. The writers here were undoubtedly making veiled commentary on Nazi racism.[15]

The Jesuits were also interested in the "new world order," which they contended should be a Catholic one. This explains why they rejected all other ideologies that in the twentieth century were attempting to control the world's governance: Soviet Russian Bolshevism, Italian Fascism, and German National Socialism. Their criticisms encompassed politics, economics, and philosophy simultaneously.[16]

It turns out, then, that while the official and semi-official Catholic publications in Spain condemned racist theory, they did not openly oppose antisemitic attitudes. Until 1941, the Jewish question was barely discussed. Furthermore, the Jesuits in Spain did not concern themselves with the persecution of the Jews, despite their declared anti-racist position. The Jesuit organization in Rome, Civiltà Cattólica, also made numerous expressions of antisemitism through to the end of the Second World War.[17]

The Holocaust and Its Repercussions in Spanish Catholic Action (Acción Católica Española, ACE)

An approach similar to the one taken by the Jesuits also developed in *Eclessia*, the official journal of Acción Católica, the secular branch of the Church. In June 1941, the Germans invaded the Soviet Union and began systematically murdering Jews. In 1942, this mass extermination took the form of slaughter in gas chambers specially constructed to accelerate that process. Reports of this began to reach the Allied countries and their media in the middle of 1942; in November of 1942 the reports of this mass extermination were finally confirmed, then reconfirmed in December by the Allies.[18] In Spain it would have been difficult for the Spaniards to receive news about the magnitude of the extermination before the end of 1942, even though they surely received at least some information from their consulates. (See Lisbona, chapter 8, in this volume about Spanish diplomatic communiqués regarding the mass murder of Jews.)

For Spain and Spanish Catholicism, in the second half of 1941, attention to crises in the international sphere naturally concerned affairs other than the fate of European Jewry. The German invasion of the Soviet Union had fostered a new hope of destroying communism, considered a bitter enemy of Catholic Spain. The "crusade" against communism was publicized in the media of the Catholic youth, which called for people to enlist in the Blue Division. They saw this as a means to reward Germany for its cooperation in the Civil War as well as to fight a common enemy. (On the Blue Division, see chapters 23 and 24 by Kovalev and Tejada López in this volume.)

The Jewish question raised its head only sporadically in print. But as early as June 1942, before the German invasion of the Soviet Union, it was broached in *Ecclesia* in an editorial that stated the position of Spanish Acción Católica. On 13 June 1942, "necessary clarifications" were made to Catholic readers in which the editors emphasized the permanent truths of the faith that its readers should embrace. One such permanent truth was that "al pueblo de Israel le fue providencialmente señalada una misión histórica o tuvo una misión providencial en la Historia. Fue el pueblo elegido para de que de él saliera el Redentor del mundo" (the Israeli people were providentially given the sign of a historic mission or they had a providential mission in History. The people were chosen so that the world's Redeemer would emerge from them). Divine Will was manifested, according to the editor, when the rule of Law was given to them in Sinai, ending slavery there, when the sea was opened to save them, when they were fed in the desert, and when it was revealed to them that the Messiah would be born from their seed. But "[s]i, desde la muerte de Salomón, la historia de Israel y de Judá no es sino una serie de crímenes, de impiedades e idolatrías, solo algunas veces abjuradas, la crucifixión del propio Hijo de Dios corona esta historia de infidelidad" (if, since the death of Solomon, the history of Israel and of Judas is nothing but a series of crimes, of impieties and idolatry, only sometimes retracted, the crucifixion of the Son of God himself crowns this history of infidelity). Interpreting the thinking of Saint Paul and Saint Augustine, the editor claimed that "el hundimiento del pueblo judío se debió a su ingratitud para con el Señor, que le había colmado de favores" (the collapse of the Jewish people was caused by their ingratitude to God, who had granted them abundant favours). But then, to reinforce his argument based on the necessity not to deviate from interpretations taken from the Scriptures, he added his own conception of the negative world in regard to the Jews, echoing modern antisemitism by claiming:

Sin olvidar estas verdades católicas, podemos luego abrigar las justas reservas que han movido y mueven a los Estados a precaverse contra las influencias perturbadoras de los israelitas. Precisamente España, en las horas más augustas y geniales de su historia, supo fundamentar su repulsa en altos móviles no de índole física o de cualquier modo material, sino de altísima conveniencia espiritual y religiosa.

Without forgetting these Catholic truths, we can then protect the just reserves that have moved and that are moving to nation states to protect against the disturbing influences of the Israelites. Precisely Spain, in the most august and brilliant hours of her history, knew to base its highly-motivated condemnation not on physical nature or any material means, but on the highest spiritual and religious interest.[19]

Acción Católica's objective with this editorial was to reinforce the obligatory and sacred character of both the Old Testament and the New, as well as to remind its affiliates that God's choice of the Jews was the work of Divine Will and thus impossible to refute.[20]

For its followers, the Church set up clear barriers with respect to the Jewish people; there were certain bounds that Catholics could not overstep or violate. Human dignity and God's election of the Jewish people were both part of this clearly drawn boundary. Many priests insisted on differentiating religious from racist motives in their arguments, yet in their writings it is sometimes difficult to distinguish between religious and racist themes. For example, the Jesuit priest Enrique Herrera y Oria, in his book *Historia de la educación española después del Renacimiento* (*History of Spanish Education after the Renaissance*), argued in 1941 that:

> es misterio divino el espíritu del mal y la destrucción de la raza judía, se trata de una realidad que la ciencia no puede explicar ... la mentalidad de los judíos los llevó a provocar ... la catástrofe más bárbara de la humanidad ... masonería, judaísmo, socialismo y comunismo son todos hijos de la misma madre.

> it is divine mystery the spirit of evil and the destruction of the Jewish race, it has to do with a reality that science cannot explain ... the mentality of the Jews led them to provoke ... the most savage catastrophe of humanity ... Freemasonry, Judaism, Socialism, and Communism are all children of the same mother.[21]

For many Spanish Catholics at the time, the difference between a Jew and a communist was practically non-existent. After the Germans invaded Lithuania, Acción Católica, which among other things served as the mouthpiece for the ecclesiastical hierarchy, obtained information from Lithuanian sources that most of the country's communist organizations had largely Jewish memberships and that the Lithuanian population loathed them as a consequence. Lithuanian media reinforced this equating of "Jew" with "communist," drawing from traditional antisemitic prejudices, and a similar phenomenon surfaced in Spain. Spain had only a tiny Jewish population, yet their *imagined* presence and the view that they were the "real" enemy cast a long shadow. The news from Lithuania circulating in the Catholic press contended that 80 per cent of Lithuanian Communist Party members were Jews, who thus enjoyed the private confidence of the party and occupied the best positions in public administration, in factories, and in the propaganda apparatus. According to these reports – covered in the Acción Católica's youth magazine *Signo* – fifteen thousand Polish Jews had taken refuge in Lithuania and become active Communists; this explained why "con justicia se los odió, y para los lituanos 'judío' y 'ruso' quieren decir lo mismo" (the hatred towards them was justified, and for the Lithuanians, "Jew" and "Russian" mean the same thing).[22]

At the same time, the term "Pharisee" was used as a synonym for communist. Russia, it was said, did not enjoy social equality, and rich people still existed in the Soviet state; "esa raza de fariseos le ha quitado a los pobres hasta al mismo Cristo" (the Pharisee race have even taken Christ away from the poor). The identification of communists, as a political and religious enemy, with the Pharisees, synonymous with Christ killers, was fully consolidated as a concept two years after the Civil War.

In August 1941, the youth branch of Catholic Action reminded its activists who the enemies of traditional Christianity were: "En la lucha se han revelado los enemigos: el judaísmo, el paganismo, la herejía, el cisma, la falsa ciencia, la falsa política, la ignorancia y la concupiscencia." (In the struggle the enemies have been revealed: Judaism, Paganism, heresy, schism, false science, false politics, ignorance, and lust).[23] The absence of communism from this list was no accident: it would have been understood that "Judaism" folded communists into its definition.

This language we have been examining echoes the official position in terms of Catholic doctrine regarding Judaism. Yet when news about the physical extermination of Jews began to surface and circulate, most Spanish Catholics, as in other countries, did not take a stand on the issue. In rhetoric and praxis, the Catholic Church remained bound to an unadulterated continuity of traditional antisemitic content, including stereotypes; these would be modified only after the Second Vatican Council.

On 20 February 1943, *Ecclesia* took up the topic of "la expulsión de los judíos de España por los Reyes Católicos" (the Expulsion of the Spanish Jews by the Catholic Monarchs). Given that this publication served as the voice of the leadership of Acción Católica, in its selection of topics for discussion we can discern the prevailing position of the Spanish Catholic establishment in 1943 with regard to the Jewish question. In rejecting racist antisemitism, the editors presented the 1492 Expulsion as an ideal model for the treatment the Jews that should be extended on behalf of Christianity. From their point of view, Spain had resolved the Jewish problem by means of the Expulsion:

> y en ello adelantábase en muchos siglos y con evidente cordura y sensibil-
> idad a las medidas profilácticas que hoy han tomado tantas naciones para
> librarse del elemento judaico, fermento tantas veces de descomposición

nacional, del cual España se salvó efectivamente para siempre merced al referido decreto.

> and in that act, they moved forward for many centuries and, with evident good sense and sensitivity to the prophylactic means that so many nations have taken today to rid themselves of the Jewish element, so often the cause of national decomposition, of which Spain effectively saved itself thanks to the referenced decree.[24]

The consequence of that decree was that in the 1940s, within the framework of the Spanish Catholic Church, Jews were conceived as traitors who threatened the nation's stability. Protective measures needed to be implemented in order to defend the nation against the Jews. In this regard, the Catholic Monarchs had determined that expulsion was the ideal way to deal with the Jews. But that expulsion was *religious*, not racist. Furthermore, motive mattered much more than consequence. According to these criteria, expulsion based on racism was unacceptable, but when it was conducted on religious grounds, it was considered both valid and Christian. Therefore, "expeler de sí los elementos extraños y perjudiciales a su vida, y tal fué el caso de España, prueba de su recia vitalidad religiosa" (expelling from the self the foreign and dangerous elements of life was a sign of vitality, and that was the case in Spain, proof of their robust religious vitality). From there,

> que es inadecuado considerar el edicto como una medida de salvaguardia de la raza nacional, pues ello supondría creer en la España de Diego Laínez y los teólogos defensores en Trento de la doctrina de la justificación y de la igualdad esencial de los hombres, participe de la teoría que supone la supremacía humana fundada en meros motivos de color o de sangre.

> it is inadequate to consider the edict as a means of protection of the national race. Because that would suppose a belief in the Spain of Diego Laínez and the theologians in Trent who defend the doctrine of the justification and essential equality of men, part of the theory that assumes the human supremacy founded in mere motives of color or blood.[25]

All of this led to the conclusion that Spaniards were not racists and that indeed they defended the Christian doctrine of essential equality among all men.

Furthermore, it was claimed that the edict was "rotundamente popular" (wildly popular). These explanations and the religious justifications for the 1492 expulsion show the extent to which the will to hang

on to historic tradition impeded any abandonment of ancient stereotypes. The justifications for aversion towards Jews included "la riqueza
judaica y el orgullo y la sed de mando a ellas inherentes" (the Jewish
riches, and the pride, and thirst for control inherent in them), as well as

> la separación judía de los cristianos en materia alimenticia, la muerte
> de Jesús de Nazaret, el celo indiscreto de algunos frailes y el odio de
> religión, con el deseo natural en quien domina de someter a los demás a
> su religión y a su fe, los celos amorosos producidos por haber puesto los
> judíos sus ojos en las mujeres de España.

> the Jewish separation from the Christians in relation to food, the death
> of Jesus of Nazareth, the indiscrete zeal of some friars, and the hatred of
> religion, with the natural desire of those that are in power to impose their
> religion and their faith on those they control, the jealousy produced when
> the Jews set their eyes on the women of Spain.[26]

Their economic position as "arrendador o almoxarife" (landlord or
treasurer), "el abominable tráfico de esclavos" (the abominable traf-
ficking of slaves), and other Jewish occupations also contributed to the
rationalization for expulsion.

In this context, the work of the Inquisition was justified, based on
the primary objective of the Catholic Monarchs, which was the unity of
Spain. Therefore,

> [e]n el heredado problema aquellos (los Reyes Católicos) temían, sobre
> todo, el daño espiritual creado en sus súbditos por la convivencia de
> judíos y cristianos, y después de ver fracasados los métodos pacíficos y de
> convicción que de modo especial la Inquisición intentó y embriagados por
> el éxito de la destrucción del último reducto musulmán promulgan el céle-
> bre decreto expulsorio el 31 de marzo de 1492, por virtud del cual habían
> de salir de España en un plazo de tres meses cuántos hebreos rehusaran
> la conversión.

> in the inherited problem they [the Catholic Monarchs] feared, above all,
> spiritual damage created in their subjects by the cohabitation of Jews and
> Christians, and after seeing the failure of the peaceful methods and with
> the conviction that the special means that the Inquisition attempted and
> drunk on the success of the destruction of the final Muslim stronghold,
> they promulgated the celebrated expulsion decree on March 31, 1492, by
> virtue of which all Hebrews who refused conversion were forced to leave
> Spain within three months.[27]

The decree was "a no dudarlo, rotundamente popular ... y considerado como el esfuerzo más gigantesco en pro de la unidad religiosa registrado por la historia humana" (without a doubt, wildly popular ... and considered to be the largest effort in favour of religious unity registered in human history). The dominant justification for the expulsion and the Inquisition as expressions of Spanish unity resided, then, in elevated spiritual motives. The historical experience, as it had been conceived by Spanish tradition since the expulsion, continued to be a primordial factor shaping twentieth-century attitudes towards the Jews. As we have been observing, racism, an ideology foreign to Catholicism, was rejected in its absolute form.[28]

The anti-racist position regarding the Jews was reinforced when, in July 1943, *Ecclesia* showed support for the Slovakian episcopate, which had published a collective pastoral in which it protested the authorities' refusal to take into account the conversion of Jews. The Spanish interpretation, similar to the one circulated in *L'Osservatore Romano* on 6 June 1943, held that the rules of natural law should be respected and that Christian rights should be extended to all who had received the sacrament of baptism.[29]

Yet the Spanish Church overlooked the German persecution of European Jews even while it opposed the cruelty shown towards Jewish *conversos*, whom it considered Catholics. It would maintain this position throughout the war. For the Spanish Church, the main issue was the conversion of Jews – an indication of the absence of a racist criteria, but also of the situation of the Nazis' victims.[30]

The Holocaust from the Perspective of the Catholic Press 1939–1945

During the Second World War, to what extent did the Catholic press have, in spite of censorship, the freedom to express positions regarding the Jewish question? Some historians maintain that the Catholic press enjoyed total freedom and that while the censors would not have blocked antisemitic publications that reflected Franco's desire to please the Nazis, neither would they have compelled the appearance of publications that did so. According to Alfonso Lazo, all of the Catholic Church's antisemitic publications expressed the opinions of the editors. He argues that the Church's publications had to have had the blessing of the Church establishment, which makes it difficult to talk about the Church as being free from external pressures.[31]

Certainly the regime demanded the dissemination of certain slogans and entire articles, but it cannot be claimed that when antisemitic positions appeared in Catholic publications, they had been imposed from above. The Spanish press was aware of the antisemitism of the Romanian, Italian, and German Fascist movements, as well as the differences among them. The Catholic as well as the Fascist and Monarchist presses reported on antisemitic measures adopted in various European countries. An examination of ninety-eight reports about antisemitic policies published between 1939 and 1944 in the Spanish Nationalist press reveals the extent of the articles and editorials about anti-Jewish actions in Europe. In thirty-three of them, the text merely transmits information, but sixty-five of them express acceptance of many antisemitic prejudices. Between 1939 and 1945, by contrast, we find no criticisms of the anti-Jewish persecutions taking place in Europe.[32]

Moreover, in the Catholic Nationalist press one can often discern a tone of admiration for the methods adopted against Jews in some countries. That antisemitic tone is perceptible in *El Correo de Andalucía*, which reported on the methods taken in Bohemia-Moravia with regard to Jewish goods: the freezing of property and the prohibition against Jews acquiring furniture or charging rent for their property. Even before the war broke out, the journalistic attitude towards Germany seemed plainly enthusiastic.[33] *El Correo de Andalucía* also reported on the Slovakian decree that resulted in Jews being expelled from the military, and on the expropriation of Jewish goods in Danzig before the outbreak of the war. The article is solely informative and lacks even the slightest compassion for the victims of the decrees.[34] In September 1939, when the war broke out with the German invasion of Poland, the magazine *Signo* (of Acción Católica's youth division) adopted a careful attitude of neutrality, adhering to Franco's position: "Ante Europa en armas, neutralidad" (Facing Europe at war, we stay neutral).[35]

The hostile attitude towards Jews and the identification with antisemitic methods reappeared in the Catholic press after the war began. For example, in early October 1939 the *Correo* reported that Romania had expelled the Jews from public administration and that six hundred Jews had been killed in the city of Galatz after they had been accused of protesting against the government by applying for Soviet citizenship.[36] It was also reported that close to ten thousand Jews had fled Moldova after the Soviet army ran up against the Romanian army between Reni and Ungasi. This report emphasized the links between Jews and communists and took a clearly anti-Jewish position. The antisemitic legislation signed by the Romanian king enjoyed support in the Catholic press in Madrid, in the newspaper *Ya*.[37]

After the war broke out and Poland was occupied, the Catholic press supported the violence against the Jews in Warsaw, where they had been condemned to forced labour. Moreover, according to *El Correo de*

Andalucía, world peace did not depend on Germany. In October 1939, in a description of the Jewish district in German-occupied Warsaw, there is an obvious lack of sympathy for the Jewish victims, who had been brutalized and impoverished by the Nazis. The writer is utterly devoid of Christian pity:

> Cuando se baja por la Nawrek abajo va decreciendo la formación ciudadana occidental para convertirse, para degenerar en viviendas inmundas que corresponden al barrio judío. Hay casuchas que no importa que tengan tres pisos para que sean inmundas e infectas. Las "doroskas" corretean por las calles llenas de chicuelos harapientos y sucios. El caftán judío sobresale sobre toda vestimenta y las barbas abundan como el miedo a una epidemia.

> When you enter Nawrek, the image of the proper Western citizen diminishes, and the place degenerates into the filthy dwellings of the Jewish neighborhood. There are shacks – regardless of how many floors they are – that are filthy and infected. The "doroskas" run around on streets full of ragged and dirty kids. The Jewish caftan stands out above all other clothing and the beards abound like the fear of an epidemic.[38]

The Catholic press reported on and justified the segregation of the Jews, including their expulsion, as part of a proven policy that Spain had been the first to apply during the reign of the Catholic Monarchs, and that others followed in the twentieth century. In this sense, there was not much of a difference between how the Catholic press and the Falangist press broached the Jewish question during the months following the German invasion of Poland.

Reports on massacres of Jews in various countries under German domination circulated sporadically in the Catholic press, but not the news that came to light in November 1942 regarding the organized extermination of all the Jews in Europe by then being carried out by the Nazis as the "Final Solution." When *that* became public, the Alfonsian Monarchist newspaper *ABC* reported on 28 February 1943 that according to the Romanian press, world Jewry was at risk of being utterly eliminated. The Falangist press, notwithstanding its stance against antisemitism, expressed a violent prejudice against Jews in all of its publications. Also, in both implicit or direct form, these press outlets did not shy away from sustained apologies for Nazi racism and the methods of persecution that resulted from it. The Falangists, because they were Catholic, had to forge a compromise between Catholicism and racism, and they accepted racism as a basic idea of the nation and state in Spain. Two examples of this compromise can be seen in the case of Professor Luis del Valle, from Zaragoza, and Dr Vallejo Nágera. According to Vallejo Nágera, the racist spirit had always been alive and well in Spain as a means for it to achieve purity of faith, as demonstrated by the documents about the blood cleansing of Jews and Muslims.[39] Of course, this idea represented not the official voice of the Church but rather that of the Catholic Falangists.

The End of the War

Towards the end of the war, Acción Católica sporadically took on the Jewish issue within the framework of religious themes or the conversion of Jews. In February 1945, a statement attributed to Albert Einstein expressed that while the world, including the universities, maintained silence regarding Hitler, only the Catholic Church confronted him.[40]

In early 1945, news of the conversion of the Chief Rabbi of Rome, Israel Zolli, and his wife, who had converted that year after having been saved by the Vatican, received significant coverage with the intention of emphasizing the charity of the Church towards Jews who might be tempted to convert. Zolli's conversion reverberated widely. Acción Católica emphasized that according to the rabbi's own words, he "deseaba pagar una deuda para con los cristianos, ya que el pueblo judío es culpable de la muerte de Dios y él procuraba borrar la mancha al abrazar con todo su corazón el Nuevo Testamento" (wanted to pay a debt to the Christians, because the Jewish people are responsible for the death of God and he managed to erase the stain upon embracing with all his heart the New Testament). It is also significant that the Catholic press made no reference to the role the Holocaust might have played in the conversion of Jews to Christianity. Given the late date of this news – almost at the end of the war – the silencing of the Holocaust cannot be attributed to fear or to the regime's censorship.[41]

As the war drew to an end, the line followed by the Catholic Church continued to be quite cautious. An editorial in *Ecclesia* stated that Catholics were forbidden to applaud or condemn issues belonging to this world's public sphere. The same position appeared in regard to peace: happiness for the evil that came to an end, and fear for what the Pope called the evil that could reappear and threaten. The only true peace would be the triumph of the Church. The Allied victory won in part by liberals and communists gave the Church a glimpse of an uncertain future.[42]

Pla y Daniel, Cardinal Primate of Spain, explained at the end of the war why Spain had not participated in it and why that attitude had been prudent and intelligent. The primary reasons, according to him, were that Spain had just come out of the Civil War, in which almost one million men had died, and, moreover, the world war had nothing to do with Spain. According to him, the Civil War had been fought as a crusade for God and for the homeland, whereas the world war had raged beyond Spain's borders because its objective was expansion and power.[43]

Although the Francoist state cannot be considered a Catholic regime *per se*, and the Spanish Catholic Church remained subject to state censorship, it is evident that censorship functioned primarily to monitor any criticisms of the regime and did not extend to Church statements about the Jewish question as a national or religious category. The Church, which controlled the educational system and the composition and publication of textbooks, could have blocked or refused to publish antisemitic expressions. In education as in other spheres, we perceive the presence of traditional religious prejudices against Jews based on theology but also taken from the modern-day antisemitism that had infiltrated Spanish Catholicism. During Franco's government, school textbooks contained expressions of religious contempt for the Jews. The concept of the "deicide people," against the backdrop of patriotism, appeared frequently in schoolbooks through to the end of the 1960s, when, following the Second Vatican Council, the Sisters of Zion, through a meticulous examination of the textbooks, had these expressions removed from the texts because they contradicted the council document *Nostra Aetate*, which exempted Jews from collective guilt for having killed Jesus Christ.[44]

Conclusions

The Catholic influence on Franco's government was strong in the educational field, which had remained in control of the Church. Many textbooks enjoyed wide circulation, for example, two antisemitic books by Agustín Serrano de Haro, who was the General Inspector of Primary Education: *Yo soy español* and *Hemos visto al Señor* (I Am Spanish; We Have Seen God). The latter included popular Spanish stories from the Middle Ages about the blood libel, such as the story of the innocent boy Dominguito de Val, murdered by Jews. What is more, both primary and secondary textbooks were means to transmit anti-Judaism from theological sources, but they also contained modern and secular antisemitic content, which had seeped into Catholic culture and education in Franco's Spain.[45] As we have been observing, in spite of Catholic anti-racism, antisemitism continued to be part of the Church's cultural heritage. The motivations were not purely theological. Everything suggests that the anti-Jewish rhetoric that already existed in Franco's Spain in the 1930s adhered to the Church, whose centre of power resided in the social and educational sectors. Therefore, the Church refrained from criticizing Nazi Germany, it was profoundly anti-communist, it identified communism with Judaism, and it saw the Catholic monarch's Edict of Expulsion from 1492 as a positive Catholic example regarding the treatment of Jews. All of this granted – in the political context of the Second World War – relevance and currency to already deeply rooted theological and antisemitic stereotypes.

NOTES

1 Sections of this article are based on my book: *La Iglesia Católica ante el Holocausto: España y América Latina 1933–1945* (Madrid: Alianza Editorial, 2003).
2 García-Nieto and Donezar, *Bases documentales de la España contemporánea. La Guerra de España*, 353–402; idem, *Bases documentales de la España contemporánea. La España de Franco*, 12–14; 11–115. See also Hermet, *L'Espagne au XX siecle*, 177; Andrés-Gallego and Pazos, *La Iglesia en la España contemporánea*, vols. 1–2: *1800–1936*.
3 Blin, "Franco et les juifs"; Avni, *España, Franco y los judíos*; Marquina and Inés Ospina, *España y los judíos en el siglo XX*. See also Danielle Rozenberg, "Minorías religiosas," 249.
4 "El mensaje de Nuestro Presidente Nacional."
5 "El pensamiento de Codreanu"; Etayo, "La organización Guardia de Hierro."
6 "El cinema yanqui"; "La literatura del III Reich."
7 *Misión*, no. 59 (November 1939); Rozenberg, "Minorías religiosas," 248.
8 This appears in an article signed by A.A. in which an article by Father Julio Meinvielle is praised: "Los Tres Pueblos Bíblicos."
9 Ben Dror, *The Catholic Church and the Jews.*
10 "Catolicismo y Patria."
11 Pujiula, "Raza, razas, razas puras." See also Llera, "Prensa y censura."
12 Fernández Almuzara, "El judío internacional."
13 Ibid.
14 Heras, "La cuestión aria"; Izaga, "El laicismo político"; Pujiula, "Eugenesia bionómica humana."
15 "Editorial guión. Mensaje a las juventudes hispánicas."
16 Azpiazu, "Pío XII y el llamado 'Orden Nuevo.'"
17 On Pío's planned encyclical on racism and antisemitism, *Humani Generis Unitas*, see Passelecq and Suchecky, *Un silencio de la Iglesia*; on the Jesuits, see Taradel and Raggi, *La Segregazione Amichevole.*

18 Hilberg, *The Destruction of the European Jews*; Wyman, *The Abandonment of the Jews*, 42–78.
19 "Editoriales. Precisiones necesarias."
20 Ibid., 4.
21 Herrera Oria, *Historia de la educación española*, 245–56.
22 "Lituania bajo la bandera roja."
23 On the impact of the Second Vatican Council in Spain, see Andrés-Gallego, Pazo, and Llera, *Los españoles entre la religión y la polítcia*, 139–66.
24 "La expulsión de los judíos por los Reyes Católicos."
25 Ibid.
26 Ibid.
27 Ibid.
28 Ibid., 14. See also Bernardino Llorca, "La inquisición española." Bernardino Llorca was a professor of Scholastic History at the Colegio Máximo de San Ignacio in Sarriá, Barcelona.
29 "Los cristianos observarán las leyes de la Caridad."
30 Ibid.
31 See Alfonso Lazo's opinion in *La Iglesia, la Falange y el fascismo*, 186. On this topic, see also Llera, "Prensa y censura"; Andrés-Gallego, *¿Fascismo o Estado Católico?*, 30.
32 Lazo, *La Iglesia, la Falange y el fascismo*, 188, gives a list of Catholic publications.
33 *El correo de Andalucía*, 23 July 1939, cited in ibid. See also "Últimas Noticias," *El Correo de Andalucía*, 24 July 1939.
34 "Régimen autoritario en Eslovaquia," *El Correo de Andalucía*, 23 July 1939; "Últimas Noticias," *El Correo de Andalucía*, 1 August 1939. On Jewish property confiscated in Danzig, see also *El Correo de Andalucía*, 6 July 1939. On 1 August, in the Monarchic press, see also *ABC* (Madrid), and in the Falangist press, *Arriba España*.
35 "Ante Europa en armas, neutralidad."
36 "Desmovilización eslovaca," *El Correo de Andalucía*, 1 October 1939.
37 "Los judíos se manifiestan tumultuosamente." In the Monarchist press, see *ABC*, 23 January 1940; *Ya*, 8 August 1940.
38 "La paz no depende de Alemania," *El Correo de Andalucía*, 11 October 1939.
39 *ABC*, 29 February 1943. In the Falangist press, see *Arriba*, 7 December 1943. Alfonso Lazo cites a professor from Zaragoza, Luis del Valle, and Dr Vallejo Nágera as two important examples of the reconciliation between Catholicism and racism in their works. Specifically, he cites a speech given by Nágera in Madrid (in *Signo*, 10 January 1943), and Nágera, *Eugenesia de la*, 114. See Lazo, *La Iglesia, la Falange y el fascismo*, 198.
40 "Editorial: Los judíos y la Iglesia."

41 "Crónica del Vaticano." The topic appears as a subtitle under the title "Crónica del Vaticano." On the Franco policy regarding the West during the final years of the war, see, for example, Preston, *Franco, Caudillo de España.*
42 "Editorial, Nuestro deber ante la paz."
43 "Conducta de España."
44 *Amistad Judeo-Cristiana. Informe ...; Amistad Judeo-Cristiana. Segundo informe ...;* Benarroch, "La Real Academia Española"; V. Serrano, "El judaísmo."
45 Serrano de Haro, *Yo Soy Español* and *Hemos visto al Señor* (in particular the chapter on "La Sangre Inocente: Los judíos mataron a Dominguito de Val"). See Ben Dror, "'Traitors and Evildoers.'"

20 The Politics of Survival: Madrid's Pro-Jewish Propaganda and the Canonization of Francisco Franco as Benefactor of Jews

PEDRO CORREA MARTÍN-ARROYO

In April 1940, the chairman of Lisbon's Comissão Portuguesa de Assistência aos Judeus Refugiados (Portuguese Commission for Assistance to Jewish Refugees, COMASSIS), Augusto d'Esaguy, reported that "the situation of the Jews in Spain, as well as in Spanish Morocco, is getting worse every day." D'Esaguy also echoed rumours that notwithstanding the absence of general anti-Jewish measures in Spain, the Spanish interior minister – "an open advocate of racial and Nazist doctrine" – was preparing several police measures directed against Jews that would be carried out secretly in order not to alarm public opinion.[1] D'Esaguy's predictions were borne out in May 1941, when the interior minister instructed the Spanish police to conduct a census of all Jews present in Spain.[2] Also confidential was the Ministry of Commerce and Industry's ruling of October 1941, which ordered Spanish shipping companies to ban "the undesirable" Jews from Spanish vessels.[3] Other anti-Jewish policies carried out covertly included the Spanish government's internment and expulsion of Spanish Jews – many of whom it stripped of their Spanish nationality – as well as the Spanish-German joint police action against German-Jewish refugees living in Spain.[4]

That Francoist Spain deployed these antisemitic measures in secret reflects Madrid's attempt to appease an increasingly anti-Francoist public opinion within the Allied countries. As this chapter examines, the Franco government set out to whitewash its antisemitic record in the aftermath of the Second World War and to exploit Franco's self-professed rescue of Jewish refugees for its own benefit. Naturally, the reason for the Spanish government's new pro-Jewish façade was purely pragmatic: it was to use the Jewish question to dissociate itself from the Axis stigma, thereby circumventing the international isolation that the newly created United Nations had imposed on Franco's fascist government. But the echoes of Madrid's propaganda campaign continued even after the Francoist regime achieved its desired reconciliation with the West in the early 1950s. As we will see, the Spanish myth of the rescue – as exemplified by the public canonization of General Francisco Franco as rescuer and benefactor of Jews – is the result of a decades-long propaganda campaign that could not have succeeded without the support of independent Jewish organizations both within the regime and abroad.

The Birth of the Spanish Rescue Myth during the Second World War

After the downfall of Mussolini's Italy in 1943, Madrid begun to see its pro-Jewish propaganda efforts as central to the regime's survival. As the war tilted in favour of the Allies, the Spanish government realized it needed to abandon its pro-Axis sympathies in favour of a new pro-Allied attitude. The Francoist leadership understood that antisemitism was a defining feature of Nazi Germany, and it was pained by the increasingly common criticisms from Allied officials and commentators that Spain had ill-treated Jewish refugees. Unwilling to compromise the regime's international position, Madrid confronted this negative publicity by taking a propaganda line that suggested the complete opposite. These fabrications were intended to portray the Franco regime as deeply concerned about the refugee situation in general and as having engaged in rescuing and providing shelter for as many Jewish refugees as possible.

Paradoxically, the initial impetus for the spread of Franco's propaganda came from international organizations engaged in helping refugees from Nazism. The most illustrative example of this was the rapport between Rabbi Maurice Perlzweig, head of the British wing of the World Jewish Congress (WJC), and Juan de Cárdenas, Spanish Ambassador to Washington. They first met in March 1943, when the rabbi requested Madrid's authorization to allow Jewish communities in South America to send parcels to European Jewish refugees stranded in Spain, as well as Spain's cooperation in facilitating the transit of Jewish children then in Nazi-occupied countries. Ambassador Cárdenas, who saw this as a great opportunity to improve the regime's image across the Americas at virtually no cost, tried to persuade his superiors at the foreign ministry to satisfy the rabbi's requests, in vain.[5]

Interestingly, the Spanish government's refusal to cooperate with the WJC did not dissuade Rabbi Perlzweig from mentioning, in a May 1943 radio broadcast across the United States, that "some twenty thousand refugees have found both a temporary haven and security in Spain, and they have found these things in circumstances which would have denied them entrance into many other countries."[6] Rather than punishing the Franco regime for its lack of cooperation on refugee matters, Rabbi Perlzweig's approach was to praise the Franco government, hoping this good publicity would incentivize it to relax its border and refugee policies. This also seems to have been the position adopted by Moses A. Leavitt, secretary of the American Jewish Joint Distribution Committee (JDC), who on several occasions thanked Ambassador Cárdenas for the "sympathetic attitude of your government in Madrid in behalf of the refugees who have come to Spain."[7]

Unfortunately, the reality of the Jewish refugees who transited through Spain was quite different (as we have seen in Jacobo Israel Garzón's chapter 3 and Josep Calvet's chapter 5 in this volume). To begin with, the regime's hostility to foreign organizations of any kind barred private relief organizations from formally assisting refugees in Spain, despite the great demand for assistance.[8] This forced relief groups to operate on a near-clandestine basis and to live under the constant inquisition of the Spanish police. In October 1942, Dr Samuel Sequerra, the unofficial representative of the JDC in Barcelona, reported on the difficult reality of the refugee and relief situation in Spain:

> A large percentage of those trying to cross the border are being arrested by the Spanish authorities ... the Spanish police demand of us that we give them the names of those who seek our help. If we so denounced them, they would be immediately arrested ... In spite of the fact that they know of the humanitarian work that we do, they do not stop torturing us. During the month of August they took away all our files and papers and returned them only after almost a month, and then only a part ... I should also mention the anti-Semitic campaign which the Spanish press is conducting ... The Jewish organizations in Portugal are simply admitted to function, and we are barely tolerated ... We must keep our problems of assistance very quiet in order to avoid difficulties with the authorities.[9]

But more than simply concealing its treatment of Jewish refugees, Franco's propaganda during the war highlighted and exaggerated the government's good deeds towards them. In February 1944, the foreign minister broadcast news across the Americas concerning the repatriation to Spain of 365 Sephardic Jews interned at Bergen-Belsen: "Para que pueda V.E. contrarrestar campañas antiespañolas atribuyéndonos política racista" (to counter the anti-Spanish campaign which insinuates that we follow a racist policy).[10] The Nazis had spared this group of Salonikan Jews from the gas chambers because they held passports of a neutral country: Spain. That these Sephardim were Spanish subjects, and that Madrid had tried for months to avoid repatriating them, was not mentioned in this broadcast. Moreover, the Spanish government credited itself with rescuing these Jews even though Madrid had only agreed to such "repatriation" on the condition that international relief organizations would cover the whole cost of the operation and organize their departure from Spain with the shortest possible delay. (Maria Fragkou provides a close examination of the case of Greek Jews deported to Bergen-Belsen in chapter 7 of this volume; see also Lisbona, chapter 8).

Besides taking a harsh attitude towards foreign relief organizations, the Spanish government was hostile towards the Jewish community of the Spanish Protectorate of Morocco. In April 1944, the Protectorate's High Commissioner in Tetouan, General Orgaz, summoned a delegation of Jewish bankers, manufacturers, and merchants from the Tangiers and Tetouan Jewish communities. Following a series of financial and physical threats directed against their respective communities, General Orgaz coerced the Jewish representatives "to show their gratitude to Spain and give proper consideration to its work and chivalrous and aristocratic attitude" towards Jews in general, and especially towards Jewish refugees.[11]

Equally premeditated and self-interested was the Spanish government's approach when the Jewish communities of the Spanish Protectorate of Morocco were invited to send a representative to the WJC's November 1944 international convention in Atlantic City, New Jersey. After some hesitation, Madrid calculated that this was a great opportunity for "desconcertar extraordinariamente a nuestros enemigos, granjeándonos muchas simpatías y no comprometiéndonos ante nadie" (confusing our enemies, enhancing friendly attitudes towards Spain, and not compromising our position with anyone).[12] According to the foreign minister, Count Gómez-Jordana, Spain sent a Jewish spokesman with "precise instructions" regarding what to say concerning Francoist Spain's attitude towards Jews: that Spanish legislation did not discriminate against them, and that they enjoyed the same political and civil rights as all other Spaniards.[13]

Besides utilizing international Jewish organizations and the Spanish Jewish community as propaganda channels, the Francoist government boasted of its humanitarianism on state-controlled media. Thus in July 1944 the Spanish newspaper *ABC* celebrated Spain's role: "el Gobierno español y la Embajada de los Estados Unidos de Madrid han colaborado eficazmente en la ayuda a los refugiados europeos de diversas nacionalidades, judíos en su mayor parte, desmintiéndose así la campaña de la prensa izquierdista, que venía afirmando que el Gobierno español entorpece esas evacuaciones" (the Spanish government and the US Embassy in Madrid have efficiently collaborated in aiding European refugees from several nationalities, most of them Jews, proving wrong the defamation campaign of the left that assured that the Spanish government hindered these evacuations).[14] But the reality of the refugee situation did not escape Robert Briggs, who as head of Madrid's Representation in Spain of American Relief Organizations (RSARO) was the highest Allied authority in relief and refugee matters in Spain. In July 1945, for instance, Briggs was perplexed to see "how screwy" the Spanish press could be when he came across a Spanish newspaper article that spoke of Barcelona as "one of the chief transit centres for the repatriation of thousands of civilians liberated from German concentration camps."[15]

Despite the unsubstantiated nature of its claims and its dubious attitude towards Jews more generally, Franco's propaganda found a crucial ally in the US State Department. In June 1946, Assistant Secretary of State Breckinridge Long claimed that Spain had been

> uno de los países que más contribuyeron durante la guerra a aliviar el éxodo judío. España, no siendo un país rico, dió refugio a más de sesenta mil personas que cruzaron ilegalmente los Pirineos, huyendo de la invasión alemana. El Gobierno de Franco cooperó eficazmente con el embajador de Estados Unidos de Madrid y el Comité Judío de Ayuda a los Refugiados, suministrando a éstos alimentos y dinero.

> one of the countries that contributed the most to alleviate the Jewish exodus during the war. Spain, despite not being a rich country, gave refuge to sixty thousand people who crossed the Pyrenees clandestinely fleeing from German occupation. The Franco Government efficiently cooperated with the United States ambassador in Madrid and the Jewish Committee for Refugee Relief [sic], supplying them with food and money.[16]

The motives behind the State Department's embrace of Francoist propaganda are more obscure than those that drove the Jewish relief organizations and Jewish communities in Spanish Morocco. One possibility is that, by inflating the number of those allegedly rescued in cooperation with the Franco government, Breckinridge Long – who as head of the State Department's Visa Division had been repeatedly criticized for supposedly trying to halt the influx of refugees into the United States – was trying to exonerate his office's own controversial policies towards Jews.[17] Another possibility is that the US State Department was simply paving the way for a pragmatic alliance with General Franco, whose fervent anti-communism made him a convenient ally in the emerging confrontation between the two post-war superpowers: the United States and the Soviet Union.

The Francoist Propaganda Campaign: Between International Isolation and the Cold War

With the vanquishing of its former Italian and German fascist counterparts, Franco's Spain entered a period of international isolation and economic autarky that severely threatened the regime's survival in the immediate post-war years. This isolation crystallized on 12 December 1946, when the UN General Assembly voted to exclude Franco's fascist government from membership in any UN-related agency until a "new and acceptable government" took over in Spain.[18] To overturn this situation, the Franco regime set out to whitewash the regime's pro-Axis record and improve its image in the West. For obvious reasons, Madrid's alleged rescue of thousands of Jews from the Nazi Holocaust became the centrepiece of this propaganda.

Shortly after the UN's anti-Franco declaration, the Spanish foreign ministry (MFA) requested from all its diplomatic legations in countries formerly under Nazi occupation any information regarding aid given to Jews during the war. Despite the limited number of positive responses, the MFA prepared a report describing "the very ample protective efforts realized by Spain in favour of the Sephardi" and sent it to Washington and London for circulation.[19] By 1949, this report had grown into two pieces of propaganda. One was the fifty-page pamphlet *Spain and the Jews*, distributed in Spanish, English, and French.[20] The other was a five-page brochure titled *Spain and the Sephardic Jews*.[21] Besides shamelessly exaggerating Spain's humanitarian attitude towards the refugees, this propaganda literature adapted the Spanish myth of the rescue to the Cold War rhetoric of the late 1940s. Thus, Franco's propagandists chose to highlight the regime's Christian morals in an attempt to differentiate it from the "ruthless wheels of totalitarian materialism" – a term skilfully designed to conflate Franco's former patrons, Nazi Germany and Fascist Italy, with the West's new enemy, the Soviet Union: "Considered as a whole, the action taken by Spain to protect the Sephardi Jews during World War II is one of which Spain is justly proud. Such diplomatic protection of defenceless persons is not only one of the highest missions of the diplomatic purpose but also that of Christian charity to a neighbor who had been caught up in the ruthless wheels of totalitarian materialism."[22]

Alongside this attempt at whitewashing Francoist Spain's fascist nature, there was a second line of propaganda that became vital as a means to validate the regime's humanitarian achievements. To counteract National Catholic Spain's intrinsically antisemitic ideology, this new line sought to present Franco's Spain as actually philosemitic. Illustrative of this trend was the government's passing of a 1948 decree that granted the ambiguous status of "súbditos españoles en el extranjero" (Spanish subjects abroad) to a limited number of Sephardic Jews "[que] por su amor a España, se han hecho dignos de tal merced" (whose love for Spain made them worthy of such honour).[23] In practice, this decree had little real impact, as it would only grant symbolic citizenship to a limited number of Sephardim from the Balkans, most of whom had perished during the Holocaust. Moreover, the decree's pro-Jewish rhetoric contradicted two previous circular orders issued secretly towards mid-1945 to "evitar en lo posible la entrada y permanencia en España de aquellos sefarditas cuya residencia anterior fuera en el extranjero" (avoid at all cost the entry and settlement in Spain of those Sephardic Jews who previously lived in a foreign country).[24] Despite the regime's hypocrisy, Franco's new decree attained great media coverage internationally, with sensationalist headlines conveniently magnifying its scope and reach. The *Washington Post*, for example, announced on its front page Franco's determination to invite some hundred thousand Sephardim back to Spain.[25] Similarly, Jerusalem's daily the *Palestine Post* celebrated this same decree with the powerful headline "Franco Invites Jews to Return."[26]

Although these propaganda initiatives surely paved the way for Spain's reconciliation with the West, it was ultimately the bipolar nature of the Cold War that rescued Franco's Spain from ostracism. The turning point was the Communist invasion of South Korea in June 1950. As the conflict with the Soviet Union unfolded, many formerly anti-Francoist commentators in the West begun to recognize General Franco's anticommunism as an important asset to halt the spread of communism in Europe. This was the case with Alexander W. Weddell, the American diplomat who had served as US Ambassador to Spain between 1939 and 1942. Notwithstanding his description of Franco's government as "bad, unqualifiedly bad, and one which I abhor," Weddell considered that any attempt to overthrow his government would lead to another civil war, thus bringing the Iberian Peninsula closer to the Soviet Union: "of the two evils" – argued the ambassador – "I prefer the former."[27] This pragmatic position was shared by the US State Department. George Keenan, its first Director of Policy Planning and architect of Cold War policy, saw this position as in the US national interest in order to re-establish political and economic relations with Spain, "irrespective of wartime ideological considerations or the character of the regime in power."[28] The US government's renewed support for the Franco dictatorship led, in November 1950, to the abrogation of the UN's anti-Franco declaration of December 1946; this initiated the progressive re-establishment of diplomatic relations with Spain.

In Israel, as in the United States, more and more Knesset members – particularly on the political right – saw Franco's Spain as an indispensable ally in the war against communism. But the inclusion of Franco's fascist regime in the Western Bloc proved challenging for the general public as well as for some Israeli officials who had been highly critical of Franco's government in international forums. To counter anti-Franco sentiments, the conservatives of Herut launched a propaganda campaign of their own to praise Franco's role in rescuing thousands of Jews during the war. This was notably the case with Knesset member Benjamin Arditti, who published several articles in 1951 in which he claimed that Jews were indebted to Franco for his rescue of Jews of Spanish citizenship in Bulgaria during the war. Later that year, Arditti publicly praised Franco from the podium of the World Congress of Sephardic Jewry in Paris, which he attended as representative of Israel's Bulgarian community.[29]

The exploitation of the Spanish rescue myth to enlist Spain in the struggle against communism was not, however, exclusive to the Israeli right wing. In the United States, the director of the Latin American Bureau of the National Catholic Welfare Conference's Social Action Department, Richard Pattee, published a pro-Franco monograph, *This Is Spain* (1951), in which he made fantastic assertions regarding the Spanish government's humanitarian record:

> Spain can indeed be proud of this page in her contemporary history, for the evidence reveals that the Madrid government utilized every avenue and took advantage of every channel to render aid to the Jews ... Within Spain, the religious, military, and civil authorities were generous to a fault in offering a sanctuary to those fleeing the concentration camps of Nazi Europe ... In the social field, the Spanish authorities have been spending upward of a million pesetas a year on behalf of the Jewish communities for such things as free school lunchrooms, clothing for those in distress, medical aid, and special donations for Jewish religious festivities.[30]

Most of these claims were either unsubstantiated or wildly exaggerated. Yet Pattee's book was translated into three languages and saw fifteen printed editions within five years of its publication. Even more hyperbolic than Pattee's representation of the Spanish rescue myth was the one published by Norway's right-wing and highest-circulation newspaper, the *Aftenposten*, which attributed to Franco the saving of more than 300,000 Jewish lives from the Nazi gas chambers.[31]

The Canonization of General Franco as Benefactor of Jews

The Cold War logic of alliances played a decisive role in validating the Spanish rescue myth; but the impact of that myth also relied heavily on the regime's ability to substantiate words with actions. In this regard, the regime undertook a series of structural reforms in the early post-war era aimed at "defascistizing" Franco's Spain. In July 1945, the Franco government introduced the Fuero de los Españoles (Spaniards' Charter of Rights), which in theory guaranteed basic civil liberties. In the words of British historian Paul Preston, it aimed "to give the impression that the Caudillo presided over a *sui generis* democracy and was not a dicta-tor."[32] The actual implementation of that charter was extremely limited, but on paper, it introduced religious freedom as long as the practice of religions other than the Roman Catholic did not threaten "la unidad espiritual, nacional y social de España" (spiritual, national, and social integrity of Spain).[33] Narrowly defined in this way, religious freedom became a key component of Franco's new philosemitic façade. By pre-senting itself as a tolerant and multicultural society with an interest in its religious minorities, the regime hoped to sever its previous associa-tion with the Axis and validate its pro-Jewish propaganda. It would be at least two decades, however, before the Spanish Jewish community attained full legal status.

The regime now had to offer some proof, even if symbolic, that reli-gious freedom in Spain had actually been implemented. Thus in January of 1946, the Barcelona synagogue was given permission to hold Jewish prayers for the first time since it was shut by the rebel army in 1939. This first concession, however, was only achieved thanks to the intercession of the WJC representative in Lisbon, Isaac Weissman – the Franco gov-ernment had initially rejected the petition of Barcelona's Jewish com-munity.[34] Madrid's Jewish community followed in January 1949 with a synagogue of its own. Yet these two "synagogues" were no more than private houses with no visible indications that they were places of wor-ship, for Catholics were the only ones allowed to publicly display their faith.[35] The delicate situation of Spanish Jewry was best summarized by the British Orthodox Rabbi Ephraim F. Einhorn during his visit to Spain in 1951. According to Einhorn, Spanish Jews "made every effort to hide their identity" because they realized that criticism was use-less as a form of resistance; instead, they had become accustomed to the Franco regime's "psychological and refined form of antisemitism, [which] finds its expression in an under-the-surface discrimination."[36]

Over the next few years, Franco's rescue narrative was put to the test when the Jews of Egypt and Morocco – in distress owing to their pro-Israel stance in the escalating Arab–Israeli conflict – requested the dictator's assistance. As argued by Israeli historian Raanan Rein, the Spanish attitude during the wars of 1956 and 1967 in the Middle East was reminiscent of its treatment of Jewish refugees during the Second World War: humanitarian aid was restricted almost exclusively to Jews of Spanish citizenship, and the Spanish government tried to block at all cost any Jewish resettlement in Spain.[37] Moreover, as was the case during the early 1940s, this assistance owed more to the independent actions of some Spanish diplomats abroad than to any consistent refugee policy orchestrated from Madrid. Even so, these events further legitimized the Spanish rescue myth and softened the regime's image in the West. Danielle Rozenberg has pointed out that these rescue activities offered the Spanish government a way to make symbolic gestures to the Jewish world without having to formally establish diplomatic relations with Israel, which would have harmed Franco's good rapport with the Arab world.[38] Francoist Spain's cynical use of the matter of Jewish refugees was best captured by the head of Arab and Middle Eastern Political Affairs, José Felipe de Alcover, who warned the Spanish MFA that "el alma sefardí es siempre una espada de dos filos que únicamente debe ser utilizada cuando exista certeza de que no va a caer en manos extrañas" (the Sephardic soul has always been a double-edged sword that should only be brandished when there is certainty that it will not fall into foreign hands).[39]

The assistance provided to Moroccan Jews during the 1956 Suez Crisis, in particular, led to an unintended yet critical event: a private audience between General Franco and Solomon Gaon, an influential Sephardic rabbi and Hakham of the Sephardic communities of the British Commonwealth, as well as founder of the Sephardic Studies program at New York's Yeshiva University.[40] In 1957, upon Gaon's request, the World Sephardi Federation (WSF) sent Yair Behar as representative to Spain, where he confronted the delicate situation of the Spanish Jewish community. Over the next few years, Behar's efforts focused on trying to improve the situation of Spanish Jewry through cultural and educational initiatives jointly organized with the Spanish government. The most important of Behar's cultural initiatives, the World Sephardic Bibliographical Exhibition of 1959, was held in Madrid's Biblioteca Nacional to the benefit of the government's own propaganda agenda. Ironically, this exhibition had only been authorized by the Ministry of Education on the condition "that this exaltation of one facet of our own culture does not degenerate into a glorification of those aspects of Sephardic thought which are fundamentally antagonistic to the spiritual concept of the authentic Spain."[41]

The exhibition was a great success that fitted perfectly with the regime's propaganda campaign. In addition to the WSF delegates, it was attended by representatives of the World Jewish Congress, the World Zionist Organization, the Hebrew University of Jerusalem, and the Alliance Israélite Universelle. At the close of the exhibition, Franco bestowed on Rabbi Gaon one of Spain's highest civil decorations: the order of Alfonso X, the Wise. In response, Gaon gave a speech in Judeo-Spanish that was said to have touched the dictator himself. As recounted in *The American Sephardi*, General Franco declared, "wiping away his tears," that "the Spanish Government is proud to have been able to save Jewish lives during World War II and wishes to do everything possible to develop cultural bonds between the Sephardim and Spain."[42] As always, however, the regime's interest in the Jews was far from altruistic and always conservative in tone. This is illustrated by the Spanish government's refusal to take the exhibition, despite great media coverage, to various European and American capitals, fearing that Zionist propagandists would utilize this opportunity to weaken Spain's rapport with the Arabs.[43]

After this successful exhibition, the Franco government's pro-Jewish gestures became increasingly frequent and more publicly visible during the 1960s. In 1961, on the initiative of the WSF, the Spanish government founded the Instituto de Estudios Sefardíes (Institute of Sephardic Studies) for the purpose of promoting scholarly research on the language and cultural heritage of Spanish Jewry. In June 1964, this institute held its First Symposium of Sephardic Studies in Madrid, which resulted in the publication of a 781-page volume on the conference proceedings, fully underwritten by the Spanish government.[44] The same year, the regime unveiled a monument to Maimonides, the medieval Torah scholar, in Córdoba and inaugurated a library-museum at Toledo's synagogue of El Tránsito, founded by the legendary fourteenth-century Jewish scholar Samuel Ha-Levi.

But the full emancipation of the Spanish Jewish community was only achieved as a direct consequence of the Second Vatican Council (1962–5), during which the Roman Catholic Church formally acquitted the Jews of murdering Jesus Christ (*Nostra Aetate*, October 1965) and recognized religious freedom as a fundamental human right (*Dignitatis Humanae*, December 1965). Faced with these dramatic reforms within the Catholic Church, Franco's Spain had no choice but to fully recognize the Spanish Jewish communities of Madrid, Barcelona, Ceuta, and Melilla.[45] By virtue of the Law of Religious Freedom of June 1967, the regime finally enabled them to practise Judaism in private as well as publicly; this led to the inauguration of a full-fledged synagogue in

Madrid on 16 December 1968. During the inauguration ceremony, the congregation read a text prepared by the Spanish Ministry of Justice which stated that the 1492 Alhambra Decree had been implicitly abrogated by the 1967 Law of Religious Freedom. In fact, the Spanish government never formally rescinded the 1492 decree, even though this is how the Jewish press interpreted the government's ruling.[46]

In the eyes of many, the emancipation of Spanish Jewry at the close of the 1960s constituted ultimate proof of the regime's sympathy for Jews. But this was one of many steps meticulously calculated by the Francoist government to retrospectively validate Franco's alleged rescue of thousands of Jews during the Holocaust. Practically unchallenged in the absence of a more nuanced analysis of Spanish attitudes towards Jewish refugees from Nazism, the regime's propaganda continued to be taken at face value until the dictator's death in November 1975. The most illustrative example of the triumph of Madrid's propaganda campaign was the offering the editors of *The American Sephardi* made "for the repose of the soul of Generalissimo Francisco Franco" at New York's historic Sephardic synagogue. This symbolic act was accompanied by an obituary that urged Jews to "honour and bless the memory of this great benefactor of the Jewish people who neither sought nor reaped any profit in what he did."[47]

Conclusion

General Franco's alleged rescue of thousands of Jews from the Holocaust was a centrepiece of Francoist propaganda. The regime would cultivate and disseminate that myth for more than three decades, until the dictator's death in 1975. The myth's redemptive quality was first exploited at the end of the Second World War, when Francoist Spain began to milk its professed philosemitism in order to differentiate itself from the defeated Nazi Germany. In a desperate attempt to overcome the UN boycott of the Franco regime during the late 1940s, the regime expanded this propaganda and presented it to the Western democracies as proof of the regime's humanitarian nature. Fear of the Soviet Union then led many in the West to echo and magnify the regime's propaganda while advocating that Francoist Spain be included in the struggle against communism. Having achieved reconciliation with the West in the early 1950s, the Franco government continued to nurture the myth of the rescue through cultural propaganda initiatives that strengthened the regime's façade of philosemitism. Pleased with the dictator's increasing concessions towards Jews, Spanish and American Jewry engaged in a symbiotic relationship with the Franco regime. Through initiatives aimed at improving the delicate status of the Spanish Jewish community, Jewish organizations such as the WSF played an unconscious yet decisive role in galvanizing the regime's rescue narrative. As a result, the regime's propaganda was deemed historically factual and Franco himself was canonized as rescuer and benefactor of Jews. Since the death of the dictator, a number of scholars, many of whom have contributed to this volume, have produced serious historical research demystifying Franco's propaganda. Alejandro Baer, for instance, highlights not only the persistence of the Francoist rescue myth in contemporary Spain, but also how this legend is constantly being reshaped by both private parties and public institutions in the context of Spain's ongoing debates about historical memory and public memorialization.

NOTES

1 The Minister of Interior was Ramón Serrano Súñer. Augusto d'Esaguy, COMASSIS Lisbon, to HICEM Paris (5 April 1940); YIVO Institute for Jewish Research (YIVO), RG 245.4, series I, file XII, MKM-13.36#3.
2 Israel Garzón, "El Archivo Judaico del franquismo."
3 This ruling was in reaction to the lawsuit initiated by the passengers of the SS *Navemar*, a Spanish freighter that sailed from Seville on 7 August 1941 transporting 1,180 passengers, most of them Jewish refugees from the Reich. See Jesús María de Rotaeche, Ministry of Commerce's Director General, to Ministry of Foreign Affairs (MFA) (23 October 1941); United States Holocaust Memorial Museum Archives (USHMM), RG-36.001M, R-1190-83-6.
4 Although the historiography on these two cases of Spanish antisemitism is still pending, there is evidence that the Spanish government discriminated against both Spanish Sephardim and German Jewish refugees. Regarding the former, see for instance the cases of José Palomo Sagués, a Spanish-born Jew of Turkish Sephardic origin who was expelled from Spain on 22 January 1944 (Archivo Provincial de Cádiz, Gobierno Civil, 2433, 98); and Jaime Zacuto, a Salonika-born Sephardic Jew with Spanish nationality who, after a year of preventive imprisonment, was "sent back to his country of origin" on 19 June 1944 (Archivo General de la Administracion, Tratamiento Penitenciario, Caja 8, Legajo 20, 1571R). Concerning the Spanish government's treatment of German Jewish refugees, see the case files of the Klepper family, Hermann Gruenbaum, Alfred Kauffmann, Siegfried Goldenkranz, and Goetz and Margit Berger (USHMM, AFSC case files, 2002.296, cases 3505, 6209, and 13025, respectively).

5 See Bernd Rother, "Myth and Fact – Spain and the Holocaust," in Gómez-Quiñones and Zepp, eds., *The Holocaust in Spanish Memory*, 53.

6 Rother, *Franco y el Holocausto*, 384–5.

7 JDC secretary Moses A. Leavitt to Ambassador Cárdenas (30 December 1943), American Jewish Joint Distribution Committee Archives (JDC), AR193344, reel 69, folder 916.

8 This situation was partly overcome early in 1943 with the establishment of the Representation in Spain of American Relief Organizations (RSARO), an umbrella organization that allowed several relief organizations to work in Spain under the auspices of the US Embassy in Madrid.

9 Sequerra to JDC Lisbon (2 October 1942); JDC, AR193344, reel 69, folder 914.

10 Telegram from the MFA to all Spanish Embassies in the Americas except Washington, La Habana, and San Salvador (19 February 1944); Archivo General del Ministerio de Asuntos Exteriores y de Cooperación (AMAE), Leg. 1716, Ex. 1.

11 C. Burke Elbrick, Cargé d'Affaires ad interim, American Legation in Tangier, to the Secretary of State, Washington, D.C. (18 April 1944); United States National Archives and Records Administration (NARA), 881.4016.60.

12 Javier Martínez de Bedoya, press attaché of the Spanish Embassy in Lisbon, to Minister Jordana (11 April 1944); AMAE, Leg. 1716, Ex. 4.

13 Cited in Lisbona, *Retorno a Sefarad*, 123–4. My translations.

14 EFE, "España ha ayudado a la Evacuación de Refugiados Europeos," *ABC Andalucía* (23 July 1944), 9. My translation.

15 See note 8 above. Robert L. Briggs, RSARO Madrid, to JDC Lisbon (22 July 1945); YIVO, RG-335.5, reel 68, folder 727. Translated in original.

16 Breckinridge Long's declaration first appeared in New York's *Daily News* on 14 June 1946 and was reproduced in the Spanish press the following day. EFE, "España Protegió a Sesenta Mil Judíos," *ABC Madrid* (15 June 1946), 7–8. My translation.

17 For greater insight into Breckinridge Long's personality and the debate around his controversial refugee policies at the US State Department, see Erbelding, *About Time*, 40–2.

18 General Assembly of the United Nations, "Resolution 39/I."

19 MFA to Spanish Legation in London, 24 July 1948, and to the Spanish Legation in Washington, 26 July 1948; cited in Rother, "Myth and Fact …," 59.

20 MFA, *Datos sobre la protección a los judíos sefarditas* (Madrid, 1948); AMAE, Leg. 2996, Ex. 1; MFA, *Spain and the Jews* (Madrid, 1949); Leo Baeck Institute, DS 135.S7.S72. The brochure's French translation is cited in Avni, *Spain, the Jews, and Franco*, 179.

21 MFA, *Spain and the Sephardic Jews* (Washington, DC: Spanish Embassy, 1949); American Jewish Historical Society, DS135.S7.S7.

22 MFA, *Spain and the Sephardic Jews*, 5.

23 Franco Bahamonde, "Decreto-ley de 29 de Diciembre de 1948." My translation.

24 Circular Orders nos. 2083 and 2088, "Sobre Nacionalidad de Sefarditas y su Entrada en España," 24 July and 10 October 1945 (AMAE, Leg. 1672, Ex. 1); cited in Lisbona, *Retorno a Sefarad*, 123–4. My translations.

25 AP, "Sephardic Jews Invited Back by Spain: Franco Decree Involves Descendants of About 100,000 Ousted in 1492," *Washington Post*, 10 January 1949, 1.

26 AP, "Franco Invites Jews to Return," *Palestine Post*, 12 January 1949, 2.

27 Editor, "Sound Advice on Franco from Mr Weddell," *Richmond News Leader*, 11 June 1946.

28 Keenan to State Department, 24 October 1947; cited in Rein, *In the Shadow of the Holocaust*, 83.

29 *Herut* (11 May 1951); cited in Rein, *In the Shadow of the Holocaust*, 120.

30 Pattee, *This is Spain*, 396–404.

31 Previously, on 7 May 1945, *Aftenposten* had published the Nobel laureate Knut Hamsun's infamous obituary of Hitler, causing great controversy. Synnøve Stray Fischer, "Los 'judíos españoles' han escapado de las cámaras de gas de Hitler" (Spanish translation), *Aftenposten* (15 January 1953); cited in Ortí Camallonga, *The Spanish Perception*, 82–4.

32 Preston, *Franco: A Biography*, 537–9.

33 Jefatura del Estado, *Fuero de los Españoles*, art. 33.

34 Isaac Weissman to Maurice L. Perlzweig, "Our work for free exercise of religion in Spain" (31 December 1945), USHMM; RG-67.014M, reel 314, 10.027–8.

35 Rein, *In the Shadow of the Holocaust*, 16.

36 AJP, "Spain's Jews Try to Hide Identity As Anti-Semitic Tension Flourishes," *The Sentinel*, 20 September 1951, 3.

37 Rein, "Diplomacy."

38 Rozenberg, *La España Contemporánea*, 198–9.

39 José Felipe de Alcover to Fernando María Castiella, Minister of Foreign Affairs (26 January 1960), AMAE, Leg R. 5965, Exp. 40. Cited in Lisbona, *Retorno a Sefarad*, 267. My translation.

40 As chair of Sephardic studies, Rabbi Gaon also founded the journal *The American Sephardi*, published by Yeshiva University between 1966 and 1978. Despite being politically independent from the Franco regime, this journal celebrated every single one of the dictator's pro-Jewish initiatives with reverence; it even dedicated an extensive and laudatory obituary to General Franco in its last issue of 1978. Over the following years, Rabbi Gaon became an essential link between the American Sephardic community and Franco's regime. See for instance the articles by Benardete, "Spain Grants Freedom of Religion to the Jews"; and Barnett, "Sephardi Museum Inaugurated."

41 Cited in Rein, *In the Shadow of the Holocaust*, 184–5.
42 As told by Salomon and Ryan de Heredia, "In Memoriam. Francisco Franco," 216.
43 Rein, *In the Shadow of the Holocaust*, 185.
44 Hassán, Rubiato, and Romero, eds., *Actas del Primer Simposio.*
45 The *Ley de Principios del Movimiento Nacional* (17 May 1958) declared the Spanish nation subordinate to the "Law of God." According to this principle, Spanish legislation should be in harmony with the doctrine of the Catholic Church.
46 See for instance "Spanish Government Formally Rescinds 1492 Decree Ordering Expulsion of Jews," *Jewish Telegraphic Agency* (17 December 1968).
47 Salomon and Ryan de Heredia, "In Memoriam. Francisco Franco."

21 Tainted Visions of War: Antisemitic German Propaganda in Spain

MERCEDES PEÑALBA-SOTORRÍO

In September 1938, Juan Luis Beigbeder y Atienza, High Commissioner of Spain in Morocco, declared to a foreign correspondent that the antisemitism present in rebel propaganda was no more than a rhetorical toll that his country had to pay its German allies in exchange for their help.[1] Interestingly, this idea survived for decades and trickled into historical explanations of the topic, which tended to make Nazi propaganda responsible for the rhetorical display of antisemitism in Francoist Spain. However, as several experts in this volume have demonstrated, this explanation ignores and obfuscates the origins and existence of antisemitic sentiments in Spain.[2] These sentiments were especially present among the Catholic right and the Carlists, and to a somewhat lesser extent among the Falangists, long before the outbreak of the Spanish Civil War.[3] (See chapter 2 on antisemitism in Spain; chapter 18 on Francoist antisemitic propaganda; and chapter 19 on the Franco regime and the Catholic Church.) The Jewish-Bolshevik conspiracy was neither created by Nazi Germany nor imported from it, although the Nazis certainly used it to their advantage. During both the Second Republic and the Civil War that followed, German propaganda networks tapped into antisemitic sentiments already present in Spain and stoked them by funding the newspaper *Informaciones* with the help of pro-Nazi Spanish journalists like César González Ruano, Vicente Gay, and Federico de Urrutia.[4] The civil conflict allowed for an increase in propaganda materials as well as closer collaboration with Spanish authorities, especially Falange Española,[5] the Spanish fascist party, which was fascinated by the Nazi regime.

German propaganda continued to flood Spain until 1944. However, that campaign did not prioritize antisemitism, which lingered in the background but was generally not a key issue, and when it did become one, it did so via collaboration between the Falangists and German propagandists.

The Spanish Civil War saw the arrival of Wilhelm Faupel, accompanied by his propaganda team, as ambassador to Franco. More than sixty people, including at least four Spanish nationals,[6] worked for the Sonderstab, which was led by Willi Köhn, a German propagandist and member of the Ausland organization as well as the SS. Their objective was to help strengthen Franco's regime and establish strong relations between Germany and Spain. Both Köhn and Faupel were convinced that Germany could only achieve influence over Spain through the triumph of the radical Falange[7] and the subsequent emergence of a Spanish brand of National Socialism. Coincidentally, during this period, Nazi propaganda made an effort to tie antisemitic messages to the idea of the war as a crusade, tapping into the belief that the Jews and their liberal ideas were the cause of Spain's decline. In this regard, it was normal for Nationalist propagandists to refer to Republicans as *conversos*,[8] a pejorative term that remained at the core of Spanish antisemitic discourse. After the expulsion in 1492 of the Jews who had refused to convert, the Spanish monarchy developed and helped foster an obsession with false converts. Known as *conversos* – or *judaizantes* – those Jews who had converted but were suspected of secretly practising Judaism were among the main targets of the Spanish Inquisition. In the historical context, the term *converso* became equated with treason, falsehood, manipulation, and anti-Spanish tendencies. So it was not difficult for the Spanish right to integrate into its discourse the idea of the Judeo-Masonic conspiracy that had its source in *The Protocols of the Elders of Zion* (Javier Domínguez Arribas elaborates on this topic in chapter 18 in this volume).[9] Thus, when the German news agency DNB sent its communiqués on the Jewish question to various rebel newspapers or when Nazi propaganda pointed to the connections between communists, Jews, and Freemasons,[10] they were not creating a new climate of opinion in Spain but rather advancing their arguments in an environment already open to embrace antisemitism and anti-Bolshevism.

However, even though Goebbels himself had ordered the promotion of antisemitism, along with anti-Bolshevism, in Spain,[11] and Köhn's Sonderstab was hell-bent on promoting National Socialism in the country,[12] the cornerstone of their propaganda campaigns during the Spanish Civil War was anti-Bolshevism and not antisemitism. In fact, by 1939, blaming the Spanish Civil War on the Soviet Union and placing the Spanish conflict at the centre of international debates on communism were considered the main successes of Nazi propaganda in Spain.[13] That said, anti-Jewish-Freemason-Bolshevik propaganda reached its peak during the Spanish Civil War,[14] which suggests that some of the blame for the Spanish conflict was aimed at Jews as well. This idea is also found in works on the Spanish Civil War published in Germany.[15] However, antisemitism was not the sole or even main focus of German propaganda.

In fact, when Faupel and ultimately Köhn and his team were forced to step down,[16] antisemitism receded into the background of the propaganda campaigns. This change coincided with two key events: first, the arrival of Hans Lazar in Spain and his appointment as press attaché; and second, changes in the propaganda structure in Germany. In 1938, an Austrian national, Hans Josef Lazar, arrived in Spain as a representative of the German news agency Transocean. A few months later, he became press attaché for the German Embassy in Madrid and Ambassador Eberhard von Stohrer's confidant after assisting him in the dissolution of the Sonderstab and the dismissal of Köhn, whose desire to see a mimetic National Socialist regime established in Spain had endangered Hispano-German relations.[17] Lazar's stance regarding the utility of antisemitism as a propagandistic argument was quite clear in his own explanation for why the information bulletins published by the embassy did not focus on promoting antisemitism: "The Spaniards would not be at all interested in this question, they might even find it irksome since they already found their own solution to the Jewish question five hundred years ago. Neither von Stohrer nor his successors had any objections to my argument, despite constant harassment by the media and the Nazi party leadership. Not even the head of the Berlin press division, delegate Schmidt, nicknamed 'Presse-Schmidt' [objected]."[18] Although one has to be careful with these kinds of testimonies, it is certainly true that the Germans were not running an antisemitic campaign through their information bulletins. However, before exploring this question, it is important to note Lazar's mention of Paul Schmidt.

In May 1939, Hitler allowed Ribbentrop's Foreign Affairs Ministry (AA) to establish its own press division, which was placed under Paul Schmidt's direction. A few months later, a new decree sealed the AA's encroachment on Goebbels's control of propaganda, when Hitler entrusted Ribbentrop with the design of all propaganda abroad, while reserving the crafting of general guidelines for Goebbels.[19] This office, which was subordinate to the AA, would issue orders to Lazar throughout the Second World War. Those orders confirm, as Lazar had stated, that Schmidt and the AA, unlike Goebbels and Köhn, were not particularly interested in exploiting the antisemitic argument in Spain.

An analysis of the information bulletins and the correspondence between the German Embassy in Madrid and the AA's press division[20] makes it clear that between September 1939 and December 1942 the Nazi propaganda campaigns in Spain prioritized other arguments and topics. After the Bolsheviks' responsibility for the outbreak of the Spanish Civil War had been established, the Molotov-Ribbentrop pact drove a propaganda shift towards other enemies, first and foremost Britain and its empire. This anti-Western theme exploited Spain's traditional animosity towards Britain, which had deepened as a result of British support for the Second Republic. German propaganda was sharply focused on justifying the invasion of Poland (the event that started the Second World War), sowing mistrust of Britain among neutrals, and asserting German superiority. At the same time, the Nazis paid particular attention to two things: religious propaganda, in an attempt to prove the Christian character of the Nazi regime; and, up until their attack on the Soviet Union, the Spanish press's coverage of the Winter War between the Soviet Union and Finland,[21] which threatened to harm their image as well as bely their contention that the war was a defensive act. Ribbentrop himself demanded that the press be steered towards blaming Britain for the situation in Finland, while avoiding linking Germany to any Russian actions in the region.[22]

Moreover, considering the already strong ties between Spanish Communists and Spanish Jews,[23] any antisemitic campaign would be an inconvenience at the time of the Soviet–German alliance. Even after June 1941, comments and concerns about Jews continued to feature only as a background argument. Antisemitism, however, was not totally absent.

As Aristotle Kallis has pointed out, antisemitism came to be a "powerful common denominator for National-Socialist propaganda," enabling the eventual fusion of all the various propagandistic discourses aimed at Britain, the Soviet Union, and the United States.[24] In fact, on the rare occasions during those three years that Nazi propaganda in Spain did refer to the Jews, it did so to reinforce the principal arguments and leitmotivs of the propaganda campaigns. In this sense, Jews never appeared alone; they were always linked to or identified with some other enemy, be it the Western plutocracies – especially Britain and later on, the United States – Freemasonry, anti-Christianity, or communism. These references, which were neither original nor invented, used the Jew as a means to link all convenient enemies at the time. They played the same role within Spanish antisemitic discourse.[25] Interestingly, while Jews never appeared alone, references to Britain and communism that made no mention of Jews were more frequent than those that did.

Nevertheless, some expressions of antisemitism were of consequence. Although, as Lazar stated, there were no specific campaigns against Jews in the information bulletins, they missed no opportunity to highlight the implementation of antisemitic measures in other countries – especially occupied France – as well as the harmful effects of Jews in other countries, such as Hungary and Slovakia.[26] The idea, of course, was to show that Nazi Germany was justified in its treatment of Jews. But the appearance of these measures in the bulletins is especially interesting because, as noted by Domínguez Arribas, there was a connection between the increase in antisemitic comments in the Spanish press and the implementation of antisemitic measures in other countries.[27] It is doubtful that Germany was the only source of such information, however. Given that the information bulletins were being disseminated to everyone of importance in the country,[28] that Spanish correspondents in Berlin sent their articles straight through the German news agency Transocean, and that Lazar had established strong relationships with every newspaper editor in Madrid,[29] it is not far-fetched to suggest a connection between the dissemination of these news items by German sources and spikes in antisemitic propaganda in Spain. For example, when the DNB reported on demonstrations against Jewish shops in Paris at the end of August 1940, the Falangist newspaper *Arriba* stated in October that most department stores in Paris were Jewish.[30] Moreover, both Nazi and Francoist propaganda used similar arguments when violently attacking the Western powers in 1941.[31]

Yet this does not mean that Spanish propagandists were not resorting to such arguments voluntarily. As Ben Dror and Domínguez Arribas have noted in this volume, the Catholic and Falangist press reported clearly and without criticism on antisemitic policies in Germany and elsewhere. As late as the final months of 1944, the Falangist press continued to praise ghettos as a means to control the Jews.[32] Proof of Francoist Spain's voluntary commitment to the Axis perspective is the fact that Spanish authorities asked the German Embassy for lists of Jewish authors and filmmakers who should be banned from Spanish media.[33]

However, by the end of 1941, coinciding with the United States' entry into the war and the stalemate on the Eastern Front caused by the Russian winter, the German Embassy had grown concerned about the increasing presence of Allied propaganda in Spain. This motivated the launch of Nazi Germany's largest propaganda campaign on Spanish soil, the Grosse Plan, approved in January 1942 and devised by Stohrer and Lazar.[34] That plan sought to counteract enemy propaganda by intercepting it and by disseminating pro-Nazi black and grey propaganda.[35] The materials distributed by this campaign appeared as anonymous or independent publications, and none of them revealed their true origin, although in some cases they suggested a Falangist origin. Indeed, the plan relied heavily on the Falange's cooperation, as both the interception of Allied materials and the dissemination of new materials were mostly in the hands of this organization.[36] This created a symbiotic relationship between the Falangist party and the German Embassy, in that the plan served the interests of both.

Given its counter-propagandistic nature, most topics addressed by the plan were determined by enemy propaganda. They focused especially on highlighting the weaknesses of the Allied powers and convincing their audience of Germany's inevitable victory. Attacks on the Western powers continued – with Britain as the main target – while religious propaganda increased considerably and anti-communism regained its importance. In this context, antisemitism was more prominent than before.

Although more or less present from the beginning, the idea that the Jews controlled the media and that they were orchestrating a campaign against Germany figured more prominently in propagandistic publications after the second half of 1941. Jews started to be mentioned in connection with other enemies and especially in connection with propaganda and manipulation. Nazi propaganda described enemy propaganda as manipulative and deceitful and conveyed the idea that it was this way because the Jews controlled it and they were the only ones profiting from the war.[37] This insistence coincided with growing concern about the Allied propaganda that had sparked the Grosse Plan. In fact, four different leaflets published between the end of 1942 and the beginning of 1943 addressed this issue: *The German Cause in the World, Four Comments on Democracies' False Propaganda, Meditations on the Fourth Year of the War*, and the *Catholic and Anti-Communist Newssheet*.[38] In each of them, Jews were mentioned just once, but always to state that they controlled British and American propaganda. The newssheet – the only leaflet that elaborated on this argument – claimed that 75 per cent of Allied leaders were either Jews or *judaizantes*, a word intended to highlight the supposedly deceitful nature of the Jewish people and to tap into a view of Jews that was already widespread in Spain. Finally, the newssheet warned Catholics against "ciertas propagandas que periódicamente llegan a sus manos" (certain propagandistic materials that could fall in their hands).[39] It is no coincidence that the publication of these leaflets overlapped with the German defeat in the Battle of Stalingrad, which marked a turning point in the war and in the effectiveness of propaganda, since it was harder to control the narrative as Germany's losses became more apparent.

The year 1943 was one of intense developments for the Grosse Plan. The appointment of Francisco Gómez-Jordana as foreign minister several months earlier marked a shift in Spanish foreign policy, away from the Germanophile attitude of his predecessor, Ramón Serrano Suñer, and towards a more neutralist policy, one that made an effort to ensure that Spain neither favoured not disfavoured Allied or German propaganda.[40] Interestingly enough, again in 1943, the Francoist government became increasingly concerned about its image in the foreign press, which it believed was controlled by the Jews.[41] It is quite possible that the combination of Spanish anti-Jewish/anti-Freemason campaigns and German propaganda fostered an image that would make it harder for Nazi Germany to continue to influence the media. However, the Falange's continued cooperation with Lazar would aid in this mission and complicate Jordana's term in office.

Over the following months, this specific use of antisemitism featured as well in a subtler kind of propaganda. In connection with Lazar's desire to attract the Spanish Church to the German cause – or at least defuse the anti-Nazi sentiments present in strongly Catholic sectors – his collaborators started to identify priests whose sermons tended to align with German interests. In some cases, they would attend mass and print out the homilies to disseminate afterwards, as a means to prove that the Spanish Church was, if not clearly on the side of Germany, at least against the Allies. That was the case, for example, with a sermon by the Dominican priest Carino in which he warned his parishioners against any liberal, international, or democratic propaganda, which, according to him, could only come from Masonic Jews and lead to communism.[42] But this was not enough: the members of the Grosse Plan went so far as to help organize Catholic masses just to ensure that these priests reached a proper audience. This was the case with a mass celebrated in Madrid on 14 February 1943 in remembrance of the Fallen of the Blue Division.[43] The organization of masses and the use of priests' sermons as a propaganda tool continued over the following months. A look at German reports suggests that these priests did not always include antisemitic references in their homilies and that antisemitism was not a priority for them; however, this propaganda was spread orally, making it much more difficult to analyse, so we cannot ascertain the degree to which this hypothesis is correct. Then in April 1943 the Spanish press was instructed to publish antisemitic comments once again, even though such statements had been declining since the end of the Civil War, and even though in November 1942 the press had been ordered to moderate its portrayal of international events.[44] However, this short-lived revival of antisemitism did not halt the general trend.

These were not the only traces of antisemitism in the Grosse Plan. It was also common to suggest from time to time that Roosevelt was a Freemason and a Jew, or that Churchill intended to organize a Jewish army in Palestine.[45] German propagandists also distributed pamphlets targeted at specific sectors in Spain. Two of these, addressed to Catholics, exploited the religious aspect, claiming that the alliance between Britain and the Jews made the former an enemy of the Cross and that the Allied nations, all controlled by the Jewry, were against God and religion.[46] However, the main objective here was not to foster antisemitism but merely to refer to it in order to exploit religious concern in Spain – an appropriate tactic to implement in a confessional regime rife with religious and cultural antisemitism. Other pamphlets addressed to Carlists and Anglophiles, as well as a leaflet titled *Decálogo del buen español ante la Guerra Mundial* (Ten Commandments of the good Spaniard in the face of the World War) (figure 21.1), which was widely disseminated, also mentioned the Jews, but only to reinforce anti-British arguments.[47]

Antisemitism featured especially in those publications that had been crafted in collaboration with the Falangist Federico de Urrutia and with the support of the party. Urrutia had worked for *Informaciones*, the Nazi-financed newspaper, before the outbreak of the Spanish Civil War, and by 1939 he had written a book commissioned by the German Embassy on Germany's reasons for going to war.[48] A few years later, around January 1942, while he was serving as propaganda delegate for the province of Madrid, he wrote a new work titled ¡*Camarada: he aquí el enemigo!* (Comrade: This Is the Enemy!), printed by a covert publisher of the Francoist regime and distributed as part of the Grosse Plan.[49] This pamphlet did not dwell on the Jewish issue, but instead used it to link together all the enemies of the Nazi regime and to promote unity against covert enemies. It was meant to strengthen a Falangist campaign that sought to foster unity between party members and the army in response to incidents that had occurred that spring. It seems that several of the pamphlets distributed by this campaign, as well as other leaflets that Urrutia wanted to distribute among monarchists, originated in the German Embassy or at least were part of the Grosse Plan,[50] showing how strong cooperation between the Falange and Hans Lazar really was. In fact, it is possible that the German Embassy had a hand in the publication of other volumes published by Ediciones Toledo, such as *La garra del capitalismo judío* (The claw of Jewish capitalism), which also appeared in 1943, although there is no evidence of it so far.

That many antisemitic comments originated in collaboration with the Falange highlights the fact that fostering anti-Jewish sentiment was not a priority for the German Embassy. It also shows there were already antisemites in Spain who needed no further encouragement from Germany. Most importantly, it shows a symbiotic relationship between the Falange and Lazar, in that many materials produced for

DECALOGO del BUEN ESPAÑOL
ANTE LA GUERRA MUNDIAL

160

I.   Obedece al Caudillo.

II. Piensa que España y los países totalitarios tienen en la hora presente un común destino por el triunfo de la Justicia.

III. No olvides ni un momento que el mejor español es el que combate en Rusia.

IV. No lances bulos, ni intrigues, ni murmures, porque ello es una consigna criminal del Servicio Secreto inglés.

V.   No olvides que de todos los males que padeció tu Patria, sólo es responsable la Gran Bretaña.

VI. Todos los días dedica un recuerdo a Gibraltar y jura rescatarlo.

VII. Convence a tus amigos de que el capitalismo anglosajón y el comunismo ruso son una misma cosa: el judaísmo.

VIII. Cuando oigas defender hipócritamente al marxismo o a las democracias, ataja virilmente el veneno.

IX. No quieras para tus hijos un pasado de oprobio, en el que España era una colonia del judaísmo y de la masonería.

X.   Odia a Inglaterra y compadece a los ingleses.

21.1 *Ten Commandments of the Good Spaniard in the Face of the World War* pamphlet (Auswärtiges Amt / Politisches Archiv R67662).

the Grosse Plan served both the propagandistic agenda of Hans Lazar and the domestic politics of the Falangists.

The Grosse Plan made more frequent use of antisemitism than other campaigns, not with the intention of spreading it, however, but rather to reinforce arguments and attacks against other enemies, especially the Western powers and communism. Nevertheless, antisemitism did linger in the background of other propaganda campaigns. As Lazar stated, the information bulletins were "the only official propagandistic publications"[51] that did not advance antisemitic campaigns, which means there were others. The cultural collaboration between Spain and Germany allowed antisemitic and pro-Nazi publications to be imported through the Deutsch-Ausländischer Buchtausch and book exhibitions, as well as for the publication of antisemitic, pro-Nazi Spanish books by publishers secretly controlled by Germany, such as Rubiños, Nueva Época, and Persiles.[52] But this cultural propaganda, though extensive, was not as closely linked to the course of the war as the campaigns studied here.

Antisemitism was not a priority for German propaganda in Spain, even when Britain's declaration of support for Russia renewed interest in the use of antisemitism as a propagandistic leitmotiv in Germany.[53] Several factors can explain this. First of all, there were almost no Jews in Spain,[54] and the Freemasons, to whom the Jews were constantly linked, had been mostly wiped out by postwar Francoist repression. Therefore, their usefulness as propagandistic enemies had diminished.

As Domínguez Arribas has pointed out, antisemitic arguments by Francoist propagandists continued to fade from use after 1939 and had almost disappeared by the second half of 1943. Considering the close monitoring of the Spanish press that Lazar's collaborators implemented, it is easy to assume that he was aware of this change and thought it better to exploit other arguments. That was the case with anti-Bolshevism, which experienced a strong revival in 1941. Indeed, anti-communism was more useful than antisemitism. It drew on the experience of the Civil War, reminding audiences of the horrors of that conflict and the consequences of democracy and communism. In this sense, it was a more visible and identifiable enemy. Anti-British arguments were also useful, for they tapped into a centuries-old dislike for Britain among the Spanish right that had only deepened during the Spanish Civil War, while exploiting the yearning to reinstate the empire felt by the Falangists and army men. In this context, it was easier to present Britain as this potential empire's main enemy, as a nation seeking world domination.

In addition, the counter-propagandistic character of German propaganda, especially the Grosse Plan, influenced heavily the choice of topics, bringing religion, neutrality, anti-Britishism, anti-Americanism, and anti-Bolshevism to the forefront of the campaign. In connection to this, it is important to note that all of these campaigns, though designed and implemented by Lazar, were in the remit of the Press Division of the foreign ministry and not the propaganda ministry. Ribbentrop was not interested in transforming Franco's regime into a National Socialist system, but rather in protecting German war interests as the conflict developed, a very different attitude from the one held by Goebbels's envoys during the Spanish Civil War. That conflict had marked the beginning of a close relationship between Spain and Germany. Soon enough, Nazi aid to the rebel army gave way to transforming Spain into an economic stronghold (at least temporarily),[55] a base for Abwehr operations,[56] and a not-so-silent ally during the Second World War. Spanish support for the German war effort came to be endangered by the latter's setbacks on the Eastern Front and by the increasing pressure the Allies were exerting on Franco's government, which by early 1943 was shifting its position in light of German setbacks in the war. Counteracting Allied propaganda became important to ensure that Spain's assistance continued for as long as possible.

Furthermore, during the early years of the Franco regime, interest in Morocco and the prospect of expanding the African empire strengthened a certain philosephardism already present in Spain, especially on the part of military leaders present in the region. (See Isabelle Rohr's chapter 4 for further discussion of Spanish relations in North Africa during the war.) This philosephardism, which had arisen in the early years of the century during the colonial wars in Morocco, saw Jews as potential allies of the Spanish empire in Africa[57] and may have been a factor in diminishing the usefulness of the antisemitic element in Spanish and German propaganda. Also, in January 1943, Spain was asked to repatriate its Jews from occupied Europe. In this context, Spain's reluctance to do so[58] would only have increased if Nazi propaganda increased its antisemitism.

Moreover, while antisemitism was less prevalent in Spain, it was a cornerstone of propaganda for the Arab countries, where even criticism of Spain was used to foster their allegiance to Nazi Germany.[59] This shows that Nazi propaganda abroad did not consist in merely importing arguments and tropes wholesale from the Reich, but involved adapting to new audiences and collaborating with local propagandists, be they the Grand Mufti of Jerusalem or the Falangists. Adaptation and collaboration determined the prominence of antisemitism in the various propaganda campaigns. Good propagandists make choices on the basis of their profound knowledge of their audience,[60] and Lazar was a skilled one who opted for restrained use of antisemitism in order to guarantee his propaganda's effectiveness. Spanish antisemitism was born of a combination of antisemitic sentiments tied to the theory of the Judeo-Masonic conspiracy, the historical image of *conversos*, Falangist fascination with Nazi Germany that encouraged imitation, and the dissemination of Nazi cultural and propaganda materials. However, there is no reason strong enough for us to assume that Nazi propaganda bore the sole or even primary responsibility for the appearance of antisemitism in Spain.

NOTES

Research for this work has been funded by the Irish Research Council.

1 Palmero Aranda, "El discurso antisemita en España," 15.
2 See also Álvarez Chillida, *El antisemitismo en España*; Domínguez Arribas, *El enemigo judeo-masónico*; Rohr, *The Spanish Right*.
3 Álvarez Chillida, *El antisemitismo*, 183; Domínguez Arribas, *El enemigo*, 79–80.
4 Álvarez Chillida, *El antisemitismo*, 314; Domínguez Arribas, *El enemigo*, 457–61.
5 Bowen, *Spaniards and Nazi Germany*, 13–14, 26; idem, "Spanish Pilgrimages to Hitler's Germany"; Morant i Ariño, '"Una importante expresión."
6 Deutsche Pressepropaganda in Spanien, Auswärtiges Amt / Politisches Archiv (AA/PA), Botschaft Madrid 716.
7 AA/PA, Botschaft Madrid 615.
8 Rohr, *The Spanish Right*, 78–82; Álvarez Chillida, *El antisemitismo*, 166.
9 Böcker, *Antisemitismus ohne Juden*; Álvarez Chillida, *El antisemitismo*; Rohr, *The Spanish Right*.
10 Domínguez Arribas, *El enemigo*, 184.
11 Raguer, "La guerra civil vista por Goebbels," 26.
12 Schulze Schneider, "El régimen franquista," 241.
13 Waddington, "The Anti-Komintern," 584.
14 Domínguez Arribas, *El enemigo*, 161–234.
15 Ferrer Benimeli, *La masonería*, 115.
16 Ruhl, *Franco, Falange y "Tercer Reich,"* 47, 59; AA/PA R29854; Sáenz-Francés, *Entre la antorcha y la esvástica*, 152–3.
17 AA/PA/Hans Lazar Akt 8.624 and 8.627.
18 Sáenz-Francés, *Entre la antorcha*, 164–5.
19 Kallis, *Nazi Propaganda*, 50; Schulze Schneider, "El regimen franquista," 240.
20 Bundesarchiv (BArch) R901/60302–60304; Archivo General de la Administración 9 (17.12) 51/20898; AA/PA Botschaft Madrid 757 and 758.
21 December 1939 Report, Friedhelm Burbach, Bilbao, 3/1/40, AA/PA Spanien 5, R103027.

22 Telegram from Joachim von Ribbentrop to the German Embassy in Madrid, 8/12/39, AA/PA Botschaft Madrid 757.

23 This connection had been clearly established in Spain during the Spanish Civil War, as studied in Domínguez Arribas, *El enemigo,* 157–234.

24 Kallis, *Nazi Propaganda,* 49, 76.

25 Álvarez Chillida, *El antisemitismo,* 205–6; Domínguez Arribas, *El enemigo,* 406–7.

26 Information bulletins, 15/5/41, 16/10/41, 23/4/42, 30/4/42, 3/5/42, BArch R901/60303–60304.

27 Domínguez Arribas, *El enemigo,* 207–8.

28 Sáenz-Francés, *Entre la antorcha,* 162.

29 Schulze Schneider, "El régimen," 242.

30 AA/PA Botschaft Madrid 757; Domínguez Arribas, *El enemigo,* 326.

31 AA/PA Botschaft Madrid 757 and 758; BArch R901/60302–60304; Domínguez Arribas, *El enemigo,* 327–32.

32 Ibid., 186; Lazo Díaz, *Una familia mal avenida,* 183–6, 195–7.

33 Domínguez Arribas, *El enemigo,* 341–2; Diez Puertas, *El montaje del franquismo,* 242–3.

34 Ruhl, *Franco, Falange,* 41–2; Schulze Schneider, "La propaganda alemana."

35 Black propaganda hides its origin: "[It is] produced by clandestine organisations within the enemy country, not necessarily totally opposed to their government. Sometimes it pretends to come from the target audience's own authorities ... Grey propaganda is anonymous; it bears no signature and leaves the target guessing its origin." Newcourt-Nowodworski, *Black Propaganda,* 4.

36 Ruhl, *Franco, Falange,* 41–2; Schulze Schneider, "La propaganda"; Ros Agudo, *La guerra secreta,* 290–8.

37 BArch R901/60302 and 60304; AA/PA Botschaft Madrid 757 and 758.

38 AA/PA R67662, R67663.

39 Hoja de información católica y anticomunista, 28/4/43, AA/PA R676634.

40 Tusell, "La etapa Jordana," 169–89.

41 Rohr, *The Spanish Right,* 123.

42 Report from the German Embassy in Madrid to the Foreign Affairs Ministry in Berlin, 8/2/43, AA/PA R67663.

43 Ibid.

44 Domínguez Arribas, *El enemigo,* 342.

45 *Cómo veía y cómo ve Mr. Churchill a la URSS y al comunismo,* August 1942, AA/PA R676662.

46 Schulze Schneider, "La cooperación," 1183–5.

47 AA/PA R676662.

48 Domínguez Arribas, *El enemigo,* 457–61; Ruiz Bautista and Barruso Barés, "La propaganda alemana," 194.

49 AA/PA R67661; Domínguez Arribas, *El enemigo*, 376, 397–8.

50 Domínguez Arribas, *El enemigo*, 464–9; AA/PA R67661.

51 Sáenz-Francés, *Entre la antorcha*, 164–5.

52 Ruiz Bautista and Barruso Barés, "La propaganda alemana," 194; Longerich, *Propagandisten im Krieg*, 271.

53 Kallis, *Nazi Propaganda*, 125–9.

54 Avni, *Spain, the Jews, and Franco*, 45.

55 García Pérez, *Franquismo y Tercer Reich*; Leitz, *Economic Relations*.

56 Ros Agudo, *La guerra secreta*.

57 Álvarez Chillida, *El antisemitismo*, 181; Rohr, *The Spanish Right*, 7, 97.

58 Rother, *Spanien und der Holocaust*.

59 Herf, *Nazi*, 121–2.

60 Kallis, *Nazi Propaganda*, 9.

22 A Touch of Nazi Sophistication: The Promotion of Spanish Culture in Wartime Germany

MARICIÓ JANUÉ I MIRET

With the outbreak of the Second World War, German industry came to rely on supplies from Spain. As a result, Germany became increasingly interested in forging links between Spain and the Axis powers, and, accordingly, increased its investment in projects involving cultural collaboration. As we saw in the previous chapter, Spain proved to be fertile ground for Nazi cultural influence, due to its climate of intellectual isolation and autarky as well as the strongly fascist political orientation that dominated during the early years of Francoism. The signs of this cultural exchange were clear not only in the increased presence of German culture in Spain, but also in the promotion of Spanish culture in Germany. (See Joshua Goode's chapter 25 and David Messenger's chapter 26 in this volume on the presence of Germans and German culture in Spain.) This exchange can be understood as a sophisticated form of cultural diplomacy. By sending a message of interest in and concern for Spanish culture, the Nazis tried to avoid arousing any suspicions the Francoist authorities might have harboured about the initiative. Three types of activities are particularly crucial to understanding this sphere of influence: invitations extended to Falangist intellectuals, the promotion of the doctrine of *Hispanidad*, and the advancement of various forms of artistic expression.

Precursors: Cultural Relations in the Interwar Period

Spain was neutral during the First World War. Nevertheless, after Germany's defeat, Spain became a primary objective of Germany's cultural foreign policy.[1] Notwithstanding its socio-economic underdevelopment, Spain offered Germany an opportunity to display its cultural and scientific potential on the continental stage.[2] Spain also offered Germany a bridge to influence in Latin America. Germany's foreign policy interests with regard to Spain intensified, with Germany involving itself in Spanish institutions and also highlighting Spanish culture in Germany. This explains the emergence, even before the end of the First World War, of various Iberian American and German–Spanish societies in Germany. In 1917, the Hamburg Ibero-American Institut (IAI-H) was founded. In 1929, the Prussian Ministry of Science, Art, and Culture (Preußisches Ministerium für Wissenschaft, Kunst und Volksbildung) founded the Berlin Iberian-American Institute (IAI). The following year, working in close collaboration with the IAI, the Berlin German-Spanish Society (DSG) opened its doors.[3]

The National Socialists' rise to power in 1933 caused friction in the cultural relations between the two countries, a result of the mutual antipathy between the Nazis and the Second Spanish Republic. However, the outbreak of the Spanish Civil War in 1936 meant that relations between the two countries would once again take on special significance in the eyes of authorities within the German dictatorship.[4] The Nazis made an effort to establish relationships with Spanish intellectuals and academics favourable to Franco's cause, prioritizing those who had previous contact with German culture. Of these, there was a notable subgroup who had spent time in Germany and had imported ideas that would turn them into ideologues of Falangist National Socialism in Spain. The German Service for Academic Exchange (Deutsche Akademische Austauschdienst, DAAD), founded in 1925, and the Alexander von Humboldt Stiftung (Alexander von Humboldt Foundation), supported these exchanges and granted scholarships.[5] They also sponsored lectureships in Spanish language and literature at German universities.[6] However, it was the DSG that would, from its inception, carry out the most intensive and important work of promoting Spanish culture in Germany. Beginning in 1936, its president was Wilhelm Faupel, a renowned authoritarian military officer, now retired, who had been president of the IAI since 1934.[7] In the autumn of 1936, Faupel was named head of operations; later he would be appointed German Ambassador to Franco's Spain, although he would be relieved of his duties in August of 1937 for refusing to subordinate his relations with the Falange to the directives issued by Franco's new regime. As president of the DSG, Faupel used the opportunity afforded him by the Spanish Civil War to turn the society and himself into the primary contact for Spaniards in the German capital who supported the causes of Francoism and National Socialism. In this context, the headquarters of the DSG were moved to the offices of the IAI in order to facilitate collaboration with the specialists in charge of sections at the IAI.

After the Civil War, the National Socialist regime was positioned to exercise influence over Spanish politics, culture, and science. Germany's contribution to Franco's victory had left Spain with substantial debt, the payment of which Germany could demand via a bilateral agreement. In addition, the Germans could rely on the support of Germanophile academic elites. The autarky, intellectual isolation, and pronounced fascist orientation that dominated during the first years of Francoism facilitated Nazi influence in Spain.[8] During this period, the Franco dictatorship looked towards Germany and Italy in its search for cultural points of reference and in order to expand its networks in science and technology. The Convenio sobre la Colaboración Espiritual y Cultural entre España y Alemania (Convention on Spiritual and Cultural Collaboration between Spain and Germany), signed in Burgos in January of 1939, marked an important step forward in cultural relations between the two states.[9] However, that convention was never ratified due to opposition from the Vatican and the hierarchy of the Catholic Church in Spain.[10]

Invitations for Spanish Intellectuals and Academics to Visit the Reich

With the outbreak of the Second World War, Spain was incorporated into the National Socialist plan for redefining the European economic space. The German war machine became dependent on Spanish minerals (such as wolfram and tungsten) necessary for manufacturing armaments. As a consequence, Germany became increasingly interested in linking Spain to the Axis powers, and accordingly, it redoubled its efforts in the area of cultural collaboration. Spain's rejection of the German–Soviet Non-Aggression Pact, in force from the summer of 1939 to the summer of 1941, complicated the German authorities' project. This rejection was rooted in the Franco government's prioritization of anti-communism. But despite this disagreement, political and cultural relations between the two states continued to develop. In June of 1940, Spain officially embraced a policy of "non-belligerency," which meant it would not intervene militarily despite its support of the Axis powers. In September of 1940, Spain's interior minister, Ramón Serrano Suñer, travelled to Berlin. One month later, the leader of the Nazi SS, Heinrich Himmler, toured Spain. These visits underscored Spain's gratitude towards a nation that had been its ally during the Civil War; they also highlighted Spain's desire to join the National Socialist New Order.[11] Also, in October of 1940, Franco and Hitler met in Hendaya. Over the course of these visits, Spain was invited to join the recently signed

Tripartite Pact of military alliance with Italy and Japan, although it ultimately did not do so. In May of 1941, Franco carried out a reorganization of his government in which fascist circles of the Falange lost power; this shifted the balance towards more Catholic factions as well as those in the military who did not want Spain to participate in the world conflict. In this same context, however, the Falange, aware that only an Axis victory could improve its power and position within the country, opted to strengthen its relations with Berlin.[12]

During his brief tenure as head of the German Embassy in Franco's Spain, Wilhelm Faupel became aware of the need to prevent the Spanish authorities from growing suspicious of Nazi efforts to strengthen ties with the country. Spain's rejection of the friendship pact between Germany and the Soviet Union left Faupel all the more convinced of this need.[13] So after returning to the presidency of the DSG, he ordered lists to be drawn up of notable Spanish intellectuals accepted by the Franco regime and who were sympathetic towards the Reich. These individuals would be invited to Germany by the DSG, pending the approval of the German Embassy in Spain. In this task of attracting "official" Francoist intellectuals and academics,[14] prominent members of the DSG aided Faupel; they included Helmut Petriconi, a professor at the University of Greifswald and a member of the board of directors of the association since July of 1938, as well as a member of the editorial team at *Ensayos y Estudios* (*EE*), a Spanish-language journal published by the IAI beginning in January of 1939.[15] Faupel also enlisted the aid of Johannes Bernhardt,[16] director of the Hispano-Marokkanische Transport-Aktiengesellschaft (Spanish-Moroccan Transport Company Ltd HISMA), which during the Civil War had been a pillar of the system of goods exchange on which economic relations between Spain and Germany depended.

Pedro Laín Entralgo, a doctor, philosopher, and national adviser to the Falange, was one of the notable Spanish intellectuals the DSG invited to Germany. Laín had studied in Vienna and had visited Berlin in 1938. At the time he was invited to Germany by the DSG, Laín was director of publications in the Spanish Ministry of Government. His visit took place between 28 February and 21 March 1940, during which time he toured the country giving paid speeches at various institutions,[17] including the Berlin, Bremen, and Stuttgart chapters of the elitist Deutsche Ausland-Club (German Foreign Club), as well as the Frankfurter Gesellschaft für Handel, Industrie und Wissenschaft (Frankfurt Society for Commerce, Industry, and Science), where he spoke on "La nueva generación y el problema del desarrollo cultural en España" (The New Generation and the Problem of Cultural Development in Spain). Laín also visited the University of Bonn and the Munich chapter of the Deutsche Akademie (German Academy), forerunner of the Goethe Institute. At the University of Berlin, Laín spoke on "El sentimiento de la muerte en la literatura y pensamiento españoles" (The Sentiment of Death in Spanish Literature and Thought). His talk "Visión y revisión del 'Idearium español' de Angel Ganivet" (Vision and Revision of Angel Ganivet's "Idearium español"), delivered to the IAI on 8 March 1940, was published in *EE*.[18] Additionally, during Laín's stay in Germany, Goebbels received him at the Reich Ministry of Public Enlightenment and Propaganda (RMVP), and he participated in Nazi Party Day in Nuremberg and in the Reich congress of the NS-Gemeinschaft "Kraft durch Freude" (NS Community "Strength through Joy") in Hamburg.

The philologist Antonio Tovar was another old-guard Falangist who travelled to Germany during the war.[19] Tovar had continued his studies in Berlin, which is where he found himself at the outbreak of the Civil War. His paper "La idea del imperio español en la historia y en el presente" (The Idea of the Spanish Empire in History and Today), delivered at the IAI in the summer of 1940, was also published in *EE*.[20] In it, Tovar announced the upcoming release of the third edition of his book *La idea del Imperio Español* (The Idea of the Spanish Empire), likely in reference to his famous volume with a similar title, the fourth edition of which would be published the following year.[21] A few months after visiting the DSG, Tovar would be named Sub-Secretary of Press and Propaganda in the Spanish Ministry of Government. In addition, he would become vice-president of Spain's Asociación Hispano-Germana (Spanish-German Association, AHG), which would receive economic support from the RMVP. Several well-known Francoist intellectuals belonged to the AHG, including the aforementioned Laín and García Valdecasas.

Among the "official" academics to visit the DSG during the Second World War, Alfonso García Valdecasas, professor of political law, stands out. García Valdecasas was in Germany from 23 November to 7 December 1940, during which time he gave a talk on "Ser y significado del Hidalgo" (Being and the Meaning of Hidalgo).[22] García Valdecasas had participated, along with José Antonio Primo de Rivera, in the founding of the Falange in 1933. He had, moreover, been the director of the Falangist Instituto de Estudios Políticos (Institute for Political Studies, IEP) since its inception. The IEP and its official journal, the *REP*, to which Laín and Tovar also contributed, imported fascist and National Socialist ideology.[23] The DSG welcomed the IEP's principal contributors to the capital of the Reich, and several of their pieces were published in *EE*. Like Valdecasas, Laín, and Tovar, many prominent IEP intellectuals were also members of the AHG.

Similarly, in the autumn of 1941, the fascist ideologue, politician, writer, and university professor Ernesto Giménez Caballero, author of *Genio de España* (Genius of Spain)[24] and a founder of the Falange, also visited the DSG. After the Civil War, Giménez Caballero worked as national adviser to the Movimiento, prosecutor, and education minister, although his political influence later declined. During his time in Germany, between 23 and 26 October, he attended the meeting of the Europäische Schrifsteller Vereinigung (European Writers' Association) in Weimar. Goebbels presided over this meeting, and Giménez Caballero interviewed him there.[25] His paper, given at the IAI on 31 October 1941, treated the topic of "La espiritualidad española y Alemania" (Spanish Spirituality and Germany) and was also published in *EE*.[26] The strongly racist component of his arguments stands out in this article.

In early 1942, the medievalist and director of the Archivo de la Corona de Aragón (Archives of the Crown of Aragon) in Barcelona, Fernando Valls Taberner, became another visitor to the capital of the Reich. Valls had collaborated with several German Hispanophiles such as Heinrich Finke, who had spent time in Catalonia.[27] He had also published in *Spanische Forschungen der Görresgesellschaft*, an academic journal dedicated to Hispanic culture edited by the Catholic Görres Gesellschaft (Görres Society), an organization Finke presided over, and which had been banned in 1938 by the National Socialist regime.[28] Similarly, Valls maintained ties with many Spanish intellectuals who had spent time in Germany.[29] At the Exposición del Libro Alemán (German Book Expo) held in Barcelona in February 1941, Valls gave a talk on "La erudición germánica y la historia medieval española" (Germanic Erudition and Medieval Spanish History).[30] While in Germany, in addition to visiting the DSG, Valls appeared at the Universities of Leipzig and Greifswald, where he repeated the same talk on "Las relaciones entre España y el Reich alemán hasta el interregno de mediados del siglo XIII" (Relations between Spain and the German Reich until the Interregnum of the Mid-Thirteenth Century).[31] A few months later, he would be named official librarian of the AHG.[32]

Finally, the archaeologist and paleohistorian Martín Almagro Basch figured among the intellectuals and academics invited to Germany during the Second World War. From December of 1935 to July of 1936, Almagro had studied at the Universities of Hamburg, Berlin, and Marburg, and at the Prähistorisches Institut of Vienna, sponsored by Spain's Junta de Ampliación de Estudios (Council for Continuing Studies).[33] At the outbreak of the Civil War, Almagro returned to Spain and joined the Falange. Following the Civil War, he became director of Barcelona's Museo Arqueológico (Archaeological Museum) and of the Servicio de investigaciones arqueológicas (Archaeological Research Service), where he was responsible for the excavations at Ampurias.[34] On 2 February 1942, Almagro delivered a talk in German to the IAI on the subject of "Ampurias, su surgimiento y su decadencia" (The Rise and Fall of Ampurias).[35]

The Promotion of the Doctrine of the "Raza de la Hispanidad" in Germany

The doctrine of the "Raza de la Hispanidad" has its origins in the commemoration of Christopher Columbus's discovery of America on 12 October 1492. In 1913, conservative political sectors in Spain promoted the commemoration of this event as the "Fiesta de la Raza" or "Día de la Raza," and the promotion of Spain's resurgence as an imperial power became associated with the celebration. Connected to this discourse was the concept of *Hispanismo*, which stood in opposition to the usage of the term Pan-American in the English-speaking world. In 1918, a decree established the Día de la Raza as a national holiday in Spain. In the context of the Second Republic, *Hispanismo*, which thanks to Ramiro de Maeztu came to be known as *Hispanidad*, became a core element of conservative ideology.[36]

Spanish fascists adopted the conservative discourse of *Hispanidad*, emphasizing, above all, the glorification of the Empire, which they considered the precondition for the resurgence of the *patria*.[37] *Hispanidad* allowed them to express Spain's "misión" of affirming its "imperio cultural católico" (Catholic cultural empire) in Europe and throughout the world. During the early years of the Franco government, the discourse of *Hispanidad* was employed as a fundamental instrument for reinforcing the position of the dictator, both inside the country and on the international level. Within Spain, the promotion of *Hispanidad* served as a doctrinal and propagandistic means of legitimizing the dictatorial system by linking it to an "España imperial y eterna" (imperial and eternal Spain).[38] Outside the country, the politics of *Hispanidad* sought to increase the value of Spain's contribution to the new fascist Europe. In Germany, observations of the Día de la Hispanidad had become common during the interwar period.[39] The IAI, from its inception, organized and carried out these festivities in the German capital, celebrations in which the DSG regularly participated.

Following the rise to power of the National Socialists and, later, the Spanish Civil War, one of the principal objectives of the annual Fiesta de la Raza celebration became showcasing the special relationship between Nazi Germany and Francoist Spain.[40] Spain's sphere of influence was seen as a potential sphere of German influence. Additionally, the anti–North American component of *Hispanidad* dovetailed well with Axis ambitions. In the summer of 1939, the AA explicitly proposed using Spain's new political and cultural imperialism to Germany's benefit; cultural relations with Spain were to be strengthened in order to influence America through propaganda.[41] The DSG expressed similar intentions in its 1939–40 report.[42]

The rhetoric of the Fiesta de la Raza followed the same pattern in the Reich as in Francoist Spain, reproducing the symbology that represented Spain as mother to her Latin American daughters.[43] Within this framework, the IAI positioned itself as the "brother" of Spain and at the same time as the "uncle" of Iberian America. Spain also benefited from this German tactic, since it allowed Spain to present itself as Germany's companion. The celebration of the Fiesta de la Raza also symbolized an international consensus in favour of an authoritarian, hierarchical, and racist society. In any event, in 1942, after the United States entered the war against Germany and the majority of Latin American countries discontinued diplomatic relations with the Reich, the AA decided to put an end to celebrations of the Fiesta de la Raza.

The promotion of the doctrine of *Hispanidad* in Germany was also supported by various German intellectuals and academics. During the Second World War, Helmut Petriconi published an article on the image of Spain in German consciousness that had emerged from a talk he gave for the opening of the German Book Expo in Barcelona, mentioned earlier.[44] In his text, Petriconi points to the coronation of Carlos V as a decisive moment in the advancement of relations between Spain and Germany. He also emphasizes that in the most famous German literary work of the seventeenth century, "Simplicius Simplicissimus" by Grimmelshausen, "Spain" was understood as the whole of the Spanish empire. The author links the temporary and partial distancing of the two countries in the eighteenth century to the end of the Hapsburg dynasty in Spain. He notes, however, that the nineteenth century saw a new period of German enthusiasm for Spanish culture and its classics. At the time of the article's publication, the figure of King Philip II was of key interest to German historians of Spain. Petriconi points to the surge in German interest in Spanish culture that took place after the First World War, when the works of authors such as Miguel de Unamuno and Pío Baroja, who rediscovered the beauty of Castile, were translated into German. At the same time, the author laments the diminishing awareness of the essential relationship between Spain and Latin America. He concludes that in the year 1936, when Spain finally re-emerged on the world stage, only Germany and Italy were prepared to recognize Spain as an imperial nation, cognizant of its mission.

The Hispanist Hermann Hüffer, a cultural attaché to the German Embassy in Madrid, also wrote about the Spanish empire.[45] During the war, Hüffer published an article on the history of cultural relations between Germany and Spain,[46] which would later appear in Spanish in the journal *Revista de Estudios Políticos* (Journal of Political Studies, REP).[47] In that article, like Petriconi, Hüffer emphasizes that the two countries reached the peak of their spiritual connection during the time of Charles V. He associates the beginning of Spain's downfall with the end of the Hapsburg dynasty, noting that relations would take off once more in the last decade of the eighteenth century, as illustrated by the evident interest in Spanish landscape and culture in the travelogues of brothers Wilhelm and Alexander von Humboldt, and by the German Romantics' idealization of the Spanish Golden Age. Hüffer underscores the influence that the Krausist movement was to have in nineteenth-century Spain. He goes on to stress the significant cultural rapprochement between the two countries following the First World War, highlighting the founding of the IAI-H and the IAI during the interwar period. Hüffer explains that although the declaration of the Second Spanish Republic resulted in a cooling of relations, these relations would improve again thanks to Franco's Nationalist uprising – an improvement exemplified by the visits leading Falangist intellectuals made to Germany after the uprising, arranged by the DSG.

The propagation of *Hispanidad* in Germany would go hand in hand with a positive view of the way Spain had managed its empire. The Spanish empire's achievement – the spread of Christian hegemony to the American continent – was interpreted as a boon to European unity and hegemony. In modern times, Spain's imperial mission was not to recover territorial possessions in the Americas – which Germany did not consider the essential element of the Spanish empire – but rather to recover spiritual control of its empire. *Hispanidad*, which would experience a resurgence under Francoism, was consequently reinterpreted as the spreading of the European New Order to the Americas in the face of Bolshevik and Anglo-American threats. With this new interpretation, *Hispanidad* became more than a means of cultivating relations with the Franco regime. It was an idea that harmonized with Germany's geostrategic interests in Spain: namely, Spain's integration into the totalitarian New Order and the strengthening of its ties with Latin America.

The Promotion and Exhibition of Spanish Art

During the Second World War, the Nazi regime used music and art as extraordinarily effective instruments of propaganda for cementing its political alliance with Spain.[48] The regime organized a range of activities aimed at promoting and exhibiting Spanish art and music in Germany and invited prominent Spanish artists and musicians to visit the country. Specialists from various departments of the IAI, whose willingness to collaborate was influenced by the ever-increasing difficulties afflicting communication between Germany and Latin America, supported the fundamental work of the DSG. As in the other spheres we have discussed, here the Germans followed the pattern of taking into account the Franco regime's acceptance of the invited or featured artists' works and ideas, giving priority to those artists who had demonstrated sympathy for National Socialist Germany.

Throughout these years, the Franco government instrumentalized art and music as a means of spreading its ideology, evoked through imperial grandeur and the historical continuity of Spanish unity. The regime created mechanisms for regulating and administering the development of these activities within the country.[49] In music, composers who exemplified "nacionalismo musical español" (Spanish musical nationalism) enjoyed support and protection. Chief among these musicians was Manuel de Falla, who, in spite of having exiled himself to Argentina, became fundamentally important to the regime's project, along with other recent composers such as Isaac Albéniz and Enrique Granados. In Spain, as in Germany, radio was instrumental to the homogenization of musical tastes.[50] Spanish critics saw Germany as the most important country in matters pertaining to music, and Spanish–German relations would play a critical role in the rebuilding of musical life after the Civil War.[51]

Back in Germany, the head of the IAI's music division, Richard Klatovsky – an orchestra director and specialist in Incan music who had spent twelve years in Latin America – created a broadcast dedicated to Spanish music that first aired on German short wave radio (Deutsche Kurzwellensender) in May of 1939.[52] The program was broadcast once a month and offered the listener forty to sixty minutes of works by classical and modern Spanish composers. Shortly after the outbreak of the Second World War and coinciding with *Hispanidad* festivities, Klatovsky was involved in the rebroadcast of a concert the IAI and the DSG had jointly organized in which the Berlin Philharmonic and the Spanish pianist José Arriola performed a program of Spanish and Latin American music.[53] In preparation for his work with Spanish music, Klatovsky undertook several long visits to Spain between 1940 and 1942 as an envoy of the DSG.[54] Klatovsky's contacts in Spain paved the way for notable Spanish musicians interested in Germany to visit the country at the DSG's invitation. Thus, on 20 April 1940, Hitler's fifty-first birthday, the orchestra conductor José María Franco led the Berlin Philharmonic in a performance of a Concierto Español.[55] In

October of the same year, the pianist José Cubiles, a member of the AHG with ties to Spain's music administration, also performed with the Philharmonic, and the IAI and the DSG held a reception in his honour.[56] Cubiles would also participate in the Deutsch-Spanisches Musikfestival (German-Spanish Music Festival), held between 10 and 16 July at Bad Elster and organized by the DSG and the RMVP.[57] Also invited to the festival was the brilliant young Spanish pianist Ataúlfo Argenta, who, on a grant from the German government, had undertaken continuing studies in Germany.[58] Argenta gave a concert in Germany in May of 1942, and several more throughout the autumn of 1943.[59] The renowned dancer Mariemma, an exponent of Spanish dance, also performed at Bad Elster.[60] Heinz Drewes, musical director of the RMVP, attended the festival.[61] From 5 to 11 July 1942, the second Semana Musical Hispano-Alemana (Spanish-German Music Week) was held at Bad Elster and Dresden, where Cubiles again took part and Drewes delivered the opening address.[62]

Dr Gertrud Richert, director of the IAI art division, also worked intensively for the DSG. Richert had spent several years in Spain, where she taught at the University of Barcelona. Her most notable achievement during the war was the Ausstellung Spanischer Kunst der Gegenwart (Exposition of Contemporary Spanish Art), held at the Prussian Art Academy (PAK) from 19 March to 12 April 1942.[63] The exposition presented 219 works by eighty-five Spanish artists and was visited by twenty-eight thousand people, which was, according to Faupel, "a number that, in all the many events of this kind that have thus far taken place at the PAK, had never before been achieved, nor even approached."[64] Well-known Spanish painters such as the Galician Fernández Álvarez Sotomayor, director of the Museo del Prado; the Valencian Manuel Benedito Vives, a student of Joaquín Sorolla; and Francisco Núñez Losada, an internationally recognized landscape painter from Salamanca, attended the Exposition. Goebbels and Rosenburg visited as representatives of the Reich.

In the summer of 1941, the DSG decided to establish branches in several German cities.[65] The first of these was founded in Munich on 29 April 1942. In October of 1942, the second branch opened in Leipzig.[66] Finally, in February of 1943, a third branch was founded in Frankfurt. Relations between Germany and Spain were now cooling, given that the tide was turning against Germany in the war. The most notable cultural event any branch of the DSG organized was the Second Spanish Week in Frankfurt, held from 28 November to 4 December of 1943.[67] The city of Frankfurt had a tradition of celebrating classic Spanish Renaissance literature. Since 1937, no fewer than eight productions of

Lope de Vega and Tirso de Molina plays had been staged, four of them in German. The philologist Hans Schlegel, a resident of Barcelona and a specialist in the translation of classic Spanish literature into German, collaborated on the translations. The First Spanish Week in Frankfurt was held in 1938, organized by the DSG.[68] During the event, Schlegel gave a talk that was later published in *EE*.[69]

The Frankfurt Opera company had been appearing at the Liceo Opera House in Barcelona on a regular basis since 1939, mostly performing operas by Wagner, with Hans Meissner, general manager of Frankfurt's municipal theatres, as stage director. These same municipal theatres collaborated with the Frankfurt branch of the DSG to organize the Second Spanish Week, which was dedicated to the presentation of classic Spanish theatre and opera. Schlegel delivered a talk titled "El camino a Lope" (The Path to Lope). During Spanish Week, Schlegel's German translations of Lope's works *Liebe aus Neid* (*El perro del hortelano*)[70] and *Die Freundschaftsprobe* (*La amistad pagada*) were staged. The Spanish Week's program included the first performance of a Spanish opera in Germany: *Las Golondrinas* by José María and Ramón Usandizaga, translated by Schlegel as *Fahrendes Volk*. The cycle also featured a Spanish-German musical event in which German musicians played eighteenth-century Spanish chamber music and pieces by particularly well-admired Spanish contemporary composers: in addition to Albéniz and Manuel de Falla, the event featured Joaquin Turina, associated with the Francoist music administration; Jesús Guridi, who was inspired by Basque folklore; Pablo Sorozábal, composer of *zarzuelas* (a genre of musical theatre native to Spain), who had pursued advanced studies in Germany; and Ernesto Halffter, a notable student of Falla's. Argenta performed as a solo pianist in one of the concerts. Concurrently, the series held a theatrical and musical exposition on Spain in the city centre.

In spite of its brilliant program, however, Spanish Week was marked by unpleasant incidents. Just days before it began, heavy bombing had damaged Frankfurt's municipal theatres. The city's Opera House was also hit and was left half in ruins. Because of damage caused by the bombing, Celestino Sarobe, a baritone from Guipuzcoa and professor of voice at the Barcelona Liceo who had participated in the Second Spanish-German Music Week in 1942,[71] suffered an accident in which he broke a rib; as a result, Usandizaga's opera could only be performed at the end of the Week. Faupel did not attend the opening ceremony,[72] surely due to his irritation at Spanish ambassador Ginés Vidal y Saura's refusal to participate in the event despite having been invited, and the fact that the ambassador failed to send even a small group of qualified representatives from the embassy.[73]

Conclusions

After the Spanish Civil War, the National Socialist regime was favourably positioned to exert influence over Spanish politics, culture, and science. The outbreak of the Second World War increased German interest in connecting Spain with the Axis powers, and accordingly, the Germans expanded their efforts towards cultural collaboration. National Socialists considered cultural relations with Spain important to the pursuit of their foreign policy objectives, as analyses of Nazi cultural diplomacy during the interwar period have shown. Additionally, they used sophisticated modern techniques of institution building and cultural diffusion, such as the propagation of the ideas of *Hispanidad* in Germany, in an effort to overcome the suspicions of the Francoist authorities by transmitting a message of interest in and consideration for Hispanic culture.

The Nazis' plans for German-Spanish cultural relations were underwritten by a racial ideology that corresponded to their imperialist objectives. The Francoist interest in reinforcing Spain's historical unity and its ties with Latin America was, in this sense, in accord with National Socialism. Moreover, the anti-American component of *Hispanidad* was tailored to Axis ambitions. Even so, these German programs were not indifferent to questions of quality, given that they attempted to attract the most important intellectuals, academics, and artists of the moment. These people were, furthermore, vetted by the Francoists, who prioritized the participation of individuals who occupied high posts in the regime, Falangists, and figures who had demonstrated sympathies with National Socialism. The cultural elements the Nazis and the Francoists jointly promoted can in no way be considered popular or vulgar.

Ultimately, the push for National Socialist cultural supremacy in Spain was curtailed due to several factors. First, the radicalized sectors of the Falange who were the most receptive to the Nazi cultural program were in competition with other forces that supported Francoism, notably the *nacionalcatólicos*. Second, and in spite of this link between Francoists and Catholics, the markedly Catholic component of Spanish Falangism made it more compatible with Italian Fascism rather than with Nazism. Yet it is also true that when faced with a progressive loss of power and the realization that only an Axis victory could improve their situation within Spain, Axis-supporting sectors of the Falange intensified their relations with Berlin. In reality, Germany's downward spiral in the war beginning in late 1943 was the decisive factor in its loss of cultural influence in Spain: by then, Germany's cultural foreign policy had become pointless. By the summer of 1944, as Allied gains intensified, cultural contact between Spain and Germany countries had ground to a halt.

Abbreviations

AA   Auswärtiges Amt (German Ministry of Foreign Affairs)
AHG   Asociación Hispano-Germana (Spanish–German Association)
DSG   Deutsch-Spanische Gesellschaft Berlin (German–Spanish
         Society of Berlin)
EE   *Ensayos y Estudios*
GSTA   Geheimes Staatsarchiv Presussischer Kulturbesitz (Secret
         Archive of the Prussian State)
IAI   Ibero-Amerikanisches Institut Berlin (Iberian American
         Institute of Berlin)
IAI-H   Ibero-Amerikanisches Institut Hamburg (Iberian American
         Institute of Hamburg)
IEP   Instituto de Estudios Políticos (Institute of Political Studies)
LVG   *La Vanguardia*
PAAA   Polistisches Archiv des Auswärtigen Amtes (Political Archive
         of the Foreign Service)
PAK   Preussische Akademie der Künste (Prussian Academy of the
         Arts)
REP   *Revista de Estudios Políticos*
RMVP   Reichsministerium für Volksaufklärung und Propaganda
         (Reich Ministry of Public Enlightenment and Propaganda)

NOTES

1 Pöppinghaus, *Moralische Eroberungen?*; Hera Martínez, *La política cultural.*
2 Janué Miret, "Autorepresentación nacional"; "Im Spiegel der deutschen
   Wissenschaft und Kultur," in Rebok, ed., *Traspasar Fronteras*, 170–91.
3 Janué Miret, "La cultura como instrumento"; "Imperialismus durch
   auswärtige Kulturpolitik.
4 Janué Miret, "Relaciones culturales"; idem, "The Role of Culture."
5 Delgado López-Escalonilla, *Imperio de papel*, 199; Hera Martínez, *La política
   cultural* 280.
6 Rodríguez López, "La Universidad de Madrid."
7 Oliver Gliech, "Wilhelm Faupel. Generalstabsoffizier, Militärberater,
   Präsident des Ibero-Amerikanischen Instituts," in Liehr, Mainhold, and
   Vollmer, eds., *Ein Institut und sein General*, 131–279.
8 Delgado López-Escalonilla, *Imperio de papel*, 269; Carlos Sanz Díaz,
   "Relaciones científico-culturales hispano-alemanas entre 1939 y 1975," in
   Rebok, ed., *Traspasar Fronteras*, 361–80; Sesma Landrín, "Importando el
   Nuevo Orden," 252.

9 Hera Martínez, *La política cultural*, 404–31.

10 Marquina Barrio, "La Iglesia Española."

11 Sesma Landrín, "Importando el Nuevo Orden," 257ff.

12 Bernecker, "Alemania y España." 177; Delgado López-Escalonilla, *Imperio de papel*, 161ff.; Janué Miret, "La atracción del falangismo"; Saz Campos, *España contra España*, 342–3.

13 Janué "La cultura como instrument"; idem, "Imperialismus."

14 Miguel Ángel Ruiz Carnicer, "*La cultura del poder*. Propaganda en la alta manera," in Gracia García and Ruiz Carnicer, *La España de Franco*, 155–85.

15 IAI, F 00/10: 927, 25.10.1939.

16 IAI F 00/10, 928, 13.11.1939.

17 GSTA, I.HA Rep. 218, 345; IAI, F 00/10: 929, DSG report 1939–1940

18 Laín Entralgo, "'Idearium español.'"

19 IAI F 00/10, 929, DSG report 1940.

20 Tovar, "La idea del imperio español.".

21 Tovar, *El imperio de España*.

22 IAI F00/10 929, DSG report 1939–1940; IAI F 00/10 927, DSG report 1940.

23 Sesma Landrín, "Propaganda en la alta manera"; idem, "Importando el Nuevo Orden."

24 Giménez Caballero, *Genio de España*.

25 Idem, *Memorias de un dictador*.

26 Idem, "La espiritualidad."

27 GSTA I.HA Rep. 218, 218, 30.1.1942.

28 Sandra Rebok, "Deutsche Wissenschaft in Spanien: Der Beginn der institutionellen Zusammenarbeit Anfang des 20. Jahrhunderts/Ciencia alemana en España: los comienzos de la cooperación institucional en los albores del siglo XX," 108–37 in Rebok, ed., *Traspasar Fronteras*, 128–31; idem, "Las primeras instituciones científicas," 176.

29 Peláez, Guckes, Gómez, and Serrano: *Epistolario Germánico*.

30 *LVG*, 14.2.1941.

31 GSTA, I.HA. Rep. 218, 218, 31.1.1942; IAI F 00/10 927; LVG, 14.2.1942

32 *LVG* 14.7.1942.

33 Formentín and Villegas, "Aportaciones," 53–4.

34 Gracia Alonso, *Arqueologia i política*.

35 IAI F 00/10 927.

36 Maeztu, *Defensa de la hispanidad*.

37 Delgado López-Escalonilla, *Imperio de papel*, 123–4; Diffie, "The Ideology of Hispanidad"; González Calleja and Limón Nevado, *La Hispanidad como instrumento de combate*, 26–30; Saz Campos, *España contra España*, 184–5.

38 Barbeito Díez, "El Consejo de la Hispanidad"; González and Limón, 88–9; Pérez-Zalduondo, "La música en los intercambios culturales," 420.

39 Dawid Danilo Bartelt, "Rassismus als politische Inszenierung. Das Ibero-Amerikanische Institut und der Día de la Raza," in Liehr, Maihold, and Vollmer, eds., *Ein Institut und sein General*, 67–129.

40 Ibid., 86–90.

41 GSTA I.HA. Rep. 218, 216, 13.7.1939.

42 IAI F 00/10, 929.

43 Bartelt, "Rassismus als politische Inszenierung," 109–15.

44 *LVG* 12.2.1941; Petriconi, "Das Spanienbild."

45 Hüffer, *La idea imperial española*.

46 Idem, *Deutsch-Spanische Kulturbeziehungen*.

47 Idem, "Las relaciones hispanogermanas."

48 Erik Levi, "The Reception of Spanish Music in Germany during the Nazi Era," in Pérez Zalduondo and Gan Quesada, *Music and Francoism*, 14.

49 Civilotti, "Franquismo y heteromías," http://revistacombate.com/revista/franquismo-y-heteronomias-en-la-musica-espanola/ (accessed 30 November 2016); Jordi Gracia García, "Artes y Letras de supervivencia," in Gracia García and Ruiz Carnicer, *La España de franco*, 127–53; Marzo and Mayayo, "Del fascismo a la desideologización"; Moreda Rodríguez, "Fascist Spain and the Axis," http://britishpostgraduatemusicology.org/bpm9/rodriguez.html, (accessed 15 December 2016); Pérez-Zalduondo, "El nacionalismo"; idem, "La música en los intercambios culturales"; idem, "Music, Totalitarian Ideologies," http://www.cilam.ucr.edu/diagonal/issues/2011/Gemma.pdf (accessed 1 December 2016); idem, "Música, censura y Falange."

50 Levi, *Music in the Third Reich*, 126–39.

51 Moreda Rodríguez, "Fascist Spain and the Axis"; Pérez Zalduondo, "La música en los intercambios culturales."

52 IAI F 00/10, 929, DSG report 1939–40; Levi (2013), 12.

53 Levi, *Music in the Third Reich*, 12.

54 GSTA, I.HA. Rep. 218, 681; GSTA, I.HA. Rep. 218, 685; *El Alcázar*, 10 July 1940 and 20 February 1942; *Informaciones*, 20 July 1940; *Ritmo* 136, July 1940: 13; *Unidad*, 27 January 1942; *Arriba*, 15 February 1942; Javier Suárez-Pajares, "Festivals and Orchestras: Nazi Musical Propaganda in Spain during the early 1940s," in Pérez Zalduondo and Gan Quesada, eds., *Music and Francoism*, 59–95 at 60–6.

55 GSTA, I.HA. Rep. 218, 341; Levi (2013), 15; *ABC* 25.4.1940; *Ritmo* 134, 5.1940: 18; Suárez-Pajares, 64–5.

56 IAI F 00/10, 929, DSG report 1939–40; *ABC* 15 October 1940; Levi, *Music and Francoism*, 15, 17.

57 *Ritmo* 147, July–August 1941, 12–13; Hausswald, "Deutsch-Spanisches Musik Fest," 539; Civilotti, "Franquismo y heteromías"; Levi, *Music and Francoism*, 15–17; Pérez Zalduondo, "La música en los intercambios culturales," 436–46; Suárez-Pajares, "Festivals and Orchestras," 66–78.

58 Levi, *Music and Francoism*, 14, 17; Suárez-Pajares, "Festivals and Orchestras," 68, 73–4.
59 IAI F 00/10 927; GSTA I.HA. Rep. 218, 682.
60 Pérez Zalduondo, "La música en los intercambios culturales," 445.
61 Levi, *Music in the Third Reich*, 32–8; idem, *Music and Francoism*, 16; Suárez-Pajares, "Festivals and Orchestras," 75.
62 *Zeitschrift für Musik* 8 (1942): 337–49; *Ritmo* 159, October 1942: 6–7; Levi, *Music and Francoism*, 18; Suárez-Pajares, "Festivals and Orchestras," 84–8.
63 GSTA I.HA. Rep. 218, 218.
64 IAI, F 00/10: 929, Faupel's report.
65 IAI, F 00/10: 927; GSTA I.HA.Rep. 218, 395.
66 GSTA I.HA.Rep. 218, 395.
67 GSTA I.HA. Rep. 218, 682; Schweizer, "Spanische Woche," 23; Levi, *Music and Francoism*, 22–3; Suárez-Pajares, "Festivals and Orchestras," 88–93.
68 GSTA I.HA. Rep. 218, 682.
69 Schlegel, "El problema de la traducción."
70 Vega Carpio, *Liebe aus Neid*.
71 Suárez-Pajares, "Festivals and Orchestras," 85–6.
72 GSTA I.HA. Rep. 218, 782.
73 GSTA I.HA. Rep. 218, 682.

PART SIX

The Blue Division

23 The Blue Division and the National Question in the Occupied Territory of Russia, 1941–1943

BORIS KOVALEV

After Franco aligned Spain with the Axis powers, he created a volunteer fighting division that, starting in 1941, would take part in the German campaign against the Russians.

This chapter is devoted to the Spanish Blue Division, a foreign volunteer unit created for service under the German Wehrmacht that fought against the Soviet army on the Eastern Front during 1941–3. The Spanish force was integrated into the Wehrmacht as a stand-alone military entity: the 250th Spanish Volunteers Division. In June and July 1941, thousands of volunteers joined what would become known as the División Azul, at first composed of some seventeen thousand combatants. Recruits came to the units through both the Falange and the Spanish Army. Many of the volunteers had fascist sympathies, and most professed that they were keenly anti-communist. High casualties in the field required replacement forces, with the result that nearly thirty thousand more Spaniards went to Russia throughout the late autumn of 1943, first to the Volkhov front and later to the Leningrad front. All recruits spent between two and eight weeks on German soil for training before departing for the Soviet Union. Around five thousand Spanish soldiers perished in the war, and another 450 were taken prisoner by the Red Army.

This chapter discusses findings about the Blue Division drawn from documents and other materials in Russia's state and departmental archives as well as from personal interviews with witnesses to the events described. Recent Spanish research on the Blue Division, including work by the Blue Division historian Xosé Núñez Seixas, cites my monograph, *Dobrovol'cí na chuzhoj voyne. Ocherki istorii Goluboj divizii* (Volunteers in the Foreign War: Essays on the History of the Blue Division),[1] noting the value of these archival documents.[2] In the course of my research, I consulted provincial security and interior ministry files and the Russian Defence Ministry's central archive, in addition to analysing diaries, memoirs, and letters written by fallen Spaniards, some of which were later confiscated by the Soviets. The findings also stem from interviews with some fifty people who resided in areas controlled by the Blue Division, especially near Lake Ilmen and the River Volkhov in the Russian provinces of Novgorod and Leningrad. The prologue by Haim Avni and Macarena Tejada López's chapter 24 in this volume contribute different aspects of the history of the Blue Division.

During their "military voyage" to Russia, the Spaniards encountered French, Germans, Poles, Belorussians, Latvians, and Russians. Most of the Blue Division volunteers claimed to have felt aversion to the Nazis' "final solution." However, the treatment of Jewish communities did not lead to any substantive conflicts between the Spaniards and the Germans. When deployed to the city of Novgorod, the Spaniards set up a special occupation regime, which relative to that of the Nazis could be considered a milder version of occupation, for they did not engage in mass repression of Russian civilians. Unlike the Germans, the divisioners were not intentionally cruel towards civilians. In their memoirs and diaries, the Spaniards expressed a pervasive antisemitism but not the murderous racial prejudices characteristic of Nazis.

Spain Enters the War against Russia

Almost all of Europe separates Spain from Russia. Yet during the Second World War the Spanish Blue Division, as an ally of Nazi Germany, found itself in northwestern Russia. Its soldiers had to march thousands of kilometres to reach the towns of Novgorod and Pavlovsk, the village of Posad, and Krasny Bor. They crossed Spain, France, Poland, Belorussia, Lithuania, and Latvia to reach Russia. In June 1941, at the beginning of Nazi Germany's war against the Soviet Union, the Reich Ministry of Public Enlightenment and Propaganda proclaimed Europe's "Crusade against Bolshevism." At this point, Finland, Romania, Italy, Slovakia, and Hungary joined Germany's side in the war.

The Spanish government had been inspired by the news of Germany's invasion of the Soviet Union. On 24 June 1941, Spanish foreign minister Ramón Serrano Súñer notified the German ambassador, Eberhard von Stohrer, that "the Spanish Government ... [felt] the greatest satisfaction with the beginning of the struggle against Bolshevist Russia."[3] Serrano Súñer appealed to the German government to allow Spanish Falange activists to join the fight against the common enemy. Reich foreign minister Joachim von Ribbentrop notified the German representative in Madrid that "the German government will gladly give assent to Spanish Falange volunteer units."[4] On the same day, Serrano Súñer addressed Spanish Falange activists with an appeal for volunteers for the war against the Soviet Union. Franco proclaimed a "crusade against Jews and Masons, communists and homosexuals."[5] The Germans hoped that Serrano Súñer's policy would draw Spain into the war on the side of the Third Reich. But Franco was well aware that his country had not yet recovered from the Civil War and that Spanish society remained unstable. So he chose to confine himself to sending volunteers to the Eastern Front.

Agustín Muñoz Grandes, a popular general in the Spanish Army, was given command of the division. After being fitted with German uniforms, the soldiers took the oath of allegiance to Nazi Germany. From that day on, the Spanish volunteer unit became known as the 250th Infantry Division of the Wehrmacht. Many Spaniards sincerely believed they were going to Russia to liberate Russians, not to enslave them, and subsequently, they reported feeling distressed that the Russians they encountered did not understand their cause. Unlike the Germans, the Spaniards, with the Spanish Civil War still fresh in their minds, called their enemies at the front not "Russians" but "Reds."[6] In this way they revealed that they comprehended their military engagement not as a fight against the Russian people, but rather as an effort to topple the Communist regime and Stalin.

Archival materials, memoirs, and oral histories reveal how Russian civilians encountered and viewed the Spanish soldiers as well as how Spaniards understood and remembered the various populations with whom they interacted as they moved across Russian territory. What image of the Spaniards did the Russians paint in their reports about petty crimes committed by the visiting forces? What impressions did the Spaniards hold not only of the Russians, but also of the Nazis and the Jewish communities they came across? A careful analysis of reports from the archival holdings as well as interviews complicates our view of the encounters between Russian civilians, Spanish volunteers, Germans, and Jews.

Russian Civilians and Spanish Soldiers

Records and reports about petty crimes offer insights into how Russian civilians remembered the Spanish and German occupiers – in particular, the differences in behaviour between Spanish and German troops. For example, Alexandra Dmitrievna Okhapkina, a former teacher, was twelve in 1941.[7] She was an unremarkable Soviet child, a Pioneer, who lived with her elder sister's family in the town of Novgorod before the war started. They escaped from Novgorod to the Otensky monastery, 10 kilometres from the city. She describes the Spaniards as thievish but not cruel. They even displayed some sympathy for civilians: "They took away local people's pigs, cows, and cooked meat on fires." Okhapkina remembers the day that Spanish soldiers came to their cell in the monastery and, having turned everything upside down, asked:

> "Where are civilians?" They did not touch the children. The soldiers gave us [the dwellers of the monastery cells] 20 minutes to pack our things and then kicked all of us – the children and adults – out to the snow. The Spaniards lined us up, and photographed us, and drove us farther away from the front line, back to the village of Shevelyovo where they were stationed. Now I understand their forced cruelty to us, civilians. The Spaniards knew we should not stay in [the] Otensky monastery as the fighting was going on nearby. Our life was in great danger there. That is why the Spanish soldiers drove us out, so we could survive somehow. "Clear off or we'll thrash you!" they said.[8]

Spanish soldiers fought against the Red Army, killing Red Army soldiers, but occasionally they rescued civilians. Alexandra Okhapkina remembered the following incident: The Germans and the Spaniards had different grocery stores. The Germans had a warehouse in the German Colony, a village where ethnic Germans lived, while the Spaniards were stationed in the village of Shevelyovo. One day someone plundered the German grocery store. The Germans thought that the locals did it and decided to shoot them. The soldiers kicked the locals out onto the street and lined them up. The last in the line was a woman who had six children. A Spanish soldier quietly pushed her aside, out of the line, saving her life.

In their relations with the local population, Spaniards, unlike Germans, sought closer contact. Lidia Osipova, who worked as a laundress for Blue Division soldiers in 1942, described her new acquaintances in her diary:

> The Spaniards destroyed all our ideas about them as a proud, beautiful and noble people. No opera characters. They are small, nimble like monkeys, dirty and thievish like gypsies. But they are very good-natured, kind and sincere. All the German "kralechki" [pretty young women] immediately jilted the Germans for the Spaniards. And the Spaniards also show great tenderness and affection for the Russian girls. The Germans and the Spaniards hate each other, and this hatred is heated by their rivalry for women.[9]

In April 1944, a few months after the liberation of northwestern Russia from the German occupation, the Extraordinary State Commission (ESC) started to collect materials about the damage to the region. The ESC must be understood as a historical source. Commission members were interested in the facts of the crimes committed in the occupied territories and the degree of destruction suffered by the country. As the ESC was interested only in revealing crimes, no information about the humane treatment of civilians was recorded. This official inquiry took place a few months after the Spaniards departed. Some forty-eight people were questioned. It appears that most of those interviewed answered sincerely and in detail. Repeatedly, persons who answered the ESC questions noted the differences between the behaviour of Germans and that of Spaniards, recognizing the comportment of the latter as more "correct" in relation to the non-belligerent population.

The ESC documents that refer to Spanish soldiers are quite diverse. They include interviews with witnesses, statements of victims, accounts of acts of destruction, and identity checks of persons guilty of committing crimes (the material that would be transferred to the State Security Committee of the Soviet Union). It was difficult to determine the guilt of Spanish soldiers, considering that the Blue Division left the Novgorod region in the summer of 1942, a year and a half before Novgorod was liberated and two and a half years prior to the establishment of the ESC. Most of the Novgorodians did not see a significant difference between the German and Spanish occupiers, for they could not differentiate the German language from Spanish and the soldiers' uniforms were largely the same. Only those residents who had close contact with Spaniards for several months could ascertain and thus provide a record of any difference between the behaviour of the Wehrmacht soldiers and that of the Blue Division soldiers.

Anastasia Dmitrievna Mukhina, from the village of Bolshoye Zamoshye, gave the following testimony on 11 November 1944:

> When in the winter of 1942 the Spaniards were driving Russian prisoners of war, three of them, the Germans [stationed] in our village shot them at the church. In February 1942 a village lad, Sergey Fedorovich Shalavin, born in 1925, was hanged because the Spaniards suspected him of stealing sausages as he was a carrier. [I]t was the German soldiers who had broken into a box of sausages, but they accused Shalavin. He was hanged. He was even forced to thrust his head into the loop.[10]

This episode, and others similar to it, demonstrate that typically it was Germans rather than Spaniards who faced criminal accusations. But this was not always the case. For what kinds of infractions were Blue Division soldiers usually blamed? In the first place, Russians accused them of theft and robbery. Of course, the Spaniards suffered from hunger and cold. But Russian villagers lived from hand to mouth during the war, and warm clothes were often among the few items left to them. Their unwillingness to give away their animals or other belongings often had tragic consequences. Thus, it was reported that

> [i]n the village of Lukinschina in January 1942, a Spanish soldier shot with a rifle an old man, Gregoriy Izotovich Izotov, born in 1881, for refusing to give away his cow. In January 1942, in the village of Babki 70-year-old Vasiliy Ivanovich Pikalev was shot with a rifle in his house, when he resisted the Spanish soldiers who were trying to take away his felt boots right off his feet.[11]

Anna Vasilievna Sotskaya from the village of Lukinschina told the ESC members that

> [i]n our village, there were periodically Germans and Spaniards from the Blue Division ... In the winter, the Spaniards took away all the warm clothes and boots, regardless of whose and where they were. They also took a pair of my felt boots from the Russian stove.[12]

Sometimes stealing felt boots was presented as a fight against guerrillas. Viktor Mikhailovich Ivanov recalled:

> There were no partisans in our area but the Spaniards were constantly looking for them. The winter was cold. The Spanish soldiers came to us. They searched for partisans in our large Russian stove, and then we found all the felt boots we had were pinched.[13]

Alexander Petrovich Yashin, born in 1937, was living in the village of Stipenka near Novgorod in 1941–3. He remembered that when he was a little child, the Spaniards took away not only men's clothes, but women's as well:

> The Spaniards liked big downy shawls. I saw them going about like big dolls wrapped in those shawls. It was impossible to see a military uniform under those duds. The soldiers were very thievish but were afraid of the Germans, and especially the military commander.

When the Spaniards found his bread and took it away, his grandmother began to shout and threaten that she would complain to the commander's office. "The Spaniards were frightened. They said, 'Matka [woman], do not yell, do not swear!' After that, they left the loaf, and were gone."[14]

These episodes demonstrate that the Spanish soldiers stole warm clothes and fought with people who resisted being stripped of them. When stealing cattle, Spaniards preferred to lock up their owners so that they did not interfere with the "brave men" who were spiriting away their "battle trophy." When cows and chickens had been exhausted, cats became the main fare for Spanish soldiers. Misha Petrov, from the village of Ostrovok, recounted that the Spaniards caught his cat and ate it. Such cases were widespread. Alexander Dobrov, a combatant who took part in the battle near Novgorod in the winter of 1941–2, recalled the following story:

When we [Alexander Dobrov and his fellow soldiers] went into one of the courtyards, we met a very friendly, elderly, and still quite cheerful, host who said,

– I did not doubt that you would banish these warriors [Spaniards]. If you had not driven them out, it would be a disgrace to Russia. Look, you're strong to a man and you're clothed and shod well and warmly. You are not like the Spanish poor specimens in their garrison caps and thin overcoats – a disgrace to look at!

We were invited into the izba to warm up. The hosts told us that Hitler did not feed the Spaniards, but paid wages to them to buy food from the Russian population.

– And what can be bought from the poor? – complained the hostess.

They started begging. They would come and say: "Matka, give potatoes!" And I would tell them to get in the cellar and take some. "No, – they would answer, – there is a partisan. Bang-bang! They meant to shoot. So I would go downstairs to the cellar and fill a bucket to give it to the Spaniards. What could I do? They had eaten all the cats in the village. They called it "Russian hare."

It occurred to me that the old woman was talking through her hat. But the old man said that their cat had been scorched, but the Spaniards did not have time to eat it up.

– There it is at the gate.

Indeed, there was a scorched cat lying at the gate. Why it was scorched but not skinned, I did not know, and I had no intention to ask. The hostess added,

– And what made these poor wretches from Spain turn up in Russia in such clothes, ah? Our lads will boot them out all right.[15]

"Meowing hare" on Spanish soldiers' tables is well remembered by many Novgorodians. In the 1980s, Moscow historian Boris Ivanovich

Gavrilov was collecting materials about the battle on the river Volkhov in 1941–2:

> According to the stories of local residents, the Spaniards were in the village of Zamoshye allegedly on vacation. Unlike the Germans, the Spanish soldiers did not get up to mischief and did not make big requisitions. Army rations were not enough for them, and they ate village cats for lack of rabbits.[16]

If the theft of food, warm clothes, and icons[17] had at least some logic, why did Spaniards, in passing, grab cumbersome peasant property? The explanation for this is quite prosaic. What was stolen in one village often became a marketable object in another. The statement of Daniil Frolovich Kuznetsov, from the Novgorod region, reveals the following: "In addition to the Germans, there were some Spanish units. The soldiers of these units often came from house to house, stealing things. Then they resold or [ex]changed the stolen property in other villages."[18] The Russian civilian population did not like being robbed by Spaniards. Still, when compared to the crimes of Germans, Estonians, and Latvians, who killed local residents sometimes merely to take their property, Spanish soldiers' crimes come across as relatively minor. The ESC documents and Russian civilians' recollections corroborate this assessment.

Having collected the material about the deeds of Spaniards in the occupied territory of the Novgorod region, the ESC officially identified only two officers of the Blue Division as war criminals: Agustín Muñoz Grandes, division's commander, who was directly involved in the crimes against citizens of the Novgorod region; and Antonio Basco, a lieutenant in the Blue Division, who organized numerous executions of civilians and prisoners of war and who himself carried out shootings.[19] In a quantitative sense, this list is quite modest relative to the serious crimes committed by the German occupiers.

The Blue Division and the Holocaust

After the war, a considerable number of veterans of the Blue Division wrote memoirs about their time in Russia. (See Tejada López's chapter 24 in this volume for more on Spanish Blue Division narratives.) But in those accounts, there is almost no information about the plight of the Jews in German-occupied territories. One soldier summarizes:

> Most of the time we, ordinary soldiers, were on the front lines or in hospitals. We did not know about what was happening in the death camps.

Moreover, 99% of the German population knew nothing about it until the very end of the war, except the fact that the Nazi regime did not tolerate the Jewish people.[20]

Xosé Núñez Seixas explains that Spanish veterans wanted

to conceal the dark side of the Nazis' dominance of Europe, which they had also witnessed, from the use of forced labour to some of the consequences of the segregation, deportation and annihilation of the Jews. Indeed, the Holocaust was always an uncomfortable chapter within the memory of BD veterans in Spain.[21]

In an interview with a Novgorod journalist, Julio Ángel Salamanca, a veteran of the Blue Division, stated:

I can assure you as a Catholic and a Christian that my fellow soldiers did not have the slightest hint of antisemitism. There is evidence that the Spaniards opposed the German soldiers against civilians, Jews in particular. The Spaniards could not tolerate the humiliation of women, children, elderly people or helpless disabled people.[22]

In those parts of the Eastern Front where the Blue Division was stationed (the Novgorod region, and later the town of Pavlovsk near Leningrad), the Jewish population mostly managed to evacuate. Those who had not escaped behind the Soviet lines had been murdered by the Nazis before the Spaniards arrived. However, the march across Poland, Lithuania, and Belarus had exposed Spanish soldiers to the full realities of the Nazi policy; as Núñez Seixas put it, there was sporadic confrontation with "las *consecuencias* de las políticas antisemitas del nazismo" (the *consequences* of the antisemitic policies of Nazism).[23] The Spanish journalist Miguel Bas Fernández recounted this episode: "When the division was marching to the Soviet Union, a group of soldiers went AWOL in Poland. Naturally, they dressed in civilian clothes for that. And they were seized as they all were dark-haired. They were considered Jews."[24] From this, an armed clash ensued between the Spaniards and the Germans – the Spaniards started shooting in order to rescue their fellow soldiers from the Germans.

The vast majority of Spanish *divisionarios* had no knowledge of the Holocaust; however, there were some who knew that Jewish ghettos had been liquidated and that Jews were being murdered en masse. For example, in 1944, after the liberation of the town of Pavlovsk, ESC members found that "according to the statements of eyewitnesses, in

1941 the German invaders executed two groups of civilians, Jews, in the town of Pavlovsk. One of the groups consisted of sixteen people, and the other – of twenty-five people, forty-one people in total."[25] Thus, by the time Spanish servicemen appeared in Pavlovsk in August 1942, all of the town's Jews had been murdered by Nazis and their accomplices. Having spoken with the local population, the Spaniards knew it. Historian Caballero Jurado believes that

> [p]ara la casi totalidad de los voluntarios españoles, aquélla fue la primera vez que vieron un judío. Y se les distinguía perfectamente porque los alemanes los obligaban a llevar una estrella de David sobre su ropa. Antes del paso de los españoles por aquellas regiones, los Einsatzgruppen alemanes habían cometido bárbaras matanzas con ellos. Los españoles, por tanto, no fueron testigos ni de matanzas ni de deportaciones en masa de judíos. Pero sí de un trato discriminatorio y brutal para con ellos.

> for practically all of the Spanish volunteers, it was the first time they had seen Jews. Spaniards understood that those people were Jews as Germans forced them to wear the Star of David on their clothes ... Before the Spaniards had passed through those regions the Einsatzgruppen had committed barbarous slaughters of Jews. The Spaniards, therefore, witnessed neither murders nor mass deportations of Jews, but they had witnessed discrimination and [a] barbaric attitude to the Jewish population.[26]

The vast majority of Spanish volunteers were shocked by this and condemned the Germans' actions.

Dionisio Ridruejo, a Spanish poet, joined the Spanish Falange in 1933 when José Antonio Primo de Rivera was the party's leader. Ridruejo held a number of positions in the National government. He had been propaganda minister during the Spanish Civil War. He joined the Blue Division as a correspondent for the Falangist press, but on his return to Spain in 1942, he broke with the Falange and left his position.

In 1941–2, while he was in Russia, Ridruejo kept a diary. It became available to a broad readership only in 1978, after his death. Ridruejo wrote in his diary:

> El 15 de septiembre escribía: Acaso, en conjunto, nos repugnan los judíos. Pero no podemos por menos de sentimos solidarios con los hombres. Sólo tengo vagos datos sobre los métodos de la persecución, pero por lo que yernos es excesiva (...) En nuestra viva adhesión a la esperanza de Europa que hoy es Alemania, éstas son las pruebas, los escrúpulos, más difíciles de salvar. Me consta que en Grodno, en Vílna, y en algunos otros sitios,

entre nuestros soldados y los alemanes ha habido reyertas y golpes por causa de judíos y polacos, especialmente por causa de niños y mujeres eventualmente objeto de alguna brutalidad. Esto me alegra.[27]

The 15th of September I wrote: I cannot say that we found the Jews repulsive. We cannot help but feel some sympathy for these people. I have some information about their persecution, and what we see is a terrific spectacle ... We are participants in the war on the side of Germany, the hope of all Anti-Bolshevist forces, but its attitude towards Jews is very difficult to understand. I know that in the town of Grodno, in the city of Vilno, and in some other places there were quarrels and clashes between our soldiers and Germans because of Jews and Poles, especially because of children and women who became the object of German rudeness. And the behavior of Spaniards makes me happy.

Ridruejo was proud of his fellow countrymen, whose attitude towards civilians seemed humane. He expressed his attitude towards the German solution to the "Jewish question" as follows: "We – not just me – we are shocked, and scandalized by this proclivity for violence – cold, methodical, impersonal, which helps to carry out the preliminary plan to wipe Jews from the face of the earth ... I have only vague information about the methods of persecution but what we see is excessive."[28] However, the German command, though they noticed that the Spaniards were not chauvinists, nevertheless appreciated their specific way of treating Jews. Fedor von Bock wrote in his diary: "3 September 1941. All the women, in their [Spanish soldiers'] opinion, are whores and easy prey. In the town of Grodno, they organized orgies with Jewish women and then drove them in their cars."[29]

As noted earlier, the Blue Division was stationed in northwestern Russia from 1941 to 1943, in areas where few Jews lived before the war. Nevertheless, Spaniards were repeatedly arrested by Germans, who were convinced they were hiding Jews.

After 1942, the Blue Division began to enrol former Republicans released from Franco's camps. Many of these volunteers immediately defected to the Red Army, while others who remained in the ranks of the Blue Division presented themselves as enemies of fascism. General Emilio Esteban Infantes, who replaced Muñoz Grandes as commander of the Blue Division, reported that the casualties on the shores of Lake Ilmen and the Volkhov River numbered fourteen thousand. The division was stationed in that area from November 1941 until the end of August 1942.[30] The rear hospitals in the cities of Riga and Vilno were packed with Spanish wounded.

Spanish Soldiers and Baltic People

For many Spaniards the route from Novgorod to Riga resembled the path from hell to heaven. They left the field hospital near Novgorod in the village of Grigorovo, then were moved to the town of Porkhov, and from there to Riga.

Spaniards did not want to notice along the way the suffering of people whose only fault was their non-Aryan ethnicity. Spanish soldiers rejoiced at the sight of the Latvian capital and the pleasures it offered. They did not witness the killing of Jews, and the existence of a ghetto in Riga seemed just and proper to them. After all, the Hitlerites had declared the Jewish population an enemy of Germany and its allies as well as agents of Anglo-American capitalists and Bolsheviks. However, the presence of Spaniards annoyed the Latvians, who did not consider Spaniards to be good soldiers and took them for marauders. The German leadership had a more scrupulous attitude towards the Baltic peoples than towards the Russian population. Thus any aggression against Latvian civilians or theft of their property angered the Germans.

The report of the head of the Jēkabpils Auxiliary Police (southeastern Latvia) regarding the political sentiments of the locals in March 1942 reads as follows: "Large military masses are expected in the town of Jēkabpils and its neighborhood. In particular, Spanish soldiers who commit robberies and thefts just as they did in Lithuania. Therefore the stores will be closed. It is the beginning of the week but under the influence of these rumors residents of the town are trying to get their rations for the week ahead."[31] Not only Latvians became victims of theft. At railway stations near Riga, Spanish soldiers repeatedly grabbed suitcases that belonged to Reich officers.[32]

All of this led to conflicts. On a Riga tram, there was a fight between a Spanish officer and a Latvian legionnaire. This case was described in great detail in the 5 January 1943 edition of the newspaper *Tēvija*. An article titled "The punishment for the humiliation of the German officers" reported on the conflict on a tram between a Latvian legionnaire, his brother, their Russian friend, and a Spanish officer.[33] The Latvians and the Russian insulted the Spanish officer and did not listen to the conductor who asked them to behave properly. Then the Spanish officer, who was dressed in a German uniform, asked them to stop misbehaving, but the Russian continued making a row and showed the officer indecent signs with his finger. The Latvians supported the Russian and began to curse the Spanish officer and the German army. The conflict was interrupted when German soldiers arrested the troublemakers and brought them to the command's office.

In Riga, Spaniards were treated for their diseases and wounds, and rested after being at the front. They believed that the local people should treat them with great respect. But newspaper accounts indicate that the Latvians' attitude was quite the opposite.

Even after the Blue Division had left the Eastern Front, and the Blue Legion was formed in its stead, behaviour problems among Spanish soldiers continued. The presence of Spaniards at the front grew increasingly undesirable to the Germans. In February 1944 the command of Army Group North received a report from a representative of its logistical services:

> According to the order, the Spanish legion of 2,000 people should be stationed in the town of Tapa (Estonia). I've been familiar with the behavior of Spanish soldiers for more than two years. Spanish discipline behind the front line was extremely poor and in no way corresponded to the norms of civilized behavior of military men. Attacks on local residents, arsons, thefts, robberies, sexual offenses, etc. were commonplace. I've been informed recently that the discipline of Spanish soldiers has become even worse.
>
> Taking into consideration that Spaniards' misconduct in Russia had a very negative effect on local residents and caused difficulties for the German forces, and in light of the expected reaction of Estonians, accommodation of the Spaniards in Estonia seems simply unacceptable. Therefore, I ask not to send the Spanish Legion to Estonia or, if it is not possible, to limit its stay in the territory of Estonia and to ensure a quick withdrawal of the Legion from the country.[34]

This document was marked "secret." The German propaganda services wanted to show only a positive image of their allies. In their view, only soldiers of the Red Army could be marauders. The Spaniards' conflicts with the Baltic population had a negative impact on the image of Nazi Germany and its leadership.

Spanish Soldiers and the Riga Ghetto

Spanish soldiers were present in the Baltic states either in transit to or on leave from the Eastern Front. Riga, the Latvian capital, had a large hospital where Blue Division soldiers received treatment for battlefield injuries and sexually transmitted diseases. Prisoners from the Riga ghetto worked as cleaners at the hospital.

On 1 July 1941, the German Army had occupied Riga, whose inhabitants at that time included some thirty-five thousand Jews, some of them refugees from other places. Five thousand of these Jews were killed in July. On 25 August 1941, the Nazis established a ghetto for the survivors, most of them women.[35] As they walked around Riga, some Spaniards pointedly ignored the "Jewish ghetto" signs. They spoke without hesitating to the local residents, claiming that for them there were no differences between Jews, Poles, and Germans.

A few Spanish soldiers in Riga risked their lives trying to help the ghetto prisoners. In 2012, Marģers Vestermanis (a former ghetto prisoner, and founder and former director of Riga's Jewish Museum) told the author the following:

> It is safe to say that there is no documentary information about contacts of Riga ghetto prisoners with Blue Division soldiers. I can only recount what I myself [born in 1925] heard, being a prisoner of the Riga ghetto. In the winter of 1941 and the spring of 1942 Jewish young people involved in the ghetto resistance group talked a lot about contacts with Spanish soldiers from the military hospital of the Blue Division [address: Latgale 122/124, the former Jewish hospital Bikur Holim]. A group of Jewish ghetto prisoners was used in the hospital transport services.
>
> Some of the recovering Spanish soldiers preparing to leave for a vacation in Spain spoke broken Russian. They recounted that during the Civil War they fought on the Republican side, and, according to their words, were assigned to the Soviet military advisers.
>
> The Spaniards insisted that they were forced to join the Blue Division to "redeem with blood" their former political sins. According to rumors circulating in the Riga ghetto, those vacationers offered some of the young Jewish men who worked in the hospital to take the prisoners with them in the guise of shell-shocked patients.
>
> According to very obscure rumors some Jews took that risk, but later other Spaniards who had returned from leave reported that those daredevils were allegedly detained by the German Gestapo at the French–Spanish border.[36]

David Zilberman mentions the names of those prisoners who risked contact with the Spaniards in his collection of memories and interviews gathered from survivors of the Riga ghetto:

> When in the ghetto, I often heard guys complain that it was easier to sneak into some country not occupied by Germans like Spain, Sweden or the south of France than to take refuge in Riga itself. There were many desperate attempts to escape from the Riga ghetto, but most of them failed.

Boris Kaplan, a lawyer, with his friend, almost got to Spain, but they were detained at the French–Spanish border, and later they both died.[37]

These facts have something in common with the experience of Max Kaufman, who wrote the following in his 1947 memoir:

> There was also a second, so-called Spanish group, which included Boris Kaplan (a lawyer) and two other men. They worked in the unit "Kvartiramt" [provisioning service] and met a Spanish officer of the Blue Division there [in Riga]. He promised them [the prisoners] to take them to Spain. The escapees reached the Spanish border but they were captured by the Gestapo when exchanging money and they were conveyed to the Riga prison.[38]

Giving credence to, or trusting, those Spanish soldiers could only be an act of the Jewish prisoners' desperation.

The Blue Division and Antisemitic Propaganda

The pages of the Blue Division trench newsletter *Hoja de Campaña* in the early years of 1941–2 contained almost no antisemitic rhetoric; the focus was instead on anti-communist and anti-British propaganda. The publication devoted a good deal of space to describing the extreme poverty and backwardness of Soviet peasants, who were typically cast as "dirty and foul-smelling" and as victims of their corrupt Soviet regime – a stereotype informed by "literary images and icons formed by anti-communist propaganda."[39] For all the loathing and disgust the Russians aroused among the divisioners, for some Spanish volunteers the military mission on Russian soil held the promise of redeeming the Russians and returning them to Christ.

In the second half of 1943, however, antisemitic propaganda started to appear in the newsletter's articles, cartoons, and drawings.[40] On 26 September 1943, for example, *Hoja de Campaña* published a small caricature titled "Educación judía" (Jewish education). It depicted a conversation between a student and a teacher: "Ya lo sabes, Moisés, Jehová es nuestro Dios y Stalin su profeta" (You know, Moishe, Jehovah is our God, and his prophet is Stalin).[41]

On 17 October, the newspaper published an article titled "Stalin y su sombra. Los judios mandan en Rusia" (Stalin and his shadow: Jews rule Russia). The illustration to the piece depicted Stalin's profile as an ominous silhouette of Satan with the word Judaism on it.[42]

23.1 "Educación judía," *Hoja de Campaña*, 26 September 1943 (private collection of author).

23.2 "Stalin y su sombra," *Hoja de Campaña*, 17 October 1943 (private collection of author).

23.3 "¡Dos frentes tiene la Legión Azul!," *Hoja de Campaña*, 27 January 1944 (private collection of author).

On 20 October 1943, Franco decided to begin withdrawing the division from Russia as a prelude to disbanding it. The Spanish *caudillo* no longer believed that Hitler would win the war and was beginning to take small steps towards rapprochement with Britain and the United States. This would be the Blue Division's last week on the Eastern Front.

The German government did not want to lose its foreign soldiers and launched a propaganda campaign encouraging enlistment in the Spanish *Legion* of Volunteers, which would fall, in contrast to the Blue Division, exclusively under the German command. With this change from Division to Legion, antisemitic propaganda increased dramatically in the Spanish trench newsletter. More cartoons appeared, sometimes occupying up to half a newspaper page, with the text reinforcing the visuals. The meaning of these was clear: Jews were equated with communists, and communists signified the death of Spain and the civilized world. On 21 November 1943, *Hoja de Campaña* published an article titled "El comunismo interpretación materialista de la vida. Los sostenedores de la internacional bolchevique" (The Communist Materialist Interpretation of Life: The Masters of International Bolshevism).[43] The caricature accompanying the piece depicted Stalin with corpses lying under his feet, with grotesque Jewish capitalists and communists behind his back.

On 15 December 1943, *Hoja de Campaña* published a large cartoon "Contra sus tres enemigos aliados" (Against Three of Their Allied Enemies), referring to Bolshevists, Jews, and masons.[44] The last issues of *Hoja de Campaña* (published until 18 March 1944) were full of antisemitic propaganda. On 27 January 1944, the newspaper boasted: "Dos frentes tiene la legión Azul! Un solo enemigo con dos caras!" (Two fronts of the Blue Legion! One enemy with two faces!).[45] A drawing accompanying the article depicted "Lies" and "Hate" and showed Blue Legion soldiers beating and killing Jewish Reds and Jewish capitalists. The two hostile forces of Spain appear supported by a representative of the *qahal.*

The legion's most fanatical Spanish soldiers joined the ranks of the SS. They fought on Hitler's side until the spring of 1945 near the town of Narva, in Romania, and almost defeated Berlin. Some of them took the citizenship of the Third Reich. Most of the volunteers of the Blue Division seem to have felt a genuine aversion to the realities of the Final Solution. However, it cannot be said that this led to any substantive disagreements with the Germans. For more than two years Spaniards were on the Eastern Front, fighting against the Red Army. They fought clearly and unequivocally on the side responsible for the Holocaust.

NOTES

1 Kovalev, *Dobrovol'cí na chuzhoj voyne.*
2 Núñez Seixas, "Good Invaders?" On the behaviour of the Spanish *division-arios* towards the Jews they encountered in eastern Poland and the Baltic countries, see Núñez Seixas, "¿Testigos o encubridores?"
3 Chernov, *Krestovy pokhod na Rossiyu,* 333.
4 Ibid.
5 *Tsena pobedy,* http://www.echo.msk.ru/programs/victory/703276-echo/#element-text, accessed 30 June 2016.
6 Rudinskiy, *S ispantsami na Leningradskom fronte,* http://pavlovsk-spb.ru/vospominaniya-o-blokade/rudinskiy-s-ispantsami.html, accessed 20 May 2016.
7 Interview with Alexandra Dmitrievna Okhapkina, 15 March 2013.
8 Ibid.
9 Budnitskii and Zelenina, eds.,"*Svershilos. Prishli nemtsy!*" 139.
10 State Archives of the Novgorod region (GANO), Fund 173, Inventory List 1, File 23, 13.
11 Ibid., 230.
12 Ibid., 239.
13 Interview with Viktor Mikhailovich Ivanov, 12 September 2013.
14 Interview with Alexander Petrovich Yashin, 14 October 2013.
15 Dobrov, *305-ya strelkovayadivizia,* 61.
16 Gavrilov, *Dolina smerti,* 111.
17 There is a Russian Orthodox tradition to keep an "icon corner" in the house where people keep their family icons. This tradition was very strong during the war.
18 GANO, Fund P-1793, Inventory List 1, File 25, 105.
19 Ibid., 286.
20 Novrorod TV interview with Julio Ángel Salamanca, 16 May 2005.
21 "Wishful Thinking in Wartime?," 99–116 at 111.
22 Ibid.
23 Emphasis added here because it is significant that the Spaniards did not observe the mass murder of Jews. They witnessed not the liquidation or extermination of Jews but rather the aftermath of the policies of the Final Solution. Núñez Seixas, "¿Testigos os encubridores?," 261.
24 *Tsena pobedy.*
25 Central State Historical Archives of St Petersburg, Fund 9421, Inventory List 1. File 195, 35.
26 Caballero Jurado, *Atlas ilustrado,* 89.
27 Ibid.
28 Elpatievskiy, *Uchastnik «Goluboi divizii»,* 80.

29 Von Bock, *Ya stoyal u vorot Moskvy*, 156.
30 Pozharskaya, *Tainaya diplomatia Madrida*, 113.
31 Latvian State Historical Archives, Fund П-252, Inventory List 1, File 43, 31.
32 Pozharskaya, *Tainaya diplomatia Madrida*, 120.
33 *Tēvija*, 5 January 1943.
34 Bundesarhiv-Militararhiv, RH 19 III, 774, 180.
35 Yitzhak, *Oni srazhalis za Rodinu*, 273.
36 From the author's correspondence with Marǵers Vestermanis.
37 Zilberman, *Ih ty yeto videl*, 228.
38 Kaufman and Barkahan, *Khurbn Letland*, 145.
39 Núñez Seixas, "Russia and the Russians," 358, 361.
40 Compare these cartoons with those discussed by Domínguez Arribas in Chapter 18.
41 *Hoja de Campaña*, 26 September 1943.
42 Ibid., 17 October 1943.
43 Ibid., 21 November 1943.
44 Ibid., 15 December 1943.
45 Ibid., 27 January 1944.

24 Representations of the Blue Division in Memoir and Fiction

MACARENA TEJADA LÓPEZ

As we saw in the previous chapter by Boris Kovalev, the Blue Division refers to Spain's military collaboration with Nazi Germany during the invasion of Soviet Russia. That division was overwhelmingly young, comprised of men between twenty and twenty-eight. Many of them had fought in the Spanish Civil War as members of the Nationalist military or as Falangists, and they served in the Blue Division (División Azul, BD) alongside pro-regime civilians. Many of the youngest Falangists were university students affiliated with the Sindicato Español Universitario (SEU). Recruitment efforts initially found more success in Madrid and Andalusia; they were less successful in Catalonia, Navarre, and the Basque Country.[1] Among the Spaniards who went to the front, there were also women, often overlooked by the historiography on the BD, whose work as nurses in military hospitals proved valuable in terms of their capacity to provide first aid and moral support for wounded divisioners. Many of these women had been nurses during the Civil War and had enrolled in the BD to honour their fallen relatives.[2]

The Spanische Division, as it was known to the Germans, represents the most tangible, numerous, and bellicose collaboration between Spain and Germany during the Second World War. Although historical scholarship on the Blue Division abounds, to date no scholar has published an exclusively literary analysis of the divisioners' diaries and memoirs. This chapter aims to begin to fill that gap. Studying the autobiographical and literary production of the divisioners is the first step in addressing the history of the Spaniards' campaign in the Soviet Union from the perspective of its protagonists and through the lens of self-representation. In the volunteers' diaries and memoirs, shifting formations of subjectivity function as the catalyst for veterans' recall of political and ideological dispositions over a span of eight decades: from the Francoist dictatorship through to democracy (1939–2010). Specifically, we can isolate three moments when these life narratives most often appeared: (1) during the war itself (1943–5); (2) under the Franco regime (1950s); and (3) in democratic Spain (1978–present). Within this time span, the written production has been very prolific. In his introduction to the latest edition (2004) of divisioner José Antonio Hernández Navarro's *Ida y vuelta* (1946), historian Carlos Caballero Jurado surveys the literary production by and about the divisioners.[3] Caballero Jurado lists eighty-three published memoirs, novels, and diaries (a few more have been published since 2010). Moreover, surviving divisioners and their relatives continue to contribute columns to newsletters published by various *hermandades de veteranos* (veterans' associations) distributed throughout the peninsula. Blau Division, an organization of survivors and their families from Alicante (Valencia), has published newsletters uninterruptedly since 1957. According to Caballero Jurado, the volume of production merits a specific literary subgenre: the literature of the Blue Division. In addition, an unknown number of unpublished diaries and memoirs exist in private family archives, the General Archive of Salamanca, and the General Military Archive in Ávila.

How should these memoirs and diaries be read? This chapter ventures that, ironically, it is the scholarship in the field known as "Soviet Subjectivity Studies" (especially the work of Jochen Hellbeck) that proves especially fruitful in understanding the mechanisms for self-inscription in history, and thus constitutes a productive theoretical framework for examining the divisioner memoirs as ideological texts that both reflect the past self and produce – through acts of memory and writing – a variable self in the present.[4] Phillipe Lejeune's foundational writing about diary and autobiography is also informative in analysing these texts.[5] How did these ex-divisioners inscribe themselves on their own life stories as well as on the larger narrative of the adventures and challenges of a military collective during the war? Do these personal narratives function as a continuation of anti-communist propaganda after the war, or do they offer an alternative interpretation of the conflict? Kovalev's chapter considered how Russians viewed the divisioners, and vice versa; the readings that follow here offer a useful counterpoint in that they focus on how the divisioners understood themselves as *men*, as *anti-communists*, and as a *soldiering collective* both during the war and across the long decades of its aftermath.

To answer these questions, this chapter studies the following diaries and memoiristic texts: the prologue to *Con la División Azul en Rusia* (With the Blue Division in Russia, 1943) by Colonel José Martínez Esparza; *Canción de invierno en el este. Crónicas de la División Azul* (Winter's Song in the East: Chronicles of the Blue Division, 1945) by José Luis Gómez

Tello; and *Memorias de un soldado de la División Azul* (Memoirs of a Soldier of the Blue Division, 2010) by José María Blanch Sabench. The chapter then moves on to fiction: *Embajador en el infierno* (Ambassador in hell, 1955) by Torcuato Luca de Tena, and *El infierno de los inocentes* (The innocents' Inferno, 2014) by Luis Molinos. These works encompass both the very earliest and the most recent publications by former divisioners, thus framing the aforementioned time span covering distinct social and political periods in contemporary Spanish history. Together, the texts speak to diverse experiences of the divisioners, including the early withdrawal from the front and captivity in the gulags.

A preliminary reading of the memoiristic texts reveals common features that bridge the temporal gap that separates them. Antisemitic judgments, patriotic fervour, and hatred of communism count among the most frequent tropes, followed by vitiation of the Soviet soldier and reflections on a Manichaean division of Europe into West (modernity) and East (backwardness). The fictional novels echo these same tropes but with less affective intensity ascribed to them. In terms of self-representation, these divisioners embed themselves in their narratives in very different ways. For example, Gómez Tello oscillates between the first-person "I" and impersonal descriptions in which he functions as a heterodiegetic narrator:

> Dentro de dos meses, de un mes, cuando Riga viva bajo un manto de nieves boyardas y el hielo se desfleque en todos los tejados de pizarra, estará helado, y vendrán las muchachas de esta Venecia nórdica a patinar, enlazadas por el talle. Entonces *podré* contarte, Marika, nuestra historia, la más bella de las historias de amor de un español en Riga, porque no existió jamás.[6]

> In two months, or in a month, when Riga lies under a coat of Boyar snow and ice starts to flake on the slate roofs, all will be frozen, and the young women from this Nordic Venice will come to ice-skate, grabbing each other by the waist. Then *I will be able* to tell you, Marika, our story, the most beautiful love story of a Spaniard in Riga, because it never happened.

By contrast, Martínez Esparza narrates his account integrally using the collective pronoun "we," except in the prologue. Blanch Sabench uses a different strategy, deploying the *nosotros* and the *yo* forms interchangeably, sometimes in the same paragraph:

> Al levantarnos teníamos media hora de gimnasia en el patio antes de desayunar ... Allí llevábamos las piezas de artillería y aprendimos a atalajar los

caballos a las piezas. A veces nos llevaban a las Colinas circundantes ...
Gracias a sus consejos *conseguí* que al sentarme a lomos de un caballo no
pareciese [yo] un saco de patatas.[7]

Right after getting up, we had thirty minutes of physical exercise in the
patio before breakfast ... We took the artillery pieces there and we learned
to tether the horses to the artillery carts. Sometimes we were taken to the
hills nearby ... Thanks to their advice *I managed to* ride a horse without
looking like a sack of potatoes.

These excerpts display personal pronoun choices also present in some
of the diaries that Hellbeck analyses in *Revolution on My Mind*. In the
Soviet context, the collective pronoun "we" functioned as a mechanism for identifying and inscribing oneself within a collective society
that worked and advanced together. According to Hellbeck, the mixed
uses of "I" and "we" reflected the inner struggle some diarists faced to
harmonize the coexistence of their personal and social selves.[8] Stalinist
subjectivity resulted from the individual's conscious participation in
the reconstruction of his new public and private selves in an effort to
identify himself with the illiberal Soviet state as opposed to the liberal
capitalist West.[9] Ideally, Soviet citizens would subordinate their personal to their social interests, thus demonstrating the correct alignment
of their identity with the thinking of the party. The pronoun choices in
the autobiographical texts of the divisioners operate similarly despite
the radical disparity in the ideological affiliations of the Spaniards. By
means of *nosotros*, the Spanish volunteers avoided overindividualizing
their narratives and merged themselves with the division, thus allowing a degree of collective representation that has endured. This practice
surfaces again in the twenty-first-century memoirs.

While these grammar choices remain in the most recent publications,
in terms of content, discursive shifts do appear across the time span
(1939–2010). In recent works, new or altered tropes surface: the antisemitic discourse largely disappears, replaced by descriptions of tolerance and even collaboration between soldiers and the local Russian
population, a weakening conviction regarding the virtue of the military
enterprise, and, rarely, dissidence. Such changes may be motivated by
the writers' knowledge (after the war ended) of the Nazi program of
extermination and by the absence of pressure from the Franco regime
to present the Blue Division in an emphatically anti-communist fashion. Whatever the reasons for these thematic changes, literary production related to the Blue Division offers us a unique vantage point on
how feelings and beliefs towards – and knowledge about – the Second

World War and the Holocaust have developed and changed in Spain over time.

After the extensive coverage on the radio and in newspapers and newsreels that the Blue Division enjoyed during Operation Barbarossa (1941–4),[10] and later the celebrated – and televised – return on 2 April 1954 of the 194 soldiers who had survived captivity in the Soviet gulags, the division fell subject to a collective amnesia. In the introduction to his latest publication, *Camarada invierno. Experiencia y memoria de la División Azul (1941–1945)*, Spanish historian Xosé Manoel Núñez Seixas asserts almost no one in Spain today is ignorant of the Blue Division.[11] However, Núñez Seixas's claim is debatable. In Spain today, due to a long period of collective silence among divisioners as well as the continued absence of the study of the Second World War in the Spanish education system, the youngest generations do not know what the BD was. The main cause for this knowledge gap seems to be an ongoing lack of political commitment to recognize Franco's complex involvement in the war. (See Marta Simò's chapter 32 in this volume on the current state of Holocaust education in Spain.) When it comes to gauging the motivations and experiences of divisioners, and how they represented the division, the diaries and memoirs they published are indispensable.

The Blue Division in Diaries and Memoirs

The first publication of the Blue Division was a diary written by officer José Martínez Esparza, penned in the summer of 1942 and published in 1943, while the Blue Division was still at war. It is difficult to ascertain whether diary-keeping was common practice within the division, whether the divisioners received a journal to record their experiences as part of their equipment, or whether diary-keeping was practised only among the more formally educated members of the division. Given the high percentage of volunteers who came from very poor backgrounds – with consequently low levels of literacy – the third hypothesis seems most plausible. Yet many divisioners kept a personal journal during the military campaign, and some decided to publish it. For some who did not keep a journal (or who lost it in the war), the memoir was another popular mode of expression. The Second World War provides the backdrop for a writing practice whose genesis in the Western world can be traced back to fifteenth-century hagiographies. Lejeune and Hellbeck agree that, although journals enjoy a long history, it was not until the seventeenth century in Puritan New England that the journal was invested with a more personal dimension. The Puritans utilized the personal diary as a space to expiate their conscience in order to attain salvation after death. Since then, diarist practices for more mundane purposes have extended across North America and Europe.

Lejeune's *On Diary* enumerates a series of characteristics inherent to the genre, three of which in particular are pertinent to this chapter. First, unlike autobiographies, diaries allow space for change and personal growth, much like a Bildungsroman, given that they record life as it happens or, at least, in a non-linear, fluid chronology. Second, when dating the entries, the diarist focuses on the date the narration happened, whereas when incorporating the date into the narrative, the diarist puts emphasis on the actions that took place that day. Third, diaries and autobiographies accurately explore the development of modern selfhood in the Western world. Some autobiographical texts by the Blue Division exemplify this third characteristic (namely those by Dionisio Ridruejo, Antonio José Hernández Navarro, and Tomás Salvador). The earliest accounts tend to be more chauvinistic and ideologically pro-German, as opposed to those written from 1978 to the present. Divisioners who penned later accounts distanced themselves from the Axis defeat and argued that they had gone to Russia simply to defend God and fight communism. Setting aside the differences in narrative styles, these autobiographies generally record war actions chronologically: military training in Spain, followed by further training in Germany, then the march to the front, the battles on the front, and, finally, repatriation.[12]

Con la División Azul en Rusia (With the Blue Division in Russia, 1943), José Martínez Esparza Vendrell

Martínez Esparza's is the earliest account of the Blue Division's intervention at the front, written in 1942 and published in 1943. Upon his return, there was still much hope that Nazi Germany would win the war, which in this book powered a rather celebratory tone for the BD's participation. The blunt antisemitic and anti-Russia remarks, the open support for the Germanization of Poland, and the firm belief in a superior Spanish race directly descended from the *Reconquista* warriors make this memoir one of the most radical, pro-fascist ones. This title also stands out as a counterpoint to later postwar narratives that are less germanophile and more sympathetic towards Jews and Soviets.

Colonel José Martínez Esparza Vendrell (1898–1949) devoted his life to the Spanish Civil Guard and the army. He also had an impeccable service record with the Spanish Legion and the Blue Division (Regiment 269). He died in a car accident outside Madrid in 1949. Martínez Esparza's text resists cataloguing the events. On the first page of his prologue, he calls his work a "relación militar en términos simples" (military account in simple terms), "una especie de diario anecdótico" (a kind of anecdotic diary). Indeed, his work harmoniously integrates the characteristics of both genres. *Con la División Azul en Rusia* functions as a military logbook by relating the daily routines of soldiers during training and at the front, explaining how military equipment works, categorizing different combat strategies used during battle, and listing the division's fallen heroes. The logic of dates, however, likens his writing to that of diary practices from the sixteenth century. The author uses the term "diario anecdótico" to define his own account, yet the text challenges the notion of a diary that the contemporary reader might hold. When paying attention to how this "diary" addresses the passage of time, the reader realizes that it actually contains no dated entries. Only one clue situates the time of production of the text: "10 de julio de 1942, la fecha en que escribimos estas líneas" (10 July 1942, the date on which we write these lines).[13] The officer penned his memories almost six months after returning to Spain on 26 January 1942. Its rich content – names, dates, specific hours – however, suggests that Martínez Esparza kept a journal with frequent entries during the military campaign, although I have not been able to find concrete evidence of this hypothesis. How does the author remember everything in so much detail? One answer holds that this diary resulted from a collaborative effort by a group of divisioners, but again, the text itself makes no suggestion of such a process. Martínez Esparza inserts the dates into the narrative: "El día 11 de julio recibimos la orden de trasladarnos a Madrid ... El día 12 tomamos el avión y a las trece horas nos encontrábamos en la capital de España ... " (On July 11, we received orders to move to Madrid ... On July 12 we took the plane and thirteen hours later we were in the capital city of Spain).[14] Thus, the text privileges the date on which the action happened over the date on which it was recorded. According to Lejeune, fashioning the movement of time like this implies a reconstruction of events, because these were not recorded at the time they happened.[15] Retelling from memory makes the content vulnerable to critics who doubt its veracity on the basis that memory is fallible. However, for Lejeune, reconstructing from memory does not in the least affect the credibility of the narrative.

Martínez Esparza's racial and political stances are controversial. Unsurprisingly, the general defines himself as anti-communist.[16] Ulrike Pfeifer, in her unpublished thesis about the Blue Division, states that the officer's self-identification as anti-communist does not equate with anti-semitism.[17] Indeed, anti-communism and antisemitism do not necessarily go together, even if Spanish anti-communism rested firmly on a belief in a Judeo-Masonic conspiracy. However, the officer's negative references about the Jews and his appreciation of a *judenfrei* Spain since the fifteenth century confirm that he subscribed to a racialized political view:

> Explicaban, por su parte, el desastre de Polonia diciendo que este país, a pesar de su fondo católico, se había visto asaltado por una minoría de masones y judíos que se habían apoderado del mando. Los judíos precisamente eran los que allí, al ser muy numerosos, agravaban el problema [económico]; circunstancia que no existía en España, gracias a la visión política de iluminados que tuvieron los Reyes Católicos.[18]

> They explained Poland's disaster by saying that this country, despite its Catholic background, had been attacked by a Masonic and Jewish minority that had taken control. Precisely the Jews, because there were so many, aggravated the [economic] problem; this circumstance did not exist in Spain thanks to the politically visionaries and enlightened Catholic Monarchs.

Other frequent tropes include the author's comparisons between Western and Eastern Europe, the bravery of the Spanish soldiers as opposed to the cowardice of the Soviets, the serfdom of POWs, antisemitic slurs, and russophobia.

Such racist, Western supremacist remarks may be a response to Spain's long military history, which nurtured the notion that the country was entitled to an empire as great as the one recently lost. Martínez Esparza was serving in Algeciras (Cádiz) when he was appointed commander of Regiment 269, formed in Seville. His devotion to the army is palpable in the diary by how he appraises the act of serving in the Blue Division by choice, in contrast to the Soviet soldier, who was forced to serve. In the text, the decision to serve voluntarily in the division points to the natural superiority of the Spanish soldier and Spanish manhood. Here, the divisioners spontaneously sing the Falangist hymn "Cara al sol" (Face to the Sun) to celebrate that no divisioners died on the battlefield that day:

> Hasta algunos prisioneros rusos, en su deseo de hacerse gratos, balbuceaban, asombrados ante aquellas estrofas, que, desde luego, no entendían, pero a través de las cuales comprendían que quienes la cantan eran hombres que saben morir por su Patria alegremente, y no como ellos, que lo hacían por penosa obligación, a la que se sustraían en cuanto les era posible.[19]

> Even some Russian prisoners, wishing for our empathy, babbled, amazed by the verses that, certainly, they did not understand, but through which they could comprehend that those who sang them were men who knew

> how to die happily for their Fatherland; unlike them, who were forced by
> pitiful obligation, from which they fled whenever possible.

Thus, the divisioners are always defined as heroes, whereas the Soviets are cast as cowards who allow themselves to be captured so as to escape the hardships of fighting for the Red Army. Several other incidents point to a presumed Stockholm syndrome among the Soviet POWs, who seemingly preferred to be captured by the Spaniards rather than the Nazis.

The author depicts Jews and Soviet civilians with equal personal contempt: "Los judíos de Grodno, por su aspecto y sordidez, pueden contarse entre los más repugnantes que vimos" (The Grodno Jews, judging by their aspect and squalor, were among the most repugnant we had seen).[20] Further mentions of the Jews mark them as blameworthy for the destruction of Poland, where "ellos eran muy numerosos ... y entre los más sucios, más miserables y repugnantes" (they were numerous ... and among the dirtiest, most miserable and repugnant).[21] For the author, the Russians were no better. In one anecdote, he recalls how a Russian couple tried illegally to sell a cow, and how they told a German officer that the cow had been stolen to avoid retaliation. For Martínez Esparza, this exposed "la maldad de los rusos" (the wickedness of the Russians);[22] here he was stigmatizing all civilians based on the actions of two people. Other negative references to the odours of their houses, and the immorality of young Russian women going to bars alone, punctuate the officer's narrative.[23] At times, however, the author softens his opinion of the Russians by praising their "lealtad sin reservas" (unreserved loyalty).[24] This fluctuating view of the Russians suggests that the anti-communist sentiments the divisioners professed – products of the rabid anti-communist campaign in Spain – lacked total conviction. These political and racial prejudices consequently shaped the broader concept of Western and Eastern Europe. The West receives its highest praise through his representation of the Germans: clean, hard-working, and organized. They would be perfect if only they were uniformly Catholic. By contrast, he presents the East as disorganized, dirty, and ruined, mainly after Poland tried to "de-Germanize" Dantzig. In fact, Suwalki (Poland) reminds the author of Spain twenty years earlier, "antes de la Dictadura" (before the Dictatorship)[25] – that is, backwards.

Martínez Esparza's ideas demonstrate that the most ultra-Catholic, conservative, and pro-regime Spanish factions kept their faith in the war as the only option to cleanse Spain of the communist menace. His anecdotal diary testifies to his personal convictions, and by expressing himself in the collective "we," he makes the convictions of the entire Blue Division his own.

Canción de invierno en el este. Crónicas de la División Azul (Winter Song in the East: Chronicles of the Blue Division, 1945), José Luis Gómez Tello

Although ideologically aligned with Martínez Esparza, Gómez Tello's text presents a different narrative style, closer to fictional accounts of a distant Russia that evoke romantic images combined with short history lessons. José Luis Gómez Tello (1916–2003) was a novelist and journalist affiliated with the Falange. He wrote several pieces infused with political analyses for newspapers, including *Arriba* and *Fuerza Nueva*; these included chronicles of his travels around Europe. They contained cultural notes and personal experiences, which appear as well in *Canción de invierno en el este*. Despite the title, there is nothing lyrical about this text. Gómez Tello offers no explanation, but the book's elevated prose suggests that "Canción" (song) denotes the sophistication of the author as a writer as well as his desire to write an homage to the division. *Canción de invierno en el este* sets itself apart from other divisionary writings in its cultivated abstract and poetic style, replete with historical references that expose the writer's higher education.[26] As a result, this text resembles a memoir more than a diary. Unlike Martínez Esparza, who was appointed to the Blue Division due to his high rank in the military, Gómez Tello volunteered for the division and departed for Russia with the first deployment. Writing in the immediate aftermath of the war, he continues to glorify the Hispano-German collaboration. He makes no attempt to hide either his antisemitism, which he shares with Nazi Germany, or his belief in Germany's racial superiority.

His memoir is divided into three parts. In the first, "A través de cuatro países en guerra" (Through Four Countries at War), the author shares his impressions of France, Germany, Latvia, and Estonia, all of which he visits on the way to the Russian Front. The protagonists in this section are the landscape and the architecture, the latter characterized as reflecting the cleanliness and good order of the German occupation. The second part, "La Rusia soviética que yo he visto" (The Soviet Russia I Saw), focuses on Poland and Belarus and the Soviet and German occupations of those lands. "Crónicas de la División Azul" (Chronicles of the Blue Division), the third and final section, immerses the reader in the battlefield. In this part the author is no longer detached from the narrative, and in his autobiographical retelling the first-person singular predominates. The shifting pronouns mark another difference from Martínez Esparza, who always writes in the first-person plural to avoid seizing the war experience for his own, and to allow other divisioners to identify themselves with the narrative.

The leitmotifs in *Canción de invierno en el este* echo those found in the writing of Martínez Esparza. The major difference between the two resides in the level of detail devoted to military exploits: Gómez Tello does not get caught up in exhaustive descriptions of the BD's military actions. For him, the clash between West and East is over the very idea of Europe, and the Jew merits contempt:

Todos ellos son pobres entre todas las castas de Israel al lado de los judíos de Osmiana, que comercian con la miseria. Napoleón solo tendió la mano pidiendo limosna dos veces en su vida. Y se la tendió a los judíos las dos veces. Una vez a Rothschild, cuando Waterloo. A los judíos de Ashmyany, la otra.[27]

All of them are poor among all the castes of Israel next to the Jews in Ashmyany, who trade with misery. Napoleon extended his hand begging for alms twice in his life. To Jews both times. The first to the Rothschild[s] for Waterloo. To the Jews in Ashmyany the other time.

He also refers to Moscow as "el gran campamento de Israel" (the great encampment of Israel).[28] The author reverts to familiar Jewish stereotypes, perpetuating the image of the Jew as covetous and malicious. These expressions of antisemitism in the memoir had a confessional basis: the Jew was a threat not to *la españolidad* (Spanishness), but rather to Christianity. As Núñez Seixas puts it, in Spain there was "un antisemitismo sin judíos" (an antisemitism without Jews).[29] That is, the contempt of a small portion of the division – presumably high officials – towards European Jews grew primarily out of a question of faith, with minor racial connotations. Still, despite Spain's rapid shift towards philosemitism even before the end of the war (one of various Francoist political manoeuvres to bring about Spain's entrance into the United Nations), Gómez Tello's antisemitism and support of Nazism endured. (See Gonzalo Álvarez Chillida's chapter 2 on philosemitism and Pedro Correa Martín-Arroyo's chapter 20 on the Francoist myth.)

Memorias de un soldado de la División Azul (Memoirs of a Soldier of the Blue Division, 2010), José María Blanch Sabench

Memorias de un soldado de la División Azul, the most recent writing published by an ex-divisioner, is yet another example of a young Spanish man who saw in the division his chance to launch a military career. However, Blanch Sabench was not driven by the annihilation of the enemy. He understood communism as a liability to religious freedom, but that did not make the Russian people the enemy; they were just as oppressed as the people from Soviet satellite countries who suffered under communism. This memoir is characterized by an amiable paternalism with the Russians and a more open mind towards foreign customs. Whether this really reflected Blanch Sabench's attitude in 1941 or was the result of decades of thinking back on the war is a judgment left to his readers.

There is little biographical information available about José María Blanch Sabench – only that which the author includes in his memoir, which is also available on "Memoria Blau," the online forum devoted to the Blue Division.[30] According to these sources, Blanch Sabench (b. 1923) was born in Girona, Catalonia, and educated in Paris, where he lived between 1928–41. He regretted not being old enough to participate in the Civil War and saw the Blue Division as an opportunity to make up for this. He was assigned to the artillery, although he also worked as a translator because he spoke four languages: Spanish, French, German, and the Russian he learned at the front. He spent two years at war, enrolling in December 1941 and returning to Spain in November 1943. By 1943 the divisioners were being received back in Spain without ceremony, official or otherwise. The state's muted response to the returning divisioners reflected Spain's change of attitude towards Germany, whose defeat was by then foreseen. After returning from Russia, the author worked as a translator for various Spanish institutions and as an art dealer.

Blanch Sabench wrote his memoir decades later, in 2010, by which time democracy was well-established in Spain. Historian Luis E. Togores points to feelings of "frustration" as the main reason why some ex-divisioners decided to share their experiences so many decades after the Russian campaign:

> Resulta difícil hoy imaginar la frustración que tuvo que sufrir una generación entera de jóvenes soldados, al regresar a su casa, en muchos casos repletos de heridas y condecoraciones, cuando se les pidió que no las lucieran orgullosos en su pecho. La guerra había cambiado y los enemigos de ayer, vencedores hoy, iban a tener que ser los aliados de mañana.[31]

> Today, it is difficult to imagine the frustration felt by an entire generation of young soldiers when they returned home, in several cases replete with wounds and medals, when they were asked not to take pride in them. War had changed the odds and the enemies of yesterday, victors today, would become the allies of tomorrow.

Togores writes that the silence imposed by Franco's regime was the result of Germany's defeat and the need for Franco's government to maintain friendly relations with the victors: Britain, the United States, and, to a much lesser extent, the Soviet Union. The Spanish transition to democracy after Franco's death in November 1975 presented an opportunity for the ex-divisioners to break the silence that had been imposed on them and to share memories of the war while also paying homage to their fallen comrades in Russia. Literary publications of the Blue Division have increased in number since the end of the Second World War. As Blanco Corredoira, author of the novel *Añoranza de Guerra* (War Longing, 2011), pointed out in an interview, most of the ex-divisioners chose to remain silent, and the others took too long to speak, sharing their stories only among relatives or with those researchers interested in the Blue Division.[32] Christina Dupláa, in her book chapter "Memoria colectiva y lieux de mémoire en la España de la transición," contends that silence is "una reacción contraria a esa necesidad constante de denuncia" (a counter-reaction to that constant need for denunciation).[33] After returning from the Eastern Front, the divisioners were reduced to commemorating their war effort in their local *asociaciones* because the great ideal they defended in Russia had been sacrificed during Spain's shift in foreign policy.

The narratives by Martínez Esparza and Gómez Tello follow a line from Spain to Russia without digressions; Blanch Sabench's does not. This represents a challenge for the uninformed reader. The book's initial discontinuity likewise marks the presumed deterioration of the author's memory and the difference between penning memories right after the war's end and doing so decades later. Blanch Sabench begins his narration in Grafenwöhr, the training camp he attended in Germany; he then describes the march to the front, before jumping backward in time to his prior training in Spain. After this digression, the events unfold chronologically from the march to the front until his return from Krasny Bor, where the Blue Division fought its deadliest battle during the Siege of Leningrad. On the morning of 10 February 1943, the BD's positions, defended by six thousand men, were attacked by forty-four thousand Soviet soldiers, resulting in at least four thousand deaths on the Spanish side. The Spanish state is to this day working with Russia to locate and repatriate the bodies.

Writing sixty-five years after the end of Operation Barbarossa requires an effort described in this way by the octogenarian author: "Para sacar a la luz estas 'memorias inmemoriales'... he tenido que buscar hasta lo más hondo de mi alma y sacarlas a jirones" (In order to shed light on these "immemorial memories"... I had to search for them in the depths of my soul and pull them out in shreds).[34] Blanch Sabench went through an arduous process of introspection to retrieve fractured memories. His memoir tends to be less ideological than the two divisioner life narratives discussed earlier. As he writes in the preface, "las líneas que siguen no pretenden hacer un juicio moral o politico" (the lines that follow do not pretend any moral or political judgment).[35] He makes no reference to Jews, and the Russian people function as situational allies who exchange shelter for food. He justifies his presence in Russia in this way: "de pequeño siempre quería ser militar" (as a child, I always wanted to be a soldier).[36] That is, he is driven purely by military vocation, not by political conviction or by vengeance for comrades who fell during the Civil War. Blanch Sabench and Emilio Fernández Granados, another ex-divisioner, treat the Soviet civilians with kindness in their texts. Indeed, Fernández Granados dedicates his fictionalized memoir *Traición en el infierno* (Betrayal in the Inferno, 2011) to "la población rusa, tan querida y añorada, que aún sigue colocando flores en las tumbas de nuestros caídos. *Spasiva*" (the Russian population, so beloved and missed, who still place flowers on the graves of our fallen ones. Thank you).[37]

The memoirs published in the 2010s tend to lean more on anecdotes of the war than on a meticulously descriptive and defensive recounting of fascism. This change of focus from antisemitism and visceral anti-communism to reconciliation is, first, a response to the general disappointment the divisioners felt when they returned home and the Spanish government did not deign to acknowledge them or thank them for their sacrifices. Second, it marks a shift in the appraisal of Germany since the earlier publications (1940–50), mainly due to the vast increase in information now available about the war and the Holocaust. Knowledge of the crimes that Nazi soldiers perpetrated behind the lines has dismantled the notion that the Germans were heroes – which most Spaniards had earlier held – and this has invited an interrogation of that notion when it has not simply led to their exclusion from memoirs. Third, the divisioners distance themselves from the cruelty displayed by the Nazi soldiers in the occupied lands by emphasizing the good relations they themselves maintained with the Russians, but they do so without chancing a negative opinion about their brothers-in-arms or analysing the atrocities committed.

The Blue Division in Narrative Fiction

Contemporary Spanish fiction has focused more attention on the Blue Division since 2000. According to Isabel Uriarte Arbaiza, these "historic" novels are but a "gancho comercial" (a commercial hook),[38] that is, they are marketable products for new novelists to gain readers. These works have brought the division closer to the younger generations: from novels whose protagonist is the collective Blue Division itself (*El tiempo de los emperadores extraños* / The time of the foreign emperors by Ignacio Del Valle or *El infierno de los inocentes* / The innocents' inferno by Luis Molinos), to novels that include divisioners anecdotally (*El corazón helado* / The Cold Heart by Almudena Grandes; *La vida en un puño* / Life in the Fist by Silvia Ribelles). Except for the scarce "ficción divisionaria" (divisioners' fiction) from the 1950s, understood as a confirmation of stalwart ideological and political values in times of international turmoil, the publications in the twenty-first century tend to avoid Manichaean interpretations of the Russian campaign. More often than not, the circumstances of the Blue Division work as a historical scenario for love stories whose main protagonists have been separated during the Spanish Civil War and who unwillingly find themselves serving on opposing sides, Republican and fascist.

In two examples of fiction about the Blue Division, one published under the dictatorship and the other from 2014, the political context and relative distance from or proximity to the Second World War inform the novels' content and form, as is the case for the previously discussed memoirs and diaries. *Embajador en el infierno. Memorias del Capitán Palacios* (1955) overwhelms the reader with its patriotism and anti-communism. Meanwhile, *El infierno de los inocentes* (2014), a love story, delivers a multilateral impression of Soviet Russia facilitated by the two protagonists, Daniel and Rosa, whose tale highlights a dramatic and tragic episode in the division's adventures in the Soviet Union: captivity in the gulag.

Embajador en el infierno. Memorias del Capitán Palacios (Ambassador in Hell: Memoirs of Captain Palacios, 1955), Torcuato Luca de Tena

In its prologue, Luca de Tena defines his novel as "la narración histórica de un militar [capitán Palacios], transformada en reportaje por un periodista" (the historic narration of a soldier [Captain Palacios], transformed into a journalistic report).[39] The journalist is Luca de Tena himself, who worked as a reporter before enrolling in the Blue Division and after his liberation from the Soviet gulags in 1954. The writer places his personal testimony in the mind and words of an omniscient narrator who suffers in ten different gulags over eleven years of captivity (February 1943–April 1954).[40] Luna de Tena justifies this decision in the prologue, which functions as a distorted autobiographical pact as understood by Lejeune (1995). In said pact, the author identifies himself as both the narrator and the protagonist of the text, that is, the text offers an autodiegetic narration. From the reader's perspective, there is no ambiguity as to the referent for the "I" pronoun. Nevertheless, Luca de Tena wanted his novel to represent a collective experience rather than an individual one. So instead of composing a memoir narrated in the collective "we," as Martínez Esparza had a decade earlier, the writer opts for compiling and unifying the voices of "múltiples y dignísimos protagonistas de muy varias nacionalidades" (multiple and respectable protagonists of many nationalities).[41] Consequently, despite the strong (auto)biographical essence of the text, it qualifies as a novel because the multiple testimonies are fictionalized.

In the novel, Captain Teodoro Palacios (a historical figure) tells the first-person story of the captivity of his battalion, from the Battle of Krasny Bor on 10 February 1943 until the day the Red Cross ship arrived at the port of Barcelona on 2 April 1954. His is a story of bravery and insurrection against the ruthless cruelty of the Soviets, who subdued the prisoners with starvation rations, forced labour, subfreezing temperatures with unfit winter clothing, and constant beatings. The author describes the experience of forced labour in the camp at Cherepovets:

> El trabajo, en sí, era durísimo, pues había que romper el hielo con unas barras de hierro que a aquellas temperaturas quemaban la piel; después había que extraer los troncos, transportarlos, aserrarlos y cargarlos. El horario de trabajo durante estos primeros años era siempre superior a las diez horas, llegando muchas veces a doce y trece, descontando las marchas.[42]

> The work alone was extremely hard, since we had to break the ice with iron bars that, at that temperature, burned our skin; next, we had to pull out the logs, transport them, saw them and load them up. The work day during those first years always lasted over ten hours, sometimes peaking to eleven to twelve, not counting the marches.

This kind of description would not be shocking to readers of Aleksandr Solzhenitsyn's *The Gulag Archipelago* (1973) or Anne Applebaum's *Gulag* (2003).[43] The inhumane conditions that prisoners suffered in these open-air prisons and while being transported between camps resemble those of other Second World War labour camps:

> A primeros de mayo fuimos trasladados ... al campo número 27 de Moscú. El teniente Rosaleny se quedó solo en Cheropoviets ... El viaje duró ocho días. Mejor dicho, cinco, pero permanecimos tres más encerrados en los vagones con el tren parado en la estación de Moscú. Al salir de Cheropoviets nos habían dado la comida completa para el viaje, siendo cada uno libre de administrarla a su gusto.[44]

> On the first of May, we were moved ... to camp number 27 in Moscow.
> Lieutenant Rosaleny was left alone in Cheropoviets ... The journey took
> eight days. Five, to be exact, but we were left locked in the carriage for
> three days while the train was stopped in Moscow. When we departed
> from Cherepoviets, we were given all the food for the trip, each of us
> dividing it up as we wished.

This passage describes the transport of inmates from Cherepovets to
Moscow, a distance of 373 miles, traversed over eight days: five days
en route and three days locked in with meagre rations provided at the
beginning of the trip. Memoirs often exposed experiences of this kind,
and the Francoist government utilized them to denounce the savagery
of the Soviet regimen.

In the 1950s, Spain needed to bring an end to the diplomatic blockade
that had been imposed by Britain and United States as a consequence
of its collaboration with Nazi Germany. To push forward its application to join the UN, Spain strategically emphasized the anti-communist
side of the Eastern campaign, given that the Soviet Union had become
the West's enemy. With this in mind, *Embajador en el infierno* perfectly
encapsulated the evils of the socialist system but without emphasizing Spain's collaboration with Hitler. Furthermore, there is no mention in the novel of Hispano-German collaboration, nor is there any
allusion to ties between the Spanish soldiers and the Germans. Jews
appear only twice in the text. In the first reference, Palacios observes
in 1948 that the Russian Jews who had been granted permission to
immigrate to the new state of Israel were being cheated by the Soviet
state and sent to prison instead. Palacios meets his new Jewish cell-
mate, Abraham Ifimowich, who "era músico y escritor, autor de varios
libros de éxito, muy celebrados en Rusia antes de caer en sospecha de
impureza política" (was a musician and a writer, the author of several
successful books that were celebrated in Russia, before being suspected
of political impurity).[45] In the second instance, "un judío ruso llamado
Barón llegaba cada hora con una lista" (a Jew named Baron came every
hour with a list)[46] of the people who were to be tried. Neither passage
contains language that arouses suspicion of antisemitism; these Jews
are simply people whom the protagonist happens to meet but whose
fate depends on the Soviets.

In 1955, *Embajador en el infierno* won both the National Prize for
Literature and the "Ejército" Prize for Literature. José María Forqué's
1956 cinematographic adaptation, *Embajadores en el infierno*, received
considerable support and praise from the Spanish state in the form
of production funding and prizes, all further reinforcing the message

that Spain had suffered at a safe distance from the Hispano-German alliance that drove the creation of the division in the first place.

El infierno de los inocentes (The Innocents' Inferno, 2014) by Luis Molinos

Luis Molinos's fifth novel tells a love story marked by forced migrations. In it, Rosa Santacruz is one of the "niños de Rusia" (children of Russia), sent along with thousands of other children from the north of Spain to Moscow in 1937 to escape Spain's Civil War. The other protagonist, Daniel Iriarte, spends the Civil War in Valencia, where his father is executed by Republicans in the early days of the war. These two events change the course of the characters' lives, until they are reunited again on opposite sides of the war: Daniel as a divisioner and Rosa as a Red Army nurse. Before composing his novel, Molinos researched the Spanish Civil War, the Second World War, and life in Soviet Russia and the gulags.[47]

Much of the story revolves around Daniel's years of captivity in the gulag. The novel gives life to characters in a complex historical and political context in which they are active participants and make their own decisions. Daniel, for example, did not volunteer for the Blue Division out of strong anti-communist convictions. Although he wanted to avenge his father's death, he mostly wanted to see Rosa again. Consequently, the Russians or "the Reds" are not necessarily identified as enemies:

> En el trayecto se cruzaron con una columna de prisioneros rusos. Era la primera vez que veían a los soldados que iban a combatir, marchaban derrotados, cabizbajos, macilentos ... ¿Qué tenían que ver aquellos rusos a los que se iban a enfrentar, con los hombres que se llevaron a su padre? ¿Tal vez compartían una ideología? A lo mejor ni eso. Probablemente eran como él, personas atrapadas en el torbellino de los acontecimientos.[48]

> While marching, they encountered a column of Russian prisoners. It was the first time they saw the soldier that they were going to fight, and they marched defeated, dejected, gaunt ... What did those Russians they were to face have to do with the men who took his father? Maybe they shared an ideology? Maybe not even that. They were probably just like him, people trapped in the turmoil of events.

A passage with this level of self-reflection, questioning one's role in the war, would have been impossible to find in autobiographical texts or fiction under Franco's regime. That is not to say that these identity crises among divisioners did not occur, but that they could not be shared publicly. These crises resulted from exposure to the real horrors of the front, as opposed to the distorted reality of Soviet Russia, a product of the anti-communist propaganda in Spain. Understanding the complexities of the Russian people first-hand proved destabilizing for some divisioners, a trope that comes across in the memoirs.

Recalling Martínez Esparza and Gómez Tello's novels, there is only one moment in *El infierno de los inocentes* when Daniel encounters a group of Jews. Molinos's contemporary novel distances itself from the previous publications by describing the Jews more sympathetically: "con la estrella amarilla marcada sobre la ropa, demacrados y desesperanzados, que los miraban pasar con ojos tristes, con la mirada opaca del que ha perdido las ganas de vivir" (with the yellow star marked on their clothes, emaciated and hopeless, they looked [at the Spaniards] with their sad eyes, and the opaque gaze of those who had lost the will to live).[49] Nothing here suggests that their misery was deserved.

El infierno de los inocentes also allows itself the privilege of criticizing the gender inequality under Francoism. Rosa had access to an equal and gender-mixed education in Russia, then worked as a nurse and pursued a medical degree in Moscow after the war. She lived as an independent woman. But that changed when Rosa and Daniel, now married, returned to Spain in 1954, only to find that their marriage was not legal and that Rosa could not work:

(Madre de Daniel) - "¡Caramba! Mujer y médico, aquí en España no conozco a ninguna mujer médico, no sé si habrá alguna. Creo que no tendrían clientela. [...] Además, las mujeres no deben trabajar fuera de casa.

Las mujeres tenemos que consagrarnos a Dios, a la Patria y al hogar," apostilló Esperanza. Los hombres son los que deben preocuparse por el trabajo y el dinero."

[Daniel's mother] – "Heavens! A woman and a physician, here in Spain I don't know any female physicians, I don't know if there are any. I don't think they would have patients ... Besides, women should not work out of the house.

Women have to consecrate themselves to God, to the Fatherland and to the house," added Esperanza. "Men are the ones who should worry about jobs and money."[50]

Both Rosa and Daniel, unable to adjust to what they perceive as a backward way of life, decide to immigrate again, this time to Tangiers.

Embajador en el infierno and *El infierno de los inocentes* depict similar "infiernos" with nuances that highlight the differences in politics and history between their respective eras. Spain in 1955 was pursuing an agenda of collaboration with the United States and Britain, and to achieve this, membership in the UN was essential. Also, Spain needed to align itself with the West in the Cold War conflict, and the literature of the time proved a useful tool for portraying Spain's fierce anti-communism. After 1978, democratic Spain ceased to dictate what could be published in literary works, and writers and artists enjoyed more freedom to express their stories and opinions without being drafted as instruments of the state. Thus, Molinos was able to portray a less Manichaean image of the Blue Division, one that highlights the differences in opinions and viewpoints of its members rather than perpetuating the illusion of an unchanged and politically homogenous Blue Division.

Conclusions

The literature of the Blue Division has evolved. Francoist Spain defended an ideology that encapsulated political, religious, and racial stances crystalized in a fixed idea of what Europe should be: Catholic and anti-communist. Predictably, Blue Division memoirs published during the war or in its aftermath reflect this with their scornful descriptions of Soviet morality and the Soviet people. In Spain, the divisioners' accounts proved instrumental in shaping and strengthening a fascist ideology as well as legitimizing Franco's crusade against communism during the Civil War. Decades later, Blue Division fiction and memoirs are less overtly politicized, engaging with more nuanced ideas about Jews, communists, and Spain's alliances with Nazi Germany. The authors of contemporary fiction on the Blue Division strive to bring readers into a more fully real-ized human landscape during wartime, drawing comparatively multidi-mensional characters whose lives are intertwined with the events before and after the war, instead of the isolated, exclusive facts of the Russian campaign that the reader is often exposed to in memoirs from the 1940s and 1950s. These fictional characters, built from the divisioners' actual experiences, question the reasons for fighting in Russia and reassess the presumed evil of their wartime religious and political antagonists.

The literature about the Blue Division has had another agenda in terms of Spain's ongoing relationship with its historical memory. Works of fiction such as *El infierno de los inocentes*, *El corazón helado*, and *El invierno en tu rostro* (Winter in Your Visage) by Carla Montero[51] – a divisioner's granddaughter – keep the memory of the divisioners alive and attract lay readers and historians alike to the study of what remains a rather obscure episode in Spanish contemporary history. The fiction of the division reflects the changes in the subjectivity of the Spanish soldier, a figure central to the formation of historical memory. This masculine figure addresses the complex identities of the victors after the Spanish Civil War: his convictions, his hatreds and prejudices of race and class, and his hunger for war, but also his doubts, his weaknesses, his affections, and his crises of identity. Thus, the literature of the Blue Division also offers a case study for the evolution of nationalistic European masculinities across decades and in the context of Spain's remarkable transition from dictatorship to democracy.

NOTES

 1 Rodríguez Jiménez, "Ni División Azul."
 2 For more information, see Uriarte, *Las mujeres de la División Azul.*
 3 Hernández Navarro, *Ida y vuelta.*
 4 Hellbeck, "Working, Struggling, Becoming." See also for Hellbeck: "*AHR Roundtable.*"
 5 Lejeune, *Le Pact Autobiographique*; idem, *On Diary.*
 6 Gómez Tello, *Canción de invierno en el este*, 26. Emphasis added.
 7 Blanch Sabench, *Memorias de un soldado de la División Azul*, 13. Emphasis added.
 8 Hellbeck, *Revolution on My Mind*, 90–1.
 9 Ibid., 9.
10 Operation Barbarossa was the name given by the Nazi military to the invasion of the Soviet Union.
11 Núñez Seixas *Camarada invierno*, 13.
12 A few authors provide written accounts that describe the years of slave labour in Russian concentration camps after having been taken prisoner in February 1943. They include Vadillo, *La gran crónica de la División Azul*; Alonso Gallardo and González Pinilla, *Prisioneros en Rusia*; and Blanco Corredoira, *Añoranzas de guerra.*
13 Martínez Esparza, *Con la División Azul en Rusia*, 6.
14 Ibid., 22.
15 Lejeune, *On Diary*, 81.
16 Martínez Esparza, *Con la División Azul en Rusia*, 9.
17 Pfeifer, *Obras literarias de los combatientes*, 61.
18 Martínez Esparza, *Con la División Azul en Rusia*, 152.
19 Ibid., 261.
20 Ibid., 146.
21 Ibid., 153.
22 Ibid., 172–3.
23 Ibid., 190, 178.

24 Ibid., 208.

25 Ibid., 144.

26 "José Luis Gómez Tello," http://www.fnff.es/Jose_Luis_Gomez_Tello_periodista_Divisionario_941_c.htm, accessed 1 September 2016.

27 Gómez Tello, *Canción de invierno en el este*, 66–7.

28 Ibid., 72.

29 Núñez-Seixas, "¿Testigos o encubridores?," 262.

30 *Memoria Blau*, http://memoriablau.es/viewtopic.php?t=1818&p=56764, accessed 1 June 2018.

31 Blanch Sabench, *Memorias de un soldado de la División Azul*, 6.

32 Interviewed by Carlos Pérez Roldán for the website *Tradición Viva* in Madrid, July 27, 2012. (http://www.lavoz.circulocarlista.com/entrevistas/jose-maria-blanco-corredoira)

33 Christina Dupláa, "Memoria colectiva y *lieux de mémoire* en la España de la transición" in Joan Ramón Resina (Ed.), *Disremembering the Dictatorship: The Politics of Memory in the Spanish Transition to Democracy*, (Atlanta: Rodopi, 2000), 34.

34 Blanch Sabench, *Memorias de un soldado de la División Azul*, 9.

35 Ibid., 1.

36 Ibid.

37 Fernández Granados, *Traición en el infierno*.

38 Interview for *Diario Ya*, January 2013.

39 Luca de Tena, *Embajador en el infierno*, 3.

40 The Gulags were Chevropovets, Moscow, Suzdha, Oranque, Potma, Kharkiv, Borovichi, Revda, Scherbacov, and Voroshilovgrad.

41 Luca de Tena, *Embajador en el infierno*, 1.

42 Ibid., 26.

43 Solzhenitsyn, *The Gulag Archipelago*; Applebaum, *Gulag*.

44 Ibid., 32.

45 Ibid., 106.

46 Ibid., 127.

47 According the bibliography the author provides at the end of the book (383–5), historical sources include Preston, *Las tres Españas del 36*; and Iordache, *En el Gulag*. Solzhenitsyn's *The Gulag Archipelago* and the ex-Divisioners' autobiographical works also provided the author with background information on the Blue Division's experiences and life in captivity in Soviet Russia.

48 Ibid., 146.

49 Molinos, *El infierno de los inocentes*, 149.

50 Ibid., 369–70.

51 Grandes, *El corazón helado*; Montero, *El invierno en tu rostro*.

PART SEVEN

Nazis in Spain

25 Spain's Neutral Holocaust: Memories of the Axis Alliance in Francoist and Post-Franco Spain, or "The Wonderful, Horrible Life of Otto Skorzeny"

JOSHUA GOODE

In an editorial written in July 1997 for the Spanish newspaper *El País*, the eminent Spanish historian Javier Tusell described what he thought were the historical resonances of a recent attack by the Basque separatist group Euskadi Ta Askatasuna (ETA). ETA had kidnapped Miguel Ángel Garrido Blanco, a parliamentary representative from the Partido Popular, the conservative political party, and had demanded the release of ETA prisoners in exchange for his release. ETA gave a forty-eight-hour deadline, after which, if the demands were unmet, they would kill Garrido Blanco and leave his body somewhere public and out in the open. The threat began a gruelling two-day public spectacle on Spanish television and radio. The various Spanish television channels included countdown clocks running all day and night that showed the time left until Garrido Blanco's presumed assassination, an assumption born of the Spanish government's official stance not to negotiate with ETA.

Tusell's article appeared a few days after Garrido Blanco's body was found shot through the head in an open pit in northern Spain. Tusell argued that images of the scene were reminiscent of other spectacle killings in the twentieth century: mass graves, people shot in the head, bodies left to die in pits. His historical associations in fact were quite clear. He wrote: "Lo que hemos vivido en estas últimas semanas parece paralelo con aquella experiencia: idénticos los verdugos y las víctimas, semejante el impacto en el espectador" (what we've seen in the last few weeks is similar to a past experience, identical executioners and victims and similar impact on the spectator).[1] More than just the body in a pit resonated for Tusell. He felt that the victimization of Spaniards from the assault of ETA militants looked a lot like other events, and he equated the suffering of the present with suffering of the past:

> De nuevo en este punto reaparece el Holocausto. Para muchos la constancia en la denuncia de los judíos resulta pura obsesión, transcurridos

tantos años. Pero en realidad nos revelan que, como escribió Primo Levi, si aquello lo hizo un ser humano puede repetirse. Ojalá las víctimas del terrorismo no cejen en recordarnos su existencia para que no banalicemos ese Mal absoluto en que consiste.

The Holocaust has reappeared. For many the ongoing denunciation of Jews was the product of a pure obsession and as Primo Levi pointed out, if a human being has done something once, he can do it again. Let's hope the victims of terrorism never cease to remind us of their existence so that we don't become inured to this banality of absolute evil.[2]

In 1997, this association of Basque separatist violence with the Holocaust stood out as odd and discordant; after all, for a country that had not participated in the mechanisms of the Shoah, had expelled Jews five hundred years earlier, and had been isolated for most of the twentieth century from the process of coming to terms with the past that Tony Judt has described as the cornerstone of post-war history efforts in the rest of Europe, comparing this event with the Holocaust seemed out of place.[3] Alejandro Baer has recently argued – and reiterates his point in the concluding chapter of this volume – that this discordant note was precisely the point; Holocaust memory in Spain, especially in the last decade, has largely been configured around the absence of Jews. The coming to terms with the past that has defined the rest of Europe to various degrees has had in Spain a far greater internal inflection, deriving its political and cultural valence from internal Spanish conflicts rather than as a result of a sense of guilt or complicity in the actual events. Precisely because of this absence of Jews and withdrawal from the major events that had served to define post-war Europe, invocations of the Holocaust and its memory in Spain speak more to particular contemporary Spanish issues that have very little to do with the crimes and events of the Shoah.[4]

Thus, a vacuum of memory produced Tusell's inapt and idiosyncratic association. What had produced this vacuum? This chapter argues that the forces that produced Tusell's imagined link are neither unique nor particularly idiosyncratic in Spain. They are rooted in two seemingly contradictory characteristics. Spain's ostensible post-war isolation from the other cultural and political settlements of the post-war period conflicted with Spain's unique position as former ally of the Nazis during the Spanish Civil War and as its ideological fellow traveller during the Second World War. This contradictory stance has been manifested over the past twenty years in the delayed interrogation of the Spanish Civil War and its historical aftermath that has occupied Spain now that, to borrow the title of Saul Friedländer's memoir, "memory has come." The immediate post-Francoist period was known for its energetic efforts to suppress historical memory: what became known as the "pact of silence." Officially, the Amnesty Law of 1977 offered an official and legal reprieve against charges for past crimes, no retribution or restitution for families, and an overarching effort to avoid discussing the crimes, executions, and repressions during and after the Spanish Civil War. In practice, there has been a general slippage between the moniker "pact of silence" and a "pact of forgetting" that always seemed to be somewhat telling; there has been a conflation between silencing real historical investigation of the past and the desire to more comprehensively ignore and do away with the past.[5]

Either way, the result has been an active, ongoing, and deeply politicized confrontation with the events of the Spanish Civil War and its aftermath, especially over the last decade and a half. First, efforts began to dig up bodies from largely unmarked but never forgotten mass graves filled with perceived enemies of the Francoist forces during the Spanish Civil War. Then the Spanish Socialist Party government passed a Law of Historical Memory in 2007 that called for a more active engagement with the past, including the final removal of Francoist statuary from Spain's cities, and the creation of a panel to investigate and arrive at a final disposition for the Franco-era monument El Valle de los Caídos (the Valley of the Fallen). The monument had always symbolized the complexity of memory in Spain; what was officially incarnated as a memorial to all the fallen soldiers of the Spanish Civil War also was a basilica and the final resting place for Franco and the Falange party leader José Antonio Primo de Rivera, who was killed in the early years of the Spanish Civil War. As a result, the state-supported Valle de los Caídos has always been viewed far more as a monument to Franco and to his regime rather than as a national monument for the war.[6] There have been renewed and quite energetic debates among historians, politicized in a manner akin to the German *Historikerstreit*, about the causes and results of the Spanish Civil War.[7]

Amid this historical investigation, a widened frame of historical comparison that seeks to place the Spanish Civil War and its aftermath in the context of the violence and mass murder of the twentieth century in Europe has also emerged. New work has examined the Spanish Civil War, the treatment of enemies, the prison camps that long outlasted the war, and the repressions that followed as a "Holocaust" or a genocide.[8] Part of this expanded frame has included a focus on the secret and hidden world of the Nazi refugees who found asylum in Spain throughout the post-war years and created successful lives of leisure, of comfort, and sometimes of business.[9] This work, referenced in David Messenger's chapter 26 in this volume, rooted in archival work in governmental repositories in the United States, Great Britain, and Spain, has uncovered a far more complicated range of Francoist-era diplomatic relations and exchanges between Spain, the United States, NATO, and West Germany than has long been assumed.

This re-examination of the past and comparative framework for understanding the Franco regime, its ideology, and its place in the bloody pantheon of Europe's twentieth century has also unfolded outside historians' circles. Literary and cultural studies theorists have noted the lingering, ghostly presence of Spanish Jewish life in modern Spanish film and literature, noting in particular the ways in which the Shoah has occasionally served as a metaphor or a leitmotif for describing evil acts. (Stacy N. Beckwith writes about this phenomenon in recent Spanish fiction in chapter 29 of this volume.) The surprising and odd association with the Holocaust in a recent comedy, *El crimen ferpecto*, is a case in point. The first concern the film's main character harbours after murdering his boss and disposing of the body in the department store incinerator is: "¿Soy un Nazi?" (Am I a Nazi?).[10] There has also been some recent analysis of the role and image of the Holocaust in Spain and the appearance and appropriation of the lost Jewish life of Spain, ended formally in 1492 and lingering like a ghost or a void in Spanish culture, writing, and thought.[11] Here the Holocaust plays out in Spanish memory as an event that did not have an impact on or basis in Spain, but perhaps has developed as a leitmotif for Spanish suffering and as a stand-in for accounting for the unpunished crimes of the past. One might suggest that debates about the role of the Jewish past in Spain that cropped up energetically in the 1950s and 1960s had as their subconscious root a focus on the similarities between Spanish history of the medieval and early modern era and the bloody history of Germany in the 1930s and 1940s.[12] This comparison has led to a kind of "memory envy" where the delayed confrontation with Spanish misdeeds of the past and suffering can be elevated to a larger international level of pain and trauma.[13]

A particular part of this confrontation with the past has been an interrogation of the role the Nazi state played in the Spanish Civil War and Franco's Spain. Though largely undiscussed, the presence of Nazis in Spain who arrived through various rat lines or who simply remained after the war's conclusion has been the subject of recent scholarship, including David Messenger's examination in this volume.[14] Some of this research has centred on the diplomatic efforts in the immediate post-war years to deal with Nazis residing in Spain for the purpose of preventing them from being extradited back to Germany or the United States to face war crimes trials or denazification hearings.[15] In these works, the presence of Nazis in Spain was largely secret and circumstantial. These Nazi "refugees" chose Spain mainly because it was a proximate safe haven through which to escape justice. While Messenger has suggested that the Franco state had no clear official policy of resistance to Allied judicial demands to repatriate these Germans, it is also plain that town or neighbourhood police provided significant aid to Nazis attempting merely to avoid extradition and stay in Spain. At best, it seems, Nazis often enjoyed a casual acquaintance or affiliation with the regime or with particular figures within the Francoist hierarchy who would then protect their identities or keep them from being extradited back to Germany.[16] In general, however, the public presence of between five and twenty thousand Nazi refugees in Spain was kept secret and was certainly never the subject of a public accounting.[17]

As the regime pivoted away from the Second World War in the 1950s, Franco's efforts coalesced around promoting Spain as an anti-communist bulwark for the West. Spain's wartime alliances had to be diminished. Yet neither in the 1940s nor later in the 1950s were Nazi refugees ever an invisible group inside Spain. In fact, the Spanish press covered Nazi refugees in Spain and followed some of the more notorious among them as if they were celebrities: they served as a fairly flexible symbol in the Francoist press. Presented occasionally as a significant ideological link to their Falangist colleagues in the 1940s, Nazi refugees were also cast as important interlocutors in expanding Spanish commerce with West Germany.[18] In some press organs, the Nazis subtly connected the regime to its fascist roots or they could serve as a prismatic projection of the regime's future as a third path between the democratic West and the communist East. Often one figure alone could project all of these different images.

One particularly emblematic example is Otto Skorzeny, a former Waffen SS colonel and famous mostly for liberating Benito Mussolini from his mountaintop prison on the Gran Sasso mountain in the Apennines in 1943. Skorzeny was a consistent presence in the Spanish media throughout the Franco regime. His appearances in the Spanish press present the discomfiting realization that not all Nazi refugees in Spain were hidden or secret. Analysing the public presentation of Skorzeny through the censored and controlled Francoist press allows one to have a sense of the multiple roles he was able to play. Skorzeny's public presentation and the uniquely high level of approbation he received in the Spanish press testified to the protean figure he was. He served the Falangist press as a committed and faithful fascist, a good Nazi. He was also a good German, helping to expand mutual Spanish and German business interests in the era. He possessed a range of positive characteristics that conformed to Francoist military values, having already demonstrated his valiant derring-do leading the team of steely commandos who in their first assignment freed Mussolini without firing a shot.[19] The Spanish press focused attention again on Skorzeny after the Second World War as he escaped from the Allied prisoner-of-war camp in Darmstadt.[20] He was covered in the Falangist press for his ability to evade the United States and other former Allied authorities.[21] There was consistent coverage of the efforts scouring Europe to find the elusive Skorzeny as he fled from Paris to Rome, Berlin, Munich, and Vienna in 1949–50.[22]

His public reappearance in 1950 coincided with the publication of his autobiography in France and its translation into various languages. The unrest in Paris that followed the publication of his book was well documented in the Spanish press and focused on the fact that Skorzeny and his work upset the post-war political consensus in France. The riots born of the publication of his book were presented as having "disgustado profundamente a los comunistas" (profoundly irritated the communists) and were rooted in the fact that *Le Figaro* published excerpts of the book to "bother" its colleagues at the left-leaning *Liberation* newspaper.[23] This coverage of Skorzeny focused on him far more as a former Nazi thorn in the side of international communism than as a fascist ideologue and allowed his Nazism to be viewed as a kind of ardent anti-communism. Thus, he re-emerged as what one might call a "premature anti-communist," which meant that a Francoist association with this former Nazi would not tether the regime to wartime alliances as much as align it with the regime's new, contemporary image as a faithful Cold Warrior.[24]

Skorzeny perpetuated this kind of ideological repositioning of Nazism as a positive if failed alternative to communism in his own public utterances in Spain. In one interview in 1966 with a Francoist journalist and former Falange member, Skorzeny presented Hitler as a humane leader, ahead of his time. Here, the former Nazi living in Spain anachronistically superimposed the then contemporary efforts to forge a more united Europe through the European Economic Community onto Hitler's plans to "unir el continente europeo" (unify the European continent). First, Hitler was a sensitive politician who attempted to move beyond the calcified dynamics of left- and right-wing politics:

> Será preciso en el futuro, cuando las pasiones se quieten, descubrir a las generaciones de mañana la verdadera humanidad de Hitler. Ahora parece que las izquierdas tienen derecho a todo y las derechas a nada. En la

naturaleza ya hay derechas e izquierdas y también en política están las dos, juntas y equilibradas.

In the future, when the passions of the moment have quieted down, future generations will re-discover the true humanity of Hitler. Today it seems the Left can claim what it wants of the past while the Right can claim nothing. But, in nature as in politics, the left and the right exist together in equilibrium.[25]

Later in this same interview, Skorzeny referred to the idea of a united Europe locked between the United States and the Soviet Union as one that Hitler shared and had tried to implement, albeit "prematurely."

This idea of Nazism as a third path balanced between the left and the right emerged in another manner in the coverage of Skorzeny in Spain. Often Skorzeny was presented as an incarnation of a new and recovering Germany, one freed of the taint of Nazism in order to move forward. In this context, Skorzeny was positioned to demonstrate that Germans were not responsible for the crimes of the Nazi state; only German leaders bore the sole responsibility for these excesses. Skorzeny appeared as a good and noble German soldier, exemplified by altruistic acts towards the enemy during the Second World War:

Lo que hizo el regimen nacionalsocialista ha sido aireado suficientemente, y en algunas ocasiones exagerados. Ahora bien; no se comprende como personas de cierta cultura pueden identificar los sentimientos naturales de todo un pueblo con las violaciones del derecho de gentes que hayan podido cometer sus dirigentes.

What the national socialist regime did has been sufficiently discussed publicly and sometimes has been quite exaggerated. In fact, one just cannot understand how certain people can confuse what are the natural sentiments of a *pueblo* with the violations of human rights that their leaders might have committed.[26]

Skorzeny also tried to maintain his affiliations with the Spanish Falange. Throughout the 1950s and 1960s, his yearly attendance at a memorial to Mussolini, in the company of Ramón Serrano Suñer, Franco's brother-in-law and former head of the fascist party, received consistent press coverage, both in articles and in photographs.[27]

In another moment, Victor de la Serna, a Spanish journalist closely allied to the Franco regime, celebrated Skorzeny's concern for his colleagues, six former Nazi military figures who had been condemned to death in Landsberg Prison, including the SS general, Joachim Peiper. This concern for their well-being in the face of a callous death sentence demonstrated a kind of lost chivalric Europe, an end to a "Europa derrotada" (defeated Europe):

> Si un día Otto Skorzeny y sus camaradas (Guderian, Manteufel) pronuncian el "Todo se acabó", hay algo que acaba efectivamente: acaba una idea del destino de Europa, bajo la que el viejo Continente escribió páginas que empezaron en un observatorio a las orillas del Vistula, donde Copernico sentía en su corazon el ruido de la Tierra girando alrededor del Sol, siguieron en Cracovia, donde se presentía la ruta de Poniente camino de las tierras virgenes y acabaron en la soledad de un laboratorio en que un sabio modesto descubría la "germanina" contra la terrible soñera del tropic. Podrá discutirse esta idea de Europa; podrá encontrarse que una idea más estética, menos patética, es más agradable y más cómoda. Pero si Skorzeny y sus afines pronuncian el "consumatum", es cierto de toda certidumbre que se producen bajas irreparables en la escuadra de los espíritus encargados de la guardia de Occidental.

> If one day Otto Skorzeny and his comrades [Guderian, Manteufel] proclaim, "All has ended," then something else has definitively concluded: a hope for the future of Europe which had started to be imagined in an observatory on the banks of the Vistula where Copernicus felt in his heart the sound of the Earth orbiting the Sun, and then followed a route west to virgin lands and which would finish back in Krakow in the solitude of a laboratory where a modest genius discovered treatments against the terrible germs of the tropics. One can argue over this idea of Europe and discover one more aesthetic and less pathetic, nicer and more comfortable. But if Skorzeny and those like him declare their "consumatum," it is certain beyond any doubt that there are irreparable losses in the squadron of spirits that guard the West.[28]

It is interesting to note that Skorzeny returned the favour of these compliments to Victor de la Serna in his obituary for the Spanish journalist. Writing in *ABC* in 1958, Skorzeny asserted that de la Serna was an "[e]uropeo verdadero" (true European), always ready to help forge the bonds between German soldiers of the Second World War and their comrades in Spain:

> Tuvo también el valor de ser impopular y asistir a los soldados alemanes cuando todavía eran considerados como criminales en todo el mundo.

> Será inolvidable para mi como hizo suyos los problemas de los demás,
> sobre todo durante los años más difíciles de la postguerra, y puso su nom-
> bre conocido a disposición de las causas justas, sin ninguna condición.

> He always possessed the great valour to be unpopular and assist German
> soldiers who were still considered criminals throughout the world. I will
> never forget how he made other people's problems his own, especially
> in the difficult years of the postwar, and gave his name in support of just
> causes without asking anything in return.[29]

Skorzeny also worked to demonstrate his status as a wealthy and influential German businessman. He started in the early 1950s first by asserting that in the last days of the war he had managed to hide away all of
the "Nazi gold," with which he would fund a new army to raise a Fourth
Reich from a crumbling Germany.[30] He also was careful to be seen as a
good businessman, appearing throughout the 1950s as an important go-
between with the Spanish, Egyptian, and West German governments.[31]
Skorzeny cultivated this image, once remarking in 1954 to a reporter
with the *London Express* that his wartime fame was merely a conduit for
his business dealings: "[B]elieve me for some years it has been pleasant
to be known as Mussolini's rescuer. Here in Spain I feel at last I can drop
the mask ... I am working for the future."[32] The CIA operatives who kept
tabs on Skorzeny throughout the 1950s and 1960s remained consistently
dubious about Skorzeny's financial acumen, but also noted the value
these claims had for forging connections with Spanish political and military leaders.[33] Certainly, Skorzeny's marriage to the niece of Hjalmar
Schacht, the former finance minister of the Nazi state, in 1954 did add
to Skorzeny's range of contacts and seemed to leverage the financial
dealings he was able to conduct in the 1950s and 1960s.[34]

Yet neither the reality of this heroic image nor Skorzeny's intrigues
as a Svengali-like figure plotting a return of a Fourth Reich, maintaining a Nazi escape network from Europe named ODESSA, harbouring
Nazi gold, or being contracted by the Israeli Mossad to assassinate former Nazi scientists in Egypt – all the subjects of the usual coverage
of Skorzeny – matter less than how Skorzeny's image exists as a construction of the Franco regime's ideological apparatus in the 1950s and
1960s.[35] Towards the end of his life, the complicated and pliable image
of Skorzeny reappeared. Two years after the previously discussed 1966
interview with Fernando Vizcaíno Casas, Skorzeny gave an interview
to the conservative paper *ABC* in which he appeared as a charming relic
of the past, settling into a Spanish dotage. Pictured comfortably with his

wife in their Madrid apartment, Skorzeny became the put-upon "Viejo coronel … de recuerdos, de aquel lance de espada de juventud" (old colonel of memories with the sword flashes of youth) whose wife really controlled the house while appearing not to.[36] Ironically, this interview took place just a few months after another interview with Skorzeny featured on the American television program *60 Minutes* titled "The Most Dangerous Man in Europe," a moniker Skorzeny had cultivated after British intelligence gave it to him during the war. While, again, most of the interview focused on Skorzeny's daring rescue of Mussolini, the difference between this interview and the one conducted by *ABC* was apparent in the additional question posed to him by the American correspondent: did he have any regrets about the war?[37] Guilt and regret were not subjects that appeared in the Spanish press.

Ideologically, the Franco regime has long been understood best as a balancing act, with Franco's only real skill an ability to balance diverse political forces within a political coalition kept together by a police state and opportunism.[38] It is a description that works well for Otto Skorzeny. It has also become an apt description of the equilibrium between history and memory in Spain. Franco's state was never clearly anti-Nazi, nor was it so silent about its past alliances. The presence of Nazis on Spanish soil was also not a secret; Nazis were pliably deployed in the Spanish ideological apparatus. Perhaps the voids of Spanish history that allow for multiple perspectives and variable uses of the past to flourish today were not quite so empty in the past. Spaniards held multiple and contradictory attitudes and beliefs towards Nazism long before Javier Tusell's confusions of ETA and Nazism. In fact, just a month before Tusell's article appeared, Paul Preston, the eminent British historian of Spain, had exposed in the conservative newspaper *ABC* the presence of Nazi refugees in Spain, including one of the most famous, Otto Skorzeny, the Nazi "el as de operaciones especiales" (the ace of special operations), who had liberated Mussolini from his mountainside prison.[39] Even while the presence and alignments of Nazis in Franco's Spain were being discussed, the supposed confusions of history forged by voids and absences unfolded alongside them.

NOTES

1 Javier Tusell, "El reproche y la tenacidad," *El País* (Madrid), 19 July 1997 (Madrid), http://elpais.com/diario/1997/07/19/espana/869263212_850215. html, accessed 5 April 2016.
2 Ibid.

3 "As Europe prepares to leave World War Two behind – as the last memorials are inaugurated, the last surviving combatants and victims honoured – the recovered memory of Europe's dead Jews has become the very definition and guarantee of the continent's restored humanity." Judt, *Postwar*, 804.

4 Baer, "The Voids of Sepharad." Andreas Huyssen has made a similar argument for the Holocaust in general, suggesting that it has become a screen memory, a universal trope for all traumatic events, in *Present Pasts*, 14.

5 On the pact of silence versus the pact of forgetting, see Richards, *After the Civil War*, esp. 277–9; on trauma and its impact on memory, a useful introduction is LaCapra, *History and Memory after Auschwitz*.

6 See Olmeda, *El Valle de los Caídos*; and Richards, *After the Civil War*, 190–1. The symbolism of El Valle endures, despite Franco's exhumation from the monument on 24 October 2019.

7 For a recent recapitulation of the renewed politicization of the historiography of the Spanish Civil War, see Holguín, "How Did the Spanish Civil War End ..."

8 Ruiz, "A Spanish Genocide?"; Preston, *The Spanish Holocaust*; Miguez Macho, *The Genocidal Genealogy of Francoism*. See also Baer, "The Voids of Sepharad"; and Goode, *Impurity of Blood*, epilogue.

9 Collado Seidel, *España, refugio nazi*; Cantarero, *La huella de la bota*.

10 *El crimen ferpecto*, dir. Iglesia.

11 Labanyi, "History and Hauntology"; Gómez López-Quiñones and Zepp, eds, *The Holocaust in Spanish Memory*; Flesler, Linhard, and Melgoa, eds, *Revisiting Jewish Spain in the Modern Era*.

12 While an extensive bibliography touches on this topic, few directly confront this comparison head-on. Among the oblique references are the following: a prescient but subtle suggestion of this link in the long overlooked Russell, "The Nessus-Shirt of Spanish History"; Yerushalmi, *Assimilation and Anti-Semitism*; and Netanyahu, *The Origins of the Inquisition in Spain*.

13 See, in particular, Baer, "The Voids of Sepharad," 134–7.

14 On the arrival of Nazis in Spain, see Steinacher, *Nazis on the Run*, esp. 255–70; Goñi, *The Real Odessan*, 75–80; and the essays in David A. Messenger and Katrin Paehler, eds, *A Nazi Past*.

15 Messenger, *Hunting Nazis in Franco's Spain*.

16 David Messenger's work has shown there was no overarching official policy to bring Nazi refugees to Spain. See Messenger, *Hunting Nazis*, chapter 1 and 111–35. A lingering question in this work is how much the aid that individuals received from the Spanish government was the product of a top-down policy and how much was the product of the individual initiative of Francoist officials.

17 One journalist who has recently tried to promote the idea that these former Nazis played an outsized role in building the present-day neo-Nazi and far right movements in Spain seems to imply that all of these Nazis lived

in their own kind of community-based exile in Madrid or nestled in their small enclaves on the Costa del Sol. Joan Cantarero suggests that it was international efforts to track Nazi war criminals in the 1990s that led the then Socialist party government to open the archives – especially those of the Ministry of Foreign Affairs in Madrid – that initiated this reckoning with Francoist complicity in harbouring so many suspect Germans. See Cantorera, *La huella de la bota*, 26.

18 Collado Seidel, *España, refugio nazi*, ch. 2; Irujo, *La lista negra*, 217–33. Messenger points out that economic development was a two-way street. Germans in Spain had an incentive to showcase their international business connections for a Spanish government that, according to Messenger, might be persuaded to turn a blind eye to their Nazis pasts. See Messenger, *Hunting Nazis*, 110.

19 Dozens of articles in *ABC* covered this action in front-page, full-page, multi-day coverage. See, for example, *ABC*, 16 September 1943.

20 Skorzeny was accused of putting his German soldiers in US Army uniforms and of executing American soldiers en masse. He was exonerated at his trial; even so, US authorities remained convinced that he had committed the war crimes but that the evidence would never exist to prove it. See, for example, "Skorzeny liberado," *ABC*, 10 September 1947; and Otto Skorzeny, CIA name file, RG 263, entry ZZ18, box 121, NARA, College Park, MD.

21 The articles include "Pedía 400,000 marcos por un manuscrito," *El Alcázar*, 28 November 1950, 4; "Detenidos y liberados," *ABC*, 18 May 1945, Morning Edition; and "Skorzeny relata la forma en que fue rescatado a Mussolini," 18 May 1945, Andalucian Edition. Even the exiled Spanish press covered Skorzeny's movements: "España reducto fascista," *España Libre*, 7 September 1952.

22 See *ABC*, 19 September 1947; 29 July 1949; 8 October 1949, 12; 14 February 1950.

23 On "profoundly irritated," see n.a., "Notas Internacionales," *El Alcázar*, 14 April 1950: 2; on the conflicts between *Liberation* and *Le Figaro*, see Luís Calvo, "Irritación comunista contra Le Figaro pero más bién contra la libertad de Skorzeny," *ABC*, 8 April 1950, 13.

24 The best example of the focus on Skorzeny as an anti-communist is the coverage of the rumour that he had planned to assassinate Stalin. See, "Otto Skorzeny planeó matar a Stalin," *ABC*, 13 May 1961, Andalucian edition. This turn of phrase, "prematuramente anti-comunistas" (premature anti-communists), is a play on post-war US efforts to label Americans who had fought in the Spanish Civil War for the Republic "premature anti-Fascists" rather than as communist sympathizers during the Red Scare.

25 Vizcaíno Casas, *Café y copa con los famosos*, 33–4.

26 "Notas Internacionales," *El Alcázar* (Madrid), 14 April 1950, 4.

27 Beside a photograph of Skorzeny standing alongside Serrano Suñer, the caption reads: "Como todos los años, se ha celebrado en una iglesia madrileña un funeral por Benito Mussolini" (Just like every year, a mass was celebrated for Benito Mussolini in a Madrid Church). See "Skorzeny, en el funeral del Duce," *ABC*, 1 May 1963; "Misa por las almas de Mussolini y los caídos italianos," *Imperio*, 29 April 1954, 1; "Funerales por el Duce," *España Libre* 17, no. 531 (21 May 1961), n.p. Recent revelations by Joan Cantarero about Skorzeny's work with far-right groups in Spain indicate that more than just appearing as a connection to a fascist past, Skorzeny was working to develop a fascist future; see Cantarero, *La huella de la bota*, 24–36.

28 Victor de la Serna, "Los seis de Landsberg," *ABC* 12 January 1951, 1.

29 Otto Skorzeny, "Europeo verdadero," *ABC*, 27 November 1958, 27.

30 Infield, *Skorzeny: Hitler's Commando*, 170–2.

31 For example, "Llegada el ex coronel alemán Skorzeny," *ABC* 6 November 1963: 37.

32 Infield, *Skorzeny*, 170–1.

33 Skorzeny's CIA name file, at the National Archives in College Park, Maryland, contains a running account throughout his years in Spain of the rumours of his fabulous wealth, the film rights he was negotiating for his life story in 1952, and his efforts to build the Bundeswehr, a new German army to reinstitute the Fourth Reich. These rumours, which are littered throughout his file, also include near constant admonitions in dispatches back to Washington such as the following from 1951: "Skorzeny known personally to [redacted] to be psychopathic liar and congenital fraud. This view shared by late Kaltenbrunner and Walter Schellenberg who ought to know. Wish to go on record that Zacabin, irrespective of Zacactus involvement should under no circumstances be manoeuvred into position of sponsoring Skorzeny's 'intelligence' activities." See Otto Skorzeny, CIA name file, RG 263, entry ZZ18, box 121.

34 Infield, *Skorzeny*, 171.

35 Lourdes Baeza, "La leyenda nazi que fichó el Mosad," *El País*, 6 April 2016, http://internacional.elpais.com/internacional/2016/04/06/actuali-dad/1459930638_691858.html, accessed 7 April 2016.

36 Skorzeny is quoted as saying: "Quien toma las decisiones importantes en casa soy yo, amigo mío, es natural. Ahora, quien se encarga de decir cuáles son las decisiones importantes y cuáles no, es mi mujer, desde luego" (The one who makes the important decisions in the house is me, of course ... But the one who is in charge of deciding what are the important decisions,

that's my wife, of course). Tico Medina, "El ruido y las nueces: Otto Skorzeny," *ABC*, 26 April 1975, 121.

37 "The Most Dangerous Man in Europe," *60 Minutes*, 7 January 1969, https://www.paleycenter.org/collection, accessed 4 April 2016 via Paley Center Online Archive.

38 The classic description of this system remains Linz, *The Party System of Spain*, 1966.

39 Paul Preston, "Franco y los 'nocivos' alemanes," *ABC*, 7 June 1997, 33–4.

26 Nazis, Real and Imagined, in Post-Second-World-War Spain

DAVID A. MESSENGER

Introduction

As Ronald Newton has written of the German colony in Argentina, between 1933 and 1939 a major transformation occurred within the German colony in Spain, masterminded by operatives of the National Socialist Party, which resulted in a new situation whereby

> with few exceptions the communal organizations – religious, educational, welfare, musical, sport, social – had declared their formal adhesion to Hitler's New Order ... [T]eaching cadres in the larger schools came to be dominated by recently arrived apostles of the New Germany, most of them party members, the children of leftist and Jewish parents were driven off ... [the] German Labor Front organized the employees of many German firms.[1]

This pattern repeated itself across many countries. In Spain, these developments built on a history of commercial relations that dated from the turn of the century, when the Deutsches Bank helped create the Banco Hispano-Alemán and the Banco Alemán Transatlántico.[2] Following the First World War, many Spaniards as well as Germans sought to reinvigorate cultural, scientific, and economic ties between the two countries, when French and American cultural and economic elements were active on the Iberian Peninsula.[3]

In Spain, the process of Nazi influence over the German colony was well under way when the Civil War broke out in July 1936. At that point in time, one of the leading Germans in Spain, Johannes Bernhardt, managed to persuade Hitler to give air support to move Franco's troops from Spanish Morocco to the mainland. This eventually led to Hitler's dispatch of the Condor Legion, a unit of the Luftwaffe, to fight in Spain and to a rapid expansion of German economic interests in Spain. The twenty-nine months of service in Spain by members of the Condor Legion was significant for the later development of German activities in the country. Nearly nineteen thousand Germans volunteered to serve in the Condor Legion over the course of the Civil War.[4] Many had ties to Spain or had a relationship with the German colony in Spain before the war. By 1939, the ties between Germans in Spain, Nazism, and the Spanish regime of General Franco were even closer. The respective air ministries established exchange programs for officers; the Spanish fascist movement, the Falange, had formal ties to the Nazi Party; and the Gestapo established relations with the Civil Guard.[5]

Although Italy's Benito Mussolini provided the majority of Axis military support to Franco, Germany's attempt to economically colonize Spain had longer-lasting effects.[6] In October 1936, the German Plenipotentiary for the Four Year Plan, Hermann Goering, created the company ROWAK to manage German trade with Franco's zone in Civil War Spain. In 1938 Sofindus was created, and it became a holding company for all German government-owned mines, companies, and properties in Franco's Spain. Johannes Bernhardt, the instigator of German support for Franco, led this enterprise throughout the Second World War.[7] The economic power of Sofindus expanded the German presence and built upon the foundation established during the Civil War by the Condor Legion.

German economic penetration into Spain was equalled by the massive expansion of German intelligence operations, which, as with economic matters, was carried out with the complete acquiescence of Francoist officials.[8] Intelligence officers were first posted with the Condor Legion, and by 1937 a broader German military operation had begun in the course of which Abwehr agents were sent to monitor British Gibraltar.[9] By 1938–9, the Abwehr detachment in Spain, KO-Spanien, had become one of the Abwehr's largest foreign operations, with two hundred personnel and more than one thousand sub-agents as well as a close relationship with Franco's intelligence services, first in Burgos and then, after the Civil War, in Madrid through the Spanish General Staff.[10] It included sections on intelligence-gathering versus the Allies; sabotage in the vicinity of Gibraltar, Morocco, and Algiers; counterespionage versus Allied intelligence in Spain; and specific intelligence-gathering operations related to French Morocco, Allied aviation, the Atlantic coast and the Canary Islands, and Gibraltar and its strait (Operation Bodden).[11]

It was quite common for German intelligence in Spain to use Germans familiar with the country, those who had been members of the colony before 1936 or who had come into Spain with the Condor Legion or German businesses during the Civil War. Abwehr agent Richard Molenhauer first went to Spain in 1932 to work for the Spanish affiliate of IG Farben, Unica Quimica y Bluch SA of Barcelona. Evacuated at the start of the Spanish Civil War, he had returned by the end of 1936 to serve as the IG Farben's representative on Nationalist territory. He worked in Spain until recalled to Germany for military service in 1942 and in February 1944 was transferred to the Abwehr and sent back to Spain to work on translating reports from agents in Madrid.[12] Josef Boogen arrived in Spain in 1936 with the Condor Legion and by 1941 had established himself in Bilbao as a representative for several German machinery firms. His office there served as a cover for numerous German agents who passed through the area, and by 1943 he was suspected of being the primary Gestapo agent in Bilbao and of working with the lead Abwehr agent in the city, Otto Hinrichsen.[13] Hinrichsen himself had come to Spain in 1936, although he had worked in Spain in the 1920s, when he married a Spanish woman, and had two Spanish-born children. During the war he served both the Abwehr and the Nazi Party as a party leader in Bilbao. His son served in the German army during the Second World War.[14]

Military intelligence was not the only game in town: the Sicherheitsdienst (SD) – the Security and Intelligence Service of the SS – was also heavily engaged in Spain. Formal German intelligence operations in Spain began with the Police Treaty signed between Germany and Franco's Burgos-based government on 31 July 1938. The first official police attaché sent to Spain from Berlin was a representative of the Gestapo, part of the SD.[15] This was Paul Winzer, who remained in Madrid until the end of the war. Close collaboration between the SD and the Spanish Dirección General de Seguridad (DGS) was carried out on issues such as the internment of Spanish Republican activists in occupied France. Also, SD agents were dispatched to all German consulates across Spain to monitor the German colony, and after 1941, SD agents sent by its head of foreign intelligence, Walter Schnellenberg, were used to gather intelligence that was more than just of military value.[16] SD agents were placed not only in German consulates but also in a number of German firms, many with ties to the SS.[17]

The Gestapo similarly became involved in Spain. The Spanish police developed by Franco in his Nationalist zone were established on the pattern of the police organization in Germany.[18] Winzer, as noted, had been part of the Gestapo since 1935. He worked between 1937 and 1939 on having the Gestapo train the Spanish police and security service[19] to help the Franco regime maintain its control of Spain, just as the Gestapo in Germany was charged with investigating and suppressing all forms of anti-state tendencies throughout Germany and then later in the German-occupied territories. The Gestapo passed on what it knew: it was tasked with taking action against potential political opposition by operating as an information-gathering and law enforcement body that gradually assumed offensive functions and an overtly political role that was hardly subject to judicial restrictions.[20] The Gestapo represented the National Socialist regime's most important element for enforcing policy and implementing a system of terror that reinforced compliance with National Socialist doctrines and German law,[21] and the methods and tactics it used were exported to Spain. Under the guise of contributing to the struggle against world communism, Gestapo agents were dispatched to Spain[22] to train the Spanish police in its methods and procedures.[23] All of this helped reinforce the authority of the Franco regime and keep it in the Axis orbit.

Moreover, while posted in Spain, Gestapo chiefs acted in an extraterritorial capacity without being subject to Spanish authority. They occupied important commercial posts and spied on individuals perceived as hostile to the National Socialist regime, potentially taking aggressive actions against them.[24] Its agents administered "Harbor Service Departments," which represented the Gestapo's greatest sphere of influence abroad in Spain as in other foreign countries.[25] Its sub-sections were charged with supervising individuals, along with overseeing the "Returned Immigrants Department." German citizens whom the Gestapo considered to be threats to the regime were returned to Germany and were often taken either before a court or to a concentration camp after they were first arrested by the Spanish police at the instigation of German authorities. Targets for suppression included Jews, leftist politicians, and immigrants who were considered enemies of the regime,[26] especially after the Second World War began, when more and more Germans fleeing Hitler sought to enter Spain via France. This group included such luminaries as the Jewish-German literary critic Walter Benjamin, who had fled to Spain as a refugee, only to commit suicide there upon arrival in Portbou in September 1940 in reaction to the terror implied by the French government's assent to surrender German nationals wanted by National Socialist Germany.[27] The Harbor Service also enlisted the assistance of National Socialist organizations in Spain, such as the Labor Front, which pressed German employees abroad into its service, in the course of which they were closely watched regarding their individual conduct.[28] This supervision of German nationals in Spain extended to German ships arriving in Spain and the individuals on board, German pilots, and churches attended by Germans,[29] while a Gestapo official posted at the German Consulate in Salamanca was responsible for compiling a card index on all German civilians arriving in Spain.[30]

The Gestapo in Spain during the Second World War was very active among the local police, to the extent of determining whether prisoners would be held or released.[31] The head of the Gestapo in Logroño, Franz Lubs, spoke not only to German nationals in the region about National Socialism, but to Spaniards as well, especially the local detachment of the Spanish Civil Guard.[32] As the Gestapo chief of Maestranza, he exercised considerable political influence over the Spanish police as well as over the German colony there,[33] just as a member of the consulate in Bilbao, R. Konnecke, was the Gestapo's lead agent there,[34] charged with counter-espionage among German residents in Bilbao, Logroño, and Vizcaya, and supervising several SS members acting as sub-agents.[35] As the war continued, many Gestapo activities focused on relations with the German occupying force in France. A fairly large contingent of Gestapo agents was based in the principality of Andorra, on the border of France and Spain. Working with the German Consulate in Barcelona, the Gestapo in Andorra drew upon existing smuggling networks to recruit agents and focused on monitoring and stopping refugees' entry into Spain.[36] As was characteristic of the overlapping jurisdictions in National Socialist Germany among various organizations of the regime, there was a separate SS station in Barcelona that also collaborated with the Spanish police while monitoring border crossings from France into Spain; this occasionally involved requesting the security police to stop or arrest any escaping individuals who were of interest to the National Socialist regime, such as Allied prisoners of war.[37]

The impact of Germany's war effort in Europe was clearly felt in neutral states like Spain. In 1941, some seventy-five hundred Germans were resident in Spain; it is estimated that by 1944–5 that number had grown to twelve thousand.[38] These Germans consisted of a small group involved in business and other activities since the 1920s or earlier; a significant number who came during the Spanish Civil War for either military or business purposes; and a large number sent during the Second World War for military intelligence and diplomatic and cultural relations, and for economic reasons as well. Whether they belonged to the Abwehr or SD or Gestapo, they were involved in German espionage in Spain during the war. This chapter, largely drawn from American and British intelligence records created in the immediate postwar period, seeks to elaborate on the state of the German colony in Spain following the war, the fears it generated among the victorious Allies, and the ongoing fascination many have had since with the idea of Nazis in Spain.

After the War

After the war, both British and American intelligence units were assigned the dual mission of tracking German agents and diplomats and attempting to remove any Nazi influence from Spain and other formerly neutral states of Europe. With their extensive knowledge of German economic and political penetration in the region since the Civil War, Allied agents first focused on the German leadership in Spain; this included not only the staff of the German Embassy in Madrid, but also the heads of German economic firms, especially those linked to the German state. A major concern for Allied intelligence in 1945–6 was to measure the continued existence in Spain of overt Nazi activities. Allied intelligence operatives had an immediate fear of Nazi "stay-behind" or "werewolf" groups within the German colony that would continue to advocate Nazi ideology and seek to integrate it into the life of the German colony and Spanish society more generally. These werewolf groups were never large in number, nor were they ever a real threat to the Spanish state or to security in general; nonetheless, they were present and active, clearly on the lookout for favours from the Spanish government and perhaps even influence over the Franco regime on certain matters.

Interrogations of former German Embassy employees in Madrid revealed that in the last months of the war, General Eckhardt Krahmer, the air attaché in the Embassy, had accumulated some 7 to 9 million pesetas through the sale of German aeronautical equipment and that the money was earmarked for funding werewolf activities.[39] Krahmer worked with the former naval attaché at the embassy, Kurt Meyer-Doehner, to establish a group called Kampfgemeinschaft Adolf Hitler. Its base was the Erika Bar in Madrid. Using these funds, by July 1946 it had developed a list of former Nazis who had cooperated with Allied investigators and targeted them for "liquidations," although how many were actually killed or attacked is unclear from the documents.[40] In May 1946, one of the werewolf groups, "Edelweiss 88" (8 representing the letter "H" in the alphabet, so 8–8 represented "Heil Hitler!"), kidnapped a prominent German outside of Seville and robbed him, then threatened him with death if he spoke to Allied authorities or to other Germans about this incident.[41]

Over time, as these groups and their sources of money became more established, they moved from clandestine werewolf activities towards more open advocacy for their cause. The evidence of this was best summed up by a source working with American intelligence, identified only as "Eva," who reported in mid-1946 that "[t]he general tendency of the Nazis during these months has been to work more and more openly and to convince the more moderate or scared Germans that *no pasa nada* from the side of the Allies. I find the situation worse than it was a year ago, when there was a great confusion and a general feeling of insecurity among them [the Nazis]." In small talk reported to Eva, many Nazis were now willing to advise others to "keep strong because the Allies are in quarrel and our hour is near."[42]

Beyond werewolf activity, there was also a more general sense of the continued presence of Nazism within the German colony. The American Embassy in Madrid cultivated one informant, a Frenchman named Roger Tur, who had been working in the region of Zaragoza for the Allies since 1944. Tur had previously been closely affiliated with the Vichy regime in France and had many contacts within Spanish and German circles in Spain.[43] As early as October 1945, he reported that among Germans, there was general agreement to support Franco "in order to annoy the Allies."[44] These reports from Zaragoza were representative of what was being observed across Spain. Most Allied agents had overplayed the initial fear of werewolf activities and by early 1946 had come to see much of what was being reported from Germans in Spain as "pure bombast and 'wishful thinking'" and as no real threat to peace or security either internationally, within Spain, or even locally. Yet as more Germans stayed in Spain, their infiltration into Spanish life and the fear that they would influence important elements of Spanish society and politics, and thereby introduce elements of Nazi ideology into Spain, did not diminish. The involvement of these Germans in the organizing of anti-French demonstrations in Zaragoza in February 1946, when France was in the midst of debating its own policy towards Spain domestically and within the UN, was one example of this.[45]

The potential for Nazi influence in Spain was also seen in the cases of individuals who had obtained prominent positions within Spanish institutions and had begun to establish successful postwar careers in Spain. The former cultural attaché at the German Embassy, Hans Juretschke, managed to move into education, teaching German at the University of Madrid, where, in May 1946, he opened a German library. Most of the books were relics of the Nazis' propaganda ministry. The OSS report on Juretschke from late 1946 called him "the link between Nazi *Kultur* and Gestapo" and made the assessment that his postwar activities were nothing less than a continuation of Nazi cultural propaganda in Spain.[46] Dr Heinz Franz Josef Schulte-Herbruggen presented himself to the American Embassy in Madrid as an anti-Nazi in June 1945. He was a German language and literature lecturer at the University of Murcia, and he informed the embassy of the German influence within the Spanish education system. His own views, well known as anti-Nazi, led to harassment from other Germans participating in the

Spanish university system, especially from the German lecturer at the University of Madrid, the former cultural attaché Juretschke.[47]

More official ties to the Franco regime were found in the case of Hans Heinemann, a German agent in France who arrived in Barcelona in 1943, where he worked in wolfram smuggling. His close wartime ties with the Spanish government led to postwar work with the Spanish military. The liberation of France in 1944 revived the desire of Republican exiles based in France to free Spain from Franco's control, and thousands of the more politically active Spanish Republicans who had participated in the French Resistance remained armed in the hope that an assault on Spain could develop. Outside of the largest attempted incursion – in the Val d'Aran in October 1944, led by the Spanish Communist guerrilla group Unión Nacional Española (UNE) – most armed activity took the form of border skirmishes between small groups of Republicans and border guards.[48] The Spanish response was to fortify the border by moving additional troops to the region, under the direction of General Moscardo. Heinemann, a close associate of Moscardo, left his day job as a bar owner in Barcelona to work along the border two or three days per week; in particular, he brought Moscardo in touch with his contacts in the French region of Pyrenées-Orientales.[49] The United States had no interest in supporting Spanish *maquis* or disturbing the peace along the Franco-Spanish frontier; even so, the use of a former Nazi agent in the region was of concern.

The dispatch of German Catholic priests to Spain in the summer of 1945, primarily through religious orders, and their involvement in linking the Catholic Church and Germans was another concerning trend remarked upon by Tur.[50] Similar reports came from Bilbao, where prominent priests in the German community such as Father Lang had taken residence in convents and a source reported that there could be plans in the works to hide fugitive Germans within religious orders.[51] Perhaps the most important contact that US officials had within the German colony was Pastor Bruno Mohr, the head of the German Protestant Church in Madrid. Mohr regularly visited Germans held in Spanish internment camps in 1945 and 1946, when they were being considered for deportation to occupied Germany due to their wartime work. On one of these trips, in January 1946, to the camp at Carranza, which held four hundred internees, Mohr observed how monies raised for the maintenance of internees, often by Catholic priests, were being directed to certain prisoners, almost always the more vocal pro-Nazis, to administer. Thus, such monies were not simply linked to charity; their intent, in Rothe's words, was "to animate political life within the camps."[52]

The development of charitable funds to assist Germans interned throughout Spain was the primary activity of the German Catholic

Church in Spain by early 1946. The role of the German Catholic community and its charitable organizations in assisting those who had been temporarily imprisoned or who needed assistance after the war was thought to often be a cover for the continuation of Nazi Party contacts within the German colony. Fr José Maria Huber, president of the Association of German Catholics of Northern Spain in Bilbao, and Fr José Boos of the Association of German Catholics in Barcelona, were at the centre of these activities.[53] The largest fund was set up and administered by Boos. Early reports in 1946 stated that the funds raised within the German colony were being distributed primarily to the wives and families of interned Abwehr members.[54]

By 1946 and 1947, prominent former Nazis were resuming their leadership activities within the German colony and were doing so more and more overtly. The most significant sign of this change was the more public emergence of Catholic charitable activities. By 1947, several leading members of the German community – Clarita Stauffer, a Hispano-German woman active in the leadership of the Sección Femenina of the Falange, Father José Boos, and Herbert Hellman of AEG – had formed a new Hilfsverein to raise funds for the small number of Germans still interned and to advocate for their release.[55] Initially Boos had sought to launch the group publicly, but he was forbidden to do so by the civil governor of Barcelona on the advice of the US and British consulates there.[56] Nonetheless, its establishment was tolerated by Spanish officials, and by April and May 1947 it was able to promote its fundraising efforts via radio and newspaper ads, although using the term "Central Europeans" instead of "Germans" on the advice of the Spanish foreign minister and the papal nuncio.[57]

Earle Titus of the US Embassy believed that the purpose of the group, beyond its aid activities, was "fostering German nationalism and that Junker spirit of imperialism which has largely been the cause of the European disaster," and that its leadership, "known Nazi sympathizers that we have in Madrid and Barcelona [, would lead the group to become] an opposition next which may eventually become dangerous."[58] Titus quoted a slogan from the Hilfsverein's own materials stating that its goal in serving the community was to "[l]et all Germans unite; forget the past; [and] let us preserve our German nationalism."[59] In Bilbao, a group similar to Boos's Hilfsverein was established under Father Jose Maria Huber, head of the Association of German Catholics of Northern Spain, which advocated for the release of those in the camp at Miranda del Ebro.[60] The British Embassy in Madrid considered the Hilfsverein network to be the most significant example of Nazi influence on the Franco regime, concluding that it was "unwise to discount the possibility of its revival."[61]

Beyond the activities of these individuals in the Hilfsverein, Earle Titus saw signs of a Nazi revival within the German colony in the activities of other formerly prominent community members. One case was that of Ernst Jaeger, former head of the German Chamber of Commerce in Spain, who had resumed travelling around the country visiting businesses in the company of other known Nazi sympathizers.[62] Jaeger had used the chamber for many pro-Nazi propaganda initiatives during the war and by October 1947 was campaigning to be re-elected to the organization's board.[63] Also, Titus noted that Pastor Bruno Mohr, the Lutheran leader in Madrid who had assisted the Allies and had a strong anti-Nazi reputation, was by 1947 being openly criticized by many former Nazis in his parish for reading American Lutheran materials to his congregation instead of German materials. Titus took this as a sign of the more public face of a Nazi revival.[64]

Another grave concern for Titus was the effort made by the German colony to reopen Spain's German schools. In 1945, the US Embassy in Madrid made it clear that all employees of German schools that had operated under Nazism would be considered German government officials and should be removed from their positions.[65] The physical buildings of all German schools had been seized by the British–American Trusteeship in 1945; they were considered part of the German government property that the trusteeship had taken over as the Spanish representative of the Allied Control Commission (ACC) in occupied Germany. By 1947, many of those buildings had been repurposed; for example, in Bilbao, the trusteeship had given the German school to the French government, which then opened the first French school in the city there.[66] A committee emerged within the Madrid colony in spring 1947, led by Eugen Armbruster, also a member of the Hilfsverein, to petition the Spanish foreign ministry to allow the school to resume its role in educating the expatriate colony.[67] A private German school had been opened in Barcelona in the spring of 1947, and by the fall it was reported to be "a social and cultural centre for the German colony," which Titus feared would make it "a future nucleus of German nationalism."[68] This, even though the Allies had turned the former German school there into an "International School." A formal appeal to the American Embassy to open a German school in Madrid was made by Fr Boos in January 1948.[69]

Nazis Imagined

What the above survey demonstrates is that in the years immediately following the war, the German colony in Spain remained active and fairly pro-Nazi. However, that community rarely worked directly for the Spanish government and in fact Nazism had not really penetrated Spanish circles as deeply as the US government and others feared. What we can say is that Nazism in Franco's Spain remained vibrant but not overly political. Since the end of the Franco dictatorship, many authors and artists have written fictional accounts that set their stories in a postwar Spain full of Nazis, and assign them a greater amount of influence and control over daily life and social situations than the above survey demonstrates.[70] Many of these works are exaggerated and don't actually represent the sort of Nazi one found in Spain after the war. That does not mean there weren't war criminals there; indeed, the US intelligence community was well aware that war criminals *could* enter Spain, especially after the German colony in Spain, led by Clarita Stauffer, expanded its Hilfsverein operations to encompass the clandestine movement of Nazis to South America via Spain.

Stauffer carried a German passport and was a national secretary of the Falange's Sección Femenina.[71] She emerged in the fall of 1945 as a leader of the Hilfsverein, collecting clothes and food packages for Germans held at the Spanish internment camp of Sobron. Soon enough she was linked with Fr Boos, the rector of the German Catholic community in Madrid and Barcelona. Stauffer, Boos, and Herbert Hellman of AEG were members of a new Hilfsverein founded in 1947 as a public organization, as noted above. Soon enough this organization moved from assistance and fundraising to more clandestine activities, namely, hiding Germans wanted for repatriation and facilitating their journeys to the Western Hemisphere.[72] This group developed close ties with a series of pro-Nazi officials in the DG Seguridad Nacional, especially its head, Rodríguez. It petitioned officials at Seguridad Nacional to release Germans still interned in Spanish camps, including the ten released from Salamanca in March 1947. These individuals then proceeded to Stauffer's apartment in Madrid and from there to private homes or to Stauffer's own pension in Oviedo, which she rented from the Falange Femenina. Based in Madrid, by mid-1946 Stauffer was active in establishing a series of hiding places for Germans around Santander and arranging their journeys to Argentina.[73]

One such case was that of the head of the firm AEG in Spain, Karl Albrecht. Albrecht, like Bernhardt, was a Nazi Party member with purported ties to German intelligence.[74] Ultimately AEG Iberica was shut down by the Spanish government in 1948 as part of its settlement with the ACC regarding German para-state companies with ties to Nazism.[75] Yet when the war ended, Albrecht continued to live openly in Madrid and run the company. Besides heading AEG, he was president of the German Chamber of Commerce in Spain from 1941 to 1944 and head of the German schools funding agency, which was a chief arm of Nazi propaganda in Spain during the war and was believed to have taken in Nazi assets as the war ended.[76] After the war he continued leading AEG in Madrid until pressure from US investigators to meet drove him into hiding, reportedly in a monastery, in early 1946.[77] In July 1946 the AEG Iberica Board of Directors dismissed him as president for being absent for the previous six months.[78] Others in hiding included Fritz Ehlert, former head of the German Labor Front in Spain, who disappeared from Madrid in November 1945 and reportedly was living near Torrelavega; Robert Baalk, a former Gestapo agent sent to Spain in the spring of 1944, in hiding near Vigo; and former air attaché General Eckhardt Krahmer, who initially lived openly in Madrid following the war but went into hiding in February 1946.[79] Krahmer was wanted not only for his military activities but also for the transport of some two hundred works of art from France to Spain in October 1944, art that had been stolen in the name of Hermann Goering.[80]

As indicated earlier, while most of the people who wanted to move to Argentina were Spanish-based Germans from the war, there were also war criminals from Eastern Europe who came to Spain intent on pursuing the same path. In October 1947, Titus reviewed a report concerning a Major Brohmann, who had arrived in Spain from Germany in February 1947 via Paris. Travelling on a Lithuanian passport, he and his family were based at a home in Madrid known to be a residence for German military officers with false papers. While he attempted to arrange refuge in either Venezuela or Argentina, for the time being Stauffer had arranged for his employment in the Spanish war ministry.[81] It is certainly likely this individual was fleeing potential prosecution for war crimes. More notorious was the case of Walter Kutschmann, a member of the Gestapo in Poland during the war, responsible for the massacre of Jews in Lwow, who entered Vigo via Italy at the end of the conflict and remained there until 1947 under the alias Ricardo Olmo. He then moved on to Argentina, where he was discovered in the 1980s by the Nazi hunter Simon Wiesenthal.[82] This was a minority, however, of the people who sought to go to South America.

In fact, many in the German colony stayed on in Spain. Moreover, this continuation of the German colony and its European collaborators had a direct political impact on groups such as the neo-Nazi Círculo Español de Amigos de Europa (CEDADE), the first legal neo-Nazi association in Europe, founded in Madrid in 1966.[83] Key figures in this group included the Austrian SS commander Otto Skorzeny and the former Belgian fascist leader Léon Degrelle, who entered Spain after the war and remained until their deaths, in 1975 and 1994 respectively.

(See Joshua Goode's chapter 25 on Otto Skorzeny.) Others, too, like Herbert Heim, a SS doctor at the Mauthausen concentration camp, settled in Spain for most of the rest of their lives.[84] Indeed, Heim was part of an active German community in the region of Valencia, which, along with Málaga and Palma de Mallorca, became a centre of continued Nazi community after the Second World War, aided by people such as the former German Consul in Málaga, Hans Hoffmann, and his counterpart in Palma de Mallorca, Hans Dede.[85]

In most cases, the former Nazis stayed in Spain, supported Franco, and did not abandon many of their political ideas, thought they did not exploit them either. As Spain developed into a more integrated European state from the 1960s onwards, former Nazis settled into quiet, successful, and largely apolitical lives, as did most Spaniards. Federico (Friedrich) Lipperheide had established himself in Bilbao in 1921 along with his brothers, in order to become involved in the mining business.[86] During the war, using his contacts in Germany, Lipperheide added to his mining business by founding one of the largest conglomerates in the chemical industry.[87] Although he had a well-known falling out with Johannes Bernhardt, Lipperheide had been a member of the NSDAP since 1934, and according to US intelligence sources, he smuggled German propaganda films into Spain throughout the war,[88] besides doing extensive business in the mining and chemical sectors with Nazi Germany. He fought vigorously to avoid repatriation, contacting both the foreign ministry in Madrid and the US Consulate in Bilbao.[89] Although the Allies vetoed his purchasing of chemical companies being sold after the war as German assets, he stayed in Spain and negotiated a series of agreements with Bayer and other companies that allowed him to build two of the largest Spanish chemical companies during the autarkic era of Franco's Spain.[90]

From all accounts, these men thrived under the long life of the Franco regime.[91] They sought, as did many of their compatriots, to be a part of the regime that Franco was still in the process of building as the Second World War ended. They aimed to become part of Franco's "New Spain," and they eventually succeeded. In the late 1940s, their role in the Spanish Civil War and the Second World War, working mostly for the German government in Spain, had demonstrated their loyalty and commitment to Franco's new vision. All they wanted now was a place. The linkages they could make as Civil War veterans, partisans of a renewed and Catholic Spain, and anti-communists connected their Nazi and Francoist commitments; the continuation of the Franco regime after the Second World War gave them a venue for making such commitment the basis for avoiding denazification. That commitment also made them more and more Spanish as time went by, a fact officially recognized – eventually – with formal citizenship. And they, like other Spaniards, found ways to thrive under the transition and in the Spanish democracy that followed Franco.

NOTES

Sections of this chapter previously appeared in Messenger, *Hunting Nazis*, and in Szanajda and Messenger, "The German Secret State Police in Spain."

 1 Newton, "The United States," 85–6.
 2 Puig, "La conexión alemana," 4.
 3 Romero Sá and Candido da Silva, "La *Revista Médica*," 9.
 4 Locksley, "Condor over Spain," 69.
 5 Schulker-Springorum, *Krieg und Fliegen*, 225–8.
 6 Leitz, *Economic Relations*.
 7 Idem, "Nazi Germany's Struggle," 73.
 8 Rodríguez González, "El espionaje nazi," 211.
 9 Ros Agudo, *La guerra secreta de Franco*, 209–10.
10 Ibid., 210.
11 Ibid., 211–17.
12 Interrogation of Richard Molenhauer, 3 October 3, 1946, RG 84, entry 2531B, box 87, United States National Archives and Records Administration II, College Park, MD (NARA).
13 Memorandum by G.C. Howell, "Germans for repatriation," 27 February 1946, RG 226, entry 190A, box 23, NARA.
14 Ibid.
15 "Haig Files," 31 January 1946, RG 226, entry 127, box 28, NARA.
16 Ros Agudo, *La guerra secreta de Franco*, 191–201.
17 For one such case of an agent under cover in a trading firm, that of SD agent Walter Schwedke and the Hamburg-based business Harder & De Vose, see a series of memos by the OSS, RG 226, entry 190A, box 24, beginning 11 July 1946, NARA.
18 Berlin, SW 11, den 6. Dezember 1937. Betr.: Entsendung deutscher Polizeifachleute nach Spanien. Politisches Archiv des Auswärtigen Amtes, Berlin (AA), R100749.
19 Funk-Telegram. Madrid, am 4. Dezember 1939. AA, R100741; Der Reichsführer SS und Chef der Deutschen Polizei. An das Auswärtige Amt. Berlin. 5 Jan. 1940 Berlin. AA, R100749; Telegram (geh,. Ch. V.) Salamanca, den 28. November 1937. AA, R100741.
20 Gellately, "The Gestapo and German Society," 654–5.

21 Ibid., 693.

22 Peterson, *Both Sides of the Curtain*, 194; Telegram (geh. Ch. V.). Salamanca,
    den 28. November 1937. AA, R100749. Berlin; Der Reichsführer SS
    und Chef der Deutschen Polizei. Schnellbrief. An das Auswärtige
    Amt – Referat Partei – Berlin. 4 Jun. 1940, AA, R100751; Diplogerma.
    Madrid. Berlin, den 12 Jan.1940, AA, R100741; Telegram (geh,. Ch. V.)
    Salamanca, den 28. November 1937, AA, R100749; Betr.: Entsendung
    deutscher Polizeifachleute. 27. November 1937, AA, R100749. Berlin;
    Bernhard, "Origins of a Fascist Interpol." Bernhard, while in residence
    at the Jack, Joseph and Morton Mandel Center for Advanced Holocaust
    Studies at the US Holocaust Memorial Museum in 2014, conducted
    research on a project titled "Origins of a Fascist Interpol: German Police
    Collaboration with Franco's Regime During and After the Spanish Civil
    War, 1936–1943."

23 Uebersetzung. Spanischer Staat. Diplomatisches Kabinett. Eilig und
    Vertraulich, Verbalnote. Salamanca, den 25. November 1937. AA, R100749.

24 Gollomb, *Armies of Spies*, 65–7.

25 *SchwarzRotbuch-Dokumente*, 111.

26 Burns, *The Nazi Conspiracy in Spain*, 136–40, 157, 163–4.

27 Caron, *Uneasy Asylum*, 262.

28 Burns, *The Nazi Conspiracy in Spain*, 145–6, 150–1.

29 Ibid., 148–50; 156–7.

30 Interrogation Report. Schäfer. Gustav, Karl. Secret. 7. March 1946. 291/117.
    KV 2. 272. London. United Kingdom National Archive, Kew (UKNA).

31 Subject: Spain, December 6, 1941. Political, p. 2. RG 226, entry 194, box 38,
    NARA.

32 Rodríguez González, "El Espionaje Nazi," 217.

33 Franz Lubs. Gestapo chief at Logrono. KV 3. 269, UKNA.

34 Rodríguez González, "El Espionaje Nazi," 218.

35 R. Konnecke. Official German agent attached to the German consulate,
    Bilbao. KV 3. 269, UKNA.

36 19 November 1943. RG 226, entry 108B, box 233, NARA.

37 Barcelona. KV 3, 269, UKNA.

38 Collado Seidel, "España y los agentes alemanes," 436.

39 OSS Interrogation of Berndotto Freiherr von Heyden-Rynsch, 19 June
    1945, RG 226, entry 183, box 7, NARA; also NARA RG 226, entry 190A,
    box 24, Earle Titus interview of Werner Michael Schultz, Madrid, 2
    February 1946.

40 Bond to Chargé d'Affaires, US Embassy, Madrid, 8 August 1946, RG 226,
    entry 190A, box 24, NARA.

41 17 June 1946, RG 226, entry 210, box 34, NARA.

42 Marion Parks to Bond, 'Eva Reports', 12 July 1946, RG 226, entry 210, box 38, NARA.

43 Note, US Embassy Madrid, 11 December 1945, RG 84, entry 3163, box 2, NARA.

44 US Embassy Madrid to State Department, 9 November 1945, RG 84, entry 3162, box 75, NARA.

45 US Embassy Madrid to State Department, 7 March 1946, RG 84, entry 3162, box 97, NARA.

46 Memo. by G.C. Howell, 26 February 1946, RG 226, entry 190A, box 23, NARA.

47 US Embassy Madrid to State Department, 26 June 1945, RG 84 entry 3162, box 73, NARA.

48 Messenger, "'Our Spanish Brothers,'" 61.

49 Memo. by G. C. Howell, 27 February 1946, RG 226, entry 190A, box 23, NARA.

50 US Embassy to State Department, 19 January 1946, RG 84, entry 3162, box 97, NARA.

51 "Note from Recent Haig Reports (Incoming British)", RG 226, entry 127, box 2, NARA.

52 Rothe Report, 16 January 1946, RG 226, entry 210, box 35, NARA.

53 Earle Titus, Madrid to Nelson Park, Barcelona, 18 November 1946, RG 84, entry 3162, box 98, NARA.

54 Harold Rhodes, Commercial Attaché, US Embassy Madrid to Richard Ford, US Consul-General, Barcelona, 21 January 1946, RG 84, entry 3162, box 97, NARA.

55 Memo. by Titus, 11 March 1947. RG 226, entry 190A, box 24, NARA.

56 Ibid.

57 Memo. by Titus, 15 May 1947, RG 226, entry 190A, box 24, NARA.

58 Memo. by Titus, 1 May 1947, RG 226, entry 190A, box 24, NARA.

59 Memo. by Titus, 11 March 1947, RG 226, entry 190A, box 24, NARA

60 Titus to Consulates of the United States in Spain, 8 November 1946, RG 84, entry 3175, box 18, NARA.

61 Howard to Bevin, 19 June 1947, FO 371/67902B, TNA.

62 Memo. by Titus, 15 May 1947, RG 226, entry 190A, box 24, NARA.

63 Memo. by Titus, 30 October 1947, RG 226, entry 190A, box 24, NARA.

64 Memo. by Titus, 12 January 1948, RG 226, entry 190A, box 24, NARA.

65 US Embassy Madrid to State Department, 14 July 1945, RG 84 entry 3162, box 75, NARA.

66 Randall to Wardlaw, 18 September 1947, RG 84, entry 3175, box 22, NARA.

67 Memo. by Titus, 15 May 1947, RG 226, entry 190A, box 24, NARA.

68 Memo. by Titus, 18 November 1947, RG 226, entry 190A, box 24, NARA.

69 Memo. by Titus, 12 January 1948, RG 226, entry 190A, box 24, NARA.

70 See, for example, the film by Agustí Villarronga *Tras el cristal* (1987), or the novel by Clara Sánchez, *Lo que esconde tu nombre* (2010). Stacey N. Beckwith discusses the latter in chapter 29 of this volume.

71 Memo. by G.C. Howell, 27 February 1946, RG 226, entry 190A, box 23, NARA.

72 Memo. by Titus, 11 March 1947, RG 226, entry 190A, box 24, NARA.

73 Memo. by G.C. Howell, 27 February 1946, RG 226, entry 190A, box 23, NARA.

74 Ibid.

75 Spanish Foreign Ministry to Allied Control Council, July 5, 1948, R/004209/7, Archives du Ministère des Affaires Étrangères, Paris (MAE).

76 Memo. by G.C. Howell, 27 February 1946, RG 226, entry 190A, box 23, NARA.

77 US and UK Embassies to Ministry of Foreign Affairs, Apr. 9, 1946, R 2159/6, MAE.

78 Memo. by G.C. Howell, 27 February 1946, RG 226, entry 190A, box 23, NARA.

79 Ibid.

80 Goñi, *The Real Odessa*, 75.

81 Memo. by Titus, 22 October 1947, RG 226, entry 190A, box 24, NARA.

82 Rolland, *Galicia en guerra*, 159–61.

83 Cantarero, *La huella de la bota*, 23.

84 Ibid., 25–6.

85 Ibid., 47.

86 "Los Lipperheide y la industria petroquimica vasca" CyberEuscadi, 5 January 2009 https://ganazia.com/lipperheide, accessed 14 May 2019).

87 Puig, "La Conexión Alemana," 7.

88 Agent 23715/C to 23700, 4 December 1945, RG 226, entry 127, box 2, NARA.

89 Lipperhedie to Hawley, 4 February 1946, and Hawley Memo of conversation with Lipperheide, 29 January 1946, RG 84, entry 3175, box 18, NARA.

90 Puig Raposo and Alvaro Moya, "Misión Imposible?"

91 See Isabel Estrada's treatment of the documentary *Hafners Paradies* about just one such "thriving" former Nazi in Spain in chapter 28 of this volume.

PART EIGHT

The Holocaust in Contemporary Spanish and Ladino Culture

27 Memory and the Ethical Imagination: The Holocaust and Deportation to Mauthausen in Twenty-First-Century Spanish Theatre

MARILÉN LOYOLA

Chaim Kaplan wrote the following in his diary on 2 November 1940, two years before perishing in the Treblinka death camp: "I will write a scroll of agony in order to remember the past in the future."[1] Kaplan's determination had less to do with his own survival than it did with the survival of the memory of the horror he was witnessing. It was memory's erasure in the future that Kaplan's "scroll of agony" was resisting. Theatre has a similar capacity "to remember the past in the future" in that it hinges on spectators' imaginations and on their complicity in the lived, performative act of bearing witness. In *Performing European Memories: Trauma, Ethics, Politics* (2013), Milija Gluhovic explains how the goal of mourning and reparations in twentieth-century European theatre that addresses experiences of genocide, forced displacement, and mass incarceration compels a creative experience of the past that enables new ways for audiences to imagine the future:

> Forcing their audiences to become excavators of these repressed paths, these artworks challenge their audiences' historical imagination and renew their affective engagement with Europe's past ... The main ethical impetus behind their engagement with the past arises from their need to bear witness and to mourn. The work of mourning may never dissolve all melancholy or heal all wounds, but it is to be hoped that it may disclose unrealized possibilities within the past and create new openings for the future.[2]

Concern with how a traumatic past links to the future has particular resonance in Spain's memory politics. Almost eighty years after Spain's Civil War, debates continue to surface over whether to remember, whom to remember, and where and how to stage Spain's acts of remembering.[3] Theatre in Spain has responded to historical shifts regarding how to address the nation's violent recent past with a compelling transition of its own. No longer attached to the realism of historical theatre, playwrights in twenty-first-century Spain have turned especially towards what José Sanchis Sinisterra calls "teatro de la memoria" (theatre of memory), "uno de esos rincones en los que se pretende conjurar el olvido, *revisitar* el pasado para entender un poco más el presente, y quizás para ayudarnos a escoger un futuro ... o incluso para luchar por él" (one of those corners where we can conjure up oblivion, *revisit* the past in order to understand the present better, and perhaps help us choose a future ... or even fight for it).[4]

That theatre circles in twenty-first-century Spain are increasingly promoting historical memory plays indicates a growing refusal within the theatre community to echo the silencing efforts of the Franco era and the post-Franco transition period.[5] Max Aub was the first playwright writing in Spanish to depict the danger facing the Jews on the eve of the Holocaust. A moving example is Aub's *De algún tiempo a esta parte* (*For Some Time Now*, 1939), a post-Anschluss, pre-Second-World-War monologue set in Austria, which Ignacio García directed and Carmen Conesa performed at the Teatro Español in Madrid in early 2016. The year 2016 also saw the production at Madrid's Teatro Real of the children's opera *Brundibár* (libretto by Adolf Hoffmeister, 1938) by Hans Krása, which had been performed by the inmates of Terezín for the Red Cross in 1944 as part of the Nazis' "beautification" campaign. *Himmelweg* (*Camino del cielo*) (*Way to Heaven*, 2004), one of playwright Juan Mayorga's most widely translated and internationally represented plays, derives contextually from this same 1944 Red Cross visit to Terezín.[6] Complementing these Holocaust-themed works in Spain are those that address the memory of the approximately seven thousand Spanish Republicans who fled to France after the Spanish Civil War and were deported to Mauthausen by the Nazis after Franco refused to recognize them as citizens.[7] This chapter explores this turn towards memory in Spanish theatre by analysing the theatrical tools used in three twenty-first-century plays in Spain to address the links between the past, present, and future through the staged exercise of memory and the imagination. The first two plays, *El triángulo azul* (The Blue Triangle, 2014) by Laila Ripoll and Mariano Llorente and *J'attendrai* (I Will Wait, 2017) by José Ramón Fernández, feature Spanish political prisoners who had been deported to the Nazi concentration camp Mauthausen at the beginning of the Second World War, while the third play, Juan Mayorga's *El cartógrafo. Varsovia, 1: 400.000* (The Cartographer: Warsaw, 1: 400,000, 2017), takes place on the grounds of what was the Warsaw Ghetto and deals directly with the Holocaust and its repercussions.[8]

Ripoll and Llorente's *El triángulo azul* was the first play in Spain to represent Spaniards' struggle for survival in Mauthausen in a major national theatre, in April–May 2014 at the Teatro Valle Inclán of the Centro Dramático Nacional (CDN). Ripoll and Llorente's introduction to the play on the CDN's website criticizes Spain's lack of "un triste monolito" (a single sad monument) to remember these victims.[9] Works such as *El triángulo azul* and those discussed in this chapter resist this absence of commemoration by shifting the public discourse towards visibility, mourning, and accountability.[10] *El triángulo azul* takes place in the Mauthausen camp and features a historical figure who recalls his place in the camp and his role in the Spaniards' plight. José Ramón Fernández's *J'attendrai* similarly commemorates the lives of the victims at Mauthausen. The play takes place in present-day France and features characters – one French, one Spanish – who passed through Mauthausen: one survived and the other became a victim of Nazi horror.[11] Engaging a similar dynamic in the context of the Holocaust is Juan Mayorga's *El cartógrafo. Varsovia 1: 400.000.*[12] *El cartógrafo* is structured around two parallel plots that begin at different points in time. One plot begins in present-day Warsaw, where a Spanish diplomat's wife perceives the absence of the Holocaust past on Warsaw's city streets and proceeds to map it. The other begins in the Holocaust-era Warsaw Ghetto, where an aging cartographer teaches his young granddaughter the art of map-making.

These three works are by no means exhaustive of plays in Spain that address the Holocaust and Nazi repression, nor are they comprehensive of each author's memory or historical theatre, but they do share one key element. Beyond their common thematic thread, each play collapses the distance between two moments in time. In all three plays, characters from the past or present venture into a different time period, whether through their imaginations, physically, metaphorically, or as the ghosts of their former selves, and are compelled to engage the past through a sense of justice.[13] Through these imaginative, temporal devices, these plays perform a theatrical convergence of memory and what I refer to as the ethical imagination. I define the ethical imagination as the intellectual and visual mechanism used by the remembering subject who, in response to ascertaining past atrocity and injustice, employs creative and performative means of seeing the past and calling for accountability. Far from eroding memory, the ethical imagination in the following works complements and even nurtures the performance of bearing witness, working, much like Chaim Kaplan's "scroll of agony," to resist oblivion and "remember the past in the future."

Memory, Performance, and the Ethical Imagination

In *The Fantastic: A Structural Approach to a Literary Language* (1975), Tzvetan Todorov argues that the fantastic in literature works to occupy the space of incomprehension when what has occurred in the lives of characters defies the laws that rule the familiar world.[14] He identifies two possibilities. The person who has experienced the incomprehensible event is either "the victim of an illusion of the senses, of a product of the imagination – and the laws of the world then remain what they are; or else the event has indeed taken place, it is an integral part of reality – but then this reality is controlled by laws unknown to us."[15] The relevance of this distinction for the performance of the memory of atrocity is twofold. Theatre allows for the fantastical to coexist with reality – for the past, the present, and the future to mingle on a single stage, and for the living and the dead to engage in dialogue in the theatrical present. But when it comes to the performance of an unthinkable, traumatic past, the relevance runs deeper. Freddie Rokem suggests that atrocities such as those committed during the Holocaust exemplify Todorov's second possibility:

> Testimonies of survival from the Holocaust, as they have been represented on stage and screen, communicate the sense that the victims in the ghettos and in the camps were living in a world controlled by laws unknown or incomprehensible to them. This in turn implies that their testimonies must also be viewed as expressions of the fantastic, a position which these performances in different ways also attempt to reproduce in their relationship to the spectator-participants.[16]

In the plays discussed here, present-day characters who face the memory of Nazi atrocities and its victims do so by imagining time and space as if they were governed by an alternate set of laws, in this case, made extraordinary through theatre. These same characters question and demand accountability for the past in the present, thus fostering commemoration and mourning and paving the way for an imagined future in which the victims of the Holocaust and the Nazi cruelties at Mauthausen will never be forgotten.

El triángulo azul (2014) by Laila Ripoll and Mariano Llorente

El triángulo azul is set in two places and two periods of time: in Mauthausen during the Second World War and in Cologne, Germany, in 1965. The latter is the year from which Paul Ricken, the real-life SS photographer who managed the photography lab in Mauthausen, narrates his recollections of the events he witnessed in the camp and his role in them. The play fluidly shifts between locations and time periods, sometimes overlapping them simultaneously and with little if any change of scenery. *El triángulo azul* opens in 1965 with Ricken speaking into a microphone attached to a cassette player. He addresses his children and the future, confessing that he had supported the Nazis' horrifying, murderous campaign of extermination:

> Sé, ahora lo sé, que nada me disculpa, que mi sacrificio nunca será entendido, que vosotros, queridos hijos, a los que he procurado alejar del horror y la barbarie, jamás comprenderéis cómo vuestro padre, vuestro amoroso padre, pudo participar en esa orgía de sangre.

> I know, I now know, that nothing justifies my actions, that my sacrifice will never be understood, and that you, my dear children, whom I have tried to protect from horror and barbarism, will never understand how your father, your loving father, could have participated in that orgy of blood.[17]

In his confessional account, Ricken uses his memories to venture into the past and account for his inaction. While he retells the story of what he did and didn't do and why, Ricken also marks the point of incomprehension in Todorov's sense, where he cannot explain further and his children will never understand. Ricken's character exists in 1965 – his present day – but he also circulates through the scenes in the play that take place in Mauthausen between 1940 and 1945, invisible to the other characters and observing the horror he witnessed as though through a new, ethical lens.

Among the scenes juxtaposed with the play's concentration camp setting are playful musical interludes performed by cabaret musicians, singers, and dancers. These are both funny and grotesque, a performative irony that is purposefully shocking for spectators, who may not know that in the Nazi concentration camps such as Mauthausen and Terezín (known by the Nazis as Theresienstadt), music and performance played a vital role beyond entertainment.[18] As director Raina Ames writes: "Art has the power to transform lives, but in Terezín the arts were a mode of survival."[19] In *El triángulo azul*, there is a catchy, playful dialogue about death that takes place between the nameless prisoners, the same ones who sing in the cabaret. Prisoner #3 confidently asserts: "La calavera es el muerto y la cara es la muerte y lo que llamáis morir es acabar de morir y lo que llamáis vivir es morir viviendo. En este lugar hay tantas muertes como personas. ¿Qué miras?" (The skull is the dead man and the face is death and what you call dying is to finish dying and what you call living is to die while alive. In this place, there are as many deaths as there are people. What are you looking at?).[20] In their spirited singing and dancing, the prisoners survive for the moment but seem to anticipate and, as if through a kind of tragic irony, perform their own living death sentences.

As resident SS photographer of the Mauthausen camp, Ricken's work required him to observe, witness, and capture with his camera any prisoner and SS activities. But above all he had to protect the images themselves, making only the prescribed number of copies of each photograph. In the camp's photography lab are two Spaniards, Toni and Paco, who challenge Ricken's ability to carry out his duties. Toni is an older, more seasoned prisoner, intolerant of the young and precocious Paco, a new arrival at the camp. Paco yearns to see and understand the horror that surrounds them and at the same time questions all that Toni strives to teach him. In the 2014 CDN performance, when Paco impulsively jumps up on a ledge to investigate through a small window the shooting sounds of an execution, Toni harshly warns: "Está terminamente prohibido mirar" (Looking is strictly prohibited).[21] Spectators may recognize that Paco's character represents Catalan prisoner/resister and photographer Francesc Boix, who smuggled nearly twenty thousand negatives out of Mauthausen, at the risk of death. (See chapters 14, 15, 17, and 28 for more on Boix.)[22] Boix, along with a few helpers including Antoni Garcia, on whom Toni's character is based, managed to preserve negatives that would later, during the Nuremberg Trials, provide critically important evidence of the Nazis' crimes. In *El triángulo azul*, Paco is aloof, deceptively jovial, and mildly annoying, so that spectators only gradually realize that he is engaged in a perilous, high-stakes operation that involves making and hiding one additional copy of each photograph, then successfully smuggling them all out of the camp. Paco's ethical imagination comes through in his capacity to conceive of what could happen without this proof – as he tells the young Yugoslavan woman Oana, a camp prostitute: "Si sale bien nunca podrán negar lo que sabemos que van a negar. Todo, todas las atrocidades que han hecho, los asesinatos ... todo está en ese paquete" (If everything goes well, they will never be able to deny what we know they'll deny. Everything, all the atrocities they've committed, the executions ... everything is in that package).[23]

In the play's final moments, after a monologue reflecting on what he witnessed but neglected to act upon, the 1965 Ricken asks one of the singing and dancing Spaniards, "¿Qué va a ser de mí? ¿Qué va a ser de nosotros? Español, ¿qué es lo que nos espera?" (What will happen to me? What will happen to us? Spaniard, what awaits us?), to which the prisoner responds, almost jubilantly, "Para ustedes la noche. Y para nosotros, el día" (For you, the night. And for us, the day).[24] Thirty seconds later and still onstage, Ricken shoots himself in the head. With the sound of Ricken's pistol, the music ends and the curtain falls. The play's unlikely encounter between 1940–5 and 1965 culminates in this final scene, in which the Ricken of the 1960s is no longer an invisible bystander to the concentration camp prisoners onstage, but rather a living memory who must account for his refusal to act ethically in the face of the horror of which he formed an integral part. Ricken's only recourse is to condemn himself before the eyes of the camp prisoners who had feared him, before the ears of his children, and before the spectators.[25]

J'attendrai (2017) by José Ramón Fernández

José Ramón Fernández's *J'attendrai* takes its title from the French *chanson* recorded by Rina Ketty in 1938, popularized during the Second World War and often played by the Nazis in the concentration camps to accompany their most atrocious executions.[26] The lyrics allude to the longing associated with waiting for someone who will never return and to the experience of mourning in that person's absence. Fernández's appropriation of this song in *J'attendrai* recasts it in terms of the present day (as he specifies, sometime between 2005 and 2010), drawing audiences into this same performative waiting and mourning while looking to the past. In *J'attendrai*, the encounter between past and present happens in part through the fantastical onstage presence of two ghosts, Claude ("el Pájaro") and Patricia, and through an encounter between Claude and Pepe ("el Gafas"), an octogenarian Spaniard who had survived Mauthausen. Claude, a young French soldier killed in Mauthausen, appears as a ghost dressed in a tattered concentration camp uniform with the letter F sewn onto a red triangle patch that identified him as part of the French Resistance. In 1937, prior to being detained and sent to Mauthausen, Claude had fallen in love with Patricia at a village dance shortly after she arrived in La Rochelle, France, after fleeing the Spanish Civil War. Patricia lived to old age, still longing and waiting for Claude to return from the war.[27] During the play, Claude is invisible to all except Patricia and eventually Pepe, who initially senses but is not entirely conscious of Claude's presence until, in the final scenes, Pepe is able to see and talk to him. The play opens with Pepe and his grandson arriving at an inn in rural France run by Claire, Patricia's middle-aged granddaughter, who has inherited the letters and mementos that tell most of the love story between her grandmother and Claude. Pepe's grandson, the French-born Vincent, is a young man in his twenties who is largely unaware of what his grand-father had suffered in Mauthausen. Vincent reacts with annoyance at his grandfather's insistence that they stop at what seems to him a random inn on their way to a Mauthausen memorial event in Paris.

The play culminates in a theatrical collapsing of time and memories. First, Pepe and Claude re-enact the moment of their first encounter at Mauthausen, revealing to the audience how Pepe had offered to take Claude under his wing by "training" him to be a metalworker as a means of survival.[28] Then the living (Pepe) and the dead (Claude) finally meet in the present day and account for all the painful experiences in and after Mauthausen that both separate and unite them.[29] This unlikely encounter between the living and the dead, however, produces another quite necessary one between Pepe and Vincent, in which Pepe recognizes the fear and guilt that he feels as a survivor and finally tells his grandson the story of what he lived through.[30] When Claude interrupts Pepe, goading him to tell his stories in more detail, Pepe responds only to Claude: "Pero yo no tengo fuerzas para recordar esas cosas. Ya no tengo fuerzas para recordar" (But I don't have the strength to remember those things. I no longer have the strength to remember), to which Vincent responds, "No hace falta que me cuentes nada. He visto mucho ya. He visto miles de fotos" (There is no need for you to tell me anything. I have seen a lot already. I have seen thousands of photos).[31] Except, of course, that Vincent does need his grandfather's testimony. Vincent cannot truly understand what his grandfather experienced except through the old man's stories. A similar moment of realization occurs when Pepe reveals to Claire that, while in Mauthausen, he had befriended Claude, the love of her grandmother's life. Pepe explains to Claire that he had seen the Nazis hang Claude in the central plaza of Mauthausen as punishment for his attempt to escape, and that during the execution, the musical strains of "J'attendrai" rang through the camp.

In a fascinating dynamic of authorial imagination, however, Fernández includes one additional character – a fragmented, semi-autobiographical, authorial Yo who performs before audiences in multiple voices, all emerging from the ambivalence the playwright experienced while writing the play.[32] This voiced Yo appears interspersed in periodic *stasimos* that break the onstage action, allowing for Yo to speak directly to the audience. Fernández has a personal link to this plot – as one Yo describes it, the author's uncle, Miguel Barberán, had survived Mauthausen, but this authorial Yo had never been bold enough to ask his uncle about it directly.[33] Fernández indicates in his stage direction that Yo can be played by one actor or by several, by the living characters already onstage or even by audience members.[34] By opening the character of Yo to any combination of actors, Fernández creates a theatrical voice that speaks the lines and intentions of many, including contemporary audiences. Yo gives voice to his/her/their/our ethical imagination, demanding, as he does repeatedly, that the horrors his uncle and others experienced in Mauthausen never be forgotten.[35] After years of research and a mustering of bravery, it is Yo's ethical imagination that ultimately writes and "remembers" this past, imagining through the creation of these characters a sort of meeting of memories – those memories that both link the survivors of Mauthausen and separate them from its victims, and the older generations from the younger. The encounters between Pepe and modern-day characters Claire and Vincent establish a bridge to the future, leaving spectators with a sense that both Mauthausen's survivors *and* its victims demand that future generations be aware of and never forget what happened there. As the authorial Yo asserts:

> Si la obra que escribo vale la pena como literatura, como arte, será leída dentro de veinte años, cuando yo ya esté muerto, cuando los hijos de esos españoles de Mauthausen sean ancianos o hayan dejado de existir ... Porque eso servirá para algo. Servirá para que un espectador que se emocione con esta pequeña historia de amor busque en los libros. Para que un espectador no se olvide de aquellos locos españoles del triángulo azul.

> If the play that I write is worth anything as literature, as art, it will be read in twenty years, when I am already dead, when the children of the Spaniards of Mauthausen are old or have ceased to exist ... Because then this play will serve a purpose. It will serve its purpose if there is a spectator who, moved by this small love story, goes searching in books; if there is a spectator who does not forget those crazy Spaniards of the blue triangle.[36]

The encounters between Pepe and the ghosts and Pepe and the younger generation, together with the interspersed ponderings of the authorial Yo of the *stasimos*, are extraordinary theatrical tools. Both Yo and Pepe use their ethical imaginations to push through the terrible pain of silence, resist oblivion, and commit to transmitting a collective Spanish memory of Nazi persecution and terror.

El cartógrafo. Varsovia, 1: 400.000 (2017) by **Juan Mayorga**

Over the course of four years, four hundred thousand Jews died behind the ten-foot walls of the Warsaw Ghetto, the vast majority from starvation, disease, execution, or deportation to Treblinka. In *El cartógrafo. Varsovia, 1:*

400.000, Mayorga constructs the act of map-making as a mode of urgent, ethical seeing necessitated by the invisibility, danger, and concealment that made the Holocaust possible. In their introduction to *A Thousand Plateaus: Capitalism and Schizophrenia* (1987), Gilles Deleuze and Félix Guattari examine the rhizome as a metaphor for a meaningful engagement with reality, one whose closest tangible manifestation is maps. In their words, a map is "open and connectable in all its dimensions; it is detachable, reversible, susceptible to constant modification. It can be torn, reversed, adapted to any kind of mounting, and reworked by an individual, group or social formation. It can be drawn on a wall, conceived of as a work of art, constructed as political action or as a meditation."[37] In *El cartógrafo,* maps are useful precisely because they are unconventional, have multiple entry points, change over time, and represent something other than what is visible, but also because they do things. As the aging cartographer in this play insists, "¡Cuántas catástrofes han comenzado con un mapa! Buenos tiempos para el cartógrafo, tiempos difíciles para la humanidad" (So many catastrophes have begun with a map! Good times for the cartographer, difficult times for humanity).[38]

El cartógrafo opens in present-day Warsaw, where a Spanish couple, Blanca and her husband Raúl, are discussing why Blanca missed Raúl's diplomatic event at the embassy. She explains that she had become distracted on her walk and, curious, entered an old synagogue where workers were preparing an exhibit of Holocaust-era photographs. Each image had a caption specifying the street and location where it was taken. Intrigued, Blanca marked each photo's location on her map and ventured into Warsaw's streets to reproduce the photographer's tracks. On her walk, Blanca sees some small monuments or plaques as well as a museum commemorating the history of Polish Jews. Overall, however, there is little sign of former Jewish life, and she is struck by the erasure and absence of this past.[39] Realizing that their apartment is within what were once the ghetto's walls, Blanca decides she will draw a map each day onto the area's sidewalks, much like the detective who draws white chalk lines to outline the now absent body of a cadaver, the circumstances of whose death he or she must reconstruct by working back from the present. Blanca's dynamic, determined engagement with the past frames Mayorga's play as a moving, fluid map of the imagination. Driving her search is the local legend of an old cartographer who, too frail to do so himself, taught his granddaughter how to survey the ghetto undetected. Among the most important lessons he had taught her was that a good cartographer only includes what is most essential: "¿Qué es lo importante cuando hay cuatrocientos mil vidas en peligro? Sal a la calle y pregúntate qué debe ser recordado. Serás tú quien salve o condene. En eso yo no voy a ayudarte." (What is important when there are four hundred thousand lives in danger? Go out there and ask yourself what you must remember. You will be the one to save or condemn. In that, I will not help you).[40]

In the January–February 2017 performances of *El cartógrafo* at the Las Naves del Español/Matadero de Madrid theatre, Mayorga directed his two actors, Blanca Portillo and José Luis García-Pérez, to play the roles of all the characters in the play, whether living in the present or the past and whether young or old. Blanca Portillo played Blanca, the modern-day adult character, and at the same time played the little girl, looking wide-eyed at her grandfather while learning and practising his sobering lessons and looking more deeply into the horrors surrounding them in the ghetto. Similarly, actor José Luis García-Pérez moved fluidly between playing the aging cartographer, a modern-day diplomat, Blanca's husband Raúl, and an archivist or a cartographer's supervisor in the intervening years. This strategy has an effect similar to the Yo in Fernández's *J'attendrai*, wherein one actor performs two or more time periods or characters, a technique that invites spectators to participate in a theatrical convergence between the past and the present in a single space and moment. Like Blanca, spectators are compelled to look beyond what is immediately visible and to consider the danger, violence, and fear within the space that a map of atrocity can represent. With the help of the audience's imagination and her grandfather's guidance, the little girl creates an unconventional map in the air that is invisible onstage but nevertheless intended to serve and warn future generations confronted with other human catastrophes.[41]

In the play's final scenes, Blanca makes contact with Deborah, a retired cartographer. Blanca suspects that Deborah is the now-adult granddaughter whom spectators have observed in previous scenes as she evolves through her adult life. By the time Blanca meets her, the audience knows that Deborah has established a career of making maps that strategically undermine regimes bent on controlling information and imposing their "truths" at the expense of the innocent. In a final encounter with Blanca, Deborah initially denies but in her final monologue reveals that she is indeed the little girl from the legend of the old cartographer in the ghetto. As they prepare to take a walk, Deborah explains:

Camino haciendo memoria, como si luego tuviese que contar lo que veo a alguien que me espera. La gente me mira mal, el que camina despacio y mirando es sospechoso. Tengo tiempo, todo el tiempo del mundo, pude morir a los diez años. Nunca voy derecho, avanzo y retrocedo, doy vueltas alrededor, miro el lugar a distintas horas, intento recordar qué hubo antes allí. Desconfía de tus ojos, lo que tus ojos ven oculta cosas. Quédate quieta mientras todo se mueve, échate a un lado, échate atrás. No basta mirar, hay que hacer memoria, lo más difícil de ver es el tiempo. Si te fijas, verás señales a punto de perderse.

While I walk, I make memory, as if later I had to recount what I have seen to someone who is waiting for me. People give me strange looks. Someone who walks too slowly while looking around is always suspect. I have time, all the time in the world. I could have died when I was ten. I never go straight. I go forward and I go back, I take turns and go in circles. I see the same place at different times of day. I try to remember what was there before. Don't trust your eyes; what your eyes see hides things. Stay still while everything moves, move to the side, move back. It is not enough to see – you have to make memory. The most difficult thing to see is time. If you notice, you will see signs about to disappear.[42]

With this, Deborah offers Blanca her method of creating maps as an exercise of the imagination that allows her to bridge the past, present, and future. This conflation of timescapes mimics the method that Blanca had exercised throughout the play to understand her own painful past and to make visible the memory of the Holocaust in present-day Warsaw. Near the end of the 2017 stage production of *El cartógrafo* in Madrid, Blanca and Raúl outlined each other's bodies on the black stage using wide white tape, leaving an empty, outlined image of each – a map of absence, a "Cartografía de la ausencia," as the title of Deborah's book reads. This visual exercise compels audiences to imagine the space of pain and loss ethically. In order to "see" what these maps communicate, spectators must question and investigate the past guided by a sense of justice similar to Blanca's. They must learn to see through the lens of their ethical imagination just as the old cartographer taught his granddaughter to see. Only then will no one forget.

Conclusion

In her posthumous *Our Faithfulness to the Past: The Ethics and Politics of Memory* (2014), philosopher Sue Campbell argued that sharing memory is fundamental to our interrelatedness – what she has called "relational remembering" (2003).[43] "Sharing memory is our default," writes Campbell:

When we are silent about our pasts, when memory is guarded, protected, too traumatized to be articulable, without resources for expression, or privately treasured, these experiences have some of their meaning in relation to our natural habit of sharing the past ... Where I look for memory, I find relation and its influence on an ever-shifting sense of individual and communal pasts and identities.[44]

El triángulo azul, J'attendrai, and *El cartógrafo* perform a sharing of memory through the theatrical encounter between the past and the present as well as the characters' insistence that future generations remember past victims' suffering. The ethical imagination emerges as a performative tool for characters to bear witness to the past and mourn its victims, but also to creatively resist the disappearance of memory. Cathy Caruth writes that bearing witness to a traumatic past takes on the destruction of the memory itself – that the remembering subject encounters "a history constituted *by the erasure of its own witness,* a history that burns away the very possibility of *conceiving* memory, that leaves the future itself, in ashes" (italics in the original).[45] In Ripoll and Llorente's *El triángulo azul,* Ricken's ethical imagination compels him to leave his children with the truth of his actions and to venture back in his memory to a Mauthausen in which he demands his own accountability. Similarly, the authorial Yo of Fernández's *J'attendrai,* struggling to tell an impossibly difficult story, creates the characters Pepe and Claude, who use their imaginations to reveal their painful experiences of the past to each other and the next generation. Their stories work to heal and bridge the decades of loss and misunderstanding that had separated them. And it is the ethical imagination in Mayorga's *El cartógrafo* that allows Deborah, Blanca, and eventually Raúl to see and imagine a different, more humane and compassionate map of the past, one that might one day save lives, even perhaps their own. Far from heralding memory's erasure or destruction, these works insist on the infinite creative capacity of the ethical imagination, memory's means of living and breathing amidst the ashes.

NOTES

1 Kaplan, *Scroll of Agony,* 218.

2 Gluhovic, *Performing European Memories,* 2.

3 For more on contemporary memory politics, see Amago and Jerez-Farrán, eds., *Unearthing Franco's Legacy;* and Fernández Aguilar and Payne, *Revealing New Truths.*

4 Sanchis Sinisterra, "Una propuesta del autor," in *Terror y miseria en el primer franquismo,* 187–8. All translations in this essay are mine unless otherwise indicated. On historical memory in Spanish theatre, see Avilés-Diz, "Fosas de la identidad perdida"; Rimoldi, "De memoria histórica"; Boukraa, *Teatro español y memoria histórica;* Floeck, "Del drama histórico," 189–207.

5 Aub, *De algún tiempo a esta parte*, in *Tres monólogos y uno solo verdadero*. Aub's classic Jewish tragedy, *San Juan. Una tragedia*, was at the Centro Dramático Nacional in 1998 (dir. Juan Carlos Pérez de la Fuente). On Aub, see Alonso, ed., *Actas del congreso internacional*; Aznar Soler, *Los laberintos del exilio*; and Doménech, *"De algún tiempo a esta parte: El comienzo;"* 9–10.

6 Mayorga, *Himmelweg (Camino del cielo). Himmelweg* debuted in Madrid at the Teatro María Guerrero on 18 November 2004 (dir. Antoni Simón). Raimon Molins directed its most recent Madrid production in February–March 2017 at the Teatro Fernán Gómez. On *Himmelweg,* see Aznar Soler, "Memoria, metateatro y mentira"; and Francisco Rodó, "El tiempo de los vencidos."

7 See chapters 11, 14, and 15 in this volume on Mauthausen.

8 Llorente and Ripoll, *El triángulo azul*; Fernández, *J'attendrai*; Mayorga, *El cartógrafo.*

9 See *El triángulo azul* and its April–May 2014 production at the Centro Dramático Nacional. Please visit the play's dossier: http://cdn.mcu.es/ wp-content/uploads/2014/03/DOSIER-triangulo-azul.pdf, 3.

10 See Brenneis, *Spaniards in Mauthausen.*

11 *J'attendrai* enjoyed both a dramatic reading and a full-length onstage production in 2015 and 2016 at the Téâtre de l'Horizon in La Rochelle, France. *J'attendrai*'s publication (Alupa Editorial, 2017) coincided with the first dramatic reading of the play in Spain in November 2017 for the XXI Ciclo SGAE Lecturas Dramatizadas, a festival of contemporary theatre held at the Sala Berlanga in Madrid.

12 *El cartógrafo* had its first full onstage production in November 2016 at the Teatro Calderón in Valladolid, Spain, followed by a full run in January–February 2017 at the Naves del Español's Sala Fernando Arrabal in Madrid, with Mayorga as director.On cartography in Mayorga's theatre, see Brizuela, "Una cartografía teatral"; Colombo, "La memoria en el espacio"; and Alberto Sucasas, "Cartografía teatral," in Mayorga, *El cartógrafo,* 107–28. Mayorga's other Second World War– and Holocaust–themed works include short plays and adaptations such as "Job (A partir del Libro de Job ...)"; "JK" and "Wstawac: Homenaje a Primo Levi." On the Holocaust in Mayorga's works, see Floeck, "Die Shoah im Zeitalter der Globalisierung."

13 For Mayorga, "esa anulación del tiempo representa en sí misma la idea de que los hombres somos contemporáneos: más allá de la condición histórica hay la condición humana, la humanidad" (that annulment of time represents in itself the idea that we humans are contemporaneous: beyond the historical condition is the human condition, humanity). "La representación teatral del Holocausto," 165.

14 Todorov, *The Fantastic*, 25.

15 Ibid.

16 Rokem, "On the Fantastic in Holocaust Performances," 43–4.

17 Llorente and Ripoll, *El triángulo azul*, 19.

18 See Fialdini Zambrano, "*El triángulo azul*"; García-Pascual, "Francoist Repression," 439–68.

19 Qtd in Humphries Mardirosian, "Giving Voice to the Silenced," 263. See also Rovit, "Cultural Ghettoization and Theater"; Roig, *Els catalans als camps nazis*.

20 Llorente and Ripoll, *El triángulo azul*, 31.

21 Ibid., 40.

22 Bermejo, *Francisco Boix*. On Boix, see Herrmann, "Camera Caedens, Camera Vindex"; and Brenneis, *Spaniards in Mauthausen*, 59–76.

23 Llorente and Ripoll, *El triángulo azul*, 106.

24 Ibid., 124. These lines, a slight variation of the published version, were taken from the video-recorded on-stage performance of *El triángulo azul* that took place on 13 May 2014.

25 Ricken's suicide in the play is apocryphal: in actuality, he died uneventfully in 1964 (Rubio, Colombo, and Landa, *El fotógrafo de Mauthausen*, 140).

26 Fernández, *J'attendrai*, 77.

27 Ibid., 21–2.

28 Ibid., 55–7.

29 Ibid., 62–7.

30 Ibid., 69.

31 Ibid., 72.

32 Fernández explains he owes a literary debt to playwright Tadeusz Kantor for his use of intermittent *stasimos* as a way of speaking directly to the audience. As one Yo reflects: "Si por fin hubiera sido capaz de escribir esta obra; si esto fuera una obra de teatro, podría presentar un personaje que se llamase Yo y que dijera todas estas cosas. Es algo sencillo y ya no es original. Es un recurso que se encuentra en Tadeusz Kantor" (If I had finally been capable of writing this play; if this were a play, I could present a character named Yo who would say all of these things. It is something simple and no longer original. It is a strategy found in Tadeusz Kantor) (34). See Romanska, *The Post-traumatic Theatre*.

33 Fernández, *J'attendrai*, 26–7.

34 Ibid., 17.

35 Ibid., 8.

36 Ibid., 95.

37 Deleuze and Guattari, *A Thousand Plateaus*, 12.

38 Mayorga, *El cartógrafo*, 28.

39 Ibid., 15.
40 Ibid., 44.
41 Ibid., 49. On the strategies of Jewish artists to hide their work or conceal messages, see Roth, "On Seeing the Invisible Dimensions."
42 Mayorga, *El cartógrafo,* 101.
43 Campbell, *Our Faithfulness to the Past;* idem, *Relational Remembering.*
44 Campbell, *Our Faithfulness,* 3.
45 Caruth, *Literature in the Ashes of History,* 81.

28 Audiovisual Production on the Republican Deportation and Spain as Haven of the Nazis

ISABEL ESTRADA

The audiovisual production that engages with historical links between Spain, the deportation of Spaniards to Nazi camps, and the Holocaust has to be understood in the context of the so-called *recuperación de la memoria histórica* since the mid-1990s.[1] Documentary film and investigative reports broadcast on television have raised public awareness of the traumatic experience of the Spanish Civil War and the Francoist dictatorship. This body of work has embraced the mission of civic associations – such as the Asociación para la Recuperación de la Memoria Histórica – that have demanded reparations for the war's victims and for those who suffered repression under the dictatorship. These documentary films include Javier Corcuera's *La guerrilla de la memoria* (The Guerrilla of Memory, 2001), Manuel Palacios's *Rejas en la memoria* (Prison Bars in Memory, 2004), Mercedes Álvarez's *El cielo gira* (The Sky Turns, 2004), and *El tren de la memoria* (The Train of Memory, 2005) by Marta Arribas and Ana Pérez, as well as the controversial *Memoria de España* (Memory of Spain, Fernando García de Cortázar 2004, TVE), *La memoria recobrada. Una mirada crítica de nuestro pasado más reciente* (Recovered Memory: A Critical Look toward the Past, Alfonso Domingo 2006, TVE), and Almudena Carracedo and Robert Behar's Goya award winning documentary, *El silencio de otros (The Silence of Others,* 2018).

The urgency to recover the memory of Republican prisoners who died in concentration camps has been echoed in a number of investigative documentaries made for television. The recuperation of victims' memories is accomplished mostly by giving voice to the survivors as a collectivity, thus embracing Theodor W. Adorno's contention that victims' testimony is necessary for a full comprehension of past events.[2] A key element of documentary production that informs the recuperation of memory is the testimony of the victims, particularly as the number of survivors rapidly decreases. Those testimonies become invaluable for their informative quality and also – indeed, most importantly – because oral history brings recognition to those who were stripped of their identity and dignity in Nazi camps.

These televisual reports focus on the victims' testimony, with the interviewers usually situated off-screen and the interviewees filmed mainly in interior spaces. The role of the voice-over narration is to link the archival images to the testimonies. In terms of sheer volume, the Spanish production is modest compared to the audiovisual production on the Holocaust in Germany, France, and Italy.[3] Although Spain lacks works with the evocative power and poetry of Alain Resnais's *Nuit et brouillard* (Night and Fog, 1955) or the complexity and depth of Claude Lanzmann's *Shoah* (1985), the investigative reports broadcast on regional and national television have participated in the debate on historical memory by raising public awareness.[4]

Catalan investigative reporters Montse Armengou and Ricard Belis have produced a significant body of work that has brought to light the deportation of Spanish Republicans. This chapter begins by providing an overview of their most relevant reports on Spain and the Nazi terror – specifically, their groundbreaking *El comboi dels 927* (The Train with 927 Passengers, 2004), which focuses on the train that carried 927 exiled Spanish Republicans from Angoulême in the south of France to Mauthausen, and *Ravensbrück. L'infern de les dones* (Ravensbrück: Women's Hell, 2005), a collection of testimonies by women of several nationalities who were imprisoned in that Nazi camp for women. The analysis then turns to examine two documentaries that depart from the dominant focus on collective victimhood by honing in on individual figures instead: *Francisco Boix, un fotógrafo en el infierno* (Francisco Boix, a Photographer in Hell), directed by Llorenç Soler in 2004, and *Hafners Paradies* (Hafner's Paradise) directed by Günter Schwaiger in 2007. While approaches that focus on collective victimhood have led to much-needed progress in recognizing the survivors, this chapter ultimately argues that Soler's and Schwaiger's documentaries demonstrate that historical memory is far from being a closed chapter in Spain and that the documentary genre remains a vital site for the ongoing contestation of Spain's past.

Armengou and Belis's collaboration for the Catalan regional television station TV3 since the late 1990s has resulted in several pioneering reports in which they have taken up the moral duty of telling the stories of Republican exiles whose lives ended in Nazi camps. While the journey of Republican exiles such as the poet Rafael Alberti and the communist leader Dolores Ibárruri was widely known, the dark fate of thousands of exiles had remained largely unrecognized by the general public. The average educated Spaniard may know that the poet Antonio

Machado died of natural causes shortly after crossing the French border in 1939, but very few are likely to realize that as many as ten thousand Republican exiles died between 1942 and 1945 as a result of Nazi Germany's occupation of southern France. As discussed in detail in the chapters in Section IV of this book, some Spaniards were taken prisoner while in French refugee camps, or while members of forced labour units, or after they had joined the French Resistance. Once in the hands of Nazi Germany, thousands of them met their death at camps in Mauthausen, Buchenwald, Ravensbrück, and Flossenbürg, among others.

The report *El comboi dels 927* makes the claim that the train that took 927 exiled Spanish Republicans from Angoulême in the south of France to Mauthausen was the first of the "death trains" that transported civilians from Western Europe to Nazi camps.[5] How, exactly, did more than seven thousand Republican refugees end up in Mauthausen?[6] Armengou and Belis report that in September 1940, Serrano Suñer, Franco's prime minister, sealed their fate by not allowing them to return to Spain, which left them under Nazi control. After the German army occupied the south of France, thousands of exiled Republicans living in refugee camps faced the sudden possibility of German repression. When entire families of refugees at the camp at Les Alliers learned that a train was coming for them, they believed that the French government was returning them to Spain or, perhaps, sending them to Russia. None of them thought they were being taken to Austria, to a camp where at least 90,000 prisoners died.

The structure of the report is simple: a voice-over narrates historical facts, with the visual support of photographs, archival footage, dramatization, and the testimony of several survivors. The testimonies capture the suffering, as well as the experience of death and separation that still brings tears to the eyes of these victims. *El comboi dels 927* thus migrates between two poles over the course of an hour: history and politics. A third, crucial pillar is introduced at the very end, when the survivors Juan Paredes, Ángel Olmedo, Pablo Escribano, and Manuel Huerta openly and harshly criticize the silence in democratic Spain and express the need to honour the Nazis' victims. In doing so, they vindicate their right to participate in the debate about historical memory. By merging the political with the personal, their testimonies bring to light the dual public and private nature of historical memory. By concluding with a political statement, Armengou and Belis take the side of many other audiovisual productions that declare the need to remember; the documentary argues against reports – broadcast mainly on national television – that represent the recuperation of memory as a closed process.[7]

Mauthausen was the destiny for men and teenage boys used as forced labour; women were imprisoned in another camp, Ravensbrück, near Berlin. (See chapter 12 by Gina Herrmann.) A year after the broadcast of *El comboi dels 927*, Montse Armengou and Ricard Belis produced another investigative report, *Ravensbrück. L'infern de les dones* (2005). Airing on 1 May 2005, it garnered high ratings, with a 15.5 per cent share representing 413,000 households.[8] This report reviewed the history of thousands of women from Poland, Russia, France, and the Netherlands who were forced to work for Siemens and other factories, primarily in munitions fabrication, in Ravensbrück and its many satellite camps. What was not well known was that the prisoners there included around three hundred Spanish women, Neus Català among them.[9] Català (6 October 1915–13 April 2019) had been captured by the SS after she joined the French Resistance. The report's structure resembles that of *El comboi dels 927*, with one significant difference: it opens with six testimonies unmediated by the voice-over, thus placing the women front and centre. These survivors, women from diverse nationalities, religions, and ethnicities, attest to the indiscriminate nature of the Nazi brutality. They were imprisoned for a number of reasons: they were considered "asocials" (Roma and Sinti), or "work-shy" and "race defilers"; or they had actively resisted the Nazis, professed the faith of the Jehovah's Witnesses, were daughters of single mothers, or had been deported from the Warsaw Ghetto.[10] Their words reveal the horrifying violence to which women and children were subjected, and insofar as these first-person testimonies open the report, they are intended to have a strong impact on the audience.

Of all the on-screen testimonies from the documentaries examined in this chapter, one of the most moving appears in *Ravensbrück. L'infern de les dones*, and it is worth summarizing here. Camp survivor Lise London recalls a nightmare she had after the liberation: the strong wind uncovers the twisted and burnt-out corpse of Micheline, a woman who had given birth in the camp around the same time as Lise had. Micheline rises, addresses Lise defiantly, and asks: "as a survivor, *what are you doing for us, those who will never come back?*" (my emphasis). This is indeed a highly relevant question, one that drives our work as cultural critics. The nightmare turned into an epiphany for Lise, for she realized that she owed it to Micheline to tell her story. The following morning she wrote down the life and death of Micheline. The recuperation of memory responds to Micheline's question: what are we going to do for those who will not come back?

That is the question that filmmakers and investigative reporters have repeatedly posed to their audience. In the context of the women's diverse backgrounds, it draws our attention to the fact that Spain has lagged behind in honouring its own victims of Nazi aggression. As the report was broadcast, Prime Minister Rodríguez Zapatero became the first head of a Spanish government to participate in the commemoration of the liberation, held in Mauthausen in 2005. It was the first time in democratic Spain that a head of state had publicly paid homage, remembering Spaniards who were imprisoned there. Ten thousand Spaniards had ended up in the hands of the Nazi regime, and the recuperation of historical memory could not be accomplished without a public acknowledgment of their experiences.

Ravensbrück. L'infern de les dones originally included the testimony of one male camp survivor, Enric Marco, who at the time was the president of Amical de Mauthausen, a civic organization for the family and friends of the Republican victims of Nazi repression founded in 1962. Marco claimed to have been imprisoned at Flossenbürg, the camp where some women from Ravensbrück were taken and killed. Marco's testimony recounts with the utmost vividness his eyewitness account of the arrival of some of the women. Only two weeks after Armengou's report was broadcast, the historian Benito Bermejo proved that Marco had in fact never been imprisoned in a Nazi camp and that his account was completely fabricated. Armengou explained that her production team immediately eliminated Marco's footage from the report.[11] The collective approach to victimhood was momentarily disrupted by the notoriety of this impostor, whose fabrication may have been prompted by what Cercas calls "la industria de la memoria" (the memory industry)[12] that is, the manipulation of historical memory for political, moral, symbolic, and academic gain and publicity.

The evolution of audiovisual productions relating this history reveals that the debate over how to remember and honour the experiences of Nazi victims remains open, despite agreement about the importance of this recuperative work. The two reports discussed above represent an approach that differs from that of the two additional documentaries that will be analysed. *Francisco Boix, un fotógrafo en el infierno*, directed by Llorenç Soler in 2004, and *Hafners Paradies* by Günter Schwaiger in 2007, focus on two individuals whose characterization will advance our understanding of wartime collective victimhood. The respective journeys of their protagonists take opposite directions: Boix fled Spain to take refuge in France after the Civil War, and Hafner, an SS officer, moved to Spain from his native Germany in 1937 and never returned. Their paths epitomize the historical links between Spain and Europe at the time of the Second World War.[13] Their respective representations as hero and villain serve to indicate that historical memory continues to be a site of contention and that diverging perspectives on the issue remain a constant.

Francisco Boix, a photographer and Republican prisoner in Mauthausen who was forced to work in the camp's identification department and survived to testify at the Nuremberg and Dachau trials, is the subject of the documentary *Francisco Boix, un fotógrafo en el infierno*.[14] Boix is known for having belonged to a resistance group within the camp that clandestinely copied, carefully hid, and later smuggled out of the camp thousands of film negatives shot by the camp SS that detailed the conditions and the terror of camp life and death. The film is heavily informed by a seminal book by the independent historian Benito Bermejo, *El fotógrafo del horror. La historia de Francisco Boix y las fotos robadas a los SS de Mauthausen* (The Photographer of Horror: The Story of Francisco Boix and the Stolen Mauthausen SS Photos), as we will see. Soler, the director of the acclaimed documentary *El largo viaje hacia la ira* (The Long Trip to Anger, 1969), is one of the Spain's most relevant ethnographic documentarians. "Impregnados de realidad social denunciante" (impregnated with social critique), in the words of the critic Joaquim Romaguera,[15] his documentaries blend cinematic form and content and avoid falling into easy dogmatism.

Soler's interest in the Nazi camps was evident before Franco's death in 1975, when he made the short 16 mm documentary *Sobrevivir en Mauthausen* (Surviving in Mauthausen). The filmmaker explained that the camp serves as a metaphor for the silenced, repressed existence of Spaniards both within and beyond the country's borders.[16] His goal was to combine a denunciation of the Nazi terror with a call to action against the Franco regime.[17] Soler produced both *Sobrevivir en Mauthausen* and *Francisco Boix* as responses to two moments in Spain's history – the transition to democracy in the mid-1970s, and the process of recuperation of memory in the mid-1990s – when the deportation was inextricably linked to national politics.

Francisco Boix, un fotógrafo en el infierno opens with a dramatization of a train ride that simultaneously evokes Boix's trip to the Nuremberg Trials and the production team's quest for information on Boix, who had remained virtually unknown to Spanish historians until Bermejo published his meticulous research. This use of the quest as narrative structure has been a defining feature of audiovisual production of Spain's historical memory.[18] The opening section of *Francisco Boix, un fotógrafo en el infierno* shows a fade of one of Boix's self-portraits included in Bermejo's book, that of the young photographer on a train to Paris after the liberation.[19] On his "long trip to anger" of sorts, not on a death train, but in pursuit of information, the voice-over narrator sets out to investigate the journey that took Boix to the witness stand at the Nuremberg Trials. Boix spent his final years in Paris, so the voice-over narrator (José Sacristán) sets the city as the production crew's destination, where they will investigate "los sinuosos laberintos de la memoria de aquellos que lo conocieron" (the sinuous labyrinths of the memory of those who knew him). Soler's goal is to approach history through the eyes of those who knew Boix, "a través de un cristal empañado" (through a fogged-up windowpane). The documentary includes several interviews with acquaintances of Boix, many of whom were also imprisoned in Mauthausen. The stories narrated by these eyewitnesses of the Nazi atrocities need to be preserved, their faces seen and their voices heard. Although Boix is the central figure of the documentary, the testimonies create a dialogic tension between individual and collective victimhood. Through the talking heads, Llorenç Soler aims to understand Francisco Boix's role as a resister who salvaged photographic evidence of the criminality of the camp and as a press photographer who took iconic photographs of the liberation of Mauthausen. At the same time the powerful testimony provided by camp survivors brings the audience to empathize with the suffering of those still able to recount their suffering. Close-up shots of their eyes transport the viewers into the victims' heart of darkness, as seen in figures 28.1 and 28.2.

We have become accustomed to the atrocious images of the concentration camps, but what was the role of photography for the SS? First and foremost, it was to record the activity in the camps and send the results to their superiors in Berlin as evidence that orders were being followed. Gina Herrmann, who has researched the photographs that Boix saved, has stated, "[t]he medium conformed exceptionally to the Third Reich's obsession with meticulous documentation."[20] Yet at the same time, evidence of death in the camps was to be erased by the continuous cremation of the corpses. As Hannah Arendt pointed out: "[A]ll the photographs and newsreels of the concentration camps are misleading because they show the camps at the moment the Allied troops marched in. What makes the images unbearable – the piles of corpses, the skeletal survivors – *was NOT at all typical* for the camps, which, when they were functioning, exterminated their inmates systematically ... then immediately cremated them."[21] That is, the indexical role of photography was limited to internal record-keeping. However, as evidence, the photographic image is stripped of its indexical nature; what was originally intended to serve the oppressors becomes incriminatory in the hands of the oppressed. The documentary suggests that in salvaging the photographs, Boix played an important role in the Nuremberg Trials that has not been sufficiently recognized. By focusing

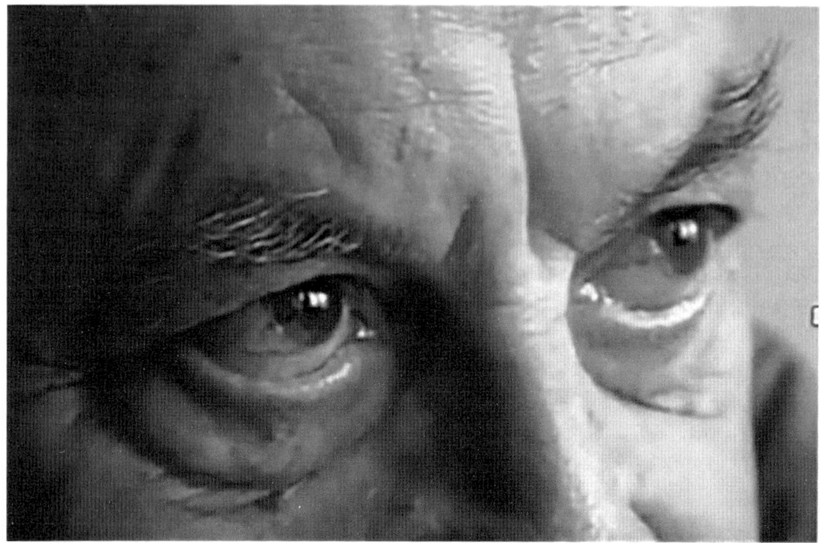

28.1 and 28.2 Stills from *Francisco Boix, un fotógrafo en el infierno* (2004, dir. Llorenç Soler). Reproduced by permission of Llorenç Soler.

on Boix, Soler highlights the contribution one Spaniard made to the process of recuperating the larger historical memory of the Nazi persecution of anti-fascists.

The documentary's concluding section renders the complexity of the camp liberation; a parallel montage of Boix on his way to Paris and the testimonies of other prisoners reveals that they were unable to experience the "liberation" as such. On the one hand, Soler provides shots of Boix and his fellow travellers in open spaces, surrounded by nature, by the river. On the other, the testimony of people like fellow prisoner Pierre Durand who bear the physical and psychological scars of the repression continues to evoke the horror. Once he settled in Paris, Boix identified and classified thousands of photographs, publishing some of them in the Communist magazine *Regards*; so he stated on the witness stand at the Nuremberg Trials. He was hired as a reporter for the Communist publication *L'humanité*; he died from kidney disease when he was only thirty years old.

From our vantage point as researchers of the Spanish Civil War and its complex connections with the Nazis' persecution of political enemies, as well as with the Holocaust, it seems hard to grasp that many of these valuable photographs have been lost. While Soler's documentary does not provide a specific answer, Benito Bermejo explains that some publishers in the United States had made Boix generous offers to purchase the photographs but that he declined, as he thought they should end up in the archives of victims' associations.[22] Bermejo adds that neither the priorities of the Spanish Communist Party in exile nor the political climate in 1950s France provided circumstances that would have allowed the photographs to be salvaged.

The journey of the photographs that did survive – those Boix either developed or took himself – resembles the fate of other photographic acts documenting genocides. For example, Vicente Sánchez-Biosca has traced the migration of mug shots of Khmer Rouge detainees at the S-21 torture centre in Phnom Penh.[23] Due to their itinerant nature, the photographic subjects were successively enemies and victims of the perpetrators, *objects trouvés* of the barbarism displayed at the Museum of Genocidal Crimes, and forensic evidence in the trial of Duch, the S-21 director. As the author indicates, "These meaning-charged objects make up a nomad archive, one in continuous migration, decomposition and re-composition."[24] Boix's photographs faced a similar fate.

Should Boix be hailed as a hero, as some have argued?[25] The parallel montage at the end of the documentary directs the viewer's gaze to Boix's privileged status. The voice-over narrator quotes Margarite Duras as stating that all photographs are self-portraits in a way: "Toda fotografía es, de algún modo, la de uno mismo" (each photograph is, in some way, a photograph of oneself). Boix's own image suffers from overexposure, thus creating a distinct opposition between Boix's glowing smile and the tears of those who recount their victimization by the SS. Boix spent most of his captivity at Mauthausen within the relatively privileged space of the photography identification lab. He did not have to face the almost inevitably lethal labour assignment of the dreaded "cantera" or quarry, where so many Mauthausen prisoners lost their lives. The photographs of his post-war life in Paris, the freedom suggested by the open spaces, and his constant smile appear in sharp contrast with the testimony of those, such as his fellow camp prisoner Manuel Azauste, who were traumatized, recount years of nightmares, and point to the scars on their chin and their forehead caused by beatings by the SS. While the singularity of Boix's experience constitutes the backbone of the documentary, it is the testimony of the survivors, filmed in enclosed spaces and close-up shots, that remains as indelible in our memory as the scars on their bodies. I contend that the visual representation of Boix by Llorenç Soler is not solely enjoined to present Boix through the lens of heroism; rather, the director is forcing the audience to compare his privileged position (sheltered labour assignment, youth, handsome looks, valued witness to the war crimes trials, not to mention Boix's twenty-first-century fame) to that of those men who survived to old age, still broken and brutalized by Nazi atrocities.[26] Ultimately, *Francisco Boix, un fotógrafo en el infierno* reveals that although Boix died prematurely, he remains somehow frozen in photographs as a young man who escaped the *infierno* even while so many others remained trapped in it by the trauma of the violence.

As Bermejo states, other communists vilified Boix, accusing him of being complicit with Nazi repression in order to maintain his status. But one would be hard pressed to say he is a villain. Paul Maria Hafner, the subject of Günter Schwaiger's documentary to which this chapter now turns, most definitely was. Schwaiger is an Austrian filmmaker with a long-standing commitment to repairing the memory of the victims of the Civil War and the Holocaust. He was the force behind the release of the documentary film series *Imágenes contra el olvido* (Images against forgetfulness) in 2010, which included works from Spain, Germany, Austria, and the United States.[27] *Hafners Paradies* focuses on the daily routine of Hafner, a former SS officer and fifty-year resident of Spain, followed by a two-day trip to Marbella, his paradise, where he tries unsuccessfully to contact other SS officers who have long resided there – Honsik, Jugler, and Soucek among them. It premiered at the Locarno Film Festival on 6 August 2007 and was subsequently included in the documentary film festival Seminci in Valladolid in October of that same year. The story of Hafner as presented in this documentary merits comparison to the discussions of other former SS and Nazis living in post-Second-World-War Spain as explored in the chapters in section VII by Joshua Goode and David Messenger.

Like Soler's documentary, *Hafners Paradies* marks a significant departure from the dominant focus on collective victimhood not only because it focuses on an individual figure but also because it is a stark reminder that the recuperation of historical memory in Spain cannot be considered a fait accompli and that the Nazi-friendly qualities of Franco's regime still need to be addressed at the beginning of the twenty-first century. Hafner epitomizes the abject not only because of his self-righteousness and his ruthless defence of Hitler's ideology, but also because of the impunity with which he lived in Spain. As the filmmaker explains: *"Hafner's Paradise* is not just a psychological portrait of an extremist; it also makes clear the close relation between Franco's Spain and the Third Reich, particularly after the Second World War, when Spain gave refuge to so many Nazis on the run."[28] That is, the documentary reveals that Spain has been a haven to those who perpetrated crimes against humanity. It draws our attention to the fact that the Franco regime not only allowed Spaniards to be deported to camps but also welcomed their executioners.

Unlike many historical documentaries, *Hafners Paradies* lacks a voice-over narration. Rather, Hafner himself becomes the main source of information. While most documentaries rely on images of the victims, Schwaiger allows Hafner the victimizer to tell us his story. The visual absence of the victims contrasts with Hafner's overpowering presence. The film opens with footage of him filmed with the camera placed at a low angle. Hafner is dressed in a dark-brown suit and tie, adding to his dignified characterization. In a tight kitchen space, Hafner explains that he became wealthy after he invented the old, worn-out yogurt maker he is holding. The profit for this prosaic invention amounted to 1 million pesetas. He goes on to explain that he later made a living by raising pigs near Madrid, that the business boomed, and as a consequence this particular breed is being successfully raised all over Spain. Proudly, he adds that he has managed to keep it a secret that they are *German* pigs. In addition to the pejorative meaning of the phrase "German pigs," easily discernible to an attentive audience, the pigs become a meaningful visual presence. For instance, as Hafner shows Schwaiger photographs of his sisters, including a close-up shot of their legs, suggesting lewdness, Hafner's voice-over discusses incest, which he considers as common among humans as among animals. The shot is immediately followed by footage of the pigs on one of Hafner's farms.

He further elaborates on his sexual desires by boasting about his extramarital affairs while we look at footage of two pigs copulating, which adds to his animalization and his characterization as a predator.

The German pigs are of a superior breed, Hafner explains: they have sixteen ribs as opposed to the fourteen ribs of the average Spanish pig. As he goes on to describe the business of their raising, he states that crossbreeding always results in the decline of a particular strain. The camera cuts to a close-up shot of the cover of the book Hafner is reading, none other than Hitler's *Mein Kampf.* He goes on reading a passage where Hitler states that by exterminating Jews, he is complying with God's will. As he closes the book, Hafner goes on to praise Hitler as one of the most reasonable figures in the history of mankind. This is one of several occasions when he explicitly expresses his admiration for the Führer.

The audiovisual production that memorializes the victims of fascism has incorporated hundreds of photographs of naked corpses, agonized prisoners, and famished bodies stripped of any humanity. Hafner's initial characterization stands in opposition to these visual referents: he is tall and well dressed and watches his diet in order to attain longevity. However, Schwaiger gradually strips him of his dignity as the film progresses. After swimming in Marbella, footage of Hafner's stark naked body reveals the inevitability of aging (see figure 28.3).

Hafner's attempts to contact other SS officials in Marbella fail, as his calls are not returned. The climax of the documentary takes place upon his arrival back in Madrid, when he converses with Hans Landauer, a Dachau camp survivor who addresses Hafner's denial of the Holocaust. As they retrace their own steps, they come to the realization that Hafner was an SS official at Dachau while Landauer was imprisoned there. While they both look at photographs of piled corpses, Hafner complains about his dentures and takes them in and out. Several close-ups of the expression of pain in his face, without his dentures, expose Hafner's own fragility and physical deterioration. However, these shots will hardly elicit empathy from the audience. Rather, the images represent the inevitability of Hafner's defeat and demise and serve as a stark reminder of the brutality of Nazi ideology.

It would be legitimate to challenge the relevance of a documentary film that portrays a Holocaust denier who has found his paradise in sunny Spain. In addition, the cruelty and political views expressed by other figures in the film are bound to offend audience members. For instance, Joachim Heyroth, an acquaintance of Hafner and long-time Madrid resident, reminisces about his participation in the Condor Legion sent by Hitler to Franco's aid in 1937. He not only boasts of the bombing of Guernica but also chuckles as he relays the experience. In addition to Hafner's praise of Hitler, some of his associates

28.3 Still from *Hafners Paradies* (2007, dir. Günter Schwaiger). Reproduced by permission of Günter Schwaiger.

glorify both Franco and Leon Legrelle at a meeting of Fuerza Nueva, a radical right-wing political party, where its well-known leader Blas Piñar (1918–2014) is in attendance. Piñar and Fuerza Nueva, reincarnated as the Frente Popular since the 1980s, have remained recalcitrant defenders of the Francoist legacy. Extremist, right-wing groups have demonstrated consistent resistance against the recuperation of memory since the mid-1990s, and their protests have found in the Valle de los Caídos, Franco's resting place until his exhumation on 24 October 2019, their most powerful symbol. Despite Franco's disinterment, the status of the Valle de los Caídos as a monument to the dictator is one of the most pressing unresolved matters of the Ley de la Memoria Histórica, which was passed in 2007 by the Socialist cabinet, led by Rodríguez Zapatero, as a result of heightened awareness as well as pressure from civil organizations. The law granted reparation to victims but failed to grant financial support for the disinterment of those buried in mass graves. To this day, there is no federal approval for the disinterment of mass graves, nor is there financial support for that action.[29] The law rightfully aimed to repair the memory of the victims of the war, but it did not achieve national reconciliation. *Hafners Paradies,* which was produced the same year the law passed, serves as an alarming reminder of the deep-rooted fascist ideology that aims to thwart the reparation of the victims' memory.

28.4 The reinternment of Francisco Boix in the Père Lachaise cemetery in Paris in 2017, shown in a tweet by Anne Hidalgo, the mayor of Paris.

The audiovisual productions examined above prove that investigative reports and documentary films remain crucial political forums, contested sites of historical memory. Impostors, heroes, victims, and villains populate documentaries and investigative reports that suggest that the memory of Francoism and Nazism remains relevant to many, including a new generation of filmmakers. While this body of work has been highly instrumental in bringing public awareness to collective victimhood, investigative reporters have also brought to light the lives of villains and heroes, executioners and victims, as well as the barbarity and cruelty that troubles audiences with divergent political views. Audiences are exposed to images that migrate and metamorphose over time. Armengou, Belis, Soler, and Schwaiger bring the link between Spain, the deportation of Republicans, and the Nazi extermination of European Jewry front and centre, even while these crossroads and connections remain a blind spot in the context of audiovisual productions about the recuperation of historical memory in Spain. The projects by Armengou, Belis, and Soler reflect the need to vindicate the victims' memory, while Schwaiger's documentary turns its censoring, even humorous and debasing eye on the few Nazis still among us and stands out therefore as the strongest political statement by placing the inhumanity of the Holocaust not beyond, but within Spanish borders.[30]

In June 2017, Boix's remains were moved to the Père Lachaise cemetery in Paris, an initiative – twelve years in the making – of the local Amicale de Mauthausen. The ceremony was presided over by Anne Hidalgo, mayor of Paris and the daughter of Republican exiles (see figure 28.4). The interim mayor of Barcelona was in attendance; so were Boix's relatives and Ramiro Santiesteban, a Mauthausen survivor. Spain's central government was not represented at the ceremony. Spain's prime minister Mariano Rajoy happened to be in Paris at the time yet did not attend, an absence that points to the continued battle between the need to remember and state-sanctioned forgetting.

NOTES

1 See Estrada, *El documental cinematográfico*.
2 Adorno, "What Does Coming to Terms ...?," 116–17.
3 For information about the lesser-known Italian production, sec Perra, *Conflicts of Memory*.
4 See Estrada, "To Mauthausen and Back: The Holocaust as a Reference in Spanish Civil War Memory Studies," in Gómez López-Quiñones and Zepp, eds, *The Holocaust in Spanish Memory*, 37–50.

5 The relevance of Armengou's and Belis's investigations, also published in book form, is illustrated by the fact that other television stations have subsequently broadcast reports on the very same topic: *El convoy de los 927-Mauthausen* (Documentos TVE) was broadcast only a few months later, also in 2004, and *Los últimos andaluces de Mauthausen* (The last Andalusians of Mauthausen, Canal Sur Andalucía) was broadcast as recently as 5 May 2015, on the seventieth anniversary of the camp's liberation.

6 See Brenneis, *Spaniards in Mauthausen*.

7 In the past I have been critical of Armengou's equating this train with the Nazi death trains that formed part of the extermination machine. However, it is undeniable that the Armengou-Belis team has greatly contributed to the national debate about historical memory. See Estrada, "The Recuperation of Memory."

8 I am grateful to Sandra Rierola of the *30 minuts* production team for providing the data.

9 See Herrmann, chapter 12 in this volume.

10 "Holocaust Encyclopedia: Ravensbrück," United States Holocaust Memorial Museum, https://www.ushmm.org/wlc/en/article.php?ModuleId=10005199, accessed 18 July 2018.

11 I am deeply grateful to Montse Armengou for giving me access to the discarded footage and discussing the issue with me at the King Juan Carlos Center in May 2017.

12 Cercas, "Prólogo," in Bermejo, *El fotógrafo del horror*, 4.

13 Another figure to have come to light recently is the diplomat Ángel Sanz Briz, who prevented the deportation to Auschwitz of four thousand Jews from Nazi-occupied Budapest. He has been portrayed in *La encrucijada de Sanz Briz* (The Crossroads of Sanz Briz), a documentary co-produced by Hungary and Israel in 2015, directed by José Alejandro González; and in *El ángel de Budapest*, a television miniseries directed by Luis Oliveros in 2011. Sanz Briz's diplomatic interventions are discussed in chapter 8 of this volume.

14 See chapter 14 by Brenneis, chapter 15 by Marín-Dòmine, chapter 17 by Toran, and chapter 27 by Loyola for additional readings of the figure of Boix.

15 Romaguera i Ramió and Soler de los Mártires, *Historia crítica y documentada*, 395.

16 Llorca, "Las raíces documentales del holocausto," 203.

17 Ibid., 210.

18 See Estrada, *El documental cinematográfico*.

19 Bermejo, *Francisco Boix*, 182.

20 Herrmann, "Camera Caedens, Camera Vindex," 116.

21 Qtd in Sontag, *Regarding the Pain of Others*, 84.

22 Bermejo, *Francisco Boix*, 232.

23 Sánchez-Biosca, "Perpetrator Images."

24 Ibid., 113.

25 Armengou in Herrmann, "Camera Caedens," 121.

26 Aside from the documentary productions about Boix, *El fotógrafo de Mauthausen* (2018) is a major biopic directed and produced by Mar Targarona, producer of the blockbuster *The Orphanage*. See also the graphic novel by Rubio, Colombo, and Landa, *El fotógrafo de Mauthausen*.

27 The series includes *Santa Cruz … por ejemplo* (Santa Cruz … for example, Günter Schwaiger and Hermann Peseckas, 2005); *La mala muerte* (The Bad Death, José Manuel Martín and Fidel Cordero, 2003/04); *La columna de los ocho mil* (The Column of 8,000, Ángel Hernández García, Antonio Navarro, Fernando Ramos, and Francisco Freire, 2005); *Presos del silencio* (Prisoners of Silence, Mariano Agudo and Eduardo Montero, 2004); *Los héroes nunca mueren* (Heroes Never Die, Jan Arnold, 2004); *Muerte en El Valle* (Death in the Valley, Christina Hardt, 1996); *España, última esperanza. Apuntes de una odisea* (Spain, Last Hope: Notes from an Odyssey, Karin Helml and Hermann Peseckas, 2006); *Una inmensa prisión* (A Huge Prison, Carlos Ceacero and Guillermo Carnero Rosell, 2006); *Los alzados de Palma* (The Revels of Palma, David Baute and Cirilo Leal, 2006); and *La memoria es vaga* (Memory Is Vague, Katie Halper, 2004). For further information, visit http://imagenescontraelolvido.com.

28 Schwaiger, "Hafner's Paradise," http://www.mosolov-p.com/comentarios-del-director.html, accessed 19 July 2018. For an overview of the German colony in post-war Spain, see Messenger's chapter 26 in this volume, where he concludes that, although National Socialism remained active as an ideology, it did not impact politics as much as US intelligence had feared.

29 Rapidly shifting political winds have made the status of the Valle de los Caídos a point of virulent debate: the Socialists heading the Spanish government accomplished the removal and reburial of Franco's remains on 24 October 2019, though plans for the monument and the removal of additional victim remains are an open question. See Minder, "Franco's Remains Are Exhumed and Reburied after Bitter Battle," https://nyti.ms/33V3TvB.

30 Other works on Nazis in Spain include fiction and non-fiction: Villaronga, *Tras el cristal* (Through the Windowpane, 1986), Sánchez, *Lo que esconde tu nombre*, winner of the 2010 Premio Nadal, published in English as *The Scent of Lemon Leaves*; and Messenger, *Hunting Nazis in Franco's Spain* on the fate of Nazi spies and diplomats who stayed in Spain after the Second World War.

29 With Sepharad as a Void: Recent Reckoning with the Holocaust in Spanish Fiction

STACY N. BECKWITH

In the mid-1950s, a fictional Holocaust survivor of Sephardic ancestry arrived in Spain for university study from Tangiers, where he and his father had found refuge from Nazi persecution in Budapest. Hoping not to have to "guardar luto perpetuo" (be in mourning any longer) for family and community members decimated in Hungary and Poland, Isaac Salama indeed found hardly any Holocaust resonance in the Spanish capital:

> Si uno miraba a su alrededor, en una taberna de Madrid, en una aula de la universidad, si caminaba por la Gran Vía y entraba en un cine un domingo por la tarde, no encontraba por ninguna parte rastros de que todo aquello hubiera sucedido, podía dejarse llevar hacia una existencia más o menos idéntica a la de los demás, sus compatriotas, sus compañeros de curso, los amigos que no le preguntaban a uno por su origen, que no sabían apenas nada de la guerra europea ni de los campos alemanes.

> If you looked around, in a tavern in Madrid, in a classroom at the university, if you walked along the Gran Vía and went into a movie theater on a Sunday afternoon, you wouldn't find a hint that any of it had happened, you could let yourself be borne off to a life more or less like that other people lived, his compatriots, classmates, and the friends who never asked about his past, who scarcely knew anything about the European war or the German camps.[1]

Such apparent unawareness of the Holocaust in mid-twentieth-century Spain might read like a passing indication of atmosphere in the midst of Antonio Muñoz Molina's umbrella novel, *Sefarad* (*Sepharad*, 2001), whose component narratives explore a range of real and invented personal identities upended by Nazi, Soviet, and Francoist discrimination and pursuit. More revealing than just a contextual note, however, Salama's impression of the Holocaust's distance from Madrid in the 1950s mirrors its continuing, substantive absence from Spanish education and collective memory into the 2000s (See chapter 32 by Marta Simó and chapter 33 by Alejandro Baer and Natan Sznaider for more on these absences.)

In sociologist Alejandro Baer's estimation, Spain's meagre public engagement with Europe's Jewish genocide has been primarily cultural. Since 1945, events during and related to the Holocaust have had a "weak reception" in the country, even though memory of Nazi-induced Jewish and Spanish Republican extermination might productively be in dialogue. Baer observes that Spain's "practically *judenrein* [environment] for the past five centuries" has impeded such mutual resonance and illumination, since "the voids, the silences, and the abiding prejudices regarding Judaism," though worse under Franco, have not completely dissipated under democracy.[2] At the same time, however, and particularly since the five-hundred anniversary of Spain's expulsion of the Jews in 1492, the Spanish touristic, commercial, and popular literary imagination has accelerated, filling in any void surrounding pre-exilic Jewish experience in Iberia. There has been growing and diversifying scholarly focus on contemporary Spanish fascination with Sephardic customs and lifestyles that are regularly commodified today in connection with trace medieval Jewish quarters or streets in cities and towns throughout Spain.

Indeed, successful mass-market historical fiction such as Catalan author Chufo Lloréns's *Saga de los malditos* (Saga of the damned, 2003) highlights both the tenacity and the reproducibility of skewed Jewish traits with pre-modern origins in contemporary Spanish culture. This novel was much heralded for its two complementary plots that match Sephardic persecution around Catholicizing medieval Spain with a replica circuit around Hitler's expanding Reich in 1930s and '40s Europe. Such facile duplication may seem able to bring a sense of Jewish victimization in the Holocaust to Spanish readers today, given the familiar Semitic touchstones that link Iberia and Nazi Europe thematically and diegetically in Lloréns's novel.

As a compound thriller fuelled by familiar preconceptions, however, his work does not create a space for Spanish readers to become acquainted with diasporic, unscripted Sephardic engagement with loss stemming from both 1492 and 1942,[3] as do Muñoz Molina's *Sefarad* and *Velódromo de Invierno* (Winter velodrome) by Juana Salabert, also published in 2001. While Muñoz Molina's Isaac Salama sees no signs of Holocaust awareness in 1950s Madrid, contemporary Spanish readers are looking at popular public spaces in their capital not through an insidious

Jewish gaze, as might be anticipated, but rather through one traversed by currents of remembered trauma and nostalgia that move in several intergenerational and transnational directions at once. Through reflections on family and collective loss by Salabert's Sephardic and Spanish Republican Holocaust survivor, Sebastián Miranda, readers perceive medieval Jewish Spain not as a "practised place," to borrow from Michel de Certeau,[4] but as a void at the core of twentieth-century Spain.

Throughout Salabert's novel the dates 1492, 1942, and 1992 mingle and evoke one another's distinct, yet emotionally linked moments in and regarding Spain, as a home forcibly abandoned, then remembered and re-explored by Mediterranean Sephardic descendants such as Miranda and by a family of uprooted German Jews with no ancestral links to Iberia. Had Sepharad as a ground zero been manifest for these characters, it might have been comparable with the ruins of the Warsaw Ghetto as African American writer W.E.B. Du Bois looked on them when he visited them in 1949. Recently, in advancing his concept of "multidirectional memory," the comparative Holocaust scholar Michael Rothberg has explored Du Bois's contemplation of the ghetto ruins to illustrate how one people's memory can spontaneously evoke and illuminate another's in such intrinsically articulate terrain. [5] The ensuing article, which Du Bois published in *Jewish Life* in 1952, highlights the communicative "mnemonic labor" that philosopher Avishai Margalit considers possible and necessary in environments where individual memories within one or more societies might not "simply aggregate [*sic*]," but also "integrate and calibrate the different perspectives of those who remember [given] episode[s]."[6]

In their recent Holocaust-related fiction, the 1930s–90s Spanish, European, and Mediterranean milieux that Antonio Muñoz Molina and Juana Salabert re/create bring diverse but experientially relatable memories of Nazi, Francoist, and/or Soviet communist oppression into dialogue for and with contemporary Spanish readers. As Spanish Research Council literary scholar Pilar Nieva de la Paz wrote of these novels in 2002, "la irrupción directa de los sucesos y las gentes del mundo real en los textos" (the direct irruption of events and people from the real world into the texts)[7] is crucially undergirded by many thematic and ethical ties to historic Sepharad and its destruction, as both a genetic Jewish and an ontological Spanish question that still resists vivid answers. What this enduring question for Spanish national character impels, particularly in Muñoz Molina's *Sefarad*, are distinct narratives that move in multiple directions involving the Holocaust, including towards a community of former Nazi SS members hosted in an exclusive and undisturbed "Berghof" on an Andalusian coastal cliff. An unsuspecting Spanish physician stumbles upon them just as a pregnant and drifting Spanish thirty-year-old finds herself ensnared by a post-Mauthausen "hermandad" (brotherhood) in a similar seaside enclave near Valencia, in author Clara Sánchez's 2010 novel *Lo que esconde tu nombre* (*The Scent of Lemon Leaves*).[8]

A cipher raised in contemporary Spain with minimal exposure to Holocaust history, Sánchez's protagonist, Sandra, is rapidly educated through happenstance involvement with the former Nazis on one hand and a Republican Mauthausen survivor with a recently deceased Jewish spouse on the other. Emblematic of Sandra's dialectical learning between these two poles, she eventually names her newborn after her Nazi-hunting tutor, frequently calling the child by the diminutive "Janín," or "Little Janus." In Antonio Muñoz Molina and Juana Salabert's novels, too, a metonymic figure of a child emerges to reflect a staid Spain that has been, and a more broadly informed one that might be. Both Muñoz Molina's lone and anonymous girl painted by Velázquez, and Salabert's "hijo del misterio" (child of mystery)[9] confound with their unfathomable genetic make-up. More crucially, they also reflect each author's and their readers' reckoning with diverse Holocaust experiences and memory over the course of each novel, via Sepharad as a cultural and ethical void of comparable ilk that continues to indict the modern nation.

Sepharad as a Practised Place

Since Spain's expulsion of her medieval Jewish population at the end of the fifteenth century, Spaniards have had more ongoing contact with recycled and largely negative Jewish images than with actual Jews.[10] At the same time, in various towns or cities in every Spanish region, generations of residents have lived amid ancient Sephardic material remains such as repurposed synagogues, cemeteries, and once marginalized streets. Since the mid-1980s, and particularly since the 1992 fifth centenary of 1492, old Jewish quarters and the Catholic streets and spires that historically hemmed them in have inspired a range of novelists to research and revive ancient Sephardic ways of life and local Inquisition dramas for contemporary national readers. Since most of this literature develops from authors' and readers' affection for their hometowns, and from an almost genetic curiosity about their *pueblo*'s partly visible medieval contours, both these spaces and the historical fiction that carries Spaniards back to them today have become "practised places" in Michel de Certeau's terms.

In differentiating between "space" as relatively "ambiguous" before being ordered, and "place" as "an indication of stability" once architectural and cultural delineation ensues,[11] de Certeau could be describing many of the early Sephardic tableaux that are now familiar within Spain's very popular historical novel genre. In his exploration of Jewish involvement in financing structural defences for the Roman and later medieval Catalonian town of Besalú, for example, "bestselling" author Martí Gironell has a tenth-century local teenage Jewess defy her rabbi's insistence on protective communal insularity. She shows a young Catholic stranger (eyes and ears for a Spanish reader today) "cómo es la vida a este lado de la ciudad" (what life is like on this side of the city.)[12] Apart from the rock and fluvial formation that furnished a *mikveh*, or ritual bath, for which Besalú is still renowned, the dubiously named Jezebel takes her companion through a generic and generalizable Jewish quarter. Its colourful main street leads to a butchering area, where she explains Jewish dietary laws. Then a step inside the synagogue allows for an overview of the Torah and how it is studied in the adjacent religious school. Jezebel's family kitchen, busy with Sabbath preparations,[13] rounds out Gironell's quick succession of typical Sephardic dioramas for time-travelling Spanish readers, who can also find a version of them in the medieval sections of Chufo Lloréns's *Saga de los malditos*.

Like Gironell, Lloréns also starts with specifics of place: how Toledo's Jewish streets cluster around the edifices of late fourteenth century protective Christian royalty. From here, ecclesiastical intrigue that undermines the king's wealthy rabbinic advisor and spurs the sacking of the latter's community is also punctuated with edifying Jewish life cycle scenes. Contemporary Spanish readers visit a Sephardic wedding and then a burial, at both events sampling transliterated Hebrew terms that convey universal Jewish ritual detail. Incongruously, Lloréns's young Sephardic heroine seems to modernize after these scenes, demanding and eventually obtaining a divorce. In this way, self-liberated Esther recalls Martí Gironell's boundary-pushing Jezebel as well as some of prominent historical novelist Toti Martínez de Lezea's male-challenging protagonists in a 2009 anthology of brief narrative glimpses at "judías, moras, y cristianas" (Jewish, Moorish, and Christian women) in eighth-through fifteenth-century Iberia.[14]

Besides including feminist anachronisms in his ancient plot, as noted above, Lloréns also explicitly shuttles readers between 1390s Spain and 1930s–40s Europe. And it is not only medieval Esther's daring that allows one to segue easily into the anti-Nazi stridence of German-born Hannah Pardenvolk, as she imperils herself by returning from family refuge in Vienna to her native Berlin in the late 1930s. Hannah's geopolitical surroundings become a mirror of Esther's in *Reconquista* Spain, with Toledo akin to Hitler's capital, with Cordoba and Seville already incorporated into Iberian Christendom just as Prague and Vienna have been into the Reich; and with Moorish Granada seemingly ripe for conquest and beckoning, like Paris. This autarkic cartography admits only back and forth, medieval/modern confirmation of the perennially cursed nature of all of the saga's Jewish or partly Semitic players. Lloréns does not venture out of this clamshell structure into any multi-directional exploration, with broader humanistic resonance, of why or how these characters might be experiencing their sliding fates.

Instead, the Jewish life cycle moments or weekly rituals that punctuate the parallel and intercutting action in both of Lloréns' theatres are also ethnically and superficially tautological. To the wedding and funeral noted above can be added a kosher Sabbath Eve dinner that readers observe early on in Berlin, where they learn the Hebrew term for the butcher who furnished the meat. Later, in Budapest, an invocation of "Adonai"[15] is not only a salient Semitic marker, but also a familiar cue to Spanish audiences, who hear this divine address in Hebrew throughout Lloréns's medieval chapters and routinely in many other Iberian Sephardic and crypto-Jewish dramas recast today. Lloréns hardly needs Ángel Sanz Briz, Spanish emissary in 1940s Budapest, to predictably discover a genetic link between Hannah's family and that of a friend of Esther's, in order to underscore the umbilical passage between Sepharad as a regularly practised place in the Spanish imaginary, and his Holocaust spin-off. (For more on Ángel Sanz Briz, Spanish diplomat, see José Antonio Lisbona's chapter 8 in this volume.)

Antonio Muñoz Molina's "Girl by Velázquez"

Ángel Sanz Briz also figures in the sixth novel in Muñoz Molina's compendium, *Sefarad*, in which his bureaucratic timing in 1944 Budapest saves only Isaac Salama and his father out of a larger Sephardic family from Nazi deportation. Scholars at the intersection of Judaic and Spanish studies have paid particular attention to Salama, whose life stages the author describes with relative fullness and contiguity. There is an almost magnetic repulsion between the character's "cornerstone"[16] sense of radiating a Jewish otherness forced on him in Nazi Europe, and how he imagines shedding this salience in a "proverbial" Sephardic return to Spain.[17] As Tabea Linhard discusses, however, Spain in the 1950s seems to actively, if not treacherously, preclude any acknowledging welcome.[18] Salama is physically and inwardly crippled from his sojourn there. He ends up in a nexus of Iberian disappointments and paternal Holocaust grief in Tangiers. Inherited mourning duties bring him to the railway tracks which alone mark the site of his family's concentration camp demise in Poland. There and in Morocco, Salama belatedly realizes the connective value of his Jewishness, which now links him to no real kindred community.[19] Nor are the scraps of a cultural program, neglected and defunded by Spain at her flagship institute in Tangiers, forthcoming. From his work at the Institute, Salama has no reciprocated sense of belonging vis-à-vis Iberia, by virtue of his family's indigeneity there.

Isaac Salama's intertwining Sephardic and Holocaust tragedies alone might induce an "empathic unsettlement" in Spanish readers,[20] particularly with Sepharad stripped of any modern redemptive capacity for this aging nostalgic, in addition to lacking any pseudo-medieval Semitic flare. Antonio Muñoz Molina also lifts a hyper-Sephardic overlay off the Jewish neighbourhood in his hometown of Úbeda in his last component novel, the only chapter that he titles "Sefarad," like his work overall. As Linhard notes, he does open here echoing some "stereotypes that shape perceptions in Spain of Sephardic Jews and Sephardic history."[21] In effect, rather like the way Chufo Lloréns launches the medieval half of his saga from the Jewish homes adjacent to Toledo's royal residence, Muñoz Molina starts his last musings amid some fifteenth-century once-Sephardic structures that abut Úbeda's historic citadel. At first his thoughts also run to negative Semitic traits made classic in historical novels like Lloréns's – greed, miserliness, and an alleged penchant for Catholic host desecration and ritual child murder.[22] Muñoz Molina interrupts this litany, however, when he sees two Stars of David engraved on an erstwhile Sephardic home and recalls a school rhyme about the Catholic kings' double campaign against Jews and Granada's Moors in 1492.

Muñoz Molina's movement here, from Semitic stereotype to sudden ambient reminders of Spain's loss-inducing hegemony in the late fifteenth century, is more revealing than his plot turns that compound Isaac Salama's family and personal nadirs. For the author's image switching, from Sepharad as familiar to Sepharad as painfully void, begins to illustrate more fully how he cultivates in his audience "an affective, disturbing response to the traumatic experience of others," as Herzberger adapts from historiography and trauma scholar Dominick LaCapra.[23] Throughout *Sefarad*, Muñoz Molina's resounding goal for his domestic readers is "an exposure [of] the self to involvement or implication in the past, its actors, and its victims."[24] The past in question is pointedly dual: a thematic and moralistic coupling of "purity of blood" fanaticism in historic Iberia with its extremes in Holocaust Europe. Yet counter-intuitively, almost bookending *Sefarad* as a whole, Muñoz Molina starts his first and last chapters by echoing a series of anti-Jewish tropes to which many Spaniards may have become inured over centuries of cultural entrenchment. Indeed, the author relays instances of personally encountering, recalling, and/or perpetuating such Sephardic stigmatizing through family and local custom. With their implication of national familiarity, these seemingly regressive moments in Muñoz Molina's writing feel designed, conversely, to help Spanish readers segue into more self-reflexive contact with his wider gallery of Jewish Holocaust victims, particularly those who are Sephardic.

As he opens *Sefarad* in his first narrative, "Sacristán," for example, Muñoz Molina situates himself among fellow, now urbanized Úbeda natives commuting home from Madrid for family visits, especially during Holy Week. Even as the narrator regrets that "nuestros hijos" (our children) are being increasingly captivated by new tastes and diversions during the religious parade, he still lifts them, just as he was hoisted, to view one of Úbeda's "más espectaculares" (most spectacular) floats, that of the Last Supper.[25] Its most "conventionally expected"[26] figure is that of Judas, who is always focused greedily on his coins with his "cara ... siniestra," or sinister Semitic features, which are lit in a "verde amarillo de malhumor hepático" (a bilious green).[27] Both intergenerational and body memory come into play here: the author's moments of parental lifting and pointing out as the float goes by suggest how families in local parishes around Spain may also have inculcated the Passion's underlying Pharisaic deviousness from one era into the next. Indeed, Muñoz Molina himself reiterates Judas's repulsiveness with the same phrasing three times before suddenly sharing local gossip about how the statue once became a precise, if an "exageración cruenta de la caricatura" (cruel exaggeration of the caricature) of the new town tailor, following communist destruction of the Holy Week figures during the Civil War. For publicly hounding Úbeda's "escultor ... bohemio" (bohemian sculptor) in order to collect on the distinctive shirts and waistcoats the artist steadily commissioned but never paid for, the clothier beheld his unmistakable likeness in Holy Week's new wooden Judas. Meanwhile, the town cobbler, who never called in the sculptor's debts, shone out from the carving of Matthew. The clash between guile and fealty on the Last Supper float transferred to Úbeda's streets as meetings between tailor and cobbler invariably caused the former to withdraw and brood; his demeanour, like his nose, registering as "más semítica que nunca" (more Semitic than ever) around the town.[28]

More than just a "historia ... sabrosa" (juicy story) many an old compatriot could tell Muñoz Molina decades later,[29] this tale moves his Spanish readers from gospel to modern Sephardic stereotyping without missing a familiar medieval reference, either in wood or in flesh. With his laughable parries for remuneration and his subsequent sulks, moreover, the tailor clearly began to exhibit what social anthropologist Paul Connerton has described as "the unease of those who feel that their bodies betray them and who regard their bodies, as it were, from the outside and through the appraising eyes of others, surveying and [attempting to] correct their practices."[30]

Throughout *Sefarad* such corporeal calibration also attends awareness that one has become publicly classified as Jewish in Holocaust Europe, derailed from the personal and professional routines of an otherwise innocuous bourgeois. What the Holy Week pageant and character incarnations in Úbeda underscore, however, is historian and Iberian antisemitism specialist Gonzalez Álvarez Chillida's finding that Spaniards have traditionally had more practice recognizing and pointing out bodily signs of Semitic otherness than intuiting how such essentializing appraisal might feel from inside a Jewish recipient's affect.[31] By implication, Muñoz Molina's Spanish readers may readily perceive the parallels in Semitic typecasting and ostracizing as they embark with him for the edges of the Nazi "univers concentrationnaire,"[32] from his overheard yarn about mid-twentieth-century Andalusian locals equating a Jewish-seeming town tailor with Judas. How to begin reckoning with the import of such a Spain-to-Holocaust segue by immersing oneself in the trauma-beset nerves of Ashkenazic victims, in particular, may be less apparent.

For where, in historiography, Dominick LaCapra finds "full identification" with the traumatized a less apropos or effective goal than cultivating "empathic unsettlement" vis-à-vis their experiences,[33] Muñoz Molina can seem equally focused on the former endeavour and hardly instructive in his continual prodding to convince Spanish readers that "eres" (you are) each of his invented and authentic Nazi targets.[34] Moreover, from urban cafés in 1920s–40s Europe, to lobbies or accommodations in train stations or hotels, the author's invented Jewish figures all exhibit the same identity-divulging physicality and growing sensations of entrapment. These Muñoz Molina also grafts onto the varying biographies of the real intellectuals and political functionaries whom he imports into his blended fictional and historical universe of those undone by both Soviet communism and Nazism. The result is a continent-wide patina of what quickly become generic responses to mid-twentieth century authoritarian pinioning. While this may be a victims'-side-up inversion of the Semitic stereotyping that Muñoz Molina portrays as still an Iberian cultural overlay, it gives Spanish readers few homegrown entrées into the onset of Holocaust trauma that he discernibly keeps urging them to experience in connection with national history.

By contrast, Primo Levi's transport to Auschwitz becomes more individually relatable after a note about his ancestors' 1492 departure from Spain to Italy.[35] When, in *Sefarad's* final chapter, the author repeats this historic Spanish tie-in, Primo Levi seems like a familial stepping stone to philosopher Jean Améry's sudden awareness of being Jewish in 1930s Vienna and to his post-Auschwitz writings, which Muñoz Molina explicitly recommends as essential.[36] By the same token, the incidental Sephardic surname of a book reviewer at a writer's luncheon in Copenhagen, the house key that reaches Isaac Salama's family from a forefather driven out of Toledo, and similarly surviving keys that the author imagines for ancestral Jewish homes in Úbeda, are also conjunctive revenants from Sepharad as a void. For they do not just trigger degrees of multidirectional wistfulness in contemporary Sephardic characters such as journalist Camille Safra or Spanish cultural attaché in Tangiers Isaac Salama. Iberian Jewish family names and guarded house keys are hallmarks of presumed intergenerational Sephardic memory in Spain, and their iconic familiarity ushers readers into Muñoz Molina's most substantive and thematically dialogic Holocaust narratives.

The shared Iberian genealogical pull of these traces from historic Sepharad is also confirmed when Muñoz Molina ends his work amid the non-taxonomic collection of Stone Age through twentieth-century material, literary and artistic testaments to Spanish richness through diversity in Upper Manhattan's Hispanic Society of America. Here he is introduced to the small, unassuming portrait of an anonymous girl by Velázquez, one who represents neither a religious nor any aristocratic notable. Still, as Muñoz Molina consistently refers to her as the "niña de Velázquez" (the little girl in the Velázquez painting),[37] the inclusive humanistic ethos she radiates from canvas or postcard also has some national specificity, encapsulating how the author's Holocaust explorations seem more accessible and pointed for Spanish readers with some domestic cultural pairing.

Juana Salabert's "Child of Mystery"

Indeed, the wide-ranging Hispanic Society displays become synesthetically personal for Muñoz Molina when he touches the raised rooster in a ceramic bowl and his thoughts slip from a similar design by Picasso to the same emblem on dishes from his childhood and the regional foods these always served.[38] For memory scholar Jan Assman, this would represent a move out of archived, "cultural memory," whose reach into a society's past exceeds the century or less of possible intergenerational sharing posited by sociologist and foundational collective memory theorist Maurice Halbwachs. Muñoz Molina enters the latter, more limited ambit of "communicative memory" as he holds the earthenware bowl and becomes aware of the Hispanic Society's expatriate Spanish curator behind him, voicing similarly inspired thoughts of home.[39] Their informal back and forth resembles how Juana Salabert brings Spanish readers into more sustained, at once intimate and polyphonic contact with the Holocaust in her 2001 novel, *Velódromo de Invierno.*

Salabert's work consists primarily of one wide-ranging conversation that takes place in central and northern Spain, in 1992, between the adult son of a young girl who escaped mass Jewish detention in Paris's winter cycling arena in July 1942, and the Sephardic Salonikan who orchestrated her Pyrenees crossing into Spain. The latter inherited his ancestors' anguish over their Iberian exile in the 1490s. Sebastián Miranda then lost all his contemporary family when the Nazis deported his relatives from Greece to Treblinka. Capture following leftist participation in the Spanish Civil War led to his own slavery in Auschwitz, after youthful "dreams of the mythical, always nostalgic return to Sepharad" originally drew him to Spain in the mid-1930s.[40]

In her recent side-by-side study of Sebastián Miranda and Antonio Muñoz Molina's Isaac Salama, Tabea Linhard explores how both characters are affected by ancestral and individual nostalgia vis-à-vis twentieth-century Spain, which they each initially perceive as the outer membrane of a deeply recessed and dwindled, yet still communicative Sephardic vitality within. Drawing on comparatist Svetlana Boym's articulation, Linhard follows each character's susceptibility to reflective and/or restorative Iberian nostalgia. The first involves imaginative travel into personal versions of Spain's Sephardic recesses, while the second urges their regeneration in some form.[41] More pertinent for Spanish readers' nationally resonant exposure to the Holocaust, though, is aging Miranda's genetically communicative memory. It exudes a symbiosis of 1492 and 1942 "limit-experiences"[42] as he talks at length in and around Madrid, en route to the fictional hub of his Holocaust child rescue organization, and in the northern town of Finis's preserved centre, close to its tourist-highlighted old Jewish quarter. Miranda's mental forays into late-fifteenth- and mid-twentieth-century Toledo, and to the Castilian birthplace of his family's "ruidosa tribu" (noisy tribe),[43] make for an even more productive conversational "reciprocity"[44] he has with 1490s and 1940s Spain, from his shifting national environs in 1992.

In effect, apartment thresholds, and living room and taxi windows, as well as café tables and a bill total that sounds to Miranda like the amount of daily dead or his own identity number being called in the concentration camp,[45] are among contemporary peninsular portals to his various Holocaust pasts. They bring readers into immediate contact with Jewish communal and family extermination and with some

Spanish Republican suffering, as well. Contributing more pointedly to such associative transport, Finis seems geographically configured by the state-consolidating and aggrandizing agents of 1492, with its main boulevard named after the Catholic Monarchs and both a street and hotel called "Colón." In the latter, present luxury is tinged with the building's doubly nuanced history as the seat of local management and propaganda for both the Inquisition and an anarchist militia during the Civil War.[46] By contrast, sights such as the Hebrew inscriptions that border the ceiling of Toledo's famed main synagogue, or just the feel of an everyday object like a copper coffee pot found in Madrid's Calle de Toledo, cause a recently vibrant Sephardic world to flash into Miranda's memory with brief, sensory precision.[47] Sounds and smells from the Salonika of his childhood, along with the typical behaviour and Ladino sayings of his female elders there, afford a taste of pre-Holocaust Sephardic liminality suffused with Iberian precedent: a fleeting sense of home through communal continuity, ahead of existential voids re/imposed.

In her endeavour to "devolver la voz a algunas víctimas del Holocausto" (give a few Holocaust victims their voices back), Juana Salabert includes some contemporary Spanish cameo listeners in her novel.[48] As they overhear stretches of Sebastián Miranda's "actividades de cicerone" (Ciceronian discourse), or help to steady him physically at one point,[49] a Cuban-born taxi driver and the hotel elevator attendant in Finis seem to represent more everyday Spaniards for whom such a manifold survivor of Jewish and Republican annihilation in Spain and Europe could be uniquely and cohesively enlightening. Indeed, catering to what he presumes are the sightseeing tastes of his two Puerto Rican–sounding passengers, the taxi driver takes them on a meandering country drive from Finis's regional airport into the town. Early on he turns down Tito Puente and other singers with "esa tropical voz" (that tropical voice) so he can journey syncretically with Miranda from pre-Holocaust Salonika to imagined scenes of Sephardic departure from medieval Toledo, and thence to the floor of a Treblinka gas chamber as it receives a handful of medieval Iberian soil from a treasured family pouch.[50] By the time the driver brakes in front of the Hotel Colón he has also looked out on postwar Paris, Lisbon, and São Tomé in haunted, multidirectional contemplation.[51] One feels that it is not only the unusual French name on his business card that suggests he is "otro hijo del misterio" (another child of mystery.)[52] The driver's proxy experience of so much of his elderly passenger's Iberian and Holocaust-induced trauma and nostalgia has clearly affected and complicated him as a run-of-the-mill, incidental listener.

Clara Sánchez's "Little Janus"

Midway through Antonio Muñoz Molina's *Sefarad* one Spanish bystander's impromptu initiation into national connections with the Holocaust resonates with how Juana Salabert's taxi driver happens to pick up on a range of them. Perhaps in synecdochial relation to a placid, contemporary Spain as a whole, Muñoz Molina's middle-aged doctor enjoys marital relations and family life to the fullist while vacationing on the Andalusian coast. However, he dreads having to inform a patient that the AIDS virus is invading his healthy cells. While still on holiday, the physician is drawn to some neolithic cave paintings atop a cliff overlooking the beach, and in search of these finds himself amid a row of German tourists' houses that seemed unobtrusive from below. The name "Berghof" in gothic letters beside one door rings a very dim bell: "Había leído ese nombre en alguna otra parte, en un libro, pero no recordaba en cuál" (I had read that name somewhere, in some book, but I didn't remember which one).[53] Like the virus subtly starting to infiltrate his patient's body, the name of Hitler's Bavarian residence steals obscurely into the doctor's enchantment with his sleeping wife after he redescends to their hotel. The name only turns noxious when a subsequent summer's return to that beach and clifftop instantaneously corrects an apparent lifetime of vague awareness of Holocaust history: "Berghof" is put into glaring relief when the doctor is dragged into the private SS shrine of an inexplicably choking former Nazi leader.

Clara Sánchez's 2010 novel *Lo que esconde tu nombre* features a sophomoric, early-middle-aged drifter who stumbles into a similar ex-perpetrator enclave on the Valencian coast. A solitary character, Sandra initially responds to the apparent kindness of two elderly German-speaking Norwegians who revive her after a bout of morning sickness on the beach. As with Muñoz Molina's physician, Sandra seems to have retained only generalities from what schooling she received on the Holocaust, which keeps her from pointedly questioning Fred Christensen's overwhelming physique or his wife's perpetual "sonrisa diabólica" (diabolical smile.)[54] Per literary scholar Fidel López Criado, Sandra resembles "muchos jóvenes ... que desconocen un pasado sin el cual no se entiende el presente" (many young people ... who don't know the past without which there is no understanding the present). Such ignorance leads her into a servile friendship with the pair that becomes a "laberinto histórico y moral" (a historical and moral labyrinth). Sandra's ensuing bildungsroman seems steeped in Genesis as recurring biblical images chart her growing knowledge of good, in the form of Republican Mauthausen survivor Julián, and evil, in what his former camp torturers cannot erase beneath their studied normality. As Sandra joins Julián in his last feasible endeavour to rout "un nido de Nazis" (a nest of Nazis),[55] one way her transformation from inside informant to hostage in the Christensens' home evinces itself is through her increasingly sinister interpretation of its furnishings. Instead of coming from quarries in Almería, for example, the marble in their bathtub seems Austrian, from a quarry like the one in which Julián "había estado encerrado como la pobre gente que tantas veces había visto en los documentales" (had been locked up like all those other poor people I'd sometimes seen in documentaries).[56]

Echoing Muñoz Molina, here Clara Sánchez emphasizes the transformational impact of a measure of personal contact with Holocaust trauma, perpetrated or endured, over negligible recall of indistinct images from contemporary Spanish education or cultural literacy. This urges a more nuanced reading of the author's culminating image for her novel than López Criado proposes. He sees Sandra's eventual nickname for her son, "Little Julián," also "Little Janus," as inculcating the need to look to the past so that the future can be faced more holistically.[57] In their recent literary reckoning with the Holocaust, Antonio Muñoz Molina, Juana Salabert, and Clara Sánchez are first concerned with *how* they might artistically facilitate such critical learning from history. Each of these writers, as well as Chufo Lloréns, uses correlations between Iberian history and dimensions of the Nazi genocide as a way of organically connecting Spanish readers with a range of Jewish and Republican experiences during the Holocaust. Lloréns simply extends a staid Semitic "practised place" from Spanish *Reconquista* to German Reich, however. By contrast, portraying Sepharad as a void in contemporary Spain, Muñoz Molina's and Salabert's works offer Spanish readers more un/familiar places in which to practise personally and nationally enlightening movement in and between Spanish history and the Holocaust. Through its local simulation of a slight measure of Nazi entrapment, such a place for reader proxy experience is what Clara Sánchez's novel provides, as well.

NOTES

All English translations are my own except for quotations from Muñoz Molina, *Sefarad*, and Sánchez, *The Scent of Lemon Leaves*. For those I use existing English translations.

1 Muñoz Molina, *Sefarad*, 156–7; *Sepharad*, trans., 103.
2 Baer, "The Voids of Sepharad," 136, 143.

3 I juxtapose these dates following Juana Salabert's novel, *Velódromo de Invierno*. In the text, 1492 and 1942 mingle and evoke each other, and their inverted numerals signal fifteenth- versus twentieth-century environmental and circumstantial difference.

4 Certeau, *The Practice of Everyday Life*, 117.

5 Rothberg, *Multidirectional Memory*, 111–15.

6 Margalit, *The Ethics of Memory*, 51.

7 Nieva de la Paz, "*Sefarad* de Antonio Muñoz Molina," 367, 368n12.

8 Sánchez, *Lo que esconde tu nombre*, 257ff.

9 Salabert, *Velódromo de Invierno*, 90ff.

10 Álvarez Chillida, *El antisemitismo en España*, 73ff.

11 Certeau, *The Practice of Everyday Life*, 117.

12 Gironell, *El puente de los judíos*, 82.

13 Ibid., 82–9.

14 Lloréns, *La saga de los malditos*, 253–65, 589, 651–7; Irisarri and Martínez de Lezea, *Perlas para un collar*.

15 Lloréns, *La saga de los malditos*, 27, 922.

16 Herzberger, "Representing the Holocaust," 91.

17 Linhard, *Jewish Spain*, 59.

18 Ibid., 56–64.

19 Herzberger, "Representing the Holocaust," 91.

20 LaCapra, *Writing History, Writing Trauma*, 41 and throughout.

21 Linhard, *Jewish Spain*, 63.

22 Muñoz Molina, *Sefarad*, 541–2.

23 Herzberger, "Representing the Holocaust," 87.

24 LaCapra, *Writing History, Writing Trauma*, 102.

25 Muñoz Molina, *Sefarad*, 21, 26; *Sepharad*, trans., 8–9, 12–14.

26 Connerton, *How Societies Remember*, 35.

27 Muñoz Molina, *Sefarad*, 21, 27; *Sepharad*, trans., 9, 12.

28 Muñoz Molina, *Sefarad*, 28, 27, 31; *Sepharad*, trans., 14, 13, 16.

29 Muñoz Molina, *Sefarad*, 27; *Sepharad*, trans., 13. I have adapted the wording in the Spanish and English versions of the novel here. Muñoz Molina's Spanish reads, "Godino me explicó la historia, no sin prometerme que me contaría otras aún más sabrosas ..." Sayers Peden's translation reads, "Godino told me the story, not without promising that he would tell me others even juicier."

30 Connerton, *How Societies Remember*, 91.

31 Álvarez Chillida, *El antisemitismo en España*, 73, ff.

32 David Rousset, cited in Moyn, "From *l'Univers Concentrationnaire*," 279.

33 LaCapra, *Writing History, Writing Trauma*, 102.

34 Muñoz Molina, *Sefarad*, 443ff.; *Sepharad*, trans., 288ff. This direct address appears intermittently throughout the novel.

35 Muñoz Molina, *Sefarad*, 448.
36 Ibid., 550–2.
37 Muñoz Molina, *Sefarad*, 589, 590; *Sepharad*, trans., 378.
38 Muñoz Molina, *Sefarad*, 581–2.
39 Assmann, "Collective Memory," 125–7.
40 Linhard, *Jewish Spain*, 50.
41 Ibid., 40–1, 47, 49–51.
42 Rothberg, *Multidirectional Memory*, 139.
43 Salabert, *Velódromo de Invierno*, 35.
44 Maurice Halbwachs discussed in Assmann, "Collective Memory," 126.
45 Salabert, *Velódromo de Invierno*, 206.
46 Ibid., 108, 121.
47 Ibid., 40, 34.
48 Juana Salabert, cited in Luis García Jambrina, "La recuperación," 152.
49 Salabert, *Velódromo de Invierno*, 120.
50 Ibid., 91.
51 Ibid., 90–108.
52 Ibid., 109. Throughout Salabert's novel the epithet "child of mystery"
    applies primarily to Sebastián Miranda's visitor, Herschel, son of German
    Jewish Ilse Landermann, who reached Miranda after her chance escape
    from the Paris Velodrome in July 1942. The identity of Herschel's father
    remains a mystery despite his Iberian investigations.
53 Muñoz Molina, *Sefarad*, 288; *Sepharad*, trans., 191.
54 Sánchez, *Lo que esconde tu nombre*, 258; *The Scent of Lemon Leaves*, trans., 181.
55 Sánchez, *Lo que esconde tu nombre*, 247; *The Scent of Lemon Leaves*, trans., 172.
56 Sánchez, *Lo que esconde tu nombre*; *The Scent of Lemons Leaves*, trans., 181.
57 López Criado, "De Mauthausen a Denia," 193.

30 "Only Writing Matters": Anne Frank in/and Spanish Holocaust Poetry, 1966–2004

PAUL CAHILL

Spain and the Holocaust

In his volume on Spain for the *Life Magazine World Library* series, historian Hugh Thomas states that in Francoist Spain "[c]ensorship results in such general ignorance of outside events that a high court judge in Madrid heard of Hitler's massacre of the Jews only at the time of the Eichmann trial in 1961."[1] In a column published in the 29 November 1962 issue of *La Nueva España* (Oviedo), Guy Bueno discusses Thomas's book and highlights some of the inaccuracies he sees in it, specifically the example cited above:

> Hugh Thomas ha descubierto en Madrid a un alto magistrado que tan sólo se enteró en 1961 de la existencia de los campos de concentración alemanes de Buchenwald y Belsen. Sin poner en duda esta información, cabe señalar empero que si el magistrado en cuestión realmente ignoró, hasta 1961, dicha existencia, es porque lo quiso. En 1944 cualquier madrileño que pasara por la Cibeles hubiera podido comprar en los quioscos de «turistas» la información necesaria.[2]

> Hugh Thomas has discovered a high court judge in Madrid who only became aware of the existence of the German concentration camps at Buchenwald and Belsen in 1961. Without casting doubt on this information, it is worth noting that if the judge in question truly did not know, until 1961, about their existence, it is because he did not want to know. In 1944 any resident of Madrid who passed through the Cibeles plaza could have bought the necessary information in the "tourist" kiosks.

Information about the camps also appears after the war, including in newspapers affiliated with Franco's government, as was the case with *La*

Nueva España.[3] While these references usually take the form of informing readers about war crimes trials rather than serving as exposés on the Holocaust, these accounts of the trials often include specific details about the Holocaust and frame it in terms of crimes committed against Jews.

The series of war crimes trials held at Lüneburg and Nuremberg, the trial of Adolf Eichmann, and the Auschwitz trial in the mid-1960s received significant coverage in Spanish newspapers between 1945 and 1965. This coverage included detailed and occasionally graphic descriptions of wartime atrocities. What stands out in the press is the wide range of ways that these stories discuss the camps and the roles played by the accused. At each of these key moments between 1945 and 1965 one finds articles that employ an objective rhetorical style alongside others that engage the tropes and questions associated with sceptical attitudes towards the Holocaust, including some that verge on Holocaust denial. This proves to be the case particularly with the coverage of the Eichmann and Auschwitz trials.[4]

Given the range of different perspectives on the Holocaust present in Spain in the mid- to late 1960s, the earliest texts written by Spanish poets about the Holocaust did not appear in a vacuum and have the potential to contribute to this dialogue even today. There is also a retrospective value to this work, since even if Spanish poetry about the Shoah did not enjoy a large readership when published, we can consider what roles these poetic texts might play in the cultural and literary archive of reactions to the Holocaust in Spain from the Franco era to today.

Spanish Holocaust Poetry, 1961–2013

The authors who have produced Holocaust poetry in Spain include poets from some of the most important groups of writers in the twentieth and twenty-first centuries, including the Generation of 27 (León Felipe and Jorge Guillén), the Generation of 36 (José García Nieto), the Generation of the 1950s (Carlos Barral, José Manuel Caballero Bonald, José Ángel Valente), the *novísimos* (Marcos Ricardo Barnatán, Antonio Martínez Sarrión, José-Miguel Ullán, and Jorge Urrutia), and the post-Franco era (Antonio Crespo Massieu, Antonio Méndez Rubio, Juan Carlos Mestre, Isabel Pérez Montalbán, and Jorge Riechmann). This work has received rather scant critical attention and remains largely overlooked both by critics who study Holocaust poetry in other national contexts and by critics analysing Spanish poetry unrelated to the Shoah.[5]

The decade of the 1960s saw the first examples of Spanish poetry that discussed the Holocaust in the case of poems by Carlos Barral and José Manuel Caballero Bonald. These initial examples were followed by work by León Felipe, José García Nieto, Gabriel Celaya, Marcos Ricardo Barnatán, José Alberto Santiago, and José Ángel Valente. The next significant wave began in the 1990s with the work of poets like Juan Carlos Mestre and Isabel Pérez Montalbán. The first and second decades of the twenty-first century saw an even larger increase in interest in the Holocaust and in particular the first book-length poetic engagements with the Holocaust published in Spain. Poetic works like J. Jorge Sánchez's *Del Tercer Reich* (Of the Third Reich, 2002), Félix Grande's *La cabellera de la Shoá* (The hair of the Shoah, 2010), Antonio Crespo Massieu's *Elegía en Portbou* (Elegy in Portbou, 2011), Ana Vega's *Auschwitz 13* (2013), and Marifé Santiago Bolaños's *Nos mira la piedad desde las alambradas* (Pity looks at us from the barbed wire, 2013) present sustained, nuanced, and often provocative engagements with the Holocaust that occupy entire collections instead of isolated poems.

The types of knowledge upon which Spanish poets rely to craft these representations encompass a wide range of forms, ranging from existing written and visual representations and documentation, to physical objects and spaces that act as stimuli in the present, to accounts of visits to concentration camps. They also refer to key figures associated with the Holocaust like Primo Levi, Paul Celan, and the focus of this study, Anne Frank.

Anne Frank in Spain

Readers of the weekly magazine *Blanco y Negro* would have read in the 7 December 1963 issue that worldwide Anne Frank's *Diary* had sold more than 4 million copies and had been translated into twenty-one languages. These same readers would also have found the following description of the *Diary* as "un diario escrito en un cuaderno, en el que Ana Frank narraba las angustias, temores, esperanzas y desesperanzas durante los veinticinco meses de terror que ella y los suyos habían pasado escondidos en un granero de Amsterdam" (a diary written in a notebook, in which Anne Frank narrated the anguishes, fears, hopes, and desperation during the twenty-five months of terror that she and her loved ones had endured hidden in a barn in Amsterdam).[6] This description is both detailed and limited, as the inaccurate description of Frank's hiding place indicates.

While the most readily available edition in Spanish of Anne Frank's *Diary* at the moment is the current Plaza & Janés edition translated by Diego J. Puls (originally published in 2000), earlier translations of Frank's stories and diary (published both individually and together by this same publisher) completed by Juan Cornudella and Ana María de la Fuente had been available in Spain since 1962. The earliest translation into Spanish (and published in Spain) available in the Biblioteca Nacional de España collection is *Las habitaciones de atrás* (The Back Rooms), translated by María Isabel Iglesias and published in 1955 by Garbo (Barcelona).

A number of references to Anne Frank appeared in Spanish periodicals in the 1950s and 1960s, particularly in publications like *Blanco y Negro* and *¡Hola!* In addition to references to testimonies of those who knew her and the opening of the Anne Frank museum, there have also been numerous references to the adaptations of her *Diary* for the stage and the screen. The details surrounding her death also appear as part of a trivia game featured in the satirical magazine *La Codorniz*.

One of the most important articles that appeared during this time was a series of three features on Anne Frank written by Lies Goslar Pick (with Stanley Frank) and published by *¡Hola!* in January 1959.[7] The features' title, "Yo conocí a Anna Frank" (I met Anne Frank) draws attention to Frank's name by printing it in all capital letters. The second instalment of this feature includes a section about Bergen-Belsen, in which the author describes an encounter with Frank in the camp:

> La emoción me impide recordar lo que siguió en los primeros minutos de nuestro encuentro. Creo que me explicó que había estado escondida y que la enviaron a Auschwitz cuando la Gestapo descubrió a toda la familia. Yo me esforzaba por verla en la oscuridad. Conforme mis ojos se acostumbraban a las sombras, pude darme cuenta de que vestía un harapiento uniforme, lo que me hizo avergonzarme de mis ropas, que los guardianes me habían permitido conservar. Estaba tan depauperada que sus ojos parecían dos pedazos de carbón colocados en las cuencas de una calavera. De pronto comprendí por qué había pensado en una calavera. Le habían afeitado la cabeza.[8]

> Emotion stops me from remembering what followed during the initial minutes of our meeting. I think she explained to me that she had been hidden and that they sent her to Auschwitz when the Gestapo discovered her whole family. I tried hard to see her in the darkness. As my eyes got used to the shadows I realized that she wore a tattered uniform, which made me ashamed of my clothing, which the guards had allowed me to keep. She was so debilitated that her eyes seemed like two pieces of coal placed in the eye sockets of a skull. I suddenly understood why I had thought of a skull. They had shaved her head.

This vivid account of the author's encounter with Anne Frank paints a partial picture for Spanish readers at the time of the conditions in Nazi concentration camps. Taken together, these texts provide information regarding Anne Frank's writings, their popularity, and how they were adapted, as well as an account of her time and experience in Bergen-Belsen. They provide readers with information – of varying degrees of accuracy – while simultaneously assuming that these same readers already possess certain knowledge of the subject. The three poems that will be discussed in the next section aim to expand on how imagination and information inform Spanish poetic representations of Anne Frank in poems dating from the 1960s and from the first decade of the twenty-first century.

Anne Frank in Spanish Poetry: 1966, 1968, 2004

The earliest evidence of the impact of Anne Frank on the work of Spanish poets appears in the 1960s in the form of texts by José García Nieto (1914–2001) and Antonio López Luna (1944–2014). Both of these poems incorporate Anne Frank and her writing into the text by way of a connection to the poetic speaker's personal experience, and one could argue that they are as much about Anne Frank as they are about what Anne Frank and her writing mean to the speaker. Both poems rely on a confessional tone and structure, employing the rhetoric of autobiography to frame the speaker's discovery of Anne Frank. Although these poems seek to come to terms with and find a place for Anne Frank's legacy in the context of the speaker's life, both end up exhibiting a fairly superficial engagement with Frank and her diary. A later engagement with the figure of Frank appears in a prose poem by Jorge Urrutia (1945–) published in 2004. The Anne Frank discussed in Urrutia's poem is one mediated by Primo Levi's discussion of the significance of her writing and legacy. Urrutia's text explores the ethical and theoretical implications of violence, suffering, and representation, using Frank as a case study.[9]

1966: José García Nieto

The awarding of the Premio Cervantes to José García Nieto in 1996 celebrated his status as one of the most prominent poets in postwar Spain. García Nieto is best known for his early work and the magazine it was associated with, *Garcilaso. Juventud creadora. Verso y prosa* (1943–6). The initial framing of *Garcilaso* and *garcilasismo* was built around the convergence of several different discourses: the commemoration of the four-hundredth anniversary of Garcilaso de la Vega's death in 1936, the beginning of the Spanish Civil War, and a reaction to the experimental aesthetic tendencies of the 1920s and 1930s.[10]

García Nieto's work would at first glance seem an unlikely place to look for poems about the Holocaust, given his penchant for writing poetry considered to be disengaged from social concerns or even implicitly supporting conservative political interests. *Memorias y compromisos* (Memories and Commitments, 1966) represents a significant departure from this dominant view of the poet, in both formal and thematic terms. Unlike most of the work of García Nieto, whose numerous sonnets reflect the neoclassical *garcilasista* style for which he is best known, the poems that make up *Memorias y compromisos* exhibit a blending of free verse and prose poetry.

"Carta para Ana Frank" (Letter for Anne Frank), a poem included in *Memorias y compromisos*, is simultaneously a letter *to* Anne Frank, as the title indicates, but is also a letter *about* Anne Frank to the readers of García Nieto's text. There is thus a multi-pronged effort in place here – to address Anne Frank, to reflect upon the experience of reading her diary, and to inform readers of what her diaristic text says but also what happened collectively during the Holocaust. The basic thematic progression of García Nieto's poem is the following. After an initial address to Anne Frank the speaker goes on to recount his reading process, the impact this process had on him, and what he seeks to accomplish after reading the *Diary*. A tension between what the speaker did and did not know takes up much of the poem, which ends with a series of things the speaker will not forget. These tensions and motifs are marked by anaphora, and in the case of the tension between knowledge and ignorance, these form part of an explicit logical structure. This poem ends up painting a mixed picture of Anne Frank and her writing. On the one hand, the poem and its speaker highlight the significance and impact of Frank's work. At the same time, however, the poem devolves into patronizing language and problematic comparisons that minimize Frank's symbolic power.

García Nieto's poem begins with a statement directed to Anne Frank that involves hope, one of the key concepts that will be identified in her work:

> Tú has hecho válida la letra,
> tú has hecho posible la palabra;
> tú has hecho del lenguaje la más patética dimensión de los hombres,
> y nos has dejado mudos si ya no nos atrevemos a ir un poco más lejos que
>   tú en la esperanza.[11]

> You have made the letter valid,
> you have made the word possible;
> you have made language the most pathetic dimension of men,

> and you have left us mute if we no longer take the risk of going a little
>   farther than you in hope

These verses bring together both the medium ("letter," "word," and "language") and the content ("hope") of Frank's writing, and they do so while positing a "we" affected by this writing. This "we" seems to be an expansive one, made up of "mankind" (or perhaps just "men"). In the next sentence this collective group gives way to the experience of just one person, the poem's speaker, and his reading of Anne Frank's *Diary*: "He leído de prisa, he leído tarde, he cerrado ahora tu Diario como quien cierra la caja de un muerto querido" (I have read quickly, I have read late, I have closed your Diary just now, like someone who closes the casket of a deceased loved one).[12] This speaker, moved by his reading, feels compelled to add his own contribution to Frank's legacy:

> Y ahora que sigue sonando tu voz y me golpea como la pata de un
>   animalillo doméstico que de tan claro no entendemos, de tan cercano
>   no sentimos,
> yo quiero dejar unas letras en unas cuartillas para que haya una doliente
>   piedra más en el edificio que has levantado y en el que alojaste tu
>   comunicativa soledad. . .

> And now that your voice keeps sounding and hits me like the paw of a
>   house pet that is so clear that we don't understand it, so close that we
>   don't feel it,
> I want to leave some letters on some pages so that there may be one more
>   aching stone in the building that you've raised and in which you
>   housed your communicative loneliness. . .[13]

The speaker's contribution is presented as one building upon an already existing structure ("edificio") and is seemingly framed as but a modest contribution to this legacy. These words also walk a fine line between celebrating the impact of Anne Frank's words and at the same time taking away their (intellectual) value or at least casting doubt on her authorial intentions, in particular when we look at the simile in which her voice is compared to the paw of a pet. The words left by García Nieto's speaker employ anaphora to build an explicit logical structure populated by a discussion of what he did and did not know, what he learned (by reading Anne Frank's *Diary*), and what he can now conclude regarding the significance of Frank's writing.

A potential pitfall associated with this effort to educate and inform readers is the amount of imagination required for this to take place. The clearest instance of this appears when García Nieto's speaker describes events not covered in the *Diary*:

> el final de tu esperanza con nosotros era llegar a caminar desnuda entre el hambre y la miseria de un campo de concentración, con la cabeza rapada, guardando memoria de los dedos de Robert que jugaban con tus cabellos bajo los tejados sin luz y sobre el silencio temeroso de los canales de Amsterdam o el estruendo de los bombardeos

> the end of your hope with us was ending up walking naked among the hunger and misery of a concentration camp, with your head shaved, guarding the memory of Robert's fingers that played with your hair beneath the dark roofs and above the scared silence of the canals of Amsterdam or the tumult of the bombings[14]

What, then, could we say this poem adds to the "building" or archive created by Anne Frank? From a purely practical standpoint, García Nieto's poem introduces readers previously unfamiliar with Anne Frank to her writing and includes vivid images of persecution. García Nieto's poem aims to reach readers through imagery based not on Frank's own documented memories, but instead on an imagined scenario like the one described in the passage cited above. One could argue that in a cultural context like Spain's, in which images of the Holocaust were scarce, such representations and extrapolations might be necessary to inform readers about what took place in Nazi concentration camps, but the fact remains that García Nieto's poem also offers a fabricated (but perhaps not improbable) image to readers, thus dehistoricizing Anne Frank even while it writes her into the historical record and collective imaginary.

1968: Antonio López Luna

Antonio López Luna published only two books of poetry (the second one, *Monstruorum artifex* [1977] under the pseudonym Alascok-Ish de Luna). While other Spanish poets born between 1939 and 1951 ended up being more prolific, López Luna's first collection does form part of an important subset of Spanish poetry in the 1960s. *Memoria de la muerte* (Memory of death, 1968) received an *accésit* (runner-up) for the Premio Adonáis de poesía. Submissions that received *accésits* or the prize itself were published in the prestigious Adonáis series. This prize, which still exists, played an especially important role in the 1960s. Collections by important poets like Marcos Ricardo Barnatán (1946–), Pureza Canelo (1946–), Antonio Colinas (1946–), Félix Grande (1937–2014), Antonio

Hernández (1943–), and Diego Jesús Jiménez (1942–2009) received the prize or an *accésit* between 1963 and 1970.

Although the Holocaust is not a central thematic focus of "Tiempo de origen" (Time of Origin), Anne Frank, her experience, and her writing *do* still play a central role in the origin traced in López Luna's poem. This long poem – it has more than 350 verses – recounts a sort of non-existent origin that nonetheless influences the experience and identity of the poem's speaker and his generation. Included in *Memoria de la muerte*, this poem revolves around the idea of a lack of direct experience of the past:

> No estábamos allí: nosotros, jóvenes
> de ahora, generación de la posguerra,
> muchachos que nacimos por los años
> cuarenta. [...].[15]

> We weren't there: we, youth
> of today, generation of the post-war,
> young men who were born in the
> 1940s.

These verses posit and construct a specific subset of people as the ones who make up the "we" in question. The "we" that was not there during the Spanish Civil War is made up of the youth of "today," the generation of the post-war born in the 1940s. The shifters used to craft this "we" and its distance from the Spanish Civil War hinge primarily on temporal questions. This "lack" of specific experiences appears later in the poem in the context of the Second World War and the Holocaust.

Although the poem uses the same construction to introduce Anne Frank and the Holocaust – a declaration that "we" were not there when the events to be recounted took place – in this instance it is not merely a question of temporal distance. Even if the members of this generation had been alive at the time they still would not have been aware of Anne Frank's experience until years after the fact. Regardless of this increased distance, the events recounted play a telling role in the way this generation understands its identity. There is also a greater specificity to this absent yet present experience, since it centres on a specific figure associated with the Holocaust.

Reiterated throughout the poem, this lack of experience creates an intriguing tension with the emphasis on the importance of what was not experienced. What was not experienced vis-à-vis the Holocaust is an already mediated occurrence that relies on a symbol of the

Holocaust: Anne Frank and her diary. The lacking experience sought by the speaker is thus one that is negotiated by writing and a synecdoche that has come to represent the Holocaust for many:

[...] y no estábamos
allí cuando Ana Frank, niña, esperando
su cumpleaños mensual, tenía
en su menor edad horas más largas
que la vida normal de un mes, y estaba
esperando el amor aunque escribía
el testamento de una raza entera,
el legado de amar Jerusalén,
el libro de los últimos deseos,
en un blanco diario inacabado
y con su letra azul de colegiala.[16]

and we weren't
there when Anne Frank, a child, awaiting
her menstrual birthday, had
at her young age longer hours
than the normal life of a month, and was
awaiting love although she was writing
the testament of an entire race,
the legacy of loving Jerusalem,
the book of final wishes,
in a white, unfinished diary
and with her blue schoolgirl handwriting.

The opening verses highlight a sense of hope and expectation marked by failure. This disillusionment at such a young age becomes doubly tragic, especially when the poem goes to such lengths to draw attention to these two elements by referring to her as a "niña", "esperando / su cumpleaños mensual," who "estaba / esperando el amor aunque escribía / el testamento de una raza entera." The poem creates the sensation that Frank was experiencing things that were overwhelming for someone her age. After referring to her as a "niña" in an appositive, the text juxtaposes her "menor edad" and the "horas más largas / que la vida normal de un mes" that she experienced. A similar juxtaposition seems to be taking place between what her writing meant to her and what it has come to mean to others. The "aunque escribía" that introduces the "testamento de una raza entera" also presents a further description of her text and its effects. What she was writing was thus a testament, legacy, and book written in a diary with the blue handwriting of a schoolgirl. How do we reconcile the grandeur and transcendence of the greater future impact of her writing with the naivety that López Luna's text attributes to her writing process?

Despite including an extended allusion to Anne Frank and her diary, "Tiempo de origen" does not describe what happened to Anne Frank or other victims of the Holocaust. Without knowing anything else about Anne Frank or the Holocaust, one would not even know that Anne Frank had died in a Nazi concentration camp, nor could one be entirely sure which "raza entera" she was writing about. All we would have would be a sense of tragedy, a youth marked by hardship, and an unfinished diary that speaks to what could have been. "Tiempo de origen" thus relies on a certain amount of knowledge brought by the reader to be able to flesh out and activate the text. Given the amount of information already available in Spain about the Holocaust in general and Anne Frank in particular, it is not unreasonable to assume that most readers would be able to fill in any necessary blanks. Providing so little information about Anne Frank as López Luna's poem does could also have the effect of positing and presenting her as a sort of universalized symbol of injustice and human cruelty and as a result eliding and obscuring her specificity and Spain's long history of antisemitism.

2004: Jorge Urrutia

The complex relationship between experience, writing, and mediation in the case of Anne Frank becomes even more complex when the "Anne Frank" referred to by a poem is one discussed in the writings of others. In a poem from his 2004 collection *El mar o la impostura* (The Sea or Slander), Jorge Urrutia (Madrid, 1945–) refers to the "Anne Frank" discussed in Primo Levi's *The Drowned and the Saved* (1986). Spanish translations of Levi's Auschwitz Trilogy were posthumous, appearing in 1987–9 (one volume each year). All three books are currently available in a single volume.[17]

Jorge Urrutia's first poetry collection was published in 1966. Engaging with surrounding social reality and in particular social injustice has been a key to much of Urrutia's poetry, including poems that allude to the Holocaust, the Vietnam War, refugees, and the second Iraq War. Urrutia is known for both his poetry and his scholarly work; his poetry has received awards including the Premio Jaime Gil de Biedma (for *El mar o la impostura*) and has been included in a number of anthologies.

Urrutia's poem "(Porque sólo soy verbo)" ([Because I'm only a Verb/ the Word]) opens with the following epigraph from Levi's text: "Una sola

Ana Frank nos conmueve más que las innumerables personas que sufri-
eron igual que ella. Y así quizá deba de ser: si tuviésemos y pudiésemos
compartir los sufrimientos de todas las personas, no podríamos seguir
viviendo"[18] (A single Anne Frank excites more emotion than the myriads
who suffered as she did but whose image has remained in the shadows.
Perhaps it is necessary that it can be so. If we had to and were able to
suffer the sufferings of everyone, we could not live).[19] Urrutia's engagement with the genocide relies on existing texts as a vehicle for extending
critical thought about the Holocaust. In this instance the text is already a
reflection on the representation of the Holocaust rather than on an autobiographical account. By attributing the quote to Levi, Urrutia situates
his text within a certain tradition of texts reflecting upon the Holocaust,
and thus it serves as a commentary of the epigraph:

> Este parrafito puede tener dos comentarios que interesan desde el punto
> de vista semiótico.
>
> No importa tanto, para conmover, para convulsionar, para reclamar la
> acción, el sufrimiento como el signo del sufrimiento. A través de su diario,
> la joven Ana se convirtió en eso, en signo de la maldad, no ya sufrida,
> sino ejercida sobre el ser humano. A la ética no le afecta la maldad por el
> sufrimiento, sino por el acto.
>
> Pero, para convertirse en símbolo, Ana Frank precisó de la escritura.
> Sin ésta no habría existido Ana, y sin Ana carecería de expresión el dolor
> sufrido y la injusticia ejercida.
>
> Luego, terriblemente (y digo bien «terriblemente»), sólo la escritura im-
> porta. A la postre, sólo la escritura es.[20]

This short paragraph can have two interesting commentaries from the
semiotic point of view.

It doesn't matter so much, to move, to convulse, to demand action, suffering as the sign of suffering. Through her diary, the young Anne became
that, the sign of evil, no longer suffered, but rather exerted upon the human being. Evil doesn't affect ethics through the suffering but rather the
act.

But, to become a symbol, Anne Frank needed writing. Without this
Anne would not have existed, and without Anne the pain suffered and
the injustice exerted would lack expression.

Therefore, terribly (and I'm right to say "terribly"), only writing matters. In the end, only writing is.

In this poem Urrutia uses an epigraph from Primo Levi's *The Drowned
and the Saved* to frame his poem and then employs an extended and

explicit logical structure to unpack Levi's quote and explore the meaning of both Anne Frank and the representation of trauma and injustice more broadly. Urrutia's poem seeks to define ways to create a positive impression in the wake of social injustice and atrocity. The three actions posited as desired outcomes appear in the poem's second paragraph: "conmover," "convulsionar," and "reclamar la acción." The poem begins with what *does not* matter to or help accomplish these goals: "el sufrimiento como el signo del sufrimiento" (suffering as the sign of suffering). The poem juxtaposes two ways of looking at these sorts of signs. The first sees them through the lens of evil as pain suffered by human beings while the second focuses instead on evil as a result of the violence perpetrated upon human beings. This same juxtaposition is applied to how we see things in ethical terms. The poem privileges the unjust or violent act over the suffering that results from it. Grammatically, this interplay is represented by past participles used as adjectives, thereby combining the explicit descriptive function of an adjective with the perfected nature of the actions and the suffering they engender.

What matters in the end, according to Urrutia's speaker, is writing. It is through writing that "Anne Frank" becomes "Anne," symbol of both suffering and the violence that causes suffering. Without her diary "Anne" would not exist, and neither would the testimony of suffering and injustice. The explicit logical structure in this poem is scaffolded by the following terms: "(no) importa" (it doesn't matter), "para" (to), "pero" (but), and "luego" (therefore) and employs polysyndeton to highlight each of the three future actions mentioned in the second paragraph. This gesture of using an account of past injustices and atrocities as a springboard for action in the present also appears in earlier poems written by Urrutia. As I have discussed elsewhere, "Poema ardiente" (Burning Poem) from his 1968 collection *La fuente como un pájaro escondido* (The Fountain like a Hidden Bird) employs a similar repeated logical structure (including the verb "importar") and instances of past injustice (including the Holocaust) to ultimately make the case for resolve and action in the present.[21]

What remains unclear is whether a similar belief in resolve and action is present in "(Porque sólo soy verbo)." What matters in the end is writing, this poem tells us, but it is equally important to look at precisely how it is that writing matters. This fact – that *only* writing matters, that *only* writing exists – is framed by the repetition of the adverb "terribly." Writing, by this account, is both sufficient and insufficient; it is able to reach wide audiences, especially in the case of Anne Frank, but for as much as it represents there is much more that it does not and cannot represent. Writing is, then, but *only* writing is.

The Testament of an Entire Race?

A close look at Spanish newspapers and magazines published during the Franco regime reveals that much more information about the Holocaust was available than one might imagine, given the strictures of Francoist censorship. From accounts of war crimes trials to stories about historical figures like Anne Frank, readers at the time could certainly have found information regarding the names and locations of camps as well as certain of the atrocities perpetrated by Nazis and their collaborators. Spanish poets writing during that time likewise contributed to both the dissemination and the framing of this information. The poems they wrote do not necessarily exhibit deep or extended engagements with figures like Anne Frank (and her writing) but they do present her as an important figure and offer her *Diary* as a text that merits the attention of Spanish readers. Both García Nieto's and López Luna's texts posit Anne Frank's writings as foundational for the crafting and development of each poetic speaker's persona. In both "Carta para Ana Frank" and "Tiempo de origen" Anne Frank serves an identity-conferring role in how these speakers see themselves and the world in which they grew up or into which they were born. As I have argued above, a more nuanced negotiation with the person and symbol of Frank – and her significance for other authors – is the focus in Jorge Urrutia's more recent "(Porque sólo soy verbo)." In all three of these poems, nevertheless, *writing* takes centre stage. Anne Frank's words and their ability to circulate through different linguistic, temporal, and national spaces and contexts allow Spanish poets and readers to reflect upon the meaning of her work, even while these Spanish poems proffer Frank as but a starting point on a journey of exploration into Spanish social and historical identities as they may find meaning through the Holocaust.

NOTES

1 Thomas, *Spain*, 116. The 1966 edition of Thomas's study appears to be a reprint of the original 1962 edition.
2 Bueno, "Aparece un nuevo libro sobre España," 3. The story Bueno alludes to appears in this later, 1966, edition.
3 In his thorough study of antisemitism in Spain between 1912 and 2002, Gonzalo Álvarez Chillida discusses the coverage of the Holocaust in *ABC*, NO-DOs, and books. While this coverage included some details of the Holocaust, including references to the number of people killed and to the

camps where these deaths took place, these sources also tended to minimize the impact of genocidal violence by way of comparisons with other atrocities. In virtually all cases, images of camps and victims were strictly censored. Álvarez Chillida, *El antisemitismo en España*, 414–20.

4 In May 1961, *La Nueva España* ran a multipart series from Paul Rassinier's *The Lie of Ulysses*. The series was framed by the large-print headline "Lo que nadie se atreve a decir sobre El caso Eichmann" (What nobody dares to say about the Eichmann case).

5 Some of the studies that do look at this work include those by Cahill, "Globalizing Good and Evil"; and Luis Martín-Estudillo, "Death's Twilight Kingdom: Antonio Martínez Sarrión's *Cantil*," and Sultana Wahnón, "Graves of the Jews: The Holocaust in Post-war Spanish Poetry," both in Gómez López-Quiñones and Zepp, eds, *The Holocaust in Spanish Memory*.

6 "Cuatro millones de ejemplares del 'Diario de Ana Frank.'"

7 In *Anne Frank: The Book, The Life, The Afterlife*, 57, Francine Prose provides additional background on and corroboration of this story.

8 Goslar Pick, "Yo conocí a Anna Frank," 17.

9 See Tabea Alexa Linhard's discussion of Anne Frank in chapter 6 of this volume.

10 Urrutia, "El concepto de Garcilaso," 131.

11 García Nieto, *Memorias y compromisos*, 91.

12 Ibid., 91.

13 Ibid., 93.

14 Ibid., 92–3.

15 López Luna, *Memoria de la muerte*, 45.

16 Ibid., 51.

17 Levi, *Trilogía de Auschwitz*.

18 Urrutia, *El mar o la impostura*, 13.

19 Levi, *The Drowned and the Saved*, 56.

20 Urrutia, *El mar*, 13.

21 Cahill, "Globalizing," 465–7.

31 The Words That Replace the Elusive Past: Some Recent Ladino Poetic Responses to the Holocaust

SHMUEL REFAEL

A growing number of researchers are delving into the significance of the poetry written after Auschwitz, especially now that more than seventy years have passed since smoke stopped rising from the crematoria. There is increasing recognition in the research literature on the philosophical examination of the poetics of the Holocaust that Auschwitz will soon fade away and will be replaced by the word: words that will replace the past, will give it a new presentation, and will attempt to offer a cure to the oblivion that is gnawing savagely at the memory of the Holocaust. Alvin H. Rosenfeld, in *The End of the Holocaust*,[1] devotes the first section of his book to a discussion of this issue, and bases his findings on the perceptions of a few of the well-known Holocaust documenters, such as Claude Lanzmann, who has commented that works of art are a more powerful means for preserving the elusive historical past. All that remains in the end is the work of art. Rosenfeld's words ring all the more true in light of the fact that the last Holocaust survivors – those who suffered the indignities of Auschwitz – are departing this world. This is particularly tangible in the dramatic decline in the numbers of Ladino-speaking Holocaust survivors, who from the outset were a small minority among all the survivors. Even so, the voice of the survivors from Salonica and other Sephardic Balkan communities in the historical documentation of the Holocaust has increased its pitch in recent years.[2] This voice has been raised out of a strong desire to return Sephardim – who suffered from being relegated to the margins of history and from being labelled as "not belonging" to the Holocaust narrative – to the centre stage of research and documentation.[3] Among this group of historical documenters are also poetic documenters: we have a large corpus of poems written in Ladino that constitute an unrecognized response to the subject of the Holocaust and the Sephardic experience.[4]

These poets sought, after it was all over, to arouse interest in the experiences of Ladino-speakers (Sephardim) during the Holocaust.

In recent years we have witnessed an exceptional phenomenon of some writers whom I define as culture agents: those who do not necessarily have first-hand experience of the events and the incidents, but who seek to be a mouthpiece for those who are no longer with us, for those whose stories can no longer be heard. These culture agents are taking the place of the Ladino Holocaust survivors. Why do certain authors choose to write poetry in Ladino on the subject of the Holocaust? What is behind this need? Why are they choosing writing? Rosenfeld examined writing as a difficult and unrelenting obligation when he dedicated a chapter in his book to the writings of Primo Levi – a Holocaust survivor who used his writing to bring an awareness of Auschwitz to millions, but who, despite his prolific writing about Auschwitz, never felt that his writings brought him any release from his distressing past.[5]

In the past decade there has been a measure of progress in both research and debate about poetic Ladino Holocaust literature.[6] There has also been increased activity in the poetic corpus composed in Ladino and featuring the Holocaust experience of Sephardim. The circle of Ladino Holocaust poets has grown as well, although two of the poets have produced only one or two works, while a third has written a series of long, narrative poems. Yacob Nahmias, one of the most interesting poets among the culture agents, has in particular attempted to amplify the voices of Ladino Holocaust poetry in his work, while turning himself into a mouthpiece for the victims. A. Isaac Habib, B. Leon R. Arouh, and Nahmias are just a few of the Ladino poetic voices that have emerged in the past decade.

A. Isaac Habib was born in 1951 in Lubumbashi, to parents who were natives of Rhodes and immigrated to Congo. Two of his poems were published in *Los Muestros*, and their narrative is connected to the Jews of Rhodes during the Holocaust.[7] In his poem "A los que se salvaron" (To those who were saved) which is written in simple, direct language, he laments the rapid loss of the Jewish community in Rhodes and paints a heart-wrenching parallel between pregnancy, which culminates with childbirth, and the nine months during which the Jews of Rhodes were annihilated. In his poem "La sinagoga shalom" (The shalom synagogue), he extends a literary invitation to his readers to visit the orphaned synagogue of the Rhodes Jewish community. Although this synagogue has become a tourism destination, the Jewish community life that once resounded within its walls has been silenced forever.

B. Leon R. Arouh was born in 1943 to Refael and Alegra Arouh in Athens. His parents left Salonica for Athens in 1942, during the German occupation. Leon Arouh was active in the community life of

Jewish Salonica, participated in cultural initiatives, and was the editor of *El Avenir* magazine, which was published under the auspices of the Salonican Jewish community. Between 2003 and 2008 he set his hand to writing poetry, and the fruits of his labours appeared in the booklet "Un poko de riir un poko de yorar" (A Little Laughter a Little Weeping). One short, untitled poem by Arouh that appeared in an edition of *El Avenir* is a brief depiction of the narrative of his family in Salonica during the Holocaust.[8] He died in Salonica in 2009, the same year that poem was published.

C. Yacob Nahmias, born in 1933 in Salonica to Rachelle and Meir Nahmias, moved to Eretz Israel with his parents when he was barely three months old. He was raised and educated in Eretz Israel and later in the State of Israel, with full exposure to Hebrew. A book of his poems, *Poemas*, was published in 2012, when the author was seventy-nine.[9] This book has an abundance of bilingual poems (Ladino and Hebrew), and an entire section of Holocaust poems that will form the focus of this chapter.

Winds of the Traumatic Past:
The Holocaust Poems of Yacob Nahmias

Nahmias's Holocaust poetry epitomizes Dominick LaCapra's statement in *Writing History, Writing Trauma* that the dangers of trauma hover not only over those individuals who experienced it personally, but also over the society touched by those experiences in any manner, which is revisited by the winds of the traumatic past.[10] Nahmias was born in Salonica but spent his entire life in a Hebrew-speaking milieu and in Israeli society; he never personally experienced the horrors of the Holocaust. Writing poetry was not a lifelong pursuit for him, but rather a talent he discovered in his later years, when he decided to give expression to the voices of the Ladino speakers who had perished. While his poems are a tribute to the Jews of Salonica who were murdered in the Holocaust, they also gave him release from the spirit of the traumatic past – of his lost relatives who died in the Holocaust – which gave him no peace. Nahmias is the most prolific of the poets who have written Ladino Holocaust poetry in recent years.

Nahmias's collection is powerful, both in the volume of the poems and considering that it came seemingly out of a vacuum, for the author had no previous works. Nahmias was not a Holocaust survivor and Ladino was not an active language for him. Nevertheless, his poems were written not from a position of distance, but rather from a position of complete identification with the communal catastrophe. He wrote in the first-person plural, and anyone unfamiliar with his biography might mistakenly assume that these are poems by a Holocaust survivor, as they are exceptionally detailed. The full descriptions seem to fulfil Nahmias's need to be faithful to the historical narratives. One might ask, how could someone who was not "there" write as if he had actually been there?

Nahmias's cycle of Holocaust poetry consists of eight lengthy narrative poems. The full volume of fifty poems is not dedicated solely to the topic of the Holocaust; that said, these eight long poems in the first half have a marked effect on the entire book.[11] They were written over the course of several months, between the autumn of 2009 and the summer of 2010, and appear in the book as a representation of the unfolding history of Salonican Jewry during the Holocaust, from the Nazi conquest of the city to the liberation of the extermination camps. The opening poem of the cycle is "Plaza de la Libertad," which relates the assembling of Salonica's Jews in Liberation Square, where they had to register for future work assignments and eventual transport to the camps in Poland. The closing poem is "Marcha de la muerte," which treats the death marches immediately prior to the liberation of Salonica's Jews from the concentration and extermination camps.

Nahmias's poetry is unique in that it seemingly restores repressed memories. These are not his personal memories, but rather those of members of his community, to whom he never had the opportunity to bid farewell because he was so young when his parents permanently departed the city of his birth, Salonica. He throws off the mantle that envelops and protects those who did not personally suffer the indignities of the Holocaust, and who could have refrained from the obsessive preoccupation with the past; he chooses instead to confront memories that are not his, out of the desire to give them expression, form them into words and afford them poetic representations. He dismantles emotional experiences that ostensibly do not belong to him, and acquires them for himself through the penning of long, complex strophes of poetry. One gains the impression that the painful experiences exist within him as memories that he is willing to adopt in order to give them expression. Thus, paradoxically, he turns forgotten remembrances into memorable memories. These memories were acquired over many decades and accumulated until they formed a rich and full-bodied narrative poem totality. The traumatic past that was the lot of his relatives, whom Nahmias could have chosen to forget because they were not part of his life experience, erupts from the subconscious and makes the memory of the past accessible. From this perspective it is possible to assert that Nahmias serves as a medium for memory, a liaison who mediates between those who experienced the trauma (but could not speak about it) and those who did not experience it (but sought to speak on behalf of others). Nahmias did not recoil from addressing that trauma as an intensely negative emotional experience,[12] but rather exhibited a willingness to integrate it into the story of his life. The poet heard his relatives speaking about their traumatic experiences, engraved them on his own consciousness, and stored them in his inner being; then later, as if they were latent memories that resurface at the final station in the life of the sufferer, he processed them in a torrent of creativity that resulted in Holocaust poetry. These poems effectively seal a hole that gaped in the souls of those tormented by the memories, and who could not express their experiences. In this way, Nahmias gives voice to his relatives' muteness.

In her comprehensive article on the role of forgetting in working through the Holocaust trauma within poetic language, Israeli researcher Rina Dudai suggests three main paradigms of forgetting: deep forgetting, shallow forgetting, and cathartic forgetting.[13] Deep forgetting is hidden, inaccessible, and sometimes seems to have fallen into the abyss of oblivion. The traumatized person prefers not to arouse the memory, in order not to contend with painful events from the past.[14] Poetic texts that are built from extractions from deep memory into the literary medium employ extreme caution, without raising the events of the past and without bringing them into confrontation with the new reality.[15] Those who use the coping method of shallow forgetting – the second category – lead a double life. On the one hand they live with the trauma as a continuous experience, while on the other they live life outside the trauma. The forgetting mechanism is flexible, which facilitates this double life.[16] Poetic texts whose construction employs shallow forgetting also use the psychological tension that exists between the buried story and the obsessive need to save it from the abyss of oblivion, and retell it. This type of writing could be likened to poor-quality photography in that the literary text contains poor-quality fragments of the memory narrative. The third and final category of forgetting is cathartic forgetting, which Dudai stresses is the result of the processing of the traumatic memory, in order to gain release from it.[17] In this context it is noteworthy that literary works based on the processing of trauma in order to gain release from it raise the memory in fine detail, in a form of inner reflection that ultimately liberates the sufferer from the bonds of the memory and that can result in cathartic forgetting.[18]

Nahmias's flurry of writing that resulted in a copious quantity of texts is consistent with the third category presented by Dudai – cathartic writing that is characterized by the fine details of materials that the trauma victim conjures from his memory. In Nahmias's case, however, this process is somewhat paradoxical, for he did not experience the traumas but rather acted as the liaison between those who experienced the Holocaust and his readership. In this sense, Nahmias's writing is aimed at attaining a different sphere of coping: one of consolation and compassion. These are poems that Nahmias wrote during the final stage of his life, as if he were asking himself (and his relatives who perished) to repay an old debt that for many years had languished in the gloom of deep forgetting, and had been drawn up from those depths only after immense effort. From this perspective, one can say of Nahmias that he passed through the three stages Dudai enumerates in her article, from deep forgetting to full catharsis.

In the preface to his book, Nahmias relates that throughout the Second World War he and his family (who were living in Eretz Israel) had no knowledge of the fate of their relatives who had been sent from Salonica to Auschwitz:

> Durante los años de la guerra mondiala pasimos tiempos muy muy duros, especialmente porque no teníamos ninguna noticia ni informaciones de la vasta familia de mi padre, ni de mi nona y de toda la familia de la parte de mi madre. No se puede comparar muestra[19] situación en Israel entonces con lo que pasaron los judiós y otros en Europa al mismo tiempo.[20]

> We endured a very difficult period during the war years, especially due to the fact that we had no news or information from our extended family on my father's side, from my grandmother, or from my mother's side. There is no comparison between the situation in Israel and what the Jews and other nations in Europe went through during that same period.

This lack of information necessary to later process the mourning led Nahmias to a form of deep forgetting in the sense expressed by Dudai. For many years Nahmias also distanced himself from the Judeo-Spanish world, with all its symbols and linguistic expressions. He too found it difficult to cope with the trauma of the Holocaust suffered by his relatives who were left behind in Salonica, even if perhaps there was no reason for his distress. Nahmias lived with this feeling for many years. An in-depth examination of his poems, however, and an examination of the preface to his book, reveals that alongside the deep forgetting, he also lived with what Dudai describes as a dual identity. On the one hand he was an Israeli, but on the other hand he felt – even if in a repressed fashion – that he was the continuation of the Greek Jewish world. His father spoke several languages, and the songs in his home were in Greek, from the culture of Salonican Jewry.

Also, the general atmosphere in his family was Judeo-Grecian, as he describes in his preface:

> Los cuatro hermanos mos crecimos en la cultura judía y grega, hemos mantenido la tradición judía en oraciones y cantos religiosos, pero la música grega era la dominante en muestra casa. Mi padre tenía una hermosa y agradable voz, y a mosotros no mos mancaba: dos de mis hermanos tocaban la guitarra y la casa estaba siempre llena de alegría.[21]

> We four brothers were raised in the Jewish and Greek cultures. We kept the Jewish traditions of prayer and religious songs, but Greek music was very dominant in our home. My father had a very pleasant voice, which we were not lacking either. Two of my brothers played the guitar and our house was always filled with joy.

Nahmias refers to the atmosphere in his home not as Judeo-Spanish, but rather as Judeo-Grecian. Thus the Greek aspect covered and to some extent concealed his true identity, which was Sephardic, and this ultimately found expression in the cathartic stage in Dudai's paradigm. During this stage Nahmias wrote his poems in Judeo-Spanish (Ladino). Furthermore, these poems would be published in Spain, thereby closing the great circle in the author's reconciliation with his identity – a process that began with a deep repression and ended with the author's return to the crucible of his culture, Spain, via the language he acquired anew in his later years, through study and his exposure to dictionaries. In his preface, he describes his writing process in his later years:

> A la edad de 69 años me retirí después de laborar 55 años llenos de actividad gozosa y productiva. Hoy día soy estudiante en la Universidad Bar-Ilan, en el centro Naime y Yehoshua Salti de Estudios de Ladino. Allí topí de muevo mis raíces y torní a hablar el ladino de mi casa de antes de las guerras. Agora, teniendo más tiempo líbero, escribí en esta lengua mis poemas para dejarlos en herencia a las generaciones que vendrán, en la lengua que una vez no me placía, ma que fue la lengua de mi chiquez.[22]

> At age 69 I retired, after 55 years of blessed and productive activity. Today I am a student at Bar Ilan University, at the Naime and Yehoshua Salti Center for Ladino Studies. There I discovered my roots and began speaking the Ladino of my home before the war. Now that I have more free time, I have written my poems in that language, for the benefit of future generations – in this language that I disliked for a time, but which was the language of my childhood.

Bringing the Past to Eternal Rest by Collapsing the Distance between "There" and "Here"

The transition process between the three paradigms as described by Dudai enabled Nahmias to collapse the distance between "there" and "here." His readers gain the impression that these poems are a singular attempt by an older author not only to extract a deep trauma and bring it to a resting place in a cathartic process of sweeping and extensive writing, but also to use his writing to collapse the distance between what was happening "there" (in the extermination camps, where he was not part of that experience) and what was happening "here" (in Eretz Israel, when the poet was a small boy living safely with his family). In this context LaCapra says, in the spirit of Freud's assertion, that:

> the traumatic memory can include temporality and an incubation period between a previous true or imagined event and a later event that is somehow reminiscent and activates repression or renewed rejection and invasive behavior, but when the past is revived in an uncontrollable manner, there is seemingly no difference between the past and the present.[23]

Thus Nahmias apparently required a long incubation period that culminated in the collapse of times and places. In his poems, Nahmias becomes a Jew from Salonica who has joined those assembled at Liberty Plaza; is loaded onto a railcar of death; descends at the final station in Auschwitz-Birkenau; is chosen to work at back-breaking jobs (including the work of the *Sonderkommandos*); and towards the end is sent on the death marches, during which thousands of camp inmates died. These were events that Nahmias was re-experiencing in their totality. In LaCapra's parlance, the self was haunted by the traumatic "being there," compulsively returned to it and not always able to signify it or address it appropriately within the framework of language, or at least not as the critical liaison in any controlled fashion: "These processes are vital to anyone who wants to bring the spirits of the past to their final Real Estate, to renew an interest in life and activate memory in ways that can be examined critically."[24]

Nahmias's decision to open his cycle of Holocaust poems with "Plaza de la Libertad" was by no means arbitrary. Going to this square was akin to going back in time, to a place in which Salonica's Jews still lived and worked, before the commencement of the terrible tragedy. In Nahmias's poem, this square takes on a human character, through the author's use of the literary device of anthropomorphism. Even so, this human form has no voice, no ears, no face. It holds only spirits from the past who wish to return to the body that will give them verbal representation:

Plaza de la Libertad, tu nombre, ¿por qué?,
¿qué gloria vites que así te llaman?
No me respondes, tu voz, tus orejas, muertos.
Memorias cuentas de mi chiquez,
plaza de encontro forzado.
Lo veo,
parado, su cabeza elevada, de orden,
sus ojos pesgados, la luz apagada.
[...]
Nube blanca sobre la plaza, figuras en la nube,
las veo, miles,
todas escuras como manchas sobre blanco,
retornando de los fornos.
La ceniza en sus lados, vuela,
no permite enterrarlos, abominación eterna.
Retornando veo, sí, otra vez
a ti, plaza, que Libertad en ti no hay.[25]

Liberty Square, that is your name, but why?
What glory have you seen, that you are thus called?
You will not answer me, because your ears are blocked
You tell memories of my childhood,
O square of forced meetings.
I see
his head raised, responding to an order
his eyes despondent, their light extinguished
[...]
White snow on the square, figures in the snow
I see them in their thousands,
all dark, like stains on the whiteness
returning from the ovens,
The ash beside them flies up,
Making their burial impossible, eternal shame
They return to you once more, O square,
to you who has no liberty.

Nahmias's decision to return to the square exemplifies the principle of a trauma victim's need to return to the location of a traumatic experience in order to be healed from it. This poem is an example of a conscious return, and one gains the impression that the person returning to the past can still control it, without the past causing him to lose his sense of self. Nahmias's return to the square is clearly the return of a visitor, as his position is obvious: The poet stands on one side of the square, while the other side of the square is filled with ghostly figures. There is no loss of control in this poem, and the manner in which the poet addresses the past is measured and under control. From this perspective, it is patently evident that Nahmias returns to the square in order to extract the trauma that was seared in his memory in the distant past, or in what Dudai terms the deep forgetting. This forgetting has only blurred senses, which Nahmias expresses with the words "figures en la nube," ghosts that are visible through a fog.

The return to the square could also enable Nahmias to embark on the process that modern psychologists refer to as delayed grief. Delayed grief is forced on people who were unable to grieve at the appropriate time for the death of a close relative. Writing from the distance of so many years after his relatives died brought the poet to return to his childhood days in Salonica, a process that modern psychologists call STUG, or subsequent, temporary upsurge of grief.[26] Any reminder, such as a date, a piece of information, an important event, or a fragrance or flavour can arouse a delayed upsurge of grief, especially in someone who did not manage to undergo a proper mourning process, specifically the Jewish mourning process, which dictates that a son or daughter mourn a parent for an entire year. Delayed grief floods the consciousness with memories, not in order to return to the past, but rather to be able to move forward and look straight towards the future.

The commencement of delayed grief is also expressed in the poems through situations of self-accusation, a form of self-flagellation for the poet's childhood, which was far better than that of those who had no possibility of being saved and were dispatched on the death trains. One example of this appears in "Vagones en Varonish," whose opening lines describe a grandmother (Hana Bibas) who is forced to board the death train, while her children and grandson (the future poet) boarded a ship bound for Eretz Israel and were saved:

Mi nona, Hana Bibas,
en Varonish de Salónica nació.
En su cuartier toda su vida vivió.
Mis padres con barco, a Palestina,
ella, abandonada la dejaron en el molo.
Sus lágrimas,
la alma perforan.

En mi chiquez, sólo sueños tuve,
doloroso estó,
que nada tengo de recodrar,
sólo memorias contadas,
de su lloro.
Años pasaron,
sin pueder enviar certificato.
Mientras, nubes escuras
en el horizonte y sobre Salónica,
aire de rumores,
¿a ónde mos llevan?
Temor silencioso,
mosca volando, grande sonido.
Vagones de vacas esperaban.
Con miedo de muerte, mi nona
arriba al vagón, como que escala tuvo.
Lleno el vagón,
apretados, ahogando,
sin pueder hacer paso.
Mi nona, apenas arribó a Auschwitz,
la tiraron, la mataron.
Mis pruebas, escondidas en mi corazón.
Contadas, no calman mi dolor,
sólo amargura y aborrecimiento me vienen,
perdonar, no perdono.[27]

My grandmother Hana Bibas,
was born in Varonish, in Salonica.
She lived her life in this neighborhood.
My parents boarded a ship bound for Palestine,
and she was left alone on the quay.
Her tears
made holes in her soul.
In my childhood I had only dreams
It pains me
that I remember not even one.
only memories have I been told,
about her tears.
Years went by,
with no way of sending a visa,
while dark clouds
filled the horizon of Salonica,

and the air filled with rumors.
Where are they taking us?
Fearful silence
The buzzing of a fly is deafening
Cattle cars stood waiting.
With the fear of death upon her, my grandmother
climbed up to the railcar, as if she had a ladder.
The car filled up
crammed in, with no air,
with no room to move an inch.
My grandmother, when she arrived in Auschwitz,
was shot, was murdered.
The testimonies hide inside my heart.
Retelling them does not lessen my pain,
only bitterness and loathing remain within me.
Forgiveness? I will not forgive.

This poem allows the writer to connect to characters from the past and commune with them. From the third poem in the cycle of Holocaust poems onward, Nahmias alters his point of view. He is writing no longer from a position of distance, as one who overlooks the events, but rather from a standpoint of maximum proximity. The poet switches to the first-person plural and is effectively writing the poems as if he himself was a Holocaust survivor conjuring up his memories. The following are a few examples:

Ahí estuvimos recogidos,
día de verano, nube oscura, los cielos en furor.[28]

There we gathered,
on a summer day, dark clouds, an angry sky.

En vagones esperando, olvidados,
al camino salimos.
La hermosura de llanos, y olor de bosques,
no son consuelo,
sin saber, a ónde mos llevan.
Súbito, se para el vagón,
sólo adivinaciones tenemos,
sin ver ninguno,
excepto de la gente del vagón.[29]

Waiting in the railcars, forgotten
we set out
the beauty of the plains and the fragrance of the forests
are no consolation,
for we know not where we are being taken,
Suddenly the car stopped.
We could only guess what awaited us.
We could see no one,
except the people in the car.

Día de esclavitud atrás de nos.
En escuridad salimos, escuro el retorno.
Saco vacío, pobre de contenido, sobre canapé cae,
olor de muerte alderredor,
muestro cuerpo tormentado, amenazado,
luchando.[30]

A day of work is already behind us
In darkness we left, in darkness we returned.
A worn out sack, empty of any content, collapses on the bunk.
The smell of death is all around.
Our tortured, threatened body
fights back.

Writing in the first-person plural turns Nahmias into a participant in the experience, and he forces his readers to listen to his memories of it. This is not easy listening, as the lines are heavy with detailed descriptions that are difficult to digest and flood the reader with emotions. Dori Laub has explained the process of listening to a trauma:

The person listening to a traumatic event participates in the event and shares its intensity; as one would expect of a listener, he himself experiences the trauma, even if only partially. His relationship to the victim of the traumatic event therefore affects the manner in which the listener perceives the event – and he feels the hurt, the helplessness, the confusion, the terror and the internal conflicts that torment the trauma victim.[31]

Nahmias's poems pose a double challenge. The reader becomes the audience to the trauma to which someone else (the poet) listened, and it is he who transmits the trauma to us, as if these were his experiences. In this context, LaCapra says that during testimonies the survivor in his position as a witness, often relives the traumatic events and is controlled by the past. These are the most difficult parts of the testimony for the survivor, for the interviewer and for the observer of the testimonies. The testimony requires a response, but the interviewer or the observer could feel embarrassment or confusion with respect to the fitting response or the appropriate way to express their response in words.[32]

Indeed, Nahmias's poems are likely to arouse a certain embarrassment in the reader when he realizes that he is reading poetic second-hand testimony. Nahmias apparently was seeking only to produce a new poetic voice from the voices of those who had perished: as a means to crystallize his lost identity; to "return and commune" with his murdered relatives; to strengthen the Judeo-Spanish narrative towards the subject of the Holocaust in Israeli society and Spanish society; and to conduct a dialogue with this narrative, in order to bring about his own cathartic redemption that would release him, once and for all, from the suffering of the terrible past and, mainly, from the guilt that he had survived while his relatives had perished.

The Return to Ladino as a Healing Process

Nahmias's poems are written in Ladino, the language of the Sephardic Jews who lived in Salonica and in the Mediterranean countries after the expulsion from Spain in 1492. He is well aware that he is returning to the language of his forefathers after many years of abandonment, and he expresses his mixed feelings towards this language and the return to it. In the opening poem of the Holocaust cycle, he writes:

Felicidad y sentimiento es lo que
en muestro muevo encontro siento,
ladino.
En mi chiquez tuve
primer encontro,
recordos de que te amaba, no tengo,
lo que recordo son tus esfuerzos
de acercarte y mi indiferencia,
que era tropiezo, mal pasado.
Siempre eras caliente y cercana.
A veces tanto te acercabas,
que te aborrecía,
excusas, no tengo.[33]

A feeling of joy and happiness
from our renewed meeting,
Ladino.
In the days of my childhood I had
my first meeting,
memories of love for you – I have none,
I will remember your efforts
to be liked by me,
that I endear you, in the face of my indifference.
A type of obstacle that I did not overcome.
You were always warm and close.
Sometimes you came so close to me
that I abhorred you.
I have no excuse.

The return to the language of his forefathers is the motivating factor behind Nahmias's decision to write his book of poetry. Writing poetry was not a lifelong pursuit for Nahmias, and certainly not in Ladino. To this end he had to learn the art of poetic writing in a language with which he was largely unfamiliar. His extant Ladino vocabulary was insufficient for the writing of an impressive corpus of poems. To meet this challenge, he also mastered Spanish via language lessons and sought the assistance of a group of friends and relatives who ultimately aided him with the poetic texts in Ladino. Despite these efforts, he remained saddened by the fact that Ladino is a language that is slowly fading into the past. He (like many others who have written poetry or other literary texts in Ladino, especially in recent years) viewed himself as the last author in this language, and as someone who was genuinely extending the life of Ladino, which seems doomed to death. He expressed these thoughts as follows:

Lo que me da tristeza,
es saber, que lo que estó,
trabajando en mis poemas,
es sólo por alargar
tu agonía.
Hoy día, que ya puedo pensar
en ladino, sé que estás en estado
de morirte.
Y renacimiento, no creo que atorne,
en tus últimos días,
cuando de ti tomo una profunda arrogancia,

y ayuda para componer mis poemas,
que son curas para mi abatida alma.
Pedrida te veo en el mundo,
caminando y despariciendo.
Ladino, hoy que sé,
que tanto preciosa sos para mí,
obligado estó de guadrarte,
por alargar tu vida.[34]

Sorrow grips me,
with the knowledge
that the travail of my poetry
is only for the sake of
prolonging your demise.
Now that I can think
in Ladino, I know that you will soon
pass away.
I do not believe in resurrection
at the end of your days.
I take from you a deep pride
and help with the lines of my poems.
I see you lost in this world,
walking away and disappearing
Ladino - today when I know
how precious you are to me,
I am committed to preserving you,
to prolong your life.

Nahmias, like other literary creators who voice their concerns for the future of Ladino, dares to break down into components his Israeli identity, built so painstakingly by his parents, who covered the shame of their Judeo-Spanish past with so many layers. Nahmias, along with many others in Israel and in the Sephardic world, those whom I call Ladinoists, yearn for and cling to the images of the childhood their parents enjoyed in the Judeo-Spanish Ladino-speaking communities in the eastern Mediterranean. In his poetry, Nahmias removes the layers of forgetting and the abandonment of the Judeo-Spanish world in favour of Hebrew and Israeli culture. He is well aware that the Ladino language will never again be the primary language of Sephardic Jews in the full and broad sense of the word, but he, like many others, does not cease to yearn for this language and glorify it. He views himself, as well as his relatives who spoke Ladino and perished in the

Holocaust, as unofficial bridges between Spain as a distant homeland and Ladinoland as an imagined homeland. Nahmias lived his physical life in Israel, but his mental life was closely connected to Salonica and even Auschwitz-Birkenau, where Salonica's Jews and Nahmias's family met their deaths in the Holocaust. His preoccupation with Salonica and its past, via the writing of poems in flawed Ladino, for him represented the re-establishment of the homeland that had been stolen from his forebears. He attempted to use the Ladino poems to re-establish the continuity of the Jewish people. Nahmias left Salonica when he was eighty days old and until the age of eighty was a lost man, even though he learned to live in another land and even though he seemed to have integrated well. Thus for Nahmias, Salonica and Ladino were his homeland as well as the place from which came his mobile language. The Spanish exiles carried the language with them along the paths of the exile to the Ottoman Empire; the inhabitants of the empire carried it in their memories for many generations; those exiled to the extermination camps carried it in the death trains, and the immigrants to Israel brought it in bundles of memory, struggling against its final disappearance. Nahmias the Israeli, the Sephardi, the Greek Jew, took the initiative to fight the waves of globalization in a world in which his mother's and father's language no longer had much meaning. Via his poems, Nahmias declared that he was not prepared to wrench his mobile homeland, and with it his imperfect mother tongue, from within him, just because his language is not polished and might not meet academic standards. On the contrary, he believed in the old, the cracked, the unpolished. He was unwilling to allow Ladino to exist on the margins, not even those of consciousness, just because the learned historical researchers pointed out that Ladino was dying.

Herman Lewis has written that "[t]he first principle of healing is the empowerment of trauma victims. They must be the instigators of their healing and its controllers. Others can provide counselling, support, assistance, affection and concern, but not healing ... No intervention that takes power away from the victim can promote his recovery, no matter what the immediate good it may do."[35] Nahmias's choice to write his poems in Ladino was particularly symbolic; it also demonstrated a power to cope with trauma. By controlling the process, Yacob Nahmias was also using his poetry to heal himself.

Afterward

In March 2018, Yacob Nahmias published a novelistic memoir in Hebrew in which he shared his childhood memories as a Salonican youth in Tel Aviv.[36] That work to a certain extent completed the poetry therapy process he had begun with the writing of his poems and their publication in Ladino, by a publishing house in Spain. In that book too, as in his book of poetry, Nahmias assumed the role of the narrator – not always of himself, but at times also of the generations that preceded him, of those for whom he sought to be a storytelling medium. He wrote about this in his preface to the book: "I wanted with all my might to revive the conceptual world of my childhood, the dream that was full to brimming with the traces left by the generation of my childhood, which I tried to understand; to agree with or to dispute. I wrote out of curiosity and out of passion for the focal point of the life that I lived, that has passed but is still a central avenue in their memory ... That time capsule that I have revived with words, I would like to grant to you, to touch it, and if I were to know that I have touched your hearts, that would be my greatest reward."[37] Nahmias died on 4 June 2019.

NOTES

1 Rosenfeld, *The End of the Holocaust* (Hebrew).
2 On Salonican Jews aided through Spanish diplomatic interventions, see chapters 7 and 8 in this volume by Fragkou and Lisbona, respectively.
3 Rodrigue, "Sephardim and the Holocaust."
4 Refael, *Un grito en el silencio.*
5 Rosenfeld, *The End of the Holocaust*, 135–54.
6 See Agnieszka, "The Representations of Kurtijo"; Balbuena, *Homeless Tongues.*
7 Habib, *Poesie.*
8 Arouh, "Marso 1943."
9 Nahmias, *Poemas.*
10 LaCapra, *Writing History* (Hebrew), 15–16.
11 Nahmias, *Poemas*, 30–55.
12 Herman, *Trauma and Recovery* (Hebrew).
13 Dudai, "Forgotten, Remembered, and Re-Forgotten," 112.
14 Ibid., 115.
15 Ibid., 120.
16 Ibid., 123.
17 Ibid., 128.
18 Ibid., 129.
19 In most dialects of Ladino this is *muestra*, but following the re-Hispanization of ancient Ladino, we are seeing a return of the *m* to an *n* in some words.
20 Nahmias, *Poemas*, 6.

21 Ibid.
22 Ibid., 6–7.
23 LaCapra, *Writing History*, 117.
24 Ibid., 117–18.
25 Nahmias, *Poemas*, 30–1.
26 Rando, *Treatment of Complicated Mourning*.
27 Nahmias, *Poemas*, 32–3.
28 Ibid., 35.
29 Ibid., 37.
30 Ibid., 41.
31 Felman and Laub, *Testimony*, 67 (Hebrew).
32 LaCapra, *Writing History*, 122.
33 Nahmias, *Poemas*, 9.
34 Ibid., 9–11.
35 Herman, *Trauma and Recovery*, 163.
36 Nahmias, *Yacobico* (Hebrew).
37 Ibid., 8–9.

32 Teaching and Learning about the Holocaust in Spain

MARTA SIMÓ

Introduction

The Holocaust is a topic that encompasses history and memory, and its transmission is necessary and difficult. Public institutions – in particular, educational institutions – are frequently tasked with carrying out this dissemination.[1] To flesh out the multiple valences of the history and the idea of the Holocaust as they impact Spanish society, it is crucial that we analyse the state of education and communication about the Holocaust in present-day Spain.

This chapter first briefly describes the specific context of Holocaust memory in Spain and how it influences the educational process. Then it moves to a discussion of the current state of education in Spain. The subsequent section explores the latest pedagogical initiatives as well as the most recently developed materials in the country. The chapter concludes with a more panoramic perspective on the topic and offers some ideas to keep in mind when approaching Holocaust education in the future.

Holocaust Memory

In 1998, the philosopher Reyes Mate wrote: "Aquí no hay rastro de lo que pudiéramos llamar una cultura del Holocausto. España ha vivido de espaldas a ese acontecimiento singular, el más significativo del siglo XX" (There are no traces here of what we could call a culture of the Holocaust. Spain has lived with its back turned to this singular event, the most significant of the twentieth century).[2] Along the same lines, Anne Menny suggests that the official memory of the Holocaust is an appropriation of forms of European commemoration more than a unique national memory. As such, she considers the collective memory of the Holocaust in Spain to be a foreign concept, a sort of delayed memory.[3] How can we explain the absence of the Holocaust in Spain's collective memory?

In 1953, President Eisenhower visited Spain and signed a military cooperation agreement with General Franco. From that moment on, the regime was able to successfully create the idea that Spain had maintained neutrality during the Second World War and that the country had no connection whatsoever with the Holocaust (Pedro Correa Martín-Arroyo addresses this myth in chapter 20 of this volume). At that time, Spain's educational system was being developed under the auspices of National Catholicism, rooted in the Catholic Church, which was far removed from the fascist and antisemitic ideas that were present in the early years of Francoism.

During the early post-war years in Spain, as in the large majority of European countries, specific references to the Holocaust were largely absent from the national narrative. (See Marín-Dòmine, chapter 15, and Cahill, chapter 30, on early mentions of the Holocaust in the Spanish press.) The important role the Catholic Church performed as the only educational institution alongside the small and silenced Jewish community did nothing to help the development of Holocaust memory in Spain.[4]

It was not until the 1970s that the political and economic transformation of the country required a more modern education system, one that would facilitate the democratic transition and allow Spain to join the European Community. In the context of historical memory, this transition from dictatorship to democracy took place under what is known as the *pacto del olvido* (Pact of Forgetting), in which many Spaniards – on both the right and the left – benefited from the opportunity the pact afforded to rewrite or forget history. There was little interest in verifying the complex relationships between fact and fiction, and the country as a whole was turning its back on the past in order to focus on the transition process, and as a consequence, this revised history suppressed certain elements and altered others, with the worst episodes being entirely omitted from historical texts. In the absence of a truth and reconciliation commission and with many Francoists from the previous military and political spheres still in power, it was, for many, a real opportunity to alter uncomfortable personal and collective versions of history to make them more palatable.[5] During this period, the Amical de Mauthausen played an important role as the only organization that helped uphold the memory of the Republicans deported to Nazi camps. However, the Amical's focus remained on the Spanish deportees, not on the memory of the Jewish genocide.[6]

By the 1980s, the need to belong to the European Union – which Spain joined in 1986 – had put pressure on the political establishment to participate in the search for a European history and a common, collective European memory. That same year, Spain finally established diplomatic relations with Israel, bringing knowledge of the Jewish medieval past into focus. As Martina L. Weisz and Raanan Rein detail at the beginning of this volume, Spain's complex relationship with the Jewish people continues to evolve. As an outgrowth of the contemporary desire to present Spain as a democratic and European country that has broken with its dictatorial past, the Holocaust has come to be a symbol of Spain's shared European identity – of values and obligations it holds in common, or "objetivo moral" (moral objective) as Tony Judt calls it.[7]

Since the early 2000s, a number of events have demonstrated Spain's incorporation into the transnational framework of a globalized and collective memory of the Holocaust.[8] In December of 2004, the Spanish government declared 27 January as Holocaust Remembrance Day. (The parliament of the Autonomous Community of Madrid had been marking *Yom Hashoah* in April since 2000.) In 2006, the Centro Sefarad-Israel was founded in Madrid. In 2008, the centre would represent Spain as a member of the Holocaust Remembrance Alliance (IHRA). From that point on, and for the first time, Holocaust education with an interdisciplinary approach would be included in the country's educational curriculum. During the 2008–9 school year, the government declared the Holocaust an obligatory topic in the social science curriculum. In December of 2013, with the Ley Orgánica para la Mejora de la Calidad Educativa (Organic Law for the Improvement of Educational Quality, LOMCE), the country's parliamentary body added an additional ruling on the "Prevención y resolución pacífica de conflictos y valores que sustentan la democracia y los derechos humanos" (Peaceful prevention and resolution of conflicts and values that sustain democracy and human rights), which established that the study of the destruction of the European Jews or the Shoah would be included at different stages in the primary and secondary school curriculum.

But as Alejandro Baer and Natan Sznaider ask in the concluding chapter of this volume, what is understood in Spain as the Holocaust? Is it the genocide of European Jews (the Shoah) or the Nazi crimes committed between 1933 and 1945 in broader terms? And was the Holocaust unique or was it comparable to other atrocities in the past and present? These two questions have specific implications in Spain, particularly in the education sector, in that the perspective chosen determines the emphasis and focus of teaching and learning about the Holocaust. To approach the Holocaust as a unique event would be to differentiate Nazism from fascism. To consider deported Spanish Republicans as victims of the Holocaust might amount to equating

Nazism with Francoism.[9] To include *all* victims of Nazism under the rubric "Holocaust" would be to ignore that exterminating Europe's Jews was the central and driving force to that project.[10] Furthermore, the more than thirty years during which Spanish Republican prisoners never had the opportunity to complete their grieving process can lead to what Geoffrey Hartman calls "memory envy."[11] In some discourses surrounding Republican memory, this sense of envy has sometimes elicited – not necessarily from the deportees themselves but from others who have worked with these memories – the idea that the Jewish geno-cide has been given too much prominence.[12] My examination of current practices regarding Holocaust pedagogy in Spain will detail how these opposing memory paradigms are borne out in the classroom.

Current State of Holocaust Education in Spain

When it comes to understanding Holocaust education in Spain, it is important to keep in mind that the Spanish education system is relatively decentralized. The autonomous communities or the central government make most of the decisions concerning education in Spain (approximately 43 and 16 per cent, respectively), and individual schools make around one quarter of the decisions. Regional authorities are responsible for organiz-ing and providing education and maintaining schools, as well as for mak-ing financial determinations and assessments regarding the curriculum, among other functions. Thus the education system is not homogenous across the country. Groups dedicated to promoting Holocaust education exist in practically all of the autonomous communities; however, I will focus on two such communities: Madrid and the Catalan autonomous community which have most well-developed programs.

Two organizations in Madrid and Catalonia have become centres of Holocaust and Spanish Republican memory in Spain. The Centro Sefarad-Israel in Madrid organizes seminars, conferences, debates, workshops, exhibits, concerts, homages to victims, trips, and training for teachers both in Spain and abroad. It works with organizations such as the Shoah Memorial in Paris, Yad Vashem in Jerusalem, the Wannsee Conference House in Berlin, the Anne Frank House in Amsterdam, and the Auschwitz-Birkenau Memorial and Museum in Poland, among other institutions with common educational purposes.

In Catalonia, the Memorial Democràtic is a public organization whose mission is to recover, commemorate, and develop the dem-ocratic memory of Catalonia during the period encompassing the Second Republic, the Generalitat Republicana, the Civil War, and the early Spanish transition. Its mission is to represent victims of the Franco dictatorship, including Republican exiles and deportees to Nazi concentration camps.

There is no specific university department or academic group for Holocaust Studies in Spain; however, a series of empirical studies have provided an initial sense of the situation of Holocaust education in the country.[13] Using quantitative and qualitative methods, I analysed high school students' feelings towards and level of knowledge about the Holocaust, as did the Grupo Eleuterio Quintanilla.[14] I conducted the first study in Catalonia with 196 students; the Grupo Eleuterio Quintanilla conducted the second in Asturias with 862 students. In each case, the investigation was based on an analysis of the curricula and textbooks as well as a survey of the students about their knowledge and feelings. These studies set out to measure the students' knowledge of the events, to evaluate the sources of that knowledge, and to identify the students' ethical and moral positions vis-à-vis both Nazism and Judaism. While the projects were entirely separate, the results were similar. They revealed that students had minimal knowledge of the historical events related to the Holocaust and that films and literature were their principal sources of knowledge. In some of the responses, open as well as hidden antisemitic tendencies were encountered, including a case of Holocaust denial and familiar negative stereotypes about Jews. That said, most students demonstrated their opposition to National Socialism and classified the Nazis as bad. Other students expressed a moral position from which they saw themselves as defenders of equality and favoured the idea that differences between human beings do not exist. In explaining how the Holocaust could have happened, some contended that Nazism had been a mental illness and classified the Nazis as insane, savage, and illiterate.

The most recent empirical studies were carried out in 2013 and 2015. Montserrat Richou and colleagues conducted a study of textbooks in Catalonia for the social sciences course for the fourth year of compulsory secondary education in 2013, examining their treatment of the Republican deportation and the Holocaust.[15] The authors quantitatively and qualitatively analysed the textbooks and their relation to the official Catalan curriculum. The investigators found that overall, there was a very basic didactic approach to issues surrounding the Republican exile and deportation and a somewhat more developed approach to the Holocaust. They also found that the textbooks did not relate Nazi ideology to anti-Judaism or antisemitism from earlier historical periods, did not explain the previous life of diverse Jewish communities in Europe, and did not differentiate between the East and the West. There was no clear reference to the diversity of the victims, nor was there to the Nazi regime's varied policies towards the groups they targeted (genocide, ethnic cleansing, etc.). The textbooks did not include any references to the Righteous Among the Nations. The distinct periods in the process of the destruction of the Jews were not sufficiently explained; nor was the role in the Holocaust played by other countries. This was especially notable in regard to the Franco regime's treatment of the Jewish population and Republican political prisoners.

Another researcher, Jack Jedwab, carried out a study in Canada, the United States, Germany, and Spain in 2015 in which he asked people to evaluate the strength of their knowledge of the Holocaust.[16] The surveys' primary objective was to observe the relationship between the perceptions people had of their knowledge of the Holocaust and their preoccupation with antisemitism, as well as to see how readily those surveyed accepted social diversity. The results revealed that knowledge about the Holocaust was highest in Germany, at 84 per cent, followed by Canada (78.4 per cent) and the United States (72.8 per cent). Spain had the lowest rate of knowledge about the Holocaust (57.4 per cent). But of greatest relevance was the gap among populations in Spain as it related to age: 47.8 per cent of young people between 16 and 24 demonstrated a knowledge of the Holocaust, compared to 72.9 per cent of people between 45 and 54, which approaches the Canadian and United States averages.

Individuals with a strong knowledge of the Holocaust were more likely to agree that antisemitism was a problem in society; Germany, however, was an exception – there was no correlation.[17] Also, in Germany there was no significant correlation between the respondent's level of knowledge about the Holocaust and whether he or she considered anti-Muslim prejudice a serious problem. In the United States and Spain, the study found significant differences between those who viewed themselves as having strong knowledge of the Holocaust and those who believed that prejudice against Muslim populations was a problem: 75 per cent of those with strong knowledge versus less than 50 per cent of those with weak knowledge of the Holocaust identified negative beliefs about Muslims as a problem. But where the differences were perhaps starkest was at the intersection of two factors: level of knowledge about the Holocaust and level of social distance between Jews and Muslims.[18] In general, in most countries, those surveyed believed they shared more values with the Jewish population than with the Muslim population. In Spain, only 24.9 per cent felt that they shared values with Muslims.

Finally, the study revealed a relationship between knowledge about the Holocaust and acceptance of diversity. In all four countries, the investigators observed that people with a higher level of knowledge about the Holocaust believed that people with ethnic and religious backgrounds distinct from the majority of the country make an important contribution to the national culture. With respect to whether immigrants would have to abandon their customs and traditions and appear more like the rest of the population, no correlation was observed between those with either a strong or a weak knowledge of the Holocaust.

In a 2015 empirical study, Peter Carrier sought to document the ways the Holocaust was present in the curricula and textbooks for secondary school social science courses in twenty-six countries on five continents.[19] The study was based on 272 curricula and on eighty-nine textbooks published since 2000. In Spain, Carrier's sample consisted of one history textbook and four social science textbooks published between 2008 and 2011 for use by sixteen-year-olds. All of the textbooks dealt with the Holocaust for between three to six pages in the sections devoted to the Second World War, except for one, which placed the Holocaust in a section titled "Fascismo y Nazismo" (Fascism and Nazism). Another textbook also had a subsection dedicated to "Genocidios, Deportaciones y otras consecuencias de la Guerra" (Genocides, Deportations, and Other Consequences of War), and yet another had a subsection titled "Los Campos de Concentración" (The Concentration Camps). Collectively, the textbooks generally did not date the Holocaust clearly: some framed the event between 1933 and 1942, while others mentioned the pogrom of 1938 (*Kristallnacht*). The textbooks tended to locate the Holocaust in Germany and Europe, while one related it to Spain by including a photograph of Spanish Republicans imprisoned in Mauthausen. All of the textbooks focused on Jewish victims, but none of the books dealt with Jewish history before 1933 or after 1945. In terms of the perpetrators, Hitler featured in all textbooks: one included the testimonies of German bystanders; and another mentioned German resistance as well as people who collaborated with the Nazis in territories occupied by Germany. All but one book used the terms "Holocausto" and "genocidio," pointing towards their interpretive paradigms. Other textbooks referred to "exterminio" (extermination), "exterminio físico de los judíos" (physical extermination of the Jews), "masacre" (massacre), "deshumanización total" (total dehumanization), or "genocidio de la población judía o de los judíos" (genocide of the Jewish population or of the Jews). The textbooks included a wide range of supporting materials such as photographs, posters, maps, propaganda, drawings, excerpts of historical documents, film stills, and caricatures. Although they made use of the relevant terminology, discussions of the manifestations of Nazi ideology in the camps and of the types of persecution were not consistent among the textbooks. The didactic focus of all the textbooks resided in exercises that included source analysis, critical reflection, explanation of the camps, or reflections on links between the Holocaust and present-day "limpiezas étnicas" (ethnic cleansing). More generally, the textbooks explicitly encouraged reflection on the Holocaust's links to mass violence and genocide, albeit without explaining those links. Finally, with respect to national idiosyncrasies prevalent in Spain, links between the Holocaust and the Spanish Civil War were rare in the textbooks, and none of them raised the issue of the Allies' failure to act in defence of the Republicans in 1937 or of the victims of the Holocaust. One merely stated that the German invasion of Spain provided a venue to "probar armas" (test weapons) to be used later during the Second World War, while another depicted Republican prisoners in Mauthausen making victory signs with their hands at the moment of their liberation.[20] Ultimately, the results of the two studies of textbooks, while focused on different autonomous communities, were very similar.

New Pedagogical Initiatives and New Materials

Teacher Training

The Centro Sefarad-Israel has enabled more than four hundred teachers throughout Spain to receive training at Yad Vashem. The centre, along with the Ajuntament de Barcelona and B'nai B'rith, under the direction of Professor Xavier Boltaina, also organized a course about the Holocaust for teachers, educators, and administrative personnel in Barcelona.[21] The course consists of thirteen two-hour sessions led by different professors and specialists. As of 2019, more than 225 people had participated in eight sessions.

In addition, Professors Alfredo Hidalgo and Graciela Kohan have taught distance learning courses about the Holocaust and antisemitism at the UNED Foundation in which more than ninety students have participated. "Educación en el Holocausto. Educando para prevenir y no olvidar" (Holocaust Education: Educating to Prevent and Not Forget) is intended for primary and secondary teachers and other educators. Other courses offered include "La Justicia durante el nacionalsocialismo en Alemania y la Europa ocupada" (Justice during German National Socialism and Occupied Europe) and "La medicina durante el nacionalsocialismo y el Holocausto" (Medicine during National Socialism and the Holocaust).[22]

In addition to these courses, a significant number of working groups exist, although they are not always active.[23] The "Exili, Deportació i Holocaust" (Exile, Deportation, and the Holocaust) working group in Barcelona was launched nine years ago by a group of secondary school teachers, university professors, researchers, and administrative workers under the umbrella of the Departament d'Educació de la Generalitat de Catalunya (Department of Education of the Generalitat of Catalonia) and the Memorial Democràtic.[24] Among other activities, this group organizes the International Holocaust Remembrance Day with groups of high school students, ages fourteen to seventeen, from various schools in Catalonia. It generally follows the proposals set out by the "Holocaust and the United Nations Outreach Programme, and the Holocaust Memorial Day Trust (HMDT) from the United Kingdom."[25] The group compiles materials for teachers and students and receives training through a collaboration with the Wannsee House in Berlin and other organizations in Europe.

Student Training

Professor Esteban González of the Medical School at the Universidad Autónoma de Madrid offers "El Holocausto, una reflexión desde la medicina" (The Holocaust, a Reflection from the Field of Medicine), the only elective course on the Holocaust at the university level available since 2012. More than 270 students have taken this class.

In the realm of non-governmental organizations, the Amical de Mauthausen provides training for secondary students via activities organized through Mai més (Never Again), a network dedicated to the preservation of memory and the prevention of fascism. The organization is comprised of thirty schools and is supported by twelve local governments and other entities. The Amical de Mauthausen offers talks given by survivors or descendants; trips to memory sites such as Mauthausen and Buchenwald; and support for research projects – which all students in the final year of high school must complete – through its specialized library as well as a database on deported Republicans.

Didactic Materials

Various entities have created didactic materials on the Holocaust and the Republican deportation over the last few years. The Exile, Deportation, and Holocaust working group develops materials based on activities and concrete topics related to International Holocaust Remembrance Day. The first of these was a free pamphlet for all secondary schools in Catalonia on "El coratge de salvar" (The Courage to Save).[26] The text's goal is to provide resources for professors as well as pedagogical materials for students to deepen their knowledge of the Republican exile of 1939, political deportees, and the Holocaust. It also aims to promote reflection and analysis of the human values of those who risked their lives for others (the Righteous Among the Nations). Memorial

Democràtic produced the didactic video "Camins" (Paths), which was translated into six languages, recounting the intersecting journeys of two families between 1933 and 1945: one was a Polish-Jewish family; the other was the family of a deported Austrian politician who fought in the International Brigades.[27]

Another recent example is the "Guía didáctica de la Shoá" (Shoah Didactic Guide), edited by the Comunidad de Madrid in 2015. Raúl Fernández Vítores, director of the Centro Territorial de Innovación y Formación "Madrid Sur" (South Madrid Regional Centre for Innovation and Training), coordinated the guide, which was designed for teachers and has been distributed to primary and secondary education centres in the Community of Madrid.[28] In addition, this centre boasts a specialized library with more than seven hundred titles on the Holocaust.[29]

Other Projects

Other projects, while not conducted in the context of formal education, have nevertheless contributed to knowledge about the Holocaust in Spain. The first example, Perseguits i Salvats (Persecuted and Saved), was conducted within the framework of the European Union under the program Europe for Citizens. The project's objective was to recover the memory of 120,000 people who crossed the Pyrenees to escape the Nazi terror. Many were Jews, but there were also Allied soldiers, pilots, and resistance fighters from various European countries (Germany, France, Poland, Czechoslovakia, Yugoslavsia, etc.). Perseguits i Salvats defines and remembers this moment in European history, disseminating it through an educational initiative. (Josep Calvet, one of the scholars who participated in this project, details a number of its findings in chapter 5 in this volume.)[30]

The second example has been driven by civil society and local activism: the Stolpersteine Project.[31] Created by the German artist Gunter Demnig, this endeavour currently encompasses twenty-one countries and more than fifty thousand commemorative stones. In April 2015, for the first time in Catalonia and Spain, Demnig installed five *Stolpersteine* to commemorate the fates of five Republicans who were deported to Mauthausen. This initiative was made possible thanks to the Projecte trencant els silencis (Breaking Silences Project), carried out to recover local historical memory in the Municipality of Navàs, a small city north of Barcelona. As of May 2019, Demnig has installed 164 *Stolpersteine* across Spain, including 138 in Catalonia, with one marking the life of Neus Català, discussed by Gina Herrmann in her chapter on Spanish and Catalan women active in the resistance and deported to Ravensbrück.[32]

Conclusions and Perspectives

In recent years we have seen progress in the number of groups – personal and collective initiatives – that support more robust knowledge about the Holocaust. Nevertheless, the political engagement in this endeavour continues to be to a certain extent ambiguous and discontinuous. This is apparent in the fact that a university-level department of Holocaust Studies in Spain still does not exist. Along these same lines, there is a complete lack of empirical studies that analyse the impact and value of the various actions now taking place to reclaim the historical memory of the Holocaust and the Republican deportation in Spain.

Although there are no scientific results to prove it, after more than fifteen years of experience with Holocaust education in Spain, teachers still exhibit a notable discomfort and fatigue when approaching the topic. In addition, there are very high social expectations attached to Holocaust instruction: it is commonly proposed as a useful tool to approach the current debates on Holocaust denial and the extreme right. It is also considered useful as a tool for preventing stereotypes, prejudices, and racism. While there is no doubt about its function, Holocaust education does not always have the desired effect, and this generates more reticence on the part of teachers to teach it and students to learn about it.

At the same time, Spain's role in the Second World War is a topic that continues to generate controversy, as we have seen throughout this volume. The historical memory of these events has become wrapped up with political identities and their respective narratives. Furthermore, the Franco regime has yet to be publicly condemned for its responsibility for the deportation of some ten thousand Republicans to Nazi concentration camps – a controversial topic with important implications for Holocaust education. The same is true regarding the role that representatives of the regime played in offering only limited aid to groups of Jewish refugees and Sephardic Jews in occupied Europe, the role of the Spanish diplomats as Righteous Among the Nations,[33] and the Franco government's direct collaboration with Nazi Germany during the war. (The chapters in Section II, "Spain and the Fates of Jewish Communities," as well as Pedro Correa Martín-Arroyo's chapter 20 on the Franco myth, examine these issues in depth.) This association can be seen in the cases of the Blue Division (see chapters 23 and 24), of labourers who went to work in Germany – contracted in an agreement between the two governments – and of Spain's provision of raw materials for the Nazi war machine. Furthermore, once the war was over, the Franco regime helped various Nazi officials or collaborators escape to

Spain, not an inconsiderable number of whom remained as permanent residents. (See chapters 25 and 26.) Even though in recent years various historians have uncovered these details,[34] translating these revelations for the educational sphere continues to be difficult.

Some members of the general public as well as some teachers still consider Holocaust education to be less relevant or necessary in countries that were not occupied by the Germans and that did not take an active part in the Second World War. Furthermore, the existence of diverse memories, sometimes causing "memory combat" or "divided memories," represents a challenge for Holocaust education and memory. Another problem not unique to Spain but relevant to all countries that were considered neutral is the lack of significant places of memory. In Spain, there has been a recent effort to memorialize the border crossings, as we have seen in Tabea Alexa Linhard's chapter 6 in this volume, as well as in the work of Josep Calvet.[35] The Amical de Mauthausen has played an important role in developing these types of memory spaces with their memorial journeys to Mauthausen and Buchenwald.

A final aspect that is not strictly about the Holocaust but rather about its surrounding discourse does have a direct impact on Holocaust education in Spain. In debates surrounding the phenomenon of a new antisemitism, camouflaged as anti-Zionism – habitually expressed by groups on the left that end up trivializing the Holocaust – there are frequent comparisons to the Israel-Palestine conflict. Without an open and calm debate, these groups occasionally face accusations of antisemitism.[36] We must also consider the emergence of new forms of neo-Nazism that are characterized not only by racism and xenophobia but also forms of banalization and Holocaust denial, undeniably present in certain spheres of political discourse today.[37]

Education about and through knowledge of the Holocaust in Spain answers the ongoing need to remember the Shoah by recognizing and respecting the memory of its various victims, by considering its specificity and singularity among victims of the Holocaust and Nazi persecution, and by attracting new generations to transmit these memories. One recent initiative to this end is the proposal by the Catalan Parliament for a program in which diverse representatives of victims' collectives (the Exile, Deportation and Holocaust group, and the Parliament's Department of Education, together with six secondary schools and representatives of Catalonia's school system) will jointly prepare the ceremonies for the International Holocaust Remembrance Day.

It will be essential to establish a dialogue between new academic research about the Holocaust and its connections with the Spanish State – elaborated throughout this volume – and the educational system.

This ongoing conversation has the potential to highlight links between local/national history and universal history, as well as foment specific knowledge about the culture and history of the Jews among young people. Initiatives such as the Educashoah Conference, organized by Miguel Angel Ballesteros of the University of Seville in July of 2018, in which almost 150 teachers from throughout Spain met to share their experiences regarding the teaching and study of the Holocaust, show that the Holocaust continues to be a theme at the forefront of educators' minds.

Finally, one must keep in mind that pedagogy about the Holocaust allows, in addition to an examination of the past – still crucial in a nation such as Spain, which is marked by an absence of memory – an examination of the present and, above all, of the future. This type of Holocaust education can be used as an example of the consequences of discrimination, oppression, and lack of respect towards fundamental human rights.

NOTES

1 Eckmann and Heimberg, *Memoire et Pedagogie.*
2 "En el Día del Holocausto," *El País*, 23 April 1998.
3 Menny, "Un país neutral."
4 Simó, "Challenges for Memory."
5 Russell, *Postmemory.*
6 Amical de Mauthausen brings together Spanish Republicans who were deported to Nazi camps, including family members and friends of the survivors and those who perished. The association takes its name from the camp to which the greatest number of deportees were sent. For more information, visit http://www.amical-mauthausen.org as well as Chapters 11, 14 and 17 in this volume.
7 Judt, Cuellar, and Gordo del Rey, *Posguerra.*
8 A. Baer, "Los vacíos de Sefarad," 507–8.
9 See the concepts of literal memory and exemplary memory in Todorov, *Los abusos de la memoria*, 38–41.
10 A. Baer, "Los vacíos de Sefarad," 511–13.
11 Hartman, *Scars of the Spirit.*
12 Ibid.
13 This information comes from the Education Research Project (ERP) conducted by the IHRA.
14 See Simó, "Teaching about the Holocaust in Catalonia."
15 Richou and Simó, "La deportación republicana."
16 Jedwab, "Measuring Holocaust Knowledge."
17 In Germany, those who considered themselves to have little knowledge of the Holocaust still thought that antisemitism was a problem in German society.

18 Here the term "social distance" reflects the extent to which those surveyed think that there are shared values between the Jewish population and the Muslim population.

19 Carrier, "The International Status of Education."

20 Ibid., 142–14.

21 Seminari de formació per al professorat i altres agents educatius, organized by the City Council of Barcelona, Institut Municipal d'Educació, B'nai B'rith, and Centro Sefarad-Israel under the direction of Professor Xavier Boltaina. Since 2018 the course has been organized by the UIMP (Universidad Internacional Menendez Pelayo).

22 http://www.fundacion.uned.es/publico_actividad/5328

23 There are organized working group networks in Barcelona, Girona, Gijón, Madrid, Oviedo, Trujillo, Sevilla, Santiago de Compostela, and Valencia, among others.

24 The author of this chapter is a member of this working group and maintains a first-hand familiarity with its activities.

25 http://www.un.org/en/holocaustremembrance/2015/calendar2015.html and http://hmd.org.uk

26 http://memorialdemocratic.gencat.cat/ca/publicaciones/ material_educatiu/QDMD_02.-El-coratge-de-salvar-durant-lHolocaust

27 http://memorialdemocratic.gencat.cat/ca/publicacions/ material_educatiu/QDMD_03.-Camins

28 http://www.elmundo.es/cultura/2014/01/26/52e55081268e3ec7108b456e. html

29 http://ctif.madridsur.educa.madrid.org/index. php?ltemid=39&id=7&option=com_content&view=article

30 www.perseguits.cat

31 www.stolpersteine.eu

32 http://www.ccma.cat/324/neus-catala-homenat- jada-amb-una-llamborda-de-la-memoria-historica/ noticia/2833715/

33 A. Baer and Correa, "The Politics of Holocaust Rescue Myths in Spain," in Guttstadt et al., eds, *Bystanders, Rescuers, or Perpetrators?*, 205–16.

34 Rother, *Franco y el Holocausto*; Ros Agudo, *La guerra secreta de Franco*; Leitz, *Sympathy for the Devil*; Bowen; Calvet, *Huyendo del Holocausto*, among others.

35 Visit the Lleida government's project: www.perseguitsisalvats.com.

36 See the controversy surrounding Pagès y Casas i Vilalta's book, *Republicans i republicanes als camps de concentració nazis* in "El trabajo de la memoria o el testimonio como categoría didáctica," *Enseñanza de las ciencias sociales* (Barcelona: Universitat Autònoma de Barcelona, 2006), 5, 115–24.

37 Monique Eckmann, "Specific Challenges for Memory and for Teaching and Learning about the Holocaust in Switzerland," in Guttstadt et al., eds, *Bystanders, Rescuers, or Perpetrators?*, 275–87.

Afterlives: Holocaust Appropriations in Spain

33 Between "No Pasarán" and "Nunca Más": The Holocaust and the Revisiting of Spain's Legacy of Mass Violence

ALEJANDRO BAER AND NATAN SZNAIDER

For a long time, Spain was known for its successful transition from dictatorship to democracy. It has served as a model, showing how a society can move from authoritarianism to freedom, integrate into Europe, and modernize within a short period of time and without revenge and retribution against those responsible for the previous chapter. That seemed to change in the year 2000 when civil society associations started to exhume the mass graves of victims of executions behind the front lines of the Civil War and victims of repressive violence against civilians during the ensuing Franco dictatorship. As a result of the emergence of a surprisingly strong social movement centred on the Asociación para la Recuperación de la Memoria Histórica (Association for the Recovery of Historical Memory, ARMH), the opened graves and the corpses of the executed victims they contained generated an unprecedented level of public exposure and opened up intense debates about the way Spain had dealt with the dictatorship and its victims. The success of the much lauded *Transición* was grounded in the assumption that the past could *remain* the past and that silence over the past was key to the democratization process.[1] The exhumations of the 2000s challenged this assumption in significant ways. Observers of Spanish politics started to identify the fundamental flaws and deficiencies of a period that was stained by a so-called *pacto del olvido* (pact of oblivion). Especially critical were those who had been mere children when Franco died, who had no direct experience of the dictatorship, and who had not participated in the political pacts and compromises of the transition years, such as 1977 Amnesty Law and the 1978 Constitution.[2]

Yet more than politics was at stake here; so was theory. The opening of graves ushered in new ways of thinking that reframed the discussion in terms of an international language of transitional justice, human rights, traumatic memory, and victimhood. "Verdad, Memoria, y Justicia"

(Truth, Memory, and Justice) became a rallying cry for many Spaniards in the new millennium and has since become a universal prescription for how democracies must address their dark and painful pasts. This interpretative frame for understanding political violence and state terror has clear links to Argentina's human rights and memory movement, which was a fundamental source of inspiration for the Spanish memorialists. The Argentine discourse, however, borrowed (and continues to do so) from the language and symbolism of the Holocaust. We argue in this chapter that *through* Argentina as well as through Spain's Europeanization, the Holocaust has found its way to the mass graves of Francoism. A new generation started to look at Spaniards' past as Europeans and global citizens. An exceptionalist approach gave way to a universalist understanding of how a society should confront a past of extreme violence and state terror. The Holocaust has been translated into the Spanish context as a memory paradigm, a cultural script that is not always visible to the social actors but that shapes new victim identities and trauma self-definitions and the public articulation of these through political, judicial, and cultural action. Would the memorialists' claims have won such public weight and extraordinary moral and political significance without the Holocaust becoming a European and global narrative? Would this powerful and far-reaching revisiting of the Spanish past and the questioning of its transitional model ever have occurred?

In this fundamental paradigm shift regarding remembrance of what had previously been deemed a divisive past, the concept and theory of trauma (understood as social trauma or a traumatized society, metaphors of the open wound, and the return of the repressed) have played a crucial role. In this new stance on Spain's past, the identities of victims and of perpetrators are demarcated anew and the ascription of responsibilities has changed as well. The generation of the "fathers of the constitution" interpreted Spain's past in terms of a civil war that called for "reconciliation" and "starting a new chapter"; whereas today, the imperative of remembrance is linked with the nature of the crimes that were committed by the Franco regime during the war and – importantly – under a forty-year dictatorship. No longer is it the fratricidal battles of a civil war that have been "thrown into oblivion" – the term coined by historian Santos Juliá in his passionate defence of the agreements and balances struck during the transition; rather, it is the crimes against humanity (for some, even genocide) committed by the victors in that war and swept under the rug during Francoism as well as during the transition. Memorialists contend, with the support of recent historiography, that the crimes committed by Franco were no different from those of the Nazis in Europe or the military junta in Argentina.[3] Why should those be remembered and ours be forgotten? Given that they fall into the same category, such crimes cannot even be actively forgotten as an act of political maturity. A higher morality anchored in the victims' rights deems such a pact – trading memory and accountability for political stability – treacherous and inadmissible. These crimes call for the amendment and even repeal of the legislation that ignored them and for the fullest possible restitution. In legal terms, crimes against humanity are not subject to a statute of limitations; in moral and political terms, they are characterized by their constant posing of questions to the present. In this light, such crimes haunt Spanish society to this day. Affect, pathos, and trauma metaphors construct a victim-centred narrative that often lacks comprehensiveness, historical accuracy, or complexity. Such memory narratives erase the intricacies of political conflict; they become legitimized through an emphasis on the innocence of those who are seen as victims because their rights were violated. It is no coincidence that the universalized model and paradigm for these narratives – the Holocaust – has left its stamp on the methods the social actors involved in memory work have chosen as a means to relate to the past and project it into the public sphere.

Becoming European: Never Again *Franquismo*

Catching up with Europe in the late 1970s and 1980s meant breaking loose from a repressive and conservative society, and thus involved overcoming Francoism through forgetting it. But at a generational remove, things look different. In the present day, becoming European has come to mean actively remembering Francoism. Memory work – with the mass grave exhumations at its centre – addresses both Spain's democratic shortcomings and its incomplete Europeanization.[4] For Spain's memorialists, becoming a citizen in a modern democracy has meant a belated integration with Western Europe's memory of Nazism and fascism. Spanish memorialists assiduously invoke the established and uncontested public memory of the Nazi regime in Germany. In this model, Spain would *join* Germany (ironically, a symbol of modernity and the embodiment of "Europe") and other Western European states by developing a culture of memory as a means to acknowledge and confront the crimes of Hitler's peninsular ally through memorials, state-sponsored museums, and the school curriculum. Memorialists understand their work in relation to the standards of an imagined European community that takes pains to fold the evils of the Holocaust and Nazism/fascism into its political culture. But in Spain today,

Francoism is not actively and unequivocally remembered as the cautionary counter-image of democratic Spain. This points to Spaniards' contested and still divided memories of the Franco dictatorship. For memorialists, moreover, it is a symptom of not having fully joined Europe, since a European country today cannot be democratic without being explicitly anti-fascist.[5]

The defenders of the transition, however, contest this line of thinking and argue that the refusal to redress the past has not in the least hindered the founding of a successful democracy. Quite the contrary – according to them, Spain's democracy is not inferior to that of countries in which the transition from dictatorship to democracy followed a different path, one that involved investigations and prosecutions.[6]

The progressive incorporation of legal language into the political debate about the past in Spain is clearly a consequence of the interventions of the *memoria histórica* movement. Human rights and memorial organizations in Spain have borrowed freely from their Latin American and especially Argentinian counterparts to conceptualize "forced disappearances" – a crime against humanity under international human rights law – in Spain.[7] Thus, the term *desaparecidos*, with its clear Latin American connotations, depoliticized meaning, and subtext of Holocaust victimhood, has become a central reference point for Spanish human rights organizations that want to place the Spanish victims of the Franco regime in context.[8] European and Latin American fascism served as a template for this reassessment. The significance of the conceptual and symbolic transfer of the Latin American discourse to the Spanish case cannot be understated: the *paseados* – the local term used for those who were "taken for a walk" to be executed under the Franco regime and now lie in mass graves throughout the country – have been retroactively redefined as *desaparecidos*.[9]

The transference of meaning from one continent to the other takes place in different dimensions and planes by way of strategies of visibilization and "multidirectional activism," in which visual imagery (such as portraits and silhouettes of *desaparecidos*) and rituals of contestation (such as the Plaza de Mayo protests) are adopted from the successful experiences of Argentinian human rights activists and applied in the Spanish context, and through legal action inspired and backed by the international human rights regime.[10] In 2002, ARMH succeeded in including Spain in the UN Working Group on Enforced or Involuntary Disappearances, founded in 1980 to investigate disappearances in Chile.[11] As a result, the Spanish state slowly incorporated demands that originated in the fruitful interaction between global symbolic repertoires and local, nationally framed meaning systems. Further evidence of such "recursive cosmopolitization" can be located in the ways in which human rights memories, couched in the powerful rhetoric of anti-impunity, have become more consequential and found greater resonance at the domestic level.[12] Cultural and political sensitivities had shifted by the new millennium, and institutional changes, however timid, would ensue in Spain in its first decade.

Landscapes of Traumatic Memory

Memory activists are anchored in the present and feed off contemporary ways of theorizing and successfully embedding memories of mass violence in the public debate. Theories, metaphors, categories, and cultural frames connected to Holocaust history and the discussion about its (im) possible representation play an important role in these processes.

The politics of memory of the recovery movement are rooted in a philosophy of history that claims that history must be "undone" so as to incorporate the perspective of the victims.[13] It is no coincidence that it is philosophers and cultural theorists – rather than political scientists or historians – who have provided the theoretical foundation of the memorialist narrative.[14] Walter Benjamin's metaphors prove to be extraordinarily relevant – in particular, his notion of memory as a theory of knowledge that illuminates the blind spots of visible reality (factuality) and whose task it is to "brush history against the grain." Benjamin thought that the present could not be deciphered without examining its foundations in the lost battles of the past. New generations in the present would thus inherit a "messianic power" from their predecessors, which would in turn oblige them to remember their suffering and lost struggles. Benjamin's formulation resonates strongly among the *memoria histórica* generation.[15] We might even say that in the new millennium, Spain has been visited by Benjamin's Angel of History. Its gaze, encompassing horror and melancholy but also hope, has been adopted by the memorialist movement. Where we see modern cities, memorialists see suffering and despair; where we see picturesque villages, memorialists point to the unquiet abandoned graves below. As in Claude Lanzmann's film *Shoah*, which begins with the survivor Simon Srebnik returning to his native Poland and identifying the site of the mass killings in the midst of placid prairies and forests, *memoria histórica* locates an elderly witness or survivor who can point to the ground and say to the younger generations: this is the place. In an op-ed in *El País* titled "El deber de memoria" (The Duty of Memory), philosopher Reyes Mate defined the approach with precision: "La mirada de la víctima permite conocer una parte de la realidad que sin ella sería inaccesible" (the look of the victim allows [us] to know a part of reality that would be inaccessible without it).[16] *Memoria histórica* thus symbolizes the Angelus Novus; in Hebrew, "angel," *malach,* also means "messenger,"[17] an unwelcome messenger who will alter perception and make us attentive to the dark side of a factuality that is built on ruins, or, in Benjamin's words, on "wreckage upon wreckage." What we deem as progress in a modernized Spain – the subsequent waves of economic development built upon the foundations of the so-called *desarrollismo,* the boom period of late Francoism in the 1960s – has its roots in unspeakable barbarity. The time of memory questions that of history. There is in this vision an idea of justice, but one that draws its force and meaning from the dead. Thus the actions of the memorialists are an unmistakable acknowledgment of the past's unrealized possibilities. Just like the *desaparecidos* in Argentina or the vanished Jews of pre-war Europe, the forgotten and rediscovered victims of the Spanish mass graves become premonitory spectres or warning signs, as well as bearers of an imagined ethical and political reconstruction in society. Recovery of historical memory is a task of visibilization and "rescue," a term often used by memorialists: rescued from oblivion and reintegrated, through memory work, into society.

Survivor testimony also plays a role in the recovery process and complements forensic practices. The discovery and identification of the victims and the testimonies of survivors and relatives turn bones into concrete stories of loss and suffering but also resilience. In this regard, the collection of testimonies and the creation of oral and audiovisual history archives goes beyond the mere collection of historical information. It is the very act of bearing witness that comes to the forefront in these projects. The term "moral witness,"[18] as opposed to the judiciary or historical form of witnessing and documenting, is relevant in these contexts. What matters are the moral effects of the witnesses' discourse. Stories of survivors must be collected, treasured, and widely communicated. Thus it is a call to a new generation to bear "witness to the witness" – a formulation Ulrich Baer employs in the context of Holocaust survivor testimony[19] – and this call is particularly imperative at a time in which direct witnesses are dying out. As Annette Wieviorka has emphasized regarding Holocaust testimony, testimony's mission is not just to bear witness to often inadequately known events; it is also "to keep them before our eyes."[20] The various video-testimony undertakings are restitution projects, and their digital collections and archives represent moral containers: symbols of past tragedy and present homage. Holocaust testimony projects, such as Spielberg's Survivors of the Shoah and the Fortunoff Archive at Yale University, have served as a model and methodological template that has inspired a number of video testimony initiatives for victims of Francoism, such as the Memorial Democràtic in Barcelona and the Aranzadi testimony archive in the Basque Country.[21] The language surrounding such testimony collection projects is very telling for the way it conflates individual and collective memory processes. It also amounts to the unequivocal adoption of a Holocaust model in what we may call therapeutic remembrance politics. Several oral history projects related to victims of Francoism have employed the formulation "se buscan donantes de memoria" (we seek memory donors).[22] The analogy to blood donors is significant, for it implies a vital need. Stories and testimonies of an unsettling violent past serve as the sap that permits life and leads to healing, both for the individual who overcomes trauma and for traumatized society at large.

But there is another perspective on this recovery process, one in which closure is viewed as an unwarranted option. As Jennifer Sime has eloquently argued, exhumations do not have to lead towards the liberation of memory and thereby to the healing of Spain's lingering traumas, to solace and closure. Rather, they can facilitate "modes of encounter with the past – indeed with the dead" – in which the past remains open and asserts its rights in the present.[23]

Between *No Pasarán* and *Nunca Más*: Anti-Fascism Meets Auschwitz

In the article "Icons of Memory Juxtaposed," historian Dan Diner points out that anti-fascist memory of the Civil War (embodied in the watchword "No Pasarán," the slogan of the heroic defence of Madrid) has gone from being a European icon to being a purely national one.[24] The global memory of the Spanish Civil War as an icon of anti-fascism, which was predominant in the postwar years among the left in Western Europe, has been substituted by another global icon: the Holocaust (Never Again). The irony in Diner's argument is that it also applies to present-day Spain, where, as we have seen, representations of *memoria histórica* are highly conditioned by the standards of the Holocaust. However, anti-fascist memory has not entirely vanished from Spanish memory politics.[25] The conflict and negotiation between these two memory paradigms plays out most clearly in the tensions and differences between the ARMH and the communist Foro por la Memoria. These two groups share the imperative of locating mass graves and investigating the crimes, but they are not in accord regarding the political approaches to exhumations and the overall significance of recovering the memory of the defeated. ARMH represents an ethics of "Never Again." It embraces the category of "victim" and emphasizes the humanity of the dead and the rights of families.[26] Foro por la Memoria invokes the revived, politicized memory of the Spanish Civil War as a struggle between the left and the right and criticizes ARMH for treating exhumations as a family affair. Indeed, if it can be claimed that current memory politics has made the Holocaust the dominant time frame of memory, subordinating the political memory of the Civil War to its new paradigm, then the Foro wants to re-establish a pre-Holocaust memory frame: the ever-present struggle between fascism and socialism, which first played out on a global scale in the Spanish Civil War, fought between 1936 and 1939.[27] As we argue, much of the human rights frame of the ARMH is, in contrast, driven by Holocaust memory. Part of this frame is mediated by family concerns and the notion of trauma, while at the same time sustaining and nurturing the mentioned ways of productive encounter with the past. The Foro, for its part, argues that recovering historical memory entails explicitly politicizing the exhumations, that is, vindicating the political identities and (it follows) the ideals and the political project for which the exhumed individuals were killed.[28] In the exhumations conducted by the Foro, political affinity (of party or union members) is a form of kinship, one that trumps family ties. It is not the "family tear" but the "political tear" that should be shed.[29]

Despite these differences, "Never Again" and "No Pasarán" are not completely separate memory frames. They intersect and sometimes blur in the work and outlook of the memorialists. In a fascinating overlap of distant temporalities and contrasting time worlds, the Foro defines itself as the Frente Popular de la memoria (the Popular Front of memory),[30] which continues the struggle against Francoism "sustituyendo el fusil y la bayoneta por el pico y la pala, la cámara de video, las charlas pedagógicas, la denuncia, la atención a las víctimas, los libros y exposiciones, las iniciativas legislaticas y un largo etcétera de instrumentos pacíficos de lucha" (substituting the gun and the bayonet with the pick and shovel, the video camera, the pedagogical lectures, the denunciation, the attention to the families, the books and the exhibitions, the legislative initiatives and a long etcetera of peaceful instruments of struggle).[31] To a certain extent, we see in this language the creative combination of the two paradigms: a discourse that ties together militant politicization with human rights concerns, epic homage to the martyrs of an ideological struggle, and the pedagogical remembrance of a criminal state that failed to protect their rights.

The Foro illustrates this in the "who we are" section of its website:

Justicia con las víctimas y sus familias, que llevan años sufriendo vejaciones y silencio, justicia con el pueblo español, que desconoce su verdad histórica y, por lo tanto, ha perdido sus señas de identidad y, por último, justicia con la izquierda, que dio lo mejor de sus militantes para combatir las desigualdades y defender las libertades democráticas y los derechos humanos.

Justice with the victims and their relatives, who have suffered humiliation and silence for years. Justice with the Spanish people, who do not know its historic truth and, therefore, have lost its signs of identity. And justice with the left, which has sacrificed the best of its militants to combat inequity and defend democratic freedom and human rights.[32]

These examples also show that there has been a reconfiguration of the political left through memorial and human rights activism. This implies going back and forth between a "radical nostalgia" – the term Peter Glazer has used for the memorialization of the Abraham Lincoln International Brigades in the United States[33] – and judicial activism for victims' rights. In Spain the *nietos*, the grandchildren, regain both victim and political identities through *memoria histórica* and find new spaces for subjective identification and collective action.

Private mourning and political allegiance blend into rituals that involve direct relatives as well as the "memory community" at large. Nostalgia combines with the Benjaminean idea of the redemptive power of a lost struggle. These notions underpin an interpretative frame for a new generation, to a large extent orphaned by the left, that searches in the past for a meaningful socio-political identity. At times one might ask whether, rather than the warped inheritance of an original injury, it is *longing* that connects the grandchildren with the imagined genera-tion of the Civil War vanquished.

Holocaust Remembrance: Spanish Readings

The Holocaust has entered Spain top-down, in the form of transna-tional initiatives of commemoration, global media, and European Union standards in the school curriculum, and it has interacted in both conflicting and supportive ways with the bottom-up memory move-ment in its re-evaluation of the Civil War and the Franco era. In this last section, we highlight some of the salient aspects of how the Holocaust has been memorialized in contemporary Spain.[34]

In January 2000, Spain joined the Stockholm International Forum on the Holocaust and signed a commitment with most other EU member states to develop appropriate forms of Holocaust commemoration and ways of transferring information, knowledge, and ethical mobilization to younger generations. While commemoration efforts followed in several Spanish regions, it was not until the Socialist Party replaced the conservative government of the Partido Popular (People's Party) in the 2004 elections that Spain began to hold an annual Holocaust remembrance ceremony sponsored by the central government. In 2005 it declared 27 January the Día Oficial de la Memoria del Holocausto y Prevención de Crímenes contra la Humanidad (Official Day of Holocaust Memory and Prevention of Crimes against Humanity). In 2008, Spain became a member of the International Task Force for Holocaust Education Remembrance and Research.

Public Holocaust commemoration in Spain is extraordinarily revealing with regard to exploring how supra-national memory discourses, rooted in institutional programs to promote Holocaust remembrance and education, are reinterpreted and adapted, and how they interact with the internal memory conflicts we have highlighted so far. How is the Holocaust understood, contextualized, and rendered meaningful by different political actors in these ceremonies? Polarized partisan interpretations of the Holocaust are a critical component in understanding the influence of global memory constellations on the self-understanding of Spaniards vis-à-vis their own history, and they are key to assessing the process by which the country adopts and resignifies Western Europe's memory narratives.[35]

The Holocaust Remembrance Day ceremony initiated by the Socialist government in 2005 brought together representatives of the Jewish, Spanish Republican, and Gypsy communities, who lit six memorial candles, echoing the lighting of a candle for each of the six million murdered Jews, as is done in many *Yom Hashoah*, the Jewish Holocaust Remembrance Day ceremonies. Now, however, two of the candles were lit "En memoria de las víctimas españolas asesinadas en los campos de concentración" (in memory of the Spanish victims who died in the concentration camps) and "En memoria de las víctimas del pueblo gitano y de otros colectivos perseguidos por los nazis" (in memory of the victims from the Gypsy community and other groups persecuted by the Nazis).[36] Hence, the ceremony, which is Jewish in its origins, symbolically incorporates the new Spanish memories of the Holocaust. When the term "Holocaust" is semantically opened to refer to Nazi atrocities other than the Jewish genocide, this distant past is linked to Spain. Republican presence in these ceremonies is not simply a *novum*; it inescapably probes a tender spot in Spanish memory politics. The Holocaust remembrance ceremony of 2006 deserves special attention. Present on that occasion was King Juan Carlos I, who in his speech chose his words carefully, referring to the Republican victims as "Sons of Spain," while avoiding the word "Republican." Nine years later, in the 27 January 2015 ceremony, King Felipe VI would acknowledge the Republican victims by their proper name and weave into his speech the fate of Sephardic Jewry, interpreting that fate, unprecedentedly, as a loss for Spain as well: "España [...] también se desangró con las víctimas: por un lado los miles de sefardíes asesinados en los campos, por otro, los exiliados republicanos españoles que el próximo mes de mayo conmemorarán el 70 aniversario de su liberación del campo de Mauthausen. Ambos, sefardíes y españoles exiliados [...] son hermanos de patria y de desdicha" (Spain also bled out with the victims: on the one side, with the thousands of Sephardim assassinated in the camps; on the other, with the exiled Republicans who next May will commemorate the 70th anniversary of their liberation of the Mauthausen camp. Both, Sephardim and Spanish exiles ... are brothers in fatherland and in misfortune).[37] Two historically marginalized memories – Sephardic Jewry and Republicans – were now merged and uttered in one breath by the highest representative of the Spanish state. It is ironic that in the context of bitter negotiations over Spain's Francoist past, it is the globalized version of (Jewish) Holocaust memory – conveyed top-down by institutional initiatives – that has paved the way for the public and official recognition of the memories of Republican deportation.

A comparison with France offers interesting insight into the novelty of this process. As Annette Wieviorka and Samuel Moyn have extensively documented, the fate of Jews was first subsumed in post-1945 France – they were only remembered through the anti-fascist rhetoric of the French Resistance. Annette Wieviorka quotes a French Auschwitz survivor who put it this way: "We made a deal: I'll lend you my gas chamber, and you'll give me your resistance."[38] In Spain, where anti-fascist and resistance narratives were first suppressed by the dictatorship and had little social relevance even after the country's transition to democracy, it is the Jewish-victim-driven globalizing Holocaust discourse that has "lent" the concentration camp, and the Holocaust as such, to Spanish Republicans. The particular case of the Spanish Republican victims of Nazism, and its relation to the memory of the destruction of European Jewry, can thus be seen as the productive, intercultural dynamic that Michael Rothberg calls "multidirectional memory." The interaction of different collective memories within the public sphere is a productive cross-fertilizing dynamic rather than a zero sum game in which the remembrance of one history erases others from view.[39]

Holocaust memorialization in Spain builds on two different universalist approaches: anti-fascism and global Holocaust memory. Whereas the former attempts to subsume the murder of the Jews within a broader definition of fascist crimes, the later presents the specifics of the Shoah in a universal language so as to draw from the event universalizing lessons. In reality, however, these two universalist approaches become the expression of particularistic memory politics rooted in Spain's specific political landscape. Whereas anti-fascism serves the left by reinserting the left-right division into the present political scenario, global Holocaust memory acts as a convenient screen memory for the conservatives. This shows again that the meaning of Holocaust remembrance is inevitably situated and contextual. In Germany, the *Historikerstreit* (the "historians' dispute") showed there was a plainly self-critical element to the emphasis on the singularity of the Holocaust. Meanwhile, putting the Nazi genocide into perspective and signalling that other nations also perpetrated atrocities (Stalin's crimes in particular) implied deflection and self-exculpation. Yet for Nazi Germany's allies (such as Spain and Italy) and for its sympathizers, the opposite is the case. Highlighting the singularity of the Holocaust results in self-exculpation regarding their fascist and Francoist pasts respectively. In this sense, whether the Holocaust is presented as a unique event, or as comparable to other atrocities, it has become an expression of where one is positioned in regard to the Spanish memory conflict.

Public memory of Nazi crimes in Spain has long been uncomfortable for the Spanish political right, and it is no coincidence that official Holocaust commemoration was started during the Socialist administration. At first, global Holocaust memory was not well received by Spanish conservatives, for it criminalized Franco as one of Hitler's allies and promoted sympathy and dignified remembrance for the victims of Nazism, who included Spanish Republicans. Holocaust memory drew attention to past events that had been "pushed to oblivion" during the transition, which were now being brought back into memory, given political significance, and instrumentalized by the political adversary on the left. To bypass this problem, Spanish conservatives sought to highlight the uniqueness of the Holocaust in order to draw a fundamental distinction between Nazism and Francoism, to which the People's Party is inextricably linked by birth.[40] In this respect, the paradigm of Shoah uniqueness frames the speeches by representatives of the People's Party at Holocaust remembrance ceremonies, at the state, provincial, and local levels. As much as the Shoah, and not the Holocaust or the crimes of European Fascism in an even broader sense, becomes the object of remembrance, such speeches will in most cases mention only the Jewish victims.

This perspective has even enabled ways to make an apology for Francoism, which explains the conservatives' shift from rejection of or indifference towards Shoah memory, to full embrace of it over the last two decades. Several conservative authors have attempted to undermine the increasingly dominant narrative linking Spain's authoritarian past to fascism and Nazism, and to promote simple but politically useful interpretations rooted in the maxim that "not everything about Franco was bad." The popularization of Holocaust rescue myths is a clear example of how the Spanish right has capitalized on Holocaust memory to restore a more positive memory of Francoism. These accounts have tried to substantiate the legend promoted by Franco's own propaganda during the 1940s, which claimed that the Francoist government had saved thousands of European Jews from the Holocaust. (See chapters 8 and 20 in this volume.) Although this legend has been repeatedly debunked by historiography, it is still influential, considering that publications echoing this myth are able to reach a greater audience than scholarly history books.[41] This rather paradoxical phenomenon has also been identified by Italian scholars.[42] In this approach, fascism is being retroactively validated – or at least whitewashed – through the creation of Holocaust rescue and survival narratives. The figure of the "righteous gentile," for instance, has been popularized in both Spain and Portugal through film and television in order to articulate a Manichaean narrative that juxtaposes the evil German with the good Italian (i.e., Giorgio Perlasca) and Spaniard (i.e., Ángel Sanz Briz and other diplomats who saved Jews). Their progressive counterparts have attempted to define General Franco as an indisputable partner of the Nazis in the Holocaust through similar reductionist and speculative claims.[43]

In sum, the Spanish left has underscored Franco's role as a collaborator and linked the memory of the Spanish Republicans to that of the Shoah. If the deported Republicans are "Holocaust victims," the connection between Hitler and Franco (which the partisan-driven discourse of singularity intentionally precludes) can be firmly established. For their part, conservatives have retaliated by highlighting certain aspects of the Holocaust in an attempt to dissociate Francoism from Nazi Germany.

Conclusion

When Spain escaped the grip of Franco's dictatorship, the country's democracy was rebuilt on the margins of the prevailing European cultural memory, in which the Second World War and the Nazi crimes had for decades occupied a central place as a negative reference point. Spain's progressive absorption into the wider European debate about the remembrance of war and genocide in recent decades has made the general public certainly more aware of its symbolic significance, and discussions of the Holocaust have gained presence in Spanish public life over the last two decades. The Holocaust as a focal point of European memory politics contributed to raising awareness among a new generation of scholars, artists, journalists, and above all civil society actors regarding Spain's troubled past. This has impacted the emergence of new debates around the nature and significance of the memories of extreme violence; it has also considerably shaped the form and specific meaning these memories have taken. *Memoria histórica*, we have argued, is intimately tied to developments connected to the impact on Spain of a globalized Holocaust discourse. But within *memoria histórica* we have also identified different ways to situate Francoist crimes in dialogue with World War II and the Holocaust, "No Pasarán" and "Nunca Más" being distinct and sometimes overlapping modes of engagement with this past that respectively espouse militant antifascism and cosmopolitan human rights advocacy work. But there are also particular *memoria histórica* politics implemented in Catalonia and the Basque country by nationalist governments. In Catalonia, the history of the Spanish Civil War is at the same time Europeanised and nationalized through (regional) state sponsored museums, memorials and the school curriculum as these establish direct connections between anti-Catalan/anti-Republican Francoist repression, the Second World War, and the Holocaust.[44]

The Spanish case illustrates that the Holocaust has multiple meanings determined within the parameters of cosmopolitanization and renationalization. The Holocaust exists as a memory paradigm but not as a shared memory, since particularistic readings override the universal openings that the notion of a European self-reflective and critical memory could potentially provide. It is a powerful element in the context of an open conflict over acknowledgment and redress. In Spain, the Holocaust has enabled discursive opportunities for seeking parallels and analogies through which to bring the crude reality of Francoist violence into the open. It allowed revisiting and reframing local pasts by way of metaphorical bridging to the paradigmatic event of political violence in Europe. Yet elements of that same memorial culture – i.e., the emphasis on the singularity and uniqueness of the Nazi extermination plan (the Shoah paradigm) – have served political actors on the opposite side of the political spectrum to deflect the *memoria histórica* claims and demands under the motto: Francoism was *not* Nazism.

NOTES

This chapter is based on the following publications by the authors: Baer and Snazider, *Memory and Forgetting*; idem, "Ghosts of the Holocaust"; and Baer, "The Voids of Sepharad."

1 See Ben-Ze'ev, Ginio, and Winter, *Shadows of War*, for the general context.

2 The Amnesty Law shields those who are considered criminals under transitional justice terms from judicial prosecution. It is now highly contested, and there are intense debates regarding whether it violates international humanitarian law. For the general context, see Davis, "Is Spain Recovering its Memory?"; Encarnación, *Democracy Without Justice in Spain*.

3 See Moreno Gómez, *El genocidio franquista en Córdoba*; Míguez Macho, *The Genocidal Genealogy of Francosim*.

4 See Ferrándiz, "The Return of Civil War Ghosts, 7–12; idem, *El pasado bajo tierra*; Renshaw, *Exhuming Loss*; and Rubin, "Transitional Justice against the State," among others.

5 See, for instance, Escudero's argument along these lines in the introduction to his *Diccionario de memoria histórica*, 9.

6 Pradera and Estefanía, *La Transición española y la democracia*, 19. For an empirical assessment of the effect of transitional justice mechanisms on democracy and human rights scores, see the important body of scholarship by L. Payne, *Unsettling Accounts*; and Sikkink, *The Justice Cascade*.

7 Schindel, "Los intelectuales latinoamericanos y el Holocausto," 3; Ferrándiz, "De las fosas comunes"; Gatti, "De un continente al otro," 201.

8 The Holocaust subtext in the Argentinian state's memorial narratives can be traced back to the *Nunca Más* (Never again) truth commission report, which established, on the narrative level, the figure of the *desaparecido* as an innocent victim of state terror. As Emilio Crenzel has pointed out in his work, the distinctive feature of the disappearances is found in the report in the shaping of a "humanitarian narrative" that omits the victim's political predicaments and "avoid[s] historicizing the causes of the political violence": Crenzel, *La historia política del Nunca Más*, 102. Also, the title *Nunca Más* was chosen after one of the report's authors had seen the phrase written in several languages on the monument at the Dachau concentration camp in Germany: Crenzel, *Memory of the Argentina Disappearances*, 71.

9 See Ferrándiz, "De las fosas comunes."

10 See the work of Capdepón, *Vom Fall Pinochet*.

11 Davis, "Is Spain Recovering its Memory?"; Renshaw, *Exhuming loss*.

12 Levy, "Recursive Cosmopolitization."

13 See Silva et al., eds, *La memoria de los olvidados*.

14 The renowned philosopher Reyes Mate and his research group Filosofía después del Holocausto at the Spanish Research Council have played an important role in nurturing this theoretical underpinning of the memorialist narrative. Interestingly, the group started out by reflecting not on the Spanish past but rather on the Holocaust. Since the late 1990s it has held an interdisciplinary research seminar where the canon of Holocaust literature and theory is discussed and also partly translated. The group has published a number of books and journal special issues that have at their

core the centrality of Auschwitz as a referent for rethinking the relationsip between politics and violence.

15 Benjamin, *Illuminations*.

16 Mate, "El deber de memoria," http://elpais.com/diario/2011/01/27/opinion/1296082805_850215.html.

17 Handelman, *Fragments of Redemption*.

18 Margalit, *The Ethics of Memory*. See also A. Baer, *El testimonio audivisual*.

19 U. Baer, ed., *Niemand zeugt für den Zeugen*.

20 Wieviorka, *The Era of Witness*.

21 See Egilior, "El testimonio ante la cámara."

22 See, for instance, the projects "Donantes de Memoria," https://donantesdememoria.wordpress.com and "Todos ... los Nombres," http://www.todoslosnombres.org.

23 Sime, "Exhumations," 39.

24 Dan Diner, "Icons of Memory Juxtaposed," in Gómez López-Quiñones and Zepp, eds, *The Holocaust in Spanish Memory*.

25 If there is a memory that has totally vanished from the Spanish memory movement, it is that of the anti-totalitarianism of POUM, the Trotskyists who were crushed by Stalin in Spain. See Sherry, "'Claws of Stalinism in Spain.'"

26 See also Ferrándiz, *El pasado bajo tierra*; Bevernage and Colaert, "History from the Grave?"

27 The logo of the Madrid chapter of Foro por la Memoria is explicit in this respect: a tree with the colours of the Republic on its leaves and the slogan "No Pasarán."

28 Ferrándiz, *El pasado bajo tierra*; Rubin, "Transitional Justice against the State."

29 Ferrándiz, "From Tear to Pixel."

30 The Popular Front was formed in 1936 by a coalition of left-wing republican parties and constituted the last government of the Spanish Second Republic.

31 Quoted in Ferrándiz, *El pasado bajo tierra*, 64.

32 Pedreño Gómez, "Recuperando La Memoria Histórica," http://www.foroporlamemoria.info/documentos/recuperando_construyendo.htm. The organization by the Foro por la Memoria of a conference on *Victims* (our emphasis) of Francoism in 2008 is a telling development that speaks to the force of the Never Again paradigm. The term generally used until recently by organizations was "represaliados" (persecuted), which involved agency.

33 Glazer, *Radical Nostalgia*.

34 For an in-depth discussion of this subject, see Baer, *The Voids of Sepharad*.

35 For a comparative longitudinal study of Holocaust commemoration addressing this research question see Karakaya and Baer, "Such Hatred has Never Flourished on our Soil."

36 Programa Día Oficial de la Memoria y Prevencion de Crimenes contra la Humanidad (Official Day of Memory and Prevention of Crimes Against Humanity Program), 26 January 2012.
37 Palabras de Su Majestad el Rey en el Día Oficial de la Memoria del Holocausto y la Prevención de los Crímenes contra la Humanidad (Words of His Highness the King on the Official Holocaust Remembrance and Prevention of Crimes Against Humanity Day), 27 January 2015, http:// www.casareal.es/ES/Actividades/Paginas/actividades_discursos_detalle. aspx?data=5426.
38 Wieviorka, *The Era of Witness*, 38–9, qtd in Alan Astro, "Revisiting Wiesel's Night," 142.
39 Rothberg, *Multidirectional Memory*, 2–3.
40 The Partido Popular was founded in 1989 as a new incarnation of Alianza Popular (People's Alliance), a party led and founded by Manuel Fraga Iribarne, a former Minister of the Interior and Minister of Tourism during the Franco dictatorship.
41 A. Baer and Correa, "The Politics of Rescue Myths in Spain," in Guttstadt et al., eds., *Bystanders, Rescuers, or Perpetrators?*, 205–16.
42 Perra, "Legitimizing Fascism through the Holocaust?"
43 See, for example, Martín de Pozuelo, *El Franquismo*.
44 David Messenger points to public memory spaces such as the Fossar de la Pedrera in Barcelona: "While the main foci of the site are the mass graves and the individual grave of former Catalan President Lluis Companys, at the edge of the space there are also seven black tombstone-like rock-outcroppings. Each one has the name of a Nazi concentration camp that operated during World War II." See Messenger, "Contemporary Memory Politics in Catalonia," 56.

Bibliography

List of Archives

American Jewish Historical Society Archive
American Jewish Joint Distribution Committee Archives (JDC)
Archiv der KZ-Gedenkstätte Mauthausen (AMM) [Archive of the Mauthausen Concentration Camp Memorial]
Archives of the International Tracing Service, Bad Arolsen, Germany (ITS)
Archiv der Mahn- und Gedenkstätte Ravensbrück [Archive of the Ravensbrück Memorial]
Archives du Ministère des Affaires Étrangères, Paris (MAE) [Ministry of Foreign Affairs Archives]
Archives Municipales de Bordeaux (AMB) [Municipal Archives of Bordeaux]
Archives of Bages, Manresa, Catalonia
Archives of the Alliance Israélite Universelle, Paris (AAIU)
Archives of the American Jewish Joint Distribution Committee (JDC)
Archives of the Ministère des Affaires Etrangères Français (MAEF) [Archives of the French Ministry of Foreign Affairs]
Archivo General de la Administración, Alcalá de Henares, Spain (AGA) [General Archive of the Administration]
Archivo General del Ministerio de Asuntos Exteriores y de Cooperación (MAEC or AMAE) [Archives of the Ministry of Foreign Affairs and Cooperation]
Archivo General Militar de, Ávila, Spain [General Military Archive of Ávila]
Archivo General Militar de Guadalajara, Spain [General Military Archive of Guadalajara]
Archivo Histórico Amical de Mauthausen [Historical Archive of the Amical de Mauthausen]
Archivo Histórico Nacional (AHN) [National Historic Archive]

Archivo Oficina Información Diplomática, Madrid (AOID) [Diplomatic Information Office]

Archivo Provincial de Cádiz, Spain [Provincial Archive of Cádiz]

Arxiu Històric de Girona i Arxiu Històric de Lleida [Historical Archives of Girona and Lleida]

Arxiu Nacional de Catalunya (ANC) [National Archives of Catalonia]

Auswärtiges Amt / Politisches Archiv (AA/PA) [Diplomatic Archive of the German Ministry for Foreign Affairs]

Biblioteca Nacional de España, Madrid (BNE) [National Library of Spain]

Bibliothèque Nacional de France (BnF) [National Library of France]

Bulgarian Central State Archives (CSA)

Bundesarchiv (BArch) [German Federal Archives]

Central State Historical Archives of St Petersburg

Centre de Documentation Juive Contemporaine, Paris (CDJC) [Center of Contemporary Jewish Documentation]

Centro Documental de la Memoria Histórica, Salamanca (CDMH) [Documentary Center of Historical Memory]

Centro Sefarad - Israel, Madrid (CSI)

Geheimes Staatsarchiv Presussischer Kulturbesitz (GSTA) [Secret Archive of the Prussian State]

Germaine Krull Archives

Hellenic Ministry of Foreign Affairs (MFA)

Ibero-Amerikanisches Institut Berlin (IAI) [Iberian-American Institute of Berlin]

KZ-Gedenkstätte Neuengamme Archiv [Neuengamme Concentration Camp Memorial Archive]

Latvian State Historical Archives

Lavon – Labor Party Archive, Mercaz Hapoel

Leo Baeck Institute Archives

Museu d'Història de Catalunya (MHC) [History Museum of Catalonia]

Paul V. Galvin Library, Illinois Institute of Technology (PVGL IIT)

Politisches Archiv des Auswärtigen Amtes, Berlin (AA) [Federal Foreign Office Political Archive]

Public Record Office, Kew London, UK (PRO)

The State Archives of the Novgorod Region (GANO)

United Kingdom National Archive, Kew (UKNA)

United States Holocaust Memorial Museum Archives (USHMM)

United States National Archives and Records Administration, College Park, Maryland (NARA)

Yad Vashem Archives (YVA)

YIVO Institute for Jewish Research, New York (YIVO)

Secondary Sources

Abitbol, Michel. *The Jews of North Africa during the Second World War.* Detroit: Wayne State UP, 1989.

Adorno, Theodor W. "What Does Coming to Terms with the Past Mean?" In *Bitburg in Moral and Political Perspective,* edited by Geoffrey Hartman, 114–29. Bloomington: Indiana UP, 1986.

Agnieszka, August-Zarebska. "The Representations of *kurtijo* and Their Function in Contemporary Judeo-Spanish Poetry." In *Ashkenazim and Sephardim: A European Perspective,* edited by Aleksandra Twardowska, Andrezej Katny, and Izabela Olszewska, 245–68. Frankfurt am Main: Peter Lang, 2013.

AJP. "Spain's Jews Try to Hide Identity as Anti-Semitic Tension Flourishes." *Sentinel,* 20 September 1951.

Alcheh Saporta, Isaac. *Los españoles sin patria de Salónica.* Madrid: La Lectura, 1916.

Alegre Calero, Sergio. "Las imágenes de la División Azul: Los vaivenes de la política exterior e interior de Franco a través del cine." In *Historia Contemporánea de España y Cine,* edited by Aitor Yraola and José María Caparrós Lera, 69–84. Madrid: Ediciones de la Universidad Autónoma de Madrid, 1997.

Alemany, Josep. "Martorellencs als camps d'extermini de Hitler." *Solc: Martorell,* no. 29 (September 1975): 15–19.

Alexy, Trudy. *La mezuzá en los pies de la Virgen. Los marranos y otros judíos secretos.* Madrid: Siglo XXI, 2000.

Alfaya, Javier. *Españoles en el Tercer Reich.* Madrid: Cuadernos para el Diálogo, 1970.

Aliberti, Davide. "Sefarad une communauté imaginée (1924–2015)." PhD diss., Université d'Aix–Marseille and Universitá L'Orientale of Napoli, 2015.

Allen, Michael Thad. *The Business of Genocide: The SS, Slave Labor, and the Concentration Camps.* Chapel Hill: U North Carolina P, 2002.

Almog, Shmuel. "What's in a Hyphen?" *SICSA Report: Newsletter of the Vidal Sassoon International Center for the Study of Antisemitism* (Summer 1989). Web.

Alonso, Cecilio, ed. *Actas del congreso internacional: "Max Aub y el laberinto español." Celebrado en Valencia y Segorbe del 13 a 17 de diciembre de 1993.* 2 vols. Valencia: Ayuntamiento de Valencia, 1996.

Alonso Gallardo, Félix, and Ángel González Pinilla. *Prisioneros en Rusia.* Madrid: Ediciones Esparta, 2015.

Álvarez Chillida, Gonzalo. "El antisemitismo en España." In *El judaísmo en Iberoamérica,* edited by Reyes Mate and Ricardo Forster, 197–220. Madrid: Trotta, 2007.

– *El antisemitismo en España. La imagen del judío (1812–2002)*. Madrid: Marcial Pons, [2002] 2009.

– *José María Pemán. Pensamiento y trayectoria de un monárquico (1897–1941)*. Cádiz: Universidad de Cádiz, 1996.

– "Zaragoza en la guerra civil. La memoria de un judío aragonés." *Raíces*, no. 54 (Spring 2003): 43–7.

Álvarez Chillida, Gonzalo, and Ricardo Izquierdo Benito. *El antisemitismo en España*. Cuenca: Ediciones de la Universidad de Castilla–La Mancha, 2007.

Amago, Samuel, and Carlos Jerez-Farrán, eds. *Unearthing Franco's Legacy: Mass Graves and the Recovery of Historical Memory in Spain*. Notre Dame: U of Notre Dame P, 2010.

Amat, Jordi. *El llarg procés*. Barcelona: Tusquets, 2015.

Amat-Piniella, Joaquim. "Eutanàsia." *Antologia dels fets, les idees i els homes d'occident* 1, no. 7 (November 1947): 52–9.

– "La fam." *Per Catalunya. Bulletin d'information des Catalans en exili* (August 1945): 3–4.

– *K.L. Reich*. Introduction by Ignacio Martínez de Pisón. Madrid: Libros del Asteroide, 2014.

– *K.L. Reich*. Translated by Robert Finley and Marta Marín-Dòmine. Waterloo: Wilfrid Laurier UP, 2014.

– *K.L. Reich: Novela* [1963]. Barcelona: Club Editor, 2013.

Amistad Judeo-Cristiana. Informe sobre revisión de libros de texto de enseñanza primaria, Madrid, June 1967.

Amistad Judeo-Cristiana. Segundo informe sobre revisión de libros de texto, Madrid, 31 October 1968.

Andrade, Jaime de [pseud., Francisco Franco]. *Raza. Anecdotario para el guión de una película*. Madrid: Delegación Nacional de Propaganda, 1942; Barcelona: Planeta / Fundación Nacional Francisco Franco, 1997.

Andrieu, Claire. "Réflexions sur la Résistance à travers l'exemple des Françaises à Ravensbrück." *Histoire@Politique* 5, no. 2 (2008): 3.

Andrés-Gallego, J. *¿Fascismo o Estado Católico? Ideología, religión y censura en la España de Franco 1937–1941*. Madrid: Ediciones Encuentro, 1997.

Andrés-Gallego, J., and A.M. Pazos, *La Iglesia en la España contemporánea*, vols. 1–2: *1800–1936*. Madrid: Ediciones Encuentro, 1999.

Andrés-Gallego, J., A.M. Pazos, and L. de Llera. *Los españoles entre la religión y la política*. Madrid: Unión Editorial, 1996.

Ángel, Miguel. *Los guerrilleros españoles en Francia (1940–1945)*. Havana: Instituto Cubano del libro, 1971.

"Ante Europa en armas, neutralidad." *Signo*, no. 50, 10 September 1939: 1.

Antelme, Robert. *L'espèce humaine*. Paris: Editions de la Cité Universelle, 1947.

Applebaum, Anne. *Gulag: A History*. New York: Doubleday, 2003.

Arasa, Daniel. *Los españoles de Stalin*. Barcelona: Belacqva, 2005.

Armengou, Montse, and Ricard Belis (dirs). *El comboi dels 927*. Televisió de Catalunya, 2004. Film.

– *El convoy de los 927*. Barcelona: Plaza y Janés, 2005.

– *Ravensbrück. L'infern de les dones*. Televisió de Catalunya, 2005. Film.

Arouh, R. Leon. "Marso 1943." *El Avenir* (2009) 37: 17. Thessaloniki: Jewish Community Thessaloniki.

Artero Rueda, Manuel, and Pilar Larrea. "Españoles en París, 60 años después." *Radio Televisión Española*, 4 September 2004.

Assmann, Jan. "Collective Memory and Cultural Identity." Translated by John Czaplicka. *New German Critique* 65 (1995): 125–33.

Astro, Alan. "Revisiting Wiesel's Night in Yiddish, French, and English." *Partial Answers: Journal of Literature and the History of Ideas* 12, no. 1 (2014): 127–53.

Aub, Max. *De algún tiempo a esta parte* [1939]. Seville: Renacimiento, 2018.

– *San Juan. Una tragedia* [1942]. Barcelona: Editorial Anthropos, 1992.

– *Tres monólogos y uno solo verdadero* [1939]. Mexico City: Tezontle, 1956.

Avilés-Diz, Jorge. "Fosas de la identidad perdida. Representaciones de la memoria histórica en el teatro español contemporáneo." *Hispanófila* 170 (January 2014): 73–95.

Avni, Haim. *España, Franco y los judíos*. Madrid: Altalena, 1982.

– "Los judíos en la España contemporánea. Entre emancipación y aceptación." In *La gobernanza de la diversidad religiosa. Personalidad y territorialidad en las sociedades multiculturales*, edited by Francisca Pérez-Madrid and Montserrat Gas i Aixendri, 139–65. Navarra: Thomson Reuters Aranzadi, 2013.

– *Spain, the Jews, and Franco*. Translated by Emanuel Shimoni. Philadelphia: Jewish Publication Society of America, 1982.

Aznar Soler, Manuel. *Los laberintos del exilio. Diecisiete estudios sobre la obra literaria de Max Aub*. Sevilla: Editorial Renacimiento, 2003.

– "Memoria, metateatro y mentira en *Himmelweg*." Ciudad Real: Ñaque Editora, 2011.

Azpiazu, Joaquín. "Pío XII y el llamado 'Orden Nuevo.'" *Razón y Fe*, no. 532 (May 1942): 496–519.

Bachoud, Andrée. *Franco ou la réussite d'un homme ordinaire*. Paris: Fayard, 1997.

Baer, Alejandro. *Holocausto. Recuero y representación*. Madrid: Losada, 2006.

– *El testimonio audiovisual. Imagen y memoria del Holocausto*. Madrid: Centro de Investigaciones Sociológicas, 2005.

– "Los vacíos de Sefarad." *Política y Sociedad*, 48, no. 3 (2011): 501–18.

– "The Voids of Sepharad: The Memory of the Holocaust in Spain." *Journal of Spanish Cultural Studies* 12, no. 1 (March 2011): 94–120.

– "The Voids of Sepharad: The Memory of the Holocaust in Spain." In *Revisiting Jewish Spain in the Modern Era*, edited by Daniela Flesler, Tabea Alexa Linhard, and Adrián Pérez Melgoa, 124–49. London: Routledge, 2013.

Baer, Alejandro, and Natan Sznaider. "Ghosts of the Holocaust in Franco's Mass Graves. Cosmopolitan Memories and the Politics of Never Again." *Memory Studies* 5, no. 2 (2015): 328–44.
– *Memory and Forgetting in the Post-Holocaust Era: The Ethics of Never Again.* London: Routledge, 2017.
Baer, Ulrich, ed. *Niemand zeugt für den Zeugen. Erinnerungskultur nach der Shoah.* Frankfurt am Main: Suhrkamp, 2000.
Baeza Mancebo, Antonio. *La hora de Gibraltar.* Madrid: Ediciones Toledo, 1942.
Balbuena, Monique. *Homeless Tongues: Poetry and Languages of the Sephardic Diaspora.* Stanford: Stanford UP, 2016.
Balfour, Sebastian. *The End of the Spanish Empire 1898–1923.* Oxford: Clarendon Press, 1997.
Barbeito Díez, Mercedes. "El Consejo de la Hispanidad." *Espacio, Tiempo y Forma,* serie V: *Historia Contemporánea,* no. 2 (1989): 113–40.
Barnett, Richard D. "Sephardi Museum Inaugurated in Toledo, Spain." *The American Sephardi* 5, nos. 1–2 (1971): 143–5.
Bauer, Yehuda. *American Jewry and the Holocaust: The American Jewish Joint Distribution Committee, 1939–1945.* Detroit: Wayne State UP, 1981.
Bautista Vilar, Juan. "L'Ouverture à l'Occident de la communauté juive de Tétouan 1860–1865." In *Mosaiques de Notre Mémoire. Les Judéo Espagnols du Maroc,* edited by Sarah Leibovici, 85–119. Paris: U.I.S.F., Centre d'etudes Don Isaac Abravanel, 1982.
Belenguer Mercadé, Elisenda. *Neus Català. Memòria i lluita.* Barcelona: Fundació Pere Ardiaca, 2006.
Ben Dror, Graciela. *The Catholic Church and the Jews: Argentina 1933–1945.* Lincoln and London: Nebraska UP and Vidal Sassoon International Center for the Study of Antisemitism, Hebrew U of Jerusalem, 2008.
– *La Iglesia Católica ante el Holocausto. España y América Latina 1933–1945.* Madrid: Alianza Editorial, 2003.
– "'Traitors and Evildoers': Antisemitism in Spanish Textbooks during Franco's Regime." *Moreshet: Journal for the Study of the Holocaust and Antisemitism* 11 (2014): 144–82.
Benardete, Maír José. "Spain Grants Freedom of Religion to the Jews ... An Excursion into the Realms of the Imagination and Vision." *The American Sephardi* 1, no. 2 (June 1967): 26–30.
Benarroch, Carlos. "La Real Academia Española y los judíos." *Boletín Amistad Judeo-Cristiana,* no. 31 (June–July–August 1967): 8–11.
Benet, Claude. *Passeurs, Fugitifs et Espions. L'Andorre dans la 2e Guerre mondiale.* Toulouse: Le Pas d'oiseau, 2010.
Benjamin, Walter. *Illuminations.* New York: Harcourt, Brace & World, 1968.

Benroubi, Nina. *Life Is Sweet and Bitter*. Athens: Modern Horizons, 2004.

Ben-Ze'ev, Efrat, Ruth Ginio, and Jay Winter. *Shadows of War: A Social History of Silence in the Twentieth Century*. Cambridge: Cambridge UP, 2010.

Bergen, Doris L. *War and Genocide: A Concise History of the Holocaust*. Lanham: Rowman and Littlefield, 2016.

Bermejo, Benito. *El fotògraf de l'horror. La història de Francesc Boix i les fotos robades als SS de Mauthausen*. Barcelona: RBA, 2015.

– *Francisco Boix, el fotógrafo de Mauthausen*. Barcelona: RBA Libros, 2002.

– "Los republicanos españoles en los campos nazis." *Cuadernos republicanos* 54 (2004): 161–77.

– "La Vicesecretaría de Educación Popular (1941–1945): un «ministerio» de la propaganda en manos de Falange." *Espacio, Tiempo y Forma[/ital], serie V: Historia Contemporánea*, no. 6 (1991): 73–96.

Bermejo, Benito, and Sandra Checa. *Libro memorial. Españoles deportados a los campos nazis (1940–1945)*. Madrid: Ministerio de Cultura, Subdirección General de Publicaciones, Información y Documentación, 2006.

Bernadac, Christian. *Les 186 marchés*. Paris: France-Empire, 1974.

Bernardino Llorca, SJ. "La inquisición española." *Ecclesia*, no. 80, (23 January 1943): 17–18.

Bernecker, Walter L. "Alemania y España en la época del nacionalsocialismo." In *España y Alemania. Percepciones mutuas de cinco siglos de historia*, edited by Miguel Ángel Vega Cernuda and Henning Wegener, 155–81. Madrid: Editorial Complutense, 2002.

Bernhard, Patrick. "Origins of a Fascist Interpol." Paper for Lessons and Legacies XIII conference, 30 October–2 November 2014, Boca Raton, Florida.

Berthelot, Martine. *Cien años de presencia judía en la España contemporánea*. Barcelona: KFM, 1995.

– *Memorias judías (Barcelona 1914–1954). Historia oral de la Comunidad Israelita de Barcelona*. Barcelona: Riopiedras, 2001.

Bevernage, B., and L. Colaert. "History from the Grave? Politics of Time in Spanish Mass Grave Exhumations." *Memory Studies* 7, no. 4 (2014): 440–56.

Blanch Sabench, José M. *Memorias de un soldado de la División Azul*. Madrid: Galland 2010.

Blanco, José Luis. "Mariano Constante, un aragonés superviviente de Mauthausen." *El Europeo*, 14 February 1976.

Blanco Corredoira, José María. "José María Blanco Corredoira: Autor de libro *Añoranza de guerra*." Interview by Carlos Pérez-Roldán. "Tradición Viva." Web.

Blandin, Norbert. "La population de Tanger en 1940." *Revue Africaine* 88 (1944): 89–115.

Blin, Pascale. "Franco et les juifs du Maroc. Une approche historique." In *L'Espagne contemporaine et les juifs*, edited by P.L. Abramson and M. Berthelot, 33–57. Perpignan: Univ. de Perpignan, 1991.

– *Franco et les Juifs. Paroles et actes. De sa rencontre avec les Juifs à la reconnaissance de la communauté juive d'Espagne (1968). Un itinéraire controversé.* PhD diss., Université de la Sorbonne Nouvelle–Paris III, 1992.

Böcker, Manfred. *Antisemitismus ohne Juden. Die Zweite Republik, die antirepublikanische Rechte und die Juden. Spanien 1931 bis 1936.* Frankfurt am Main: Peter Lang, 2000.

Boor, J. [pseud.]. *Masonería.* Madrid: Gráficas Valera, 1952.

Borwicz, Michel. *Écrits des condamnés à mort sous l'occupation nazie.* Paris: Gallimard, 1996.

Bosch, Alfred, and Gustau Nerín. *El imperio que nunca existío.* Barcelona: Plaza & Janés Editors, 2001.

Boukraa, Leïla. *Teatro español y memoria histórica.* Tunis: Centre de Publication Universitaire, 2011.

Bowen, Wayne H. *Spaniards and Nazi Germany: Collaboration in the New Order.* Columbia: U of Missouri P, 2000.

– "Spanish Pilgrimages to Hitler's Germany: Emissaries of the New Order." *The Historian* 71, no. 2 (2009), 258–79.

Bowman, Steven. *The Agony of Greek Jews, 1941–1945.* Stanford: Stanford UP, 2009.

– *Jewish Resistance in Wartime Greece.* Athens: Central Board of Jewish Communities in Greece, 2012.

Brenneis, Sara J. "Carlos Rodríguez del Risco and the First Spanish Testimony from the Holocaust." *History and Memory* 25, no. 1 (2013): 51–76.

– *Genre Fusion: A New Approach to History, Fiction, and Memory in Contemporary Spain.* West Lafayette: Purdue UP, 2014.

– "Moral Ambiguity in Mauthausen: Mercè Rodoreda's 'Nit i boira.'" *Letras femeninas* 38, no. 2 (2012): 217–29.

– *Spaniards in Mauthausen: Representations of a Nazi Concentration Camp, 1940–2015.* Toronto: U of Toronto P, 2018.

Brizuela, Mabel. "Una cartografía teatral." In *Un espejo que despliega. El teatro de Juan Mayorga*, edited by Mabel Brizuela, 9–24. Córdoba: Universidad Nacional de Córdoba, Facultad de Filosofía y Humanidades, 2011.

Budnitskii, O.V., and G.S. Zelenina, eds. *"Svershilos. Prishli nemtsy!" Ideinyi kollaboratsionizm v SSSR v period Velikoi Otechestvennoi voiny* ["It happened. The Germans came!" Ideological Collaboration in the USSR during the Great Patriotic War.] Moscow: RUSSPEN, 2012.

Bueno, Guy. "Aparece un nuevo libro sobre España." *La Nueva España* (Oviedo), 29 November 1962.

Buggeln, Marc. *Arbeit und Gewalt. Das Außenlagersystem des KZ Neuengamme.* Göttingen: Wallstein, 2009.

– "Building to Death: Prisoner Forced Labour in the German War Economy –
The Neuengamme Subcamps, 1942–1945." *European History Quarterly* 39,
no. 4 (2009): 606–32.

– *Slave Labor in Nazi Concentration Camps.* Oxford: Oxford UP, 2015.

Burns, Emile. *The Nazi Conspiracy in Spain.* London: Victor Gollancz, 1937.

Caballero Jurado, C. *Atlas ilustrado de la División Azul.* Madrid: Susaeta, 2009.

Cahill, Paul. "Globalizing Good and Evil in the Poetry of Jorge Urrutia and
Jorge Riechmann." *MLN* 125, no. 2 (2010): 457–76.

Calcerrada Guijarro, Enrique, and Florencio Pavón Mariblanca. *Republicanos
españoles en Mauthausen-Gusen.* Benalmádena: Caligrama, 2003.

Calvet, Josep, ed. *Barcelona, refugi de jueus (1933–1958).* Barcelona: Angle
Editorial, 2015.

– "Història del Consolat Honorari de Polònia a Barcelona (1939–1944).
La tasca en favor dels refugiats de la Segona Guerra Mundial."
Polonesos a Barcelona. Un munt d'històries. Barcelona: Ajuntament de
Barcelona, 2008.

– *Huyendo del Holocausto. Judíos evadidos del nazismo a través del Pirineo de Lleida*
[2014]. Lleida: Editorial Milenio, 2015.

– *Las montañas de la libertad. El paso de refugiados por los pirineos durante la
Segunda Guerra Mundial, 1939–1944* [2008]. Translated by Lourdes Bigorra i
Cervelló. Madrid: Alianza Editorial, 2010.

Calvet, Josep, Annie Rieu, and Noemí Riudor. *La Bataille des Pyrénées. Résaux
d'information et d'évasion alliés transpyrénéens.* Toulouse: le Pas d'oiseau,
2013.

Camons Portillo, Lucas. "Diario de mi vida." n.d. Unpublished manuscript.

Campbell, Sue. *Our Faithfulness to the Past: The Ethics and Politics of Memory.*
Edited by Christine M. Koggel and Rockney Jacobsen. New York: Oxford
UP, 2014.

– *Relational Remembering: Rethinking the Memory Wars.* Lanham: Rowman and
Littlefield, 2003.

Cantarero, Joan. *La huella de la bota. De los nazis del franquismo a la nueva
ultraderecha.* Madrid: Temas de hoy, 2010.

Capdepón, Ulrike. *Vom Fall Pinochet zu den Verschwundenen des
Spanischen Bürgerkrieges. Die Auseinandersetzung mit Diktatur und
Menschenrechtsverletzungen in Spanien und Chile.* Bielefeld: Transcript, 2015.

Caplan, Jane. "Gender and the Concentration Camps." In *Concentration Camps
in Nazi Germany: The New Histories,* edited by Jane Caplan and Nikolaus
Wachsmann, eds, 82–107. London and New York: Routledge, 2009.

Carbos, Toni, and Javier Cosnava. *Prisionero en Mauthausen.* Alicante:
Ediciones de Ponent, 2011.

Caron, Vicki. *Uneasy Asylum: France and the Jewish Refugee Crisis, 1933–1942.*
Stanford: Stanford UP, 1999.

Carrier, Peter. *The International Status of Education about the Holocaust: A Global Mapping of Textbooks and Curricula.* Braunschweig: UNESCO–Georg Eckert Institute, 2015.

Carulla, Jordi, and Arnau Carulla. *La guerra civil en 2000 carteles. República – guerra civil – posguerra.* Barcelona: Postermil, 1997.

Caruth, Cathy. *Literature in the Ashes of History.* Baltimore: Johns Hopkins UP, 2013.

Castañon, José Manuel. *Diario de una aventura (con la División Azul 1941–1942).* Madrid: Fundación Dolores Medio, 1991.

Castro, Alfonso. *El problema judío.* Madrid: Ediciones Rubiños, n.d. [1939 or 1940].

Català, Neus. *De la resistencia y la deportación. 50 testimonios de mujeres españolas* [Adgena, 1984]. Barcelona: Península, 2000.

"Catolicismo y Patria. Carta Pastoral sobre el valor de patria y del catolicismo, de S.E. El Cardenal Arzobispo de Toledo." *Razón y Fe*, no. 500–1 (September–October 1939), 141–68.

Cayrol, Jean. *Lazare parmi nous.* Paris: Éditions du Seuil, 1950.

– "Les rêves concentrationnaires." *Les Temps Modernes,* no. 36 (September 1948), 520–35.

Centro de Información Administrativa de la Presidencia del Gobierno. "España y los sefardíes. Nota sobre concesión de nacionalidad española a los judíos sefarditas." In *Actas del I Simposio de Estudios Sefardíes,* 581–611. Madrid: Instituto Arias Montano-CSIC, 1970.

Cercas, Javier. "Prólogo." In *El fotógrafo del horror. La historia de Francisco Boix y las fotos robadas a los SS de Mauthausen,* edited by Benito Bermejo, 3–8. Barcelona: RBA Libros, 2002.

Certeau, Michel de. *The Practice of Everyday Life.* Translated by Steven Rendall. Berkeley: U of California P, 1984.

Cesarani, David, and Eric J. Sundquist, eds. *After the Holocaust: Challenging the Myth of Silence.* New York: Routledge, 2011.

Chaouat, Bruno. "Jorge Semprún's Remembrance of Jewish Fate." *Yale French Studies* 129 (28 June 2016): 23–40.

Chernov, M. *Krestovy pokhod na Rossiyu* [Crusade against Russia]. Moscow: Iauza, 2005.

Choumoff, Pierre-Serge. *Les assassinats nationaux-socialistes par gaz en territoire Autrichien 1940–1945.* Vienna: Mauthausen-Studien, 2000.

– *Les chambers à gaz de Mauthausen.* Paris: ADM, 1972.

"El cinema yanqui y los países totalitarios." *Misión,* no. 60 (November 1939): 11.

Civilotti, Diego. "Franquismo y heteromías en la música española." *Combate,* 11 February 2015. Web.

"Climen [sic] contable en Mauthausen. Joan Pagés, 50 meses preso en Mauthausen." *Por Favor*, 11 November 1978.

Climent i Sarrión, Casimir. "Ya es hora ..." *Hispania* 54 (II época) (April–May 1976): 11.

Cohen, Claudine Naar. "Españoles sin patria." *Revue d'histoire de la Shoah, Le Monde Juif* 169 (May–August 2000): 216.

Cohen, Stanley. *States of Denial: Knowing about Atrocities and Suffering.* Cambridge: Polity, 2001.

Collado Seidel, Carlos. *España, refugio nazi.* Madrid: Planeta, 2005.

– "España y los agentes alemanes, 1944–1947. Intransigencia y pragmatismo político." *Espacio, Tiempo y Forma*, serie V: *Historia Contemporánea*, no. 5 (1992): 431–82.

Colombo, Pamela. "La memoria en el espacio. Cartografías del gueto en Varsovia." *Cuadernos de filosofía latinoamericana* 33, no. 107 (2012): 127–47.

Colomé, Gabriel, and Jeroni Suerda. *Deporte y relaciones internacionales (1919–1939). La Olimpiada popular de 1936.* Barcelona: Centre d'Estudis Olímpics UAB, 1994. Web.

"Conducta de España en la guerra y en la paz. Carta Pastoral del Arzobispo Primado." *Ecclesia*, no. 200 (12 May 1945): 5–6.

Connerton, Paul. *How Societies Remember.* Cambridge: Cambridge UP, 1989.

– "Seven Types of Forgetting." *Memory Studies* 1, no. 1 (2008): 59–71.

Constante, Mariano. "Historia de una vergüenza." *Andalán*, no. 174 (14 July 1978): 10, 16.

– *Les années rouges. De Guernica à Mauthausen.* Paris: Mercure de France, 1971.

– *Los años rojos. Españoles en los campos nazis.* Barcelona: Martínez Roca, 1974.

– *Tras Mauthausen.* Barcelona: Círculo de lectores, 2007.

– *Yo fui ordenanza de los SS.* Barcelona: Martínez Roca, 1976.

Cook, Matthew, and Micheline Van Riemsdijk. "Agents of Memorialization: Gunter Demnig's Stolpersteine and the Individual (Re-)Creation of a Holocaust Landscape in Berlin." *Journal of Historical Geography* 43 (2014): 138–47.

Corredoira, Blanco. *Añoranzas de guerra.* Madrid: La esfera de los libros, 2011.

Crémieux-Brilhac, Jean-Louis. "L'engagement militaire des Italiens et des Espagnols dans les armées françaises de 1939 à 1945." In *Exils et migration. Italiens et Espagnols en France, 1938 à 1946*, edited by Pierre Milza and Denis Peschanski, 579–92. Paris: L'Harmattan, 1994.

– *La France Libre. De l'appel du 18 Juin à la liberation*, I. Paris: Éditions Gallimard, 1996.

Crenzel, Emilio. *La historia política del Nunca Más. La memoria de las desapariciones en Argentina.* Buenos Aires: Siglo XXI Editores, 2008.

– *Memory of the Argentina Disappearances: The Political History of Nunca Más.* New York: Routledge, 2012.

"Los cristianos observarán las leyes de la Caridad con los judíos convertidos. Pastoral colectiva del episcopado eslovaco." *Ecclesia*, no. 104 (10 July 1943): 12.

"Crónica del Vaticano. ¿Porqué se convirtió el gran Rabino de Roma?" *Ecclesia*, no. 192 (17 March 1945): 18–19.

Cruz, Rafael. "¡Luzbel vuelve al mundo! Las imágenes de la Rusia soviética y la acción colectiva en España." In *Cultura y movilización en la España contemporánea*, edited by Rafael Cruz and Manuel Pérez Ledesma, 273–303. Madrid: Alianza, 1997.

"Cuatro millones de ejemplares del 'Diario de Ana Frank.'" *Blanco y Negro*, 7 December 1963.

Cullá i Clará, Joan B. "Crónica de un reencuentro. Los judíos en la Cataluña contemporánea." In *La Cataluña Judía*, 216–31. Barcelona: Àmbit Serveis Editorials and Museu d'Història de Catalunya, 2002.

Davis, Madeleine. "Is Spain Recovering Its Memory? Breaking the 'Pacto del Olvido.'" *Human Rights Quarterly* 27, no. 3 (2005): 858–80.

Delbo, Charlotte. *Auschwitz et après, II, Une connaissance inutile*. Paris: Éditions de Minuit, 1970.

Deleuze, Gilles, and Félix Guattari. *A Thousand Plateaus: Capitalism and Schizophrenia*. Translated by Brian Massumi. Minneapolis: U of Minnesota P, 1987.

Delgado López-Escalonilla, Lorenzo. *Imperio de papel. Acción cultural y política exterior durante el primer franquismo*. Madrid: CSIC, 1992.

Didi-Huberman, Georges. "Ouvrir les camps, fermer les yeux." *Annales. Histoire, Sciences Sociales* 61, no. 5 (2006): 1011–49.

Diez Puertas, Emeterio. *El montaje del franquismo. La política cinematográfica de las fuerzas sublevadas*. Barcelona: Laertes, 2002.

Diffie, Bailey W. "The Ideology of Hispanidad." *Hispanic American Historical Review* 23, no. 3 (1943): 457–82.

Dios Amill, José de. *La verdad sobre Mauthausen*. Barcelona: Sírius, 1995.

Dobrov, A. *305-ya strelkovayadivizia 1-go formirovania v boyakh pod Novgorodom: 1941–1942* [305th Infantry Division of the First Formation in the Battles near the Town of Novgorod, 1941–2]. Edited by V.V. Demidov. Veliky Novgorod: n.pub., 2011.

Doménech, Ricardo. *"De algún tiempo a esta parte:* El comienzo." *Ínsula* 678 (June 2003): 9–11.

Domínguez Arribas, Javier. *El enemigo judeo-masónico en la propaganda franquista (1936–1945)*. Madrid: Marcial Pons, 2009.

– *L'ennemi judéo-maçonnique dans la propaganda franquiste (1936–1945)*. Paris: Honoré Champion, 2016.

– "La propaganda anti-judeo-masónica durante el primer franquismo. El caso de Ediciones Toledo (1941–1943)." In *La masonería en Madrid y en España del siglo XVIII al XXI*, vol. 2, edited by José Antonio Ferrer Benimeli, 1165–94. Zaragoza: Gobierno de Aragón, 2004. Republished in *Hibris*, n. 65–6, September–December 2011, 17–41.

Dreyfus-Armand, Geneviève. *L'Exil des républicains espagnols en France. De la Guerre Civile à la mort de Franco*. Paris: Albin Michel, 1999.

– *El exilio de los republicanos españoles en Francia. De la Guerra Civil*. Barcelona: Editorial Crítica, 2000.

– "Les mots de la souffrance. Les camps français dans la mémoire des républicains espagnols." In *Jeu. Histoire et mémoires vivantes* 8 (December 2016): 47–61.

– "Les républicains espagnols pendant la Seconde Guerre mondiale." In *La Guerre d'Espagne. L'histoire, les lendemains, la mémoire. Actes du colloque "Passé et actualité de la guerre d'Espagne,"* edited by Roger Bourderon, 145–60. Paris: Tallandier, 2007.

Dreyfus-Armand, Geneviève, and Émile Temime. *Les camps sur la plage. Un exil espagnol*. Paris: Autrement, 1995.

Dreyfus-Armand, Geneviève, and Odette Martinez-Maler. *L'Espagne, passion française, 1936–1975. Guerres, exils et solidarités*. Paris: les Arènes, 2015.

Driessen, Henk. *On the Spanish Moroccan Frontier: A Study in Ritual Power and Ethnicity*. Oxford: St Martin's Press, 1992.

Dublon-Knebel, Irith. *German Foreign Office Documents on the Holocaust in Greece (1937–1944)*. Tel Aviv: Tel Aviv University, 2007.

Dudai, Rina. "Forgotten, Remembered, and Re-forgotten: The Role of Forgetting in Working through the Holocaust Trauma within Literary Texts." *Dapim Studies: Journal on the Holocaust* 23 (2009): 109–32. Haifa: U of Haifa P.

Dupláa, Christina. "Memoria colectiva y lieux de mémoire en la España de la transición." In *Disremembering the Dictatorship: The Politics of Memory in the Spanish Transition to Democracy*, edited by Joan Ramón Resina, 29–42. Atlanta: Rodopi, 2000.

Dwork, Deborah, and R.J. van Pelt. *Flight from the Reich: Refugee Jews, 1933–1946*. New York: W.W. Norton, 2009.

Eckmann, Monique, and Charles Heimberg. *Memoire et Pedagogie*. Geneva: Éditions IES, 2011.

"Editorial: Los judíos y la Iglesia," *Ecclesia*, no. 189 (24 February 1945): 4.

"Editorial guión. Mensaje a las juventudes hispánicas." *Razón y Fe*, no. 528 (January 1942): 5–10.

"Editorial, Nuestro deber ante la paz," *Ecclesia*, no. 197 (21 April 1945): 3.

"Editoriales. Precisiones necesarias." *Ecclesia*, no. 48 (13 June 1942): 3–4.

Egilior, Sabin. "El testimonio ante la cámara. Memoria de los fusilados y desaparecidos durante la Guerra Civil Española." *Papeles del CEIC. International Journal on Collective Identity Research*, no. 2 (2010).

Elpatievskiy, A.V. "Uchastnik 'Goluboi divizii' o Rossii" [Volunteer of the "Blue Division" about Russia]. *Vestnik arkhivista* [Archivist Bulletin], no. 6 (1995).

En los campos nazis. Supervivencia, testimonio y arte de los republicanos españoles. Organized by the Centro Documental de la Memoria Histórica. Salamanca: Ministerio de Cultura, 2010. Web.

Encarnación, Omar Guillermo. *Democracy without Justice in Spain: The Politics of Forgetting.* Philadelphia: U of Pennsylvania P, 2014.

Erbelding, Rebecca. *About Time: The History of the War Refugee Board.* PhD diss., George Mason U, 2015.

Eschebach, Insa, ed. *Homophobie und Devianz. Weibliche und männliche Homosexualität im Nationalsozialismus.* Berlin: Metropol, 2012.

Escudero, Rafael. *Diccionario de memoria histórica. Conceptos contra el olvido.* Madrid: Los Libros de la Catarata, 2011.

España, Rafael de. "Antisemitismo en el cine español." *Film-Historia* 1, no. 2 (1991): 89–102.

Estrada, Isabel. *El documental cinematográfico y televisivo contemporáneo. Memoria, sujeto y formación de la identidad democrática española.* Woodbridge: Tamesis Books, 2013.

– "The Recuperation of Memory in Regional and National Television Documentaries: The Epistemology of *Les fosses del silenci* (2003) and *Las fosas del olvido* (2004)." *Journal of Spanish Cultural Studies* 11, no. 2 (2010): 191–209.

Etayo, Jesús. "La organización Guardia de Hierro acaudillada por Corneliu Codreanu." *Misión,* no. 60 (November 1939): 13.

Eudes, Dominic. *Les kapetanios. La guerre civile grecque de 1943 à 1945.* Paris: Fayard, 1970.

"La expulsión de los judíos por los Reyes Católicos." *Ecclesia,* no. 84 (20 February 1943): 13–14.

Eychenne, Émilienne. *Pyrénées de la liberté. Les évasions par l'Espagne 1939–1945.* Toulouse: Éditions Privat, 2000.

Fancourt, Daisy. "Spain's Musical Politics during World War II." *Music and the Holocaust,* n.d. Web.

Fatal-Kna'ani, Tikva. "Grodno." In *Lost Jewish Worlds: The Communities of Grodno, Lida, Olkieniki, Vishay,* edited by Shmuel Spector and Bracha Freundlich, 15–190. Jerusalem: Yad Vashem, 1996.

Felman, Shoshana, and Dori Laub. *Testimony: Crisis of Witnessing in Literature, Psychoanalysis, and History.* Tel Aviv: Resling, 2008.

Fernández, José Ramón. *J'attendrai.* Valencia: Alupa Editorial, 2017.

Fernández Aguilar, Paloma, and Leigh A. Payne. *Revealing New Truths about Spain's Violent Past: Perpetrators' Confessions and Victim Exhumations.* New York: Palgrave Macmillan, 2016.

Fernández Almuzara, E. "El judío internacional." *Razón y Fe,* no. 496 (May 1939): 94–103.

Fernández Granados, Emilio. *Traición en el infierno.* Buenos Aires: Deauno Documenta, 2010 [Kindle edition, 2016].

Fernández López, José A. *Historia del campo de concentración de Miranda de Ebro (1937–1947)*. Miranda de Ebro: n.pub., 2003.

Ferrán, Ofelia, and Gina Herrmann. *A Critical Companion to Jorge Semprún: Buchenwald, Before and After*. New York: Palgrave Macmillan, 2014.

Ferrándiz, Francisco. "De las fosas comunes a los derechos humanos. El descubrimiento de las desapariciones forzadas en la España contemporánea." *Revista de Antropología Social*, no. 19 (2010): 161–89.

– "From Tear to Pixel: Political Correctness and Digital Emotions in the Exhumation of Civil War Mass Graves in Spain Today." In *Engaging the Emotions in Spanish Culture and History*, edited by Luisa Elena Delgado, Pura Fernández, and Jo Labanyi, 242–61. Nashville: Vanderbilt UP, 2015.

– *El pasado bajo tierra. Exhumaciones contemporáneas de la Guerra Civil*. Barcelona: Anthropos, 2014.

– "The Return of Civil War Ghosts: The Ethnography of Exhumations in Contemporary Spain." *Anthropology Today* 22 no. 3 (2006): 7–12.

Ferrari Billoch, Francisco. *Andanzas del Bulo. Apuntes para su historia*. Madrid: Ediciones Toledo, 1942.

– *La masonería al desnudo. Las logias desenmascaradas* [1936]. Madrid: Ediciones Españolas, 1939.

Ferrer Benimeli, José A. *La masonería*. Torrejón de Ardoz: Alianza, 2001.

– ed. *La masonería en la España del siglo XX*. Toledo: Universidad de Castilla–La Mancha / Cortes de Castilla–La Mancha, 1996.

Fialdini Zambrano, Rossana. "*El triángulo azul*. El teatro como recurso de sobrevivencia y espacio de memoria." *Revista canadiense de estudios hispánicos* 40, no. 1 (Fall 2015): 109–31.

Figueras i Vallès, Miquel. *Las raíces judías de Franco*. Barcelona: Agil Offset, 1993.

Fine, Ruth. "El entrecruzamiento de lo hebreo y lo converso en la obra de Cervantes. Un encuentro singular." In *Cervantes y las religions. Actas del Coloquio internacional de la Asociación de cervantistas*, edited by Santiago López Navia and Ruth Fine, 435–51. Madrid: Iberoamericana Vervuert, 2008.

Fittko, Lisa. *Mi travesía de los Pirineos*. Barcelona: El Aleph, 1988.

Flesler, Daniela, Tabea Alexa Linhard, and Adrián Pérez Melgosa. "Introduction: Revisiting Jewish Spain in the Modern Era." *Journal of Spanish Cultural Studies* 12, no. 1 (2001): 1–11.

Flesler, Daniela, Tabea Alexa Linhard, and Adrián Pérez Melgosa, eds. *Revisiting Jewish Spain in the Modern Era*. London and New York: Routledge, 2015.

Floeck, Wilfried. "Del drama histórico al teatro de la memoria. Lucha contra el olvido y búsqueda de identidad en el teatro español reciente." In *Tendencias escénicas al inicio del siglo XXI*, edited by José Romera Castillo, 185–210. Madrid: Visor, 2006.

– "Die Shoah im Zeitalter der Globalisierung. Juan Mayorga und das spanische Erinnerungstheater." *Forum Modernes Theater* 26, no. 1 (2011): 53–72.

Fondation pour la mémoire de la déportation (France). *Le Livre-Mémorial des déportés de France arrêtés par mesure de répression et dans certains cas par mesure de persécution: 1940–1945.* Paris: Ed. Tirésias, 2004.

Formentín, Justo, and María José Villegas. "Aportaciones de algunos pensionados y científicos de la Junta para la Ampliación de Estudios." In *La Junta para ampliación de estudios e investigaciones científicas 80 años después. Simposio internacional Madrid, 15–17 de diciembre de 1987*, vol. 2, edited by José Manuel Sánchez Ron, 47–80. Madrid: Consejo Superior de Investigaciones Científicas, 1988.

Fox, Soledad. *Ida y vuelta. La vida de Jorge Semprún.* Barcelona: Debate, 2016.

"Francesc Boix. Més enllà de Mauthausen." Produced by the Museu d'Història de Catalunya, commissioned by Rosa Toran, June 2015.

Francisco Rodó, Alicia. "El tiempo de los vencidos en *Himmelweg* de Juan Mayorga. El teatro histórico como teatro político." *Anagnórisis. Revista de investigación teatral,* no. 16 (December 2017): 220–44.

Franco Bahamonde, Francisco. "Decreto-ley de 29 de Diciembre de 1948 por el que se reconoce la condición de súbditos españoles en el extranjero a determinados sefadíes, antiguos protegidos de España." *Boletín Oficial del Estado* 9 (9 January 1949).

– *Papeles de la guerra de Marruecos. Diario de una bandera. La hora de Xauen. Diario de Alhucemas.* Madrid: Fundación Nacional Francisco Franco, 1986.

Friedman, Michal. "Reconquering 'Sepharad:' Hispanism and Proto-Fascism in Giménez-Caballero's Sepharadist Crusade." *Journal of Spanish Cultural Studies* 12, no. 1 (March 2011): 35–60.

Friedman, P. "Hashmadat Yehudei Vitebsk." In *Vitebsk*, edited by Baruch Karuh, 444–52. Tel Aviv: Irgun 'ole Viṭebsḳ yeha-sevivah be-Yiśra'el, 1957.

Fusi, Juan Pablo, and Jordi Palafox. *España: 1808–1996. El desafío de la modernidad.* Madrid: Espasa Calpe, 1997.

Gaida, Peter. *Camps de travail sous Vichy. Les "Groupes de travailleurs étrangers" (GTE) en France et en Afrique du Nord, 1940–1944.* PhD diss., University of Bremen, 2014.

Garbe, Detlef. "Ein schwieriges Erbe. Hamburg und das ehemalige Konzentrationslager Neuengamme." In *Das Gedächtnis der Stadt. Hamburg im Umgang mit seiner nationalsozialistischen Vergangenhei,* edited by Peter Reichel, 113–34. Hamburg: Dölling, 1997.

Garcia, Betsabé. *Con otros ojos. La biografía de Montserrat Roig.* Barcelona: Roca Editorial, 2016.

García Figueras, Tomás. *Marruecos. La acción de España en el Norte de África.* Barcelona: Ediciones FE, 1939.

García Jambrina, Luis. "La recuperación de la memoria histórica en tres novelas españolas." *Iberoamericana* 4 no. 15 (2004): 143–56.

García Nieto, José. *Memorias y compromisos*. Madrid: Editora Nacional, 1966.

García Nieto, María Carmen, and Javier María Donézar. *Bases documentales de la España contemporánea. La Guerra de España, 1936–1939*. Madrid: Guadiana, 1974.

– *Bases documentales de la España contemporánea. La España de Franco: 1939–1973*. Madrid: Guadiana, 1975.

García-Pascual, Raquel. "Francoist Repression and Moral Reparation in the Theatre of Laila Ripoll." *UNED. Revista Signa* 27 (2018): 439–68.

García Pérez, Rafael. *Franquismo y Tercer Reich. Las relaciones económicas hispano-alemanas durante la Segunda Guerra Mundial*. Madrid: Centro de Estudios Constitucionales, 1994.

García Seror, Antonio. *Los Seror en España. La saga de los Seror*. Guadalajara: Aache Ediciones, 2009.

Gaspar Celaya, Diego. *La guerra continúa. Voluntarios españoles al servicio de la Francia libre (1940–1945)*. Madrid: Marcial Pons Historia, 2015.

Gatti, Gabriel. "De un continente al otro. El desaparecido transnacional, la cultura humanitaria y las víctimas totales en tiempos de guerra global." *Política y Sociedad* 48 no. 3 (2011): 519–36.

Gavrilov, B.I. *Dolina smerti. Tragedia i podvig 2-i Udarnoy armii* [Death Valley: The Tragedy and Heroism of the 2nd Shock Army]. Moscow: Institute of Russian History of RAS, 2006.

Gellately, Robert. "The Gestapo and German Society: Political Denunciation in the Gestapo Case Files." *The Journal of Modern History* 60, no. 4 (1988): 654–94.

General Assembly of the United Nations. "Resolution 39/I. Relations of Members of the United Nations with Spain." Fifty-Ninth Plenary Meeting of the General Assembly of the United Nations, 12 December 1946.

Gigliotti, Simone. *The Train Journey: Transit, Captivity, and Witnessing in the Holocaust*. New York: Berghahn Books, 2009.

Gildea, Robert. *Fighters in the Shadows: A New History of the French Resistance*. London: Faber & Faber, 2015.

Giménez Caballero, Ernesto. *¡Despierta Inglaterra! Mensaje a Lord Holland*. Madrid: Ediciones Toledo, 1943.

– "La espiritualidad española y Alemania." *Ensayos y Estudios*, Year III, September–December, no. 5–6 (1941): 290–4.

– *Genio de España. Exaltaciones a una resurrección nacional y del mundo*. Madrid: Ediciones de "La Gaceta Literaria," 1932.

– *Memorias de un dictador*. Barcelona: Planeta, 1981.

Gimeno Font, Edmon. *Buchenwald, Dora, Bergen-Belsen, vivències de un deportat*. Barcelona: Amical de Mauthausen, 2007.

Gironell, Martí. *El puente de los judíos*. Barcelona: Random House Mondadori, 2008.

Glazer, Peter. *Radical Nostalgia*. Rochester: U of Rochester P, 2010.

Gluhovic, Milija. *Performing European Memories: Trauma, Ethics, Politics*. Basingstoke and New York: Palgrave Macmillan, 2013.

Goldhagen, Daniel. *Hitler's Willing Executioners: Ordinary Germans and the Holocaust*. New York: A.A. Knopf, 1996.

Goldschläger, Alain, and Jacques Ch. Lemaire. *Le complot judéo-maçonnique*. Brussels: Éditions Labor / Espace de Libertés, 2005.

Gollomb, Joseph. *Armies of Spies*. London: Macmillan, 1939.

Gómez, Francisco Moreno. *El genocidio franquista en Córdoba*. Barcelona: Editorial Crítica, 2008.

Gómez Bravo, Gutmaro. *El exilio interior. Cárcel y represión en la España franquista (1939–1950)*. Madrid: Taurus, 2009.

Gómez López-Quiñones, Antonio, and Susanne Zepp, eds. *The Holocaust in Spanish Memory: Historical Perceptions and Cultural Discourse*. Leipzig: Leipziger UP, 2010.

Gómez Tello, José Luis. *Canción de invierno en el este. Crónicas de la División Azul*. Madrid: Atalaya, 1945.

Goñi, Uki. *The Real Odessa: How Perón Brought the Nazi War Criminals to Argentina*. London: Granta, 2002.

González, José Alejandro, dir. *La encrucijada de Sanz Briz*. I'm FILM, 2015. Film.

González-Arnao Conde-Luque, Mariano. "Los héroes de Budapest." *La Aventura de la Historia*, no. 5 (March 1999): 21–8.

González Calleja, Eduardo, and Fredes Limón Nevado. *La Hispanidad como instrumento de combate. Raza e imperio en la prensa franquista durante la Guerra Civil española*. Madrid: Consejo Superior de Investigaciones Científicas, 1988.

González García, Isidro. *Los judíos y la Guerra Civil española*. Madrid: Hebraica, 2009.

– *Los judíos y la Segunda República (1931–1939)*. Madrid: Alianza, 2004.

– *El retorno de los judíos*. Madrid: Nerea, 1991.

Goode, Joshua. *Impurity of Blood: The Idea of Race in Spain, 1870–1930*. Baton Rouge: Louisiana State UP, 2009.

Goslar Pick, Lies. "Yo conocí a Anna Frank." *¡Hola!* 752 (1959): 16–17.

Gottlieb, Moshe. "The American Controversy over the Olympic Games." *American Jewish Historical Quarterly* 61, no. 3 (March 1972): 184–5.

Gracia Alonso, Francisco. *Arqueologia i política. La gestió de Martín Almagro Basch al capdavant del Museu Arqueològic Provincial de Barcelona, 1939–1962*. Barcelona: Publicacions i de la Edicions Universitat de Barcelona, 2012.

Gracia García, Jordi, and Ruiz Carnicer, Miguel Ángel. *La España de Franco (1939–1975). Cultura y vida cotidiana*. Madrid: Síntesis, 2001.

Grand, Evelyne. *Le deuxième groupe. Les juifs espagnols internés au camp de Bergen Belsen 14 Avril 1944–9 Avril 1945*. Jerusalem: EMN, 1994.

Grandes, Almudena. *El corazón helado*. Barcelona: Tusquets, 2007.

Grupo Eleuterio Quintanilla. *Pensad que esto ha sucedido*. Asturias: Tercera Prensa S.A., 2007.

Guttstadt, Corry, Thomas Lutz, Bernd Rother, and Yessica San Román, eds. *Bystanders, Rescuers, or Perpetrators? The Neutral Countries and the Shoah*. Berlin: Metropol Verlag & IHRA, 2016.

Habib, Isaac. *Poesie. Los Muestros*, no. 78 (2008).

Halstead, Carolyn, and Charles Halstead. "Aborted Imperialism: Spain's Occupation of Tangier, 1940–1945." *Iberian Studies* 7, no. 2 (Autumn 1978): 53–71.

Handelman, Susan A. *Fragments of Redemption: Jewish Thought and Literary Theory in Benjamin, Scholem, and Levinas*. Bloomington: Indiana UP, 1991.

Harrison, Joseph, and Alan Hoyle, eds. *Spain's 1898 Crisis: Regenerationism, Modernism, and Post-Colonialism*. Manchester: Manchester UP, 2000.

Hartman, Geoffrey. *Scars of the Spirit: The Struggle against Inauthenticity*. New York: Palgrave Macmillan, 2002.

Hassán, Iacob M., Teresa Rubiato, and Elena Romero, eds. *Actas del Primer Simposio de Estudios Sefardíes*. Madrid: Instituto Arias Montano, 1970.

Hausswald, Günter. "Deutsch-Spanisches Musik Fest in Bad Elster 10–16. Juli." *Zeitschrift für Musik* 8 (1941): 539.

Hazan, Katy, and Serge Klarsfeld. *Le sauvetage des enfants juifs pendant l'Occupation dans les maisons de l'OSE 1938–1945*. Paris: Ed. Somogy, 2008.

Hellbeck, Jochen. "AHR Roundtable: Galaxy of Black Stars: The Power of Soviet Biography." *American Historical Review* (June 2009): 615–24.

– *Revolution on My Mind*. Cambridge, MA: Harvard UP, 2006.

– "Working, Struggling, Becoming: Stalin-Era Autobiographical Texts." *The Russian Review* 60 (July 2001): 340–59.

Helm, Sarah. *Ravensbrück: Life and Death in Hitler's Concentration Camp for Women*. New York: Doubleday, 2014.

Hera Martínez, Jesús de la. *La política cultural de Alemania en España en el período de entreguerras*. Madrid: CSIC, 2002.

Heras, Enrique Heras. "La cuestión aria." *Razón y Fe*, nos. 510–11 (July–August 1940): 288–322.

Herf, Jeffrey. *Nazi Propaganda for the Arab World*. New Haven: Yale UP, 2009.

Herman, Judith. *Trauma and Recovery*. Tel Aviv: Am Oved, 2014.

Hermet, Guy. *L'Espagne au XX siecle* [1986]. Paris: Presses Universitaires de France, 1992.

Hernández de Miguel, Carlos. @*deportado4443*, 2015. Twitter account.

– *Los últimos españoles de Mauthausen*. Barcelona: Ediciones B, 2015.

Hernández de Miguel, Carlos, and Ioannes Ensis. *Deportado 4443. Sus tuits ilustrados*. Barcelona: Ediciones B, 2017.

Hernández Navarro, José Antonio. *Ida y vuelta*. Madrid: Actas, 2004.

Herrera Oria, Enrique. *Historia de la educación española después del Renacimiento.* Madrid: Ediciones Veritas, 1941.

Herrmann, Gina. "Camera Caedens, Camera Vindex: Francesc Boix and Photography at Mauthausen." In *The Holocaust in Spanish Memory: Historical Perceptions and Cultural Discourse,* ed. Antonio Gómez López-Quiñones and Susanne Zepp, 115–38. Leipziger Beiträge zur jüdischen Geschichte und Kultur [Leipzig Studies on Jewish History and Culture], vol. 7. Berlin: Leipziger Universitätsverlag GmbH, 2010.

Herzberger, David K. "Representing the Holocaust: Story and Experience in Antonio Muñoz Molina's *Sefarad.*" *Romance Quarterly* 51 no. 2 (2004): 85–96.

Higginbotham, Virginia. *Spanish Film under Franco.* Austin: U of Texas P, 1988.

Hilberg, Raul. *The Destruction of the European Jews.* Chicago: Quadrangle Books, 1961.

Hirsch, Marianne. *Generation of Postmemory: Writing and Visual Culture after the Holocaust.* New York: Columbia UP, 2012.

Hoare, Samuel. *Ambassador on Special Mission.* London: Collins, 1946.

Holguín, Sandie. "How Did the Spanish Civil War End ... Not So Well." *American Historical Review* 120, no. 5 (December 2015): 1767–83.

Hormigón, Juan Antonio. "Sachsenhausen: un testimonio del exterminio nazi." *Triunfo,* no. 658 (10 May 1975): 48–52.

Hoyo, Teresa del, ed. *Memorial de las españolas deportadas a Ravensbrück.* Barcelona: Amics de Ravensbrück, 2012.

Hüffer, Hermann J. *Deutsch-Spanische Kulturbeziehungen in alter und neuer Zeit.* Munich: Universitäts-Buchdruckerei, 1942.

– *La idea imperial española.* Madrid: Conferencias dadas en el Centro de Intercambio Intelectual Germano-Español XXXV, 1933.

– "Las relaciones hispanogermanas durante mil doscientos años (un resumen)." *Revista de Estudios Políticos,* no. 56 (1951): 43–75.

Humphries Mardirosian, Gail. "Giving Voice to the Silenced through Theater." In *The Power of Witnessing: Reflections, Reverberations, and Traces of the Holocaust,* edited by Nancy R. Goodman and Marilyn B. Meyers, 255–66. New York: Taylor & Francis, 2012.

Huyssen, Andreas. *Present Pasts: Urban Palimpsests and the Politics of Memory.* Stanford: Stanford UP, 2003.

– *Twilight Memories: Marking Time in a Culture of Amnesia.* New York: Routledge, 1995.

Iglesia, Álex de la, dir. *El crimen ferpecto.* Madrid: Warner Sogecines, S.A., 2004. Film.

Infield, Glenn B. *Skorzeny: Hitler's Commando.* New York: St Martin's Press, 1981.

Iordache, Luiza. *En el Gulag. Españoles republicanos en los campos de concentración de Stalin.* Barcelona: RBA Libros, 2014.

Irisarri, Ángeles de, and Toti Martínez de Lezea. *Perlas para un collar. Judías, moras, y cristianas en la España medieval.* Madrid: Santillana, 2009.

Irujo, José María. *La lista negra. Los espías nazis protegidos por Franco y la Iglesia.* Madrid: Aguilar, 2003.

Isenberg, Sheila. *A Hero of Our Own: The Story of Varian Fry.* New York: Blackinprit.com Editions, 2005.

Israel Garzón, Jacobo. "El Archivo Judaico del franquismo." *Raíces. Revista judía de cultura,* no. 33 (Winter 1997–8): 57–60.

– "El exilio republicano y el final de la vida intelectual y comunitaria judía en España." In *Judaísmo y exilio republicano de 1939,* edited by José Ramón López García and Mario Martín Gijón, 15–51. Madrid: Hebraica, 2014.

Israel Garzón, Jacobo, and Alejandro Baer, eds. *España y el Holocausto (1939–1945). Historia y testimonios.* Madrid: Hebraica, 2007.

Israel Garzón, Jacobo, and Uriel Macías Kapón. *La comunidad judía de Madrid. Textos e imágenes para una historia 1917–2001.* Madrid: Comunidad Judía de Madrid, 2001.

Izaga, Luis. "El laicismo político." *Razón y Fe,* no. 507 (April 1940): 345–64.

Janué Miret, Marició. "La atracción del falangismo a la causa nacionalsocialista por parte de la Sociedad Germano-Española de Berlín durante la Guerra Civil Española." In *Falange. Las culturas políticas del fascismo en la España de Franco (1936–1975). Comunicaciones,* edited by Miguel Á. Ruiz-Carnicer, 240–61. Zaragoza: Institución "Fernando el Católico" (C.S.I.C) / Excma. Diputación de Zaragoza, 2013. CD-ROM.

– "Autorepresentación nacional y conflicto socio-político. Alemania en la Exposición Internacional de Barcelona de 1929." *Spagna Contemporanea* 31 (2007): 113–36.

– "La cultura como instrumento de la influencia alemana en España. La Sociedad Germano-Española de Berlín (1930–1945)." *Ayer* 69 (2008): 21–45.

– "Imperialismus durch auswärtige Kulturpolitik. Die Deutsch-Spanische Gesellschaft als 'zwischenstaatlicher Verband' unter dem Nationalsozialismus." *German Studies Review* 31, no. 1 (2008): 109–32.

– "Relaciones culturales en el 'Nuevo orden.'" La Alemania nazi y la España de Franco." *Hispania* vol. 75, no. 251 (2015): 805–32.

– "The Role of Culture in German–Spanish Relations during Nationalsocialism." In *Nazi Germany and Southern Europe, 1933–45: Science, Culture, and Politics,* edited by Clara Fernando and Cláudia Ninhos, 84–104. London: Palgrave Macmillan, 2015.

Jedwab, Jack. "Measuring Holocaust Knowledge and Its Relationship to Attitudes towards Diversity in Spain, Canada, Germany, and the United States." In *As the Witnesses Fall Silent: 21st Century Holocaust Education in Curriculum, Policy, and Practice,* edited by Zehavit Gross and Doyle Stevick, 321–34. Cham: Springer, 2015.

Jefatura del Estado. *Fuero de los Españoles*, 18 June 1945, art. 33.

Jennings, Eric T. "'The Best Avenue of Escape': The French Caribbean Route as Expulsion, Rescue, Trial, and Encounter." *French Politics, Culture, and Society* 30, no. 2 (Summer 2012): 33–52.

Jensen, Geoffrey. "Toward the 'Moral Conquest' of Morocco: Hispano-Arabic Education in Early Twentieth-Century North Africa." *European History Quarterly* 3, no. 2 (2001): 205–29.

Jímenez, Victor José, and Malo de Molina. *De España a Rusia, 5,000 kms. Con la División Azul.* Madrid: Editorial Mediterráneo, 1943.

Joan i Tous, Pere, and Heike Nottebaum. *El olivo y la espada. Estudios sobre el antisemitismo en España (siglos XVI–XX).* Tübingen: Max Niemeyer Verlag, 2003.

Joaquín Estrada, José. *Cuando Inglaterra quedó sola ...* Madrid: Ediciones Rubiños, 1940.

"José Luis Gómez Tello, periodista Divisionario." *Fundación Nacional Francisco Franco.* Web.

Jouin, Ernest, ed. *Los peligros judío-masónicos. Los Protocolos de los Sabios de Sión.* Madrid: Ediciones Fax, 1932.

"Los judíos y la Iglesia," *Ecclesia*, no. 189, 24 February 1945, 4.

Judt, Tony. *Postwar: A History of Europe since 1945.* New York: Penguin Books, 2005.

Judt, Tony, Jesús Cuellar, and Victoria E. Gordo del Rey. *Posguerra. Una historia de Europa desde 1945.* Madrid: Taurus, 2006.

Juliá, Santos. *Camarada Javier Pradera.* Barcelona: Galaxia Gutenberg, 2014.

Junco, Álvarez. *Mater dolorosa. La idea de España en el siglo XIX.* Madrid: Santillana, 2001.

Kaienburg, Hermann. "Funktionswandel des KZ-Kosmos? Das Konzentrationslager Neuengamme 1938–1945." In *Die nationalsozialistischen Konzentrationslager: Entwicklung und Struktur,* edited by Ulrich Herbert et al., 259–84. Göttingen: Wallstein, 1998.

Kallis, Aristotle. *Nazi Propaganda and the Second World War.* New York: Palgrave Macmillan, 2005.

Kaplan, Chaim A. *Scroll of Agony: The Warsaw Diary of Chaim A. Kaplan.* Translated and edited by Abraham I. Katsh. New York: Macmillan, 1965.

Kaplan, Joseph. "Jews and Judaism in the Political and Social Thought of Spain in the Sixteenth and Seventeenth Century." In *Antisemitism through the Ages,* edited by Shmuel Almog, 153–60. Oxford: Pergamon Press, 1988.

Kaplan, Marion A. *Dominican Haven: The Jewish Refugee Settlement in Sosúa, 1940–1945.* New York: Museum of Jewish Heritage, 2008.

Karakaya, Yagmur, and Alejandro Baer. "Such Hatred Has Never Flourished on Our Soil. Holocaust Memory Politics in Turkey and Spain." *Sociological Forum* 34, no. 3 (September 2019).

Karay, Felicja. *Hasag-Leipzig Slave Labour Camp for Women: The Struggle for Survival Told by the Women and Their Poetry*. Portland: Vallentine Mitchell, 2002.

– "Women in Forced Labor Camps." In *Women in the Holocaust*, edited by Dalia Ofer and Lenore J. Weitzman, 289–305. New Haven: Yale UP, 1998.

Kaufman, Max, and Menachem Barkahan. *Khurbn Letland: Unichtozhenie evreev v Latvii* [Khurbn Letland: Extermination of Jews in Latvia]. Riga: Shamir, 2012.

Kerényi, Karl. *En el laberinto*. Madrid: Siruela, 2006.

Kirschenbaum, Lisa. "Exile, Gender, and Communist Self-Fashioning: Dolores Ibárruri (La Pasionaria) in the Soviet Union." *Slavic Review* 71, no. 3 (Fall 2012): 566–89.

Kogon, Eugen. *The Theory and Practice of Hell: The German Concentration Camps and the System behind Them*. London: Macmillan, 2006.

Kohnstam, Pieter. *A Chance to Live: A Family's Journey to Freedom*. Sarasota: Bardolf & Co, 2006.

Kovalev, Boris. *Dobrovol'cí na chuzhoj voyne. Ocherki istorii Goluboj divizii* [Volunteers in the Foreign War: Essays on the History of the Blue Division]. Veliki Novgorod: Novgorod State UP, 2014.

L'Espagne et les Juifs. Madrid: Bureau d'Information Diplomatique, 1949. Pamphlet.

La Capra, Dominick. *Writing History, Writing Trauma*. Baltimore: Johns Hopkins UP, 2014.

La garra del capitalismo judío. Sus procedimientos y efectos en el momento actual. Madrid: Ediciones Toledo, 1943.

"La literatura del III Reich." *Misión*, no. 59 (November 1939): 2.

La masonería en acción. Madrid: Ediciones Toledo, 1941.

La masonería femenina. Madrid: Ediciones Toledo, 1942.

Labanyi, Jo. "History and Hauntology; or, What Does One Do with the Ghosts of the Past? Reflections on Spanish Film and Fiction of the Post-Franco Period." In *Disremembering the Dictatorship: The Politics of Memory in the Spanish Transition to Democracy*, edited by Joan Ramon Resina, 65–82. Amsterdam and Atlanta: Rodopi, 1994.

LaCapra, Dominick. *History and Memory after Auschwitz*. Ithaca: Cornell UP, 1998.

– *Representing the Holocaust: History, Theory, Trauma*. Ithaca: Cornell UP, 1994.

– *Writing History, Writing Trauma*. Tel Aviv: Resling, 2006.

Lacave, José Luis. "Los estudios hebraicos en España, desde Amador de los Ríos hasta nuestros días." In *Los judíos en la España contemporánea. Historia y visiones, 1898–1998*, edited by Uriel Macías, Yolanda Moreno Koch, and Ricardo Izquierdo Benito, 115–33. Cuenca: Universidad de Castilla–La Mancha, 2000.

Laharie, Claude. *Le camp de Gurs, 1939–1945, Un aspect meconnu de l'histoire du Bearn*. Biarritz: Infocompo, 1985.

Laín Entralgo, Pedro. "'Idearium español' de Angel Ganivet." *Ensayos y Estudios* 2, nos. 3–4 (May–July 1940): 67–121.

Laskier, Michael M. *The Alliance Israélite Universelle and the Jewish Communities of Morocco, 1862–1962*. Albany: SUNY P, 1983.

– *North African Jewry in the Twentieth Century: The Jews of Morocco, Tunisia, and Algeria*. NYU P, 1997.

Laub, Dori. "Bearing Witness or the Vicissitudes of Listening." In *Testimony: Crises of Witnessing in Literature, Psychoanalysis, and History*, edited by Shoshana Felman and Dori Laub, 57–66. New York: Routledge, 1992.

Lazo Díaz, Alfonso. *Una familia mal avenida. Falange, Iglesia y Ejército*. Madrid: Síntesis, 2008.

–*La Iglesia, la Falange y el fascismo (Un estudio sobre la prensa española de posguerra)* [1995]. Sevilla: Universidad de Sevilla, 1998.

Le Livre-Mémorial des déportés de France arrêtés par mesure de répression et dans certains cas par mesure de persécution: 1940–1945. Paris: Ed. Tirésias, 2004.

Leguineche, Manuel. *El precio del paraíso. De un campo de exterminio al Amazonas*. Madrid: Espasa Calpe, 1997.

Leitz, Christian. *Economic Relations between Nazi Germany and Franco's Spain, 1936–1945*. Oxford: Oxford UP, 1996.

– *Nazi Germany and Neutral Europe during the Second World War*. Manchester: Manchester UP, 2000.

– "Nazi Germany's Struggle for Spanish Wolfram during the Second World War." *European History Quarterly* 25 (1995): 71–92.

– "Spain and the Holocaust." *Holocaust Studies* 11, no. 3 (2005): 70–83.

– *Sympathy for the Devil. Neutral Europe and Nazi Germany in World War II*. New York: NYU P, 2001.

Lejeune, Philippe. *On Diary*. Honolulu: The U of Hawai'i P, 2005.

– *Le Pact Autobiographique*. Paris: Seuil, 1995.

Lengyel, Olga. *Souvenirs de l'au-delà*. Paris: Editions du Bateau Ivre, 1946.

Levi, Erik. *Music in the Third Reich*. London: Palgrave, 1994.

Levi, Primo. *The Drowned and the Saved*. [New York: Simon and Schuster, 1988] Translated by Raymond Rosenthal. New York: Vintage, 1989.

– *If This Is a Man*. Translated by Charles Woolf. New York: Abacus, 1991.

– *Se questo è un uomo*. Torino: F. DeSilva, 1947.

– *Si c'est un homme* [1947]. Translated by Martine Schruoffeneger. Paris: Julliard, 1993.

– *Trilogía de Auschwitz*. Translated by Pilar Gómez Bedate. Barcelona: El Aleph Editores, 2011.

Levin, Dov, ed., and Pinkas Hakehillot. *Encyclopedia of Jewish Communities from their Foundation until after the Holocaust*, vol. 8: *Lithuania*. Jerusalem: Yad Vashem, 1996.

Levy, Daniel. "Recursive Cosmopolitization: Argentina and the Global Human Rights Regime." *The British Journal of Sociology* 61, no. 3 (2010): 579–96.

Lévy, Sam, ed. *Les Cahiers Séphardis*. Paris: Cahiers Séphardis, 1947–8.

Lichtenstein, Joseph Jacob. "The Reaction of West European Jewry to the Reestablishment of a Jewish Community in Spain in the 19th Century." PhD diss., Yeshiva U, New York, 1962.

Liehr, R., G. Mainhold, and G. Vollmer, eds. *Ein Institut und sein General. Wilhelm Faupel und das Ibero-Amerikanische Institut in der Zeit der Nationalsozialismus*. Frankfur am Main: Vervuert, 2003.

Linhard, Tabea Alexa. *Jewish Spain: A Mediterranean Memory*. Stanford: Stanford UP, 2014.

Linz, Juan J. *The Party System of Spain*. New York: Free Press, 1966.

Lion Lewin, Juanita. "Madrid, años cuarenta." *Raíces. Revista judía de cultura*, no. 31 (Summer 1997): 34–5.

"Los Lipperheide y la industria petroquimica vasca." *CyberEuscadi*, 5 January 2009. Web.

Lisbona, José Antonio. *Más allá del deber. La respuesta humanitaria del Servicio Exterior frente al Holocausto*. Madrid: Ministerio de Asuntos Exteriores y de Cooperación, 2015.

– "Presiones internas y externas a favor de las relaciones Hispano-Israelíes durante la democracia (1976–1986)." In *España e Israel veinte años después*, edited by Raanan Rein, 123–36. Madrid: Dykinson, 2007.

– *Retorno a Sefarad. La política de España hacia sus judíos en el siglo XX*. Barcelona: Riopiedras Ediciones, 1993.

– "Se pudo hacer mucho más." *La Aventura de la Historia*, no. 5 (March 1999): 19.

"Lituania bajo la bandera roja." *Signo*, no. 77 (5 July 1941): 1.

Lleonart Ansélem, Alberto José. "El ingreso de España en la ONU. Obstáculos e impulsos." *Cuadernos de historia contemporánea*, no. 17 (1995): 101–19.

Llera, Luis de. "Prensa y censura en el Franquismo 1936–1966." *Hispania Sacra: Revista de Historia Eclesieástica*, 47, no. 95 (January–June 1995): 5–36.

Llorca, Germán. "Las raíces documentales del holocausto." In *La mirada comprometida. Llorenç Soler*, edited by Miquel Francés, 199–218. Madrid: Biblioteca Nueva, 2012.

Lloréns, Chufo. *La saga de los malditos*. Barcelona: Debolsillo, 2011.

Llorente, Mariano, and Laila Ripoll. *El triángulo azul*. Madrid: Centro Dramático Nacional, 2014.

Locksley, Christopher C. "Condor over Spain: The Civil War, Combat Experience, and the Development of Luftwaffe Airpower Doctrine." *Civil Wars* 2, no. 1 (1999): 69–99.

Longerich, Peter. *Propagandisten im Krieg. Die Presseabteilung des Auswärtigen Amtes unter Ribbentrop*. Munich: R. Oldenbourg, 1987.

López Criado, Fidel. "De Mauthausen a Denia. La desmemoria histórica en *Lo que esconde tu nombre*, de Sánchez." *Letras históricas* no. 10 (Spring–Summer 2014): 175–95.

López Luna, Antonio. *Memoria de la muerte*. Madrid: Ediciones Rialp, 1968.

Louis-Panné, Jean. *Jorge Semprún. Le fer rouge de la mémoire*. Paris: Gallimard, 2012.

Lovenheim, Barbara. *Survival in the Shadows: Seven Jews Hidden in Hitler's Berlin*. London: Random House, 2003.

Luca de Tena, Torcuato. *Embajador en el infierno. Memorias del Capitán Palacios*. Madrid: Kamerad, 1955.

Lustiger, Arno. *¡Shalom libertad! Judíos en la Guerra Civil Española*. Barcelona: Flor del Viento, 2001.

Maeztu, Ramiro de. *Defensa de la hispanidad*. Madrid: Cultura española, 1946.

Marcuse, Harold. "The Afterlife of the Camps." In *Concentration Camps in Nazi Germany: The New Histories*, edited by Jane Caplan and Nikolaus Wachsmann, 186–211. London: Routledge, 2010.

Margalit, Avishai. *The Ethics of Memory*. Cambridge, MA: Harvard UP, 2002.

– *The Ethics of Memory*. Cambridge, MA: Harvard UP, 2002.

Marino, Andy. *A Quiet American: The Secret War of Varian Fry*. New York: St Martin's Press, 1999.

Marquina, Antonio, and Gloria Inés Ospina. *España y los judíos en el siglo XX. La acción exterior*. Madrid: Espasa-Calpe, 1987.

Marquina Barrio, Antonio. "La España de Franco y los judíos." In *Los judíos en la España contemporánea. Historia y visiones, 1898–1998*, edited by Carlos Carrete Parrondo, Uriel Macías Kapón, Yolanda Moreno Koch, and Ricardo Izquierdo Benito, 191–200. Cuenca: Ediciones de la Universidad de Castilla–La Mancha, 2000.

– "La Iglesia española y los planes culturales alemanes para España." *Razón y Fe*, 975 (1979): 354–70.

Marsálek, Hans. *Die Geschichte des Konzentrationlagers Mauthausen. Dokumentation*. Vienna: Mauthausen Komitee Österreich, 2006.

Martí, Carme, and Ana Herrera. *Cenizas en el cielo: la vida de Neus Català*. Barcelona: Roca Editorial de Libros, 2012.

Martí, Carme, and Neus Català. *Un cel de plom*. Badalona: Amsterdam Llibres, 2012.

Martín Corrales, Eloy. "Represión contra cristianos, moros y judíos en la Guerra civil en el Protectorado español de Marruecos, Ceuta y Melilla." In *El Protectorado español de Marruecos. Gestión colonial e identidades*, edited by F. Rodríguez Mediano and H. de Felipe, 111–38. Madrid: CSIC, 2002.

Martín de la Guardia, Ricardo Manuel, José Vidal Pelaz López, and Pablo Pérez López. "Prensa y masonería en Castilla durante el primer franquismo (1939–1945)." In *Masonería y periodismo en la España contemporánea*, edited by José Antonio Ferrer Benimeli, 295–322. Zaragoza: Universidad de Zaragoza, 1993.

Martín de Pozuelo, Eduardo. *El Franquismo, cómplice del Holocausto*. Barcelona: La Vanguardia, 2012.

Martínez Esparza, José M. *Con la División Azul en Rusia*. Madrid: Ediciones Ejército, 1943.

Martorell i Gil, Encarnació, Salvador Domènech i Domènech, and Matuca Fernández de Villavicencio. *Con ojos de niña. Un diario de la Guerra Civil española*. Barcelona: Plaza & Janés, 2009.

Marzo, Jorge Luís, and Patricia Mayayo. "Del fascismo a la desideologización del arte (1939–1951)." In *Arte en España (1939–2015). Ideas, prácticas, políticas*, edited by Jorge Luís Marzo and Patricia Mayayo, 19–146. Madrid: Cátedra, 2015.

Massaguer, Lope, and María Ángeles García-Maroto. *Mauthausen, fin de trayecto. Un anarquista en los campos de la muerte*. Madrid: Fundación Anselmo Lorenzo, 1997.

Mayorga, Juan. *El cartógrafo. Varsovia, 1: 400.000*. Segovia: Ediciones La uÑa RoTa, 2017.

– *Himmelweg (Camino del cielo)*. Edited by Manuel Aznar Soler. Guadalajara: Ñaque, 2011.

– "JK." In *Maratón de monólogos 2006*, 71–4. Madrid: AAT, 2006.

– "Job (A partir del Libro de Job y de textos de Elie Wiesel, Zvi Kolitz y Etti Hillesum)." In *La autoridad del sufrimiento. Silencio de Dios y preguntas del hombre*, edited by Fernando Bárcena Orbe, 115–36. Barcelona: Anthropos, 2004.

– "La representación teatral del Holocausto." In *Elipses. Ensayos 1990–2016*, 165–72. Segovia: Ediciones La uÑa RoTa, 2016.

– *Way to Heaven*. Translated by David Johnston. London: Oberon Books, 2005.

– "Wstawac: Homenaje a Primo Levi." In *El perdón, virtud política. En torno a Primo Levi*, edited by Eduardo Madina et al., 35–56. Barcelona: Anthropos, 2008.

Mazower, Mark. *Inside Hitler's Greece: The Experience of Occupation*. New Haven: Yale UP, 1993.

– *Salonica, City of Ghosts. Christians, Muslims, and Jews 1430–1950*. New York: Alfred A. Knopf, 2005.

Megargee, Geoffrey P. *The United States Holocaust Memorial Museum Encyclopedia of Camps and Ghettos, 1933–1945*. Bloomington: Indiana UP, 2009.

Melenchón i Xamena, Joanna María. *Mauthausen, des de l'oblit*. Barcelona: Amicron, 2008.

Mèlich Sangrà, Joan-Carles. "El trabajo de la memoria o el testimonio como categoría didáctica." *Enseñanza de las ciencias sociales. Revista de investigación*, no. 5 (2006): 115–23.

Menny, Anne. "Un país neutral, un pasado neutral, una memoria neutral? El caso de España. Bystanders, Rescuers or Perpetrators? The Neutrals

and the Shoah – Facts, Myths and Countermyths." Madrid: Conference
Presentation, 24–6 November 2014.

"El mensaje de Nuestro Presidente Nacional, Manuel Aparici." *Signo*, no. 56
(8 December 1939): 1.

Messenger, David A. "Contemporary Memory Politics in Catalonia:
Europeanizing and Mobilizing the History of the Spanish Civil War." In
The Changing Place of Europe in Global Memory Cultures, edited by Christina
Kraenzle and Maria Mayr, 49–62. Palgrave Macmillan, 2017.

– *Hunting Nazis in Franco's Spain*. Baton Rouge: Louisiana State UP, 2014.

– "'Our Spanish Brothers' or 'As at Plombières': France and the Spanish
Opposition to Franco, 1945–1948." *French History* 20, no. 1 (2006): 52–74.

Messenger, David A., and Katrin Paehler, eds. *A Nazi Past: Recasting German
Identity in Postwar Europe*. Lexington: U of Kentucky P, 2015.

Miccoli, Giovanni. *I dilemmi e i silenzi di Pio XII. Vaticano, Seconda guerra
mondiale e Shoah*. Milano: Rizzoli, 2000.

Míguez Macho, Antonio. *The Genocidal Genealogy of Francoism: Violence,
Memory, and Impunity*. Eastbourne: Sussex Academic P, 2016.

Milton, Sybil. "Women and the Holocaust: The Case of German and German-
Jewish Women." In *When Biology Became Destiny: Women in Weimar and
Nazi Germany*, edited by Renate Bridenthal, Atina Grossmann, and Marion
Kaplan, 297–333. New York: Monthly Review Press, 1984.

Moga Romero, Vicente. *Las heridas de la historia. Testimonios de la Guerra Civil
española en Melilla*. Barcelona: Bellaterra, 2004.

Molho, Michael, and Joseph Nehama. *In Memoriam: Dedication to the Memory
of the Jewish Victims of Nazism in Greece*. Thessaloniki: Jewish Community of
Thessaloniki, 1974.

Molinos, Luis. *El infierno de los inocentes*. Spain: n.pub. [Kindle edition], 2014.

Montero, Carla. *El invierno en tu rostro*. Madrid: Plaza Janés, 2016.

Montseny, Federica. *Pasión y muerte de los españoles en Francia*. Toulouse:
Espoir, 1969.

Morales Ruiz, Juan José. *El discurso antimasónico en la Guerra Civil española
(1936–1939)*. Zaragoza: Gobierno de Aragón, 2001.

Morant i Ariño, Antonio. *"Una importante expresión de amistad hispano-alemana."
Les visites de Pilar Primo de Rivera l'Alemanya nacionalsocialista, 1938–1943.'*
Paper presented at the I Encuentro de Jóvenes Investigadores de la
Asociación de Historia Contemporánea, Zaragoza, 26–8 September 2007.

Morcillo Rosillo, Matilde. "La diplomacia española y las comunidades
sefardíes de Grecia durante el primer tercio del siglo XX." *Cuadernos
Judaicos*, no. 31 (2014): 116–41.

– "Spain and Sephardim of Thessaloniki, 1913–1945: Diplomatic Issues
Concerning the Citizenship of Sephardim after the Liberation of
Thessaloniki." In *Greece–Spain 1936*, edited by Dimitris Filippis, 183–94.
Athens: Vivliorama, 2007.

Moreda Rodríguez, Eva. "Fascist Spain and the Axis: Music, Politics, Race, and Canon." BPM 9 (2008). Web.

Moreno Gómez, Francisco. *El genocidio franquista en Córdoba*. Barcelona: Editorial Crítica, 2008.

"The Most Dangerous Man in Europe." 60 Minutes. Aired 7 January 1969. Accessed via Paley Center Online Archive. Web.

Moyn, Samuel. "From *l'Univers Concentrationnaire* to the Jewish Genocide: Pierre Vidal-Naquet and the *Treblinka* Controversy." In *After the Deluge: New Perspectives on the Intellectual and Cultural History of Postwar France*, edited by Julian Bour, 277–300. Lanham: Lexington Books, 2004.

Muñoz Molina, Antonio. *Sefarad*. Madrid: Alfaguara, 2001.

– *Sepharad*. Translated by Margaret Sayers Peden. Orlando: Harcourt, 2003.

Nágera, Vallejo. *Eugenesia de la Hispanidad y regeneración de la raza*. Burgos: n.p., 1937.

Nahmias, Yacob. *Poemas*. Barcelona: Tirocinio, 2012.

– *Yacobico: Salonican Childhood in Tel-Aviv*. Tel Aviv: Milim Medabrot, 2018.

Netanyahu, Benzion. *The Origins of the Inquisition in Spain*. New York: Random House, 1995.

Newcourt-Nowodworski, Stanley. *Black Propaganda in the Second World War*. Stroud: Sutton, 2005.

Newton, Ronald. "The United States, the German-Argentines, and the Myth of the Fourth Reich, 1943–47." *Hispanic American Historical Review* 64, no. 1 (1985): 81–103.

Nieto, Felipe. *La aventura comunista de Jorge Semprún*. Barcelona: Tusquets, 2014.

Nieva de la Paz, Pilar. "*Sefarad* de Antonio Muñoz Molina. La historia convertido en mito." In *Judaísmo hispano*, edited by Elena Romero, vol. 1, 363–78. Madrid: Junta de Castilla y León, Consejo Superior de Investigaciones Científicas, 2002.

Novitch, Miriam. *Le passage des barbares. Contribution a l'historie de la déportation et de la résistance de Juifs grecs*. Nice: Presses du Temps Present, 1967.

Núñez Seixas, Xosé. *Camarada invierno. Experiencia y memoria de la División Azul (1941–1945)*. Barcelona: Crítica, 2016.

– "Good Invaders? The Occupation Policy of the Spanish Blue Division in Northwestern Russia, 1941–1944." *War in History*, 7 July 2017: 1–26.

– "Russia and the Russians in the Eyes of the Spanish Blue Division Soldiers, 1941–44." *Journal of Contemporary History* 52, no. 2 (2016): 352–74.

– "¿Testigos o encubridores? La División Azul y el Holocausto de los judíos europeos. Entre Historia y Memoria." *Historia y Política* 26 (2011): 259–90.

– "Wishful Thinking in Wartime? Spanish Blue Division Soldiers and Their Views of Nazi Germany, 1941–44." *Journal of War & Culture Studies* 11, no. 2 (May 2018): 99–116.

Núñez Targa, Mercè. "1982. Una carta de Mercedes Núñez Targa." *Faro de Vigo*, 5 May 2016. Web.

– *Cárcel de Ventas*. Paris: Éditions de la Librairie du Globe, 1967.

– *El carretó dels gossos. Una catalana a Ravensbrück*. Barcelona: Edicions 62, 1982.

– *El valor de la memoria: De la cárcel de Ventas al campo de Ravensbrück*. Translated and edited by Ana Bonet Solé and Pablo Iglesias Núñez. Sevilla: Renacimiento, 2006.

O'Donoghue, Samuel. "Carlos Barral and the Struggle for Holocaust Consciousness in Franco's Spain." *History & Memory* 30, no. 2 (Fall–Winter 2018): 116–46.

Ojeda Mata, Maite. *Identidades ambivalentes. Sefardíes en la España contemporánea*. Collado Villaba: Sefarad, 2012.

Olascoaga, Alfredo. *El Norte de Africa cabeza de puente ¿de quien?* Madrid: n.pub., 1943.

Oliveros, Luis (dir.). *El ángel de Budapest*, 2011. Film.

Olmeda, Fernando. *El Valle de los Caídos*. Barcelona: Atalaya, 2009.

Ortega, Manuel. *Los hebreos en Marruecos*. Madrid: Compañía Ibero-Americana de Publicaciones, 1919.

Orth, Karin. "Die nationalsozialistischen Konzentrationslager." In *Speziallager in der SBZ. Gedenkstätten mit "doppelter Vergangenheit,"* edited by Peter Reif-Spirek and Bodo Ritscher, 20–61. Berlin: Links, 1999.

Ortí Camallonga, Salvador. *The Spanish Perception of the Jewish Extermination, 1945–2005*. PhD diss., Cambridge University, 2013.

Pagès, Joan, and Montserrat Casas i Vilalta. *Republicans i republicanes als camps de concentració nazis*. Barcelona: Institut de'Educació de l'Ajuntament de Barcelona, 2005.

Paldiel, Mordecai. *Diplomat Heroes of the Holocaust*. Jersey City: Ktav, 2007.

Palmero Aranda, Fernando A. "El discurso antisemita en España (1936–1948)." PhD diss., Universidad Complutense de Madrid, 2016.

Papo, Isaac. *Viaje en el ocaso de una cultura ibérica*. Barcelona: Tirocinio, 2006.

Papo, José. *En attendant l'aurore. Acrivité de la Communauté Sephardite de Paris pendant l'occupation 1940–1945*. Paris: Avril, 1945.

Pappalettera, Vicenzo, and Luigi Pappalettera. *Los SS tienen la palabra*. Barcelona: Editorial Laia, 1972.

Passelecq, Georges, and Bernar Suchecky. *Un silencio de la Iglesia frente al fascismo. La encíclica de Pío Xi que Pío XII no publicó*. Madrid: PPC, 1997.

Pattee, Richard. *This Is Spain*. Milwaukee: The Bruce, 1951.

Payne, Leigh A. *Unsettling Accounts: Neither Truth nor Reconciliation in Confessions of State Violence*. Durham: Duke UP, 2008.

Payne, Stanley G. *Franco and Hitler: Spain, Germany, and World War II*. New Haven: Yale UP, 2008.

– *The Franco Regime, 1936–1975*. Madison: U of Wisconsin P, 2011.

Pedreño Gómez, José María. "Recuperando la Memoria Histórica. Construyendo Izquierda." *Foro por la Memoria*, 3 December 2002. Web.

Peláez, M.J., A.B. Guckes, M.E. Gómez, and C. Serrano. *Epistolario Germánico de Ferran Valls i Taberner 1911–1942*. Barcelona: Cátedra de Historia del Derecho y de las Instituciones, 1997.

Pennell, C.R. *Morocco since 1830: A History*. New York: NYU P, 2000.

"El pensamiento de Codreanu." *Signo*, no. 43 (9 November 1940): 6.

Pere Ferreres, Josep Noguer. "El deporte dribló a la muerte en Mauthausen." *424*, 7 July 1978.

Pérez Domínguez, Andrés. *El violinista de Mauthausen*. Seville: Algaida, 2009.

Pérez López, Pablo. "Prensa, poder político y religión durante el primer franquismo." In *Presse et pouvoir en Espagne 1868–1975*, edited by Paul Aubert and Jean-Michel Desvois, 257–72. Bordeaux: Maison des Pays Ibériques / Madrid: Casa de Velázquez, 1996.

Pérez Vidal, Alejandro. "Censura y oídos sordos ante la literatura sobre los campos de la muerte en la postguerra europea: Joaquim Amat-Piniella y Primo Levi." *Hispania nova* 1 extra. (2019): 234–56.

Pérez Zalduondo, Gemma. "Música, censura y Falange. El control de la actividad musical desde la vicesecretaría de educación popular (1941–1945)." *Arbor* 187, no. 751 (2011): 875–86.

– "La música en los intercambios culturales entre España y Alemania (1938–1942)." In *Cruces de caminos: Intercambios musicales y artísticos en la Europa de la primera mitad del siglo XX*, edited by Gemma Pérez-Zalduondo and María Isabel Cabrera García, 407–49. Granada: Universidad de Granada, 2010.

– "Music, Totalitarian Ideologies, and Musical Practices under Francoism (1938–1950)." *Diagonal: Journal of the Center for Iberian and Latin American Music* 7 (2011). Web.

– "El nacionalismo como eje de la política musical del primer gobierno regular de Franco (30 de enero de 1938–8 de agosto de 1939)." *Revista de Musicología* 18, nos. 1–2 (1995): 247–74.

Pérez Zalduondo, Gemma, and Germán Gan Quesada, eds. *Music and Francoism*. Belgium: Brepols, 2013.

Perra, Emiliano. *Conflicts of Memory: The Reception of Holocaust Films and TV Programmes in Italy, 1945 to the Present*. Bern: Peter Lang, 2010.

– "Legitimizing Fascism through the Holocaust? The Reception of the Miniseries Perlasca: Un Eroe Italiano in Italy." *Memory Studies* 3 no. 2 (2010): 95–109.

"Perseguits i salvats," prod. La Xarxa de Comunicació Local and Diputació de Lleida, 2017. Film.

Peschanski, Denis. *Les camps français d'internement (1938–1946)*. PhD diss., Université Panthéon-Sorbonne–Paris, 2000.

Peterson, Maurice. *Both Sides of the Curtain: An Autobiography*. London: Constable, 1950.

Petriconi, Helmut. "Das Spanienbild im deutschen Bewusstsein." *Geist der Zeit. Wesen und Gestalt der Völker. Organ des deutschen Akademischen Austauschdienstes* 19, no. 2 (1941): 65–75.

Petrovna Pozharskaya, Svetlana. *Tainaya diplomatia Madrida. Vneshnyaya politika Ispanii v gody vtoroi mirovoi voiny* [Secret Diplomacy of Madrid: Spain's Foreign Policy during the Second World War]. Moscow: Mezhdunarodnye otnosheniia, 1971.

Pfeifer, Ulrike. *Obras literarias de los combatientes de la Divisón Azul. Rasgos germanófilos e influencias nacionalsocialistas durante la Segunda Guerra Mundial*. Palma de Mallorca: Memoria d'investigació, 2012.

Phillips, Caryl. *The Nature of Blood*. Toronto: Vintage Canada, 1998.

Pike, David Wingeate. *In the Service of Stalin: The Spanish Communists in Exile, 1939–1945*. Oxford: Oxford UP, 1993.

– *Spaniards in the Holocaust: Mauthausen, the Horror on the Danube*. London: Routledge, 2000.

Planelles, Manuel. "Ayudar a las sombras." *El País* (Andalucía), 16 May 2005.

Poncins, Léon de. *Las fuerzas secretas de la revolución. Fr.·. M.·. Judaísmo* [1928]. Madrid: Fax, 1932.

Pons Prades, Eduardo. *Morir por la libertad. Españoles en los campos de exterminio Nazis*. Madrid: Vosa, 1995.

Pons Rovira, Juan. "En defensa del nacionalsocialismo." *Por Favor*, 2 November 1978.

Pöppinghaus, Erns-Wolfgang. *Moralische Eroberungen? Kultur und Politik in den deutsch-spanischen Beziehungen der Jahre 1919 bis 1933*. Frankfurt am Main: Vervuert, 1999.

Porch, Douglas. *The French Foreign Legion: A Complete History of the Legendary Fighting Force*. New York: Harper, 1991.

Poznanski, Renée. *Jews in France during World War II*. Translated by Nathan Bracher. Waltham: Brandeis UP, 2001.

Pradera, Javier, and Joaquín Estefanía. *La Transición española y la democracia*. Madrid: Fondo de Cultura Económica de España, S.L., 2014.

Preston, Paul. *Franco: A Biography* [HarperCollins, 1993]. London: Basic Books, 1994.

– *Franco: Caudillo de España* [Grigalbo Mondadori, 1998]. Barcelona: Debolsillo, 2004.

– "Franco and Hitler: The Myth of Hendaye 1940." *Contemporary European History* 1, no. 1 (March 1992): 1–16.

– *The Last Stalinist: The Life of Santiago Carrillo*. London: Williams Collins, 2014.

– *The Spanish Holocaust: Inquisition and Extermination in Twentieth-Century Spain*. New York: W.W. Norton, 2012.

– *Las tres Españas del 36*. Barcelona: Plaza y Janés, 1998.

Printer, A.D. "Spanish Soldiers in France." *The Nation* 156, no. 14 (3 April 1943): 488–90.

"Projecte Stolpersteine a Navàs." Ed. Generalitat de Catalunya Memorial Democràtic. Navàs: Ajuntament de Navàs, 2015. Web.

Prose, Francine. *Anne Frank: The Book, the Life, the Afterlife*. New York: Harper, 2009.

Puig, Nuria. "La conexión alemana. Redes empresariales hispano-alemanas en la España del Siglo XX." *VIII Congreso de la Asociación Espanola de Historia Económica* (2005): 1–28.

Puig Raposo, Núria, and Adoración Alvaro Moya. "Misión Imposible? La expropiación de las empresas alemanas en España (1945–1975)." *Investigaciones de Historia Económica* 7 (2007): 101–30.

Pujiula, Jaime. "Eugenesia bionómica humana." *Razón y Fe*, no. 531 (April 1942): 375–83.

– "Raza, razas, razas puras." *Razón y Fe*, no. 496 (May 1939): 57–64.

Pujiula, Jordi. "Olotins i el III Reich." *Olot Misión*, September 1978.

Pulido, Ángel. *Españoles sin patria y la raza sefardí*. Madrid: Tipogr. de E. Teodoro, 1905.

Quintà, Alfons. "Joan Pages, un català a Mauthausen. 30 anys després de la desfeta nazi." *Presència*, no. 373 (7 June 1975): 16–18.

Raguer, Hilari. "La guerra civil vista por Goebbels." *Historia 16*, no. 153 (1989): 25–31.

Rando, Therese A. *Treatment of Complicated Mourning*. Champaign: Research P, 1993.

Razola, Manuel, and Mariano Constante Campo. *Triángulo azul. Los republicanos españoles en Mauthausen, 1940–1945*. Translated by Janine Muls de Liarás. Barcelona: Edicions 62, 1979.

Razola, Manuel, and Mariano Constante Campo. *Triangle Bleu. Les républicans espagnols à Mauthausen, 1940–1945*. Paris: Gallimard, 1969.

Rebok, Sandra. "Las primeras instituciones científicas alemanas en España. Los comienzos de la cooperación institucional en los albores del siglo XX." *Arbor* 187 (2011): 169–82.

– ed. *Traspasar Fronteras. Un siglo de intercambio científico / Über Grenzen Hinaus. Ein Jahrhundert Deutsch-Spanische Wissenschaftsbeziehungen*. Madrid: CSIC/ DAAD, 2010.

Reboul, Marie-France. "La Résistance dans les camps de concentration nationaux-socialistes." *Académie de Poitiers Pôle civisme et citoyenneté*. Web.

Refael, Shmuel. *Un grito en el silencio. La poesía sobre el Holocausto en lengua sefardí – estudio y antología*. Barcelona: Tirocinio, 2008.

Rein, Raanan. "Diplomacy, Propaganda, and Humanitarian Gestures: Francoist Spain and Egyptian Jews, 1956–1968." *Iberoamericana* 6, no. 23 (2006): 21–33.

– *Franco, Israel y los judíos*. Madrid: CSIC, 1996.
– *In the Shadow of the Holocaust and the Inquisition*. London: Frank Cass, 1997.
– "Una minoría tolerada. Los judíos en la España de Franco." In *Encuentros and Desencuentros: The Spanish-Jewish Cultural Interaction*, edited by Carlos Carrete Parrondo et al., 659–75. Tel Aviv: Tel Aviv U Projects, 2000.
– "Past Images, Cultural Codes, and Spain's Attitude towards the Jews in the Inter-War Period." In *Jews and Jewish Europeans between the Two World Wars* [Hebrew], edited by Raya Cohen, 109–41. Tel Aviv: Tel Aviv U, 2004.
Rein, Raanan, and Martina Weisz. "Ghosts of the Past, Challenges of the Present: New and Old 'Others' in Contemporary Spain." In *A Road to Nowhere? Jewish Experiences in Unifying Europe*, edited by Julius H. Shoeps and Olaf Glöckner, 103–20. Leiden and Boston: Brill, 2011.
Renshaw, Layla. *Exhuming Loss: Memory, Materiality, and Mass Graves of the Spanish Civil War*. Walnut Creek: Left Coast Press, 2011.
Richards, Michael. *After the Civil War: Making Memory and Re-Making Spain since 1936*. Cambridge: Cambridge UP, 2013.
Richou, Montserrat, and Marta Simó, "La deportación republicana y el Holocausto en los libros de texto de ciències sociales en la ESO." *Enseñanza de las ciencias sociales. Revista de investigación*, forthcoming.
Rimoldi, Lucas. "De memoria histórica y de las posibilidades representacionales del Holocausto." *Gestos* 43 (April 2007): 55–73.
Río Cisneros, Agustín del.*Viraje político español durante la II Guerra Mundial 1942–1945. Réplica al cerco internacional 1945–1946*. Madrid: Ediciones del Movimiento, 1965.
Robin, Pierre. *Résonances françaises de la guerre d'Espagne*. Agen: Amis du Vieux Nérac-Édition d'Albret / Ancrage, La Mémoire des métissages du Sud-Ouest / Mémoire de l'Espagne républicaine-Lot-et-Garonne, 2011.
Rodogno, Davide. *Fascism's European Empire: Italian Occupation during the Second World War*. New York: Cambridge UP, 2006.
Rodrigo, Javier. "Exploitation, Fascist Violence, and Social Cleansing: A Study of Franco's Concentration Camps from a Comparative Perspective." *European Review of History* 19, no. 4 (2012): 553–73.
Rodrigue, Aron. "Sephardim and the Holocaust." *Ina Levine Annual Lecture*. Washington, DC: United States Holocaust Memorial Museum, 2004.
Rodríguez del Risco, Carlos. "Yo he estado en Mauthausen. Carlos R. del Risco relata en exclusiva para 'Arriba' sus siete años de aventura en el exilio." *Arriba*, 20 April–1 June 1946.
Rodríguez González, Javier. "El espionaje nazi." In *War Zone. La Segunda Guerra Mundial en el noroeste de la península ibérica*, edited by Emilio Grandio Seone and Javier Rodríguez González, 209–42. Madrid: Eneida, 2012.
Rodríguez Jiménez, José Luis. "El discurso antisemita en el fascismo español." In *Los judíos en la historia de España*, edited by Javier Tusell Gómez and José

Antonio Ferrer Benimeli, 89–129. Calatayud: Diputación Provincial de Zaragoza, 2003.
- "Ni División Azul, ni División de Voluntarios. El personal forzado en el cuerpo expedicionario enviado por Franco a la URSS." *Cuandernos de Historia Contemporánea*, no. 31 (2009): 265–96.
Rodríguez López, Carolina. "La Universidad de Madrid como escenario de las relaciones hispano-alemanas en el primer franquismo (1939–1951)." *Ayer*, no. 69 (2008): 101–28.
Rohr, Isabelle. *La derecha española y los judíos, 1898–1945. Antisemitismo y oportunismo*. Valencia: Universitat de València, 2010.
- "'Spaniards of the Jewish Type': Philosepharadism in the Service of Imperialism in Early Twentieth-Century Spanish Morocco." *Journal of Spanish Cultural Studies* 12, no. 1 (March 2011): 61–75.
- *The Spanish Right and the Jews, 1898–1945: Antisemitism and Opportunism*. Portland: Sussex Academic P, 2007.
Roig, Montserrat. *Els catalans als camps nazis* [1977, 1980]. Barcelona: Edicions 62, 2001.
- "Una generación romántica. Españoles en los campos nazis." *Triunfo*, no. 532 (9 December 1972): 34–7.
- "Jorge Semprún, en un vaivén." *Triunfo*, no. 570 (1 September 1973): 32–5.
- *La lluita contra l'oblit. La lucha contra el olvido*. Barcelona: Amical de Mauthausen, 2001.
- *Noche y niebla: Los catalanes en los campos nazis*. Barcelona: Ediciones Península, 1978.
Rokem, Freddie. "On the Fantastic in Holocaust Performances." In *Staging the Holocaust: The Shoah in Drama and Performance*, edited by Claude Schumacher, 40–52. Cambridge: Cambridge UP, 1998.
Rolland, Eduardo. *Galicia en guerra. Espías, batallas, submarinos e volframio*. Vigo: Edicions Xerais, 2006.
Romaguera i Ramió, Joaquim, and Llorenç Soler de los Mártires. *Historia crítica y documentada del cine independiente en España. 1955–1975*. Barcelona: Laertes, 2016.
Romanska, Magda. *The Post-Traumatic Theatre of Grotowski and Kantor: History and Holocaust in "Akropolis" and "The Dead Class."* London and New York: Anthem Press, 2012.
Romero Sá, Magali, and André Felipe Candido da Silva. "La Revista Médica de Hamburgo y la Revista Médica Germano-Ibero-Americana. Diseminación de la medicina germánica en Espana y América Latina (1920–1933)." *Asclepio. Revista de Historia de la Medicina y de la Ciencia* 42, no. 1 (2010): 7–34.
Ros Agudo, Manuel. *La guerra secreta de Franco (1939–1945)*. Barcelona: Crítica, 2002.

Rosado Orquín, Amalia, and Baltasar Garzón. *Virtudes Cuevas: una supervivente del campo de concentración alemán de Ravensbrück*. Castelló de la Plana: Universitat Jaume I, 2018.

Rosenfeld, Alvin H. *The End of the Holocaust*. Jerusalem: Magnes and Yad Vashem, 2013.

Roth, John K. "On Seeing the Invisible Dimensions of the Holocaust." *Holocaust and Genocide Studies* 1, no. 1 (1986): 147–53.

Rothberg, Michael. "Introduction: Between Memory and Memory: From Lieux de Mémoire to Noeuds de Mémoire." *Yale French Studies* 118–19 (2010): 3–12.

– *Multidirectional Memory: Remembering the Holocaust in the Age of Decolonization*. Stanford: Stanford UP, 2009.

Rother, Bernd. *Franco y el Holocausto*. Translated by Leticia Artiles Gracia and Gonzalo Álvarez Chillida. Madrid: Marcial Pons Historia, 2005.

– *Spanien und der Holocaust*. Tübingen: M. Niemeyer/Verlag, 2001.

– "Spanish Attempts to Rescue Jews from the Holocaust: Lost Opportunities." *Mediterranean Historical Review* 17 (2002) 47–68.

Rousset, David. *L'univers concentrationnaire*. Paris: Editions du Pavois, 1946.

Roux, Catherine. *Triangle rouge*. Paris: Éditions France-Empire, 1968.

Rovit, Rebecca. "Cultural Ghettoization and Theater during the Holocaust: Performance as a Link to Community." *Holocaust and Genocide Studies* 19, no. 3 (Winter 2005): 459–86.

Rozenberg, Danielle. *L'Espagne contemporaine et la question juive. Les fils renoués de la mémoire et de l'histoire*. Toulouse: Presses Universitaires du Mirail, 2006.

– *La España contemporánea y la cuestión judía. Retejiendo los hilos de la memoria y de la historia*. Madrid: Marcial Pons-Casa Sefarad Israel, 2010.

– "Minorías religiosas y construcción democrática en España (Del monopolio de la Iglesia a la gestión del pluralismo)." *Revista española de investigaciones sociológicas*, no. 74 (April–June 1996): 245–68.

Rubin, Jonah S. "Transitional Justice against the State: Lessons from Spanish Civil Society-Led Forensic Exhumations." *International Journal of Transitional Justice* 8, no. 1 (2014): 99–120.

Rubio, Javier. *La emigración de la Guerra Civil de 1936–1939. Historia del éxodo que se produce con el fin de la IIa República Española*. Madrid: Editorial San Martín, 1977.

– "Francia, La acogida, Los campos de internamiento." In *Emigración y exilio en Francia, 1936–1946*, edited by Josefina Cuesta and Benito Bermejo, 87–116. Madrid: Eudema, 1996.

– "Población española en Francia, 1936–1946. Flujos y permanencies." In *Emigración y exilio. Españoles en Francia, 1936–1946*, edited by Josefina Cuesta and Benito Bermejo, 32–60. Madrid: Eudema, 1996.

Rubio, Salva, Pedro Colombo, and Aintzane Landa. *El fotógrafo de Mauthausen*. Barcelona: Norma, 2018.

Rudinskiy, V. *S ispantsami na Leningradskom fronte* [With Spaniards at the Leningrad Front]. Web.

Ruhl, Klaus-Jürgen. *Franco, Falange y III Reich. España en la Segunda Guerra Mundial*. Madrid: Akal, 1986.

Ruiz, Julius. "A Spanish Genocide? Reflections on the Francoist Repression after the Spanish Civil War." *Contemporary European History* 14, no. 2 (2005): 171–91.

Ruiz Bautista, Eduardo, and Pedro Barruso Barés. "La propaganda alemana en España durante la II Guerra Mundial." In *El ocaso de la verdad: propaganda y prensa exterior en la España franquista (1936–1945)*, edited by Antonio C. Moreno Cantano. Gijón: Trea, 2011.

Ruppert, Andreas. "Spanier in deutschen Konzentrationslagern. Spuren einer vergessenen Geschichte." *Tranvía. Revue der Iberischen Halbinsel* 28 (1993): 5–9.

Russell, Matthew B. *Postmemory, the Holocaust, and the Re-moralization of the Spanish Civil War in Contemporary Spanish Cultural Producción*. Davis: U of California–Davis, 2013.

Russell, P.E. "The Nessus-Shirt of Spanish History." *Bulletin of Hispanic Studies* 36, no. 4 (October 1959): 219–25.

Sáenz-Francés, Emilio. *Entre la antorcha y la esvástica. Franco en la encrucijada de la II Guerra Mundial*. Madrid: Actas, 2009.

Sala Rose, Rosa. *La penúltima frontera. Fugitivos del nazismo en España*. Barcelona: Papel de liar, 2011.

Salabert, Juana. *Velódromo de Invierno*. Barcelona: Seix Barral, 2001.

Salinas, David. *España, los sefarditas y el Tercer Reich (1939–1945). La labor de diplomáticos españoles contra el genocidio nazi*. Valladolid: Universidad de Valladolid, 1997.

Salomon, Herman P., and Tomás L. Ryan de Heredia. "In Memoriam: Francisco Franco (1892–1975), Benefactor of the Jews." *The American Sephardi* 9 (1978): 215–18.

Sánchez, Clara. *Lo que esconde tu nombre*. Barcelona: Ediciones Destino, 2010.

– *The Scent of Lemon Leaves*. Translated by Julie Wark. Richmond: Alma Books, 2012.

Sánchez-Biosca, Vicente. "Perpetrator Images, Perpetrator Artifacts: The Nomad Archives of Tuol Sleng (S-21)." *Cinéma&Cie: International Film Studies Journal* 15, no. 24 (Spring 2015): 103–17.

Sánchez Montoya, Francisco. *Ceuta y el norte de África. República, guerra y represión 1931–1944*. Granada: Nativola, 2004.

Sanchis Sinisterra, José. *Terror y miseria en el primer franquismo*. Madrid: Cátedra, 2003.

Santarcángeli, Paolo. *El libro de los laberintos*. Madrid: Siruela, 1997.

Saz Campos, Ismael. *España contra España. Los nacionalismos franquistas*. Madrid: Marcial Pons, 2003.

Schammah Gesser, Silvina. "La imagen de Sefarad y los judíos españoles en los orígenes vanguardistas del fascismo español." In *España e Israel. Veinte años después,* edited by Raanan Rein, 67–76. Madrid: Dykinson, 2007.

Schindel, Estela. "Los intelectuales latinoamericanos y el Holocausto. Notas para una investigación." Edited by Sandra Carreras. *Der Nationalsozialismus Und Lateinamerika. Institutionen, Repräsentationen, Wissenskonstrukte* 3 (2005): 21–35.

Schlegel, Hans. "El problema de la traducción de los clásicos del teatro español. Conferencia celebrada con motivo de la Semana Española 1938 en Frankfurt." *Ensayos y Estudios* 2, nos. 1–2 (January–March 1940): 24–45.

Schönemann, Sebastian, and Reimer Möller. "Der Bestand der Effekten ehemaliger Häftlinge des KZ Neuengamme in Verwahrung des ITS." In *Freilegungen. Auf den Spuren der Todesmärsche,* edited by Jean-Luc Blondel et al., 251–62. Göttingen: Wallstein, 2012.

Schramm, Hanna, Barbara Vormeier, and Irène Petit. *Vivre á Gurs. Un camp de concentration français, 1940–1941.* Paris: F. Maspero, 1979.

Schulker-Springorum, Stefanie. *Krieg und Fliegen. Die Legion Condor im Spanische Burgerkrieg.* Paderborn–Munich–Vienna–Zurich: Ferdinand Schonigh, 2010.

Schulze Schneider, Ingrid. "La cooperación de la Alemania nazi en la lucha franquista contra la masonería." In *La masonería en la España del siglo XX,* vol. 2, edited by José A. Ferrer Benimeli. Toledo: Universidad de Castilla–La Mancha – Cortes de Castilla–La Mancha, 1997.

– "La propaganda alemana en España 1942–1944." *Espacio, tiempo y forma,* serie V, *Historia contemporánea,* no. 7 (1994): 371–86.

– "El régimen franquista y la propaganda nazi en España (1939)." Paper presented at the II Encuentro de Investigadores del Franquismo, Alicante, 11–13 May 1995.

Schwaiger, Günter. "Hafner's Paradise: Director's Statements." MOSOLOV-P & GSF Film Production Companies. Web.

– (dir.). *Hafners Paradies.* Never Land Films, 2007. Film.

SchwarzRotbuch-Dokumente über den Hitler-Imperialismus. Barcelona: Asy Verlag, 1937.

Schweizer, Gottfried. "Spanische Woche in Frankfurt a.M." *Musik im Kriege* 2, nos. 1–2 (1944).

Seghers, Anna. *Briefe an Leser.* Berlin: Aufbau, 1970.

Segura Nieto, Juan. *¡Alerta! ... Francmasonería y Judaísmo.* Barcelona: Felipe González Rojas, 1940.

Seidemann, Henny. *Berlin–Barcelona–München. Eine Münchner Jüdin erzählt.* Norderstedt: Books on Demand, 2006.

Semprún, Jorge. *La escritura o la vida.* Translated by Thomas Kauf. Barcelona: Tusquets Editores, 1995.

– *L'écriture ou la vie: roman* [1994]. Paris: Gallimard, 1996.
– "Estalinismo y Fascismo." *Pensar en Europa*. Barcelona: Tusquets, 2006.
– *Exercises de Survie*. Paris: Gallimard, 2012.
– *Le grand voyage* [1963]. Paris: Gallimard, 2011.
– "Interview by Lila Azam Zanganeh – The Art of Fiction No. 192." *The Paris Review* 49, no. 180 (Spring 2007). Web.
– *Le langage est ma patrie: Entretiens avec Franck Appréderis*. Paris: Libella, 2013.
– *El largo viaje*. Translated by Jacqueline Conte and Rafael Conte. Barcelona: Seix Barral, 1976.
– *Literature or Life*. Translated by Linda Coverdale. New York: Viking, 1997.
– *The Long Voyage*. [London: Panther Books, 1966; New York: Grove Press, 1964] Translated by Richard Seaver. New York: Tusk Ivories/Overlook Press, 2005.
– *Le mort qu'il faut* [2001]. Paris: Gallimard, 2004.
– *Quel beau dimanche!* Paris: Grasset, 1980.
– *Une tombe au creux des nuages*. Paris: Climats/Flammarion, 2010.
– *What a Beautiful Sunday!* Translated by Alan Sheridan. London: Secker & Warburg, 1983.
Serrano, Secundino. *Maquis. Historia de la guerrilla antifranquista*. Madrid: Temas de hoy, 2001.
Serrano, Vicente. "El judaísmo en los libros de enseñanza religiosa en España." *El Olivo*, nos. 7–8 (December 1978): 7–28.
Serrano de Haro, Agustín. *Hemos visto al Señor*. Madrid: Madrid Escuela Española, 1940.
– *Yo Soy Español*. Madrid: Madrid Escuela Española, 1940.
Serrano Suñer, Ramón. *Entre el silencio y la propaganda. La historia como fue. Memorias*. Barcelona: Editorial Planeta, 1977.
– *Entre Hendaya y Gibraltar*. Barcelona: Nauta, 1973.
Sesma Landrín, Nicolás. "Importando el Nuevo Orden. El Instituto de Estudios Políticos y la recepción de la cultura fascista y nacionalsocialista en España (1939–1942)." In *Rebeldes y reaccionarios. Intelectuales, fascismo y derecha radical en Europa*, edited by Ferran Gallego and Francisco Morent e Valero, 243–80. Mataró: El Viejo Topo, 2011.
– "Propaganda en la alta manera e influencia fascista. El Instituto de Estudios Políticos (1939–1943)." *Ayer*, no. 53 (2004): 155–78.
Setton, Guy. *Spanish–Israeli Relations, 1956–1992: Ghosts of the Past and Contemporary Challenges in the Middle East*. Eastbourne: Sussex Academic P, 2016.
Setton, Guy, and Raanan Rein. "La diplomacia franquista y los judíos, 1956–1975. La preferencia por el judaísmo diaspórico." *Historia del Presente*, no. 27 (2016): 49–60.
Shandler, Jeffrey, and Barbara Kirshenblatt-Gimblett. *Anne Frank Unbound: Media, Imagination, Memory*. Bloomington: Indiana UP, 2012.

Shaw, Donald L. *The Generation of 1898 in Spain*. New York: Barnes & Noble, 1975.

Sherry, Jonathan. "'Claws of Stalinism in Spain': Totalitarianism and the Spanish Civil War." In *The Holocaust Metaphor: Cultural Representations of Traumatic Pasts in the 20th Century*, edited by Chiara Tedaldi and Anna Rosenberg, forthcoming.

Shinan, Nitai. "Ingratitud y fanatismo. Razón de estado y deber cultural. José Amador de los Ríos y la elaboración del discurso moderado sobre el pasado judío de España." In *Los judíos de España. Estudios históricos, políticos y literarios*, edited by José Amador de los Ríos, 7–168. Pamplona: Urgoiti, 2013.

– *Victims or Culprits: The History of the Jews as Reflected in Modern and Contemporary Spanish Historiography (1759–1898)* [Hebrew]. Jerusalem: Yad Itzhak Ben-Zvi Institute, 2001.

Sikkink, Kathryn. *The Justice Cascade: How Human Rights Prosecutions Are Changing World Politics*. New York: W.W. Norton, 2011.

Silva, Emilio, Asunción Esteban, Javier Castán, and Pancho Salvador, eds. *La memoria de los olvidados. Un debate sobre el silencio de la represión franquista*. Valladolid: Ámbito, 2004.

Sime, Jennifer. "Exhumations: The Search for the Dead and the Resurgence of the Uncanny in Contemporary Spain." *Anthropology and Humanism* 38, no. 1 (2013): 36–53.

Simó, Marta. "Challenges for Memory, Teaching and Learning about the Holocaust in Spain." In *Bystanders, Rescuers or Perpetrators? The Neutral Countries and the Shoah*, ed. Corry Guttstadt, Thomas Lutz, Bernd Rother, and Yessica San Román, 301–9. Berlin: Metropol Verlag & IHRA, 2016.

– "Teaching about the Holocaust in Catalonia." MA thesis, Jagiellonian University Krakow, 2005.

Simon, Daniel. *K.L.-Mauthausen. Un carnet de notes*. Luxembourg: Amicale des Anciens Prisonniers Politiques Luxembourgeois de Mauthausen, 2006.

Sinca Vendrell, Amadeo. *Lo que Dante no pudo imaginar. Mauthausen-Gusen, 1940–1945*. Barcelona: Editoriales, 1980.

Sinova, Justino. *La censura de prensa durante el franquismo (1936–1951)*. Madrid: Espasa-Calpe, 1989.

"La situación política." *La Libertad* (Madrid), 7 February 1936: 3.

"Sobre 'Holocausto.'" *Canigó*, 7 July 1979.

Soler, Llorenç (dir.), *Francesc Boix: un fotógrafo en el infierno*. Prod. Oriol Porta/ S.A.V., 2000. Film.

Solzhenitsyn, Aleksandr I. *The Gulag Archipelago*. New York: Harper & Row, 1973.

Sommer, Robert. *Das KZ-Bordell. Sexuelle Zwangsarbeit in nationalsozialistischen Konzentrationslagern*. Paderborn: F. Schöningh, 2009.

Sontag, Susan. *On Photography*. New York: Farrar, Straus & Giroux, 1977.

– *Regarding the Pain of Others*. New York: Picador, 2003.

Soo, Scott. *The Routes to Exile: France and the Spanish Civil War Refugees, 1939–2009*. Manchester: Manchester UP, 2013.

Steinacher, Gerald. *Nazis on the Run*. Oxford and New York: Oxford UP, 2011.

Steindling, Dolly. *Hitting Back: An Austrian Jew in the French Résistance*. Bethesda: UP of Maryland, 2000.

Strebel, Bernhard. *Das KZ Ravensbrück. Geschichte eines Lagerkomplexes*. Paderborn: F. Schöningh, 2003.

Stuart, Graham H. *The International City of Tangier*, 2nd ed. Stanford: Stanford UP, 1955.

Suderland, Maja. *Inside Concentration Camps: Social Life at the Extremes*. Cambridge: Polity Press, 2013.

Suñer Aguas, Raimundo. *De Calaceite a Mauthausen. Memorias de Raimundo Suñer*. Alcañiz, Spain: Centro de Estudios Bajoaragoneses, 2006.

Szanajda, Andrew, and David A. Messenger. "The German Secret State Police in Spain: Extending the Reach of National Socialism." *International History Review* 40, no. 2 (2018): 397–415.

Szpilman, Władysław. *Śmierć miasta*. Warsaw: Spółdzielnia Wydawnicza Wiedza, 1946.

Taguieff, Pierre-André, and Renée Neher-Bernheim. *Les Protocoles des Sages de Sion. Faux et usages d'un faux*. Paris: Berg International, 1992.

Taradel, Ruggero, and Barbara Raggi. *La Segregazione Amichevole. "La Civiltà Cattólica" e la questione ebraica 1850–1945*. Roma: Editori Riuniti, Gennaio, 2000.

Targarona, Mar (dir). *El fotógrafo de Mauthausen*. Rodar y Rodar, 2018. Film.

Téllez Solá, Antonio. *La red de evasión del grupo Ponzán*. Barcelona: Virus Editorial, 1996.

The Encyclopedia of the Righteous Among the Nations. Rescuers of Jews during the Holocaust. Europe and Other Countries (Part I). Jerusalem: Yad Vashem, 2007.

The Ravensbrück Women's Concentration Camp: History and Memory. Berlin: Metropol Verlag, 2013.

Thomas, Hugh. *Spain*. New York: Time, 1966.

Tidd, Ursula. *Jorge Semprún: Writing the European Other*. London: Legenda, 2014.

Tobin Stanley, Maureen. "Mujeres silenciosas, mujeres silenciadas: Reality and Representation of the Female Republican Struggle against Francoist and Hilterian Nationalism." *Vanderbilt e-Journal of Luso-Hispanic Studies* 6 (2010): 119–46.

Todorov, Tzvetan. *Los abusos de la memoria*. Barcelona: Ediciones Paidós, 2000.

– *The Fantastic: A Structural Approach to a Literary Genre*. Ithaca: Cornell UP, 1975.

Toran, Rosa. *Amical de Mauthausen. Lucha y recuerdo. 1962–1978–2008*. Barcelona: Amical de Mauthausen y otros campos y de todas las víctimas del nazismo de España, 2008.

– "Entorn de la deportació als camps nazis (I). Testimoni i militància." *L'Avenç*, no. 261 (September 2001): 8–14.

– "Entorn de la deportació als camps nazis (II). Testimoni i militancia." *L'Avenç*, no. 262 (October 2001): 8–15.

– *Joan de Diego. El tercer secretari a Mauthausen.* Barcelona: Ediciones 62, 2007.

– *Vida i mort dels republicans als camps nazis.* Barcelona: Proa, 2002.

Toran, Rosa, and Margarida Sala. *Crónica gráfica de un campo de concentración.* Barcelona: MHC–Viena Edicions, 2002.

Touboul Tardieu, Eva. *Séphardisme et hispanité. L'Espagne à la recherche de son passé (1920–1936).* Paris: Université Paris–Sorbonne, 2009.

Tovar, Antonio. "La idea del imperio español en la historia y en el presente." *Ensayos y estudios* 2, nos. 3–4 (May–July 1940): 121–38.

– *El imperio de España.* Madrid: A. Aguado, 1941.

Trallero, Mar. *Neus Català. La dona antifeixista a Europa.* Barcelona: Mina, 2008.

"Los Tres Pueblos Bíblicos." *Signo*, no. 5 (17 February 1940): 3.

"Tsena pobedy: «Golubaya divizia» i drugie ispantsy" [The Cost of Victory: The Blue Division and Other Spaniards]. *The Echo of Moscow.* 16 August 2010. Radio program script.

Tusell, Javier. "La etapa Jordana (1942–1944)." *Espacio, Tiempo y Forma*, serie V: *Historia Contemporánea*, no. 2 (1989): 169–90.

Uriarte, Isabel. *Las mujeres de la División Azul. Una valerosa retaguardia.* Madrid: Ediciones Barbarroja, 2012.

Urrutia, Federico de. *¡Camarada: He aquí el enemigo!.* Madrid: Ediciones Toledo, 1942.

– *La paz que quiere Hitler.* Madrid: Blass, 1939.

– *Por qué la Falange es católica.* Madrid: Ediciones de la Vicesecretaría de Educación Popular, 1942.

Urrutia, Jorge. "El concepto de Garcilaso en la España del siglo XX." In *Reflexión de la literatura*, 115–44. Sevilla: Publicaciones de la Universidad de Sevilla, 1983.

– *El mar o la impostura.* Madrid: Visor, 2004.

Vadillo, Fernando. *La gran crónica de la División Azul. Los prisioneros.* Madrid: Ediciones Barbarroja, 1999.

Valentín, Manu. *Voces caídas del cielo. Historia del exilio judío en Barcelona (1881–1954).* Barcelona: Editorial Comanegra, 2019.

Van Vree, Frank. "Indigestible Images: On the Ethics and Limits of Representation." In *Performing the Past: Memory, History, and Identity in Modern Europe*, 257–83. Amsterdam: Amsterdam UP, 2010.

Vega Carpio, Lope Félix de. *Liebe aus Neid oder Des Gärtners Hund Komödie in drei Aufzügen.* Translated by Hans Schlegel. Berlin: Widukind-Verl, 1941.

Vernon, Kathleen. "Re-viewing the Spanish Civil War: Franco's Film *Raza*." *Film and History* 16, no. 2 (1986): 26–34.

Viadiu, Francesc. *Andorra. Cadena de evasion.* Barcelona: Ediciones Martínez Roca, 1974.

Vilanova, Antonio. *Los olvidados.* Paris: Ruedo Ibérico, 1969.

Vilanova Vila-Abadal, Francesc, and Mireia Capdevila Candell. *Nazis a Barcelona. L'esplendor feixista de postguerra (1939–1945).* Barcelona: Ayuntament de Barcelona / L'Avenç, 2017.

Villarronga, Agustí (dir.). *Tras el cristal.* T.E.M. Productores S.A., 1986. Film.

Viñas, Ángel. "Natural Alliances: The Impact of Nazism and Fascism on Franco's Domestic Policies." In *Interrogating Francoism: History and Dictatorship in Twentieth-Century Spain,* edited by Helen Graham, 139–58. New York: Bloomsbury Academic, 2016.

Vives i Clavé, Pere. *Cartes des dels camp de concentració.* Barcelona: Edicions 62, 1972.

Vizcaíno Casas, Fernando. *Café y copa con los famosos* [1968]. Barcelona: Planeta, 1990.

Volkov, Shulamit. *Germans, Jews, and Antisemites: Trials in Emancipation.* Cambridge: Cambridge UP, 2006.

Von Bock, F. *Ya stoyal u vorot Moskvy* [I Stayed at the Gates of Moscow]. Moscow: IAuza, 2006.

Wachsmann, Nikolaus. *KL: A History of the Nazi Concentration Camps.* London: Little, Brown, 2016.

Waddington, Lorna. "The Anti-Komintern and Nazi Anti-Bolshevik Propaganda in the 1930s." *Journal of Contemporary History* 42, no. 4 (2007): 573–94.

Wagner, Jens-Christian. "Work and Extermination in the Concentration Camps." In *Concentration Camps in Nazi Germany: The New Histories,* edited by Jane Caplan and Nikolas Wachmann, 139–60. New York: Routledge, 2010.

Weinberg, Gerhard L. "Two Separate Issues? Historiography of World War II and the Holocaust." In *Holocaust Historiography in Context: Emergence, Challenges, Polemics, and Achievements,* edited by David Bankier and Dan Michman, 379–401. Jerusalem: Yad Vashem, 2008.

Weiss, Ruth. "*Shoah, Khurbn,* Holocaust." *The Modern Jewish Canon.* New York: Free Press, 2000.

Wiesel, Elie. *All Rivers Run to the Sea.* New York: A.A. Knopf, 1995.

– *Night.* Translated by Marion Wiesel. New York: Penguin Books, 2006.

Wieviorka, Annette. *The Era of Witness.* Ithaca: Cornell UP, 2006.

Wieviorka, Olivier. *Histoire de la Résistance, 1940–1945.* Paris: Perrin, 2013.

Winter, Jay. "Thinking about Silence." In *Shadows of War: A Social History of Silence in the Twentieth Century,* edited by Efrat Ben-Ze'Ev et al., 3–31. Cambridge: Cambridge UP, 2010.

Wisse, Ruth R. "The Individual from the Ashes: Hitler and the Genre of the Holocaust Memoir." *The Weekly Standard* (1997): 29–35.

Wyman, David. *The Abandonment of the Jews: America and the Holocaust 1941–1945*. New York: Pantheon Books, 1984.

Yerushalmi, Yosef. *Assimilation and Anti-Semitism: The Iberian and the German Models*. New York: Leo Baeck Institute, 1982.

Yitzhak, Arad. *Oni srazhalis za Rodinu. Evreii Sovetskogo Soyuza v Velikoi Otechestvennoi voine* [They Fought for Their Country: The Jews of the Soviet Union in the Great Patriotic War]. Jerusalem and Moscow: Mosty kul'tury, 2011.

Yovel, Yirmiyahu. *The Other Within*. Princeton: Princeton UP, 1999.

Yusta Rodrigo, Mercedes. "Rebeldía individual, compromiso familiar, acción colectiva. Las mujeres en la resistencia al franquismo durante los años cuarenta." *Historia del Presente* 4 (2004): 63–92.

Zilberman, David. *Ih ty yetovidel* [And You Saw It]. Moscow: Polimed, 2012.

Zucotti, Susan. *The Holocaust, the French, and the Jews*. New York: Basic Books, 1993.

Contributors

Gonzalo Álvarez Chillida is an associate professor of History of Thought and of Political and Social Movements at the Complutense University in Madrid. He wrote *El antisemitismo español. La imagen del judío (1810–2002)* (Spanish Antisemitism: The Image of the Jew [1910–2002]) in 2011 and collaborated on *Handbuch des Antisemitismus. Juden feindschaft in Geschichte und Gegenwart* (Handbook of Antisemitism: Hostility towards Jews in History and the Present, 2008–11).

Haim Avni is a professor emeritus of Modern and Contemporary Jewish History at the Hebrew University of Jerusalem. He was the founder and Head of the Division for Latin America, Spain, and Portugal of the Avraham Harman Institute of Contemporary Jewry (1967–2009) and served as the academic director of the Central Zionist Archives (2000–8). Among his many publications is the groundbreaking *Spain, the Jews, and Franco* (1982).

Alejandro Baer is an associate professor of Sociology and director of the Center for Holocaust and Genocide Studies at the University of Minnesota. His publications include *Holocausto. Recuerdo y representación* (Holocaust: Remembrance and Representation, 2006), *España y el Holocausto (1939–1945). Historia y testimonios* (Spain and The Holocaust: History and Testimonies, 2007), edited with Jacobo Israel Garzón, and *Memory and Forgetting in the Post-Holocaust Era: The Ethics of Never Again* (2017), co-written with Natan Sznaider.

Stacy N. Beckwith is a professor of Hebrew and Judaic Studies and director of Judaic Studies at Carleton College. She is the editor of *Charting Memory: Recalling Medieval Spain* (2000). She has contributed to *Religious*

Perspectives in Modern Muslim and Jewish Literatures (2006) and *Sephardism: Spanish Jewish History and the Modern Literary Imagination* (2012).

Graciela Ben Dror was a researcher at the Stephen Roth Institute for the Study of Contemporary Antisemitism and Racism, a lecturer at the University of Haifa, the Director of Moreshet, Mordechai Anielevich Memorial, and is the editor of the *Moreshet Journal for the Study of the Holocaust and Antisemitism.* Her publications include *La Iglesia Católica ante el Holocausto. España y América Latina, 1933–1945* (The Catholic Church Confronting the Holocaust: Spain and Latin America, 1933–1945 [2003]).

Sara J. Brenneis is a professor of Spanish and affiliated faculty in European Studies and Film and Media Studies at Amherst College. She is the author of *Genre Fusion: A New Approach to History, Fiction, and Memory in Contemporary Spain* (2014) and *Spaniards in Mauthausen: Representations of a Nazi Concentration Camp, 1940–2015* (2018).

Paul Cahill is an associate professor of Spanish at Pomona College. In addition to publishing the article "Globalizing Good and Evil in the Poetry of Jorge Urrutia and Jorge Riechmann" in *Modern Language Notes* (2010), he prepared a critical edition of *Tabula rasa* and *El sueño del origen y la muerte* by Jenaro Talens (2013).

Josep Calvet is a historian affiliated with the History, Patrimony, and Documentation Research Group at the University of Lérida, Spain. He is the author of *Las montañas de la libertad. El paso de refugiados por los Pirineos durante la Segunda Guerra Mundial* (The Mountains of Liberty: The Passage of Refugees through the Pyrenees during the Second World War, 2010) and *Huyendo del Holocausto. Judíos evadidos del nazismo a través del Pirineo de Lleida* (Fleeing the Holocaust: Jews Escaping Nazism over the Pyrenees in Lérida, 2014).

Juan M. Calvo Gascón is a historian and member of the board of directors of the Amical de Mauthausen in Barcelona. He published *Itinerarios e identidades. Republicanos aragoneses deportados a los campos nazis* (Itineraries and Identities: Republicans from Aragón Deported to the Nazi Camps) in 2011 and *Dentro de poco os podré abrazar. Supervivientes aragoneses de los campos nazis* (Soon I Will Be Able to Embrace You: Aragonese Survivors from the Nazi Camps) in 2019.

Robert S. Coale is a professor of Hispanic Studies and chair of the Département des Langues Étrangères Appliquées at the Université de Rouen-Normandie. He contributed "From Antifascistas to PAF: Lexical and Political Interpretations of American International Brigaders in Spain during the Second World War" to *Rethinking Antifascism: History, Memory and Politics 1922 to the Present* (2016). His research into the Spanish Loyalists who served in the Leclerc Division is the basis for Paco Roca's graphic novel *Los surcos del azar* (*Twists of Fate*, 2019).

Pedro Correa Martín-Arroyo is a Leverhulme Trust Early Career Fellow at the Holocaust Research Institute (Royal Holloway, University of London). He contributed an article co-authored with Alejandro Baer to *The Politics of the Neutrals during the Shoah* (2016), and his essay "Franco, Savior of the Jews? Tracing the Genealogy of the Myth and Assessing Its Persistence in Recent Historiography" appears in *Lessons and Legacies of the Holocaust XIII* (2018).

Javier Domínguez Arribas is an associate professor of Hispanic Civilization at the Université París XIII. He published *El enemigo judeo-masónico en la propaganda franquista, 1936–1945* (The Judeo-Masonic Enemy in Francoist Propaganda, 1936–1945) in 2009, with an edition in French in 2016.

Geneviève Dreyfus-Armand is a historian and president of the Centre d'études et de recherches sur les migrations ibériques (Centre for Studies and Research on Iberian Migrations). Her books include *L'exil des républicains espagnols en France. De la Guerre civile à la mort de Franco* (The Exile of the Spanish Republicans in France: From the Civil War to the Death of Franco, 1999); *L'Espagne, passion française, 1936–1975. Guerres, exils et solidarités* (Spain, French Passion, 1936–1975: Wars, Exiles, and Solidarities, 2015) with Odette Martínez-Maler; and *Septfonds 1939–1944. Dans l'archipel des camps français* (Septfonds 1939–1944. In the Archipelago of French Camps, 2019).

Isabel Estrada is an associate professor of Spanish at the City College of New York. She is the author of *El documental cinematográfico y televisivo contemporáneo. Memoria, representación y formación de la identidad democrática española* (The Contemporary Cinematographic and Television Documentary: Memory, Subject, and Formation of the Spanish Democratic Identity, 2013).

Soledad Fox Maura is a professor of Spanish and Comparative Literature and affiliated faculty in the Jewish Studies Program at

Williams College. She published *Jorge Semprún: The Spaniard Who Survived the Nazis and Conquered Paris* in 2017.

Maria Fragkou is a Junior Research Fellow at the University of Bern Institute of History. Her book, *Spaniards and Sephardites in 20th Century Europe: An Intercommunity Sociality and International Relations, 1900–1940*, was published in 2019.

Joshua Goode is an associate professor in the departments of History and Cultural Studies and the director of the Museum Studies program at Claremont Graduate University. He is the author of *Impurity of Blood: Defining Race in Spain, 1870–1930* (2009) and contributed to *Empire's End: Transnational Connections in the Hispanic World* (2016).

Andrea Hepworth is a lecturer in Spanish and Latin American Studies at Victoria University of Wellington, New Zealand. She has published "Site of Memory and Dismemory: The Valley of the Fallen in Spain" in the *Journal of Genocide Research* (2014) and "From Survivor to Fourth-Generation Memory: Literal and Discursive Sites of Memory in Post-Dictatorship Germany and Spain" in the *Journal of Contemporary History* (2017).

Gina Herrmann is an associate professor of Romance Languages affiliated with Judaic Studies at the University of Oregon. She is the author of *Written in Red: The Communist Memoir in Spain* (2010) and co-editor of *A Critical Companion to Jorge Semprún: Buchenwald, Before and After* (2014) with Ofelia Ferrán.

Jacobo Israel Garzón is a scholar of Spanish Judaism. He founded *Raíces. Revista judía de cultura* (Roots: Magazine of Jewish Culture) and was its director from 1994 to 2005. His books include *Escrito en sefarad. Aportación escrita de los judíos de España a la literatura, la erudición, la ciencia y la tecnología contemporáneas* (Written in Sepharad: A Written Approach to the Jews of Spain in Contemporary Literature, Erudition, Science, and Technology, 2005) and *España y el Holocausto (1939–1945). Historia y testimonios* (Spain and the Holocaust (1939–1945): History and Testimonies), written with Alejandro Baer in 2007.

Marició Janué i Miret is an associate professor in the Department of Humanities of the Universitat Pompeu Fabra in Barcelona. She was director of the Jaume Vicens i Vives University Institute of History from 2013 to 2016. She published *España y Alemania. Historia de las relaciones* *culturales en el siglo XX* (Spain and Germany: History of Cultural Relations in the Twentieth Century) in 2008.

Boris Kovalev is a professor and head of the Novgorod scientific sector at the St Petersburg Institute of History of the Russian Academy of Sciences. In 2014, he published *Dobrovol'cy na chuzhoj vojne. Ocherki istorii Goluboj divizii* (Volunteers in the Foreign War: Essays on the History of the Blue Division).

Tabea Alexa Linhard is an associate professor of Spanish, Comparative Literature, and International Studies at Washington University in St Louis. She is the author of *Jewish Spain: A Mediterranean Memory* (2014) and co-editor of *Revisiting Jewish Spain in the Modern Era* (2013) with Daniela Flesler and Adrián Pérez Melgosa.

José Antonio Lisbona is a political scientist and specialist in international relations in Spain. He is the author of *Retorno a Sefarad. La política de España hacia sus judíos en el siglo XX* (Return to Sepharad: Spain's Policy towards Its Jews in the Twentieth Century, 1993) and *Mas allá del deber. La respuesta humanitaria del Servicio Exterior frente al Holocausto* (Beyond Duty: The Foreign Service's Humanitarian Response to the Holocaust, 2015), which he condenses here.

Marilén Loyola is an assistant professor of Spanish at Rockford University. She has published an online prologue to Juan Mayorga's *Animales nocturnos* (2014) and in 2016 presented on Holocaust theatre in Spain at the Second International Conference on Twenty-First-Century Hispanic Theatre held at the University of Strasbourg.

Marta Marín-Dòmine is an associate professor and director of the Centre for Memory and Testimony Studies at Wilfrid Laurier University in Ontario, Canada. She published the first English translation of Joaquim Amat-Piniella's *K.L. Reich*, co-translated with Robert Finley, in 2014.

David A. Messenger is a professor of History and chair of the Department of History at the University of South Alabama in Mobile. He is the author of *War and Public Memory: Case Studies in Twentieth-Century Europe* (2019), *Hunting Nazis in Franco's Spain* (2014), and *L'Espagne Republicaine: French Policy and Spanish Republicanism in Liberated France* (2008). He is co-editor, with Katrin Paehler, of *A Nazi Past: Recasting German Identity in Postwar Europe* (2015).

Mercedes Peñalba-Sotorrío is a lecturer in Modern History at Manchester Metropolitan University. She is the author of *La Secretaría General del Movimiento. Construcción, coordinación y estabilización del régimen franquista* (The General Secretariat of FET y de las JONS: Construction, Coordination, and Stabilization of Franco's Regime, 2015).

Shmuel Refael is the director of the Salti Institute for Judeo-Spanish (Ladino) Studies at Bar-Ilan University, Israel. Among his publications are *Un grito en el silencio. La poesía sefardí sobre el Holocausto. Estudio y antología* (A Cry in the Silence: Poetry about the Holocaust in the Sephardic Language: Study and Anthology, 2008) and *La vida de Adolf Hitler: el Haman Moderno. Salonica (1933). Text and Context of a Ladino Booklet* (The Life of Adolf Hitler: The Modern Haman, 2015).

Raanan Rein is the Elias Sourasky Professor of Latin American and Spanish History and Vice-President of Tel Aviv University. Among his publications are *In the Shadow of the Holocaust and the Inquisition: Israel's Relations with Francoist Spain* (1997) and *Guerra Civil y Franquismo. Una perspectiva internacional* (Spanish Civil War and Francoism: An International Perspective, 2016), co-edited with Joan María Thomàs. The Spanish King Felipe VI awarded him the title of Commander in the Order of the Civil Merit in 2016 for his contribution to Spanish historiography and to Spain's relations with Israel.

Isabelle Rohr holds a PhD in history from the London School of Economics and is the Archives Project Specialist at the American Jewish Joint Distribution Committee. She is the author of *The Spanish Right and the Jews (1898–1945): Antisemitism and Opportunism* (2007), which was also published in Spain in 2010.

Marta Simó received her PhD from the Universitat Autònoma de Barcelona, where she is a member of the Research Group of Sociology and Religious Studies. She is also a member of the Multilingual Expert Team of the International Holocaust Remembrance Alliance for the Education Research Project. She contributed to *Bystanders, Rescuers, or Perpetrators? The Neutral Countries and the Shoah* (2016) and *Research in Teaching and Learning about the Holocaust: A Dialogue Beyond Borders* (2017).

Natan Sznaider is a professor of Sociology at the Academic College of Tel-Aviv-Yaffo in Israel. His books include *Erinnerung im Globalen Zeitalter. Der Holocaust* (2001), co-authored with Daniel Levy, which was expanded and translated as *The Holocaust and Memory in the Global Age*

(2006); *Jewish Memory and the Cosmopolitan Order* (2011); and *Memory and Forgetting in the Post-Holocaust Age*, with Alejandro Baer (2017).

Macarena Tejada López is a PhD candidate in Romance Languages and Literatures at the University of Oregon. Her dissertation focuses on the cultural production of the Spanish Division of Volunteers in diaries, memoirs, and films. She published "A Spanish Schindler in Budapest" in *The Volunteer* (2011).

Rosa Toran is a historian and a vice-president of the Amical de Mauthausen in Barcelona. Among her publications are *Montserrat Roig, la lluita contra l'oblit. Escrits sobre la deportació* (Montserrat Roig, the Fight Against Oblivion. Writing about the Deportation, 2001), *Vida i mort dels republicans als camps nazis* (Life and Death of the Republicans in the Nazi Camps, 2002) and *Mauthausen. Crònica gràfica d'un camp de concentració* (Mauthausen: Graphic Chronicle of a Concentration Camp, 2002) with Margarida Sala.

Martina L. Weisz is research coordinator at the Vidal Sassoon International Center for the Study of Antisemitism in Jerusalem. Her publications include "Micro-physics of Otherness: Jews, Muslims, and Latin Americans in Contemporary Spain," in *Antisemitism International* (2010) and "Splitting the Soul: Spanish Conservatives, Anti-Secularism and the 'Enemizing' of Islam," in *International Journal of Iberian Studies* (2015). Her book, *Jews and Muslims in Contemporary Spain: Redefining National Boundaries*, was published in 2019.

Index

TORONTO IBERIC

Co-editors: Robert Davidson (Toronto) and Frederick A. de Armas (Chicago)

Editorial board: Josiah Blackmore (Harvard); Marina Brownlee (Princeton); Anthony J. Cascardi (Berkeley); Justin Crumbaugh (Mt Holyoke); Emily Francomano (Georgetown); Jordana Mendelson (NYU); Joan Ramon Resina (Stanford); Enrique Garcia Santo-Tomás (U Michigan); Kathleen Vernon (SUNY Stony Brook)

1 Anthony J. Cascardi, *Cervantes, Literature, and the Discourse of Politics*
2 Jessica A. Boon, *The Mystical Science of the Soul: Medieval Cognition in Bernardino de Laredo's Recollection Method*
3 Susan Byrne, *Law and History in Cervantes' Don Quixote*
4 Mary E. Barnard and Frederick A. de Armas (eds), *Objects of Culture in the Literature of Imperial Spain*
5 Nil Santiáñez, *Topographies of Fascism: Habitus, Space, and Writing in Twentieth-Century Spain*
6 Nelson Orringer, *Lorca in Tune with Falla: Literary and Musical Interludes*
7 Ana M. Gómez-Bravo, *Textual Agency: Writing Culture and Social Networks in Fifteenth-Century Spain*
8 Javier Irigoyen-García, *The Spanish Arcadia: Sheep Herding, Pastoral Discourse, and Ethnicity in Early Modern Spain*
9 Stephanie Sieburth, *Survival Songs: Conchita Piquer's* Coplas *and Franco's Regime of Terror*
10 Christine Arkinstall, *Spanish Female Writers and the Freethinking Press, 1879-1926*
11 Margaret Boyle, *Unruly Women: Performance, Penitence, and Punishment in Early Modern Spain*
12 Evelina Gužauskytė, *Christopher Columbus's Naming in the* diarios *of the Four Voyages (1492-1504): A Discourse of Negotiation*
13 Mary E. Barnard, *Garcilaso de la Vega and the Material Culture of Renaissance Europe*
14 William Viestenz, *By the Grace of God: Francoist Spain and the Sacred Roots of Political Imagination*
15 Michael Scham, Lector Ludens: *The Representation of Games and Play in Cervantes*
16 Stephen Rupp, *Heroic Forms: Cervantes and the Literature of War*